# APPALACHIA
# A REGIONAL GEOGRAPHY

## Land, People, and Development

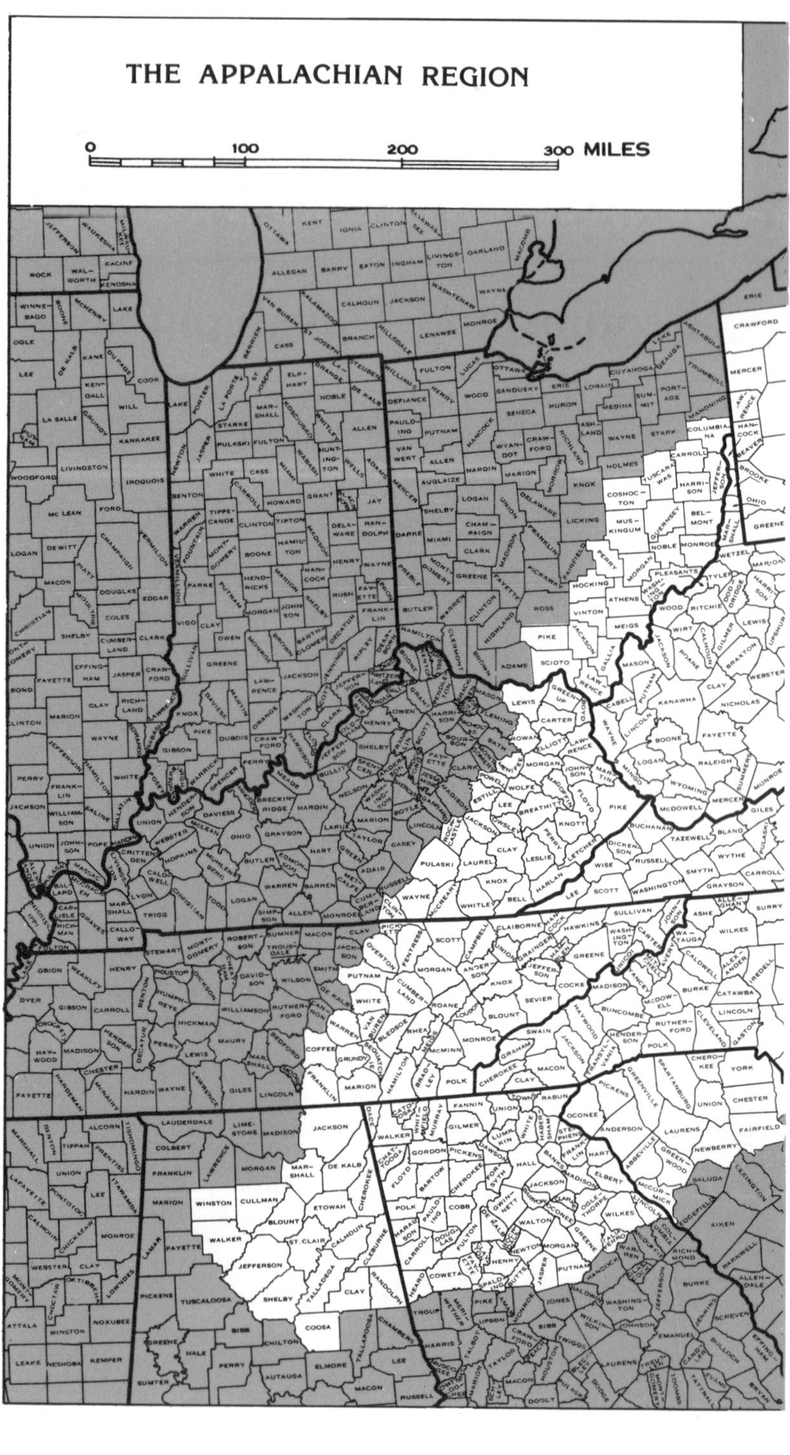
THE APPALACHIAN REGION
0
100
200
300 MILES

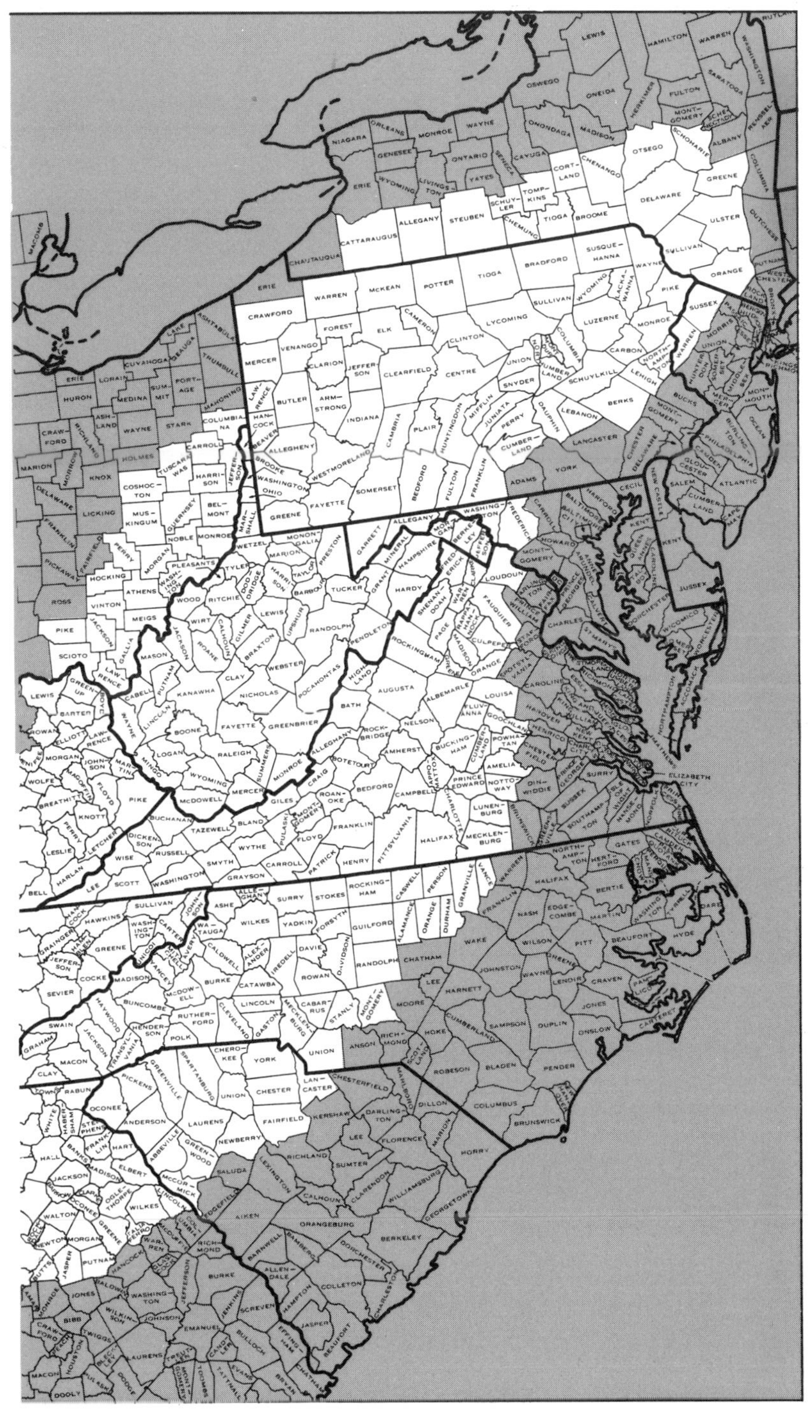

LEWIS
HAMILTON
WARREN
WASHINGTON
OSWEGO
ONEIDA
FULTON
SARATOGA
HERKIMER
MONTGOMERY
SCHENECTADY
RENSSELAER
NIAGARA
ORLEANS
MONROE
WAYNE
ONONDAGA
MADISON
ALBANY
GENESEE
ONTARIO
SENECA
CAYUGA
CORTLAND
CHENANGO
OTSEGO
SCHOHARIE
COLUMBIA
ERIE
WYOMING
LIVINGSTON
YATES
SCHUYLER
TOMPKINS
GREENE
DELAWARE
ULSTER
DUTCHESS
CHEMUNG
TIOGA
BROOME
CATTARAUGUS
ALLEGANY
STEUBEN
CHAUTAUQUA
SULLIVAN
ORANGE
PUTNAM
WESTCHESTER
ERIE
WARREN
MCKEAN
POTTER
TIOGA
BRADFORD
SUSQUEHANNA
WAYNE
PIKE
SUSSEX
CRAWFORD
FOREST
ELK
CAMERON
SULLIVAN
WYOMING
LACKAWANNA
LYCOMING
LUZERNE
MONROE
MERCER
VENANGO
CLARION
JEFFERSON
CLEARFIELD
CLINTON
CENTRE
UNION
COLUMBIA
CARBON
NORTHAMPTON
NORTHUMBERLAND
SNYDER
SCHUYLKILL
LEHIGH
MORRIS
UNION
HUNTERDON
SOMERSET
MIDDLESEX
MONMOUTH
ERIE
LORAIN
CUYAHOGA
GEAUGA
LAKE
ASHTABULA
TRUMBULL
PORTAGE
SUMMIT
MEDINA
HURON
MAHONING
LAWRENCE
BUTLER
ARMSTRONG
INDIANA
CAMBRIA
BLAIR
HUNTINGDON
MIFFLIN
JUNIATA
PERRY
DAUPHIN
LEBANON
BERKS
BUCKS
MONTGOMERY
MERCER
OCEAN
CRAWFORD
RICHLAND
ASHLAND
WAYNE
STARK
COLUMBIANA
HANCOCK
BEAVER
ALLEGHENY
CARROLL
CUMBERLAND
LANCASTER
CHESTER
DELAWARE
PHILADELPHIA
BURLINGTON
MARION
MORROW
HOLMES
TUSCARAWAS
WESTMORELAND
GLOUCESTER
CAMDEN
KNOX
COSHOCTON
HARRISON
JEFFERSON
BROOKE
WASHINGTON
BEDFORD
FULTON
FRANKLIN
ADAMS
YORK
SALEM
ATLANTIC
DELAWARE
LICKING
MUSKINGUM
GUERNSEY
BELMONT
OHIO
SOMERSET
FAYETTE
CECIL
NEW CASTLE
CUMBERLAND
CAPE MAY
FRANKLIN
NOBLE
MONROE
MARSHALL
GREENE
GARRETT
ALLEGANY
WASHINGTON
FREDERICK
CARROLL
BALTIMORE
HARFORD
KENT
WETZEL
MONONGALIA
PRESTON
MORGAN
BERKELEY
JEFFERSON
HOWARD
PERRY
MORGAN
PLEASANTS
TYLER
MARION
MINERAL
HAMPSHIRE
MONTGOMERY
PICKAWAY
HOCKING
WASHINGTON
DODDRIDGE
HARRISON
TAYLOR
TUCKER
GRANT
HARDY
LOUDOUN
ANNE ARUNDEL
KENT
SUSSEX
ROSS
VINTON
ATHENS
WOOD
RITCHIE
BARBOUR
SHENANDOAH
WARREN
CLARKE
FAUQUIER
ARLINGTON
FAIRFAX
PRINCE GEORGES
CALVERT
CAROLINE
DORCHESTER
PIKE
JACKSON
MEIGS
WIRT
GILMER
LEWIS
UPSHUR
RANDOLPH
PAGE
RAPPAHANNOCK
PRINCE WILLIAM
CHARLES
WICOMICO
WORCESTER
CALHOUN
ROANE
BRAXTON
PENDLETON
MADISON
CULPEPER
STAFFORD
SOMERSET
SCIOTO
GALLIA
MASON
JACKSON
ROCKINGHAM
ORANGE
ST. MARYS
LEWIS
GREENUP
LAWRENCE
PUTNAM
CLAY
WEBSTER
POCAHONTAS
HIGHLAND
SPOTSYLVANIA
CAROLINE
ACCOMACK
NORTHAMPTON
KANAWHA
CABELL
NICHOLAS
AUGUSTA
ALBEMARLE
LOUISA
BARTER
WAYNE
LINCOLN
BATH
FLUVANNA
GOOCHLAND
HANOVER
HENRICO
ROWAN
ELLIOTT
LAWRENCE
BOONE
FAYETTE
GREENBRIER
ROCKBRIDGE
NELSON
BUCKINGHAM
CUMBERLAND
POWHATAN
CHESTERFIELD
MATHEWS
MORGAN
JOHNSON
MARTIN
LOGAN
RALEIGH
SUMMERS
ALLEGHANY
AMHERST
APPOMATTOX
AMELIA
PRINCE GEORGE
SURRY
ELIZABETH CITY
WOLFE
MAGOFFIN
FLOYD
MINGO
WYOMING
MONROE
BOTETOURT
CRAIG
BEDFORD
PRINCE EDWARD
NOTTOWAY
DINWIDDIE
BREATHITT
PIKE
MCDOWELL
MERCER
GILES
ROANOKE
CAMPBELL
CHARLOTTE
LUNENBURG
SUSSEX
ISLE OF WIGHT
NANSEMOND
NORFOLK
KNOTT
PERRY
BUCHANAN
TAZEWELL
BLAND
MONTGOMERY
PULASKI
FLOYD
FRANKLIN
PITTSYLVANIA
HALIFAX
MECKLENBURG
BRUNSWICK
GREENSVILLE
SOUTHAMPTON
LESLIE
LETCHER
DICKENSON
RUSSELL
WISE
SMYTH
WYTHE
CARROLL
PATRICK
HENRY
HARLAN
LEE
SCOTT
WASHINGTON
GRAYSON
BELL
NORTHAMPTON
HERTFORD
GATES
CAMDEN
CURRITUCK
SULLIVAN
HANCOCK
HAWKINS
WASHINGTON
JOHNSON
ASHE
ALLEGHANY
SURRY
STOKES
ROCKINGHAM
CASWELL
PERSON
GRANVILLE
VANCE
WARREN
HALIFAX
BERTIE
GRAINGER
GREENE
CARTER
WATAUGA
WILKES
YADKIN
FORSYTH
GUILFORD
ALAMANCE
ORANGE
DURHAM
FRANKLIN
NASH
EDGECOMBE
MARTIN
WASHINGTON
TYRRELL
DARE
JEFFERSON
UNICOI
MITCHELL
AVERY
CALDWELL
ALEXANDER
IREDELL
DAVIE
DAVIDSON
RANDOLPH
CHATHAM
WAKE
WILSON
PITT
BEAUFORT
HYDE
COCKE
MADISON
YANCEY
BURKE
CATAWBA
ROWAN
LEE
JOHNSTON
WAYNE
GREENE
LENOIR
CRAVEN
PAMLICO
SEVIER
BUNCOMBE
MCDOWELL
LINCOLN
CABARRUS
MOORE
HARNETT
JONES
HAYWOOD
RUTHERFORD
CLEVELAND
GASTON
MECKLENBURG
STANLY
MONTGOMERY
CUMBERLAND
SAMPSON
DUPLIN
ONSLOW
CARTERET
SWAIN
JACKSON
HENDERSON
POLK
ANSON
RICHMOND
HOKE
GRAHAM
MACON
TRANSYLVANIA
UNION
SCOTLAND
ROBESON
BLADEN
PENDER
CLAY
CHEROKEE
YORK
SPARTANBURG
LANCASTER
CHESTERFIELD
MARLBORO
TOWNS
RABUN
PICKENS
GREENVILLE
UNION
CHESTER
DILLON
COLUMBUS
NEW HANOVER
OCONEE
ANDERSON
LAURENS
FAIRFIELD
KERSHAW
DARLINGTON
BRUNSWICK
WHITE
HABERSHAM
STEPHENS
FRANKLIN
HART
ABBEVILLE
GREENWOOD
NEWBERRY
LEE
FLORENCE
MARION
HORRY
HALL
BANKS
MADISON
ELBERT
MCCORMICK
SALUDA
RICHLAND
SUMTER
JACKSON
CLARKE
OGLETHORPE
LEXINGTON
CALHOUN
CLARENDON
WILLIAMSBURG
GEORGETOWN
WALTON
OCONEE
WILKES
LINCOLN
EDGEFIELD
AIKEN
ORANGEBURG
BERKELEY
NEWTON
MORGAN
GREENE
COLUMBIA
RICHMOND
WARREN
MCDUFFIE
BARNWELL
BAMBERG
DORCHESTER
BUTTS
JASPER
PUTNAM
HANCOCK
GLASCOCK
BURKE
ALLENDALE
COLLETON
CHARLESTON
JONES
BALDWIN
WASHINGTON
JEFFERSON
JENKINS
SCREVEN
HAMPTON
JASPER
BIBB
WILKINSON
JOHNSON
EMANUEL
BULLOCH
EFFINGHAM
BEAUFORT
CRAWFORD
TWIGGS
HOUSTON
BLECKLEY
LAURENS
TREUTLEN
CANDLER
EVANS
BRYAN
CHATHAM
MACON
DOOLY
PULASKI
DODGE
MONTGOMERY
TOOMBS
TATTNALL

To
Martha and Margaret,
Carol and Karen

# APPALACHIA
# A REGIONAL GEOGRAPHY

## Land, People, and Development

Karl B. Raitz and
Richard Ulack

with Thomas R. Leinbach

Westview Press / Boulder and London

Unless otherwise credited, all photos appearing in this book were taken by Karl B. Raitz.



Published in 1984 in the United States of America by Westview Press, Inc., 5500 Central Avenue, Boulder, Colorado 80301; Frederick A. Praeger, Publisher

Library of Congress Cataloging in Publication Data
Raitz, Karl B.
Appalachia, a regional geography.
Bibliography: p.
Includes index.
1. Appalachian Region—Historical geography.
2. Appalachian Region—Economic conditions. 3. Appalachian Region—Social conditions. 4. Appalachian Region—Description and travel. I. Ulack, Richard, 1942- . II. Leinbach, Thomas R., 1941-
III. Title.
F106.R22 1984 917.4 83-16965
ISBN 0-86531-075-0

Printed and bound in the United States of America

10 9 8 7 6 5 4 3 2 1

# CONTENTS

*List of Tables and Figures* . . . . . xi
*List of Photographs* . . . . . xv
*Acknowledgments* . . . . . xvii

Introduction . . . . . 1

**PART 1**
**THE BOUNDARIES OF APPALACHIA**

1 **Regional Definitions** . . . . . 9

Defining Appalachia as a Region . . . . . 9
A New Appalachian Region . . . . . 29
Notes . . . . . 33

**PART 2**
**REGIONAL DIVERSITY AND**
**THE BASES FOR DEVELOPMENT**

2 **Appalachia's Physical Geography** . . . . . 39

Geology and Physiography . . . . . 40
Climates . . . . . 51
Water: Quantity and Quality . . . . . 57
Soil Patterns . . . . . 63
Natural and Modified Vegetation . . . . . 67
Mineral Resources . . . . . 73
Conclusion . . . . . 84
Notes . . . . . 84

3 **Coming to the Land** . . . . . 87

Indian Tradition . . . . . 87
European Encroachment . . . . . 90

Land: Survey, Speculation, and Sale ........................ 92
Routeways and Settlement Expansion........................ 94
The Evolving Economy ........................ 100
Notes........................ 109

4 **Settlement and Culture Patterns** ........................ 113

German and Scotch-Irish Cultural Traditions .............. 117
Building and Farming Techniques........................ 122
Nineteenth- and Twentieth-Century Migrants .............. 125
Blacks in Appalachia........................ 129
Religious Patterns........................ 130
Regionalization of Speech Habits ........................ 136
Folk-Music Traditions........................ 138
Distilling, Bootlegging, and Prohibition........................ 140
Implications of a Complex Cultural Heritage............... 143
Notes........................ 146

5 **Population Growth and Characteristics**........................ 151

Population Distribution and Density ........................ 151
Population Change........................ 155
Socioeconomic Characteristics........................ 172
Racial Composition........................ 178
Summary ........................ 184
Notes........................ 184

6 **Resources: Renewable and Nonrenewable**........................ 189

Renewable Resources—The Forests........................ 190
Renewable Resources—Agricultural Production............. 199
Renewable Resources—Water ........................ 211
Nonrenewable Resources—Coal ........................ 217
Summary ........................ 229
Notes........................ 230

**PART 3**
**ISSUES, PROBLEMS, AND SOLUTIONS**

7 **Recreation and Development**........................ 235

A Recreational Tradition ........................ 236
Contemporary Recreational Development ........................ 244
The Government as Recreational Developer................ 246
Private Recreational Development: Form and Process ...... 251
Implications of Recreational Development ................ 262
Notes........................ 267

**8 Manufacturing** . . . . . 271

The Spatial Distribution of Manufacturing . . . . . 273
Change in Manufacturing: 1958–1977 . . . . . 277
The Structure of Manufacturing . . . . . 281
Selected Industries . . . . . 285
Summary . . . . . 298
Notes . . . . . 299

**9 Transport Patterns, Progress, and Issues** . . . . . 303
***Thomas R. Leinbach***

Highways in Regional Development . . . . . 304
The Rail System . . . . . 309
Inland Waterways in Appalachia . . . . . 320
The Role of Air Service in the Region . . . . . 325
Additional Concerns . . . . . 329
Notes . . . . . 331

**10 Regional Development: Past, Present, and Future** . . . . . 335

Explanations for Appalachian Poverty . . . . . 336
Evaluation of Development Programs . . . . . 346
Whither the Region? . . . . . 352
Notes . . . . . 355

*Bibliography* . . . . . 359
*Index* . . . . . 375
*Other Titles of Interest from Westview Press* . . . . . 397
*About the Book and Authors* . . . . . 398

# TABLES AND FIGURES

## Tables


1.1 The Appalachian Region: Number of Counties, Area, and Population by State, 1980 .................. 32

2.1 Average Flow for Streams Leaving the Appalachian Region .................. 58

4.1 Selected Dates in Scotch-Irish Expansion .................. 117
4.2 Whiskey Distilled in 1810 .................. 142
4.3 Moonshine Still Seizures: 1972 .................. 143

5.1 Population, Area, and Density of Population by State and Urban-Rural Residence, 1980 .................. 152
5.2 Population by SMSA: Central (or largest) County and Peripheral Counties, 1980 .................. 154
5.3 Population, Area, and Density of Population by Physiographic Province, 1980 .................. 156
5.4 Population Change in Appalachia, 1950–1980 .................. 158
5.5 Net Migration, 1950–1970 .................. 166
5.6 Leading State and State Economic Area Origins and Destinations of Migrants for North Carolina SEA 1, 1965–1970 .................. 168
5.7 Leading State and State Economic Area Origins and Destinations of Migrants for Kentucky SEA 9, 1965–1970 .................. 169
5.8 Leading State and State Economic Area Origins and Destinations of Migrants for Pennsylvania SEA 6, 1965–1970 .................. 170
5.9 Appalachian Counties with at Least 1 Percent American Indian Population, 1980 .................. 183
5.10 Appalachian Counties with People of Spanish Origin by Population Rank, 1980 .................. 183

6.1 Percentage Change in Pulpwood Production: 1963 to 1979 .................. 197

6.2 Farm Size, Farm Size Change, Value of Land, and Value of Products Sold by Physiographic Province..... 200
6.3 Selected Agricultural Characteristics: 1978............... 204
6.4 Regional Electric Generating Capacity: 1980............. 214
6.5 Change in Bituminous Coal Production: 1960 to 1978........................................ 220
6.6 Bituminous Coal Producing Counties Experiencing Rapid Production Growth: 1960 to 1978.............. 223
6.7 Bituminous Coal Production by Type of Mine in 1978 .............................................. 226

7.1 Recreational Visits to Selected Appalachian National Parks and Recreation Areas................. 236
7.2 Visits to Tennessee Valley Authority Reservoirs and Associated Sites ................................ 250
7.3 Changes in the Number of Hotels and Motels and Number of Employees in Selected Appalachian Recreational Areas.................................. 256
7.4 Changes in Seasonal Housing........................... 258
7.5 Changes in the Value of Farmland and Buildings in Selected Appalachian Recreational Areas.............. 264

8.1 Manufacturing Employment, Manufacturing Establishments, and Value Added by Manufacture for Leading SMSAs, 1977 ............... 272
8.2 Percentage Change in Manufacturing Employment, Manufacturing Establishments, and Value Added by Manufacture by State and Urban-Rural Areas, 1958–1977....................... 279
8.3 Manufacturing Establishments by SIC Code, 1977........ 282
8.4 Percentage Change in Total Manufacturing Establishments by SIC Code for Appalachia and the United States, 1958–1977 ................... 285
8.5 Employment, Establishments, and Value Added in Primary Metal Industries (SIC Code 33) for Ten Leading SMSAs, 1977.............................. 289
8.6 Average Hourly Earnings of Production Workers in Manufacturing Industries for Selected States and SMSAs, 1950 and 1980 ......................... 292

9.1 Appalachian Development Highway System and Access Roads.......................................... 308
9.2 Rail Mileage Within the Appalachian Region, by State.................................................. 310
9.3 Major Rail Firm Mileage Operated, by State ............ 311
9.4 Total Volume of Shipments Originated or Terminated by the Appalachian Region's Rail System............. 315

9.5 Appalachian Waterways: 1972 Total Annual Traffic and Principal Commodities .......... 324
9.6 Tons of Coal Moved by Transport Mode: 1974 .......... 329

10.1 Land and Mineral Rights Ownership in Selected Counties .......... 344

**Figures**

General Map .......... 4

1.1 Physiographic Regions of Appalachia .......... 15
1.2 Regionalizations by Geographers .......... 17
1.3 The Campbell and Ford Regions .......... 20
1.4 The A.R.C. Region and Subregions .......... 25
1.5 The Cognitive Appalachian Region .......... 27
1.6 Appalachia as Perceived by Insiders, Cognitive Outsiders, and Residential Outsiders .......... 28
1.7 The Raitz-Ulack Region .......... 31

2.1 Physiographic Divisions of Appalachia .......... 44
2.2 Average Annual Temperature .......... 52
2.3 Growing Season .......... 54
2.4 Average Annual Precipitation .......... 55
2.5 Rivers .......... 61
2.6 Soil Groups .......... 64
2.7 Appalachian Forest Regions .......... 69
2.8 Selected Mineralized Areas .......... 76
2.9 Mineral Resources of the Appalachian Region .......... 78
2.10 Generalized Cross Sections of Pennsylvania Anthracite .......... 80

3.1 Native Tribal Territories of Appalachia and Adjoining Lands About 1700 .......... 88
3.2 Roads and Routeways .......... 96
3.3 Expansion of Settlement into Appalachia: 1790 to 1820 .......... 99
3.4 Urban Growth: Selected Appalachian Cities, 1800 to 1900 .......... 102

4.1 Diffusion of Folk Cultures .......... 114
4.2 Generalized Routes of Scotch-Irish Expansion, 1720–1770 .......... 118
4.3 Mid-Atlantic–Upland South Culture Area, ca. 1835 .......... 120
4.4 Appalachian Religious Groups .......... 131
4.5 Speech Areas of the Eastern States .......... 137
4.6 Shape Note Harmony Singing .......... 139
4.7 Music Source Areas .......... 141
4.8 Counties Prohibiting Sale of Distilled Spirits, 1980 .......... 144

5.1 Appalachian SMSAs as of December, 1977 .............. 153
5.2 Population Change, 1960–1970 .......................... 161
5.3 Population Change, 1970–1980 .......................... 162
5.4 Per Capita Money Income, 1977.......................... 174
5.5 Percentage Increase in Per Capita Money
Income, 1969–1977.................................. 175
5.6 Median Education Levels for Persons 25 Years
or Older, 1970..................................... 177
5.7 Percentage Black, 1980.................................. 179
5.8 Percentage Black Population Change, 1970–1980 ......... 181

6.1 Lumber and Wood Processing Establishments, 1977...... 193
6.2 Softwood and Hardwood Cut for Pulp, 1979 ............ 196
6.3 Commercial Farms as a Proportion
of All Farms, 1978................................. 209
6.4 Percentage Change in Market Value
of Agricultural Products Sold, 1959–1978 ............. 212
6.5 Bituminous and Anthracite Coal Production,
1978 ............................................... 218
6.6 Bituminous and Anthracite Coal Mining
Employees, 1978 .................................... 221

7.1 Traditional Appalachian Resort Areas and
Visitor Sheds, ca. 1810 to 1860 ...................... 237
7.2 Appalachia's Thermal Springs ........................ 240

8.1 Location Quotients: Total Manufacturing
Employment, 1977 ................................. 274
8.2 Value Added Per Manufacturing Employee, 1977......... 276
8.3 Percentage Change in Total Manufacturing
Employment, 1958–1977............................. 278
8.4 Textile Mill Product Establishments, 1977............... 291
8.5 Apparel and Other Textile Product
Establishments, 1977 ............................... 294
8.6 Furniture and Fixture Establishments, 1977 ............. 296
8.7 Stone, Clay, and Glass Products
Establishments, 1977 ............................... 297

9.1 Appalachian Roadway System.......................... 305
9.2 Appalachian Development Highway System ............. 306
9.3 Appalachian Rail Connections—CSX ................... 312
9.4 Appalachian Rail Connections—Norfolk &
Western, Southern .................................. 313
9.5 The Tennessee-Tombigbee Waterway Project............. 322
9.6 Small Hub and Nonhub Air Service
Communities in Appalachia ......................... 327

10.1 Isolation in Eastern Kentucky.......................... 338
10.2 Zones of Appalachia Lying Outside Metropolitan
Commuting Zones .................................. 340

# PHOTOGRAPHS

From "A New Map of the English Empire in America," 1719 .......... 10
"Carte De La Nouvelle France . . . ," 1732 .......... 12
"A Map of the British Empire in America . . . ," 1733 .......... 13
A hillside "farm" in Ashe County, North Carolina .......... 30

The western margin of the Ridge and Valley in Pendleton County, West Virginia .......... 47
The North Fork of the Shenandoah River, showing meander loops cut into the limestone of the Great Valley floor .......... 66
Structural marble is produced by numerous quarries like this one in the north Georgia marble belt of Cherokee and Pickens counties .......... 74
The Ducktown Desert of Polk County, Tennessee .......... 77
Anthracite mining in parallel valleys in Schuylkill County, Pennsylvania .......... 81
Bituminous-coal mining at Dunham in Letcher County, Kentucky .......... 83

The Golden Triangle at Pittsburgh .......... 97
The North Carolina mountain town of Saluda on the Saluda Trail .......... 97
Owego, New York, at the junction of the Owego River and the Susquehanna River .......... 104
Cumberland, Maryland, at the point where the Potomac River changes from northeast to southeast at the Maryland–West Virginia border .......... 106

An Amish farm just south of Menno, Pennsylvania, in the Kishacoquillas Valley .......... 116
An Augusta County, Virginia, farmstead showing Pennsylvanian modification of an English Georgian house .......... 125
Johnstown, Pennsylvania, in the Little Conemaugh River valley .......... 128

A church sign at the edge of Charleroi, Pennsylvania, on the Monongahela River . . . 132
A church sign in Pelzer, a textile-mill town . . . 134

Company-built houses in Pelzer, South Carolina . . . 156
Neon-Fleming, a coal town in Letcher County, Kentucky . . . 157
The business district of Greenville, South Carolina . . . 160
Staunton, a Great Valley town in Augusta County, Virginia . . . 164

Black-walnut logs harvested from the North Carolina Blue Ridge . . . 194
A feeder cattle farm at Hightown, central to Highland County in the Ridge and Valley of Virginia . . . 203
Marshall County, Alabama, a major poultry-producing area . . . 206
Burley-tobacco harvest in Yancey County, North Carolina . . . 208
Norris Dam on the Clinch River in Campbell County, east Tennessee . . . 215
The Keystone Electric Energy Plant in Indiana County, Pennsylvania . . . 216
The Pevler Mine preparation plant in Martin County, Kentucky . . . 225
Bituminous-coal strip mining in Indiana County, Pennsylvania . . . 225

The Bedford Springs Hotel, an early spa in Bedford, Pennsylvania . . . 241
The relict Hotel Armenia in Haines Falls, New York . . . 244
A crossroads grocery store in Towns County, Georgia . . . 245
Tourists provide a ready market for North Carolina fruit growers . . . 248
Local efforts to curtail land transfers in response to rapid recreational development . . . 266

Rolling mills encroach on the business district in Johnstown, Pennsylvania . . . 288
A complex of steel mills near Duquesne, Pennsylvania . . . 289

Pineville, Kentucky, at the point where the Cumberland River cuts a water gap through Pine Mountain . . . 320
The New River, which flows north and west from western North Carolina across the Ridge and Valley into West Virginia . . . 321

# ACKNOWLEDGMENTS

If we, as outsiders to the region, have been able in this brief volume to communicate some understanding of the wondrously complex physical and cultural character of Appalachia, it is largely to the credit of a group of people whose published work, observations, or research help we were able to utilize.

Geographers whose writings on the region gave us clues to some of the key questions and sources include John Fraser Hart, E. Willard Miller, Ted Schmudde, Stanley Brunn, Ole Gade, Jeffrey Neff, Lisle Mitchell, Robert Mitchell, Milton Newton, Fred Kniffen, E. Estyn Evans, Edgar Bingham, and Wilbur Zelinsky. Henry Glassie's work on central and southern Appalachian folk culture was invaluable, as were the sociological and political interpretations made available to us by Thomas R. Ford, James S. Brown, Dwight Billings, Ron Eller, Helen Lewis, David Walls, and David Whisnant. Harry Caudill's writings have stimulated in us a concern for an understanding of the complexity that diverse historical processes have created across the region. Our special thanks go to Peirce Lewis, who encouraged our efforts with his words and letters and an intensive field experience in the folded hills of central Pennsylvania, and to John Stephenson, director of the Appalachian Center at the University of Kentucky, who has not only kindled our interest in the region but has helped guide our research with constructive criticism and direction. We also want to thank R. T. Hill of Concord College for organizing the first Appalachian Geography Studies Conference, which allowed geographers with interests in the region to exchange ideas in the spectacular setting of the New River country of West Virginia.

The Tennessee Valley Authority and the Appalachian Regional Commission have been very generous in locating rare and unpublished materials and records for us, and the Island Creek Coal Company supplied valuable information on mining technology. The library resources on Appalachia are voluminous but scattered and not always accessible. Anne Campbell, director of the University of Kentucky Appalachian Collection, lent her considerable skills to our efforts in locating numerous materials in the regional library system. At the

American Geographical Society Library Collection at the University of Wisconsin–Milwaukee, Christopher Baruth aided immeasurably in our search for historic regional maps.

Manuscript preparation was enthusiastically handled by Donna Vallance, Sylvia Henderson, and Cene Nash. Judy Hermann skillfully managed the preparation of the final draft. Special acknowledgments must go to Gyula Pauer, Cartographic Laboratory director at the University of Kentucky, for his map designs and cartographic work, and to Joseph Watts, whose editing, organizational, and cartographic skills were critical to final completion of this project. We also wish to thank Lynn Arts of Westview Press for her professionalism and Libby Barstow for her superb efforts in copy editing.

*Karl B. Raitz*
*Richard Ulack*

# INTRODUCTION

This book is about the human geography of one of America's most paradoxical and enigmatic regions: Appalachia. We have written the book for a variety of reasons, not least important of which is that there is no other volume on the geography of the region as a whole. In fact, only a few geographers have published work in any form on any part of Appalachia, and of them only a few are primarily concerned with adding to the general knowledge of Appalachia and its subregions. Our book draws on their limited work, but we have also used many other information and data sources in order to present, for the first time, a comprehensive geography of this extensive region. Because members of academic disciplines such as sociology, anthropology, and folklore have been more prolific and have contributed significantly to the considerable body of literature on Appalachia, these fields—as well as groups or individuals representing government, politics, the media, religion, music, and the arts—have contributed much to our perceptions of and knowledge about Appalachia and its people.

The ten chapters that follow have been written with two major themes in mind. First, we believe that the Appalachian region, however defined, is very diverse geographically. For example, the Upland Piedmont of western South Carolina is very different from Virginia's Blue Ridge or from central Pennsylvania's Ridge and Valley country. Cultural artifacts, dialects, diets, and music all vary throughout the region, although in a systematic way that appears to relate to historic streams of movement. There is significant spatial variation in the region's population, social, and economic characteristics, and broad differences exist between the urban and the more traditional rural areas. In the early chapters of the book we examine the reasons for this regional diversity via a review of the character of the subregions that constitute Appalachia.

The second theme that undergirds the book is that of development. The topic of Appalachian social and economic development has been pervasive in literature and planning practices. Early popular writers, missionaries, resource developers, academics, the media, government agencies, and politicians all directly or indirectly dealt with questions of the region's development. Our concern will be principally with the more recent social and economic development of the region, especially that which has occurred since the 1930s. We will explore and evaluate both formal, coordinated development efforts (e.g., the Tennessee Valley Authority and the Appalachian Regional Commission) and less formal and essentially uncoordinated efforts (e.g., recreational development and industrialization).

The tactic is simply to attempt first to understand something of the region's diversity and then to examine the question of recent development in the context of this diversity. One implication of ordering our book in this way is that applied development efforts and strategies, if they are to be effective, must address the important differences in what we might term "developmental ecology," or the total product of change rendered across the diverse areas these efforts are designed to affect.

The volume is divided into three major parts. Part 1, "The Boundaries of Appalachia," includes but one chapter, which examines the various geographical delimitations given the Appalachian region. These definitions come from several perspectives, including physical geography, history, sociology, and government. Appalachia's boundaries, much like those of the American Midwest, have been a matter of debate for quite some time. We do not attempt to select a "best" definition, as that seems a rather empty exercise. We do, however, provide a regional delimitation that aids in understanding the impact of the dual themes of diversity and development. Briefly, Appalachia as delimited in this book extends from the Hudson and Mohawk valleys in New York State south and west to northern Alabama. It includes all of West Virginia and portions of 12 other states.

Part 2, "Regional Diversity and the Bases for Development," includes five chapters all with the central purpose of providing the reader with an adequate description and evaluation of the land and its resources, people, and economy. Predominant throughout this section is the theme of diversity in Appalachia. Chapter 2 examines the physical geographic base: the geomorphology, drainage patterns, climate, soils, and flora of the region. Clearly, one cannot adequately appraise the development of the region until one has some background of the physical geography and its diversity. An understanding of the settlement and cultural history of the region is also central to our two major themes, and in Chapter 3 we investigate the sequence of settlement of Appalachia. Though we discuss pre-European populations and recognize the significance of their contributions to regional character, our major interest is with the period beginning about 1700. This is the time at which large numbers of English, Scotch-Irish, and German immigrants began arriving in the Atlantic seaports, especially Philadelphia and Baltimore, and began traveling west and then southwestward into and through Virginia's Great Valley. The cultural diversity and development of the region today is largely a function of the attributes of the descendants of these early European immigrants and to a lesser extent of later African immigrants.

The characteristics and diversity of Appalachia's cultural landscapes are the subject of Chapter 4, in which major national and racial groups and their cultural attributes are identified. Chapter 5 addresses the region's population geography. In it we identify socioeconomic subregions, note urban and rural population differences, and examine post–World War II migration trends, including the most recent phenomenon of return migration to central and southern Appalachia. Chapter 6 discusses the primary sector of the region's economy: forestry, mining, and agriculture. This is a key background chapter to subsequent discussions of development.

Part 3, "Issues, Problems, and Solutions," includes the final four chapters, each of which examines a major aspect of twentieth-century development in Appalachia. Chapter 7 reviews regional amenities and recreation. Both have long been recognized in the region, but with the advent of improved transportation the recreational potential of the region has begun to develop in a rather controversial manner. Debate centers on such issues as dramatic increases in tourism, seasonal housing and retirement living in the region, and the future direction and intensity of these developments. Chapter 8 examines the role that industries and industrialization have played in regional development efforts. In Chapter 9 we discuss the pattern of transportation development. This topic, important to regional development in any area, is perhaps of special significance because of the historic isolation of much of Appalachia's population and the generally rugged topography of the region. We use Chapter 10, the concluding chapter, to examine the more formal, coordinated development efforts and discuss the impacts of such federal agencies as the Tennessee Valley Authority and the Appalachian Regional Commission. The perception of Appalachia as an "internal colony" is addressed, as well as the implications of such a characterization. Finally, we examine new and future strategies and return to the question of development strategies and regional diversity.

The General Map shows the states to be examined in detail in this book, as well as immediately surrounding states. Cities on the map are the ones referred to in the book, unless another state is specified for a city of the same name.

Initially, we felt we were rather presumptuous to even discuss coauthoring such a book, let alone doing so. None of us are from the Appalachian region, and until recently none of us have had long-term commitments to either research in, or the teaching of, the region. However, our interest in the region began to build approximately four or five years ago. Since that time, one of us has designed and now regularly teaches a course on the "Geography of Appalachia"; another has offered graduate seminars on Appalachian topics; each of us is involved with Appalachian research projects. Specifically, our research questions examine regional perceptions, nonmetropolitan industrialization, return migration, and company towns. Additionally, we have traveled

**General Map.** Cities indicated are the ones referred to throughout book, unless otherwise specified. Boundary of Raitz-Ulack region (Figure 1.7) is superimposed on state and county boundaries.

extensively throughout most of the region over the past four years (indeed, many of the photographs included in this volume have resulted from our field trips).

We decided to undertake the writing of this monograph because we find the region intensely interesting and wish to better understand some of its enigmatic economic, cultural, and demographic complexities. And, frankly, we also believed that the region continues to receive short shrift in the geographical literature, especially in textbooks that cling to timeworn stereotypes of regional character and yet offer little in the way of contemporary perspective on regional problems. Perhaps more than any other area of the country, Appalachia provided the trial ground for the experimentation and technical evolution that fostered the modernization of U.S. industry. Mechanical processes and labor practices that were to form the basis for America's industrial growth were nurtured there, and the land and people continue to pay for the indulgences of an era of unfettered exploitation. It is hoped that as comparatively new students of the region we can be somewhat more objective about it than others who have lived there or have studied it for some time. Additionally, it seemed that our own varied specialties in geography (population-social, cultural-historical, and economic) would facilitate the completion of a project such as this. Finally, our location at the University of Kentucky (which is not in the Appalachian region) has afforded us opportunities not found elsewhere to study the region: We are located within a day's drive of most parts of the region; the university library includes an excellent Appalachian special collection; and the Appalachian Studies Center at the University of Kentucky is unquestionably the best of its kind anywhere—its resources, personnel, and visitors afford unparalleled opportunities for learning of the diverse aspects of the Appalachian milieu.

We view this book about land, people, and development in Appalachia as a monograph for anyone interested in the problems of, and prospects for, one of America's most important, least understood, and least appreciated regions.

# PART 1

# THE BOUNDARIES OF APPALACHIA

# CHAPTER 1

# REGIONAL DEFINITIONS

A basic task in regional geography is delimitation of appropriate boundaries. This essential step in regional study is difficult and often not fully acceptable to all critics. That areas can be carved into parcels as many different ways as there are persons to do the carving is not surprising, since there are an almost infinite number of criteria upon which to base a regionalization. The criteria used, of course, depend upon the purpose of the regionalization. Thus, the boundary lines we create might enclose areas that are somewhat homogeneous in terms of culture, physiography, climate, agriculture, or planning jurisdiction. In short, a region is a mental construct: an area that has been bounded in accordance with the goals of those delimiting the region. In a sense, regions do not have truth—they have only utility.

Some areas seem particularly enigmatic and therefore difficult to delimit. In the United States, for example, the Midwest and the South are two such regions. Joseph Brownell and Wilbur Zelinsky have discussed the difficulties in delimiting these two regions and have provided us with solutions. Zelinsky offered the "settlement landscape" (the aggregate pattern of all structures and assemblages of structures in which people house their activities) as a way to bound the South.[1] The solution given by Brownell for the Midwest was based upon responses from postmasters as to whether or not they considered themselves to be located in that rather nebulous region.[2] Clearly, the use of other criteria would have provided very differently bounded regions.

Another major American region for which different regionalizations exist is Appalachia. Our ultimate goal in this chapter is to delimit an Appalachian region that will best suit our purposes. There should be some natural basis for doing this, and in that context it seems appropriate that we begin by discussing the various regionalizations of Appalachia that have been introduced by others.

## DEFINING APPALACHIA AS A REGION

Many characteristics could be used to set Appalachia off as a separate region in America. The mere mention of the word *Appalachia* conjures

A segment of a 1719 map by John Senex, titled "A New Map of the English Empire in America," shows the "Apalitean Mountains" extending from north Florida to the Pennsylvania border. The "Large Savana" in western Carolina may be a section of the Great Valley that was reported to have been cleared by Indian burning. (From the American Geographical Society Collection of the University of Wisconsin–Milwaukee.)

up a variety of impressions depending upon one's perspective or purpose: Appalachia has been variously described as a region of mountains, coal mining, poverty, unique culture, tourism, welfarism, isolation, and subsistence agriculture. Any of these characteristics, or others, could be used to define the Appalachian region.

## Physical Geographic Definitions

Some of the earliest regionalizations of the United States were based upon one physical feature or a combination of several features. Natural vegetation, climatic patterns, and especially physiography have been used to delimit physical, or natural, regions. That Appalachia is often defined on the basis of its physiography is not at all surprising, given that it has a high relief relative to the areas surrounding it. Indeed, this high relief has been an effective barrier to historic migrations and according to many writers has been responsible in part for some of the region's less desirable characteristics like "isolation, poverty, and a retarded civilization."[3]

There is evidence to suggest that the Appalachians were first named in the sixteenth century by Spanish explorers (possibly even by Hernando De Soto, one of the first to explore the southern part of the Appalachians) who, so the theory goes, took the name from an Indian tribe (or village), the Apalachee of northern Florida. From that time until the Civil War, *Appalachia* was simply a term for the physiographic mountain system.[4] It was not until the latter part of the nineteenth century that Appalachia began to be viewed as a distinctive social, cultural, and economic region.

Physical geographers—more specifically, geomorphologists—have long been interested in the question of regionalization, and they have developed a number of physiographic regions for the United States. All such physical regionalizations include an Appalachian region. The first of these regional delimitations came from "the geographer Arnold Guyot in 1861 [who] is credited with establishing scientific and popular usage for the entire mountain range."[5] Guyot used the term *Allegheny* on his map (although his paper is entitled "On the Appalachian Mountain System") and discussed the east-to-west division of the system into parallel mountain ranges.[6] He also proposed dividing the system north to south into three subregions. The northern one included that area from the Gaspé Peninsula in southeastern Quebec Province (geologically, the Appalachian system extends from Newfoundland through Oklahoma to Texas) south to the Adirondack Mountains of New York; the middle section extended from the Mohawk River south to the New River; and the southern section included the area from the New River south to Alabama. The entire area covered a north-south distance of some 1,400 mi (2,252.6 km).

Another major effort to define the region was that of John Wesley Powell in 1895.[7] His was the first attempt to divide the entire United States into physiographic regions. Powell delimited three separate regions that, taken together, are generally considered today to be physiographic Appalachia. From east to west Powell named the three subregions the Piedmont Plateaus, the Appalachian Ranges, and the Allegheny Plateaus.

Part of a 1732 map by Zacharie Chatelain, titled "Carte De La Nouvelle France . . . ," shows the "Mont. d'Apalaches" in Northern Florida reaching north to "Mariland." River names and place-names north of Ste. Marie d'Apalaches on Florida's Gulf Coast may have been derived from local Indians. (From the American Geographical Society Collection of the University of Wisconsin–Milwaukee.)

Detail from "A Map of the British Empire in America . . . " by Henry Popple, 1733. The "Apalachean Mountains" are shown in western North Carolina and extend north into Pennsylvania. The Potomac River rises west of the mountains, and the "Hohio River" apparently originates just south of Lake Erie. (From the American Geographical Society Collection of the University of Wisconsin–Milwaukee.)

Together they encompassed an area that extends southwestward from the Hudson and Mohawk valleys in New York to northern Georgia and Alabama.

To geographers perhaps the best-known physical regionalization of the United States is that by Nevin Fenneman. Originally discussed in 1913 at the annual meeting of the Association of American Geographers, the culmination of Fenneman's regional work came with the publication of his *Physiography of Western United States* in 1931 and *Physiography of Eastern United States* in 1938.[8] Basically, Fenneman's geomorphic regions of the United States are defined by existing differences in topography and elevation as affected by the three control factors of structure, process, and stage. Simply stated this means "that given a certain geologic framework [type of rock], the topographic condition or expression of an area is largely determined by its geomorphic history."[9] Fenneman included eight major physiographic divisions in the United States; one of them he called the Appalachian Highlands. This region includes six provinces and extends from the Gulf Coastal Plain to the St. Lawrence River (including the Adirondacks and New England) and from the Atlantic Coastal Plain west to the Central Lowland (Figure 1.1). The Appalachian Highlands takes its name from its most prominent features, but it is by no means all high altitude. Indeed, subdivisions of the region differ greatly and each of these has considerable internal diversity as well (see Chapter 2). As Fenneman stated, "So far as this extensive region has unity, it is found in the results of repeated uplifts, involving for the most part greater altitude and stronger relief than that of adjacent regions."[10] Although Fenneman included six provinces within the Appalachian Highlands, our discussion of physiographic Appalachia will be limited to four of these: the Piedmont, the Blue Ridge, the Ridge and Valley, and the Appalachian Plateaus provinces. These provinces conform more closely with other regional delimitations of Appalachia, including our own (see the last section of this chapter).

Other physiographic, or natural, regions of the United States that have been introduced by geologists and physical geographers correspond very closely to the regional delimitation devised by Fenneman. Two such examples include the physiographic provinces of Atwood and the natural regions discussed by Hunt.[11]

Our review of twelve regional textbooks on North America and the United States published between 1934 and 1979 revealed how geographers have delimited the Appalachian region for heuristic purposes. Virtually all of the works include a map showing the physiographic regions of the United States, and in each case Appalachia appears as a distinct, major physiographic region. Generally, these physiographic regions closely follow the Fenneman definition and include the Piedmont, the Blue Ridge, the Ridge and Valley, and Plateau provinces as the major subregions.

There is much less agreement among these twelve regional texts as to the way in which the United States is carved into the geographic

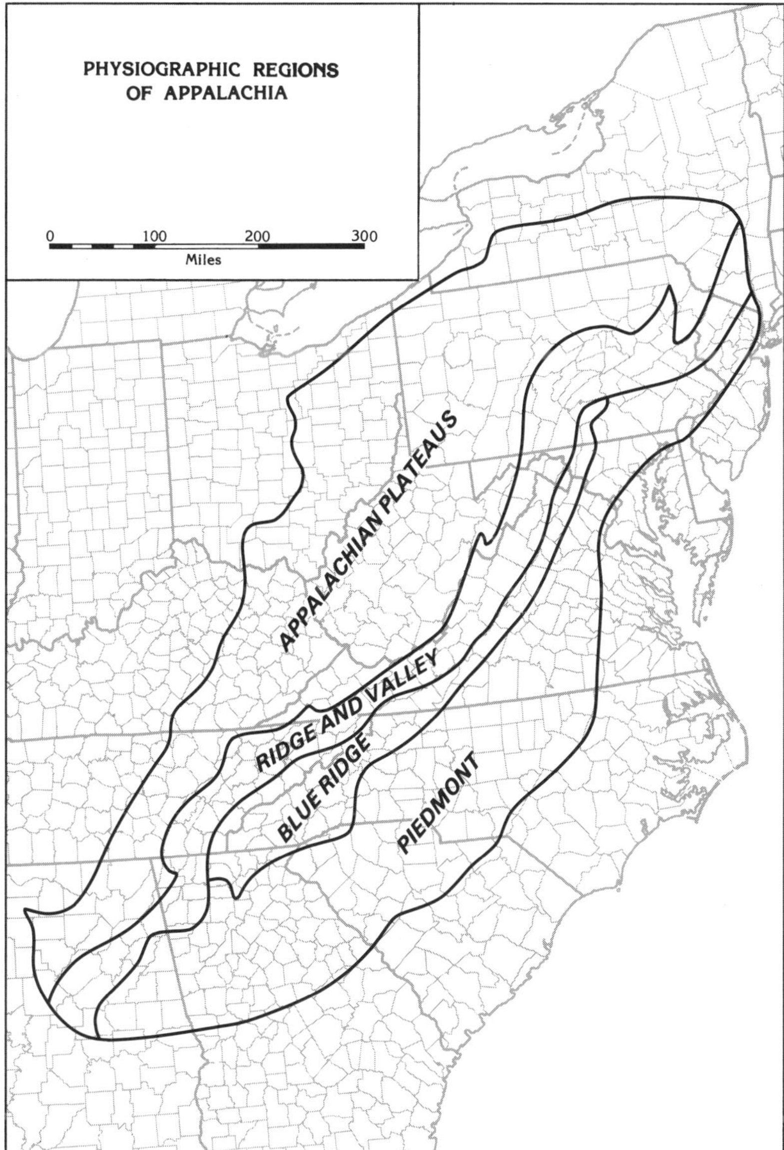


**Figure 1.1**
After Nevin M. Fenneman, *Physiography of Eastern United States* (New York: McGraw-Hill, 1938), Plates I, II, and III.

regions that are ultimately discussed. Only six of the twelve books included Appalachia as a major region for discussion and devoted at least one entire chapter to the region. Of these six, four texts apparently delimited Appalachia principally on the basis of physiographic criteria, although it is evident that other, nonphysical criteria were considered as well.[12] A fifth delimited Appalachia and the other regions of the United States based on "the total environment both physical and cultural."[13] It was not possible to determine Appalachian regional boundaries for the sixth text because no map of the regions discussed was included. The regionalization in this case was based on the author's selection of whatever criteria he felt best expressed the "personality" of a region. Thus "cultural origins, climate, space relationships, and livelihood are likely to be involved and are given coherence by the writer's perception that they compose an entity."[14]

A composite map comparison of four of the five different Appalachian regions delimited in the texts clearly demonstrates significant variations in boundary definition, even among the three that bound a physiographic region (Figure 1.2).[15] The region used for comparison here was the smallest area that was labeled "Appalachia." The boundary used by Birdsall and Florin excludes the Pittsburgh metropolitan area, which is included in most other regional delimitations of northern Appalachia. The eastern boundary of this regionalization generally lies farther west than any of the other three and clearly excluded the Piedmont area from Appalachia. The exclusion of both Pittsburgh and the Piedmont suggests that urban and topographic criteria were both important in determining the regional boundaries. The Piedmont, as we shall see in the next chapter, has generally lower average elevations than the three other physiographic provinces. Two of the other regionalizations shown also exclude most of the Piedmont Province.

The northern boundaries of the four Appalachian regions shown generally correspond and in all four cases lie south and west of New York's Hudson and Mohawk valleys. Even though physiographic Appalachia extends north of this area into Canada, geographic definitions of Appalachia that consider nonphysical criteria in drawing regional boundaries rarely extend north of this valley area. At the opposite end of the region the southern boundaries also show some degree of correspondence. Where they do not, the reason is much the same as for disagreement on the eastern boundary: the question of whether or not to include the Piedmont Province. The gently rolling nature of much of the Piedmont has allowed rather extensive farming; additionally, a number of Piedmont cities—Atlanta, Columbia (South Carolina), and Charlotte—are experiencing dynamic growth and change. According to some definitions, such socioeconomic characteristics differentiate this part of physiographic Appalachia from its other provinces.

Except that the Ozark-Ouachita Uplands of southern Missouri, northern Arkansas, and eastern Oklahoma are included within the boundary used by Griffin et al., the western boundaries of the Appalachian region

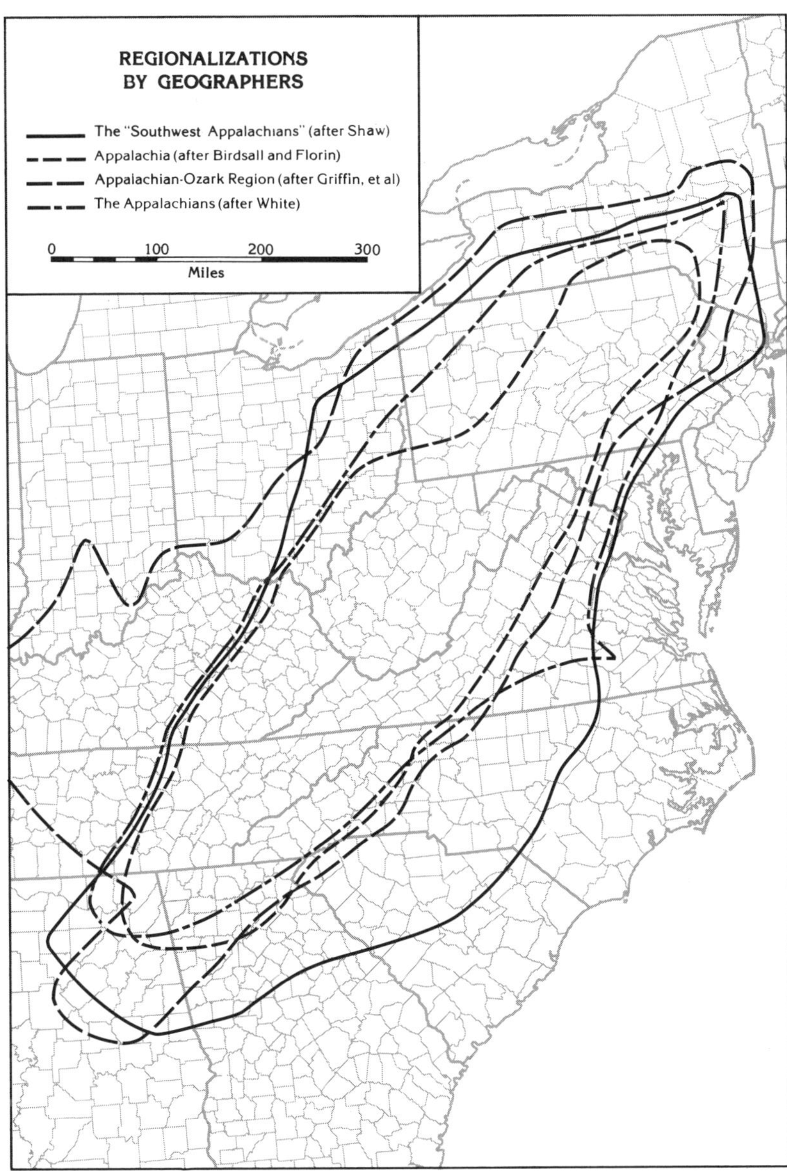
REGIONALIZATIONS
BY GEOGRAPHERS
The "Southwest Appalachians" (after Shaw)
Appalachia (after Birdsall and Florin)
Appalachian-Ozark Region (after Griffin, et al)
The Appalachians (after White)
0
100
200
300
Miles

**Figure 1.2**

correspond the most closely. In fact, three boundaries virtually overlap in Tennessee and Kentucky. These boundaries clearly are based on the sharp structural differences between physiographic provinces along the "knob" belt and Highland Rim that form the western edge of the Appalachian Plateaus Province.

The regionalization by Griffin, the "Appalachian-Ozark Region," maintains contiguity between the Appalachians and the Ozarks, and thus the western boundary differs from the other three regionalizations. The idea that the Ozarks and Ouachitas should be included as part of the Appalachian physiographic region has some merit, because structurally the two areas are very similar. The Ozark-Ouachita Uplands are also similar to the Appalachians in terms of various nonphysical criteria, and there is both precedent and justification for grouping the two areas together. As there seems to be little physiographic justification, however, for including the area between the Appalachians and the Ozarks within the regional boundaries, apparently the authors wanted to maintain contiguity. The physiographic area included, known as the Interior Low Plateaus, is a gently rolling upland with elevations generally less than 1,000 ft (304 m), considerably less than even the Upland Piedmont. It includes Nashville, Tennessee, and Louisville, Kentucky.

It is clear, then, that the Appalachian region can be delimited on the basis of physiographic (structural) characteristics: The mountains and associated geologic structures extend southwestward from Newfoundland in the north and disappear under the Gulf Coastal Plain to reappear in the Ouachita Mountains of Arkansas and as far west as the Marathon Basin region in western Texas. For sociocultural reasons, however, geographic definitions of the region have generally excluded that part of physiographic Appalachia north and east of the Hudson and Mohawk valleys. Generally, the Plateaus, the Ridge and Valley, the Blue Ridge, and at least a portion of the Piedmont (the upland section) are included within the region's boundaries by geographers. Although the Ozark-Ouachita area is sometimes included we will not consider this area to be a part of Appalachia.

## Sociocultural Regionalizations

Appalachia was not recognized as a distinct sociocultural region until the latter part of the nineteenth century. During the 1870s the region began to be popularized through what has been termed the local color movement.[16] Many romantic and colorful accounts of distinctive people and lifeways in the area appeared as novels and as popular-magazine articles. Authors used adjectives such as *isolated, quaint, independent, self-sufficient, violent, poor, simple,* and *strong* to describe the region's residents. It was a time when writers and other visitors from outside the region began to give Appalachia its distinctive reputation. Supplanting the color writers were preachers and teachers who came to Appalachia from elsewhere with their various missions intended to contribute to the health and education of the mountain people.

Gradually, more precise sociocultural definitions of the Appalachian region began to appear in the academic literature. In most cases the early studies that included regionalizations dealt only with the southern portion of physiographic Appalachia, the mountainous areas of West Virginia, Virginia, Kentucky, Tennessee, North Carolina, Georgia, and Alabama—the same areas that the local color writers had found quaint and interesting. According to David Walls, "The first person to give a precise geographic definition to the southern Appalachians as a cultural region was William G. Frost."[17] In 1894 Frost and a former student identified 194 counties in Maryland, West Virginia, Virginia, Kentucky, Tennessee, North Carolina, South Carolina, Georgia, and Alabama that were included in what was later called the Mountain Region of the South, or Appalachian America.[18]

Certainly the most widely recognized of the early sociocultural delimitations of the southern Appalachia region is that of John C. Campbell, which appeared in *The Southern Highlander and His Homeland* in 1921.[19] Campbell called the region the Southern Highlands and included 254 counties in the Blue Ridge, the Allegheny-Cumberland Plateaus, and the Greater Appalachian Valley of 9 states (Figure 1.3). Interestingly, Campbell used historic and political criteria, as well as physical, to arrive at his boundary:

> The lines by which the Southern Highlands are defined are not chosen arbitrarily. They correspond for the most part with boundaries of natural divisions; on the east with the face of the Blue Ridge, which defines the western margin of the Piedmont Plateau, on the south with the upper limits of the Coastal Plain, and on the west with the western escarpment of the Allegheny-Cumberland Plateau. The northern line [known also as the Mason and Dixon Line], in part purely political, was in its beginning a surveyor's line to determine a boundary dispute of long standing, growing out of the claims of [William] Penn and Lord Baltimore.[20]

The next major nongovernmental attempt to delimit boundaries for Appalachia was funded by the Ford Foundation. The results of this study, which reported on the population, economic, political, educational, religious, and folk characteristics of southern Appalachia, were published in 1962 under the editorship of sociologist Thomas R. Ford.[21] Titled *The Southern Appalachian Region: A Survey,* the study bounded a region that included 190 counties in 7 states (Figure 1.3). Unlike the Campbell region, the Ford region did not include any counties in Maryland or South Carolina. The eastern, western, and southern boundaries of the Ford region generally move inward from the region defined by Campbell by one row of counties. For both regions, of course, county boundary lines yield the precise regional definition. The Ford definition was unique in that it made "use of the new concept of state economic areas [SEA], developed jointly in 1950 by the Bureau of the Census and the U.S. Department of Agriculture"[22] (a state economic area is a grouping of counties whose social and economic characteristics are

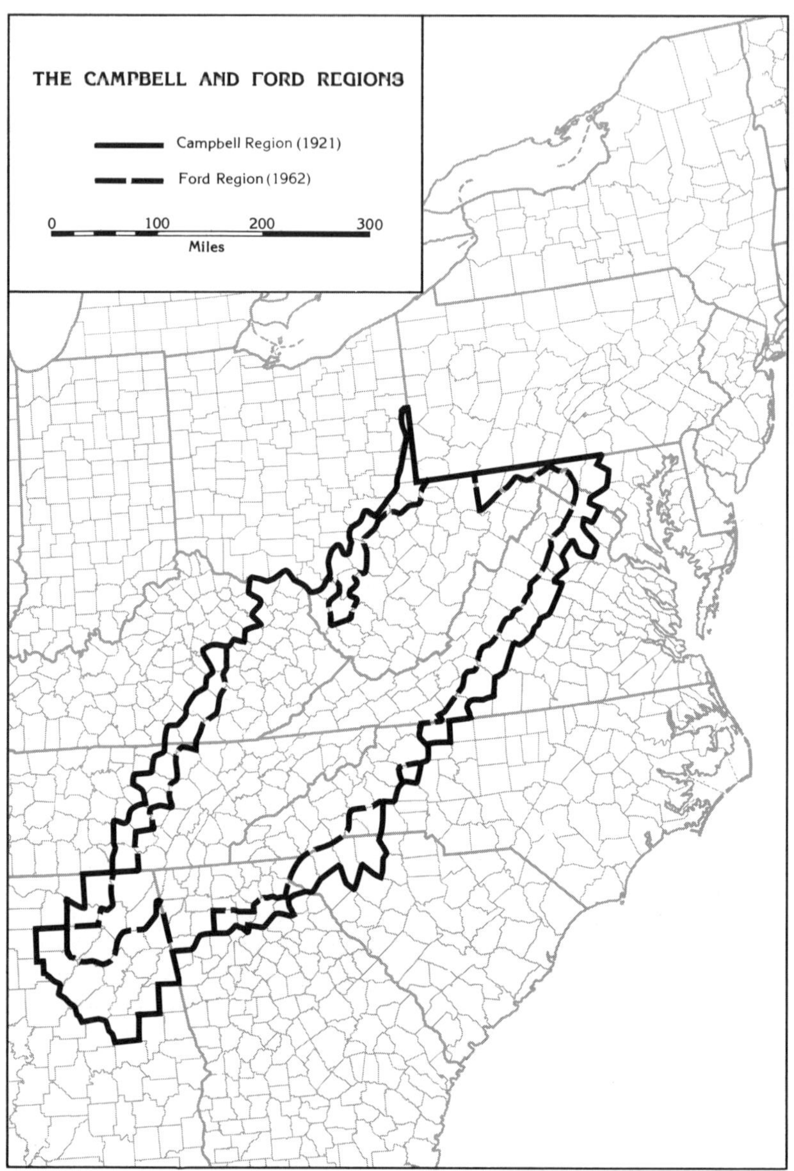
THE CAMPBELL AND FORD REGIONS
Campbell Region (1921)
Ford Region (1962)
0
100
200
300
Miles

**Figure 1.3**

similar). Some twenty-seven State Economic Areas were included in the Ford region; nineteen of these were rural-farm or rural-nonfarm SEAs, and eight were metropolitan areas. Thus, the Ford region includes the major cities of Huntington, Charleston, Roanoke, Asheville, Knoxville, and Chattanooga. Notably, it excludes Birmingham, Alabama, which is a part of the Appalachian region in virtually all other regional delimitations. The Appalachian region presented in the Ford study is the smallest of the various regional delimitations and according to one author, it "reduced the region to a heartland of Appalachia."[23] This "small" region is more than 600 mi (965.4 km) long and almost 250 mi (402.3 km) across at its widest point and encompasses an area of some 80,000 sq mi (207,200 sq km).

To our knowledge, no cultural geographers or other cultural regionalists have explicitly delimited an Appalachian culture region. Most cultural regionalists, however, do recognize a distinctive "upland" culture subregion, at least in the southeastern portion of the United States. Such a subregion is usually a part of the larger South and is given the name Upland South, Upper South, or sometimes Yeoman South, to distinguish it from the Lowland, or Plantation, South. One of the best-known cultural regionalizations of the United States is that by geographer Wilbur Zelinsky, which appeared in *The Cultural Geography of the United States.*[24] In his regional delimitation, Zelinsky identified a major subregion of the South that he called the Upland South, which "comprises the Southern Appalachians, the Upper Appalachian Piedmont, the Cumberland and other low interior plateaus and the Ozarks and Ouachitas. . . . Within the Upland South, the Ozark segment might legitimately be detached from the Appalachian."[25] Zelinsky's culture areas are defined as "a naively perceived segment of the time space continuum distinguished from others on the basis of genuine differences in cultural systems."[26] The two characteristics that differentiate this type of region from others are the great variety of ways in which it manifests itself on the landscape (e.g., house type, religion, dialect, dietary preferences) and a self-consciousness on the part of the participants.

Northern physiographic Appalachia (south and west of the Hudson and Mohawk valleys) is included in the two major culture regions that were called the Midland and the Middle West by Zelinsky. The pertinent subregions, for our purposes, are portions of the "Pennsylvania region" and the "New York region" in the former and the extreme eastern segment of the "Lower Middle West" in the latter. The modern cultural imprint of northern Appalachia, as well as southern Appalachia (the Upland South) is largely European in origin and can be traced to two "nuclear nodes along the Atlantic Seaboard: . . . the Midland, based in the Delaware and Susquehanna valleys; and Chesapeake Bay."[27] Philadelphia and Tidewater Virginia were thus the important origins for Appalachian settlers beginning about 1700.

A second cultural regionalization of the United States was that by Raymond Gastil, who acknowledged the valuable assistance of Zelinsky's work. Gastil's regions were defined "primarily by variations in the cultures of the peoples that dominated the first settlement . . . , and secondarily by variations in the cultures of the peoples that dominated later settlements, as well as cultural traits developed subsequently."[28] Basically, physiographic Appalachia south of the Hudson and Mohawk valleys is a part of three of Gastil's major U.S. cultural divisions: New England, Pennsylvania, and South. Unlike Zelinsky's regional delimitation, Gastil included New York State in cultural New England (rather than with Pennsylvania) and, interestingly, specifically labeled the southernmost "district" (the Southern Tier counties of New York) in this region "Appalachian." Two districts in Pennsylvania, called simply Western and Central Pennsylvania, also correspond to physiographic Appalachia. In the South, Gastil included a "Mountain" (Appalachian and Ozark areas) district and an "Upland" district. The latter includes most of the Piedmont and the interior plateaus. In short, the regions identified are similar to those posited by Zelinsky.

The cultural regionalizations of both Zelinsky and Gastil attempt to define areas through a consideration of the totality of cultural artifacts and behavior. Other regionalizations exist that attempt to define geographic regions in the United States on the basis of fewer cultural characteristics. An example of one such study is that by Kevin Phillips, who identified regions through an examination of historic voting-behavior patterns.[29] Though the precise boundaries are not shown, Phillips's Appalachia (also referred to as the Southern Mountains) corresponds rather closely to the Ford region. The Ozarks of Arkansas, eastern Oklahoma, and southern Missouri are also included. The Southern Highlands, according to Phillips, have long been politically and culturally different from the rest of the South. Characteristics that differentiate the Southern Highlands from neighboring areas include a predominantly Scotch-Irish pioneer settlement, relative isolation (and thus little sociocultural cross fertilization), and politics based on tradition. Political independence became apparent during the Civil War when "most of the highlands opposed secession, favored the Union and thereafter voted for the Republican Party. For all practical purposes, the mountain counties were devoid of slaves. . . ."[30] This is an important part of the "tradition" upon which contemporary voting behavior is based.

It is apparent that although most cultural regionalists do not recognize the Appalachia upland areas as a primary region, a distinct "upland" culture is recognized as an important subregion within the South and a portion of the Northeast. The contemporary cultural characteristics of these upland areas can be traced to the Scotch-Irish, English, and German immigrants who came to the uplands from Philadelphia and Tidewater Virginia. Other, more recent immigrant groups who have added to this cultural milieu, and thus to the region's diversity, include East Europeans who populated the Pennsylvania coal-mining and steel-manufacturing areas and blacks who populated the Piedmont areas of Georgia, Alabama, and the Carolinas.

## Governmental Regionalization

The first attempt at geographical delimitation of Appalachia by a federal agency (and the first recognition of the region as a social problem area) is found in a 1935 publication by the U.S. Department of Agriculture in which F. J. Marschner defined the region on the basis of its physiography, soil, and climatic characteristics.[31] The three major divisions identified were the Blue Ridge Mountains (the eastern division), the Valley and Ridge (the central division), and the Appalachian Plateau (the western division). This region excludes the states of northern Appalachia. In the northern part of the Marschner region, the 3 westernmost counties of Maryland are included; however, the counties of West Virginia that border the Ohio River are excluded. At the southern extreme, the region includes much of northern Alabama to the Mississippi border; both Tuscaloosa and Birmingham are included as a part of Appalachia. In total, Marschner's Appalachia includes 236 counties in 9 states that are divided among sixteen physiographic subregions.[32]

Another attempt on the part of the federal government to delimit an Appalachian region appeared in a 1940 publication by the Works Progress Administration that identified thirty-four "rural cultural regions" in the United States.[33] One of these regions was called Appalachia and included 154 counties in Kentucky, Ohio, West Virginia, Virginia, Tennessee, North Carolina, and Georgia. A second region, called Allegheny, consisted of 125 counties in West Virginia, Pennsylvania, Ohio, Maryland, and Virginia. The basis for regionalization in this study was "type of farming as a point of departure and placed on top of farming pattern such factors as population increase, standard of living, land value, tenancy, and race."[34]

The most recent attempt at regional delimitation of Appalachia by a government agency occurred in 1965 when Public Law 89-4 (the Appalachian Regional Development Act of 1965) established the Appalachian Regional Commission (ARC) and defined, in Section 403, the Appalachian region. As originally defined, the region consisted of 360 counties in 11 states from Pennsylvania to Alabama. Section 403 also included a provision whereby contiguous New York counties could participate, and in August 1965 the commission invited New York to join. In 1967, Public Law 90-103 amended the 1965 legislation and officially added 37 counties to the Appalachian Regional Commission's region. The inclusion of 20 counties in Mississippi, 14 counties in New York, Lamar and Pickens counties in Alabama, and Cannon County, Tennessee, brought the number of ARC-region states to 13 and the total number of counties to the present 397.

The boundaries of the original ARC region were based on both natural environmental and socioeconomic characteristics. The report of the original commission set up by President John F. Kennedy in 1963 stated that the region is "a mountain land boldly upthrust between the prosperous Eastern seaboard and the industrial Middle West. . . . Below its surface lie some of the Nation's richest mineral deposits including the seams which have provided almost two-thirds of the Nation's coal supply. The region receives an annual rainfall substantially above the national average. More than three-fifths of the land is forested. Its mountains offer some of the most beautiful landscapes in eastern America. . . ."[35] In addition to rough terrain and other aspects of the region's physical geography, the president's commission discussed several socio-economic measures that presented Appalachia as "a region apart." Characteristics of the region included low income, high unemployment, lack of urbanization, deficits in education, and deficits in living standards as indicated by such measures as retail sales, savings, housing conditions, and public assistance. One study that examined how counties included in the ARC region compared with the stated criteria for inclusion observed that the original region was well conceived.[36] However well conceived this original region, subsequent additions tend to be viewed as "political logrolling."[37] In short, "ARC's boundaries . . . increased in response to increasing political pressure as federal money for Appalachia became available."[38]

The Appalachian Regional Commission region was originally divided into four subregions because it was recognized that although the region was basically homogeneous (uniform), there were identifiable subregions, each with distinctive income, population, and employment characteristics and thus with distinctive development needs. These four subregions were called Northern, Central, Southern, and Highlands Appalachia. In 1974, the counties of the Highlands subregion were merged into the other subregions, so that the ARC presently recognizes three subregions (Figure 1.4).[39] The Northern subregion includes 143 counties and is described as an old industrial-based economy undergoing modernization. Central Appalachia is characterized as the poorest of the subregions, with coal as its primary resource. It includes 85 counties in eastern Kentucky, southern West Virginia, extreme western Virginia, and a portion of northeastern Tennessee. The 169 counties of the Southern Appalachian subregion have traditionally been agrarian based but are in transition to an urban and industrial economy. In this way the ARC recognized diversity in the region it defined, with the idea that such recognition would facilitate socioeconomic development. Even so, one critic observed, "ARC Appalachia is too large and too heterogeneous physically, economically, and politically to be dealt with effectively, even if sufficient money were available."[40]

The passage of the Appalachian Regional Development Act of 1965 came about after the recognition of Appalachia as a region socio-economically apart from most of the rest of America. *Appalachia,* the 1964 report by the President's Appalachian Regional Commission (chaired by Franklin D. Roosevelt, Jr.), stated "rural Appalachia lags behind rural America; urban Appalachia lags behind urban America; and metropolitan Appalachia lags behind metropolitan America."[41] As we have seen, the history of the federal government's awareness of Appalachia

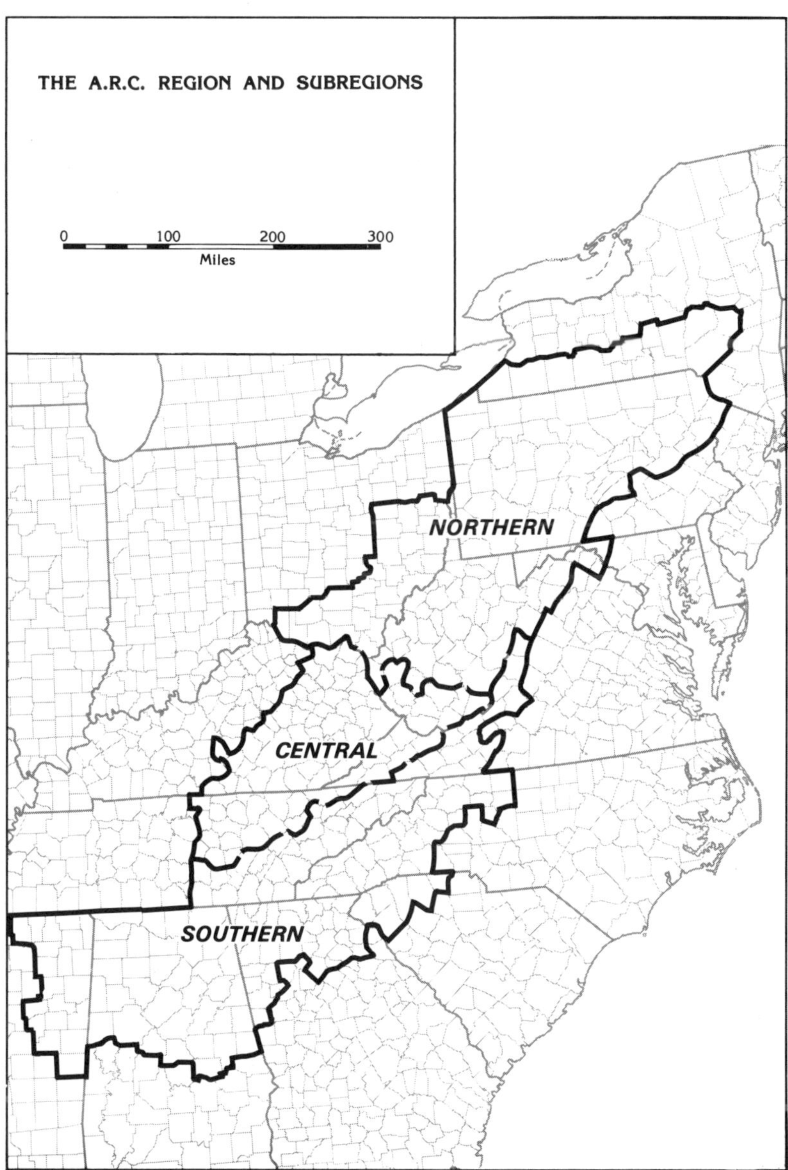
THE A.R.C. REGION AND SUBREGIONS
0
100
200
300
Miles
NORTHERN
CENTRAL
SOUTHERN

**Figure 1.4**

(or some portion of it) as a social problem area can be traced to the 1930s and to programs instituted by agencies such as the U.S. Department of Agriculture, the Works Progress Administration, and the Tennessee Valley Authority. However, it was not until the 1960s and the establishment of the Appalachian Regional Commission by President John F. Kennedy that the federal government developed a program that was focused on the entire region. The overall goal was region-wide development, so that the social and economic gap between Appalachia and the rest of America might be narrowed. The extent to which the commission has realized this goal is examined in Chapter 10. Certainly, however, we can state that one lasting impact of the Appalachian Regional Commission has been to bring about a general public awareness of the Appalachia region that did not exist before the 1960s. Although the commission appears to be in its final days as a government agency because of the Reagan administration's economic cutbacks, the region it has defined most likely will remain *the* Appalachian regional delimitation to the majority of the public who are cognizant that an Appalachian region exists.

## Cognitive Appalachia

Yet another way in which Appalachia has been delimited is through studies in regional perception. Utilizing responses from college students, a study by Kevin Cox and Georgia Zannaras developed a technique that derived perceptions of states from a ranking of state similarities.[42] Analysis of the results revealed that the student sample identified an Appalachian region centered on West Virginia, Kentucky, Tennessee, and Virginia.

In a comprehensive search for America's vernacular regions, another study by Ruth Hale found very limited recognition of the term "Appalachia" among the respondents (in this case individuals such as the county agent, postmaster, and newspaper editor were the respondents). In only two southeastern Ohio counties, Monroe and Noble, did a significant proportion of the sample state that Appalachia was the name for the region in which they lived.[43] The vernacular names given for the region in many other counties in Appalachia were primarily physiographic, such as Mountain, Piedmont, Shenandoah Valley, and Endless Mountains.

Based upon our own analysis of nearly 2,400 student respondents from sixty-three colleges and universities in and adjacent to physiographic Appalachia, we were able to construct an isopleth map that shows the percentage of students who agreed that a certain area was included in the Appalachian region (Figure 1.5). The overall regional pattern has the typical linear orientation along a northeast-southwest axis. The 10 percent cognitive-agreement line was arbitrarily selected as the minimum threshold for establishing a regional boundary. This means, of course, that at least 240 students included the area within this line as a part of the Appalachian region as they perceived it. The 80 percent agreement

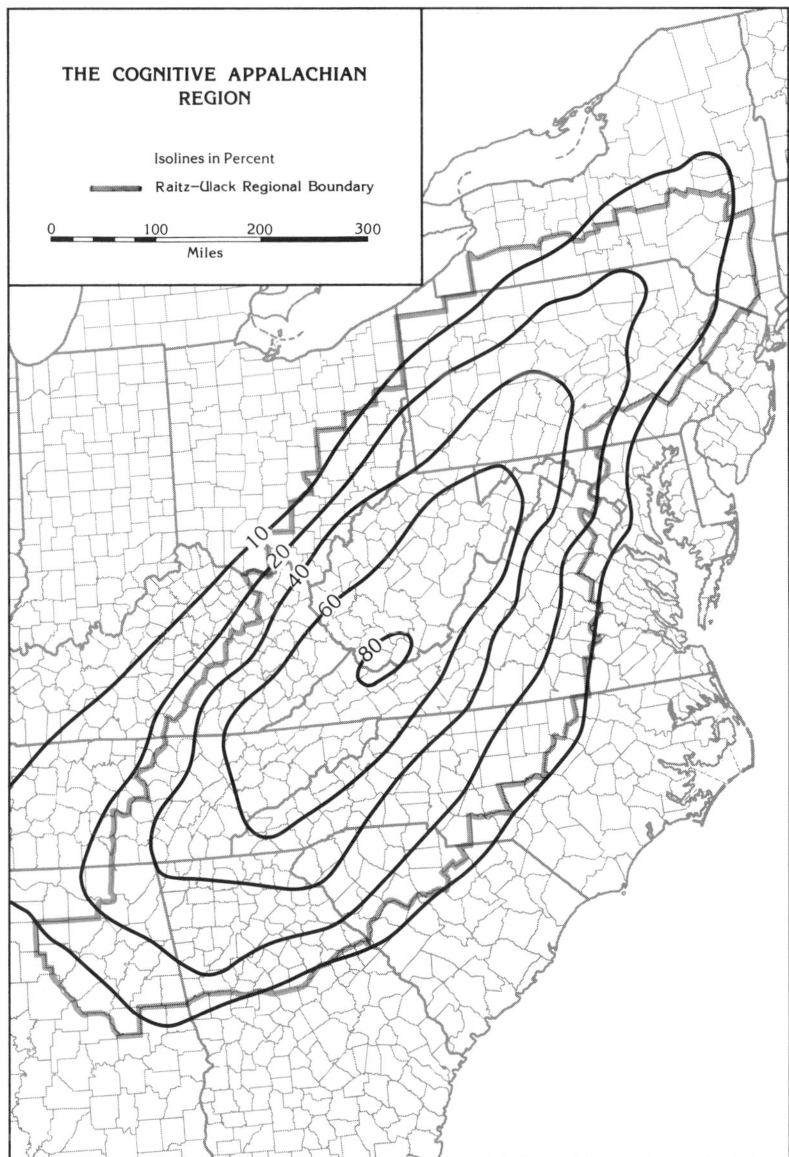


**Figure 1.5**
From Richard Ulack and Karl Raitz, "Appalachia: A Comparison of the Cognitive and Appalachian Regional Commission Regions." Reprinted with permission from the *Southeastern Geographer* 21, no. 1 (May 1981), p. 45.

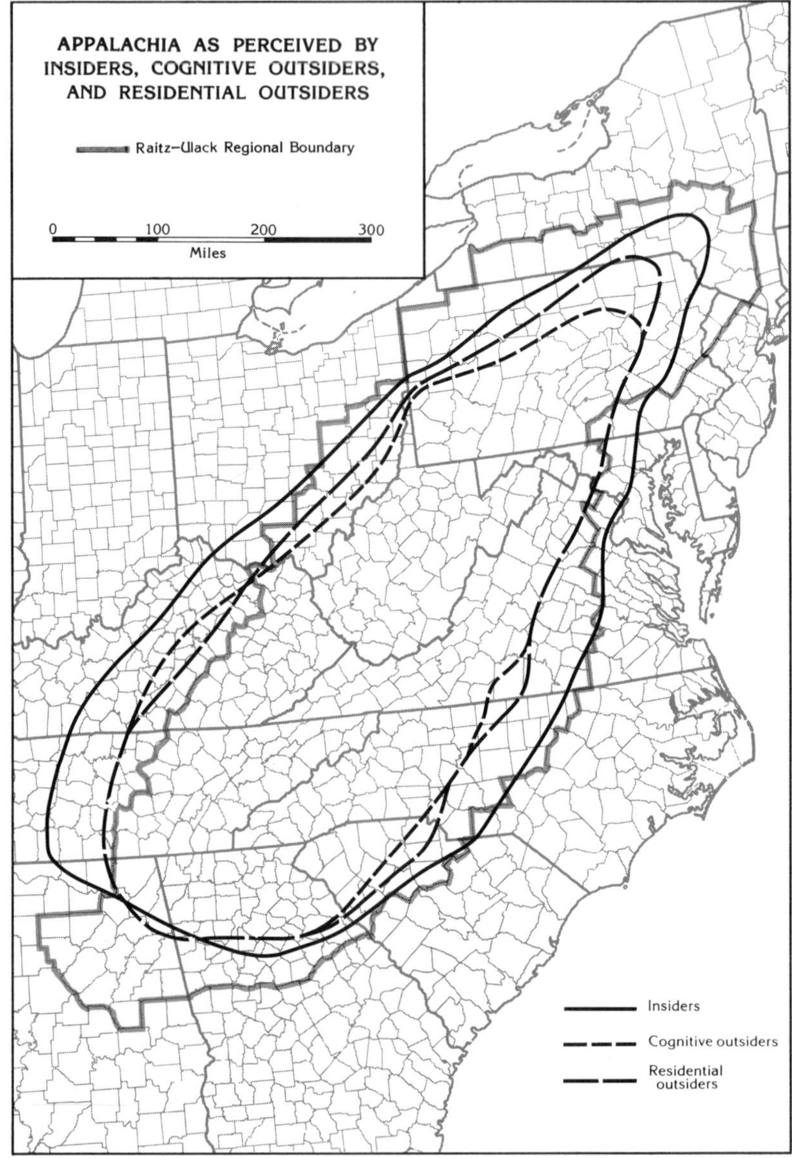


**Figure 1.6**
After Richard Ulack and Karl Raitz, "Perceptions of Appalachia," *Environment and Behavior* 14 (November 1982), pp. 742, 743, 744.

line is the cognitive core of the Appalachian region and corresponds to Mercer County, West Virginia. The cognitive Appalachian region differs substantially from the ARC region in that a significant portion of the student sample, about 40 percent, included only West Virginia, western Maryland, eastern Kentucky, western Virginia, western North Carolina, extreme northern Georgia, the western tip of South Carolina, a narrow strip in southeast Ohio, and a small portion of southwest Pennsylvania within Appalachia.[44]

By disaggregating the total respondent group we were able to examine how three subgroups that we identified, termed insiders, cognitive outsiders, and residential outsiders, perceived the Appalachian regional boundaries. The first group, *insiders,* included all those who perceived themselves as living in Appalachia. *Cognitive outsiders,* on the other hand, were those respondents who resided in physiographic Appalachia but stated they were not Appalachian. *Residential outsiders* were those who lived outside the region and stated they were not from Appalachia. Examination of the regional delimitations of each of the three subgroups reveals interesting differences (Figure 1.6). We also queried respondents as to what characteristics they associated with Appalachia (poverty and mountains were cited most often) and found, generally, that the insiders associated more positive characteristics with the region, whereas cognitive outsiders were more prone to be negative, and residential outsiders tended to fall somewhere in between.[45]

## A NEW APPALACHIAN REGION

Recently Whisnant observed that "Appalachia's boundaries have been drawn so many times that it is futile to look for a 'correct' definition of the region."[46] We have seen that there has been a variety of attempts to delimit the region. Each attempt has had a somewhat different purpose, and therefore varying criteria have been utilized. Notwithstanding Whisnant's observation and the number of Appalachian regionalizations that already exist, we offer another expanded version—the Raitz-Ulack region (Figure 1.7). Even though the principal criteria used for our regional delimitation are physiographic boundaries, political (county) boundaries, and contiguity, we are cognizant of the other important criteria that could be used. Indeed, cultural and socioeconomic characteristics were considered in our regional delimitation. For example, the Shenandoah Valley of Virginia (which is excluded from the ARC region) was included not only because it is a part of the physiographic Ridge and Valley Province but also because of its great cultural significance to the entire Appalachian region. It was the valley into and through which many descendants of Piedmont, Plateau, and Blue Ridge settlers migrated in the late eighteenth century. Indeed, contemporary cultural characteristics of all of Appalachia are intertwined closely with the post-1700 history of the Shenandoah Valley. We have carefully considered all the major attempts at regionalizing Appalachia in drawing our final regional bound-

A hillside "farm" in Ashe County, North Carolina. Rough-cut wood, steep slopes, and rock outcrops give the impression of poverty. Unfortunately, the stereotype that many Americans have of Appalachia is based on misunderstanding of such visual impressions. The three new vehicles suggest that the residents commute to jobs elsewhere and are not dependent on the farm for their income.

ary. We do not, of course, suggest this is the "best" Appalachia. We do believe, however, that it is well suited for the purposes of this volume and perhaps for other purposes as well.

The region includes 445 counties and thus is the largest nonphysiographic Appalachian region yet defined.[47] The next-largest such region, that of the ARC, includes 397 counties (Table 1.1). The southern boundary of our region corresponds rather closely to that of the Fenneman region and therefore excludes the 20 counties of Mississippi and 17 counties in central and western Alabama that are a part of the ARC region. We have attempted to keep our regional boundary within that of the Fenneman region; therefore, the western boundary of our region also excludes many of the ARC counties. For example, Clermont County, Ohio (part of the Cincinnati metropolitan area), Green County, Kentucky, and Macon County, Tennessee, are part of the ARC region but excluded from this region. The northern boundary corresponds rather closely with the ARC region and is south and west of the Hudson and Mohawk valleys. We follow more closely the Fenneman boundary than does the ARC and thereby exclude Erie County, Pennsylvania, and Chautauqua County, New York; however, the counties of New York's Catskill Moun-

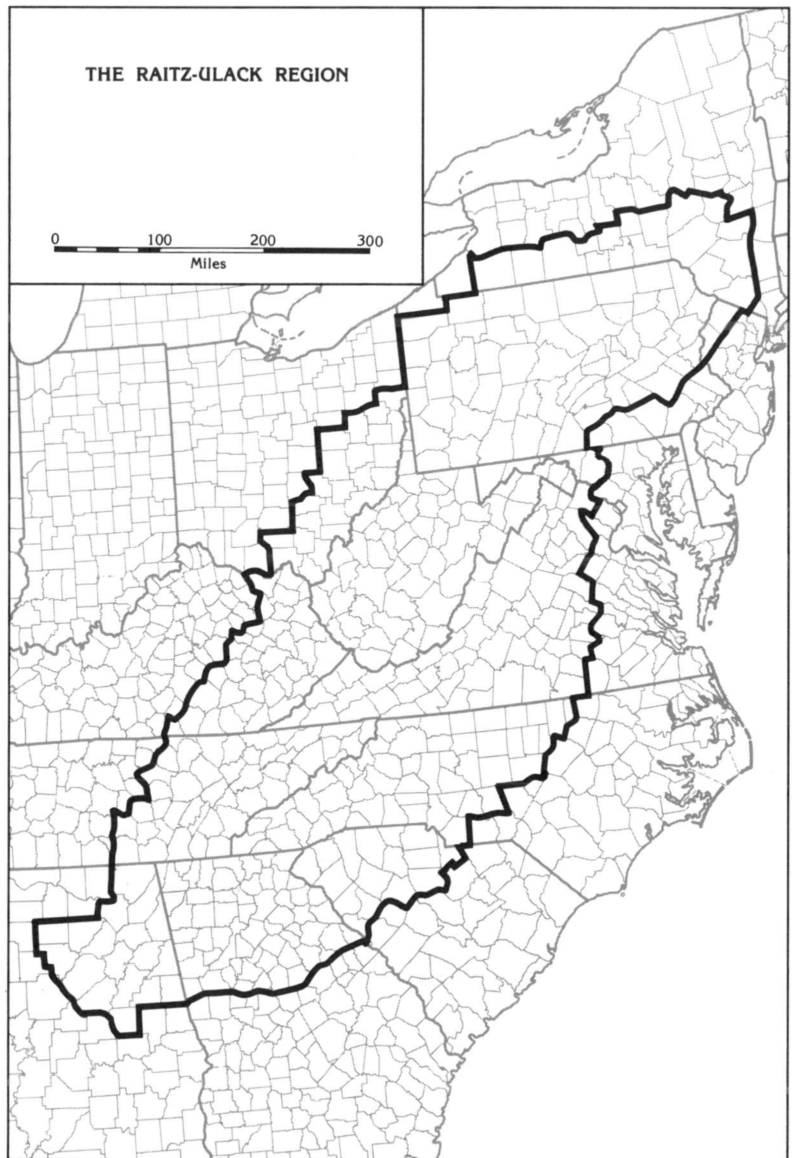


**Figure 1.7** The Raitz-Ulack regional boundary shown here is delineated on maps throughout the book.

TABLE 1.1
The Appalachian Region: Number of Counties, Area, and Population by State, 1980

| | Redefined Appalachian Region | | | A.R.C. Region | | |
|---|---|---|---|---|---|---|
| State | Number of Counties | Area (sq.mi.) | Population (000s) | Number of Counties | Area (sq.mi.) | Population (000s) |
| Alabama | 18 | 12,650 | 1,508.4 | 35 | 24,600 | 2,427.0 |
| Georgia | 59 | 17,836 | 3,087.4 | 35 | 10,804 | 1,103.9 |
| Kentucky | 36 | 12,868 | 848.7 | 49 | 16,942 | 1,077.1 |
| Maryland | 4 | 2,211 | 334.4 | 3 | 1,546 | 220.1 |
| Mississippi | 0 | 0 | 0 | 20 | 10,313 | 482.7 |
| New Jersey | 2 | 889 | 200.6 | 0 | 0 | 0 |
| New York | 17 | 14,370 | 1,514.9 | 14 | 11,806 | 1,083.3 |
| North Carolina | 52 | 22,950 | 3,513.2 | 29 | 11,884 | 1,217.7 |
| Ohio | 23 | 11,090 | 1,063.5 | 28 | 13,732 | 1,262.6 |
| Pennsylvania | 58 | 38,710 | 7,160.7 | 52 | 36,626 | 5,995.1 |
| South Carolina | 16 | 9,602 | 1,204.9 | 6 | 3,964 | 791.6 |
| Tennessee | 44 | 17,511 | 2,002.1 | 50 | 19,238 | 2,073.6 |
| Virginia | 61 | 28,450 | 2,060.1 | 21 | 9,398 | 549.9 |
| West Virginia | 55 | 24,080 | 1,949.6 | 55 | 24,080 | 1,949.6 |
| TOTAL | 445 | 213,217 | 26,448.5 | 397 | 194,933 | 20,234.2 |

tains are included. The greatest difference between our proposed region and that of the ARC is in the eastern boundary. The ARC excludes most of the Piedmont counties, whereas the majority of the counties in the Upland Piedmont are included here. Our eastern boundary corresponds closely to Fenneman's differentiation of the Piedmont and Coastal Plain along the Fall Line. We have drawn our boundary approximately one row of counties to the west of the Fall Line. Additionally, we have excluded the Lowland Piedmont counties and also those counties in the metropolitan orbits of Baltimore, Washington, D.C., Philadelphia, and New York. We did not include the mountains of Arkansas and Missouri because that area, physiographically, is not contiguous to the rest of Appalachia. We used county lines for our final boundary because they facilitate the use of census data.

The Raitz-Ulack region includes a 1980 population of some 26.5 million, or 11.7 percent of the United States total (Table 1.1). Its area is 213,217 sq mi (552,232 sq km), or 6.0 percent of that of the United States. It is an area that produces a large share of some of the nation's primary commodities, including coal, tobacco, lumber, and corn. It is also a region with important metropolitan areas that have been, and are becoming, centers of major industrial activity. Pittsburgh, Atlanta, Birmingham, Charleston, Knoxville, Harrisburg, Chattanooga, Charlotte, and Greenville are included among the region's more important cities. As has already been suggested, it is also a region with a varied physiography, a varied past, and a varied culture. In short, it is a region of great diversity, and this characteristic needs to be recognized if we hope to understand the region's past, present, and future.

## NOTES

1. Wilbur Zelinsky, "Where the South Begins: The Northern Limit of the Cis-Appalachian South in Terms of Settlement Landscape," *Social Forces* 30 (1951), pp. 172–178.

2. Joseph W. Brownell, "The Cultural Midwest," *Journal of Geography* 59 (1960), pp. 81–85.

3. Ellen Churchill Semple, *American History and Its Geographic Conditions* (New York: Houghton, Mifflin, and Co., 1903), p. 71.

4. David S. Walls, "On the Naming of Appalachia," in J. W. Williamson, ed., *An Appalachian Symposium: Essays Written in Honor of Cratis D. Williams* (Boone, N.C.: Appalachian State University Press, 1977), pp. 56–76.

5. Ibid., p. 66.

6. Arnold Guyot, "On the Appalachian Mountain System," *American Journal of Science and Arts* 31 (1861), pp. 157–187.

7. John Wesley Powell, *Physiographic Regions of the United States* (New York: American Book Co., 1895).

8. Nevin M. Fenneman, "Physiographic Boundaries Within the United States," *Annals,* Association of American Geographers, 4 (1914), pp. 84–134; Nevin M. Fenneman, *Physiography of Western United States* (New York: McGraw-Hill Book Co., 1931); and Nevin M. Fenneman, *Physiography of Eastern United States* (New York: McGraw-Hill Book Co., 1938).

9. William D. Thornbury, *Regional Geomorphology of the United States* (New York: John Wiley & Sons, 1965), p. 9.

10. Fenneman, 1938, op. cit. (footnote 8), p. 121.

11. W. W. Atwood, *The Physiographic Provinces of North America* (Boston: Ginn & Co., 1940); and Charles B. Hunt, *Natural Regions of the United States and Canada* (San Francisco: W. H. Freeman and Co., 1974).

12. Paul F. Griffin et al., *Anglo-America: A Systematic and Regional Geography* (Palo Alto, Ca.: Fearon Publishers, 1968), pp. 226–227; Earl B. Shaw, *Anglo-America: A Regional Geography* (New York: John Wiley & Sons, 1959), p. 147; J. Russell Smith and M. Ogden Phillips, *North America: Its People and the Resources, Development, and Prospects of the Continent as the Home of Man* (New York: Harcourt, Brace and Co., 1940), pp. 188–189; and C. Langdon White et al., *Regional Geography of Anglo-America,* 5th ed. (Englewood Cliffs, N.J.: Prentice-Hall, 1979), p. 98.

13. Stephen S. Birdsall and John W. Florin, *Regional Landscapes of the United States and Canada* (New York: John Wiley & Sons, 1978), p. 3.

14. J. H. Paterson, *North America: A Geography of the United States and Canada* (New York: Oxford University Press, 1975), p. 173.

15. The region defined by Smith and Phillips, op. cit. (footnote 12), is not included in Figure 1.2. Their text discussed four "regions" of Appalachia, each in a separate chapter: the Northern Piedmont, the Appalachian Ridge and Valley, the Appalachian Plateau and Upper Ohio Valley, and the Blue Ridge and the Great Smoky Mountains.

16. To appreciate the flavor of these writings, the reader is urged to sample the following examples: Will Wallace Harney, "A Strange Land and Peculiar People," *Lippincott's Magazine* 12 (1873), pp. 429–438; Rebecca H. Davis, "The Rose of Carolina," *Scribner's Monthly* 8 (1874), pp. 723–726; Edward King, "The Great South: Southern Mountain Rambles: In Tennessee, Georgia, and South Carolina," *Scribner's Monthly* 8 (1874), pp. 5–33; David H. Strother, "The Mountains," *Harper's Magazine* 51 (1875), pp. 475–485; Mary N. Murfree, "The Romance of Sunrise Rock," *Atlantic Monthly* 46 (1880), pp. 775–786; Mary N. Murfree, *In the Tennessee Mountains* (Boston: Houghton, Mifflin, and Co., 1884); J. M. Davies, "Scotch-Irish Stock in the Central South," *The Church at Home and Abroad* 2 (1887), pp. 128–129; Charles D. Warner, *On Horseback: A Tour through Virginia, North Carolina and Tennessee* (Boston: Houghton, Mifflin, and Co., 1888); and Joseph E. Roy, *Americans of the Midland Mountains* (New York: American Missionary Association, 1891).

17. Walls, op. cit. (footnote 4), p. 67. Frost was president of Kentucky's Berea College from 1892 to 1920. Berea College was established in the mid-nineteenth century as an abolitionist and multiracial institution. The college, located on the western edge of the Appalachian Plateau, has a long and active history with the Appalachian region and its people.

18. William G. Frost, *For the Mountains: An Autobiography* (New York: Revell, 1937).

19. John C. Campbell, *The Southern Highlander and His Homeland* (Lexington: University Press of Kentucky, 1969; originally published by the Russell Sage Foundation in 1921).

20. Ibid., pp. 11–12.

21. Thomas R. Ford, ed., *The Southern Appalachian Region: A Survey* (Lexington: University of Kentucky Press, 1962).

22. Ibid., p. 3.

23. Bruce Ergood, "Toward a Definition of Appalachia," in Bruce Ergood and Bruce E. Kuhre, eds., *Appalachia: Social Context Past and Present* (Dubuque, Ia.: Kendall/Hunt Publishing Co., 1976), p. 34.

24. Wilbur Zelinsky, *The Cultural Geography of the United States* (Englewood Cliffs, N.J.: Prentice-Hall, 1973), pp. 118–199.

25. Ibid., pp. 123–124.

26. Ibid., p. 112.

27. Ibid., p. 83.

28. Raymond D. Gastil, *Cultural Regions of the United States* (Seattle: University of Washington Press, 1975), p. 26.

29. Kevin R. Phillips, *The Emerging Republican Majority* (Garden City, N.Y.: Doubleday & Co., 1970).

30. Ibid., p. 253.

31. U.S. Department of Agriculture (U.S.D.A.), *Economic and Social Problems and Conditions of the Southern Appalachians,* Misc. Pub. no. 205 (Washington, D.C.: U.S. Dept. of Agriculture, 1935), p. 11.

32. The Appalachian region discussed in other portions of the U.S.D.A. report (footnote 31) includes 205 counties in 6 southern states with a total area of over 85,000 sq mi (220,150 sq km).

33. Arthur R. Mangus, *Rural Regions of the United States* (Washington, D.C.: Government Printing Office, 1940), pp. 3–5.

34. Ibid., p. 2.

35. President's Appalachian Regional Commission (P.A.R.C.), *Appalachia*

(Washington, D.C.: Government Printing Office, 1964), p. xv.

36. Ann DeWitt Watts, "Does the Appalachian Regional Commission Really Represent a Region?" *Southeastern Geographer* 18 (1978), pp. 19–36.

37. Walls, op. cit. (footnote 4), p. 71.

38. David E. Whisnant, *Modernizing the Mountaineer: People, Power, and Planning in Appalachia* (New York: Burt Franklin & Co., 1980), p. 134.

39. Appalachian Regional Commission, "The New Appalachian Subregions and Their Development Strategies," *Appalachia* 8 (1974), pp. 10–27.

40. Whisnant, op. cit. (footnote 38).

41. P.A.R.C., op. cit. (footnote 35), p. xviii.

42. Kevin R. Cox and Georgia Zannaras, "Designative Perceptions of Macrospaces: Concepts, a Methodology, and Applications," in Roger M. Downs and David Stea, eds., *Image and Environment: Cognitive Mapping and Spatial Behavior* (Chicago: Aldine, 1973), pp. 162–178.

43. Ruth F. Hale, "A Map of Vernacular Regions in America," (Ph.D. dissertation, Department of Geography, University of Minnesota, 1971).

44. The topic of congruence between ARC Appalachia and cognitive Appalachia is examined more thoroughly in Richard Ulack and Karl Raitz, "Appalachia: A Comparison of the Cognitive and Appalachian Regional Commission Regions," *Southeastern Geographer* 21 (1981), pp. 40–53.

45. See Richard Ulack and Karl Raitz, "Perceptions of Appalachia," *Environment and Behavior* 14 (1982), pp. 725–752; and Karl B. Raitz and Richard Ulack, "Cognitive Maps of Appalachia," *Geographical Review* 71 (1981), pp. 201–213.

46. Whisnant, op. cit. (footnote 38), p. 134.

47. In addition to the 445 counties there are twenty independent cities in Virginia. All data for these cities are included with the data for the county in which the city is located. In general, statements in the text refer to the Raitz-Ulack regional definition unless it is specifically stated otherwise.

# PART 2

# REGIONAL DIVERSITY AND THE BASES FOR DEVELOPMENT

# CHAPTER 2

# APPALACHIA'S PHYSICAL GEOGRAPHY

Because of Appalachia's long and complex geologic history, volumes could be written about the nuances of its physical geography and natural resources. The topic is of utmost importance, because the history of human settlement and development in the region has been so closely tied to its physical attributes. Indeed, many of the early proponents of environmental determinism, when stating the close relationship of physical character and human adaptation, rested their case on the Appalachian example.

In this brief treatment of Appalachia's physical geography we will review several outstanding features of the environment that are particularly relevant to an understanding of past, present, and future settlement and development in the region. Topics addressed in this chapter, and in future chapters, should be considered in the context of the following four points.

First, the generally rugged nature of the terrain in an otherwise relatively flat eastern United States has tended to impede or divert settlement and development. Transportation routes have largely followed the highly developed drainage network, with the earliest routes restricted to passable valleys and focused at the few mountain gaps. The pattern of the region's complex topography must be understood if one wishes to understand the variations of the region's human geography.

Second, most of the region has a very humid climate. Only two other extensive areas in the continental United States—the Gulf Coast and the Pacific Northwest—have greater annual precipitation amounts. A clean and abundant water supply is critical to continued development, as many areas of the western United States have discovered. Appalachia's abundant water supply may ultimately take on new meaning as a resource.

Third, Appalachia's rugged topography, coupled with its high annual precipitation (especially in the central and southern portions), has played a role in forming soils that are not very well suited for most types of agriculture. The thin mountain-slope soils are further reduced by erosion, and soils in the more humid parts of the region tend to be leached of their basic nutrients. Except for the Piedmont Province and the larger valleys of the Ridge and Valley Province, agriculture has not been of major commercial importance to the region. Within the Piedmont the inherently low natural fertility of the leached soils has been partly responsible for widespread farmland abandonment.

Fourth, since the eighteenth century the widespread occurrences of three resources—forests, coal, and scenic beauty—have been the keys to regional development. The proper utilization and conservation of these resources, and water, will continue to be pivotal to the region's future.

## GEOLOGY AND PHYSIOGRAPHY

In summarizing the voluminous research that has been conducted on Appalachian geology, Philip King observed that "the Appalachian chain is the most elegant on earth, so regularly arranged that its belts of formations and structures persist from one end to the other. . . . What a contrast [this is] to . . . the confusion of superposed rocks and structures in our own Western Cordillera! No wonder . . . that the Appalachians have been the birthplace of many of the great principles of . . . geology . . . [such as] the theory of geosynclines and . . . theories of folding and faulting, to name only a few! But the apparent simplicity . . . is deceiving; actually, it is full of guile, and its geology has aroused controversies as acrimonious as any of those in our science."[1] The following sections are best considered in light of this statement.

### Appalachia's Geologic History

Geologically, the Appalachian mountain system is very old; much older, for example, than the ranges of the western United States. Furthermore, today the Appalachian system is quite stable and does not experience the degree of tectonic activity (folding, faulting, or vulcanism) that is found in America's western mountains. The Appalachian mountain system has not experienced major uplift in millions of years; instead, it is an area that is being denuded relatively rapidly by heavy precipitation and human activity. This structural stability can be understood best in the context of plate tectonics, a theory based on the notion that the earth's upper crust, the lithosphere, is broken up into a series of huge segments called plates. These plates are in motion relative to each other: Some plates are moving apart from one another, others are colliding. It is in the areas where plates collide or slide past one another that the world's major zones of tectonic activity are found.[2]

Today, the Appalachian system is not located near a boundary between colliding plates, but this was not always the case. The Appalachian Mountains were formed several hundred million years ago through the repeated collision of two plates. As the plates collided, one was forced under the other in a process called subduction. As one plate overrode the other, an "orogeny," or "suturing," occurred whereby complicated folding, faulting, and vulcanism produced a high mountain range. Major orogenies affected Appalachia three times, all during the Paleozoic era, a geological time that lasted from approximately 600 million to 225 million B.P. The first Appalachian orogeny, called the Taconian, occurred at the end of the Ordovician period prior to 400 million B.P. The second major orogeny, the Acadian, occurred about 350 million B.P. when the Devonian period was ending and the Mississippian was beginning. The third major orogeny, known as the Appalachian or Alleghenian, occurred about 225 million B.P. at the end of the Paleozoic era (during the Permian period).

Prior to the Taconian orogeny the area that was to become Appalachia was a sea underlain by extensive sedimentary deposits. Between the major orogenies the area was the boundary of two lithospheric plates that pulled apart, allowing an inland sea to form. Deep layers of sediments were deposited over the area. As later uplifting of the region occurred, these sediments formed some of the most important rock types of Appalachia. The deposition, for example, of the limy and shaly sediments of the Mississippian period and the coal-bearing strata of the Pennsylvanian period (about 300 million B.P.) are of particular significance to an understanding of Appalachian lithology.

Because the Piedmont and Blue Ridge, two of Appalachia's four major physiographic provinces, were most directly affected by the repeated orogeny process, geologically they are the most complex provinces. The rock types found in these two provinces are the oldest in the region; therefore the Piedmont and the Blue Ridge are sometimes called the Older Appalachians. Ancient crystalline metamorphic rock, especially schist, gneiss, and slate, and intrusive igneous (plutonic) rock, like granite, underlies most of the Piedmont Province. The eastern part of the Piedmont is underlain by the Carolina slate belt, which accounts for some 20 percent of the province's area.[3] Granite, which accounts for another 20 percent of the Piedmont, tends to form uplands because it is particularly resistant to erosion. Numerous striking "mountains" of granite, called monadnocks, are found on the Piedmont; examples include Stone Mountain, Georgia, and Kings Mountain, North Carolina. Some 5 percent of the Piedmont's area consists of younger, sedimentary rock (mainly sandstone, shale, and conglomerate) of the Triassic period.

The Blue Ridge Province is also extensively underlain by metamorphic and plutonic rocks. The fact that the Blue Ridge has the highest mountains in Appalachia is partly related to the existence of these strongly resistant rock types. Also found in the Blue Ridge are small areas of unmetamorphosed sedimentary rock, mostly in the western Blue Ridge adjacent to the boundary with the Ridge and Valley Province. Here, where metamorphic rocks were overthrust onto younger sedimentary deposits, the overlying rock has been eroded away exposing the younger carbonate rocks. This process has produced geologic "windows" that are often called coves by the residents.[4]

The region's two westernmost provinces, the Ridge and Valley and the Appalachian Plateaus, were less affected by the three major orogenies, so their geology is somewhat less complex. Both provinces are underlain predominantly by the rock strata that were formed from sediments deposited during the Paleozoic era. The Ridge and Valley, the easternmost of the two provinces, experienced severe folding, and in cross section the sedimentary strata look like the corrugations of a washboard. The steeply pitching ridges are resistant sedimentary rocks such as sandstone (in Pennsylvania and West Virginia the Tuscarora sandstone of the Silurian period is the major ridge maker). The parallel valleys are carved into less resistant limestones and shales. The valleys, including the Great Valley, which is up to 40 mi (64.4 km) wide and runs from New York to Alabama (Virginia's famous Shenandoah Valley is a section of the Great Valley), have been most important to human migration and agricultural settlement. The ridges, on the other hand, have been a barrier to movement, and routes have diverted to points where the ridges are crosscut by water gaps and wind gaps.

The other province of the Newer Appalachians, the Plateaus, was least affected by tectonic activity, because it was farthest from the area of plate collision. Its sedimentary strata lie nearly horizontal to the surface or, at most, are only gently folded. Sedimentary rocks in the Plateaus are predominantly conglomerates, sandstones, and shales; all are interbedded with coal. Limestone is also found, but it is much less common here than in the Ridge and Valley Province. Although the eastern portion of the Appalachian Plateaus Province is quite mountainous, the entire region can best be described as an elaborately dissected plateau. The narrow valleys and sharp ridges have made internal movement and settlement difficult. Recent settlement is related in large part to exploitation of the rich bituminous-coal seams.

One additional process in the geological history of northern Appalachia must be examined before we can proceed with a discussion of the drainage and topographic pattern that characterizes the region today. This process, continental glaciation, began more than one million years ago and continued intermittently until about ten thousand years ago. This glacial period is called the Pleistocene epoch by geologists, but it is more popularly known as the Ice Age. During this period, extensive continental ice sheets, perhaps 1 mi (1.609 km) thick, moved southward from Canada. At its greatest extent the glacial ice flowed as far south as the Ohio River and covered all of New York State and northern Pennsylvania and New Jersey. The erosion and deposition caused by glaciers reshaped the topography, so that Appalachia can be divided into glaciated and nonglaciated sections. Under the ice and along the ice front large amounts of rock, sand, and silt accumulated, to be left behind after the ice retreated in formations called glacial drift, or ground moraine. The igneous boulders found in the Catskill Mountains today, for example, are of Adirondack origin but were carried south by the ice.[5] Accumulations of these deposits sometimes formed low, irregularly spaced hills called kames and drumlins.

The southward-moving ice was an extremely effective erosional agent, filling in some existing rivers and streams and scouring out other river valleys to form deep, broad trenches that later filled with water to become lakes. One of the best examples of this process is found at the region's northern margin in New York, where eleven large north-south trending lakes are found. Known collectively as the Finger Lakes, they are part of a system of "through valleys" in the west-central part of the state that are the product of erosion by both ice and glacial meltwater.[6]

The country to the south of the farthest advance of the glaciers was also affected by Pleistocene glaciation. For example, the middle portion of the ancient Teays River system, which formed over 100 million years ago, became a long and narrow lake, because the leading edge of glacial ice effectively dammed the northwestward-flowing Teays.[7] Today's Kanawha and New rivers in West Virginia, Virginia, and North Carolina are a small portion of the ancient Teays system. The lake that formed during the Pleistocene stretched from the present location of Chillicothe, Ohio, south and east to the point where the New and Gauley rivers meet to form the Kanawha in south-central West Virginia. Sedimentary deposits laid down on this ancient lake bottom can be found throughout the Kanawha Valley today and provide sand and gravel for local construction.

The rock and topography evident across the region today are products of this complex sequence of tectonic and erosional processes. The dramatic orogenies of the Paleozoic era and the gradual uplifting of the last 150 million years have rejuvenated streams by increasing their gradients. Depending on their resistance, long-buried rocks have gradually either been removed or exposed by erosion. Each of these cycles of landmass uplift and erosion has produced an extensive area of little or no relief called a peneplain. Just how many past peneplains have been produced is unclear and is a subject of debate about which there are "almost as many opinions as there are writers on the subject."[8]

## The Physiographic Subdivisions

Our previous discussion of tectonics, lithology, and erosion, together with a brief examination of each of the four major provinces and their subdivisions, outlined the diversity of topography in the region and provided a context for understanding settlement and development. As we have seen in Chapter 1, the physiographic subdivisions of Appalachia have been delimited in a number of ways. As they are discussed here, the four major physiographic regions and their subdivisions follow boundaries delimited by Fenneman (Figure 2.1).[9]

***The Piedmont Province.*** The Piedmont extends nearly 1,000 mi (1,609 km) from Rockland County, New York, to Georgia and central Alabama. The eastern boundary, which separates the Piedmont from the Coastal

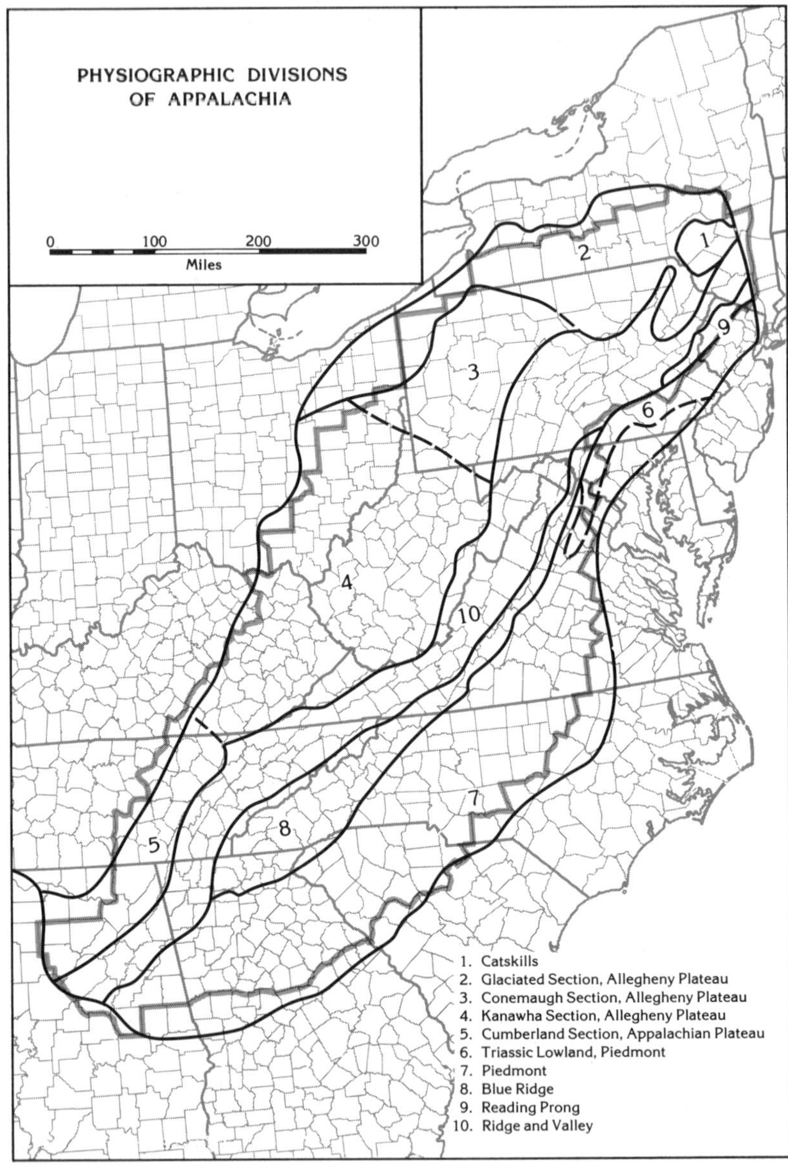


**Figure 2.1**
After Nevin M. Fenneman, *Physiography of Eastern United States* (New York: McGraw-Hill, 1938), Plates I, II, and III.

Plain Province, is known as the Fall Line. At this boundary the Piedmont's resistant crystalline rocks disappear beneath the less resistant sedimentary deposits of the Coastal Plain. Rivers such as the Potomac, Susquehanna, and Rappahannock descend over a series of falls and rapids at or near the Fall Line as they flow eastward to the Atlantic. During colonial times a number of cities were established on Piedmont rivers near the Fall Line, in part because break-in-transportation points occurred there. Examples include Philadelphia, Richmond, Columbia, Augusta, and Macon. The western boundary of the Piedmont is also sharply demarcated. In the south, where the Piedmont meets the Ridge and Valley Province, the boundary follows the Cartersville fault line. Where the Piedmont adjoins the Blue Ridge, a bold escarpment called the Blue Ridge frontal scarp marks the boundary. The escarpment is especially abrupt in North Carolina.

Internally, the Piedmont can be divided into two broad subregions, the Upland Piedmont (indicated as *Piedmont* on Figure 2.1) and the Lowland Piedmont. The Lowland Piedmont, as suggested by its name, consists of less rugged terrain of lower elevation. It is located in the northern part of the province between New York and northern Virginia, and its location corresponds closely with Triassic sedimentary rocks. We will not consider further this subregion as part of the Raitz-Ulack Appalachian region because of its low elevation and its location adjacent to the great northeastern megalopolis.

The Upland Piedmont can be described as a peneplain with a "rolling surface of gentle slopes and no great relief, say, fifty feet, more or less, cut by or bounded by valleys of steeper slope and greater depth, often several hundred feet."[10] Elevations in the subregion are lowest in the north, where they reach 800 ft (243.2 m). The Carolina Piedmont reaches elevations of 1,500 ft (456 m), and in Georgia's Dahlonega Plateau elevations of 1,800 ft (547.2 m) are not uncommon. Some areas of the Upland Piedmont, such as the Dahlonega Plateau, are punctuated with erosional remnants, or monadnocks.

That portion of the Upland Piedmont subregion north of the Virginia-Maryland boundary is excluded from the Appalachian region discussed in this volume. The counties included in that area of the Piedmont are also within the immediate metropolitan orbit of the great megalopolis that extends northeast from northern Virginia and Washington, D.C. Additionally, we have elected to eliminate from consideration those counties lying on or adjacent to the Fall Line. That portion of the Piedmont that remains in the region includes Atlanta, Greenville, Spartanburg, Charlotte, Greensboro, and Winston-Salem. In all, there are approximately 125 counties in the portions of the Piedmont included here.

***The Blue Ridge Province.*** In total area, the Blue Ridge is the smallest of the four provinces, but its mountains attain the highest elevations and its scenic beauty is perhaps the most breathtaking of any in Appalachia. The province extends some 550 mi (884.9 km) from

Cumberland County in south central Pennsylvania to northeastern Georgia. The eastern boundary of the province is the Blue Ridge frontal scarp, which reaches its maximum elevation of approximately 4,000 ft (1,216 m) near Blowing Rock, North Carolina. The elevation of the escarpment declines to the north, where it is 2,500 ft (760 m) near Roanoke, and to the south, where it is about 1,000 ft (304 m) near Gainesville, Georgia. The western boundary is marked by different rock types and is reflected in the differences in topography between the Blue Ridge and the Ridge and Valley provinces.

Fenneman divided the Blue Ridge Province into two sections at the Roanoke River. The northern section of the Blue Ridge nowhere exceeds 15 mi (24.1 km) in width. Generally, elevations are lower than to the south and only rarely do they exceed 4,000 ft (1,216 m). In addition to the Roanoke, two other major rivers—the James and the Potomac—rise west of the Blue Ridge and flow eastward, cutting across the province. Some of the water gaps formed by these rivers, as well as wind gaps formed by ancient streams, have been important routeways. Several Piedmont cities, including Roanoke and Lynchburg in Virginia and Harpers Ferry, are sited at gaps through the Blue Ridge.

The southern section begins near Roanoke, where the Blue Ridge begins to broaden. The province reaches its greatest width of between 80 and 100 miles (128.7 to 160.9 km) in North Carolina and Tennessee. The drainage of this southern section is predominantly to the west and ultimately to the Gulf of Mexico, rather than to the Atlantic Ocean. Fenneman noted that "there are said to be 46 peaks and 41 miles of divide above the level of 6,000 feet; also 288 more peaks and 300 more miles of divide above 5,000 feet" in the southern Blue Ridge.[11] The highest peak in the eastern United States, Mt. Mitchell (6,684 ft—2,031.9 m) in North Carolina, is in the Great Smoky Mountains portion of the Blue Ridge. The highest mountains of Tennessee (Clingmans Dome, 6,642 ft—2,019.2 m), Georgia (Brasstown Bald, 4,768 ft—1,449.5 m), and Virginia (Mt. Rogers, 5,719 ft—1,738.6 m) are also located within this province.

The physical characteristics of the Blue Ridge have limited both agriculture and human settlement. Only one city of the province, Asheville, North Carolina, has reached notable size. On the other hand, the extensive forests have been the basis for a significant lumber industry, and beautiful mountain scenery has drawn large numbers of tourists who have contributed to the region's economy. Many of the province's natural attractions are now within state and national parks, such as the Great Smoky Mountain and Shenandoah national parks, and are accessible by way of the Blue Ridge Parkway. Tourist resorts like Gatlinburg, Tennessee, and Cherokee and Blowing Rock, North Carolina, have developed near these parks or at other scenic areas.

***The Ridge and Valley Province.*** Physiographically this province extends from Canada's St. Lawrence Valley to central Alabama, a distance of some 1,200 mi (1,930.8 km). We will not consider here that section of

The western margin of the Ridge and Valley in Pendleton County, West Virginia, near Judy Gap. Germany Valley lies obscured by low cloud beyond the ridge in the middle distance.

the Ridge and Valley north of the Hudson and Mohawk valleys that Fenneman called the Hudson-Champlain Section. The remainder of the Ridge and Valley Province is bounded on the east by the Piedmont, Blue Ridge, and New England provinces. The latter includes the "Reading Prong," a belt of highlands 150 mi (241.4 km) long that extends southwestward from New England as far as Reading, Pennsylvania. The western boundary of the Ridge and Valley, the Allegheny Front, is a sharp dividing line separating the province from the Appalachian Plateaus. The front has been perhaps the single most imposing barrier to movement across the Appalachian system and is "the most continuous and readily recognizable interprovince boundary in the Appalachian Highlands."[12]

Internally, the Ridge and Valley Province can be subdivided into a northern section, which extends from the Hudson to the Delaware River; a middle section, which extends from the Delaware to the divide between the New and Tennessee rivers in southwestern Virginia; and a southern section, which extends into central Alabama.[13]

Portions of the middle section best typify the alternating ridges and valleys characteristic of the region. In Pennsylvania the province attains its greatest width of approximately 80 mi (128.7 km). Here are located what used to be known as zigzag mountains, named for the pattern produced by plunging anticlines and synclines. The name Endless Mountains was given to this sequence of apparently unending sandstone and conglomerate ridges by exasperated early travelers. Like the northern section of the Blue Ridge, the province is crosscut by numerous water gaps and wind gaps that effectively channeled travel along a limited number of through routes.[11]

Early travelers made their way through this middle section to Pittsburgh, the Ohio River, Kentucky, and other points west. Some saw merit in the province's fertile limestone valleys and moved no farther. The province's longest and widest major valley, the Great Valley, is also the easternmost valley and extends the length of the province. The valley varies in width, 2 mi (3.2 km) at its narrowest point to 50 mi (80.5 km) in the extreme south. It is drained by several rivers and is known by different names along its length. In Pennsylvania it is known as the Lehigh, Lebanon, or Cumberland valley; in Maryland as the Hagerstown Valley; in Virginia it is called the Shenandoah Valley in the north and the Valley of Virginia to the south; in Tennessee it is called the Valley of East Tennessee; and in Alabama, the Coosa Valley. A relatively flat to gentle rolling floor characterizes most of the Great Valley; however, there are some rugged features within it. Most notable of these is Massanutten Mountain, a 50-mile-long canoe-shaped sandstone mountain located in the Shenandoah portion of the Great Valley. This area has become important for skiing, resorts, and second-home residential development.

In Pennsylvania, two examples of important agricultural settlement in the Ridge and Valley's middle section are the 100-mile-long (160.9-kilometer-long) Nittany Valley, the westernmost valley in the province, and the smaller Kishacoquillas Valley, an area of Amish settlement. Both valleys are enclosed by ridges of Tuscarora sandstone and are floored principally with Ordovician limestone, named for the geological period in which the rock was formed. Ridge elevations in the northern and middle sections reach 1,300 to 4,500 ft (395.2 to 1,368 m) and local relief is as much as 2,500 ft (760 m). The valley floors throughout the Ridge and Valley Province vary in elevation from 400 to 2,400 ft (121.6 to 729.6 m).

The northern and southern sections of the province differ from the middle section, and from each other, in several ways. First, the northern and southern sections are narrower and do not have the marked linear arrangement of ridges and valleys, especially in the case of the southern section. There are far fewer ridges in these sections than in the middle section. For example, only two conspicuous ridges are found in the northern section, the Kittatinny and the shorter Schunemuck. Second, drainage is generally longitudinal in the northern and southern sections. That is, rivers such as the Hudson, Powell, Clinch, and Holston flow along the trend of the valleys. On the other hand, in the middle section transverse drainage is more prevalent. Third, the southern section has been affected more by faulting than either the northern or middle sections. And fourth, the northern section has been glaciated, whereas the other two sections lie south of the Pleistocene glacial advances.

A particularly noteworthy geological feature of the Ridge and Valley Province is the well-developed karst topography in those areas underlain by limestone. The Great Valley is a major karst region in the eastern United States. Much of the drainage is underground, following fractures that have been enlarged by solution. One product of the dissolving of limestone by running water is the formation of extensive cave systems such as Luray, Shenandoah, and Massanutten caves in Virginia. Other karst features include numerous sinkholes and the Natural Bridge and Burkes Garden in Virginia. The latter is an elliptical basin almost completely surrounded by a high sandstone ridge. There is one water gap through which flows the small stream that drains the 5-mile-long (8-kilometer-long) basin. Caves and other karst features are found to a more limited extent in some areas of the Appalachian Plateaus, especially in Tennessee and Alabama.

A number of hot springs and mineral springs occur along the Ridge and Valley. They are most numerous in Virginia and West Virginia but are found in other states as well. White Sulphur Springs in West Virginia, Hot Springs in Virginia, and Bedford Springs in Pennsylvania are all resorts of long and colorful history that capitalized on the supposed healing powers of their free-flowing springs. (Warm Springs, Georgia—located in the Piedmont, not the Ridge and Valley—was a favored retreat of President Franklin Roosevelt.)

In addition to the economic benefits derived from agriculture and tourism in the limestone valleys, one part of the province, northeastern Pennsylvania, has coal deposits that have been extensively developed. Four major coalfields make up what is called the Anthracite Region, an area that prospered during the early years of hard-coal production. The industry began to decline about 1930, and the local economy has been severely depressed since 1950.[15] Coal production in this area is not presently important, but earlier production had a major impact. The two largest cities in the Anthracite Region, Wilkes-Barre and Scranton, are located in the 40-mile-long (64.4-kilometer-long) canoe-shaped Wyoming Valley.

Other major cities of the Ridge and Valley Province include Allentown and Harrisburg in Pennsylvania; the tri-cities of Bristol in Tennessee and Virginia and Kingsport and Johnson City in Tennessee; and Roanoke, Knoxville, Chattanooga, and Birmingham.

***The Appalachian Plateaus Province.*** The largest of the four major physiographic provinces is the Appalachian Plateaus Province. The entire province is a structural plateau that has been so deeply dissected by streams that local relief is greater here than anywhere in Appalachia except the southern Blue Ridge. In part for this reason, much of the area is known in the vernacular as the "mountains." The eastern boundary is the formidable Allegheny Front, of which Bailey Willis, an early chronicler of Appalachia's physical geography, wrote: "As compared with the Blue Ridge, the scenery of the Allegheny Front is rugged, yes, savage. The eastern face is steep, lofty, and often crowned with a precipice of sandstone. The canyons, a thousand feet deep or more from the plateau to the rivers, are narrow, and the profiles of the opposing walls are as bold as the eastern escarpment."[16] Along the 700-mile-long (1,126.3-kilometer-long) front, elevations range from 3,000 ft (912 m) in the Catskill Mountains to nearly 2,000 ft (608 m) in Pennsylvania. South of the Potomac River in West Virginia and Virginia the front rises again to 4,000 ft (1,216 m) and reaches a maximum elevation of 4,600 ft (1,398.4 m) 20 mi (32.2 km) west of Monterrey, Virginia.[17] From there south, elevations decline and eventually the escarpment blends into the plateau. On the west, the Plateaus Province is bounded by the Central Lowland, Interior Low Plateaus, and Coastal Plain, all major physiographic provinces delimited by Fenneman. Long segments of the western boundary are known as the knobs, a reference to a segment of the Pottsville Escarpment that is marked by scattered promontories capped by resistant conglomerate rocks.

The Appalachian Plateaus Province has the largest number of internal subdivisions. The province can be subdivided into the Cumberland Plateau in the south and the Allegheny Plateau (including glaciated and nonglaciated areas) in the north. Fenneman further divided the province into the following sections (Figure 2.1). (1) The Catskill Mountains are located in the extreme northeast of the province and cover most of 4 counties in southern New York State. The Catskill section has been glaciated and is one of the highest and most dissected areas of the entire province. (2) The glaciated Allegheny Plateau, the northernmost section, includes most of Appalachian New York and much of northern Pennsylvania. Except for the changes brought about by glaciation, it is very similar to the unglaciated Allegheny Plateau. (3) In the eastern part of the province is the Conemaugh section of the plateau, which has higher elevations and has been more affected by folding because of its proximity to the zone of suturing. (4) The unglaciated Kanawha section of the Allegheny Plateau is the largest and most typical section because it is in the mature stage of erosional development. (5) To the south is the Cumberland section of the plateau, an area of nearly horizontal sandstone interbedded with bituminous coal that extends from southeastern Kentucky to the Gulf Coastal Plain in Alabama.[18]

Elevations are highest in the eastern portion of the Appalachian Plateaus Province where the Catskill, Allegheny, and Cumberland mountains sections are located. The Catskills section has the greatest relief, and there are a few summits in excess of 4,000 ft (1,216 m) and scores between 3,000 ft (912 m) and 4,000 ft. Slide Mountain, at 4,204 ft (1,281.4 m), is the highest point in the Catskills. The highest elevation in the entire Plateaus Province is found in the Allegheny Mountains section in northeastern West Virginia, where the state's highest peak, Spruce Knob Mountain (4,860 ft—1,477.4 m) is located. The Cumberland Mountains section also has summits in excess of 4,000 ft. One such is

Kentucky's highest point, Big Black Mountain (4,150 ft—1,261.6 m). In the western part of the province, elevations diminish and are less than 1,000 ft (304 m) in Alabama and Ohio, and between 1,000 and 2,000 ft (608 m) in east-central Kentucky and Tennessee.

Because of the high relief, the height and length of the Allegheny Front, and the generally rugged and dissected nature of the entire province, migration and settlement here has been more difficult than in most of the rest of the Appalachian region. The province's river valleys, water gaps, and wind gaps have somewhat facilitated movement. The best example, perhaps, is the famous Cumberland Gap, located in Cumberland Mountain at the point where the Kentucky, Virginia, and Tennessee boundaries meet. This wind gap, a part of Daniel Boone's Wilderness Trail into Kentucky, is a 1,000-foot-deep notch (1,650 ft—501.6 m—above sea level) in the otherwise even-crested Cumberland Mountain. The plateau's dendritic drainage pattern is more difficult to traverse than the trellis-type drainage of the Ridge and Valley Province, although some river valleys, such as the Greenbrier in eastern West Virginia, have been locally important routeways.

Within the Plateaus Province there are several atypical topographic features worthy of special mention. The Cumberland Mountains section, for example, is bounded by four faults. Two of these, called thrust faults, have been responsible for the formation of the ridgelike Pine Mountain on the northwest and Cumberland Mountain on the southeast. Both mountains extend southwestward from Kentucky into Tennessee. Other noteworthy topographic features include the Sequatchie Valley, Walden Ridge, and Sand Mountain. The 200-mile-long (321.8-kilometer-long) Sequatchie Valley begins in the Crab Orchard Mountains near Crossville, Tennessee, and ends at the Black Warrior coalfield near Birmingham, Alabama. The Sequatchie, similar in structure to the valleys of the Ridge and Valley Province, is separated from that province by a single fingerlike ridge located on the eastern edge of the Plateau Province, known as Walden Ridge in Tennessee and as Sand Mountain in Alabama.

Bituminous coal has had a major economic impact upon the Plateau Province. It is mined in every state except New York. Major cities have emerged both within and adjacent to the province in large part because of coal mining and its related industries, such as steel manufacturing. Pittsburgh is located in the plateau, as well as other major cities such as Charleston, Huntington, Wheeling, Binghamton, and Johnstown.

## CLIMATES

Just as Appalachia has multiple geologic and topographic personalities, it also has not one climate but many. Climatic variation is the product of several interrelated factors. The region, because of its sheer size and north-south orientation, spans 10 degrees of latitude from Alabama to New York. That distance is great enough to produce significant differences

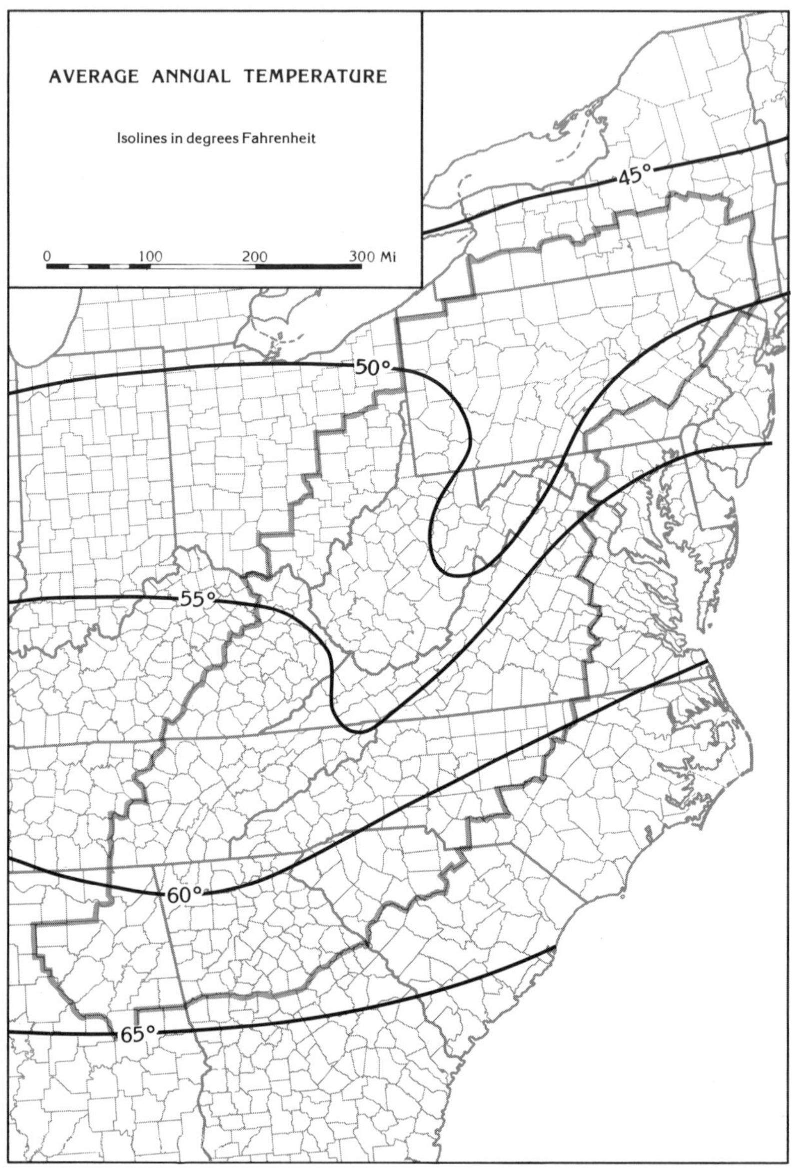


**Figure 2.2**
Source: John L. Baldwin, *Weather Atlas of the United States* (Washington, D.C.: U.S. Department of Commerce, Environmental Science Services Administration, 1968. Reprinted by Gale Research Co., Detroit, Mich., 1975).

in the range of temperatures. The average annual temperature in Alabama's northeastern highlands is about 65° F (18.3° C), but it is only 46° F (7.8° C) in southern New York (Figure 2.2). There are corresponding differences in the growing season. At lower elevations in the south, the frost-free period (the length of time between the last frost in the spring and the first frost in the fall) may reach 220 days, sufficient to grow cotton. In New York, the frost-free period is only 100 days, a period too short for corn to mature and be harvested as grain (Figure 2.3). The region's latitudinal position is in the zone of prevailing westerly winds that bring a succession of high- and low-pressure systems from autumn through spring. During the summer months, a high-pressure area over the Atlantic, several hundred miles to the east, influences the pattern of air-mass movement across the region by blocking the passage of low-pressure cells that bring drier, cooler air behind them and promoting the flow of warm, moist air from the south. Under these conditions air stagnation is common.

The great range of altitude within the region is also a factor in creating a pronounced differentiation of local climates. Part of the Piedmont of the Carolinas, for example, is 600 to 800 ft (182.4 to 243.2 m) above sea level and experiences average annual temperatures that are 12 degrees warmer than in the North Carolina Blue Ridge 120 mi (193.1 km) to the west.

Annual precipitation averages about 45 in. (114.3 cm) across the region, and although the late summer and early fall season tends to be somewhat drier, precipitation is distributed rather uniformly throughout the year.[19] The pattern of precipitation, which ranges from about 35 in. (88.9 cm) annually in western New York and Pennsylvania to a high of about 80 in. (203.2 cm) in the western North Carolina mountains, is produced by the abrupt variations in topography and the relative proximity of the region to the Gulf of Mexico (Figure 2.4). Low-pressure systems, or cyclonic storms, bring warm, moist air masses from the Gulf north and east into the region. Precipitation produced by the interaction of Gulf air and cooler, drier air from the continental interior decreases northward as the distance from the warm, moist air source increases.

Precipitation is also produced orographically when moisture-bearing air masses moving in the path of the prevailing westerlies are forced up and over a series of mountain barriers. The air is cooled as it rises, and condensation and precipitation drain the air of its moisture. The effect is higher precipitation on the windward (west-facing) slopes. The mountains of the southern Blue Ridge are the highest in Appalachia and the closest to the source region of moist air masses. Consequently, this area experiences the greatest precipitation in the Appalachians. The leeward-facing (eastern) mountain slopes are in the rain shadow and therefore receive much less precipitation. Although this effect is noticeable to some degree in most of the region's hill ranges, it is most profound

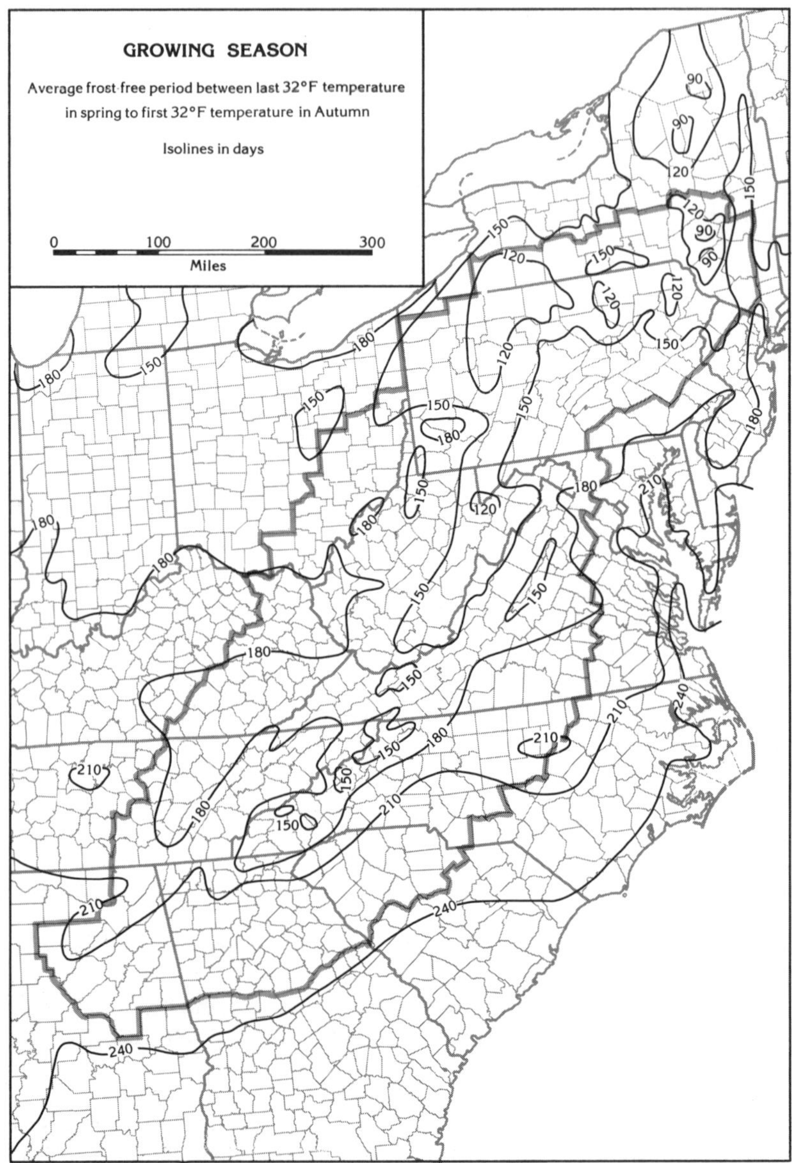


**Figure 2.3**

Source: John L. Baldwin, *Weather Atlas of the United States* (Washington, D.C.: U.S. Department of Commerce, Environmental Science Services Administration, 1968. Reprinted by Gale Research Co., Detroit, Mich., 1975).

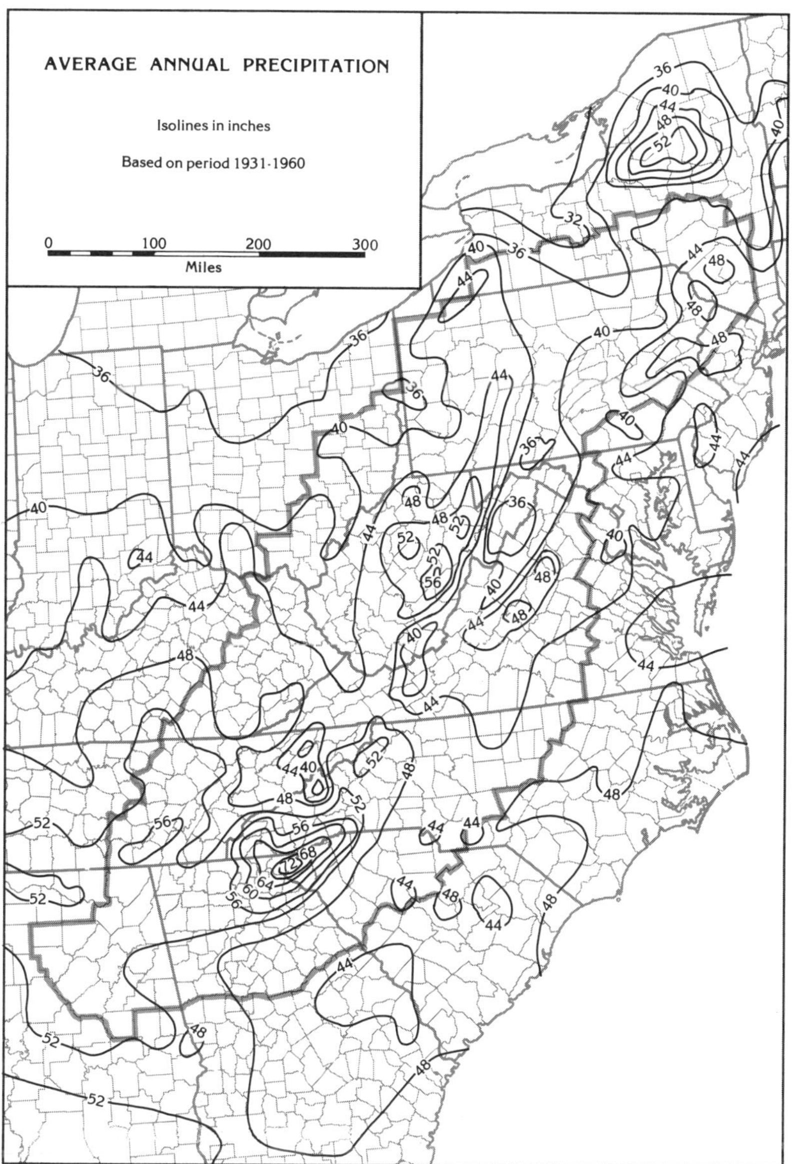


**Figure 2.4**
Source: John L. Baldwin, *Weather Atlas of the United States* (Washington, D.C.: U.S. Department of Commerce, Environmental Science Services Administration, 1968. Reprinted by Gale Research Co., Detroit, Mich., 1975).

in West Virginia and North Carolina. In the southern Blue Ridge, for example, average annual precipitation decreases from 80 in. to less than 40 in. (101.6 cm) as one travels east to the South Carolina Piedmont, a linear distance of only 50 mi (80.5 km). Precipitation gradients almost as pronounced are found in eastern West Virginia. Southern Randolph County in the Allegheny Mountains receives 66 in. (167.6 cm) of precipitation annually, but 20 mi (32.2 km) to the east the amount is only 48 in. (121.9 cm).[20]

Winters in the Appalachian highlands are somewhat more severe than in the adjacent low-lying areas, again because of topography and altitude. Snowfall is heavy in the north, especially in southwestern New York. Here, in part because air masses moving into the region from the west become recharged with water vapor as they pass over the large expanse of water in the eastern Great Lakes, snowfall can reach 100 in. (254 cm) or more. Amounts decrease southward but peak again at 126 in. (320 cm) in the Kumbrabow State Forest of east-central West Virginia. Snowfall in the higher elevations of eastern Tennessee and western North Carolina is only 12 in. (30.5 cm), but sufficient to have encouraged the development of several ski resorts. South of the Great Smoky Mountains, snowfall decreases to a regional low of 2 to 4 in. (5.1 to 10.2 cm) and provides only an inconvenience for winter travel.

In late spring and summer, most precipitation is produced by thunderstorms. This type of rainfall can be beneficial to agriculture, because the storms usually form relatively quickly, and the rain may last only minutes as the storm moves on. This gives farmers both needed precipitation and maximum sunshine. More thunderstorms occur in the south than in the north. Thunderstorm days vary from sixty per year in Alabama to thirty to thirty-five in Pennsylvania and New York.[21] Only rarely (every decade or so) are major tropical storms or hurricanes a threat to the region. Storms originating over the Gulf of Mexico travel north into the region and may bring heavy rain to the Cumberland and Allegheny plateaus. Atlantic storms, on the other hand, rarely penetrate the barrier of the Blue Ridge but do pass northward along the Piedmont. The occasional tropical storm of extraordinary size and energy that intrudes into the region constitutes a multifaceted environmental hazard of enormous proportions. Heavy rains over several days produce catastrophic floods, often over several adjoining watersheds. Rain and runoff can induce landslides and debris avalanches that strip hillsides of soil, rock, and vegetation and cover flood plains with silt.[22]

Runoff from areas of impermeable clay soils and shale bedrock is rapid. Little moisture is retained after heavy winter and spring precipitation. Consequently, streams in these areas are subject to high fluctuations in flow, with the smaller streams drying up in the fall months. By contrast, deep permeable soils overlying porous bedrock, such as limestone, will retain precipitation and release it more gradually, keeping springs and streams flowing even during the low rainfall autumn months.[23]

## WATER: QUANTITY AND QUALITY

One of Appalachia's major natural resources is water. The region receives an annual average precipitation of more than 45 in. (114.3 cm). Runoff maintains a large number of streams and rivers that carry large amounts of water from the region. The average discharge of water by all of the region's streams in cubic feet per second (c.f.s., or second-feet), the fundamental unit for measuring flow, amounts to over 300,000 c.f.s. (Table 2.1). Stated in another way, this means that on the average over 195 billion gal (738 billion liters) of water leave the region each day. Furthermore, this amount in effect is the net discharge, since only a few minor streams flow into the region.[24] Nearly two-thirds of this discharge, or 126 billion gal (476.9 billion liters) per day, flows toward the Gulf of Mexico, while one-third, or 69 billion gal (261.2 billion liters), flows eastward toward the Atlantic Ocean. Areas in the western and southern portions of the Appalachian region, because they receive the greatest precipitation amounts, have the highest average runoff. Average runoffs ranging from 20 to 25 in. (50.8 to 63.5 cm) in such areas rank among the highest runoff amounts in the United States. This pattern of runoff, of course, closely reflects the pattern of average annual precipitation; runoff amounts to as much as one-half of the annual precipitation.

There is considerable annual variation of discharge, with the greatest rates in late winter and early spring. Discharge also varies between years, in part because the Appalachian region has always been plagued by floods. The average flood recurrence interval for streams in the region is once every ten years.[25] One of the worst storms on record occurred in June 1972, when hurricane Agnes moved into central Pennsylvania. Eighteen in. (45.7 cm) of rain fell in three days over the Susquehanna River Valley. Major floods were also experienced on the Juniata, Schuylkill, and Ohio rivers. At Harrisburg, Pennsylvania, the Susquehanna crested at 16 ft (4.9 m) above flood stage and inundated the business district. Acts of men, too, can cause floods. On February 22, 1972, a flood occurred along Buffalo Creek, West Virginia, when a dam constructed from coal-mine wastes burst and 130 million gal (492.1 million liters) of water swept through a narrow crowded valley, killing more than 120 persons and leaving another 4,000 homeless.

Water quality varies with land- and water-use patterns. In some parts of the region streams have been polluted, but the total supply of usable water can be maintained by good management. Perhaps the most extensive area affected by water pollution in the region lies "in the coal mining regions of northern Appalachia where mine waste and the flow of ground water through active and abandoned mines adds a variety of solid and chemical contaminants to surface water."[26] Acid mine drainage today affects Appalachia's surface water and groundwater wherever coal is mined.

TABLE 2.1
Average Flow for Streams Leaving the Appalachian Region

| | Tributary of: | Drainage Area (in sq. mi.) | Average Flow[1] C.F.S. | Average Flow[1] In./Year[2] | Years of Records |
|---|---|---|---|---|---|
| Streams draining toward Atlantic: | | | | | |
| Susquehanna River (Harrisburg, PA) | | 24,100 | 34,530 | 19.46 | 90 |
| Savannah River (Augusta, GA) | | 7,508 | 10,200 | 18.45 | 70 |
| Potomac River (Point of Rocks, MD) | | 9,651 | 9,321 | 13.11 | 83 |
| Delaware River (Easton, PA) | | 4,636 | 9,016 | | 10 |
| Pee Dee River (Rockingham, NC) | | 6,870 | 7,997 | 15.81 | 56 |
| James River (Richmond, VA) | | 6,758 | 7,492 | 15.05 | 44 |
| Catawba River (Camden, SC) | Santee River | 5,070 | 6,372 | 17.07 | 55 |
| Broad River (Richtex, SC) | Santee River | 4,850 | 6,219 | 17.41 | 53 |
| Oconee River (Milledgeville, GA) | Altamaha River | 2,950 | 3,375 | 15.54 | 74 |
| Roanoke River (Randolph, VA) | | 2,977 | 3,076 | 14.03 | 37 |
| Ocmulgee River (Macon, GA) | Altamaha River | 2,240 | 2,740 | 16.61 | 67 |
| Saluda River (Chappells, SC) | Santee River | 1,360 | 1,979 | 19.76 | 52 |
| Rappahannock River (Fredericksburg, VA) | | 1,596 | 1,646 | 14.01 | 71 |
| Appomattox River (Matoaca, VA) | James River | 1,344 | 1,546 | 15.62 | 9 |
| Pamunkey River (Chilesburg, VA) | York River | 1,081 | 996 | 12.51 | 37 |
| Neuse River (Northside, NC) | | 526 | 516 | 13.32 | 51 |
| Deep River (Ranseur, NC) | Cape Fear River | 346 | 350 | 13.74 | 55 |
| Total | | | 107,371 | | |
| Streams draining toward Gulf of Mexico: | | | | | |
| Ohio River (Greenup Dam, KY) | Mississippi River | 62,000 | 94,420 | 20.68 | 11 |
| Tennessee River (Whitesburg, AL) | Ohio River | 25,610 | 43,690 | 23.17 | 54 |
| Coosa River (Wetumpka, AL) | Alabama River | 10,200 | 16,420 | 21.86 | 54 |
| Cumberland River (Celina, TN) | Ohio River | 7,307 | 11,690 | 21.73 | 56 |
| Black Warrior River (Northport, AL) | Tombigbee River | 4,828 | 7,879 | 22.16 | 58 |
| Chattahoochee River (West Point, GA) | Appalachicola River | 3,550 | 5,653 | 21.62 | 81 |
| Kentucky River (Winchester, KY) | Ohio River | 3,955 | 5,270 | 18.10 | 71 |
| Caney Fork (Rock Island, TN) | Cumberland River | 1,678 | 3,209 | 25.97 | 64 |
| Tallapousa River (Wadley, AL) | Alabama River | 1,660 | 2,564 | 20.97 | 55 |
| Flint River (Thomaston, GA) | Chattahoochee River | 1,220 | 1,808 | 20.13 | 11 |
| Cahaba River (Centreville, AL) | Alabama River | 1,029 | 1,608 | 21.22 | 51 |
| Licking River (Farmers, KY) | Ohio River | 827 | 1,060 | 17.41 | 40 |
| Total of streams draining toward Gulf | | | 195,271 | | |
| Total of streams draining toward Atlantic | | | 107,371 | | |
| Grand Total | | | 302,642 | | |

Sources: All figures are from various Water Resources Data reports from individual states for current years (U.S. Department of the Interior, Geological Survey).

[1]Flow is measured at gauging station nearest the region boundary, indicated by city name following river name.

[2]Inches per year runoff as a portion of total precipitation per year.

In summary, there is a huge quantity of (potentially) good-quality water available in the region. This resource has been, and continues to be, developed for hydroelectric power, transportation, industrial, and recreational purposes. The large number of dams, locks, and reservoirs constructed in the region attest to this. As a resource, water is the keystone to future regional development. Whether it will continue to be available in large quantities to the residents of the region for personal, industrial, or recreational uses depends upon how well its management is planned.

## Drainage Patterns

The direction of drainage from the Appalachian region is either toward the Gulf of Mexico or toward the Atlantic Ocean. The divide between this westward and eastward drainage follows a line along the east side of the Blue Ridge Province north into Virginia, where it cuts across the Ridge and Valley Province to the Allegheny Front. In eastern West Virginia, the divide trends north into Maryland to bisect that state's westernmost county, Garrett. The divide continues north into the Plateau Province of Pennsylvania and New York.

Whether or not drainage is toward the Gulf of Mexico or the Atlantic is important to an understanding of the region's physiography, because unequal distances from the sea affect topography. Simply stated, "it is to be expected that the more advanced stages of an erosion cycle may not be as well displayed in the area remote from the sea as in the area nearer the sea. . . ."[27] The drainage divide also has historic significance. King George III's Proclamation Line of 1763, for example, was based on the divide.[28] The country west of this line was to be held for the Crown, and the colonists were to be contained east of the divide. A second example is that during the latter part of the eighteenth century, the allegiance of settlers in areas west of the divide (such as those in the state of Kentucky) was to the Crown, or later to the United States. Their allegiance was often tested, because drainage—and therefore commerce—moved toward the Mississippi River rather than toward the established ports of the Atlantic seaboard. Thus, for a time at least, the economic interests of the people of the western country were closely tied to those of the Spanish and French.

Within the Appalachian region the pattern of drainage varies and closely reflects the region's structural geology and lithology. In parts of the Blue Ridge Province, and especially in the Ridge and Valley, the stream patterns tend to be trellised. Parallel streams between ridges are often connected by right-angle valleys through the many water gaps in the ridges. (Wind gaps, on the other hand, are notches that were formerly transversed by streams that have since been captured, or diverted elsewhere.) The stream patterns of the Piedmont, the Appalachian Plateau Province, and parts of the Blue Ridge are dendritic, and deeply incised valleys are commonly found in these areas. Examination of the road patterns on any road map of Pennsylvania demonstrates the contrasts between these two drainage patterns.

### The Region's Rivers

Nearly 60 percent of Appalachia's total water discharge is carried by three major streams: the Ohio and Tennessee rivers, which drain ultimately into the Gulf of Mexico via the Mississippi River, and the Susquehanna River, which flows southeastward into Chesapeake Bay and the Atlantic Ocean (Table 2.1).

The Ohio River begins in Pittsburgh at the confluence of the Allegheny and Monongahela rivers (Figure 2.5). The headwaters of the Allegheny are in north-central Pennsylvania, and the Monongahela flows north from central West Virginia. Pittsburgh, established as Fort Pitt in 1759 at the Forks of the Ohio River, was the initial destination for thousands of early travelers on their way west. Near Pittsburgh, the valleys of all three streams provide sites for many steel and steel-related industries that were established in the nineteenth century. From Pittsburgh, the Ohio flows southwestward to form the boundary between Ohio and both West Virginia and Kentucky, then leaves the Appalachian region west of Portsmouth, Ohio. Between Pittsburgh and Portsmouth, several important streams feed into the Ohio. These include the Big Sandy River that, with its Tug Fork tributary, forms the boundary between West Virginia and Kentucky, and West Virginia's Kanawha River, which meets the Ohio at Point Pleasant, West Virginia. The Kanawha, which flows through Charleston—where its valley is known as Chemical Valley because of the many chemical industries in place there—begins at Gauley Bridge in central West Virginia at the confluence of the Gauley and New rivers. The ancient New River, which flows north some 320 mi (514.9 km) from its headwaters in Ashe County, North Carolina, has cut spectacular gorges along its course in West Virginia—creating, so it is advertised, the Grand Canyon of the east. Eastern West Virginia's Greenbrier River, an early focus of settlement, is a tributary of the New River. Other important tributaries of the Ohio, including the Cumberland, Kentucky, and Licking rivers, all join it after they leave the Appalachian region.

Another major river that flows from the region is the Tennessee, which ultimately drains into the Ohio River near Paducah, in western Kentucky. Major tributaries of the Tennessee River include the Powell, Clinch, Nolichucky, French Broad, and Holston rivers, all of which join the Tennessee in the Ridge and Valley Province in eastern Tennessee. It was the broad, alluvial valleys drained by these rivers that attracted the first settlers who came to Tennessee from Virginia and North Carolina. The Holston River, for example, was named for Stephen Holston, who built a cabin in the valley about 1746. The early Watauga and Holston settlements were established in this area in the eighteenth century. Today a large portion of the valley is under the jurisdiction of the Tennessee Valley Authority (TVA), a federally sponsored agency

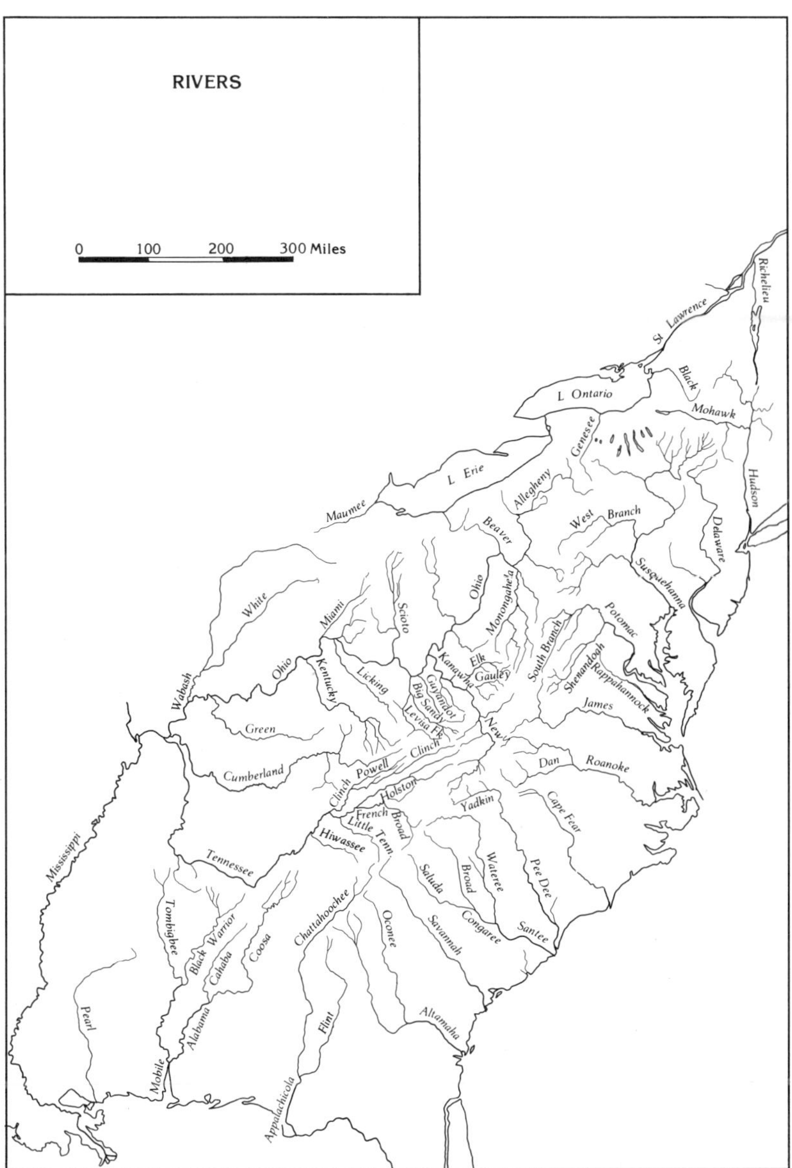
RIVERS
0 100 200 300 Miles
L Ontario
L Erie
St Lawrence
Richelieu
Black
Mohawk
Hudson
Genessee
Allegheny
Maumee
Beaver
West Branch
Delaware
Susquehanna
Ohio
Monongahela
Potomac
South Branch
Shenandoah
Rappahannock
James
White
Miami
Scioto
Wabash
Ohio
Kentucky
Licking
Guyandot
Big Sandy
Levisa Fk
Kanawha
Elk
Gauley
New
Green
Cumberland
Clinch
Powell
Clinch
Holston
Dan
Roanoke
Yadkin
Cape Fear
French Broad
Little Tenn
Hiwassee
Tennessee
Mississippi
Tombigbee
Black Warrior
Cahaba
Coosa
Chattahoochee
Oconee
Saluda
Broad
Wateree
Pee Dee
Congaree
Santee
Savannah
Altamaha
Pearl
Alabama
Mobile
Flint
Appalachicola

**Figure 2.5**

established in 1933. Major dams constructed for flood control, power generation, and navigational improvement have created numerous reservoirs in southern Appalachia. Watts Bar, Douglas, Norris, and Cherokee lakes are among the largest of the reservoirs formed by the dams that TVA has built on the Tennessee and its tributaries.

Another important river that originates in Appalachia and ultimately drains into the Gulf of Mexico is the Chattahoochee, which flows south through Atlanta and forms a part of the Georgia-Alabama border. The Chattahoochee, together with its tributary the Flint, ultimately join the Apalachicola River on Georgia's boundary with Florida.

The major river of the region that drains into the Atlantic is the Susquehanna, which rises in Otsego Lake in central New York's Otsego County and flows southward for nearly 450 mi (724.1 km) before it empties into Chesapeake Bay. Before the Susquehanna leaves the Appalachian region near Harrisburg, Pennsylvania, it is joined by the West Branch of the Susquehanna at Sunbury and by the Juniata River at Duncannon, Pennsylvania. The numerous water gaps (such as the series above Harrisburg) in the Ridge and Valley Province cut by these rivers greatly facilitated travel across Pennsylvania to Pittsburgh and the Ohio River. Roads, and later railroads, were built through the gaps. Additionally, an elaborate network of canals, built along these rivers, was constructed in the nineteenth century.[29]

A number of smaller rivers have been historic routes across the Piedmont into the Ridge and Valley. The Delaware and Potomac rivers, for example, together drain an area within Appalachia of nearly 15,000 sq mi (38,850 sq km). The Potomac rises in eastern West Virginia and flows eastward for more than 280 mi (450.5 km) before reaching the Atlantic. It leaves the Piedmont Province at the Fall Line west of Washington, D.C., where it tumbles across a series of falls and rapids including Great Falls, a 35-foot (10.6-meter) cataract. The major tributary of the Potomac is the Shenandoah River, which flows north and joins the Potomac at Harpers Ferry, West Virginia. The Shenandoah Valley is a part of the Great Valley, and beginning in the early 1700s this valley was a routeway for thousands of Scotch-Irish, English, and German immigrants from eastern Pennsylvania. Among these early settlers was the young Daniel Boone. Boone was born in Reading, Pennsylvania, in 1734; in 1750, with his parents, he migrated south up the valley and across the Blue Ridge to the forks of the Yadkin River on the North Carolina Piedmont.[30] Several years later Boone journeyed to the Valley of East Tennessee and ultimately across the Cumberland Gap, which he first crossed in 1767, into Kentucky. This route is the famous Wilderness Trail, which terminated in central Kentucky's Bluegrass region.

The route followed by Daniel Boone from Pennsylvania to Virginia, North Carolina, Tennessee, and Kentucky was one of three major routeways across the Appalachia region. A second route led across southern Pennsylvania from Harrisburg to Pittsburgh and the Ohio

River by way of river valleys and water gaps. The third major routeway across the region, known as the National Road or the Cumberland Road, led up the Potomac and across a narrow divide to the Youghiogheny River, a tributary of the Monongahela, and then on to Wheeling, West Virginia, and the Ohio River.[31]

Other important rivers that rise in the Appalachian region and flow toward the Atlantic include the James and Roanoke rivers in Virginia; the Pee Dee River of the Carolinas and its tributaries, which include the Yadkin, Catawba, Broad, and Saluda rivers, all of which flow into the Santee River in South Carolina; and the Oconee and Ocmulgee rivers, which meet to form the Altamaha River outside Appalachia near Lumber City, Georgia.

## SOIL PATTERNS

The complex processes of chemical and mechanical weathering of lithic materials across Appalachia have produced three distinct soil orders: inceptisols, alfisols, and ultisols (Figure 2.6). The inceptisols occur primarily in the glaciated area of southern New York and northwestern Pennsylvania, southern and western Virginia, eastern Kentucky, southeastern Ohio, and eastern Tennessee. These are relatively young soils that have been little modified by chemical weathering. They still retain levels of plant nutrients sufficient to support agriculture if conservation measures and fertilization are employed. These soils usually develop on a layer of deeply weathered rock or glacial till and contain a type of clay called saprolite.[32] Although inceptisols can develop on a wide range of sedimentary, metamorphic, and igneous rocks, as well as till, two processes work in concert across these diverse surfaces to produce similarly youthful soil horizons. First, many of these rocks are extremely hard and will yield only slowly to the mechanical breakdown processes of freezing and thawing. Meanwhile, a second process, erosion, continually moves soil and saprolite down steep slopes, preventing the prolonged development of deep soil accumulations.[33]

Inceptisols include a number of suborders. One, the ochrept suborder, is found over broad areas in Appalachia. Ochrepts are light colored and well drained and are usually found on steep slopes that are actively eroding. They generally have cool root zones (47° F to 59° F—8.3° C to 15° C mean annual temperature), and low fertility. Root growth is restricted by a dense clay subsurface layer. Where the natural vegetation found on these soils has been cleared for farming, the soil requires intense conservation, and agriculture is difficult at best. Dystrochrepts, a soil group in the ochrept suborder, are infertile, shallow soils developed on sandstone and shale. They are the most extensive inceptisols in Appalachia and are found from Pennsylvania south to Alabama. Dystrochrepts have developed on acid parent materials in a humid climate. The soils in turn are acid and are thoroughly leached of important plant nutrients. Although early settlers cleared large expanses of mixed con-

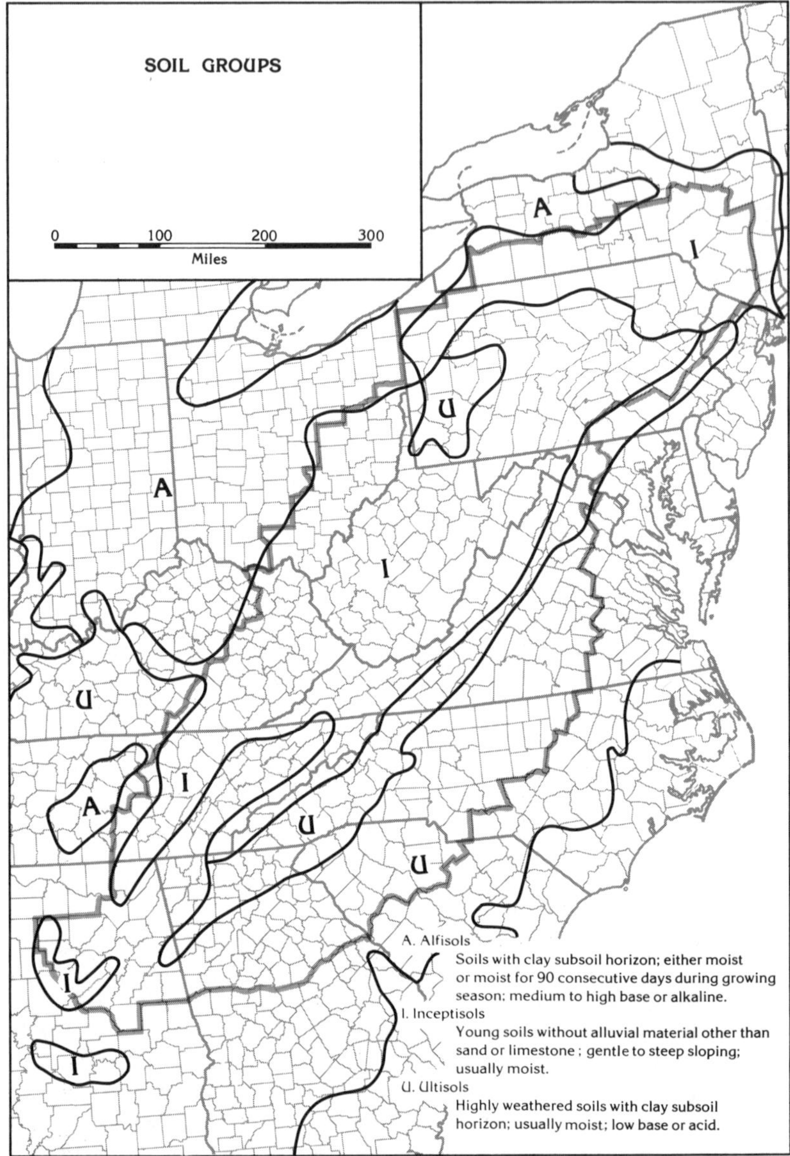


**Figure 2.6**
Generalized map after Henry D. Foth and John W. Schafer, *Soil Geography and Land Use* (New York: John Wiley & Sons, 1980), p. 38. Copyright © 1980 by John Wiley & Sons.

iferous and hardwood forests from these soils, most of the land has been abandoned and has reverted to woodland. Those farming communities that survive tend to be found on the more fertile soils of the river flood plains.[34]

In the Ridge and Valley country, the interdigitation of soils closely follows the topography and bedrock. The steep ridges are covered by inceptisols that support second-growth deciduous trees. Often the intervening valleys are floored with limestone that is readily eroded by solution and is covered with alfisols, the region's most fertile and productive soil order. The gently rolling floors of these valleys, which extend from eastern Pennsylvania through Virginia into Tennessee and Georgia, are intensively developed for agriculture. The soils are generally deep, well drained, dark red in color, and—if conservation measures are employed—high in available plant nutrients. A considerable proportion of the entire region's agricultural output comes from the alfisols and includes a diversity of products that range from grass and dairy-cattle fodder crops to orchards and truck garden crops. Alfisols occur in relatively limited areas, when one considers the region as a whole, and consequently constitute a secondary soil order.

The ultisols, the third soil type, are much greater in extent and comprise the second major soil order in the region. Ultisols have been subjected to extended periods of chemical decomposition and leaching and—geologically—are old soils.[35] Ultisols are common in low to middle latitudes. Humid climates and high mean annual root-zone temperatures (59° F to 72° F—15° C to 22.2° C) suggest that leaching of plant nutrients continues for most of the year. The soil may not freeze in the winter to temporarily halt the weathering process, and as a result the soils contain very little organic material but are high in aluminum clays. Their vivid red color indicates the buildup of iron oxides. Early settlers adapted to these soils by practicing shifting cultivation.[36] After the first two or three years of farming, when yields declined drastically, the field was abandoned, and new land was cleared of trees and planted.[37]

The soils of the Piedmont from Virginia south through Georgia are primarily ultisols. The surface is gently rolling, cut occasionally by steep stream valleys. By the Civil War much of the Piedmont had been cleared and formed a major arm of the southern Cotton Belt. The soils eroded, fertility declined, and production could be maintained only by heavy applications of fertilizer. Modern cotton production favors large-scale operations such as those in Texas, Arizona, and California. Many of the small Piedmont farms that no longer are planted to cotton now grow pine trees, which are used for pulp or lumber; others have been allowed to revert to scrub deciduous and coniferous tree stands.[38] Today, about 60 percent of the Piedmont is in trees and only about 20 percent is cultivated. North of Virginia, the proportions of land use on the ultisols are somewhat reversed. In southeastern Pennsylvania, these soils are intensively cultivated in many areas and produce livestock forage crops and truck garden and orchard crops.[39]

The North Fork of the Shenandoah River has cut meander loops into the limestone of the Great Valley floor near Woodstock, Virginia. Alfisols on the limestone support productive agriculture. In contrast, the slopes of Massanutten Mountain running diagonally across the photo have only a thin veneer of inceptisols. (U.S. Department of Agriculture photo.)

## NATURAL AND MODIFIED VEGETATION

To appreciate the complexity of the pattern of forest vegetation, as well as the wealth of species present in Appalachia, it is necessary to understand several key points about the physical and historical geography of the region. First, the northern section of the region, the Allegheny Plateau of much of southern New York and portions of northeast and northwest Pennsylvania, underwent extensive glacial modification during the Pleistocene geologic epoch. While this region was covered in ice or under the influence of periglacial climates, vegetative species are thought to have migrated south along the mountains to appropriate ecologic niches among the hills and valleys of what are now the Cumberland and Blue Ridge mountains. When the ice retreated, the barren area was colonized, in part, by species from the south. Although the glaciated topography of New York and Pennsylvania is geologically much younger than the country to the south, there is not a marked vegetation change at the glacial boundary. Instead, a gradual change occurs with a blending of species across a broad transition zone.

Second, the climate of this northern zone is cooler than that of the equivalent altitudes in the southern reaches of the region. This temperature gradient could be expected to influence the distribution of species, but it is mitigated to a large extent by a general increase in altitude from north to south. The New York and Pennsylvania plateau country varies from 500 to 1,500 ft (152 to 456 m) in elevation and in some places, before logging, was covered by a forest of spruce and fir. To the south in the Maryland Panhandle and the Allegheny Mountains, the altitude increases and spruce and fir can be found at 3,000 ft (912 m). In the southern Blue Ridge and Great Smoky mountains, spruce and fir occur at elevations above 6,000 ft (1,824 m). In other words, the climate change associated with increased altitudes of the southern mountains replicates some of the climatic characteristics of the north, with a twofold result. Northern vegetation has found an environment suitable to its requirements, 600 mi (965.4 km) south of its expected range. Further, the great variety of species that are found in the southern forests corresponds to the wide range of environmental zones to be found in the varying altitudes, slope faces, microclimates, and soil and rock types.[40]

Third, forest vegetation types do not change abruptly except along certain sharp topographic breaks. Instead, one type of vegetation association will grade into another as altitude changes and thermal conditions are altered or as species respond to the interplay of the effects of orographic rainfall and rain shadow from windward highlands to leeward valleys. One of the few abrupt vegetational boundaries occurs along the Allegheny Front, the topographic break between the Ridge and Valley and the Plateaus to the west. Here a change, especially noticeable in Pennsylvania, Maryland, and northeastern West Virginia, takes place as the oak forest of the Blue Ridge and Ridge and Valley gives way to the mixed mesophytic forest of the Allegheny Plateau.

Fourth, because of the extensive human modification of the natural vegetation over broad areas of the region, few pockets of virgin forest remain—those stands that do exist are usually found in parks or preserves. In some areas species of the original forest have reestablished themselves after a period of human exploitation. But across broad areas, the original species have been largely replaced by so-called weed trees or by extensive plantings of orchards or pines that are used for Christmas trees in west central Pennsylvania or for pulp and paper manufacturing in the Piedmont of the Carolinas and Georgia. By 1960 (the latest date for which comprehensive estimates are available), almost two-thirds of the land in Appalachia was considered forested, albeit primarily in some type of regrowth rather than in climax stands. Of some 67 million a. (27 million hectares) in timber, about 14 percent was in national forest or some form of public ownership.[41]

The original forest vegetation of the region can be divided into four major groups based on an association of tree types. The location of these forests corresponds, in a general way, to the topography of the four major physiographic provinces as well as to climate and altitude changes. A fifth group, the western mesophytic forest, is found only at the extreme western site of the Raitz-Ulack region and is not discussed here (Figure 2.7).

***Hemlock-White Pine-Northern Hardwoods Region.*** The glaciated Allegheny Plateau was originally covered by a forest of mixed coniferous trees. The pioneers who moved into the region in the early 1800s found extensive forests of white pine and hemlock, valuable as lumber, and a variety of hardwoods, including sugar maple, beech, and yellow birch. Along the edges of the numerous low-lying bogs, created by the melting of buried glacial ice blocks, were stands of red maple, sour gum, balsam fir, hemlock, and white pine. The bogs themselves were filled with a variety of sphagnum mosses and other shrub and herbaceous species, including cranberry, bog rosemary, sundew, and buckbean. This forest has been so profoundly modified, initially by pioneer clearing for farming and later by lumbering, that today it bears little resemblance to the original. As farmed land is allowed to revert back to trees, ash and hawthorn move into the old fields, initiating the slow return of the pine-hardwood forest.[42]

***Mixed Mesophytic Forest Region.*** This forest region is so named because it represents a climax association in which a number of species share dominance: beech, tuliptree (called yellow-poplar in the south), basswood, sugar maple, sweet buckeye, chestnut (before a blight killed virtually every tree in North America), red oak, white oak, and hemlock. These trees prefer moist, well-drained sites and deep soils. The mixed mesophytic forest covers almost all of the unglaciated Allegheny Plateau, all of the Cumberland Mountains in eastern Kentucky and western

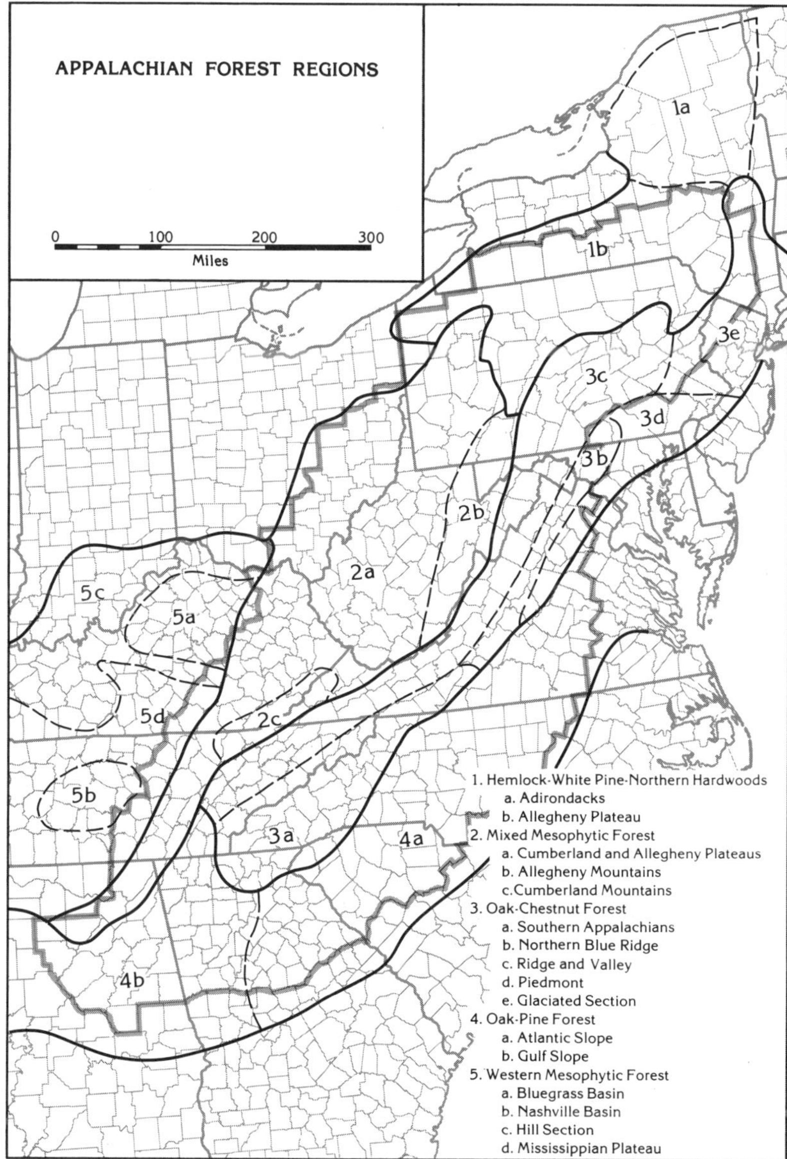


**Figure 2.7**
Source: E. Lucy Braun, *Deciduous Forests of Eastern North America* (New York: Hafner Press, 1950, reprinted 1974).

Virginia, the south end of the Allegheny Mountains, and all but the southern tip of the Cumberland Plateau. The eastern boundary lies generally along the Appalachian Front. The western boundary is coincident to the Pottsville Escarpment that marks the western edge of the Cumberland and Allegheny plateaus. Botanists regard this forest as one of the finest deciduous forests in North America because of the number of tree species, the large size of the trees, and the great variety of associated plant types. The shrub and herbaceous layer of understory plants is also distinctive and is more luxuriant and continuous than in any other forest type. Its species range from the rhododendron—found primarily along streams and rock outcrops—to ferns, flowers, and a wide range of herbs and plants of real or imagined medicinal value.[43]

Because the region covered by this forest association is so large, there is a transition of forest types horizontally and vertically. To the north, the number of beeches, sugar maples, and hemlocks gradually increases and grades into the pine and hardwood forest of central Pennsylvania. To the south, the proportion of oaks increases. Above 2,000 ft (608 m) the forest begins to give way to trees adapted to more northerly conditions. The tuliptree drops out with an increase in altitude, to be replaced by birches.

In eastern West Virginia, as elsewhere in the region where limestone bedrock replaces shale or sandstone, the lithic change is reflected in the forest vegetation. An extensive area around Lewisburg and Hillsboro along the Greenbrier River (Greenbrier and Pocahontas counties) is floored with limestone, which is now eroded into a rolling karst landscape with sinkholes and a good deal of underground drainage. The area was an island of oak-hickory forest in the mixed mesophytic forest region. The Big Levels around Lewisburg and the Little Levels at Hillsboro—as these areas were once known—were cleared by pioneers beginning in the late 1700s. Today they are among the state's principal livestock-producing areas.

A second type of anomaly in the mixed mesophytic forest coverage also occurs in West Virginia.[44] In the Allegheny Mountains of Pocahontas and Randolph counties are a number of highland bogs, or glades, as they are called locally. The glades originated in a manner different from the bogs of the glaciated region to the north. The West Virginia glades are located in topographic bowls and are the product of restricted runoff and cold air drainage from surrounding slopes. Because they are above 3,000 ft (912 m), they contain the same type of vegetation associations found in the northern bogs, including sphagnum moss, black spruce, and tamarack.[45]

The cultural vegetation occupying the area once covered by the mixed mesophytic forest today bears little resemblance to the virgin forest. Across the region, especially in the Cumberland Mountains of Kentucky and the Allegheny Mountains of West Virginia, early settlers found stands of tuliptrees, sugar maple, beech, and oak that were 5 ft (1.5

m) or more in diameter. Settlers seeking farm land were responsible for the initial cutting of these stands. Chestnut, which split easily, was preferred for rail fences, and tuliptree and oak were used in building homes and outbuildings. Beyond this, there was little opportunity to market the trees cut to clear land, so over large areas the giant logs were burned. The unglaciated Allegheny Plateau of Pennsylvania was more accessible than the highlands to the south and early on was penetrated by routes converging on the Ohio River. Extensive forests here, and in northern West Virginia, were cut to provide charcoal for the small iron furnaces that were built near the region's scattered iron-ore deposits. The extension of the railroads into the region from seaports at Baltimore and Philadelphia consumed large amounts of timber. The Baltimore and Ohio and the Chesapeake and Ohio, for example, used 2,640 hardwood cross ties per mile. Additional wood was consumed in clearing right-of-way and building bridges and as fuel.[46] Across the region, much of the land once cleared for farming has been abandoned and is beginning to revert back to forest.[47] In many areas the normal succession of vegetation back to the mesophytic forest cannot be re-established because the seed trees are gone. Instead, abandoned fields are claimed by brush and undesirable tree species.

***Oak-Chestnut Forest Region.*** A climax stand of chestnut, red oak, chestnut oak, white oak, and tuliptree once covered most of the Ridge and Valley and Blue Ridge physiographic provinces. White oak dominated tree stands in the valleys. On mountain slopes from 1,500 ft to 4,500 ft (456 to 1,368 m) chestnut predominated; it was associated with tuliptrees on the lower slopes and oaks at the upper elevations.[48] The forests of the southern Blue Ridge contain a greater variety of species than that found in the northern segment of the province. In the south, the great range of altitude and the variety of microclimates provide a diverse environment for a wide range of tree and herbaceous species. In the Unaka and Nantahala mountain ranges of eastern Tennessee and western North Carolina, for example, the chestnut forest grades into a northern hardwood–type forest between 4,500 and 5,000 ft (1,520 m). Here buckeye, silverbell, and beech blend with sugar maple and yellow birch. Between 5,500 and 6,000 ft (1,672 and 1,824 m) red spruce and Fraser fir appear.[49] Occasional "balds," or treeless mountaintops, are covered with grasses or a variety of heath shrubs and rhododendron. Periodic burning by Indians and grazing by farm livestock apparently has kept trees from colonizing the balds. When fire is controlled and grazing is no longer practiced, as in Great Smoky Mountain National Park, the mountaintops are soon reforested.[50]

The valley floors in the Ridge and Valley were cleared for farming by early pioneers. Adjacent ridges and the Blue Ridge were accessible from the Ridge and Valley to the west and the Piedmont to the east. A brisk lumbering industry flourished during the 1800s, and virtually the entire area was cut over at least once. Consequently, much of the contemporary forest is relatively young. The best-preserved remnants of the original oak-chestnut forest are in the Shenandoah National Park in Virginia.[51]

***Oak-Pine Forest Region.*** The ultisols of the Piedmont, from Virginia south through Alabama, originally were covered by an oak-pine forest. Stands of chestnut, hickory, loblolly pine, yellow pine, and white, red, black, and blackjack oak covered the interfluvial uplands, while sweetgum, sycamore, and river birch grew along the larger stream bottoms. Today the region is almost devoid of any original forest. From the earliest days of settlement, land has been alternately cleared for farming and then—as fertility was depleted by erosion and continuous cropping of tobacco, corn, or cotton—abandoned to revert back to woodland. Some farmers periodically reclear old fields as part of a multigenerational cycle of shifting cultivation. Land being cleared for farming today on the Piedmont has probably been cleared several times before, although not necessarily by the present occupants.[52] Much of the Piedmont vegetation today is an odd mix of planted pines and orchards and scrubby stands of volunteer pines and oaks. Pulp and paper companies now control vast acreages of old cotton land and have planted even-aged stands of fast-growing pines. Fruit and nut orchards have been planted extensively in Georgia and South Carolina. On old fields where trees are allowed to return, oak, hickory, and pine reclaim the land quickly. The landscape produced by this confusion of practices is one dappled by odd-shaped blocks of land, each covered with seemingly different plant associations and maturities. Tree growth is generally slow unless the stands are managed, and they provide little more than raw material for small sawmills that produce rough lumber for local construction.[53]

The combination of varied topography, a very broad range of vegetation species, and abundant precipitation and stream flow forms an exceptionally hospitable environment for wildlife. Although pioneers might have viewed such forested fastness as wilderness, the region's fauna provided the hunter with a reliable source of protein. When Europeans first entered the Appalachian woodlands they encountered the American elk, a large relative of the deer that today is found only in a few protected herds. The Pennsylvania and New York forests were browsed by the American bison and from there these hearty animals ranged as far south as Georgia. Their trails provided routeways for Indians and European settlers. Whitetailed deer were abundant in the more open portions of the region's forests, perhaps because depredations by mountain lions (known locally as panthers or painters) and timber wolves were more severe in the heavily wooded uplands. Deer have adapted to the settlement process, and they remain in numbers sufficient to be hunted, whereas the wolves and lions have almost vanished. Black bears and raccoons may have provided diversion for generations of hunters through fall nights when trained dogs pursued these animals across rugged hills. More animals than can be recounted here were on home range within the region, and many of them provided important dietary supplements for the early residents.[54]

## MINERAL RESOURCES

The distribution of Appalachia's mineral resources is a product of its geomorphic history. As discussed earlier, three of the major rock types that make up the earth's surface are found in Appalachia, often in close proximity. Igneous and metamorphic rocks of a wide range of types and ages underlie the Piedmont and the Blue Ridge. These rocks, in part products of the three stages of deformation and metamorphism of the Appalachian orogeny, range in age from Precambrian in parts of the Blue Ridge to Triassic in the Piedmont.[55] Many of these rocks were originally granites, formed under intense heat and pressure deep in the earth's crust. They contain a variety of metallic and nonmetallic mineral deposits. These ores, and the settlements that were built to exploit them, form a southwest-to-northeast band accordant to the lines of geomorphic activity. West of the Blue Ridge, the Ridge and Valley and the Plateaus are underlain by sedimentary rocks with a range of age as great as the igneous and metamorphic. In addition to their use as construction stone, these sedimentary rocks may contain a number of metallic minerals, often in the form of oxides, nonmetallic minerals, and carbon-based mineral fuels.

### Nonmetallic Minerals

Two types of sedimentary rock, limestone and sandstone, are quarried for construction stone in the region. Limestone is mined for aggregate, which is used in road construction. Because it is so widely distributed, limestone is mined near most urban areas to reduce transportation costs. Some types of limestone are basic ingredients in cement, and mining and cement manufacturing may be concentrated where these rocks appear at the surface. A major producing area runs along a valley from Cementon in Lehigh County to Portland in Northampton County in eastern Pennsylvania. Dimensional limestone, often a nonmetamorphic marble, is quarried in the Ridge and Valley of eastern Tennessee, where synclinal folds have been eroded to reveal a series of parallel limestone belts up to 16 mi (25.7 km) wide and 125 mi (201.1 km) long that follow the northeast-southwest trend of the topography. Smaller limestone beds in the Blue Ridge and Piedmont were subjected to more intense heating and pressure to produce the metamorphosed marble that is found in an area that extends from Pickens County, Georgia, to western North Carolina. Sandstones have been quarried in the Plateau country, especially from the Pottsville formation. Marbles and sandstones are used for facing buildings, floors, and decorative building trim.[56]

Slate, a metamorphosed rock derived from shale, occurs in a narrow belt that runs from Bibb and Chilton counties in central Alabama northwestward to Unicoi and Washington counties in Tennessee. This

Structural marble is produced by numerous quarries in the north Georgia marble belt in Cherokee and Pickens counties. Nelson, Georgia, was a company town, and the first group of workmen hired to quarry the stone were Italian.

slate belt coincides in a general way with the eastern boundary of the Ridge and Valley. In eastern Pennsylvania, one of the largest slate-producing areas in the country extends from Slatington and Slatedale in Lehigh County to Slateford in Northampton County. High-quality dimensional slate is produced for use as blackboards, flooring, and roofing. Lower grades are crushed and used to surface tennis courts and driveways.[57]

Gypsum was formed by precipitation out of saltwater and occurs in beds throughout the Plateaus. An extensive deposit lies in southwestern Virginia in Washington and Smyth counties, where it is mined and processed into wallboard and plaster.[58]

Quartz, one of the principal rock-forming minerals, is found in extensive deposits of sand, gravel, sandstone, conglomerate, and quartzite in the northern Plateaus and Ridge and Valley. In Pennsylvania, a major producer, the Tuscarora quartzite is used in making brick, and the Ridgeley sandstone is quarried for glass sand and numerous other uses. The highest-valued sands occur in West Virginia, where the glass industry in the Northern Panhandle uses sand quartz dredged from the Ohio River bottom and adjacent benches to manufacture fine glassware. The Oriskany sandstone in Morgan County in the Eastern Panhandle also produces high-quality sand.[59]

## Metals

Only four metals—gold, copper, iron, and zinc—have been produced in significant quantities in the Appalachians (Figure 2.8). Of these, only zinc is currently produced in large amounts.

The discovery of gold in the Piedmont of Georgia in the 1820s was responsible for the rapid settlement of the region and ultimately led to the displacement of the Cherokee Indians in the 1830s. Substantial amounts were mined from the metasedimentary rocks and associated granitic rocks that crop out in the Virginia, Carolina, and Georgia Piedmont. Peak production was reached in the late nineteenth century, and by the second decade of this century the deposits had been largely worked out.

Gold was also discovered in southeastern Tennessee near Ducktown in 1827. The search for more ore in the 1840s led to the discovery of the huge deposits of copper that have become the basis for a major extractive and copper-processing industry in the region. All minable copper in Appalachia is in the form of sulfides, such as chalcopyrite. The sulfide deposits at Ducktown, in metamorphosed Blue Ridge rocks, are the largest in Tennessee and among the largest in the world. The ore body is 6 mi (9.7 km) long and up to 2,400 ft (729.6 m) deep. Sulfur is a by-product of the copper refining process. Sulfuric acid is also produced at Ducktown for use in chemicals, fertilizers, pesticides, iron and steel, detergents, and a host of other products. Sulfuric acid has so many industrial uses that production is a reliable indicator of industry activity.[60] The processing of large quantities of copper sulfides at Ducktown released sulfur-oxide fumes into the air, killing the trees and other vegetation over a wide area. The bare land quickly eroded, and the result was scarified red hills that have become known as the Ducktown Desert.

Deposits of sedimentary iron ore are scattered across the Plateaus from Pennsylvania through West Virginia and eastern Kentucky to Alabama. Iron-rich marine sediments, mostly of Silurian age, accumulated with sand, silt, limestones, or igneous rocks. These deposits, though small and often of low quality, provided the basis for America's iron industry. Small stone furnaces were constructed near the ore workings, and the surrounding forest was cut and burned to provide charcoal. Such furnaces supplied local markets with iron as early as 1765 in Maryland and Virginia. During the 1790s, production began in Pennsylvania, Tennessee, West Virginia, and Kentucky. Ore was being mined and smelted in Ohio and Alabama by 1815.[61] But the small-scale mines of relatively low-grade ore were not competitive once the great deposits of upper Michigan and Minnesota became available after 1850. Production gradually declined in each Appalachian state except Alabama. There, near Birmingham, a happy geologic accident provided abundant Ordovician limestone, Silurian iron ore, and Pennsylvanian coal—the flux, ore, fuel, and coke required for iron production—in close proximity.

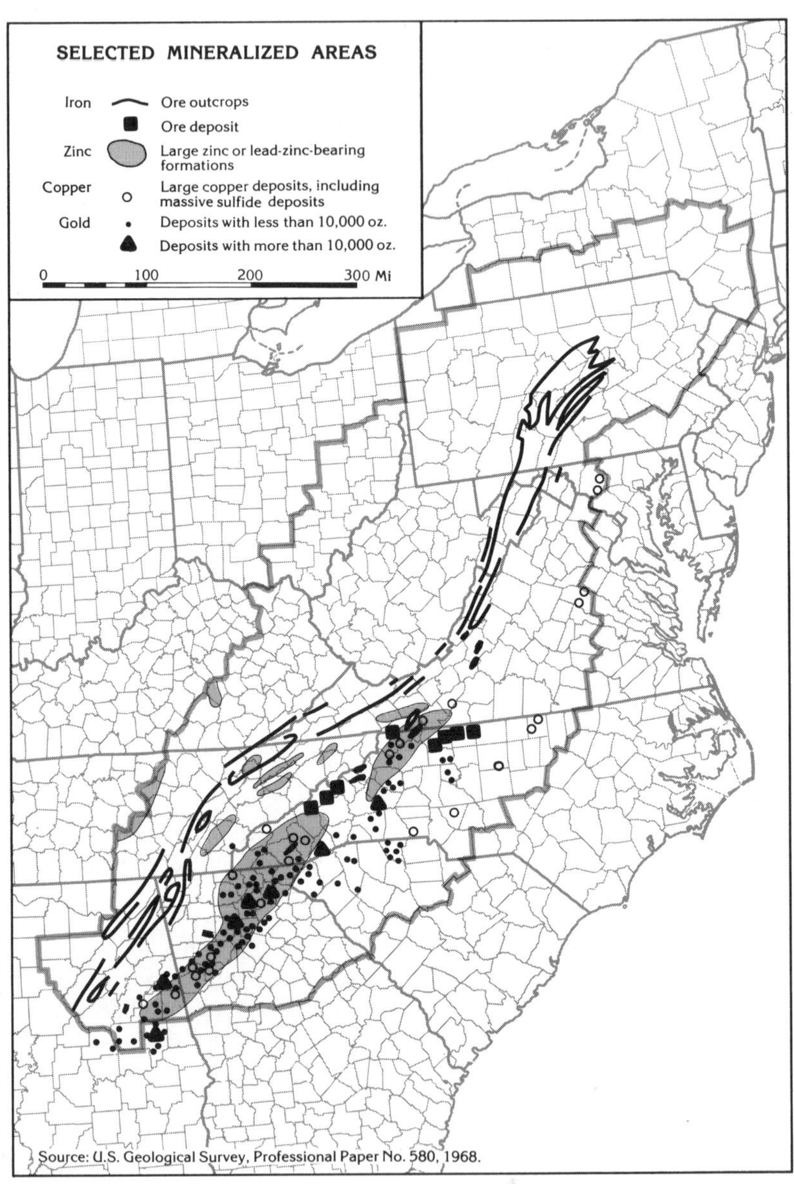
SELECTED MINERALIZED AREAS
Iron
Ore outcrops
Ore deposit
Zinc
Large zinc or lead-zinc-bearing formations
Copper
Large copper deposits, including massive sulfide deposits
Gold
Deposits with less than 10,000 oz.
Deposits with more than 10,000 oz.
0
100
200
300 Mi
Source: U.S. Geological Survey, Professional Paper No. 580, 1968.

**Figure 2.8**

The Ducktown Desert, Polk County, Tennessee. Decades of copper smelting have destroyed the vegetation, allowing severe sheet and gully erosion to scarify slopes and heavily silt stream beds. (U.S. Department of Agriculture photo.)

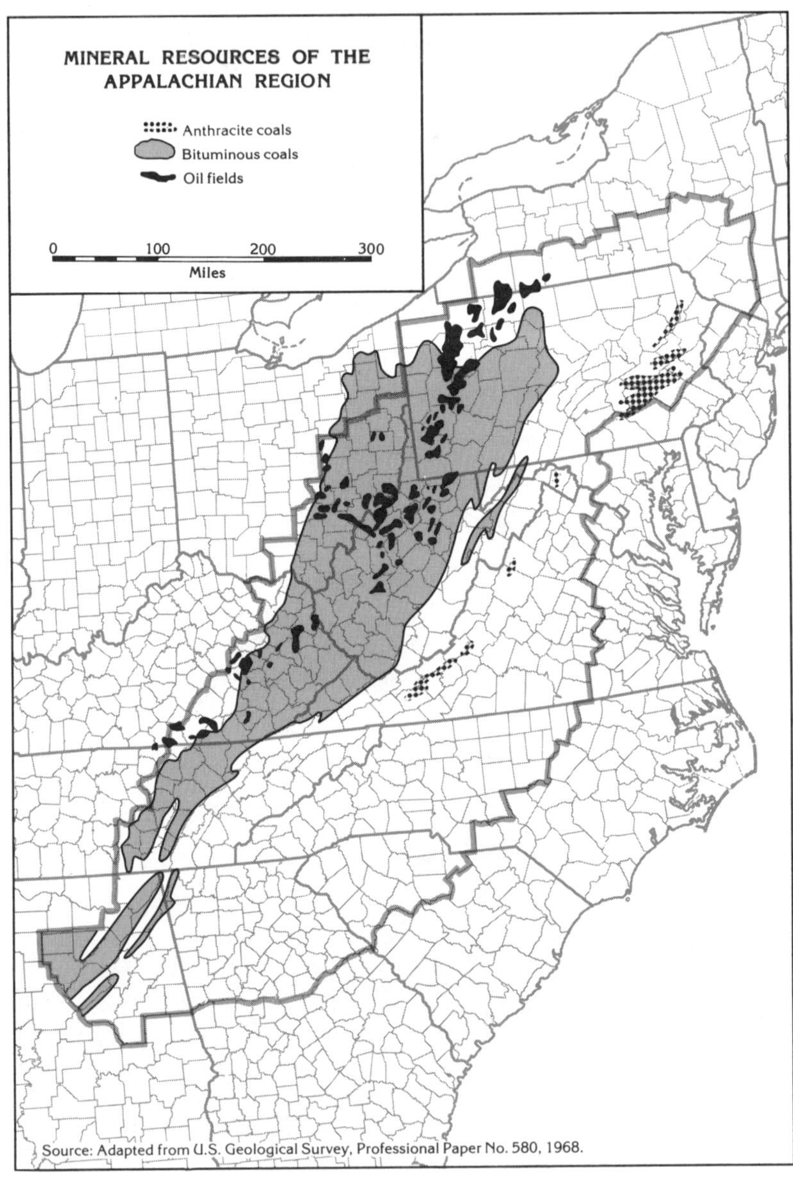
MINERAL RESOURCES OF THE APPALACHIAN REGION
Anthracite coals
Bituminous coals
Oil fields
0 100 200 300
Miles
Source: Adapted from U.S. Geological Survey, Professional Paper No. 580, 1968.

**Figure 2.9**

The ease of assembling these raw materials, in addition to Birmingham's location beyond the competitive reach of northern iron, is the basis for north-central Alabama's locational advantage in iron and steel production.

Zinc deposits often occur with lead and copper oxides in the faults and joints of Cambrian and Ordovician limestones of the Ridge and Valley. Although deposits are scattered the length of the province from Pennsylvania to Alabama, some of the largest ore bodies in the nation are found in Jefferson and Polk counties in Tennessee. Since 1950 production in Tennessee has increased rapidly; by 1978 the state produced 29 percent of the nation's zinc. Its uses are primarily for galvanizing, die castings, and the manufacture of brass. The Tennessee deposits are much larger than those found in the western states and can therefore be economically mined with large-scale equipment. Limestone rock, the waste material produced in mining, can be processed into agricultural lime or aggregate for construction.[62]

## Fuels

The most abundant and valuable mineral resource in Appalachia is coal. The region's vast bituminous-coal basin underlies 72,000 sq mi (186,480 sq km) in parts of 9 states (Figure 2.9). Anthracite is mined from an additional 484 sq mi (1,253.6 sq km) in 10 counties in northeastern Pennsylvania. Appalachian coals have been actively mined since the earliest days of white settlement. The coal has provided the energy, and profits from its use have provided the finances, for the nation's industrialization.

Most Appalachian coal was formed during the Pennsylvanian period (300 million B.P.) from extensive accumulations of vegetation in coastal swamps. Over time the Pennsylvanian swamps gradually subsided and were inundated with mud and silt washed in from eroding landmasses nearby. Between periods of subsidence the swamps reestablished themselves and more vegetative matter accumulated. Eventually these cycles came to an end as the area was covered in deep deposits of sand and silt. As the accumulation of sediments continued, the buried plant material decomposed, gases escaped, and carbon was concentrated, turning the mass from brown to black. Eventually the plant material turned to lignite and then to bituminous coal, the mud and silt turned to shale, and the sand became sandstone.[63]

Sometime after the accumulation of the Pennsylvanian deposits, the region was uplifted, and tectonic processes folded and faulted the eastern section of these deeply buried sediments (Figure 2.10). This activity had two effects. First, the coal seams in the Ridge and Valley were sharply folded and even twisted or overturned. In cross section the coals formed sets of alternating anticlinal arches and synclinal troughs. Erosion, accelerated by uplift, readily removed nonresistant sedimentary rocks from the anticlines, but the rock in many of the synclines remained below the erosional level. In this way the anthracite belts of northeastern Pennsylvania's synclinal valleys were preserved. A second process,

## GENERALIZED CROSS SECTIONS OF PENNSYLVANIA ANTHRACITE

Northern Field Near Nanticoke

Middle Field Near Shenandoah

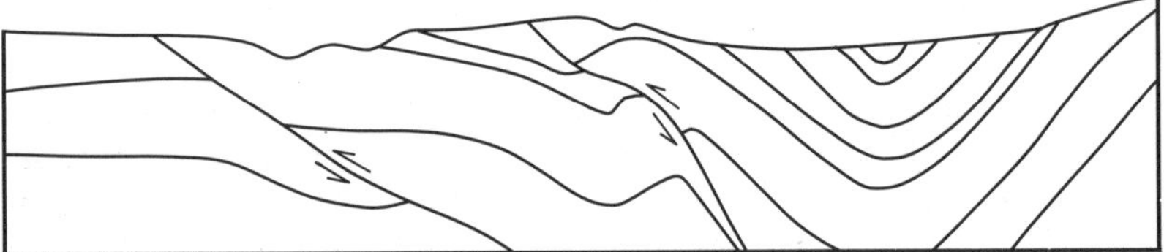

Southern Field Near Pottsville

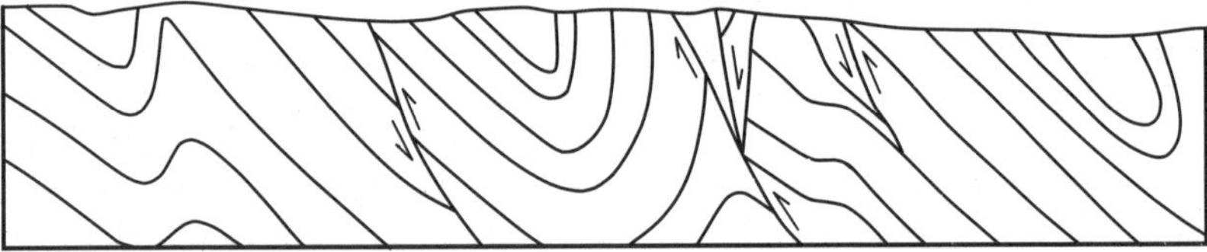

**Figure 2.10**

Source: Adapted from U.S. Geological Survey, Professional Paper No. 580, 1968.

compression of the horizontal strata into folds, also metamorphosed some rocks through heat and pressure. Coal is more susceptible to pressure and heat than many other sedimentary rocks. Consequently, Pennsylvania's northeastern coal deposits metamorphosed into anthracite, a process that drove off gases and impurities and increased the proportion of carbon. After the turn of the nineteenth century, anthracite was mined for home heating and as an industrial fuel that was coveted for its high heat output and low ash content. Mining the steeply pitching folds of anthracite is difficult at best and involves vertical and inclined underground shafts and deep, narrow excavations if mined at the surface.

The pressures that dramatically altered the Ridge and Valley coal

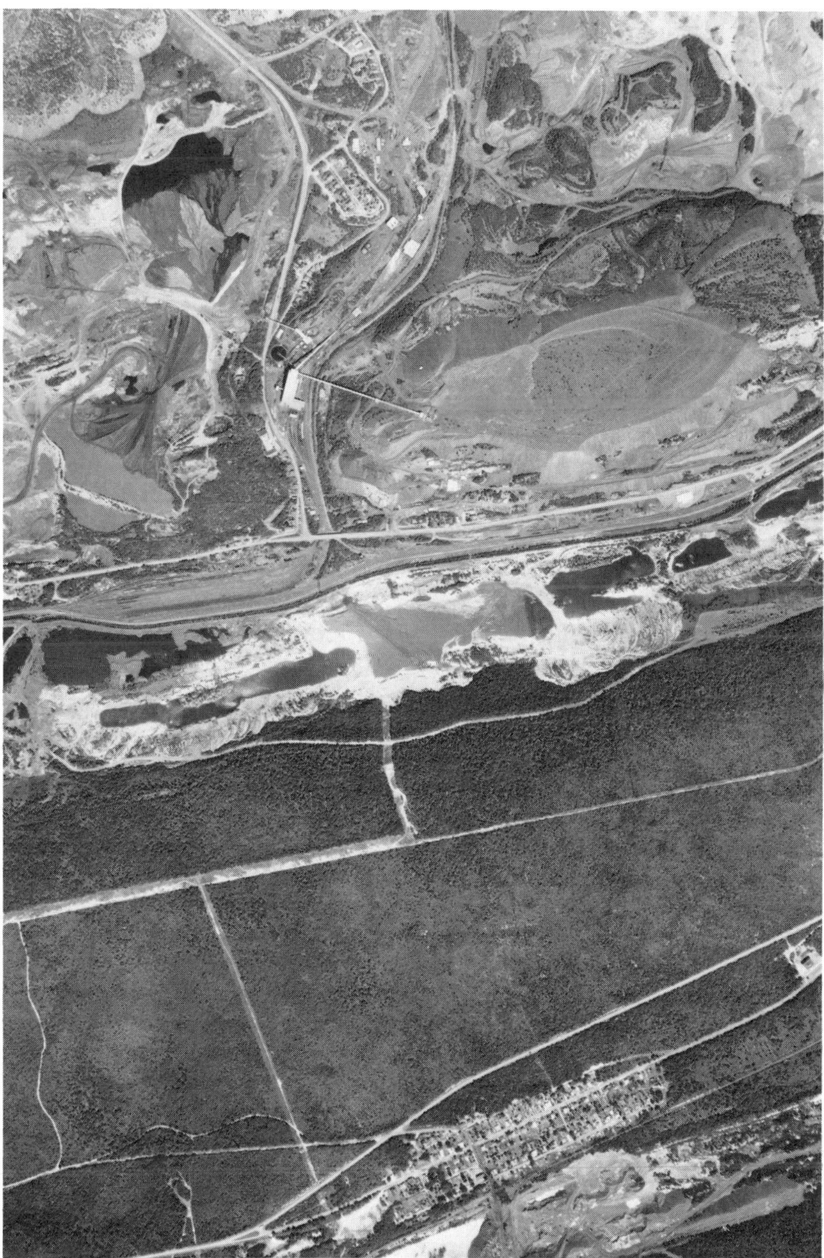

Anthracite mining in two parallel valleys in Schuylkill County, Pennsylvania, just southeast of the town of Shenandoah. (U.S. Department of Agriculture photo.)

measures decreased in intensity to the west but nevertheless altered the coals in the Plateaus. On the east edge of the bituminous-coal basin, the sedimentary rocks and coal seams dipped steeply, in some places up to 20 degrees.[64] To the west the pitch of the seams levels out and becomes nearly horizontal in western Pennsylvania, West Virginia, and eastern Kentucky. Those coals that lie in close proximity to the zone of deformation (southeastern West Virginia, for example), contain fewer volatile elements. These coals were also laid down in swamps that flourished in a cool and wet climate. These two circumstances have produced high-grade bituminous coals, low in sulfur, ash, and other impurities. Coal of this quality occurs in forty-three minable seams scattered through 4,000 ft (1,216 m) of sedimentary rock and is in high demand for metallurgical uses. To the northwest, in West Virginia and Pennsylvania, coals were the product of peat laid down in sulfur-charged water in a somewhat warmer and drier climate. Coal is mined from nineteen seams in this northern field (seven of which overlap with those in the southern field), but it is higher in volatile gases and sulfur.[65] Because the bituminous coal of the Plateaus lies in nearly horizontal beds, it can be readily mined using tunnels that follow individual seams from the surface outcrop along the side of a valley thousands of feet back under the overlying rock. Surface strip mines simply follow the coal outcrop around the contour of the mountainside.

Petroleum and natural gas rank second to coal in value of mineral commodities produced in the region. These hydrocarbons are found in porous sedimentary rock where they accumulate in traps that take the form of faults, folds, or unconformities. Because petroleum may be vaporized under the high pressures and temperatures of metamorphosis, few deposits have been found in the folded sedimentary rocks of the Ridge and Valley. Extensive deposits have been discovered west of the Appalachian Front in Pennsylvania, West Virginia, and Kentucky. Petroleum was commonly found associated with water in shallow salt and brine wells and was skimmed off for use as wheel grease, leather softener, and medicine. After the first well drilled specifically for oil at Titusville, Pennsylvania, began producing in 1859, exploration and production in the region increased steadily. Peak production was reached in the 1890s at about 40 million bbl per year.[66] By the 1960s annual production was little more than 16 million bbl. But with the oil embargo of the early 1970s and subsequent price increases, exploration for new fields is proceeding apace. Recent seismic studies have revealed that during the Appalachian orogeny portions of the Piedmont and Blue Ridge were faulted and thrust to the west, up and over younger sedimentary rocks of what became the Ridge and Valley. The sedimentary rocks under this overthrust zone are thought to contain large pockets of petroleum and natural gas, but drilling deep exploratory wells to determine whether this is the case is an expensive and high-risk venture that requires considerable geologic research.

Bituminous-coal mining, underground and surface, at Dunham in Letcher County, Kentucky. Strip mines follow the slope contour. Waste rock from a deep mine, stored in a hollow beside Elkhorn Creek, appears as a lens-shaped area at the lower left. (U.S. Department of Agriculture photo.)

## CONCLUSION

Appalachia's natural resources are diverse and widely distributed. Some, such as the fossil fuels, are abundant but nonrenewable. Others—the forests, for example—are renewable but only over a period of several human generations. But more important than resource longevity is the single overriding fact of physical geography—the form of the land, both at the surface and below it. The geomorphic processes of history have created landforms and rock associations that have strongly influenced human attempts to adapt culture, technology, and economy to its structure and complexity. At the most elementary level, the region presented not a single barrier to westward expansion of the coast-bound European colonies, but a host of them in the form of Pennsylvania's Endless Mountains or Kentucky's Cumberland and Pine mountains. When the European-American settlers began to utilize the region's vast and varied resources they possessed only elementary technologies. Their methods of farming, lumbering, and mining were crude and grew in sophistication at the expense of the land. To a considerable extent, the nation's agriculture and heavy industry, operating in a laissez faire economic milieu, used the region's resources and people to develop its technology through trial and error. The accumulated result of some 150 years of exploitation is extensive modification of the land both above and below the surface. In many areas, careless removal of resources has produced catastrophic problems as diverse as acid mine drainage, land subsidence, and soil removal through landslides or sheet erosion. Some of the central problems of Appalachian development concern the expiation of past mistakes and the establishment of plans for future use and conservation.

## NOTES

1. George W. Fisher et al., eds., *Studies of Appalachian Geology: Central and Southern* (New York: Interscience Publishers, 1970), pp. 437–438.
2. Arthur N. Strahler and Alan H. Strahler, *Geography and Man's Environment* (New York: John Wiley & Sons, 1977). See unit 23, "Plate Tectonics," pp. 150–157 and unit 59, "Ancient Mountain Roots of Appalachia," pp. 429–436.
3. Charles B. Hunt, *Natural Regions of the United States and Canada* (San Francisco: W. H. Freeman and Co., 1974), pp. 257–258.
4. Frederick A. Cook, Larry D. Brown, and Jack E. Oliver, "The Southern Appalachians and the Growth of Continents," *Scientific American* 243 (1980), pp. 160–161.
5. Hunt, op. cit. (footnote 3), p. 278.
6. William D. Thornbury, *Regional Geomorphology of the United States* (New York: John Wiley & Sons, 1965), p. 134.
7. Raymond E. Janssen, "The Teays River, Ancient Precursor of the East," *The Scientific Monthly* 77 (1953), pp. 306–314.
8. Thornbury, op. cit. (footnote 6), pp. 75–76.
9. Nevin M. Fenneman, *Physiography of Eastern United States* (New York: McGraw-Hill Book Co., 1938).

10. Ibid., p. 131.
11. Ibid., pp. 171, 173.
12. Thornbury, op. cit. (footnote 6), p. 75.
13. Fenneman, op. cit. (footnote 9), pp. 202–203.
14. See Peirce F. Lewis, "Small Town in Pennsylvania," *Annals,* Association of American Geographers, 62 (1972), pp. 333–340, for an interesting account of the effects of drainage pattern on travel to one town in central Pennsylvania.
15. George F. Deasy and Phyllis R. Griess, "Effects of a Declining Mining Economy on the Pennsylvania Anthracite Region," *Annals,* Association of American Geographers, 55 (1965), pp. 239–259.
16. Bailey Willis, "The Northern Appalachians," *National Geographic Monographs,* no. 6 (New York: American Book Co., 1895), p. 173.
17. Fenneman, op. cit. (footnote 9), p. 250.
18. Ibid., pp. 283–284.
19. William J. Schneider et al., *Water Resources of the Appalachian Region: Pennsylvania to Alabama,* Pub. HA-198 (Washington, D.C.: U.S. Geological Survey, 1965), sheet 2. Although the most recent data on climate are from the 1960s, changes in elements of climate generally occur gradually.
20. Earl L. Core, *Vegetation of West Virginia* (Parsons, W.V.: McClain Printing Co., 1966), p. 6.
21. Schneider, op. cit. (footnote 19).
22. James F. Woodruff, "Debris Avalanches as an Erosional Agent in the Appalachian Mountains," *Journal of Geography* 70, (1971), pp. 399–406.
23. Schneider, op. cit. (footnote 19), sheet 4.
24. Four streams—the Scioto, Hocking, Muskingum, and Mahoning rivers in Ohio, all tributaries of the Ohio River—flow into the region. Their total discharge, measured at gauging sites near to where they enter the Appalachian region, amounts to only 9,739 c.f.s. U.S. Geological Survey, *Water Resources Data for Ohio, Water Year 1977.*
25. Schneider, op. cit. (footnote 19).
26. U.S. Geological Survey (U.S.G.S.), *Mineral Resources of the Appalachian Region,* Professional Paper no. 580 (Washington, D.C.: U.S. Geological Survey, 1968), p. 30.
27. Thornbury, op. cit. (footnote 6), p. 80.
28. Hunt, op. cit. (footnote 3), p. 282.
29. Ibid., pp. 282–286.
30. John C. Campbell, *The Southern Highlander and His Homeland* (Lexington: University Press of Kentucky, 1969; originally published by the Russell Sage Foundation, 1921), pp. 27–30.
31. Ralph H. Brown, *Historical Geography of the United States* (New York: Harcourt, Brace and World, 1948), pp. 184–186.
32. Hunt, op. cit. (footnote 3), p. 294.
33. Henry D. Foth and John W. Schafer, *Soil Geography and Land Use* (New York: John Wiley & Sons, 1980), p. 63.
34. Ibid., p. 72.
35. Hunt, op. cit. (footnote 3).
36. John Fraser Hart, "Land Rotation in Appalachia," *Geographical Review* 67 (1977), pp. 148–166.
37. Foth and Schafer, op. cit. (footnote 33), p. 179.
38. John Fraser Hart, "Land Use Change in a Piedmont County," *Annals,*

Association of American Geographers, 70 (1980), pp. 509–516.

39. Foth and Schafer, op. cit. (footnote 33), p. 186.

40. Hunt, op. cit. (footnote 3), p. 289.

41. Schneider, op. cit. (footnote 19), sheet 1.

42. E. Lucy Braun, *Deciduous Forests of Eastern North America* (1950; reprint New York: Hafner Press, 1974), p. 397.

43. Ibid., p. 50.

44. Ibid., p. 91.

45. Core, op. cit. (footnote 20), pp. 58–64.

46. Ibid., pp. 113–114.

47. John Fraser Hart, "Loss and Abandonment of Cleared Farm Land in the Eastern United States," *Annals,* Association of American Geographers, 58 (1968), pp. 434–439.

48. Braun, op. cit. (footnote 42), pp. 197–200.

49. Ibid., pp. 206–209.

50. Phil Gersmehl, "Factors Leading to Mountaintop Grazing in the Southern Appalachians," *Southeastern Geographer* 10 (1970), pp. 67–72.

51. Braun, op. cit. (footnote 42), p. 222.

52. Hart, 1977, op. cit. (footnote 36), pp. 150–154, and Stanley W. Trimble, *Man-Induced Soil Erosion on the Southern Piedmont, 1700–1970* (Milwaukee: Soil Conservation Society of America, 1974), pp. 41–94.

53. Braun, op. cit. (footnote 42), p. 273.

54. Maurice Brooks, *The Appalachians* (Boston: Houghton Mifflin Co., 1965), pp. 295–310.

55. Cook, Brown, and Oliver, op. cit. (footnote 4), pp. 163–165.

56. U.S.G.S., op. cit. (footnote 26), pp. 193–199. Place-names in mineral-producing districts are often good indicators of industrial activity. The naming of businesses and even athletic teams for the basic economic activity of a community is common and can be evocative of regional character. For example, Northampton, Pennsylvania, lies along the Limestone Belt, and the high-school football team is called the Concrete Kids. Nearby in the Slate Belt, the Slatington team is called the Slaters.

57. Ibid., p. 205.

58. Ibid., p. 314.

59. Ibid., pp. 337–339.

60. Ibid., p. 377.

61. Ibid., p. 403.

62. Ibid., p. 465, and U.S. Department of the Interior, *Minerals in the Economy of Tennessee* (Washington, D.C.: Bureau of Mines, 1979), p. 3.

63. U.S.G.S., op. cit. (footnote 26), p. 102.

64. Ibid., p. 104.

65. S. P. Babu et al., *Suitability of West Virginia Coals to Coal-Conversion Processes,* Coal-Geology Bulletin no. 1 (Morgantown: West Virginia Geological and Economic Survey, 1973), p. 3.

66. U.S.G.S., op. cit. (footnote 26), pp. 145, 148.

# CHAPTER 3

# COMING TO THE LAND

Much of the Appalachian land from New York to Alabama was occupied by Indians upon arrival of European whites in the Atlantic colonies in the early seventeenth century. Most of the fifteen to seventeen major tribes that lived in the uplands at that time were sedentary agriculturalists and fishermen who supplemented their diets through hunting and gathering. The Indian presence—sometime antagonist, sometime adviser and benefactor—affected the manner and order in which whites were able to move into the interior, obtain and use the land, and extend their settlement perimeter. The Indians had greatly altered large acreages within the Appalachian uplands by farming and by their use of fire for hunting. Their trails often focused on river crossing points or mountain gaps and were frequently adopted by pioneers as travel routes. The mere presence of the Indians and their legal possession of the land greatly influenced the direction that white expansion could follow. To understand the sequence whereby the European came to displace the Indian in the Appalachians and to establish a culture and economy, we must place that process into the context of the Indian precedent.

## INDIAN TRADITION

The northern Appalachian uplands were occupied by two major Indian linguistic groups at the turn of the seventeenth century. The Algonquins lived along the lower Hudson Valley, the eastern third of the Mohawk lowland, and the Susquehanna basin of eastern Pennsylvania. Iroquois inhabited much of the upper Susquehanna basin (in what was to become New York) and the Ontario Plain (Figure 3.1). The Iroquois, a loose confederation of the Mohawk, Oneida, Onondaga, Cayuga, and Seneca tribes, played a pivotal role in impeding white settlement. The Iroquois tribes had probably migrated into New York from the Midwest during the fourteenth century. Their extended families lived in villages of a thousand or more people, usually located within

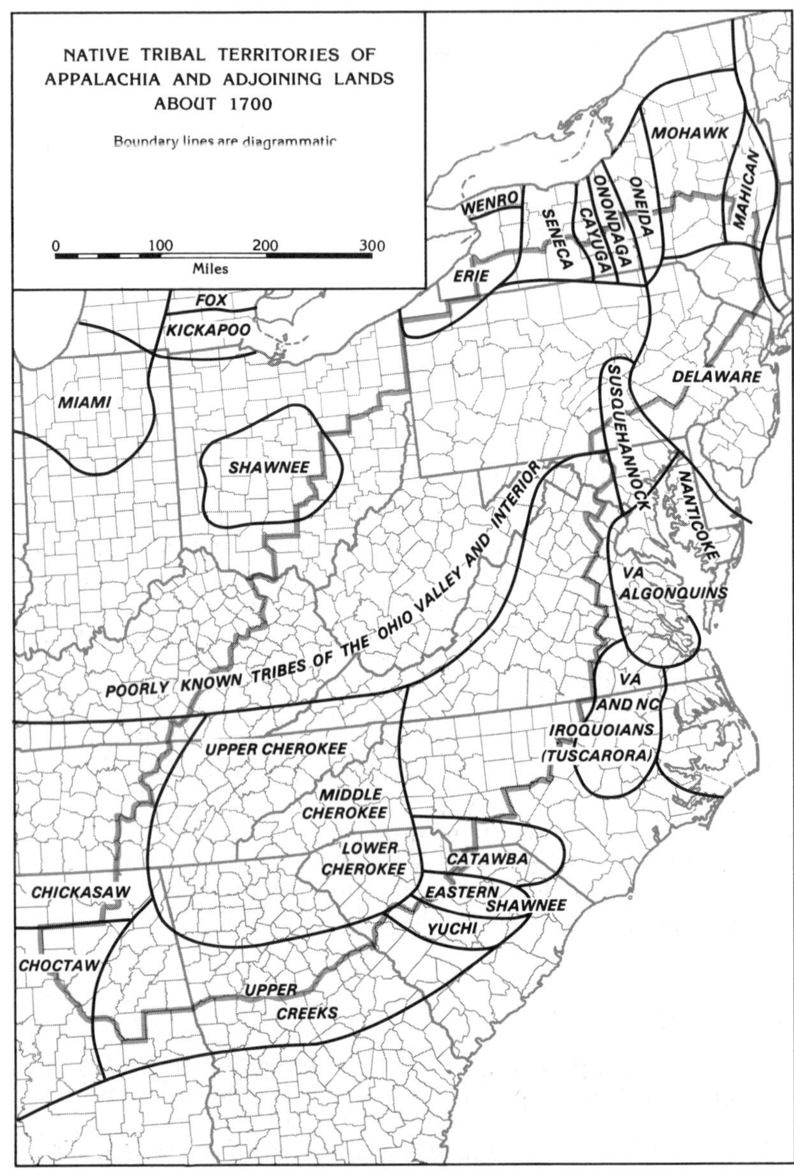


**Figure 3.1**

After Charles Hudson, *The Southeastern Indians* (Knoxville: University of Tennessee Press, 1976), pp. 6–7 (Copyright © by the University of Tennessee Press. Adaptation by permission of the University of Tennessee Press), and Bruce G. Trigger, ed., *Handbook of North American Indians,* vol. 15 (Washington, D.C.: Smithsonian Institution, 1978), p. ix.

walking distance of streams on low plains or valleys where the growing season was at least 130 days long. These locations avoided major stream confluence points—a protective measure, while allowing access to fishing, alluvial floodplain land, and trade routes.[1] The Iroquois grew maize, beans, and squash in forest clearings. As soil fertility declined and as the firewood supply from surrounding woodland was depleted, the people moved their villages to new sites and cleared land for new fields. This relocation process took place every ten to twenty-five years.[2] By the time the loosely organized Iroquois Confederacy was formed in the late 1500s, it included a population of an estimated twenty thousand people. Population densities were high only in village clusters, which were separated from each other by extensive tracts of hunting and fishing lands. The Catskill uplands and the southern plateau of New York were only thinly populated. Each group maintained long-distance trade connections with tribes on Long Island, the Inland Peninsula between Lakes Erie, Ontario, and Huron, and elsewhere. One trading trail ran from Utica, in the Mohawk Valley, westward. When adapted by whites it first became known as the Genesee Road and later as New York Highway 5.[3] The first whites to encounter the Iroquois in the early 1600s were traders dealing in furs and hides. The Iroquois tribes vied with one another and other tribes to become the middlemen in the trade relationship. They succeeded in monopolizing the Dutch trade through Albany, and they seemed to adapt to the wealth that the white colonists brought with them.[4]

To the south in Pennsylvania, three Algonquin tribes totaling about fifteen thousand people were present in the early 1600s. The Erie occupied the southeast shore of Lake Erie, and the Delaware and Susquehannocks lived along the Delaware and Susquehanna rivers. Their village sites and travel corridors, like those of the Iroquois, were largely limited to river valleys. They practiced sedentary agriculture in woodland clearings; crops included maize, beans and peas, squash and melons, and tobacco. Like the Iroquois, they moved their villages periodically as game became scarce and the soil was depleted.[5]

Increased frequency of movement by the Algonquin tribes was provoked by virtually constant conflict with the Iroquois from about 1600 to 1675. Because of the power of the Iroquois Confederation and their success in trading for guns with the Dutch, the Iroquois dominated these tribes and largely controlled much of eastern Pennsylvania. The Erie moved out of the area early on and were followed by the Susquehannocks. The latter group vacated land in the Susquehanna Valley that was subsequently taken by coastal tribes such as the Nanticokes, who were then displaced by white colonists. European settlement also forced the southern Shawnees to move into the Susquehanna Valley, and in the early 1700s, the Tuscaroras, driven out of eastern North Carolina, moved to eastern Pennsylvania as well. The Iroquois allowed these tribes to settle in the Cumberland Valley and the adjacent valleys to the west.[6]

By the time William Penn established the English colony of Pennsylvania in 1681, the Indian population was in flux. As one of the last colonies to be established, Pennsylvania became a reservoir for displaced coastal tribes. The Indian migrants were unable to readily reestablish their lifeways in eastern Pennsylvania, because a rapidly increasing European population was moving inland from Philadelphia, forcing the Indians to relocate farther and farther west. This process of sustained Indian migration prohibited the reestablishment of their sedentary agriculture system. Indian culture underwent dramatic change in a few decades: Their migrations forced a reversion to a dependence on hunting, fishing, and trapping; their contact with whites increased through trade for food, tools, and firearms. Disease introduced by the whites decimated the Indian population, increasing their vulnerability to white expansion.[7]

Much of the Ohio Valley was initially occupied by a few poorly known Indian tribes during this early period of white contact, although the Shawnee, Delaware, and Tuscarora, among others, eventually moved into northern West Virginia and Ohio. The other large concentration of Indians—Cherokees who were also of Iroquoian origin—was much farther south, centering on the Great Smoky Mountains in western North Carolina but extending into north Georgia and South Carolina on the south and the east Tennessee Ridge and Valley to the north. Like the Iroquois, the Cherokee had developed a sophisticated social and political organization by the time of white contact. They lived in palisaded villages on fertile land along rivers and creeks. The plan of each village focused on a square—a center for dancing and celebrations—and a town house—a social and political meeting place for the villagers.[8]

## EUROPEAN ENCROACHMENT

After the French and Indian War of the late 1750s and early 1760s, the British government moved to consolidate control over the Appalachians. A British proclamation in 1763 forbade all white settlements beyond the Appalachian Front. The proclamation was largely ignored in the North and in the South as well. In the early 1770s, for example, a group of North Carolinians who opposed taxes, land rents, and land grants to friends of the European aristocracy fled into the Cherokee lands after being routed from the Piedmont by British troops. In part because of the invasion of these Carolina Regulators, as they were called, and other antiroyalists, the Cherokees unwisely took the British side in the American Revolution in 1776. The British could offer them little protection, though, and the American forces repaid the Cherokee's political ambivalence by destroying more than fifty of their towns. To settle the dispute at war's end, the Cherokees ceded more than 4 million a. (1.62 million h) of land to the Americans.[9]

By the turn of the nineteenth century, the few Cherokees who remained after decimation by war and epidemic disease began to adapt to the white economy. They had modified their nucleated village pattern by building log homes near their fields. This settlement decentralization continued as more home sites were established near isolated patches of available land.[10] They diversified their agriculture, raising more livestock and trade crops such as cotton and grain. By 1827, they were using an alphabet, developed by Sequoyah, and had established a system of law based on a formal legal code with judicial districts and judges, a supreme court, and a U.S.-based constitution. Internal dissension precluded any organized resistance to white encroachment. In the North, the Iroquois had controlled the access routes into the interior by defending the Mohawk Valley, and the route was not safe for whites until the Indians were defeated in the revolution and again in the War of 1812. In the South, the Cherokee control of routeways into the interior was based as much on their legal entitlement to the land as on superior martial prowess. Strong pressure from whites continued into the nineteenth century for the Cherokee lands that remained and prompted Thomas Jefferson to establish a withdrawal policy that would remove Indians to the Louisiana Purchase, but most of them resisted the plan.

When gold was discovered on Cherokee land in northern Georgia in 1829, the Georgia legislature, supported by President Andrew Jackson, passed laws that had the effect of confiscating the Indians' land and neutralizing their ability to resist. Cherokee lands were divided into 160-acre (64.6-hectare) land lots and 40-acre (16.6-hectare) gold lots for distribution to Georgia citizens through a public lottery.[11] At Jackson's request the U.S. Congress subsequently passed a law that forced Cherokee removal.[12] U.S. military forces enforced the removal in the fall of 1838, marching the Indians across Tennessee in the winter. By the time they reached what is now Oklahoma in March of the following year, four thousand Indians—a quarter of the group that had started—had died of starvation and disease. This tragic event is still referred to by the Cherokee as the Trail of Tears. A small number of Cherokee successfully evaded capture and removal by hiding out in the virtually inaccessible interior of the Smoky Mountains. Eventually, they were allotted a small parcel of land that has become the Qualla Boundary, the reservation at Cherokee, North Carolina.

As European contact with Appalachian Indian groups increased from brief trading meetings to lengthy interaction through adjacent residence or martial confrontation and negotiation, the image of the Indian held by whites also changed. The earliest image of the Indian was that of the noble Red Man, a virtual child of nature whose social and political organization was perceived in light of the European monarchy. The Indian leadership was approved by the tribe's people, and they had individual rights and freedoms and were recognized as the source of the leader's authority, a practice not yet common in class-stratified European societies.[13] French philosophers expanded this idea into the theory that all men have inherent rights, and Thomas Jefferson incorporated the principles of "consent of the governed" and individual equality into the Declaration of Independence. As the expansion of white colonists into the hinterland of the Atlantic coast grew from a trickle to a tide and the greed for Indian land increased, this view of the Indian was most inconvenient, and the requirements of the whites were better served if the image was changed to the Indian as a ruthless and godless savage. Eventually, when the Indian had been pushed from the frontier and only small numbers remained as submissive government wards on small reservations, the image changed again. The Indian was finally seen as the lazy drunk who would not practice the ways of the whites.[14]

## LAND: SURVEY, SPECULATION, AND SALE

If the Indian presence in the Appalachians created some deviations in the progress of pioneer settlement, other—and in many cases related—problems, such as lack of secure land titles, inaccurate surveys, high land costs, and land speculation, acted to shunt population flows from one sector of the Appalachian frontier to another. Prior to the Revolution, the rights to land were often held by English development companies at the discretion of the king. In Virginia, for example, the London Company used the concept of "Head Right" in which land was given to families, 50 a. (20.2 h) per head, if they could pay for their transportation to Virginia. With the dissolution of these companies and the severance of English ties in 1776, the distribution of lands in the west fell to the states.

During the colonial period in the North, some of the better land in southwestern New York and northeastern Pennsylvania was settled in a systematic manner by New Englanders, who acquired the rights to specific blocks of land and in many cases platted towns or villages and rural holdings before settlement actually began. In the early 1770s, for example, Connecticut investors formed the Susquehanna Company and bought the Indian rights to land in Pennsylvania's Wyoming Valley. There they laid out the settlement of Wilkes-Barre as a typical New England town. Central to the 200-a. (80.8-h) town site was a square laid off for town buildings. The remaining acreage was divided into eight squares of 25 a. (10.1 h) each that in turn were divided into six individual lots of about 4 a. (1.62 h) each. Numerous town names in northeast Pennsylvania suggest other New England settlements—Windham, Litchfield, Westfield, and Salem.[15] A number of such planned settlements were established, especially in New York, but elsewhere such planning was rare; most land division was accomplished in a less formal manner, and land was occupied by individuals, not organized groups. After the Revolution and the initial defeat of the Iroquois, organized migration of New Englanders into Appalachia New York increased. Motivated by overcrowding, high land prices, and high taxes to seek western land, New England migrants were ready customers for New York land held in large blocks by European speculation companies. The speculators often developed their holdings by laying out systematic land divisions before the land was sold to settlers.[16] Other improvements were often made in the New York speculative lands. Roads were built and sawmills, taverns, and stores were erected. Potential settlers were attracted not only by these enhancements but also by the chance to obtain land with a clear title and boundaries that had been officially surveyed.[17]

In Pennsylvania, William Penn had initially insisted on providing land for settlement that was free of Indian claims and had been surveyed according to a township plan. By 1792, about thirty-three land purchases and settlement treaties had been negotiated with the Indians across the state. Penn's square townships were to contain 5,000 a. (2,020 h) each and provide land for ten families. Unfortunately, land commissioners found it easier to accommodate the demand for land by selling acreage according to the size and location desired. To attempt to control speculation and land-price inflation, individuals were prohibited from obtaining more than 300 a. (121.2 h). Although this policy was somewhat effective in the East, after 1720—when the number of immigrants from Europe increased—it was largely ignored. Many of the new arrivals were poor and could not afford to buy land. They passed through the settled communities in the southeastern counties to the backcountry, where they squatted on vacant land. Squatter settlements, made without benefit of land titles or surveys, were often located on land that was in dispute between colonial proprietors.[18] By 1726, there were an estimated 100,000 squatters in Pennsylvania.[19]

The settlement of Indian land claims was a slow process. These delays, together with the hostilities of the French and Indian War, the insecure titles on much of the fertile bottom land in the Ridge and Valley country, and the high prices of fertile land in southeastern Pennsylvania where land titles were reasonably clear, encouraged the movement of many immigrants southward along the Blue Ridge and Great Valley into Maryland and Virginia. The method of land distribution in Virginia was based on grants to soldiers and land sales and grants to speculators. Revolutionary War and French and Indian War soldiers received from 100 to 15,000 a. (40.4 to 6,060 h) depending upon rank and length of service. But squatters moved in and settled land with no title, and speculators often sold land that in fact had been given to veterans as war payments. Land was usually surveyed only on inaccurate maps. The actual land boundaries were seldom marked with permanent boundary markers, and in many cases the boundaries could not be identified. These difficulties were inherent in most of the metes-and-bounds surveys of the Virginia territory, described as "overlapping each other like shingles on a roof[;] titles were so subject to controversy that it would have been impossible to determine who were the freeholders."[20] Law suits over property ownership and boundaries strained the court system, and many settlers were forced to move elsewhere, perhaps to the frontier, because they lost their claims in legal disputes. Land titles seemed little more secure in Kentucky, the first state to be formed west of the Allegheny Front, or West Virginia, which remained a part of Virginia until 1861. During the last two decades of the eighteenth century, speculation in West Virginia, southwestern Virginia, and Kentucky was extensive. By 1805 at least 250 persons or groups, often in interlocking combinations, had acquired land grants in these areas of 10,000 a. (4,040 h) or more.[21] The Virginia land system permitted land warrant purchasers to locate their tracts before making land surveys. The result was a chaotic patchwork of irregularly shaped tracts, many of which did not include a single permanent marker and often left odd slices of land unsurveyed and orphaned between adjoining tracts.[22] The consequence of this practice may have been to discourage a large number of experienced yeomen from moving into the area. Serious farmers chose to settle where land titles were more secure. Much of the land eventually was bought up by speculators, who, as absentee owners, were primarily concerned with profits rather than long-term area development. The system is often credited with establishing the basis for large-scale economic exploitation in the late nineteenth and twentieth centuries.[23]

In the Carolinas and Georgia similar land-division practices were followed. Metes and bounds were surveyed for land deeds without reference to bordering properties or preexistent claims. So many court claims resulted that in 1839 the Georgia surveyor general investigated the land claims in 24 counties and found that although the counties contained about 8.7 million a. (3.5 million hectares) of land, maps and records in the surveyor general's office indicated that over 29 million a. (11.7 million hectares) had been granted.[24] The settlers who did migrate into the Appalachian country tended to move on after working their land a few years. This continuing displacement likely was stimulated as much by the loss of land titles in claims court as by the "need for elbow room." It is also probable that the "freedom and democracy" that settlers sought on the open frontier implied either clear land titles or the right to squat on unclaimed land as much as it suggested behavioral license.

## ROUTEWAYS AND SETTLEMENT EXPANSION

By the 1750s residents of the Atlantic colonies knew enough about the opportunities that lay in the Appalachians, and to some extent in the country farther to the west, that their routeways into the uplands had begun to focus on specific transmontane routes. Access to four large river systems that drained to the west from the Appalachian Plateaus, thereby providing some measure of water- or land-based transportation, could be obtained at three key points. The Forks of the Ohio could be reached by traveling to southwestern Pennsylvania. The Cumberland River, which led to the Nashville basin, and the Kentucky River, which led to the Bluegrass region of Kentucky, were both accessible through the Cumberland wind gap and the adjacent Pine Mountain water gap. The Tennessee River gave access to the Southwest Territory (essentially the state of Tennessee after 1796) and the Georgia Territory (which included the northern half of Mississippi and Alabama) by way of the Great Valley in east Tennessee.

A number of river and overland routes that originated in southeastern Pennsylvania and Maryland converged at the Forks of the Ohio. Forbes Road, built by British troops during the French and Indian War, was most direct, because it did not conform to the irregularities of the Ridge and Valley drainage system.[25] Laid out in 1758, it eventually connected Philadelphia to Fort Pitt and the Ohio (Figure 3.2). A few dozen miles to the south, connecting the Potomac River and later Baltimore with the Ohio, was Braddock's Road, which had been constructed during the same war.[26] After Pittsburgh was laid out in 1765 at the site of Fort Pitt, the roads were gradually upgraded by Pennsylvania and Maryland until they were passable by wagon. Improvements in road quality greatly increased the momentum of pioneer movement into southwestern Pennsylvania. Grading, bridge construction, and other improvements were especially effective on Forbes Road (later called the Pennsylvania Road), and by the turn of the nineteenth century that route was carrying a large volume of freight and passengers to the west. Although the National Road (or Cumberland Road) was completed from Cumberland, Maryland, to Wheeling on the Ohio River in 1818, the Pennsylvania Road continued as the most important routeway west. Salt, iron goods, and household goods were hauled west, and products of the western country—hides, whiskey, and herbs—were brought east on the return journey.[27] The National Road made Wheeling a competitor of Pittsburgh, but even though Wheeling had been connected by Zane's Trace through the stream-dissected country of southeastern Ohio to Limestone (Maysville), Kentucky, by 1796, the road never carried the volume of freight and passengers that the Pennsylvania Road did, as the rapid growth of Pittsburgh testified.[28] By 1800, Pittsburgh had become established as the wholesale and outfitting point for the Old Northwest. Iron industries, clothing manufacturing, and boat and raft building became important businesses within a few years.

The Cumberland Gap, some 300 mi (482.7 km) southwest of Cumberland, Maryland, was a focal point for the Wilderness Road, marked out by Daniel Boone about 1775. Once established, this route connected the Potomac River, by way of the Great Valley Road in Virginia, to the Kentucky Bluegrass settlements at Boonesborough and Harrodsburg. Initially the Wilderness Road was little more than a packhorse trail, but by 1796, as stumps were removed and streams were bridged, it became a notable route into the interior. Two major streams of migrants joined to move west along the road. One moved from Pennsylvania and Maryland southwest through the Shenandoah Valley. The second came from the Carolina Piedmont by way of the Saluda Trail and Saluda Gap to the French Broad Valley of Tennessee and finally northwest along the tributary valleys of Tennessee (Figure 3.2).[29] This latter trail was to remain important as a route for driving livestock from central

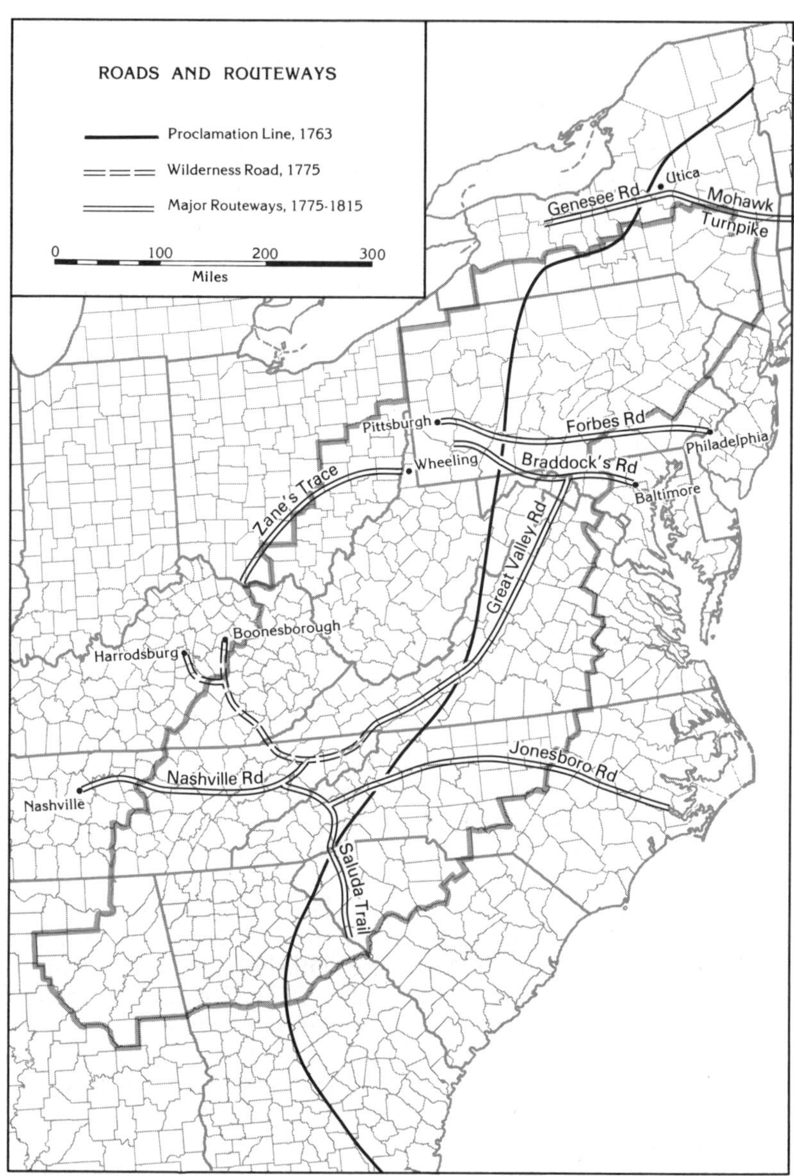
ROADS AND ROUTEWAYS
Proclamation Line, 1763
Wilderness Road, 1775
Major Routeways, 1775-1815
0
100
200
300
Miles
Utica
Genesee Rd
Mohawk
Turnpike
Pittsburgh
Forbes Rd
Philadelphia
Wheeling
Braddock's Rd
Baltimore
Zane's Trace
Great Valley Rd
Boonesborough
Harrodsburg
Jonesboro Rd
Nashville Rd
Nashville
Saluda Trail

Figure 3.2

The Golden Triangle at Pittsburgh. The Allegheny River on the left and the Monongahela on the right meet to form the Ohio. A reconstructed rampart of Fort Duquesne is visible near the approach to the bridge on the right; a Fort Pitt rampart lies beyond the highway at right. The original Monongahela wharf area lies just beyond the same bridge.

The North Carolina mountain town of Saluda was an early settlement on the Saluda Trail, which ran from the Piedmont to Asheville. The railroad (Southern) brought increased tourism to Polk and Henderson county towns.

Kentucky and the Plateaus to the cotton plantations of the southeast until railroads were built across the region in the 1840s. The route of the Wilderness Road passed through the narrowest section of the Plateaus and the consequent ease of access encouraged population increase in the Bluegrass region to the west. With the exception of the stream valleys adjacent to the road, the Plateaus Province was occupied much more slowly, and then as much through backfilling from the west or natural increase as from the routeway itself.[30]

The third focus of trans-Appalachian routes was the Valley of East Tennessee south of Cumberland Gap. Here a fertile southward extension of the Great Valley was found to hold the headwater tributaries of the Tennessee: the Holston and Watauga, the French Broad and Nolichucky. Here also Indians had farmed the alluvial valley soils, and settlers were attracted to their old fields as well as to the westward corridor itself. Between 1768 and 1773, squatters established the "Watauga settlements" (east of present-day Johnson City) in the valley, an outpost that was farther west than any other English settlement at the time.[31] By 1788, a road had been cleared westward from these settlements to Nashville on the Cumberland River (Figure 3.2). In east Tennessee, the Great Valley was sufficiently wide to offer opportunity for considerable population expansion. Yet so many people sought homes in the valley that in 1792 when a site was to be selected for a territorial capital, Knoxville, sufficient unclaimed space with proper river access could only be found some 100 mi (160.9 km) southwest of Watauga at the junction of the French Broad and the Tennessee. By 1800, the population of the East Tennessee Valley was estimated to be seventy thousand.[32]

It has been argued that salt deposits discovered in the Appalachians were the key attraction to inland migration and independence from coastal salt suppliers.[33] Salines were found in Tennessee's Holston Valley, near the Kentucky River, and in the Mohawk Valley of New York, all early settlement nodes or routes. In Pennsylvania, however, salt deposits were peripheral to the focus of settlement at the Forks of the Ohio. The settlements there, and likely the other nodes as well, developed independently of the salt supply and obtained their requirements through early trade. In Pennsylvania, at least, the early military roads and forts laid the foundation for early settlement.[34]

At the time of the first national census in 1790, the settlement frontier had expanded westward from the coast to the Catskills and a short distance up the Mohawk lowland into upstate New York (Figure 3.3). In Pennsylvania, land was settled at modest densities to the Endless Mountains. The frontier followed the Appalachian Front in Virginia for a short distance and then paralleled the Great Valley to enclose the Carolina Piedmont and a small portion of Georgia along the Savannah River. Although the frontier is portrayed on the map as a line of uniform population density, one must remember that the frontier was not a line or a wave of settlement at all but was greatly fragmented and irregular. Land along roads and navigable streams was occupied well before

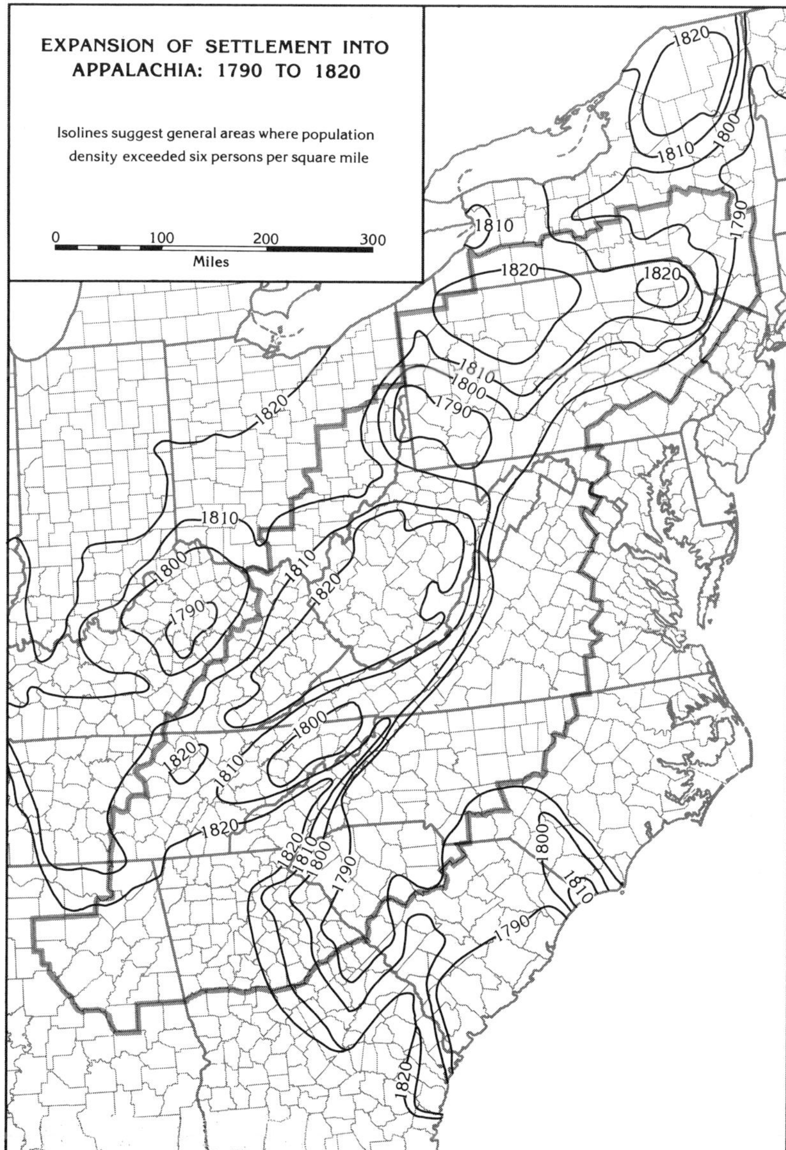


**Figure 3.3**
Information generalized from *Report on the Population of the United States,* Eleventh Census, 1890, pt. 1, 1895, maps on pp. xix–xxviii, and Randall D. Sale and Edwin D. Karn, *American Expansion* (Homewood, Ill.: Dorsey Press, 1962).

adjoining uplands. Remote but highly publicized speculative land developments were often settled earlier than more accessible lands.[35]

Early road construction had fostered the growth of three settlement clusters within or beyond the Appalachian region: the Forks of the Ohio, the Bluegrass, and East Tennessee. Each of these clusters acted as population reservoirs for the further expansion of settlement into the region. From the Forks of the Ohio, migrants moved south along the Monongahela and its major tributaries, the Tygart and Cheat rivers, into northern (now West) Virginia. Movement south along the Ohio was much more rapid, so that by 1810 the frontier had advanced well into southeastern Ohio. By that date settlement had also pressed west in New York, fed by the rapidly growing New England states and by immigrant traffic. People moved north along the Hudson and then west by way of the Mohawk Valley to the Finger Lakes and the Genesee country south of Rochester. There land-development companies blocked further expansion for a short time, a parallel to the actions of the Iroquois forty years earlier. The uplands along New York's boundary with Pennsylvania were not as desirable as the valley lands farther north and were bypassed, as were the even more rugged and remote hills of northeast and northwest Pennsylvania.[36]

In Kentucky, the settlement of the rugged Cumberland Plateau at the headwaters of the Kentucky, Licking, and Big Sandy rivers proceeded slowly, gaining as much by movements upstream from the Bluegrass and the Ohio Valley as from the Cumberland Gap routeway. An extensive area of eastern Kentucky and southern and central (now West) Virginia remained remote from easy settlement until railroads brought lumbermen and coal miners into the mountain fastness. Small settlement clusters developed along the New-Kanawha River valley by 1800, especially at the salt works near what was later to become Charleston, and a rough trail along the valley connected the Great Valley Road with the Ohio River by that date. But pioneers were not easily convinced of the merits of much of the rugged hill country to either side of the trail, when better land with fewer title problems lay to the west in the Ohio Valley. The Kentucky and West Virginia mountains remained an area to be skirted or to pass through but not to settle. From east Tennessee, pioneers moved slowly west and south along the Great Valley, whereas the central Tennessee Plateau attracted only scattered settlement before 1810. The last segment of the Blue Ridge to be occupied by whites lay in western North Carolina and north Georgia, where farmers and miners had to await the resolution of Cherokee claims before they could move in.

## THE EVOLVING ECONOMY

With the exception of scattered small-scale iron mines and furnaces, salt works, leather tanneries, and itinerant merchants and craftsmen who traveled the Appalachian frontier to sell or repair household goods, the early economy was agrarian, just as the bulk of the settlers were rural. Robert Mitchell has noted that the evolution of the economy was a gradual process that began with initial subsistence farm production and slowly progressed to greater levels of commercialization.[37] Frontier farmers in Appalachia generally did not practice specialized crop or livestock production, and they utilized crops and production techniques that had proved successful in the Atlantic colonies. In the Shenandoah Valley, for example, maize, wheat, and rye were the primary grains; cattle, horses, and swine the major livestock; flax the principal fiber; and tobacco, vegetables, and fruit the leading horticultural crops.[38] Cleared, arable land was often a small portion, 20 a. (8.1 h) or less, of the total farm acreage. As more land was cleared, small surpluses were sold locally to new settlers or travelers. Cattle, horses, hogs, and whiskey were produced in sufficient quantity to warrant taking them to eastern markets.[39] Livestock were driven long distances, in some cases from the Ohio Valley to Philadelphia or Baltimore.

The commercialization of the pioneer economy was the result of four major processes: (1) increases in agricultural specialization, (2) increasing diversification in manufacturing and services, (3) the growth of small towns as local trading centers, and (4) improved trade connections with eastern cities. All parts of the Appalachian region were not to share equally in the transition from subsistence to commercial agriculture and an economy based on surplus production and trade.[40] The limestone valleys with superior access to major routeways would merit the largest investment in land clearing, blooded livestock, and specialty crops such as tobacco and hemp. The farmers on the remote shale and sandstone hill farms would progress only slowly toward that level of production and may have abandoned their land long before the sequence had been completed. In the Pennsylvania Ridge and Valley, only scattered farms—small and poorly kept—were to be found beyond the Kittatinny Ridge by 1800. Roads were poor, if they existed at all. There were few villages offering services or trading opportunities, and grain, iron goods, and whiskey were floated down the Juniata and Susquehanna rivers to Baltimore.[41] Consequently the towns that experienced rapid growth were usually river towns, such as Sunbury and Harrisburg in Pennsylvania, both ports on the shallow Susquehanna. As coastal markets for Appalachian metals, leathers and fibers, and food products grew, regional farms, mills, and furnaces were stimulated to increase production, and the states in turn were motivated to improve the roads into the coastal hinterland. Towns grew up at major crossroads, stream crossing points, or mill sites. As new counties were formed, county-seat towns were established, all providing markets for farm products and focal points for east-coast merchants and tradesmen who wished to extend their trade connections farther into the hinterlands.[42]

Until the decade of 1810 to 1820, commercial development in Appalachia, whether agricultural or industrial, was dependent upon trade with urban consumers by way of wagons or pack animals overland or by flat boat, or "ark," on the region's streams. Freight rates were high.

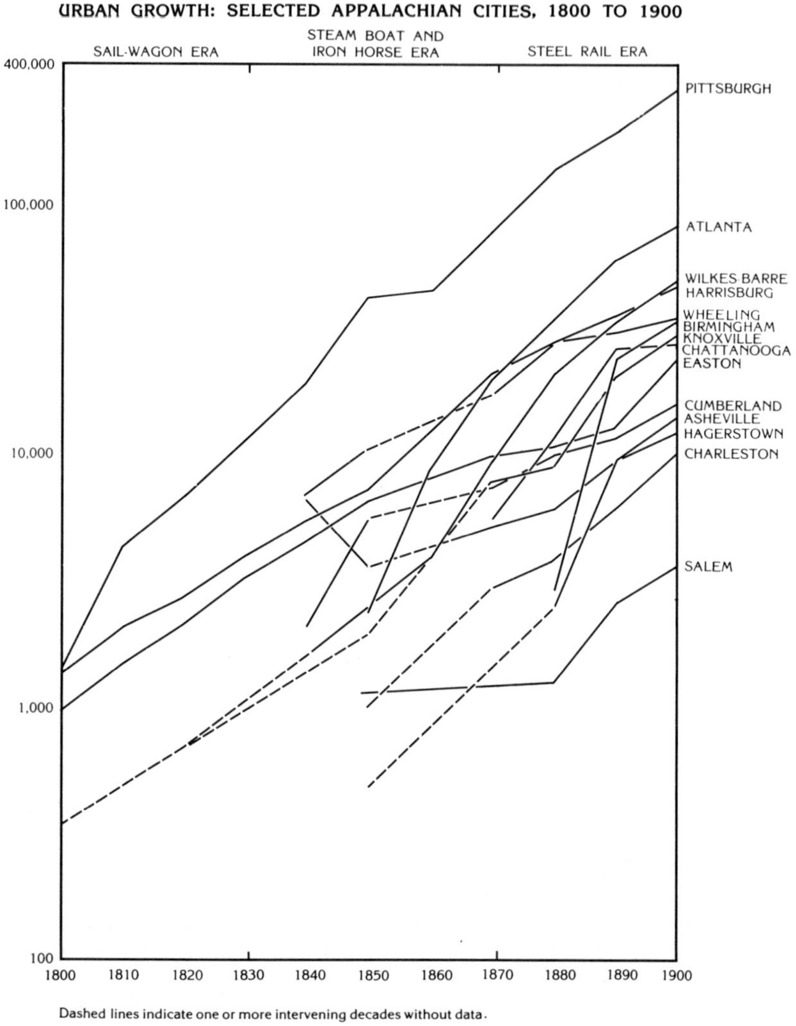

URBAN GROWTH: SELECTED APPALACHIAN CITIES, 1800 TO 1900

SAIL-WAGON ERA
STEAM BOAT AND IRON HORSE ERA
STEEL RAIL ERA

400,000
100,000
10,000
1,000
100

1800 1810 1820 1830 1840 1850 1860 1870 1880 1890 1900

PITTSBURGH
ATLANTA
WILKES-BARRE
HARRISBURG
WHEELING
BIRMINGHAM
KNOXVILLE
CHATTANOOGA
EASTON
CUMBERLAND
ASHEVILLE
HAGERSTOWN
CHARLESTON
SALEM

Dashed lines indicate one or more intervening decades without data.

**Figure 3.4**
Eras after John R. Borchert, "American Metropolitan Evolution," *Geographical Review* 57 (1967):301–325. Easton is in Pennsylvania; Salem in North Carolina.

Overland wagon freight charges in Pennsylvania and Maryland were estimated at $10.00 per ton per 100 mi ($5.63 per metric ton per 100 km). Few bulky commodities could tolerate such expense.[43] Consequently the navigable waterways such as the Potomac, Susquehanna, and Delaware were important supplementary routes to the overland roads. The sections of the region that were not agriculturally productive and were remote from major roads and rivers, such as the southern Blue Ridge, had to await the revolution in transportation brought about by the steamboat and the steam engine–powered train. Of the four major epochs of urban growth and change in U.S. cities outlined by John Borchert, the first three are especially useful in reviewing how cities in and adjacent to Appalachia responded to changes in transportation technology.[44] During the initial period, the Sail-Wagon era that lasted from 1790 to about 1830, some cities away from the Atlantic coast began to experience rapid growth, especially those that were positioned near primary resources and were on or near major inland transportation routes (Figure 3.4). Many cities in western New York and the Great Valley experienced rapid population increase during this period. Harrisburg, Pennsylvania, for example, began as a small agricultural marketing center in 1785. By 1800 the population had reached almost fifteen hundred. Situated on the Susquehanna at the mouth of a series of water gaps that led into the Ridge and Valley upstream, the town functioned as a market center for Ridgc and Valley farmers. Wheat was rafted downstream and sold to Harrisburg millers, and other farm products were processed as well. City merchants in turn sold manufactured commodities to the upcountry farmers. The city was designated the state capital in 1812. Governmental functions, together with the development of nearby iron deposits, attracted migrants and new industries, and by 1820 the population had doubled to almost three thousand.[45]

A period of canal construction, marked by the building of the Erie Canal across the Mohawk lowland in upstate New York, was initiated during the second half of the Sail-Wagon era. The canal's governmental financing was secured primarily through the efforts of politicians and entrepreneurs on the East Coat who were attempting to gain access to the lucrative markets of the rapidly developing northern Appalachian country and the Midwest. New York City, at the mouth of the Hudson River, was essentially isolated from the overland routes, the Pennsylvania Road, the new National Road, and the Pennsylvania river routes that focused on Baltimore and Philadelphia. Even the rural hinterland of New York State's Southern Tier counties shipped commodities on the Susquehanna to avoid the prohibitive freight rates of the overland turnpikes. Elmira, Owego, and Binghamton, all sited at valley junctions, had become important shipping centers to Philadelphia and Baltimore.[46] A canal constructed along the Mohawk Valley not only would give New York City access to the produce of the uplands and the fertile Ontario Plain but also—by means of a connection with Lake Erie—would allow cheap transport all the way into the heart of the Midwest by way of

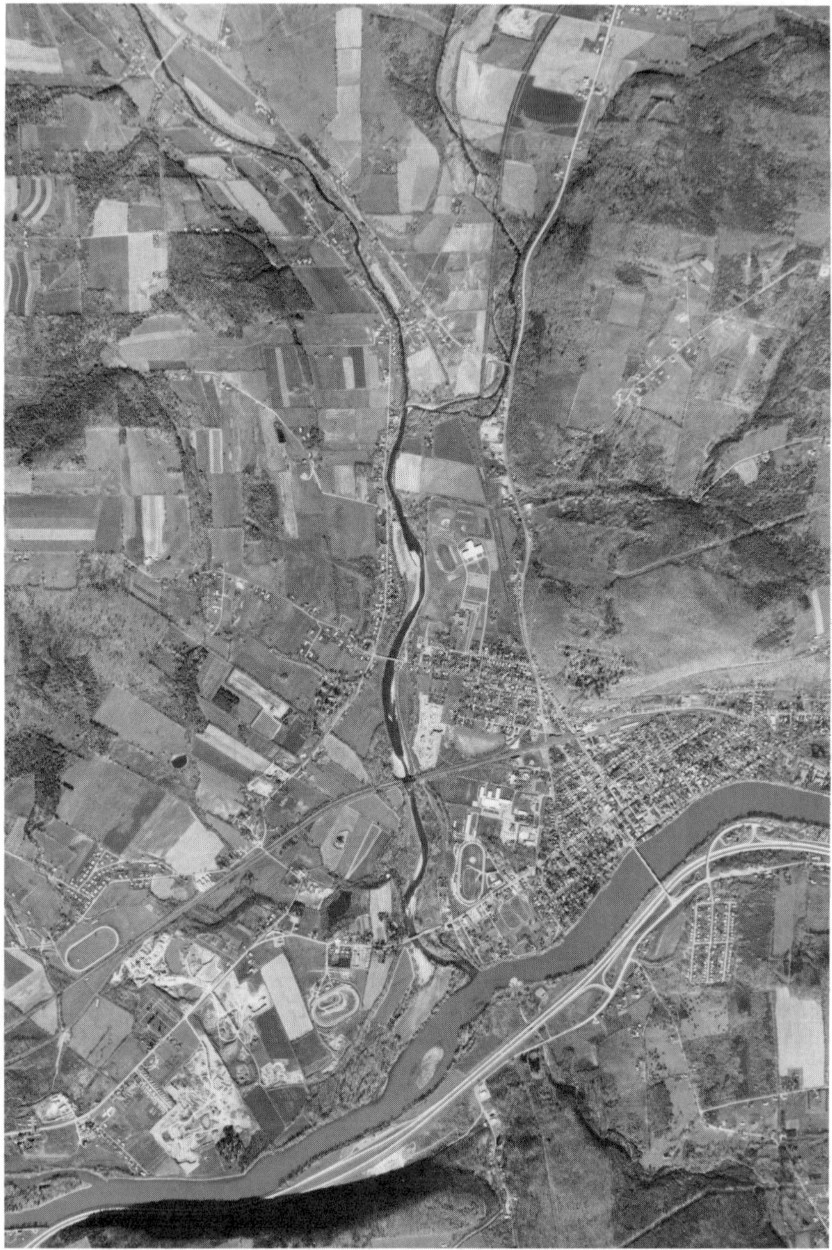

Owego, New York, lies at the junction of the Owego River and the larger Susquehanna River. Early trade routes followed the Susquehanna south to Philadelphia. The railroad, completed in the 1850s, offered alternative connections with the Hudson Valley. (U.S. Department of Agriculture photo.)

the Great Lakes system. Plans were approved in 1817, and by 1825 the 363-mile (584.1-kilometer) length of the canal was opened to Lake Erie. Freight rates were lowered from $100 to $15 per ton ($90.70 to $13.60 per metric ton) from Buffalo to New York, and travel time was reduced from twenty to eight days.[47]

The financial success of the Erie Canal and the possibility of a New York City monopoly on trade with the Midwest and upper Ohio Valley were strong motivations for bankers and merchants in Philadelphia and Baltimore to consider construction of competing canals to the Ohio Valley. Unfortunately, the Appalachian rivers that focused on Philadelphia flowed from the north, not from the west, and the barrier of the Ridge and Valley and the Appalachian Front was formidable. Nevertheless, construction on the Pennsylvania Portage and Canal System began in the 1820s and was completed by 1834. The route followed the Susquehanna upstream to the Juniata and then west to Hollidaysburg at the foot of the Appalachian Front. There a series of five inclined planes were built to hoist canalboats up the eastern face of the 2,291-foot (696.5-meter) ridge. On the west side, the canal led into the Conemaugh River at Johnstown and then connected to Pittsburgh. The route was cumbersome for freight, at best, and the system became a financial drain on its financiers.[48] Despite such realities, canal fever seemed to spread from one community to another in Pennsylvania as each town sought competitive advantage. As a result, by 1840 Pennsylvania had about 1,000 mi (1,609 km) of canals in operation.[49]

Canal construction westward from Baltimore offered even greater difficulties than those the Pennsylvania Canal had encountered. Although the eastward-flowing Potomac River could be used for part of its length, a canal would have to cross the Appalachian Front at over 2,700 ft (820.8 m). The canal, constructed by the Chesapeake and Ohio Canal Company, was initiated in 1827, but financial and engineering difficulties so hampered progress that by 1850 the canal had only reached Cumberland, Maryland, where it was stalled at the foot of the roughest portion of the traverse to the Ohio Valley. The Baltimore and Ohio Railroad had arrived eight years earlier.

The effect of these canals on the growth of Appalachian towns and cities is unclear. Some towns on the Pennsylvania Canal—Harrisburg and Johnstown, for example—did grow more rapidly than towns that did not have direct canal connections. But Pittsburgh's continued expansion may have been supported as much by its role as an outfitting center for Ohio Valley migrants as to its place as a transshipment center for goods going to eastern markets. By the close of the Sail-Wagon era in 1830, central and southern Appalachia was still a region of small towns. Trade connections with the coastal cities of Charleston, Savannah, and Norfolk (Virginia) were limited when compared to the interaction between the northern coastal cities and their hinterlands. Salem, a North Carolina Piedmont agricultural supply and trading center, did not exceed one thousand people until 1850. Knoxville, though on the Tennessee

As the Potomac River flows along the Maryland–West Virginia border, its direction changes from northeast to southeast. Cumberland, Maryland, grew up at this point and on the splice between Ridge and Valley and Appalachian Front. Cumberland was an important focus for the National Road, the Chesapeake and Ohio Canal, and the Baltimore and Ohio Railroad. (U.S. Department of Agriculture photo.)

River, was not much larger. Asheville, Chattanooga, Birmingham, and Atlanta awaited the coming of the railroads.

The steamboat and the steam-powered railroad brought drastic changes to the regional transportation network. Although steamboats had begun to travel the Ohio and its tributaries before 1820, traffic generally did not become significant until about 1830, the beginning of Borchert's Steamboat–Iron Horse era that lasted from 1830 to 1870.[50] On the Ohio River almost 190 boats hauled trade goods upstream and regional commodities down. The Falls of the Ohio at Louisville were successfully skirted in 1820, allowing boats to make the full trip between Pittsburgh and New Orleans. By 1830, steamboats had pushed beyond Pittsburgh, moving upstream along the Allegheny and Monongahela rivers. In the south, a Tennessee River steamboat succeeded in running the Muscle Shoals rapids in northern Alabama in 1825, thereby bringing a westward trade connection to Knoxville. Piedmont tobacco and cotton was shipped by boat through the port of Charleston, South Carolina, to New York and Boston. In the north, corn, wheat, and flour were shipped down the Potomac and Delaware rivers to coastal markets. Northern rivers tapped the coal fields and increasing amounts of bituminous coal and anthracite were shipped down the Lehigh, Susquehanna, and Schuylkill rivers to Philadelphia and Baltimore. Steamboats were built to burn both types of coal, and the increasing number of steam engines in use led to a boom in the anthracite fields. Wilkes-Barre, in the heart of the Luzerne County anthracite belt, had fewer than one thousand people in 1830 but increased rapidly to over forty-two hundred by 1860 as coal demand grew. Pittsburgh, already the largest city in Appalachia in 1830 with over twelve thousand people, more than tripled its size to forty-nine thousand by 1860.

The early railroads brought profound changes to the urban system evolving in the eastern states, even though limitations of brittle and fast-wearing iron track, small-scale rolling stock, and nonstandardized railroad gauges were such that the first railroads were merely short lines built between river ports and their immobile hinterlands to move farm commodities, minerals, or timber relatively short distances.[51] In the south, Richmond (Virginia), Charleston, and Savannah all sponsored the construction of railroads inland to the Piedmont in the late 1820s and 1830s. A depression in 1837 slowed the expansion of trade into northern Georgia, but by 1845 track had been laid from Macon, Georgia, north to the Chattahoochee River in the heart of the Piedmont. The small settlement that grew up around the freight depot was called Atlanta, and nearby farmers began using the line to ship cotton to Savannah and Charleston.[52] Six years later, track laid from the Tennessee River entered Atlanta from the north. Southeast Tennessee had been slow to develop after the Cherokees had been driven from the area. Soils were unproductive, and except for the occasional raft bringing Philadelphia goods downstream from Knoxville, the area was isolated. When the tiny riverbank settlement of Chattanooga was selected as the terminus for the Western and Atlantic Railroad from Atlanta, it became the center of intense land speculation and a shipping point for corn, bacon, flour, and cotton from north Alabama farms. Eventually, Chattanooga became a transshipment center with rail connections to Nashville and—when the Tennessee had been cleared of obstacles—river linkage with the Mississippi Valley.[53] Atlanta and Chattanooga were products of the railroad, as were so many other southern Appalachian cities. Atlanta grew rapidly as more rail lines tied it into a Piedmont transport manifold, and by 1860 it had become the most important rail center in the South with a population of almost ten thousand. But the city's strategic connections were too important for the Union to ignore during the Civil War, and General Sherman burned the city and destroyed the railroads.

Railroad development was somewhat slower in the North than in the South. Although the Baltimore and Ohio line, begun in the 1820s, was completed to Wheeling by 1852, construction of lines west from Philadelphia and New York lagged, in part because of the sizable investments made in canal systems. Nevertheless, the Pennsylvania Railroad from Philadelphia to Pittsburgh was completed five years after work began in 1847. In New York, a trunk line was laid from the Hudson River west across the Southern Tier counties to Lake Erie. The line, completed in 1851, was an attempt to give those counties some compensation for the Erie Canal that had bypassed them to the north and to capture the trade that was siphoned off by the Susquehanna route to Philadelphia and Baltimore.[54] Two years later, after the lifting of monopolistic regulations that allowed cross-state freight traffic only on the Erie Canal, a number of short lines were joined together along the canal route to form the New York Central Railroad.

A third period of urban growth, the Steel-Rail era, 1870–1920, was initiated by a revolutionary process that reduced the amount of carbon and silica in hot pig iron, producing high-strength steel. Henry Bessemer's discovery that high-pressure air would remove impurities from smelted iron in a bulk process allowed the iron industry to produce large quantities of steel at low prices.[55] The replacement of iron by steel in the construction of rails and railroad rolling stock resulted in greater-capacity rails, more-reliable equipment, and a significant extension of the distances that commodities could be moved. These innovations, together with the standardization of railroad gauges after the Civil War, established the revitalized and expanded rail network as the dominant transportation mode in the eastern states.[56] As the demand for coal to power increasing numbers of steam railroad engines and industrial power plants grew during this period, cities in which steel was produced and those in the western Pennsylvania coalfields expanded rapidly. Pittsburgh's population almost quadrupled between 1870 and 1900, and the population of Wilkes-Barre increased five times to fifty-two thousand in the same period.

Rail lines were extended into the central Appalachian coalfields during this era. Industrial companies in the north and Europe obtained mineral rights to millions of acres in eastern Kentucky and southern West

Virginia. Tracks were laid into the most accessible areas, and the companies built towns to house the men they hoped to employ as miners. Literally hundreds of Kentucky, Virginia, and West Virginia towns, which had not existed in 1870, had five hundred people or more within a few months after the railroad arrived.

In northern Alabama, Birmingham, which had been valley cotton fields and barren ridges as late as 1870, evolved out of a cluster of small company towns that grew up on the edge of local coal and iron-ore deposits. In 1880, three thousand people occupied the site, and by the turn of the century the population had increased ten times. Chattanooga, with important rail and river connections and access to both the minerals of northern Alabama and the timber of the southern Cumberland Plateau and Blue Ridge, increased its population five times in the same period to thirty thousand. The steel rail had a more modest impact on the towns of the Carolina Piedmont. Each county seat experienced a spurt of investment and growth when the railroad arrived in the 1880s and 1890s. For instance, lumber mills or tanning companies attracted to the stands of chestnut were established, or sufficient local capital was mustered to initiate a furniture factory or a textile mill.[57] Rail lines were built upcountry into the southern Blue Ridge only with great difficulty and expense. The chief beneficiaries in this remote area were the small highland resorts such as Tryon, Saluda, and Asheville, North Carolina, that catered to wealthy Piedmont or Coastal Plain planters escaping the summer heat. Elsewhere in the Blue Ridge, rails were laid to bring out hardwoods or minerals—mica, feldspar, kaolin—and were the initial step in reducing the isolation of many existing settlements and creating new ones. In many counties, the railroad did not arrive until as late as 1900 to 1910, but it still preceded hard-surface roads by a decade.

The growing plexus of railroads in Appalachia from 1880 to 1920 initiated a shift in economic leverage away from that enjoyed by the large coastal or gateway cities toward inland sites where agriculture and industrial production were being established. This change is best seen in southern Appalachia where, at the eve of the Civil War, there were no towns that exceeded 10,000 people.[58] By 1900, Atlanta had become the nation's forty-third largest city, and by 1910 the population of Atlanta and Birmingham each surpassed 100,000. The regional influence of long-established small towns that had idled at a mountain-gap site or a river crossing point was assured when the railroad was built through them, and although their urban growth lagged fifty years behind the rest of the country, towns like Roanoke, Charlotte, Greenville, and Knoxville became focal points for the southern Appalachian urban system.[59]

## NOTES

1. Bruce G. Trigger, "Early Iroquoian Contacts with Europeans," *Handbook of North American Indians,* vol. 15, *Northeast* (Washington, D.C.: Smithsonian Institution, 1978), p. 344, and Robert Rayback, "The Indian," in John H.

Thompson, ed., *Geography of New York State* (Syracuse, N.Y.: Syracuse University Press, 1966), pp. 113–115.

2. Elizabeth Tooker, "Iroquois Since 1820," *Handbook of North American Indians,* vol. 15, *Northeast* (Washington, D.C.: Smithsonian Institution, 1978), p. 449.

3. Rayback, op. cit. (footnote 1), p. 117.

4. Ibid., p. 119.

5. Raymond E. Murphy and Marion Murphy, *Pennsylvania: A Regional Geography* (Harrisburg: Pennsylvania Book Service, 1937), pp. 83–86.

6. Ibid., p. 87, and Francis Jennings, "Susquehannock," *Handbook of North American Indians,* vol. 15, *Northeast* (Washington, D.C.: Smithsonian Institution, 1978), pp. 364–366.

7. Murphy and Murphy, op. cit. (footnote 5), pp. 83–86.

8. Wilma Dykeman and Jim Stokely, *Highland Homeland: The People of the Great Smokies* (Washington, D.C.: U.S. Dept. of the Interior, 1978), p. 31, and Douglas C. Wilms, "Cherokee Settlement Patterns in Nineteenth Century Georgia," *Southeastern Geographer* 14 (1974), p. 50.

9. Dykeman and Stokely, op. cit. (footnote 8), p. 37.

10. Wilms, op. cit. (footnote 8), p. 52.

11. Laurence French and Jim Hornbuckle, eds., *The Cherokee Perspective: Written by Eastern Cherokees* (Boone, N.C.: Appalachian Consortium Press, 1981), p. 21.

12. Dykeman and Stokely, op. cit. (footnote 8), pp. 66–67.

13. Oliver LaFarge, "Myths that Hide the American Indian," *American Heritage* 7 (1956), pp. 5–6.

14. Ibid.

15. Lois K. Mathews, *The Expansion of New England* (New York: Houghton Mifflin Co., 1909), pp. 119–121.

16. Francis J. Marschner, *Boundaries and Records in the Territory of Early Settlement from Canada to Florida* (Washington, D.C.: Agricultural Research Service, 1960), p. 27.

17. Ray A. Billington, *Westward Expansion: A History of the American Frontier,* 3d ed. (New York: Macmillan Co., 1967), p. 255.

18. Marschner, op. cit. (footnote 16), pp. 31–32.

19. Frederick Merk, *History of the Westward Movement* (New York: Alfred A. Knopf, 1978), p. 50. The settlement of western Maryland was also hampered by land speculation and conflicting claims. See Frank W. Porter, "From Back Country to County: The Delayed Settlement of Western Maryland," *Maryland Historical Magazine* 70 (1975), p. 340.

20. Marschner, op. cit. (footnote 16), p. 40.

21. Otis K. Rice, *The Allegheny Frontier: West Virginia Beginnings, 1730–1830* (Lexington: University Press of Kentucky, 1970), p. 136.

22. Ibid., p. 41.

23. Ibid., p. 149.

24. Marschner, op. cit. (footnote 16), p. 37.

25. Ralph H. Brown, *Historical Geography of the United States* (New York: Harcourt, Brace and World, 1948), p. 184.

26. Merk, op. cit. (footnote 19), p. 83.

27. Murphy and Murphy, op. cit. (footnote 5), p. 104.

28. Ibid., p. 110.

29. Brown, op. cit. (footnote 25), p. 83.

30. John C. Campbell, *The Southern Highlander and His Homeland* (Lex-

ington: University Press of Kentucky, 1969; originally published by the Russell Sage Foundation, 1921), p. 40.

31. Merk, op. cit. (footnote 19), p. 83.

32. Brown, op. cit. (footnote 25), p. 188.

33. Frederick Jackson Turner, *Frontier and Section: Selected Essays of Frederick Jackson Turner* (Englewood Cliffs, N.J.: Prentice-Hall, 1961), p. 47.

34. John A. Jakle, "Salt on the Ohio Valley Frontier, 1770–1820," *Annals,* Association of American Geographers, 59 (1969), p. 695.

35. D. W. Meinig, "Geography of Expansion, 1785–1855," in Thompson, op. cit. (footnote 1), p. 145.

36. Ibid., p. 149.

37. Robert D. Mitchell, "The Shenandoah Valley Frontier," *Annals,* Association of American Geographers, 62 (1972), p. 475.

38. Ibid., p. 476.

39. Ibid., p. 478.

40. Robert D. Mitchell, *Commercialism and Frontier: Perspectives on the Early Shenandoah Valley* (Charlottesville: University Press of Virginia, 1977), p. 162.

41. Murphy and Murphy, op. cit. (footnote 5), p. 104.

42. Mitchell, 1972, op. cit. (footnote 37), p. 482.

43. Edward C. Kirkland, *A History of American Economic Life,* 3d ed. (New York: Appleton-Century-Crofts, 1951), p. 231.

44. John R. Borchert, "American Metropolitan Evolution," *Geographical Review* 57 (1967), pp. 301–325.

45. Murphy and Murphy, op. cit. (footnote 5), p. 105.

46. Meinig, op. cit. (footnote 35), p. 157.

47. Billington, op. cit. (footnote 17), p. 333.

48. Kirkland, op. cit. (footnote 43), p. 236.

49. Peirce F. Lewis, "Small Town in Pennsylvania," *Annals,* Association of American Geographers, 62 (1972), p. 339.

50. Borchert, op. cit. (footnote 44), p. 314.

51. Ibid., p. 315.

52. Kirkland, op. cit. (footnote 43), p. 248.

53. Gilbert E. Govan and James W. Livingood, *The Chattanooga Country: 1540–1951* (New York: E. P. Dutton and Co., 1952), pp. 116–139.

54. Kirkland, op. cit. (footnote 43), p. 248.

55. Ibid., p. 389. America's first steel-rail manufacturing plant was built in Danville, Pennsylvania, just west of the anthracite fields.

56. Borchert, op. cit. (footnote 44), p. 319.

57. Dwight Billings, *Planters and the Making of a "New South": Class, Politics, and Development in North Carolina, 1865–1900* (Chapel Hill: University of North Carolina Press, 1979), p. 53, and Ina W. Van Noppen and John J. Van Noppen, *Western North Carolina Since the Civil War* (Boone, N.C.: Appalachian Consortium Press, 1973), p. 251.

58. T. Lynn Smith, "The Emergence of Cities," in Rupert B. Vance and Nicholas J. Demersth, eds., *The Urban South* (Chapel Hill: University of North Carolina Press, 1954), p. 26.

59. Ibid., p. 32.

# CHAPTER 4

# SETTLEMENT AND CULTURE PATTERNS

The travels of Oliver Gant, one of the main characters in Thomas Wolfe's novel of life in a southern mountain community, serve as a metaphor for the long-term movement of people and ideas from the Mid-Atlantic states south and west along the trend of ridge and valley into the Piedmont and highlands. Oliver, the son of an English father and a Pennsylvania German mother, sought personal fulfillment in the Reconstruction South by moving to the Carolina Piedmont, leaving behind "the great barns of Pennsylvania, the ripe bending of golden grain, the plenty, the order, the clean thrift of the people. . . ." A subsequent move brought him eventually to a Blue Ridge resort town in western North Carolina, where he found himself among "hill and country people [who were] Scotch-Irish mountaineers, rugged, provincial, intelligent, and industrious."[1] Gant's heritage and peregrinations represent the processes of social interaction and migration whereby the six or more generations that preceded him spread from north to south, from broad valley to mountain fastness, from fat lands of bountiful production to hardscrabble hillsides.

Thus occupied by people of diverse origins, Appalachia, a region of multiple physical character, has not one national heritage but many, not a monomorphic culture but a mosaic. Sequent European immigration in the eighteenth and nineteenth centuries brought people of varied national and religious heritage to the Atlantic coast. The subsequent concentration of distinct groups in New England, the Mid-Atlantic states, and the west Chesapeake Tidewater country provided reservoirs or hearths from which people and ideas gradually moved into the Appalachians (Figure 4.1). This chapter will sketch in the major national groups that participated in this movement and the Appalachian cultural traditions that grew out of their experiences.

Each of the three coastal culture hearths was basically English in character, but by 1720 Germans and Scotch-Irish began to arrive. They were joined by Welsh, French Huguenots, Irish, Swiss, and other north Europeans. The New England area and the Dutch-settled Hudson Valley

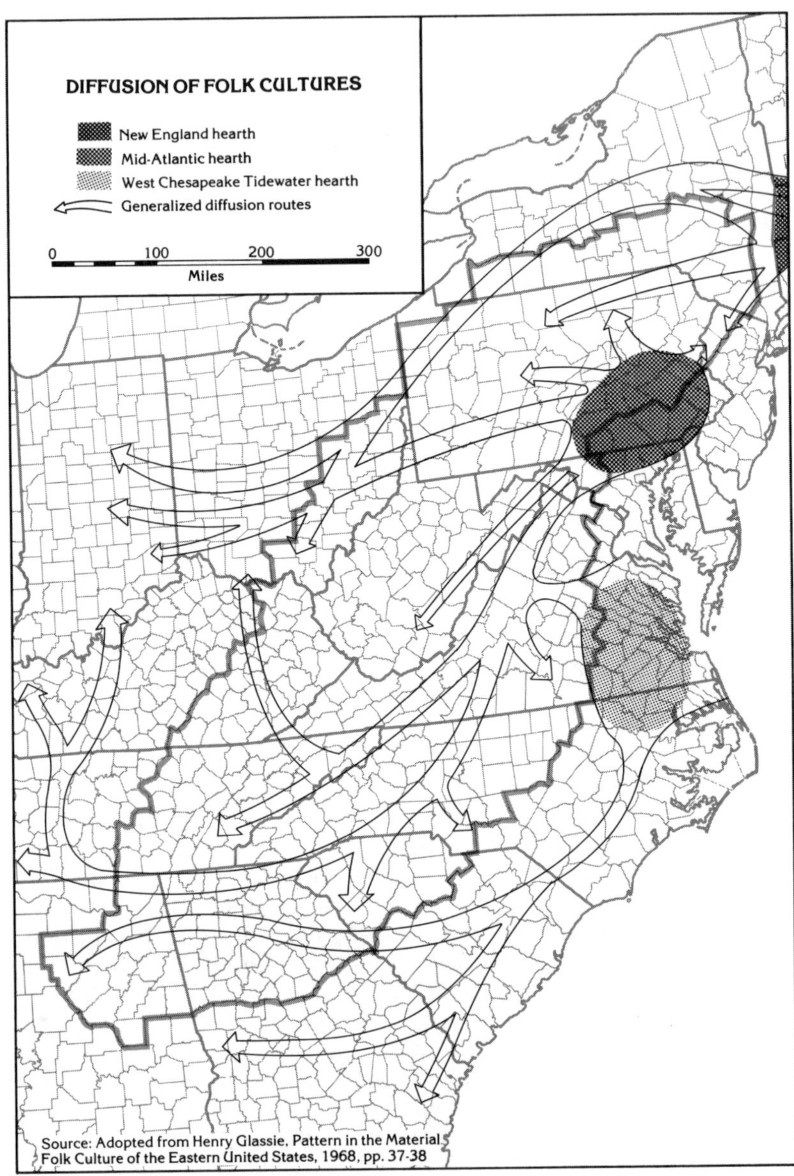
DIFFUSION OF FOLK CULTURES
New England hearth
Mid-Atlantic hearth
West Chesapeake Tidewater hearth
Generalized diffusion routes
0
100
200
300
Miles
Source: Adopted from Henry Glassie, Pattern in the Material Folk Culture of the Eastern United States, 1968, pp. 37-38

**Figure 4.1**

contributed limited numbers of settlers to northern Appalachia before the Revolution. Overland routes tended to follow stream divides or valleys, but the major rivers of New England and New York—the Connecticut and the Hudson—led north into the mountains, and westward routes across the Taconic, Berkshire, Green, and Catskill mountains were slow in developing. The one water-level corridor that penetrated a part of the Appalachian upland in New York, the Mohawk Valley, was occupied by the hostile Iroquois Confederacy, and that passage was little used until their defeat in the Revolution and the War of 1812. When this route was finally opened in the 1820s, New England influence spread into New York and the Great Lakes basin rather than filtering very far south into the Appalachians.

In the Mid-Atlantic hearth immediately to the south, land in Penn's Colony was available at reasonable prices. Many of the contentious Indians there had either moved west or north into New York, and a liberal colonial leadership encouraged those Europeans who sought tolerant attitudes toward religious practices and minimal interference in business affairs to immigrate into Pennsylvania. Philadelphia and the Delaware Valley had been a focal area for early Quaker settlers whose language and material culture gave the city and the countryside immediately to the west a distinct English flavor. Beginning in the late 1600s, small numbers of German Amish, Mennonites, Dunkards, and Pietists settled the lower Susquehanna Valley and began clearing the land for farming.[2] By 1727, immigration had increased, and the German groups (or Pennsylvania Dutch as they were later collectively called) numbered over twenty thousand. While some moved west, perhaps seeking a secure isolation in the Endless Mountains, many stayed on and consolidated their communities by infilling among earlier arrivals. These Protestant sects, some from the Rhine Valley and others from Switzerland, formed endogenous groups. They initiated some urban settlements, but many lived on small farms that—while functionally separate—retained the cohesion of village communities.[3] The immigration of Scotch-Irish Presbyterians also increased rapidly during the early 1700s, and although they were arriving at essentially the same time as some of the German groups, they were obligated to move beyond the Quaker and German settlements near Philadelphia to find cheap (or free) open land. The two groups did not readily intermix but seemed to prefer to settle among kin.

Across the Upland South the use of space in communities is generally consistent. The Pennsylvania Germans brought with them from the Palatinate, Rhenish, and Westfalian areas of Germany the individual family farm based on mixed intensive agriculture. The Scotch-Irish brought the Celtic dispersed farm with cattle grazing and kitchen garden common in Ireland and Scotland. Members of each group moved in single family units into the uplands. The Scotch-Irish often squatted on land in forested coves and mountainsides, whereas the Germans preferred the rolling valley floors. As additional settlers claimed land,

Two houses suggest that an extended family works the land on an Amish farm just south of Menno, Pennsylvania, in Kishacoquillas Valley. The 30-mile-long (48.3-kilometer-long) valley is floored with limestone and flanked by resistant ridges of Tuscarora and Bald Eagle sandstone.

farms gradually became contiguous and isolated farmsteads, by accretion, gradually became neighborhoods. The Scotch-Irish are often portrayed as individualists who sought out the isolation of the frontier. The Quakers apparently saw them as a "pernicious and pugnacious people," and German opinions were equally unflattering.[4] Nevertheless, many Scotch-Irish chose to remain in existing settlements, so that eventually they were concentrated in selected areas. Eventually Augusta and Rockbridge counties in the Shenandoah Valley of Virginia would claim to be the most Scotch-Irish counties in America.[5] With subsequent arrivals, German and Scotch-Irish settlements alternated along river valleys, and as new immigrants advanced to the frontier, the process was repeated. By the 1730s, these two groups had occupied western Maryland and the Shenandoah Valley and by 1750 had reached the Carolinas (Table 4.1).[6]

About 1724, large numbers of Scotch-Irish began arriving in the Delaware Valley ports. They crossed the Susquehanna and Shenandoah valleys and settled in the Cumberland country to the west, the area that Estyn Evans has identified as their "cradle in the New World."[7] In the parallel valleys of south-central Pennsylvania they established the townships of Antrim, Armagh, Derry, Fermanagh, and Tyrone, all

TABLE 4.1
Selected Dates in Scotch-Irish Expansion

| | Pennsylvania | Virginia | North Carolina | South Carolina |
|---|---|---|---|---|
| First Effective Settlement | 1717 | 1732 | 1740 | 1760 |
| Beginning of Steady Flow | 1718 | 1736 | 1750 | 1761 |
| First Frontier County Organized | 1729 | 1738 | 1752 | 1769 |
| First Inland Presbyterian Church | 1720 | 1740 | 1755 | 1764* |

From James G. Leyburn, The Scotch-Irish (Chapel Hill: University of North Carolina Press, 1962), p. 186. Copyright 1962 the University of North Carolina Press. By permission of the publisher.

*Date is for first church west of the Fall Line.

named for places left behind in Ulster, but movement west into the Plateaus was stifled by Indians and French, so they turned southwest, following the trend of topography and drainage into Virginia and Tennessee (Figure 4.2). Scotch-Irish immigration peaked in 1772–1773 and ebbed thereafter. By 1800, about one-sixth of the European population in America—250,000 people—was Scotch-Irish, outnumbering the Germans by an estimated 50,000. By this time, large numbers of the Ulster immigrants had moved into the Appalachian Plateaus and beyond.[8]

The Virginia (west Chesapeake) Tidewater hearth area contributed minimally to the increasing stream of people moving into the Appalachian uplands during the eighteenth century. Those planters that did move inland tended to remain on the Piedmont. Succeeding generations then carried the plantation economy and social organization into the south, finding little opportunity for large-scale farming in the mountains.

## GERMAN AND SCOTCH-IRISH CULTURAL TRADITIONS

Many of the culture elements that eventually were to diffuse into Appalachia were Indian, English, German, or Scotch-Irish. Because the Germans and Scotch-Irish often outnumbered other European groups and adopted those artifacts and practices that best suited their frontier situation, they became the principal carriers of innovation into the region. An initial differentiation between the areas occupied predominantly by Pennsylvania Germans and Scotch-Irish can be made by examining the former's preference for social contact and living in urban communities as opposed to the latter's preference for isolated farmsteads. Many of the Germans, even the farmers, were aggressive entrepreneurs and their commercial activities focused on the villages and towns. As Peirce Lewis and Ben Marsh have pointed out, the business of the Pennsylvania town was business.[9] The development of a vital urban-based economy in central and eastern Pennsylvania was fostered by the

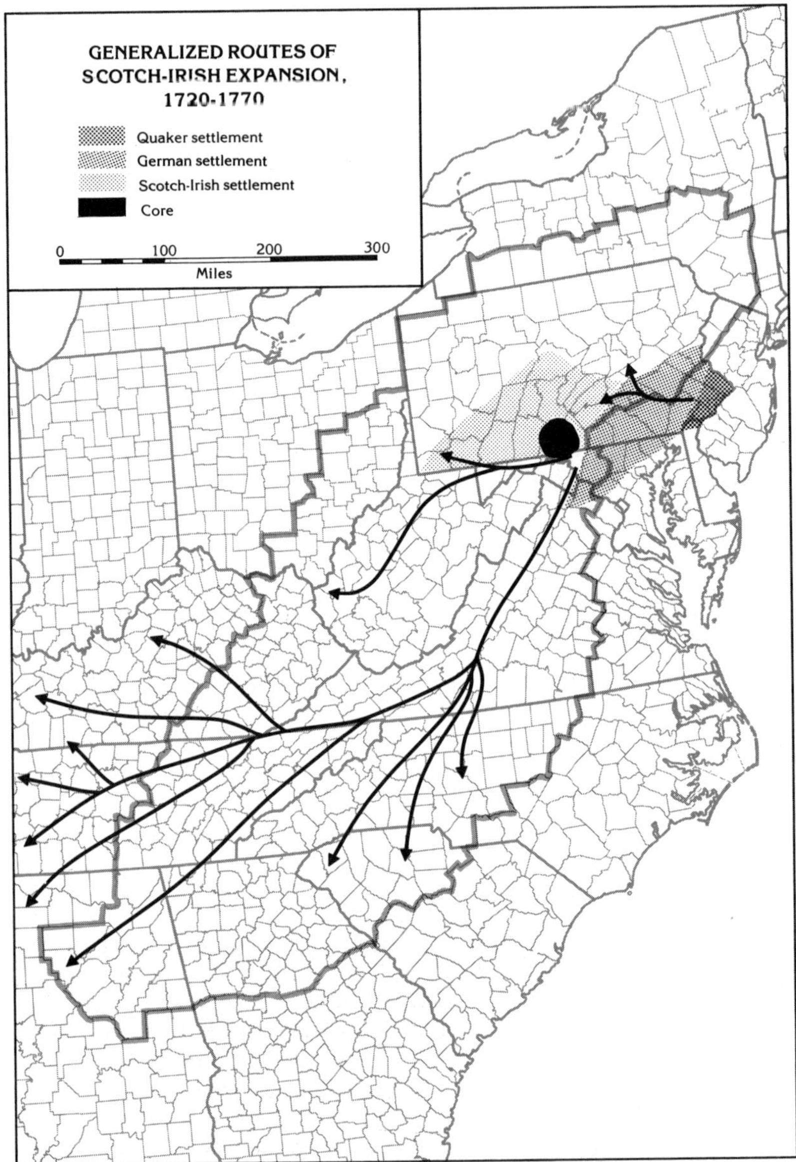


**Figure 4.2**
After E. Estyn Evans, "The Scotch-Irish: Their Cultural Adaptation and Heritage in the American Old West," in E.R.R. Green, ed., *Essays in Scotch-Irish History* (London: Routledge & Kegan Paul Ltd., 1969), pp. 70–71.

area's strategic location, its position astride relatively well developed transportation routes, its productive agriculture, newly established manufacturing industries, and a political climate that encouraged independent initiative.[10]

In the central Pennsylvania country that Wilbur Zelinsky identifies as the Pennsylvania Culture Area (PCA), an area that closely approximates the Mid-Atlantic hearth on Figure 4.1, the process of urbanization and town founding proceeded more rapidly than elsewhere in America. The PCA town took on a distinctive form replete with diagnostic characteristics that grew out of its function and the heritage of its founders. A number of attributes distinguish the Pennsylvania town. Its central residential and business area is compact, with structures often abutting one another. In many towns—Lancaster, York, and Hagerstown, Maryland, for example—the row house set on a narrow lot predominates in the original residential areas. Building density is increased by building adjacent to sidewalks and streets, thereby eliminating front yards. In part because of the German artisans' tradition of opening a shop in one of the lower rooms of their homes, the functions of the Pennsylvania town tend to be mixed, with shops and offices interspersed with dwellings while churches, cemeteries, schools, parks, and manufacturing are relegated to peripheral locations.[11] Building materials for homes, barns, commercial buildings, churches, and even sidewalks are primarily brick with much use of stone and stucco. Street geometry tends to be oriented around one or more linear main streets with side streets laid out at right angles. Alleyways are paved, frequently named, and function as streets in that they are lined with homes, shops, restaurants, and offices. The center of the Pennsylvania town often includes space for periodic public markets and community events. The space, called a diamond or a square, was created by either restricting building on the four corner lots facing the central intersection or by setting the building back from the sidewalk several feet. This distinctive town morphology is predominant in south-central Pennsylvania and extends southwest into Maryland and the Shenandoah Valley.[12]

From 1725 to 1775, German and Scotch-Irish immigrants spread along the Great Valley, through the gap in the Blue Ridge at Roanoke to the Carolina Piedmont. By the eve of the Revolution, some of the trails that they followed had been consolidated into the Philadelphia Wagon Road that connected the Delaware River settlements with Charleston, South Carolina, by way of Harpers Ferry (West Virginia), Roanoke, and Winston-Salem (Figure 4.3).[13] Milton Newton contended that many of the cultural traits carried to the frontier by these immigrants were derived from the Old World. The traits had been useful or adaptive there and fortuitously turned out to be adaptive in the Appalachian environments as well. The process of creating a distinctive Upland South culture that would come to permeate much of the Appalachian region south of the Mason-Dixon line was therefore primarily one of utilizing preadapted knowledge and skills that were appropriate to the

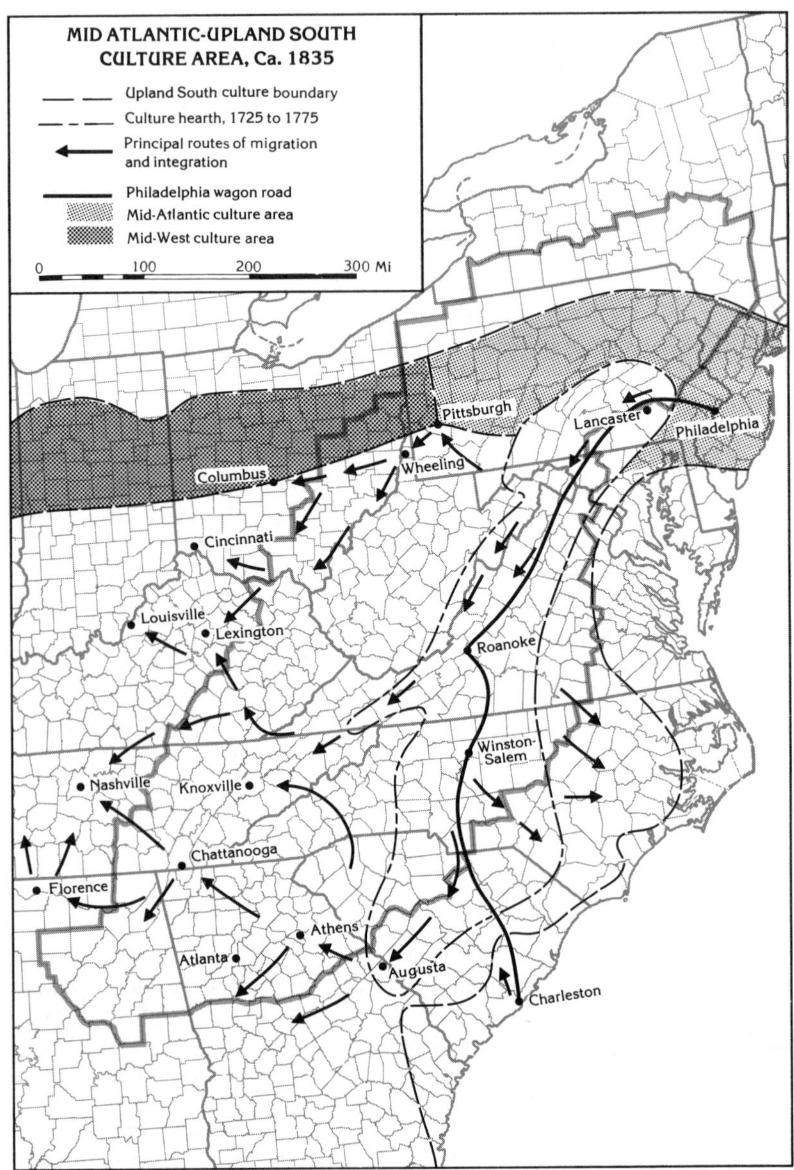


**Figure 4.3**
After Milton Newton, "Cultural Preadaptation and the Upland South," in H. J. Walker and W. G. Haag, eds., *Man and Cultural Heritage,* vol. 5, *Geoscience and Man* (Baton Rouge: Louisiana State University Press, 1974), p. 149.

new environment. Those ideas that proved successful could be passed on to neighbors. According to Newton, movement into the Appalachians and utilization of local resources was not a response to the stimulus of frontier conditions (Frederick Jackson Turner's argument), but instead was made possible by an information-diffusion process.[14] The Mid-Atlantic states, as a node of migration and information diffusion, contributed greatly to the formation of the Upland South culture hearth that extended from approximately the Fall Line west to the Appalachian Front or in the Carolinas to the Blue Ridge (Figure 4.3).

Among the dozen or more major preadaptive traits that have become characteristic of the Upland South were the courthouse-town system, which gave a clear focus to civil order and concentrated the skills of the elite, and the kinship-linked dispersed hamlet, an easily duplicated, flexible settlement that could be adapted to changing physical and economic conditions. These two settlement traits differed from New England and southern Tidewater urban traditions. In New England, the central grouping of buildings in a village clustered around a green, or common, and included a church and town hall, institutions that were seats of a single village-wide congregation and the town meeting.[15] The town's territory stretched well beyond the node of residential and commercial buildings to include farms and woodland. This town form did not enter the Mid-Atlantic or Upland South culture areas but was often recreated in upstate New York, where planned towns were occupied by Yankees who traveled and settled together in groups. The southern Tidewater plantation system was not readily adaptable to the Appalachians, so consequently few of its traits were incorporated into the Upland South culture fabric.

The first communities, whether established by Germans, Scotch-Irish, or others, were merely crossroads hamlets with schools, churches, and stores set haphazardly in open country where roads met. The hamlets had no apparent order nor fixed membership. While created by a seemingly random accretion process, these pioneer settlements had their origins in the Old World and were based on the pattern for rural republican social organization from northern Spain to western Britain.[16]

A tradition of English law had been established in New England, the Mid-Atlantic, and the South and was administered through a system of counties. The counties became the largest social units in the Upland South, each one containing a full complement of society that was generally divided into two disparate segments, the elite (businessmen, attorneys, clergy, politicians) and the rural farmers.[17] Each group produced distinctive landscape forms. The governing of each county was conducted in the county seat, usually the first town in the county and in many cases the only town for decades. Some county seats evolved from early crossroads hamlets, but many others were platted and represented a purposeful effort to establish a new town.

The layout of the county-seat town usually followed a basic morphology. A courthouse was often built on a square in the center of town and acted as a focal point for streets as well as a redoubt for the county elite. Around the square were the county law offices, surveyor's office, stores, banks, post office, a general store, and perhaps a newspaper office. Homes and churches appeared off the square. Very few farmers lived in the county seat; it was an urban place, inhabited by those employed in tertiary activities. Edward Price has shown that the courthouse square spread into the Upland South from Pennsylvania.[18] At the edge of town civil order became subsumed by traditional order, and the settlement pattern changed accordingly. Roads followed the contour of the land, and where several roads converged at a stream junction or other likely spot, a store, a few dwellings, a church, and perhaps a post office might gradually evolve into a crossroads hamlet. The hamlet might be occupied by two or three extended families that in aggregate provided the essential subsistence skills—blacksmithing, carpentry, weaving, meat curing.[19] As the upland population increased, this system was easily expanded. New counties were created as population clusters grew, and rural self-sufficiency could be reinforced by growth of crossroads hamlets.

## BUILDING AND FARMING TECHNIQUES

The Germans and Scotch-Irish employed construction techniques that allowed them to establish a subsistence economy in the Appalachian forests and that were flexible enough to permit settlers of diverse backgrounds to share common house and barn plans and building methods.[20] The evolution of the Appalachian log house and barn illustrates the movement of building technology from the Mid-Atlantic into the Upland South as well as the modifications in form and materials that occurred with contact between national groups and the requirements of suitable environmental adaptation. Along the East Coast, English settlers had built half-timber houses. The interstices between the exterior wall timbers were usually bricked in and the walls might be covered over in clapboard. Building such a house required a sizable work crew, a number of special tools, and experienced carpenters. This type of wood construction, though also used by some Germans, was largely confined to Philadelphia and the larger market towns of southeastern Pennsylvania.[21] Horizontal-log building techniques were introduced into southeastern Pennsylvania by German immigrants who had begun erecting log houses there by 1710.[22] Immigrants from different sections of Germany used somewhat different techniques, as in the notching of timbers where they joined at the corners, and variations in form. The German log house was often rectangular with three rooms, possibly a loft, and a central chimney. As new German immigrants moved farther west and south beyond the edge of the more densely settled areas, the need for speed and simplicity in erecting a log home may have overridden tradition, for the homes on the frontier were somewhat smaller and featured simpler notching techniques. This transition is reflected in the corner notching used in log houses. Among the Pennsylvania Germans, three basic types of corner-notching were commonly found: full dovetailing (*schwalbenschwanz*), V-notching, and saddle notching. The full dovetail was the strongest joint, and the angles of the horizontal cuts always carried rain water out of the notch. It required exacting measurement and was cut with a hatchet instead of the broad ax. The round log itself was often dressed to four sides, and the fit between logs was so close as to require little chinking. If time, skill, or available tools did not permit such elaborate construction, the V-notching technique was used. The building was easier to construct, but one result was a wide spacing between the logs that had to be filled with stone and lime mud. Saddle notching was usually found on the smallest temporary homes or outbuildings.[23]

Modifications of the German house form and corner timbering techniques occurred as log construction was adopted by the Scotch-Irish and carried into the Upland South by both groups. Henry Glassie and E. Estyn Evans both believed that the earliest Scotch-Irish immigrants in Pennsylvania probably built mud and stone cabins of the type they had built in Scotland and Ulster.[24] They steadily adopted German horizontal-log building techniques but modified the German house form to more closely mirror their own architectural traditions. The Scotch-Irish house was often square rather than rectangular and had one large room rather than three small rooms. In the west Chesapeake Tidewater country, English-built homes featured external chimneys. When the Tidewater English began to move west to the Piedmont about 1800, they brought their building traditions along. The external chimney, placed at the gable end of the house, was apparently adopted by the Scotch-Irish in place of the German central chimney because it could be more quickly and easily built. This small log house or cabin, usually built with trees cleared from the fields, provided the large living room to which the Scotch-Irish were accustomed. The room was then fitted with crude bedsteads, corner cupboards, hanging pegs, and shelves.[25] This was the basic house form that was carried south in the Blue Ridge, Ridge and Valley, and Plateaus.[26]

The linkage between the Pennsylvania German log-house construction tradition and the Upland south is indirect at best. The Appalachian mountain cabin is primarily English or Scotch-Irish in form and German only in construction technique. This is not the case for the Appalachian barn, which is more directly derived from German prototypes. The barn, therefore, is a more useful material indicator of the extent of Pennsylvania influence into the Upland South. The basic Pennsylvania German barn was rectangular and divided in half, each unit used to stable livestock. Each half, or crib, had a small door on the side, or gable, end. A number of variations on this basic form developed, including a barn built from two separate rectangular units separated by an open runway and covered by a common gable roof. Although barn logs were often dressed on the sides and dovetail-notched at the corners, the building was not as carefully constructed as the house.[27] As settlers moved from Pennsylvania into the valley labyrinth of Virginia and Tennessee this large barn was not easily adapted to the more limited needs of the small frontier farms. Smaller barns were built from one crib with sheds attached to the sides as stables.

In Pennsylvania, as time passed and successive generations expanded their farms and increased production, the old log barns were eventually replaced. The replacement barns, built primarily after 1850, are sometimes called Pennsylvania or forebay barns and are examples of grand-scale agrarian architecture. Built on a heavy internal timber framework, the barn was often sided with vertical boards, and the ends were brick or stone from ground to gable. Inside, the barns had two levels. Since they were often built into a hillside, the bottom level was usually only fully accessible on three sides. The lower level housed livestock in a variety of stables or pens and opened directly onto the barnyard. The second, or upper, level was usually made up of three basic units: a central threshing floor with large storage mows for grain shocks and hay on either side. Hay racks and grain wagons could be driven directly onto the threshing floor by way of a large door on the uphill side of the barn. Perhaps the most distinctive feature of these barns, aside from their sheer volume, was the overshoot of the upper-level floor, which formed a forebay (*laube*) over the first-floor doors and windows on the barnyard side. The function of the forebay has been thought to (1) afford shelter to wagons and farm implements, (2) allow the farmer to throw straw from the threshing floor into the middle of the barnyard as bedding, and (3) act as an enclosed gallery that offered weather protection for the walls, windows, and doors on the stable level.[28] Whether or not any of these explanations of forebay function is correct or not seems less important than the fact that it is part of a structure that retains its European form and interior arrangement. It was evaluated by Pennsylvania farmers, found to be functional, and then replicated on other farms throughout the Pennsylvania Culture Area. While the great forebay barn was well adapted to sheltering the herds and fodder crops of the productive farms on the broader Appalachian valleys, it was impractical in steeper land. This barn plan was carried along a selective route into the Shenandoah Valley, but it was not built on the Piedmont or in the Plateaus.

If the Scotch-Irish and Germans shared certain European experiences—religious persecution and economic instability, for example—and both groups participated in the distribution of a number of culture traits into the Appalachians, the forebay barn is an illustration of a trait that they did not share. The Scotch-Irish experience in Ulster provided a preadaptive experience that allowed them to exploit environmental niches not attractive to the Germans. Whereas German settlers preferred to select level farm sites, cut down trees, and winch stumps from the ground to create clear fields (ownership of such a parcel was then termed "free and clear") that could be systematically cultivated,

The symmetrical house facade flanked by gable-end chimneys suggests a Pennsylvanian modification of the English Georgian house. The barn has a Pennsylvania German forebay with the threshing floor projecting out over the lower level. The farmstead is in Augusta County, Virginia, north of Waynesboro.

the Scotch-Irish found the Indian technique of deadening trees by girdling and burning to be adequate. The Scotch-Irish readily adopted maize, a spring-planted Indian crop, as well as Indian planting techniques, and they preferred to make fresh clearings in their forest land or move on to new land when the productivity of their fields began to wane. Open-range livestock grazing on free woodland pastures was also a Celtic tradition that was readily adapted to the Appalachian forests. These slash-and-burn or brush-fallow farming techniques were carried into the Blue Ridge and Plateaus and in some areas are still practiced. Scotch-Irish farming was not simply an adaptation of Celtic "outfield" cultivation but instead represented a synthesis of native American, Scottish, and Irish agricultural techniques.[29]

## NINETEENTH- AND TWENTIETH-CENTURY MIGRANTS

By the second decade of the nineteenth century, the major national groups in Appalachia continued to be English, Scotch-Irish, and German with smaller numbers of Welsh, French, and other northern European groups. The accessible valleys along well-traveled routeways were filling in, and with the exception of north Georgia, central West Virginia, and northeast and northwest Pennsylvania, had population densities that exceeded two persons per square mile. A series of catastrophic events in Europe, as well as a growing demand for miners and industrial workers, especially in Pennsylvania and West Virginia, changed the population character in the northern half of the region.

Economic stress in Ireland had encouraged outmigration by the 1820s, but when the potato famines of the 1840s prevented even subsistence farming, the Irish began emigrating to America in large numbers. Some were attracted to the coal mines in Pennsylvania. By 1870, for example, over thirty-eight thousand Irish were living in the most productive part of the anthracite region, Luzerne and Schuylkill counties.[30] In the anthracite towns, the Irish were the lowest social and economic class. Most had no experience as miners, and so were relegated to the heavy work that required few skills. Irish boys left school before they were twelve to pick slate in the coal breakers. Occupational hardship and the miserable living conditions of the dingy homes provided by the coal companies broke men's spirits, and high levels of alcoholism threatened family cohesiveness. Some men worked in the mines for a decade or more and never received their wages in federal currency, but always in script redeemable only at the company store. Years of company exploitation begot unrest among the Irish miners, and they sought relief by gradually attempting to obtain political control of the region. But political and labor-organization efforts were hindered by a number of obstacles. The Irish rarely constituted over 10 percent of the population of any political unit. Further, the anthracite fields were divided by topography into several districts. A Workingmen's Benevolent Association grew to about thirty thousand members by 1869 and represented about 85 percent of the anthracite miners, but although Irish predominated, the presence of Welsh, English, and German members made cohesion difficult. Continued intransigence of the mine owners on issues of housing, job security, work week, and other problems led to the formation of a kind of Irish vigilance committee called the Molly Maguires (the Mollies).[31]

The growing militancy of the Irish and the murders and terrorist activities of the Mollies led the coal owners to look elsewhere for more-docile and more-pliant miners.[32] Recruiters were sent to Europe to publicize opportunities in the Pennsylvania mines. Immigrants from eastern Europe began to arrive in the coal and steel towns by the early 1880s and continued to come until immigration quotas were established in the early 1920s. By the 1930s, about 700,000 Ruthenian immigrants had arrived from the Ukraine and Hungary. Many moved to the anthracite region; others were attracted to the bituminous-coal mines of western Pennsylvania, Ohio, and northern West Virginia. Other immigrant groups included Poles, Czechs, Slovaks, Serbs, Croats, Ukrainians, Hungarians, and other eastern and southern Europeans. Mine and mill operators found these immigrants to be willing workers and—because of their inability to understand the language—easy to cheat at the pay desk or the company store. Many of these people had been uneducated peasant farmers. They had worked land owned by foreign landlords, paid heavy taxes, and had been subjected to long periods of military service.[33] To them the chance to work seven days a week in a coal mine may have seemed an immeasurable improvement.

The East Europeans spread from the major industrial centers of Pittsburgh and Johnstown to the smaller mining and mill towns along the Allegheny, Ohio, and Monongahela rivers. They were recruited by the large mining companies that were establishing mines and new towns in West Virginia, western Virginia, and eastern Kentucky. In the company town of Lynch, Kentucky, for example, about one-fourth of the white population was American-born when the first coal was shipped in 1917. The remainder was made up of immigrants who spoke thirty-two different languages[34] (in Monongah, West Virginia, mining instructions were posted at the mouth of the mines in seven languages). Social conditions for Slavic families in most industrial towns were poor at best. They lived in "hunky towns," paid high rents for small apartments or houses, and were discriminated against by industrial companies, landlords, merchants, schools, and even non-Slavic church parishes. Police brutality was at its worst in their neighborhoods, and their working conditions were scandalous. Labor gangs were organized into single-language groups that worked twelve hours per day, each day of the week for six to nine months of the year.[35] In some mines immigrants were hired as strike-breakers. In most mines, their willingness to work long hours helped increase productivity, but the cost in human life was catastrophic. In 1907, 3,000 coal miners were killed in the United States, a death rate two and one-half times that of British mines.[36] A large number were killed in Pennsylvania and West Virginia. Among the disasters that year was an explosion in a mine at Monongah that killed 344 miners, the worst single mining accident in U.S. history.

Today, the East Europeans are largely absent from the mining towns of Virginia, Kentucky, and southern West Virginia. During the depressed coal market of the 1920s many left the central Appalachian mining towns for northern industrial cities, and large numbers of their descendants still live in the mine and mill towns of Pennsylvania. Their Eastern Orthodox and Greek Catholic or Byzantine churches stand in the centers of their communities from Shenandoah, Hazelton, and Olyphant in the anthracite region to Johnstown, Donora, and McKeesport in western Pennsylvania. Their cemeteries—Shenandoah has fourteen ethnic cemeteries on a hill north of the city—are marked by oversized stone crosses and carved religious figures. Their neighborhoods tend to be neat and well kept despite the smoky air, culm heaps, abandoned tipples and coal breakers, and strip mines. They tend to paint their homes in earth tones, browns and grays, whereas their Irish neighbors prefer green and white. Small grottos often stand amid flowers and shrubs in tiny front yards, and fraternal clubs such as the Polish Falcons are found in each neighborhood.

Johnstown, Pennsylvania. Crowded together in the Little Conemaugh River valley, an East European neighborhood huddles against St. John the Baptist Ukrainian Catholic Church and a portion of the 8-mile-long (12.9-kilometer-long) Bethlehem Steel milling complex.

## BLACKS IN APPALACHIA

When Tidewater planters moved upcountry to open new plantations on the Carolina and Virginia Piedmont in the late 1700s, black slaves were brought along to clear and plant the land and construct buildings and fences. As cotton production rose following the boom in cotton prices in the early 1800s, the black population of the southern Piedmont steadily increased. The presence of these blacks and their role in the culture and economy of the South is well documented. The section on "Racial Composition" in Chapter 5 points out that this Piedmont crescent of the former Cotton Belt continues to hold a large proportion of Appalachia's black people.

Relatively few blacks reside in the Blue Ridge. Those who live in the Plateaus Province share with the Irish and East Europeans a similar locational *raison d'être*—coal mining. Slaves had limited application on the small farms of western Virginia or eastern Kentucky in the Plateaus, but Darold Barnum has established that blacks were used in Virginia coal mines before the turn of the nineteenth century.[37] In northern Alabama, coal was being mined near the new town of Birmingham by 1871. Within twenty years over 45 percent of the coal miners in the state were black. From Alabama and Virginia, a few black sharecroppers gradually moved into the coal mines of the southern and central Plateaus Province, marking the beginning of a three-stage relocation process that would find blacks eventually, perhaps a generation or more after leaving the Plantation South, leaving the coal camps for the industrial cities of the North. Four factors appear to have operated to attract blacks into the mining regions. First, between 1890 and 1917 there was a strong, if inconsistent, national demand for coal and consequently an increasing need for miners. Second, coal-mine operators hired blacks believing that it would forestall attempts by miners to unionize. Blacks were hired in the South as Slavs had been hired in the North: to break strikes. Some coal companies hired blacks, native whites, and immigrants hoping to promote disunity and to play each group against the other.[38] Third, the labor union had a policy of equality and through local elections was somewhat successful in electing blacks to union office. And fourth, discrimination and segregation were practiced in rural areas and coal camps alike. Many coal camps assigned black miners to a separate section of town.[39] Although the coal camps offered no respite from discrimination, they did offer wages for labor, and this was often an overriding stimulus to move to the coal camps.

From the 1920s through World War II, the number of black miners in Appalachia decreased both proportionately and absolutely. They, like the Irish and Slavs before them, tended to get the undesirable jobs. As the mines were modernized and mechanized, many of these jobs ended with layoffs. Today, strip mining accounts for more than half the coal mined in most states. Stripping is highly mechanized and employs primarily skilled and experienced heavy-equipment operators, jobs for which many blacks lack training. During World War II, many Appalachian blacks left the coal camps for steady employment in northern industrial towns. They did not return when the war ended.[40] Although little is known of black return migration into Appalachian coal counties, there is little to suggest that significant numbers of blacks have moved back in recent years. Instead, the region's black population continues to decline as older miners retire and young blacks move away.

## RELIGIOUS PATTERNS

Among the European traditions that the immigrants who settled the Appalachian region brought with them was religion, and often there was a relationship between nation of origin and religious preference. The Scotch-Irish tended to be Presbyterian. The English might be Quaker, Congregational, Methodist, or Episcopal. The Germans might be Pietists, Moravians, or Catholics. The New World provided a different context for religion, and the transfer process from Europe was not without effect. Some religions throve and grew in adherents, others faded into insignificance. To try to understand the religious diversity of the region and the mechanism whereby some religions have been more successful than others in retaining membership is also to attempt to understand some important regional differences in human character—differences that are evident if one compares the remote areas of central and southern Appalachia with the accessible lowlands.

Figure 4.4, a map of Christian denominations in Appalachia in 1971 (the most recent year for which regional data are available), illustrates vestiges of religious groupings created by the pattern of migration. In New York and Pennsylvania, Catholics were a majority or large minority in many counties. Many of the primarily rural counties may be dominated by German Catholics, whereas the urban and industrial counties may be dominated by Irish or East Europeans. The anthracite counties of eastern Pennsylvania and the industrialized river corridors of the western part of the state were strongly Slavicized by immigration around the turn of the century. Because these immigrants rarely penetrated into the Southern Highlands except into the coal camps and other Catholics were present only in very small numbers, the Roman and Greek Catholic churches were not represented in the South. Nor were the numbers of Catholics increasing in the southern mountains. About 1930, Catholics and Jews together constituted only about 2 percent of southern Appalachian religious groups, and most of them were urban or living in mining camps.[41] The proportion was little more than that in 1971.

Lutherans, primarily Germans, were majorities in a small number of counties in Pennsylvania, Maryland, and Virginia, with an outlier on the South Carolina Piedmont. This disjointed alignment roughly corresponds to the major migration route southward from Pennsylvania. Along this route were also found important minorities of other Teutonic churches including Amish, Mennonites, Moravians, and Brethren. In

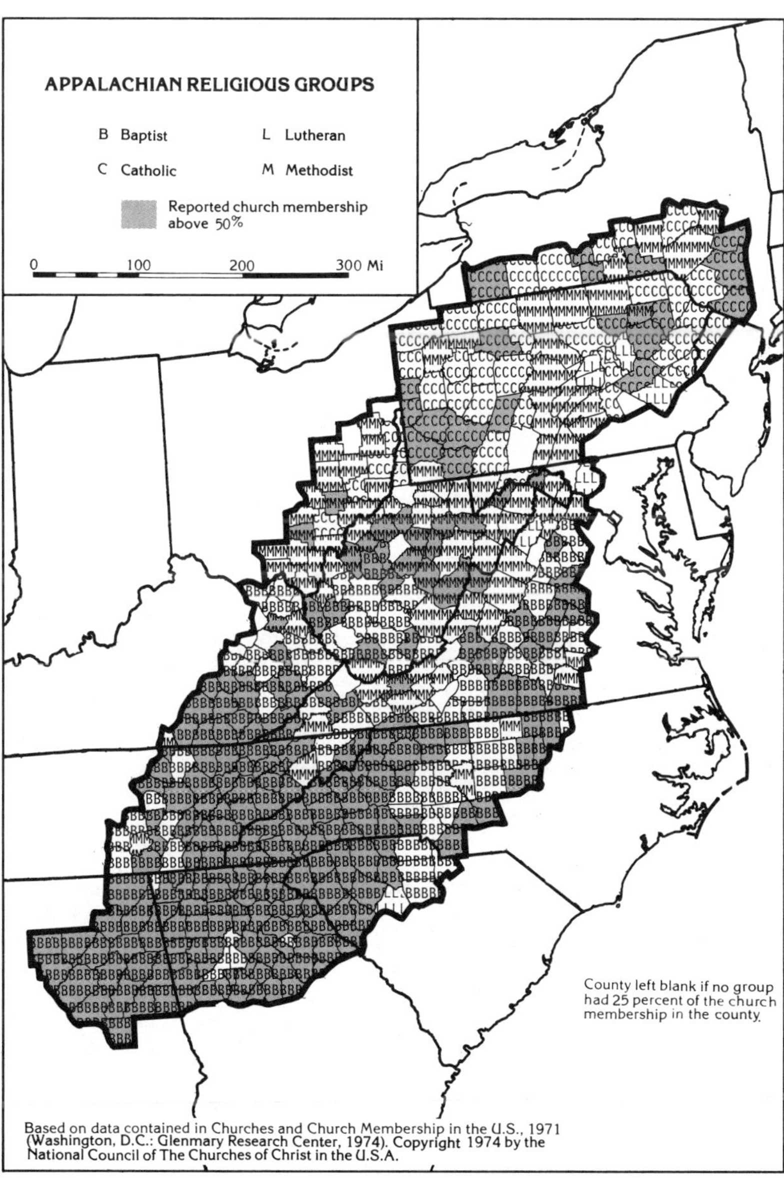
APPALACHIAN RELIGIOUS GROUPS
B Baptist
L Lutheran
C Catholic
M Methodist
Reported church membership above 50%
0
100
200
300 Mi
County left blank if no group had 25 percent of the church membership in the county.
Based on data contained in Churches and Church Membership in the U.S., 1971 (Washington, D.C.: Glenmary Research Center, 1974). Copyright 1974 by the National Council of The Churches of Christ in the U.S.A.

**Figure 4.4**

1971, the Moravians, an evangelical group that had opposed European Catholicism before the Reformation, had over fifty-seven thousand adherents nationally. A major cluster of Moravians was in Pennsylvania's Lehigh Valley. Another was in Forsyth County, North Carolina (Winston-Salem), where they made up 16 percent of all church members.[42] Forsyth County is central to a group of Piedmont counties that are distinct from the Baptist-dominated South. The area corresponds to the destination area of diverse migrant groups from the Mid-Atlantic hearth. In 1971, Forsyth County had twenty-five religious denominations; Southern Baptists and Methodists predominated, but Presbyterians, Catholics, Disciples of Christ, and Quakers were also represented.

The Church of the Brethren is one of two church groups that has a historical tradition in Appalachia (the other is the Church of God). When considered nationally, its core of adherents was there as well. The area in which this church had a large membership corresponds closely to the Pennsylvania Culture Area and the Shenandoah Valley: Pennsylvania, Maryland, and Virginia accounted for 52 percent of the group's 220,000 national adherents.

Methodism was most strongly represented in a belt from the Mid-Atlantic hearth westward. The Appalachian segment was part of a large national distribution stretching from Massachusetts to St. Louis and

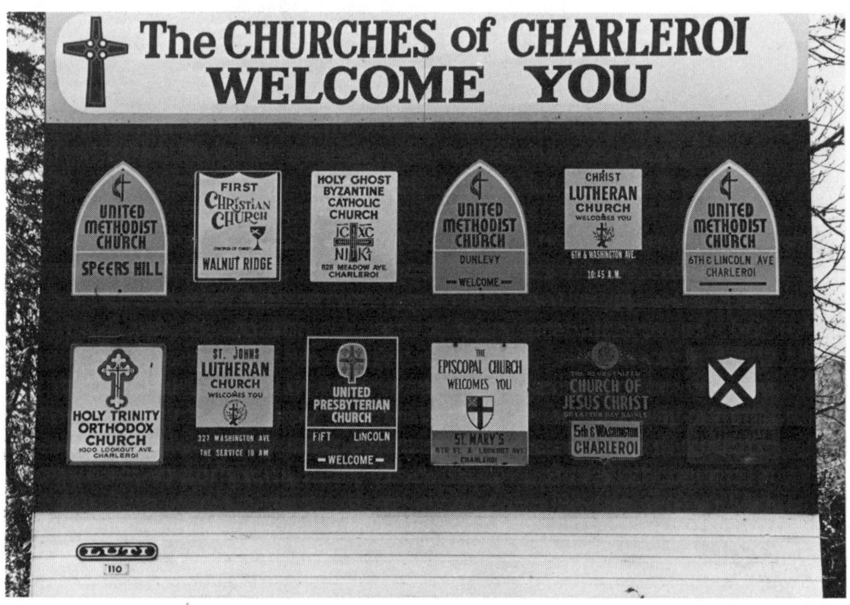


A church sign at the edge of Charleroi, Pennsylvania on the Monongahela River. The diverse selection of churches includes three Methodist and three Catholic congregations.

Des Moines. This midland corridor of Methodism included a number of other groups, with important Lutheran, Presbyterian, Dutch Reformed, and Quaker minorities. A question arises here as to why the Presbyterian church, the church of the Scotch-Irish pioneers, has not been more resilient in the midland corridor area through which so many Scotch-Irish passed. Although there was a significant Presbyterian minority in western Pennsylvania and eastern Ohio and a secondary cluster in the Carolina Piedmont, Methodism seems to have gained in the Mid-Atlantic zone and Baptists have expanded in the South. This expansion has been largely at the expense of the churches that were represented among the initial settlers: Presbyterian, Congregational, and Episcopalian.[43]

The blossoming of the Methodist and Baptist churches in central and southern Appalachia seems to be the result of two related processes—proselytism of the Great Revivals and adaptability to frontier conditions. Thomas Ford has observed that during the mid-eighteenth century, when migration into the region was just getting underway, the Presbyterian church was the most important religious body, whether measured by number of members or by influence. By the last decade of the 1700s, American Methodism under Bishop Asbury had begun to expand, and the Baptists were gaining strength on the Piedmont.[44] A series of major religious revivals within the region began in 1800 and continued for most of the century. Pioneers exposed to Methodism at camp meetings or by itinerant clergy found the concept of free grace for all members more in keeping with their democratic bent than the Calvinist (Presbyterian) doctrine of salvation primarily for those elected to it. Furthermore, the circuit-riding preachers provided frontier reinforcement for newly indoctrinated followers. The Presbyterians insisted on an educated ministry, an obligation that could not be met on the frontier, because there simply were not enough trained ministers to serve all the remote settlements.[45] The Baptists also expanded significantly during the revival period, and the growth of the church is generally attributed to a simple and straightforward gospel, a democratic congregational organization, and a dependence on lay ministers who were elected by local groups instead of being assigned by some distant church administration. Baptism moved into Appalachia from the southern Coastal Plain and Piedmont. By the early 1900s, only 6 percent of the reported church membership of central and southern Appalachia was Presbyterian. Methodist bodies had increased to 30 percent and Baptists to 40 percent.[46]

Although Baptists and Methodists gained adherents in the nineteenth century, they in turn began losing members because of schisms that divided church groups repeatedly and because of the wide appeal in the more remote and isolated mountain areas of fundamentalist sects. This body of churches is perhaps the least understood of Appalachian religious groups and yet is probably responsible for the image that many Americans have of the region as a place harboring conservative religions. Figure 4.4 shows a zone of mixed religious adherence in eastern Kentucky and Tennessee, western Virginia, and southern West Virginia, where

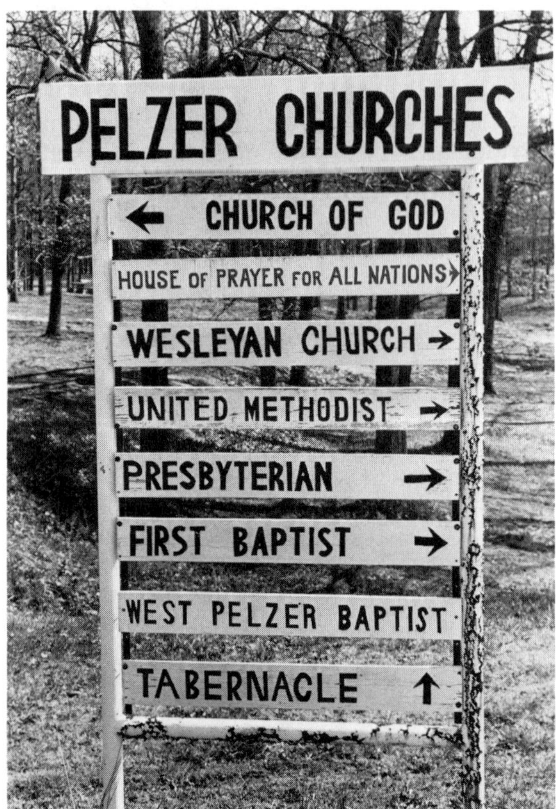


A church sign in Pelzer, a textile-mill town in Anderson County, South Carolina, about 15 mi (24.1 km) south of Greenville. The mix of Baptist, Methodist, and Fundamentalist churches is typical of this section of the Piedmont.

several counties had no single religious group that could claim more than 25 percent of county church membership. This was not an area of theological ambivalence as it might appear; rather the area was dominated by small fundamentalist churches. These groups range in heritage from splintered segments of the Baptists or other main-line denominations to localized groups with no obvious connections to larger organizations. Many of these groups meet in simple one-room churches, school houses, or private dwellings. They are known by various names that often include Primitive Baptist, Fire Baptized Baptists, Disciples of Christ, Churches of Christ, Pentacostal Holiness, and Churches of God. If fundamentalism has a core belief, it is in the literal interpretation and inerrancy of the Bible, including the Virgin Birth, Christ's miracles, and physical resurrection. Church members offer strong condemnation to those who partake of such worldly vices as drinking, dancing, gambling, swearing, playing cards, or using tobacco.[47] The highly emotional and animated worship services of some of these groups—speaking in tongues, drinking poison, or snake handling—has been sensationalized in the media and has even been the subject of a recent volume of *Foxfire*.[48]

In 1935, a U.S. Department of Agriculture report on religion in Appalachia referred to these churches as "primitive varieties [that] have been preserved in secluded nooks of the mountains just as archaic forms of plant and animal life have been perpetuated in remote islands of the ocean."[49] Regardless of their reputation or the pejorative accounting of their beliefs and practices, these churches have remained quite popular, and some were among the most rapidly growing churches in the nation. The Pentecostal Holiness churches encompass a number of revivalist Baptist and Methodist splinter groups that follow Methodist polity and believe in divine healing. Between 1952 and 1971, the group grew nationally from 41,000 to 89,000—an increase of 115 percent—with the most-rapid growth occurring in western Virginia's Blue Ridge and Great Valley. The Church of God (Cleveland, Tennessee, group) is the other denomination that, like the Church of the Brethren, had a national core in Appalachia. The Church of God was formed in 1886 and underwent a number of schisms in the 1920s. The group is made up of born-again Christians who believe in divine healing and speak in tongues. In the two decades from 1952 to 1971 their number increased from 136,000 to about 270,000, or an increase of over 170 percent. Although the Church of God had adherents scattered across the nation, their major concentration was in the Appalachian Plateaus from Alabama north through West Virginia, and it was in this area that the most significant growth took place.[50] When adherents migrate from the region to find work in northern cities, the fundamentalist church accompanies them. In Appalachian communities in Ohio—in Columbus, Dayton, or Cincinnati's Over-the-Rhine neighborhood—storefront churches of the Holiness and other fundamentalist groups can be found on almost every block.

Concern has been expressed by some social scientists and public-agency administrators that fundamentalist religion detracts from the success of self-help development strategies. Fatalism and a strong belief in predestination have been thought to mitigate motivation to pursue full employment, literacy, and proper diet and health care. But this does not appear to be the case. John Photiadis, taking a functionalist view of Appalachian religion, found that fundamentalist beliefs do help some dispossessed and alienated people to cope and adjust to rapid social change. He also found that there is no significant difference between fundamentalist groups and the members of main-line churches in orientation toward achievement, attitudes toward progress, education, or the perception of health. Where differences do exist, they seem to be primarily a function of lower socioeconomic status, not religious faith.[51] The role of religion in compromising the effectiveness of development strategy may be more in the hands of the middle-class residents of the Appalachian states who may have a Calvinist religious tradition that equates individual moral worth with worldly prosperity. As administrators of state or federal social programs they may be unsympathetic to benefits to the poor, such as welfare payments to unwed mothers, or programs such as the Job Corps.[52]

## REGIONALIZATION OF SPEECH HABITS

Speech patterns in Appalachia, as delineated by Hans Kurath, also are attributable to the settlement process by which migrants spread inland from New England, the Mid-Atlantic, and the South.[53] Drawing lines on a map of word usage to delineate speech areas is a difficult and somewhat speculative task, but there appears to be a rather strong relationship between major speech areas and the settlement routeways out of the Atlantic-coast culture hearths. The most prominent speech boundaries occur at the edges of these settlement areas (Figure 4.5). After the Revolution, New Englanders moved west into New York and northern Pennsylvania. The speech patterns of this group were sufficiently distinctive from those to the south to enable Kurath to delineate a primary speech boundary that separates this area from the Mid-Atlantic area just to the south. (North of the boundary, for example, the word used to describe corn bread is *Johnny cake,* whereas to the south it is *corn pone* or *pone bread.*)

The Mid-Atlantic speech area, which includes the Susquehanna Valley and Upper Ohio Valley areas and extends south into western North and South Carolina, was settled from Pennsylvania and Maryland before significant expansion from the Tidewater occurred. Several speech boundaries correspond somewhat to topographic barriers that were significant during settlement. The secondary boundary between the Susquehanna and Upper Ohio valleys, for example, follows the crest of the Alleghenies. Settlers from the south moved across the Coastal Plain to Piedmont river valleys and interacted with the Scotch-Irish and Germans they found there. The major speech boundary that outlines the limit of this contact (corresponding to the boundary between Speech Areas 7 and 8 on Figure 4.5) follows the Blue Ridge south to approximately the Roanoke Gap. Here the boundary moves east and south to enclose the segment of the Piedmont that was settled early on by Quakers, Moravians, and Ulster Presbyterians from Pennsylvania.[54] In western Virginia and the Great Valley section of West Virginia, the term *bottomland* is used to describe the fertile alluvial soils found along streams. This is the term used in Pennsylvania to the north. In eastern Virginia and central West Virginia the term is simply *bottoms.* Subsequently, movement of southerners into the southern sections of the Mid-Atlantic Speech Area influenced speech patterns from western North Carolina (Speech Area 9) to southern West Virginia (Speech Area 6). Here the northern edge of the Kanawha Valley watershed corresponds to a transition from southern to northern influence in the Appalachians. (Perhaps this same intermittent diffusion process explains the transition between Baptists

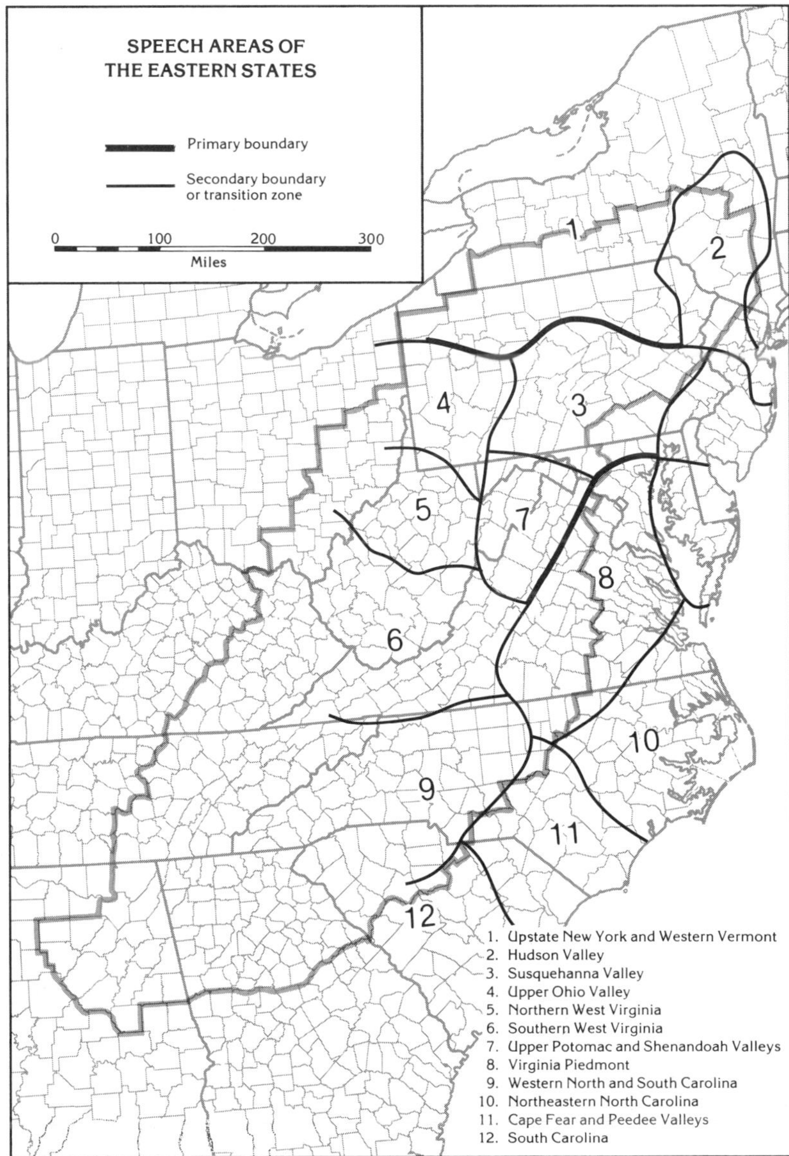


**Figure 4.5**
After Hans Kurath, *A Word Geography of the Eastern United States* (Ann Arbor: University of Michigan Press, 1949), Figure 3, p. 91. Copyright © 1949 University of Michigan.

and Methodists in West Virginia that occurs in the same area, as shown in Figure 4.4.)

The southern West Virginia and western North and South Carolina speech areas have in the past been regarded as having a rather distinctive "mountain speech" pattern with unique usage and local expressions that have been attributed to Old Elizabethan English forms preserved in the isolation of remote coves and valleys.[55] If antiquated elements of speech had been in use in the mountains at the turn of the century, they had apparently disappeared by the 1940s, because Kurath found few localized expressions. Instead, the great body of words in use there also occurred in the rest of the large Mid-Atlantic Speech Area, either in the north or the south.

## FOLK-MUSIC TRADITIONS

The folk music of Appalachia, especially in the central and southern states, has been the basis of much of the nation's contemporary country and bluegrass music, and like those of speech, religion, and material culture, the roots of the region's music lie in the Mid-Atlantic and New England hearth areas and ultimately in northern Europe. In tracing the heritage of this spontaneous and distinctive form of artistic expression, George Carney found that a large part of the early Appalachian music repertory was derived from English and Celtic folk songs.[56] The religiously conservative English colonists apparently preferred melancholy ballads to more upbeat music, with the result that a tradition of slow, sorrowful songs was passed on through the generations to become a predominate theme in the music of the highlands. The music tradition from New England and the Mid-Atlantic gradually moved into the Upland South with the migrating pioneers. Group harmony singing had been very common among German Mennonites and Dunkards in Europe, and they brought this tradition to Pennsylvania in the early 1700s.[57] The German Anabaptists and the New England colonists used a method of writing music with shaped symbols, instead of notes on a line scale, that could easily be memorized by the musically illiterate. Religious music and folk songs were written in hymn books using this shape-note technique, and shape-note harmony singing as practiced in New England was carried by Yankee singing masters into New York, Pennsylvania, and Maryland schools by the 1750s. In the early 1800s, shape-note singing spread into the South along the Shenandoah Valley to Georgia and west to Missouri (Figure 4.6).[58] After the Civil War, as the use of European music notation became more common, the interest in shape-note harmony singing declined generally throughout the Upland South except among some fundamentalist religious groups, where it has been retained. Collections of gospel music and shape-note songs are published as hymnals for church use by the Church of God (Cleveland, Tennessee) and the Primitive Baptists. It was this tradition of ballad-

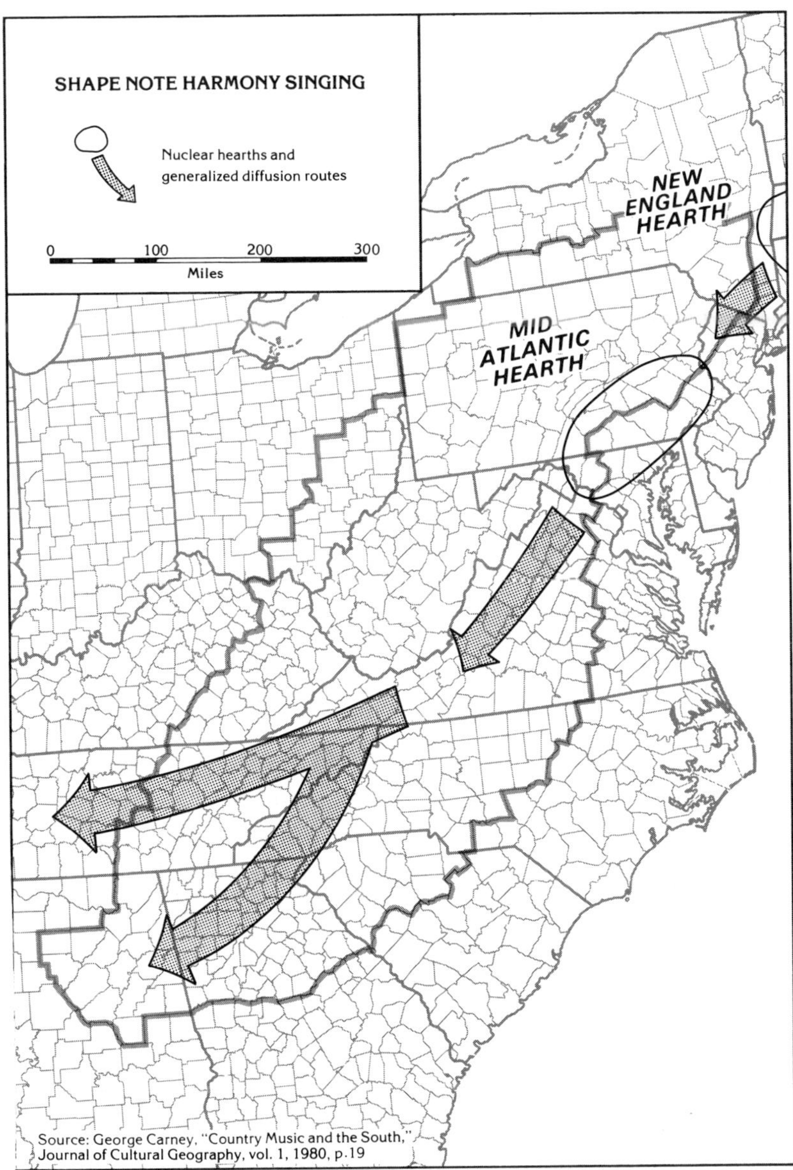
SHAPE NOTE HARMONY SINGING
Nuclear hearths and
generalized diffusion routes
0
100
200
300
Miles
NEW
ENGLAND
HEARTH
MID
ATLANTIC
HEARTH
Source: George Carney, "Country Music and the South,"
Journal of Cultural Geography, vol. 1, 1980, p.19

**Figure 4.6**

style music and harmony singing that provided the foundation for Appalachian country music.

Several instruments used in the region's folk music were derived from European prototypes, including the plucked dulcimer and the fiddle. The dulcimer was introduced into the Mid-Atlantic hearth area by Germans in the early 1700s. It was carried into the Upland South, where it was widely used as an accompaniment for ballad singers.[59] Its simplicity made it easy to play, but its low volume was inappropriate in combination with the much louder fiddle and banjo. Today it is found primarily in "mountain craft" shops where it is sold to tourists as an interior decorating item.

The traditional style of country music that evolved out of English ballads and shape-note harmony singing was found in a substyle area throughout much of Appalachia and western Kentucky and Tennessee, with core areas in the western Carolina Blue Ridge, western Virginia, southern West Virginia, and the Nashville Basin (Figure 4.7). In the 1920s, national radio networks began to carry "mountain barndance" music programming, helping to popularize it throughout the country. Early instrumentation was simple, usually a fiddle and banjo, and was secondary to the strong vocal concordance that retained a shape-note harmony singing influence.[60] Bluegrass is a second and more recent music style that has developed within the region since the 1930s. It is essentially instrumental and is played by string bands with no electrical amplification. When the music includes a vocal, it is sung in a tight, high-pitched harmony. Many contemporary performers were born in southern Appalachia, and they apparently have been influenced by the gospel music sung in mountain churches and even by Scottish bagpipe bands.

## DISTILLING, BOOTLEGGING, AND PROHIBITION

The use of a small farm still to distill "white whiskey" from grains was commonplace among the early pioneers in Appalachia. In Scotland and Ireland farm distilling represented a traditional source of income and a way to readily market otherwise bulky grains, and of course whiskey was viewed as the "water of life." When these people migrated to America and made their way to the frontier, they brought the taste for spirits and the knowledge of its manufacture with them. Most small upland communities had at least one member who regularly produced whiskey for himself and his neighbors. Early on, the federal government saw farm whiskey as a source of revenue. In the 1790s, when a federal liquor excise tax was levied on western Pennsylvania farmers, they not only refused to pay, but they attacked revenue officers sent to enforce collection. Thousands of federal militiamen were sent into the region to put down the rebellion. Although the Pennsylvania uprising apparently resulted in many distillers moving deeper into the mountains to avoid further taxation efforts, the tradition continued and expanded. By 1810,

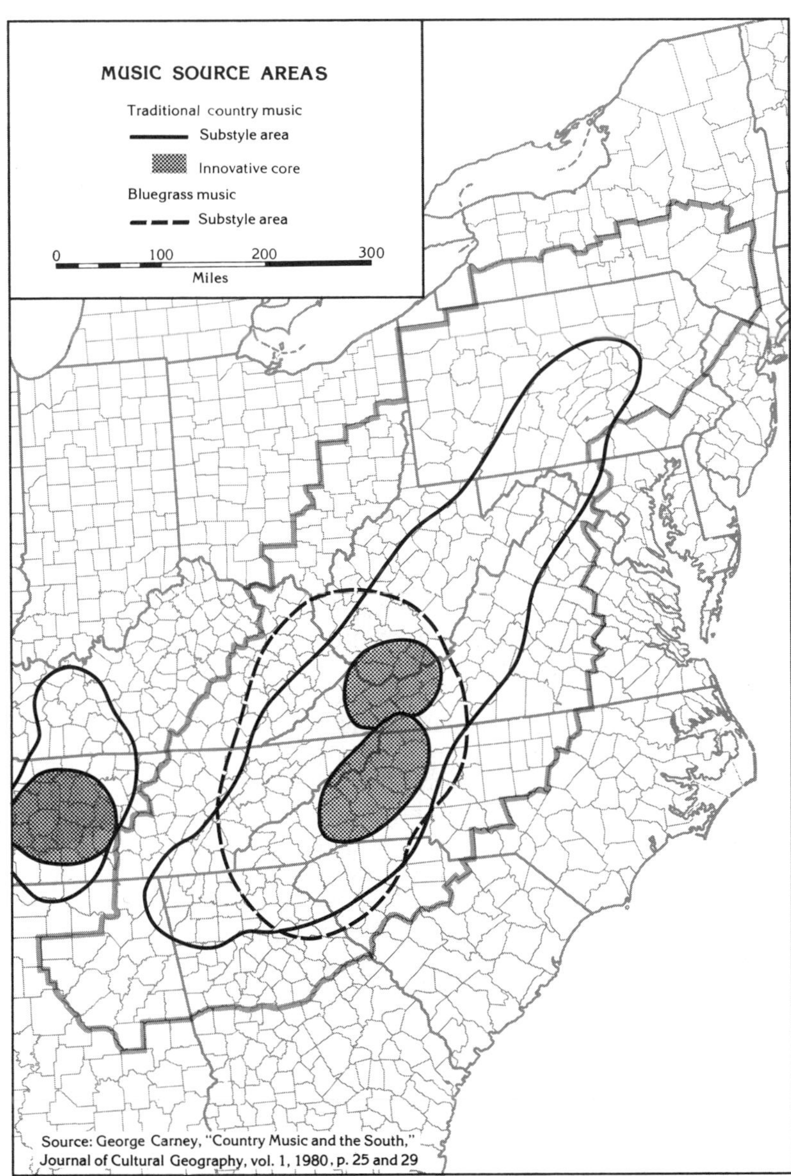
MUSIC SOURCE AREAS
Traditional country music
Substyle area
Innovative core
Bluegrass music
Substyle area
0
100
200
300
Miles
Source: George Carney, "Country Music and the South,"
Journal of Cultural Geography, vol. 1, 1980, p. 25 and 29

**Figure 4.7**

TABLE 4.2
Whiskey Distilled in 1810

| State* | Distilleries and Stills | Gallons |
|---|---|---|
| Pennsylvania | 3,594 | 6,552 |
| Virginia | 3,662 | 2,368 |
| Kentucky | 2,000 | 2,221 |
| New York | 591 | 2,107 |
| North Carolina | 5,426 | 1,387 |
| Ohio | 343 | 1,212 |
| New Jersey | 727 | 1,102 |
| Maryland | 1,509 | 733 |
| Georgia | 126 | 545 |
| South Carolina | 1,458 | 437 |
| East Tennessee | - | 335 |

Source: Tench Coxe, A Statement of the Arts and Manufacturers of the United States of America for the Year 1810 (Philadelphia: A. Cornman, 1814), page 22.

*Includes entire state except Tennessee.

about 19 million gal (71.9 million l) of whiskey were being produced in 11 of the Appalachian states (Table 4.2).

As the federal government pressed enforcement of tax laws and distilling quality standards, farm stills were secreted away to remote sites and farm distilling evolved into the illicit moonshining trade that continues to thrive in some isolated parts of the region. Illegal distilling is now comparatively rare in many traditional production areas such as eastern Kentucky and southern West Virginia. In a few remote areas, however, it still represents the only significant cash income for families that believe that making whiskey is as much their right as owning guns. The border of Alabama and Georgia north to the Tennessee state line has been a particularly resilient area for illicit whiskey production despite heavy patrolling by federal agents. Other traditional centers of moonshining activity include northeast Georgia, the mountain counties of South Carolina, and small pockets in southern West Virginia, western Virginia, and northwest North Carolina (Table 4.3).

Whereas the federal and state governments have attempted to discourage untaxed distilling by raiding stills, many county governments in southern Appalachia have attempted to legislate sobriety through prohibition (Figure 4.8). The dry county, best known for forcing asceticism on unsuspecting travelers in the Upland South, is nearly ubiquitous in Appalachian Kentucky (in many of the rural counties in the rest of the state as well) and is scattered throughout the more mountainous sections of Tennessee, Alabama, and Georgia. There appears to be a relationship in some counties between the strength of fundamentalist religion and

TABLE 4.3
Moonshine Still Seizures: 1972*

| State | Total Federal, State, and Local Enforcement Agency Seizures |
|---|---|
| Georgia | 1,722 |
| Alabama | 1,560 |
| North Carolina | 755 |
| Virginia | 415 |
| Tennessee | 387 |
| South Carolina | 293 |
| Kentucky | 53 |
| West Virginia | 27 |
| Ohio | 15 |
| Maryland | 12 |
| New York | 9 |
| New Jersey | 6 |
| Pennsylvania | 6 |

Source: Distilled Spirits Council of the United States

*Figures are for entire state.

local prohibition. Many groups counsel their members to abstain from liquor and the vices often associated with it. Almost invariably, declaring a county legally dry will not make it so but will simply put the sale of alcoholic beverages in the hands of the bootlegger, who in some cases has displaced the moonshiner as the purveyor of illegal alcohol. In some dry Kentucky counties, arrests for public drunkenness are virtually as high as in wet counties. Some dry counties have alcohol-abuse social workers and active Alcoholics Anonymous chapters. Yet this dissonant system continues in some areas, often fueled by corrupt local officials who accept or demand payoffs to allow bootleggers continued freedom to operate. The hillbilly moonshiner has been one of the more vivid image stereotypes of the Appalachian people in the minds of outsiders, although the image may be changing to that of the red-neck bootlegger.[61]

## IMPLICATIONS OF A COMPLEX CULTURAL HERITAGE

The people of Appalachia do not possess a homogeneous ensemble of cultural traditions and traits. Rather the region reflects a diverse cultural character that—to be acknowledged if not fully understood—should be viewed in the context of historic migration patterns that brought people of diverse backgrounds into a place of extraordinary environmental variety. One must then further consider the processes of adaptation and diffusion that allowed people to select the lifeways most appropriate to their situation. From the Mid-Atlantic hearth and the Pennsylvania Culture Area Germans, Scotch-Irish, and others moved

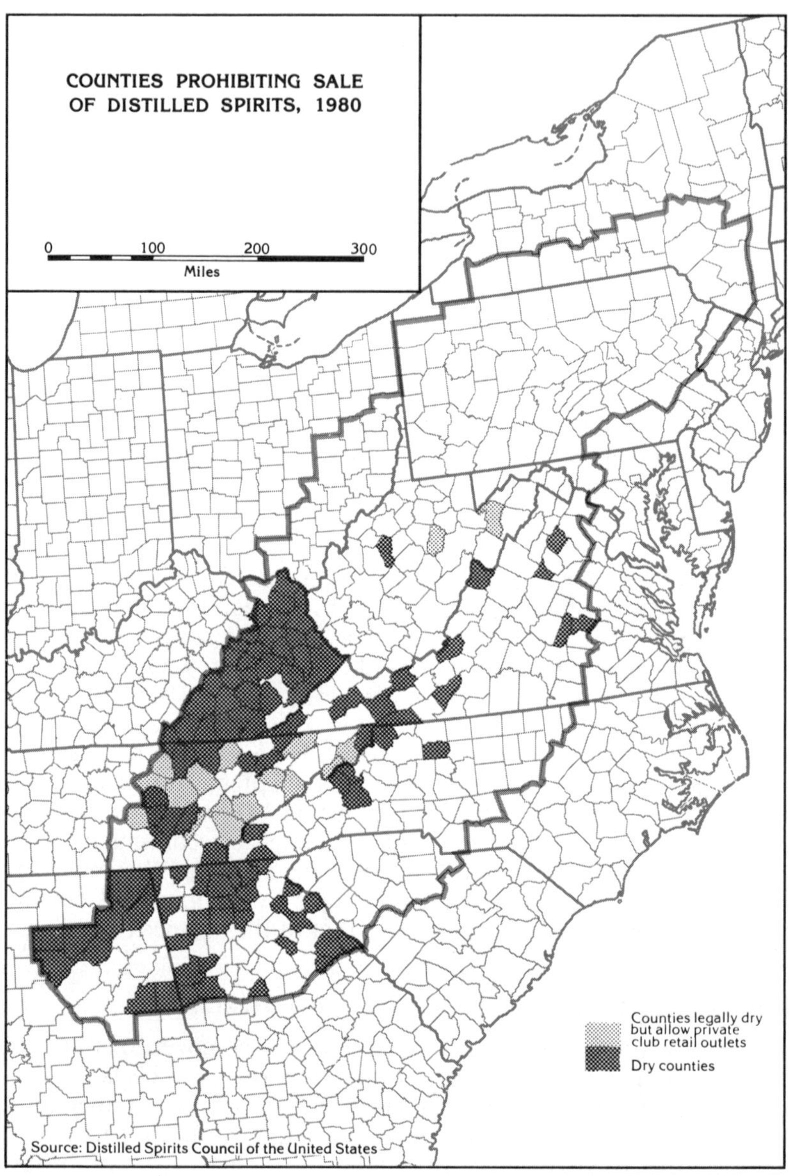
COUNTIES PROHIBITING SALE
OF DISTILLED SPIRITS, 1980
0
100
200
300
Miles
Counties legally dry but allow private club retail outlets
Dry counties
Source: Distilled Spirits Council of the United States

**Figure 4.8**

southwest, the easy routes before them shunted that direction by the maddening maze of ridges that blocked a direct westward march to the Ohio Valley. A more recent veneer of Irish and Slavic Catholics in Pennsylvania and New York was added by migrants able to utilize the toll roads and railroads that engineers had built to compromise the topographic integrity of barrier ridges and allow travel anywhere the prospect of employment was good. The migrants were attracted to industrial towns, few of which were to be found south of the Kanawha drainage in West Virginia. That watershed also seems to mark a transition into the traditional Upland South, an area characterized by small-scale farming, socially stratified counties, and mill and mine towns at sites of opportunity.

In the Upland South, many of the old folkways that made mountain life possible and that are evident in handicraft shops or magazines and books like *Foxfire* are difficult to find in current and sustained use. Further, many of the material artifacts that pass as mountain crafts are not unique to the region but may be found in relict form throughout the Upland South and Midwest. Nor are handmade southern-mountain artifacts necessarily of high quality or unusual value. Quilt collectors, for example, acknowledge that the best hand-sewn quilts in the region come from Pennsylvania, not the southern mountains where quilting is a highly publicized craft or "art form."

As a record of such "old-timey things as told by old-fashioned people . . . ," the *Foxfire* project at Rabun Gap–Nacoochee School in northeast Georgia is indeed an admirable effort. Started by English teacher Eliot Wigginton and his students as a student magazine, subscriptions grew to over 6,000 in all 50 states and a dozen foreign countries. In 1972, the group published *The Foxfire Book.* Within a year the book had sold 300,000 copies and its sequel volumes were used as textbooks in sociology, literature, history, and Appalachian-studies courses throughout the country.[62] Even though the *Foxfire* project has been a unique contribution in recording the lifeways of southern mountaineers, it is possible, as with any focused portrait of people and place, that its use may add to the already confused image of the region by outsiders by reinforcing some of their preconceptions of the region.

One distortion of regional image that may result from casual reading of this type of publication is that those with little firsthand knowledge of the region will assume that the lifeways portrayed are ubiquitous. The words and pictures therefore become a model for the entire region, not for a limited area in which such practices are rapidly disappearing. A second, and perhaps more serious, image distortion may occur for the outsider who uses this information to reduce the complex process of adaptation that has produced the present material culture and economy into a simplistic notion that the entire region is a backwater bypassed by the rest of the nation and represents a passively anachronistic and relict culture. If this kind of image accretion occurs it is unfortunate, because as Milton Newton observed, it is simply not the case. In areas of limited environmental opportunity for farming, for example, such as the southern Blue Ridge or Plateaus, the people must be cautious in adopting new techniques or machines. As farming and transport systems become more technically advanced, they also become more restricted to those environments where they function most efficiently. People living in environments that reduce the efficiency of any particular contrivance will not adopt it. Their failure to "modernize" may then give the illusion that they have not engaged in a conscious decision-making process but have simply been passive and thereby have been bypassed by the diffusion and modernization process. The valleys and ridges of the mountain South were suited to a farming technology that incorporated time-tested Indian crops and manual agricultural methods, but subsequent technical developments have not added to hill-farm efficiency. If the farms, fields, and buildings in the mountain landscape seem similar from one valley to another, it is in part a reflection of how nonfunctional or inflexible new technical systems are relative to the technology that was available when initial settlement occurred. It does not indicate that those techniques escaped assessment.[63]

Those whose views of Appalachian character are narrow and unstudied tend to have simplistic notions of a people with a restricted regional heritage and limited participation in the national culture and economy. But regional residents, north to south, have a tradition of interaction and exchange with the larger society. In some places that interchange was marked by widespread acceptance of technological or social innovation. In other places new ways were impractical. This process of interaction, sorting, and adoption or rejection of ideas is shared with the rest of America.

## NOTES

1. Thomas Wolfe, *Look Homeward Angel* (New York: Charles Scribners & Sons, 1929), pp. 6–7.

2. James G. Leyburn, *The Scotch-Irish: A Social History* (Chapel Hill: University of North Carolina Press, 1962), p. 188.

3. E. Estyn Evans, "The Scotch-Irish: Their Culture Adaptation and Heritage in the American Old West," in E.R.R. Green, ed., *Essays in Scotch-Irish History* (London: Routledge & Kegan Paul, 1969), p. 76.

4. E. Estyn Evans, "The Scotch-Irish in the New World: An Atlantic Heritage," *Journal of the Royal Society of Antiquaries of Ireland* 95 (1965), p. 41.

5. Leyburn, op. cit. (footnote 2), p. 200.

6. Ibid., p. 190. The Scotch-Irish were Scot Presbyterians who were settled in Ulster, Northern Ireland, about 1610 by King James I.

7. Evans, 1969, op. cit. (footnote 3), p. 75.

8. Ibid.

9. Peirce Lewis and Ben Marsh, "Slices Through Time: The Physical and Cultural Landscapes of Central and Eastern Pennsylvania," in Roman A. Cybriwsky, ed., *The Philadelphia Region: Selected Essays and Field Trip Itin-*

*eraries* (Washington, D.C.: Association of American Geographers, 1979), p. 27.

10. Wilbur Zelinsky, "The Pennsylvania Town: An Overdue Geographical Account," *Geographical Review* 67 (1977), p. 145.

11. Thomas J. Wertenbaker, *The Founding of American Civilization: The Middle Colonies* (New York: Charles Scribners & Sons, 1938), p. 282; Zelinsky, op. cit. (footnote 10), p. 131; and Wayland F. Dunaway, "Pennsylvania as an Early Distributing Center of Population," *Pennsylvania Magazine of History and Biography* 55 (1931), pp. 134–169.

12. Zelinsky, op. cit. (footnote 10), p. 130.

13. Milton Newton, "Cultural Preadaptation and the Upland South," in H. J. Walker and W. G. Haag, eds., *Man and Cultural Heritage,* vol. 5, *Geoscience and Man* (Baton Rouge: Louisiana State University Press, 1974), p. 148.

14. Ibid., p. 144.

15. Conrad M. Arensberg, "American Communities," *American Anthropologist* 57 (1955), p. 1148.

16. Ibid., p. 1155.

17. Newton, op. cit. (footnote 13), p. 150.

18. Edward T. Price, "The Central Courthouse Square in the American County Seat," *Geographical Review* 58 (1968), p. 41.

19. Newton, op. cit. (footnote 13), pp. 151–152.

20. Ibid., p. 152.

21. Wertenbaker, op. cit. (footnote 11), pp. 302–306.

22. E. Estyn Evans, "Cultural Relics of the Ulster-Scots in the Old West of North America," *Ulster Folklife* 11 (1966), p. 33.

23. Fred Kniffen and Henry Glassie, "Building in Wood in the Eastern United States: A Time-Place Perspective," *Geographical Review* 56 (1966), p. 59.

24. Henry Glassie,"The Appalachian Log Cabin," *Mountain Life and Work* 39 (1963), pp. 5–6, and Evans, 1969, op. cit. (footnote 3), p. 78.

25. Evans, 1965, op. cit. (footnote 4), p. 45.

26. Kniffen and Glassie, op. cit. (footnote 23), pp. 59–63.

27. Henry Glassie, "The Old Barns of Appalachia," *Mountain Life and Work* 41 (1965), p. 21.

28. Wertenbaker, op. cit. (footnote 11), p. 322.

29. Evans, 1965, op. cit. (footnote 4), pp. 47–48, and J. S. Otto and N. E. Anderson, "Slash-and-Burn Cultivation in the Highland South: A Problem in Comparative Agricultural History," *Comparative Studies in Society and History* 24 (1982), pp. 137–138.

30. James Rodechko, "Irish-American Society in the Pennsylvania Anthracite Region: 1870–1880," in John E. Bodnar, ed., *The Ethnic Experience in Pennsylvania* (Lewisburg, Pa.: Bucknell University Press, 1973), p. 20.

31. Michael P. Weber, "Occupational Mobility of Ethnic Minorities in Nineteenth-Century Warren, Pennsylvania," in Bodnar, op. cit. (footnote 30), p. 147.

32. George R. Leighton, *America's Growing Pains: The Romance, Comedy, and Tragedy of Five Great Cities* (New York: Harper and Brothers, 1939), pp. 27–31, and H. Benjamin Powell, "The Pennsylvania Anthracite Industry," *Pennsylvania History* 47 (1980), pp. 3–28.

33. Walter C. Warzeski, "The Rusin Community in Pennsylvania," in Bodnar, op. cit. (footnote 30), pp. 175–180.

34. Rose C. Feld, "What I Found in Lynch, Kentucky," *Success* (March 1926), pp. 58, 116.

35. George J. Prpic, "The Croatian Immigrants in Pittsburgh," in Bodnar, op. cit. (footnote 30), pp. 271–278.
36. Ibid., p. 270.
37. Darold T. Barnum, *The Negro in the Bituminous Coal Mining Industry,* Industrial Research Unit, Report no. 14 (Philadelphia: University of Pennsylvania, 1970), p. 16, and James W. Taylor, *Alleghania: A Geographical and Statistical Memoir* (St. Paul: James Davenport, 1862).
38. Barnum, op. cit. (footnote 37), p. 19.
39. David Bellows, "Appalachian Blacks: A Demographic Analysis" (Department of Sociology, Rutgers University, 1974, mimeographed), p. 60.
40. Barnum, op. cit. (footnote 37), pp. 31–51, and William Turner, "A Demographic Profile of Blacks in Appalachia: Selected Social and Economic Characteristics" (Department of Sociology, University of Kentucky, 1982, manuscript), pp. 2–6.
41. Bureau of Agricultural Economics, *Economic and Social Problems and Conditions of Southern Appalachians,* Misc. Pub. no. 205 (Washington, D.C.: U.S. Dept. of Agriculture, 1935), p. 169.
42. Peter L. Halvorson and William M. Newman, *Atlas of Religious Change in America: 1952–1971* (Washington, D.C.: Glenmary Research Center, 1978), p. 14.
43. Wilbur Zelinsky, "An Approach to the Religious Geography of the United States: Patterns of Church Membership in 1952," *Annals,* Association of American Geographers, 51 (1961), p. 169.
44. Thomas P. Ford, "Status, Residence, and Fundamentalist Religious Beliefs in the Southern Appalachians," *Social Forces* 39 (1960), p. 41.
45. W. D. Weatherford, ed., *Religion in the Appalachian Mountains* (Berea, Ky.: Berea College, 1955), p. 36.
46. Ford, op. cit. (footnote 44), p. 42.
47. Ibid., p. 43.
48. Paul F. Gillespie, *Foxfire 7* (New York: Anchor Books, 1982), pp. 9–279.
49. Bureau of Agricultural Economics, op. cit. (footnote 41), p. 169.
50. Halvorson and Newman, op. cit. (footnote 42), pp. 15, 18.
51. John Photiadis and B. B. Maurer, *Religion in an Appalachian State,* Appalachian Center, Research Report 6 (Morgantown: West Virginia University, 1974), pp. 24–25.
52. Frank J. Riddel, ed., *Appalachia: Its People, Heritage, and Problems* (Dubuque, Ia.: Kendall/Hunt, 1974), p. 102.
53. Hans Kurath, *A Word Geography of the Eastern United States* (Ann Arbor: University of Michigan Press, 1949), pp. 1–2.
54. Ibid., p. 2 and Fig. 90.
55. Ellen Churchill Semple, "The Anglo-Saxons of the Kentucky Mountains: A Study in Anthropogeography," *Geographical Journal* 17 (1901), p. 588.
56. George O. Carney, "Country Music and the South: A Cultural Geography Perspective," *Journal of Cultural Geography* 1 (1980), pp. 16–17.
57. George Pullen Jackson, *White Spirituals in the Southern Uplands* (Chapel Hill: University of North Carolina Press, 1933), p. 403.
58. Stanley Sadie, ed., *The New Grove Dictionary of Music and Musicians* (London: Macmillan, 1980), p. 226.
59. Carney, op. cit. (footnote 56), p. 19.
60. Ibid., p. 25.
61. See Loyal Durand, Jr., " 'Mountain Moonshining' in East Tennessee,"

*Geographical Review* 46 (1956), pp. 169–181, and Cratis Williams, "Moonshining in the Mountains," *North Carolina Folklore* 15 (1967), pp. 11–17.

62. Loyal Jones, "The Foxfire Phenomenon," *Appalachian Notes* 1 (1973), pp. 9–12.

63. Newton, op. cit. (footnote 13), p. 144.

# CHAPTER 5

# POPULATION GROWTH AND CHARACTERISTICS

In order to begin to assess problems of regional development and to determine appropriate strategies and policies for development, population growth trends and characteristics must be evaluated. In this brief overview of the region's population geography, we do not address such important topics as the age and sex structure of the region's population or mortality and morbidity trends, and we only briefly examine the important topic of fertility. This is in part because of space limitations and in part because most results of the 1980 census of population and housing results were not available in the necessary published form prior to the book's completion.

In 1980 the 445 counties of the Raitz-Ulack Appalachian region had a combined population of nearly 26.5 million, or 11.7 percent of the total population of the United States.[1] The 213,217 sq mi (552,232 sq km) of land in the region accounted for 6 percent of the United States' total land area (7.2 percent of the total excluding Alaska). This is a large segment of America that manifests considerable spatial and sociocultural variation in population characteristics; more variation, perhaps, than those unfamiliar with the region might expect.

## POPULATION DISTRIBUTION AND DENSITY

As the data in Table 5.1 show, Appalachia's population is not evenly distributed among the portions of the 13 states that constitute the region. Pennsylvania ranks first in population and area, just as New Jersey ranks last in both categories. About one-half of Appalachia's population resided in metropolitan areas as compared to the U.S. average of almost 75 percent (Table 5.1).[2] The 13.8 million urban residents of Appalachia were distributed among twenty-eight Standard Metropolitan Statistical Areas (SMSAs) located entirely within the region's boundaries and in counties of five additional SMSAs that were only partly in the region (see Figure 5.1; this and other figures in this chapter are based on data from the U.S. census). In all, there were 105 SMSA counties in the

TABLE 5.1
Population, Area, and Density of Population by State and Urban-Rural Residence, 1980[1]

| State | Number of Counties | Population | Percentage of Regional Total | Area (sq. mi.) | Percentage of Regional Total | Population Density (per sq. mi.) |
|---|---|---|---|---|---|---|
| Alabama | 18 | 1,508,430 | 5.7 | 12,650 | 5.9 | 119.2 |
| Rural | 11 | 375,455 | | 7,555 | | 49.7 |
| Urban | 7 | 1,132,975 | | 5,095 | | 222.4 |
| Georgia | 59 | 3,087,491 | 11.7 | 17,836 | 8.4 | 173.1 |
| Rural | 41 | 952,094 | | 12,730 | | 74.8 |
| Urban | 18 | 2,135,397 | | 5,106 | | 418.2 |
| Kentucky | 36 | 848,677 | 3.2 | 12,868 | 6.0 | 66.0 |
| Rural | 34 | 754,032 | | 12,357 | | 61.0 |
| Urban | 2 | 94,645 | | 511 | | 185.2 |
| Maryland | 4 | 334,395 | 1.3 | 2,211 | 1.0 | 151.2 |
| Rural | 4 | 334,395 | | 2,211 | | 151.2 |
| Urban | 0 | - | | - | | - |
| New Jersey | 2 | 200,548 | 0.8 | 889 | 0.4 | 225.6 |
| Rural | 1 | 116,119 | | 527 | | 220.3 |
| Urban | 1 | 84,429 | | 362 | | 223.2 |
| New York | 17 | 1,514,944 | 5.7 | 14,370 | 6.7 | 105.4 |
| Rural | 14 | 1,153,828 | | 12,717 | | 90.7 |
| Urban | 3 | 361,116 | | 1,653 | | 218.5 |
| North Carolina | 52 | 3,513,167 | 13.3 | 22,950 | 10.8 | 153.1 |
| Rural | 38 | 1,541,827 | | 15,987 | | 96.4 |
| Urban | 14 | 1,971,340 | | 6,963 | | 283.1 |
| Ohio | 23 | 1,063,502 | 4.0 | 11,090 | 5.2 | 95.9 |
| Rural | 18 | 735,656 | | 8,658 | | 85.0 |
| Urban | 5 | 327,846 | | 2,432 | | 134.8 |
| Pennsylvania | 58 | 7,160,728 | 27.1 | 38,710 | 18.2 | 185.0 |
| Rural | 39 | 2,388,153 | | 26,425 | | 90.4 |
| Urban | 19 | 4,772,575 | | 12,285 | | 388.5 |
| South Carolina | 16 | 1,204,863 | 4.6 | 9,602 | 4.5 | 125.5 |
| Rural | 13 | 636,105 | | 7,477 | | 85.1 |
| Urban | 3 | 568,758 | | 2,125 | | 267.7 |
| Tennessee | 44 | 2,002,115 | 7.6 | 17,511 | 8.2 | 114.3 |
| Rural | 32 | 861,796 | | 12,801 | | 67.3 |
| Urban | 12 | 1,140,319 | | 4,710 | | 242.1 |
| Virginia | 61 | 2,060,126 | 7.8 | 28,450 | 13.3 | 72.4 |
| Rural | 50 | 1,509,471 | | 23,752 | | 63.6 |
| Urban | 11 | 550,655 | | 4,678 | | 117.7 |
| West Virginia | 55 | 1,949,644 | 7.4 | 24,085 | 11.3 | 80.9 |
| Rural | 45 | 1,254,091 | | 20,854 | | 60.1 |
| Urban | 10 | 695,553 | | 3,231 | | 215.3 |
| TOTAL | 445 | 26,448,630 | 100.0[2] | 213,222 | 100.0[2] | 124.0 |
| Rural | 340 | 12,613,022 | 47.7 | 164,051 | 76.9 | 76.9 |
| Urban | 105 | 13,835,608 | 52.3 | 49,171 | 23.1 | 281.4 |

Source: 1980 Census of Population

[1]As used here urban includes all counties designated as part of a Standard Metropolitan Statistical Area as of December 1977.

[2]Totals rounded to 100 percent.

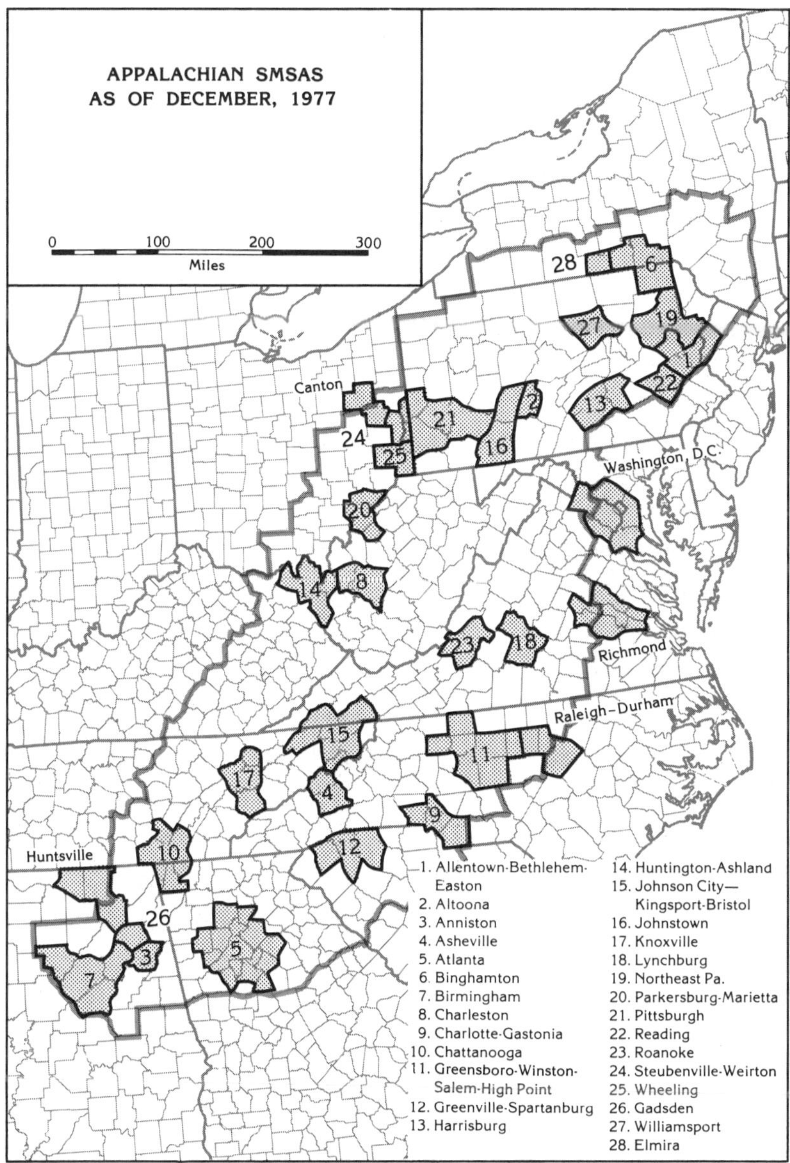
APPALACHIAN SMSAS
AS OF DECEMBER, 1977
0
100
200
300
Miles
Canton
Washington, D.C.
Richmond
Raleigh–Durham
Huntsville
1. Allentown-Bethlehem-Easton
2. Altoona
3. Anniston
4. Asheville
5. Atlanta
6. Binghamton
7. Birmingham
8. Charleston
9. Charlotte-Gastonia
10. Chattanooga
11. Greensboro-Winston-Salem-High Point
12. Greenville-Spartanburg
13. Harrisburg
14. Huntington-Ashland
15. Johnson City—Kingsport-Bristol
16. Johnstown
17. Knoxville
18. Lynchburg
19. Northeast Pa.
20. Parkersburg-Marietta
21. Pittsburgh
22. Reading
23. Roanoke
24. Steubenville-Weirton
25. Wheeling
26. Gadsden
27. Williamsport
28. Elmira

**Figure 5.1**

TABLE 5.2
Population by SMSA: Central (or largest) County and Peripheral Counties, 1980

| Population Rank | | Number of Counties | Area (sq. mi.) | Population | Density |
|---|---|---|---|---|---|
| 1 | Pittsburgh | 4 | 3,049 | 2,263,894 | 742.5 |
| | Allegheny County | | 728 | 1,450,085 | 1,991.9 |
| | Peripheral Counties | | 2,321 | 813,809 | 350.6 |
| 2 | Atlanta | 15 | 4,326 | 2,029,618 | 469.2 |
| | Fulton County | | 530 | 589,904 | 1,113.0 |
| | Peripheral Counties | | 3,796 | 1,439,714 | 379.3 |
| 3 | Birmingham | 4 | 3,358 | 847,360 | 252.3 |
| | Jefferson County | | 1,115 | 671,197 | 602.0 |
| | Peripheral Counties | | 2,243 | 176,163 | 78.5 |
| 4 | Greensboro-Winston-Salem-High Point | 6 | 3,214 | 827,385 | 257.4 |
| | Guilford County | | 655 | 317,154 | 484.2 |
| | Peripheral Counties | | 2,559 | 510,231 | 199.4 |
| 5 | Northeast Pennsylvania | 3 | 1,953 | 640,396 | 327.9 |
| | Luzerne County | | 888 | 343,079 | 386.4 |
| | Other Counties | | 1,065 | 297,317 | 279.2 |
| 6 | Charlotte-Gastonia | 3 | 1,543 | 637,218 | 413.0 |
| | Mecklenburg County | | 542 | 404,270 | 745.9 |
| | Peripheral Counties | | 1,001 | 232,948 | 232.7 |
| 7 | Allentown-Bethlehem-Easton | 4 | 1,491 | 636,714 | 427.0 |
| | Lehigh County | | 348 | 273,582 | 786.2 |
| | Other Counties | | 1,143 | 363,132 | 317.7 |
| 8 | Greenville-Spartanburg | 3 | 2,125 | 568,758 | 267.7 |
| | Greenville County | | 793 | 287,913 | 363.1 |
| | Other Counties | | 1,332 | 280,845 | 210.8 |
| 9 | Knoxville | 4 | 1,631 | 476,517 | 292.2 |
| | Knox County | | 508 | 319,694 | 629.3 |
| | Peripheral Counties | | 1,123 | 156,823 | 139.6 |
| 10 | Harrisburg | 3 | 1,624 | 446,072 | 274.7 |
| | Dauphin County | | 518 | 232,317 | 448.5 |
| | Peripheral Counties | | 1,106 | 213,755 | 193.3 |
| 11 | Johnson City-Kingsport-Bristol | 7 | 2,872 | 433,638 | 151.0 |
| | Sullivan County | | 413 | 143,968 | 348.6 |
| | Peripheral Counties | | 2,459 | 289,670 | 117.8 |
| 12 | Chattanooga | 6 | 2,109 | 426,540 | 202.2 |
| | Hamilton County | | 550 | 287,740 | 523.2 |
| | Peripheral Counties | | 1,559 | 138,800 | 89.0 |
| 13 | Reading | 1 | 862 | 312,509 | 362.5 |
| 14 | Huntington-Ashland | 5 | 1,759 | 311,350 | 177.0 |
| | Cabell County | | 279 | 106,835 | 382.9 |
| | Peripheral Counties | | 1,480 | 204,515 | 138.2 |
| 15 | Binghamton | 3 | 2,073 | 301,336 | 145.4 |
| | Broome County | | 714 | 213,648 | 299.2 |
| | Peripheral Counties | | 1,359 | 87,688 | 64.5 |
| | TOTAL | 71 | 33,989 | 11,159,305 | 328.3 |

Source: 1980 Census of Population

Appalachian region as of December 1977, and these accounted for 23 percent of the region's total land area.[3] The largest urban population was in Pennsylvania, where more than one-third of the entire region's metropolitan population resided. Four counties made up the Pittsburgh SMSA, the largest metropolitan area in the region and the nation's twelfth largest. The second-largest metropolitan area (the nation's eighteenth largest) was in Georgia—the fifteen counties constituting the Atlanta SMSA. In terms of area, the Atlanta SMSA, with 4,326 sq mi (11,204.3 sq km), was the largest in the region. The metropolitan populations of Pennsylvania, Georgia, and North Carolina accounted for nearly two-thirds of Appalachia's total urban population, and nearly one-half of all the SMSA counties were in these three states.

In Appalachia, only Pittsburgh and Atlanta—each with over 2 million people—could be considered major metropolitan centers (Table 5.2 shows Appalachia's largest SMSAs). Birmingham, the region's third-largest SMSA (it ranked only forty-fifth in the nation), had a total population of under 1 million. Many of the other, smaller SMSAs included more than one city. For example, Northeast Pennsylvania—Appalachia's fifth-largest SMSA with 640,396 people—included the cities of Wilkes-Barre in Luzerne County, Scranton in Lackawanna County, and Stroudsburg in Monroe County.

The Appalachian population density of 124 persons per sq mi (47.9 per sq km) was considerably more than the 76.1 persons per sq mi (29.4 per sq km) in the United States (excluding Alaska). Even the density in the rural Appalachian counties, 76.9 persons per sq mi (29.7 per sq km), was higher than the national average. Such high densities of population are remarkable given the rugged nature of much of the region's topography. In terms of physiographic provinces only the Blue Ridge, with 63.6 persons per sq mi (24.6 per sq km), had a population density less than the national average (Table 5.3), whereas the other three all had densities of over 100 persons per sq mi (38.6 per sq km). The Ridge and Valley Province, even though it ranked third in population and area, had the greatest population density—more than twice the national average.

## POPULATION CHANGE

The Appalachian region has been characterized as one of slow population growth or decline attributed to high rates of outmigration. It is reported that in general these outmigrants moved to metropolitan areas outside the region because of perceived economic opportunities at such destinations, coupled with an absence of opportunities in their home areas. Such a characterization was valid for much of the region in the period following World War II and until the early 1970s, although the population growth trends have varied significantly throughout the region. Since the early 1970s, however, the region has experienced a reversal in population growth trends, as much of Appalachia—and

The textile-mill town of Pelzer on the South Carolina Piedmont. Company-built houses, now owned by the residents, line the streets that focus on the centrally located mill.

especially its southern portion—has gained population at a rate significantly greater than the national average (Table 5.4). This means that those areas that have grown the most rapidly have experienced a net inmigration during the 1970s, because this trend reversal has been caused more by migration flows than by the other two components of population change, births and deaths. Migration, of course, has been the most variable (and unpredictable) of the three components in the United States since World War II. Although fertility and mortality rates have

TABLE 5.3
Population, Area, and Density of Population by Physiographic Province, 1980

| Province | Number of Counties | Population | Percentage of Regional Total | Area (sq. mi.) | Percentage of Regional Total | Population Density (per sq. mi.) |
|---|---|---|---|---|---|---|
| Piedmont | 125 | 7,901,487 | 29.9 | 54,551 | 25.6 | 144.8 |
| Blue Ridge | 39 | 948,954 | 3.6 | 14,916 | 7.0 | 63.6 |
| Ridge and Valley | 93 | 7,421,448 | 28.1 | 44,621 | 20.9 | 166.3 |
| Plateaus | 188 | 10,176,741 | 38.5 | 99,134 | 46.5 | 102.7 |
| | | 26,448,630 | | 213,222 | | |

Source: 1980 Census of Population

Neon-Fleming is a coal-company town in Letcher County, Kentucky. Many valleys in the eastern Kentucky and southern West Virginia coalfield are occupied by coal camps where houses have been built close together on small lots, creating high population densities.

TABLE 5.4
Population Change in Appalachia, 1950-1980

| State | Number of Counties | Percent Change 1950-60 | 1960-70 | 1970-80 |
|---|---|---|---|---|
| Alabama | 18 | 5.5 | 3.3 | 13.5 |
| Rural | 11 | -7.0 | 3.8 | 20.9 |
| Urban | 7 | 9.9 | 3.2 | 111.2 |
| Georgia | 59 | 21.2 | 27.5 | 24.4 |
| Rural | 41 | 3.1 | 13.5 | 19.5 |
| Urban | 18 | 34.5 | 35.4 | 26.8 |
| Kentucky | 36 | -15.7 | -7.4 | 24.4 |
| Rural | 34 | -18.0 | -9.0 | 26.4 |
| Urban | 2 | 8.8 | 5.1 | 10.6 |
| Maryland | 4* | 6.0 | 9.9 | 13.6 |
| New Jersey | 2 | 26.7 | 34.7 | 32.4 |
| Rural | 1 | 43.1 | 57.4 | 49.8 |
| Urban | 1 | 16.3 | 17.0 | 14.2 |
| New York | 17 | 12.5 | 10.0 | 11.6 |
| Rural | 14 | 11.3 | 11.7 | 16.8 |
| Urban | 3 | 15.7 | 5.9 | -2.4 |
| North Carolina | 52 | 13.4 | 14.7 | 15.1 |
| Rural | 38 | 4.9 | 9.6 | 16.6 |
| Urban | 14 | 21.6 | 19.0 | 14.0 |
| Ohio | 23 | 4.3 | -0.5 | 8.2 |
| Rural | 18 | 4.1 | -1.0 | 9.7 |
| Urban | 5 | 4.8 | 0.5 | 4.8 |
| Pennsylvania | 58 | 3.8 | 1.5 | 2.1 |
| Rural | 39 | 0.5 | 1.2 | 7.6 |
| Urban | 19 | 5.4 | 1.7 | -0.5 |
| South Carolina | 16 | 7.8 | 9.0 | 17.9 |
| Rural | 13 | 2.6 | 4.4 | 16.0 |
| Urban | 3 | 15.1 | 14.7 | 20.1 |
| Tennessee | 44 | 6.0 | 7.7 | 20.0 |
| Rural | 32 | 0.6 | 7.9 | 24.8 |
| Urban | 12 | 10.1 | 7.6 | 16.7 |
| Virginia | 61 | 3.4 | 5.9 | 16.6 |
| Rural | 50 | 0.8 | 3.7 | 16.7 |
| Urban | 11 | 12.0 | 12.5 | 16.5 |
| West Virginia | 55 | -7.2 | -6.2 | 11.8 |
| Rural | 45 | -13.1 | -8.4 | 16.1 |
| Urban | 10 | 5.0 | -2.6 | 4.8 |
| Region | 445 | 5.3 | 6.3 | 12.3 |
| Rural | 340 | -0.7 | 3.4 | 15.8 |
| Urban | 105 | 11.5 | 8.0 | 10.2 |
| United States | | 18.5 | 13.4 | 11.4 |

Source: 1950 and 1980 Census of Population

*All counties are rural in Maryland.

fluctuated somewhat, it is migration that most accounted for the dramatic regional changes that have occurred in national population trends.

In recent years national fertility rates have generally been somewhat higher than those of the Appalachian region, whereas mortality rates at the national level have been slightly lower than those of the region. In the Appalachian Regional Commission region, for example, "the average (crude) birth rate . . . for the decade [1970 to 1980] was 14.8 per 1,000, only 95 percent of the national rate, while the death rate, 9.9 per 1,000, was 110 percent of the U.S. average. As a result, natural increase added only 47 percent of the total Appalachian population gain in the ten year period, in contrast to the 60 percent that it added to the national gain."[4] An in-depth examination of the fertility rates in 190 counties in southern Appalachia only (the Ford region described in Chapter 1) reported essentially the same conclusion for an earlier time period. Analyzing four different fertility rates (crude birthrate, fertility ratio, general fertility rate, and standardized general fertility rate), the study found that whereas fertility rates were about 50 to 60 percent higher in southern Appalachia than in the nation in 1930 and 1940 and about 20 percent higher in 1950, "they were about equal to or slightly lower than national rates on all measures in 1960."[5] Considerable variation, of course, exists within southern Appalachia, and as might be expected, the counties with the lowest incomes and educational levels had the highest fertility rates. However, the stereotype of the region as an area of high fertility (the "fertile mountains," as some have called the region) is no longer completely accurate. If we assume that crude birth rates and death rates for the Raitz-Ulack region were similar to those of the Appalachian Regional Commission's region, then approximately one-half of the regional population increase, or nearly 1.5 million persons, migrated into the region between 1970 and 1980. This is a remarkable turnaround over the earlier decades.

A more detailed examination of Table 5.4 reveals that only the Appalachian portions of New Jersey and Georgia gained more rapidly than did the nation in both the 1950s and 1960s and that North Carolina grew more rapidly in the 1960s. Conversely, in the 1970s only two states, Pennsylvania and Ohio, had population gains less than the national average. The state with the greatest percentage increase was New Jersey, followed by Georgia and Kentucky. Eastern Kentucky has traditionally been among the poorest areas within Appalachia; therefore it is perhaps surprising that such substantial population gains have occurred. Although reasons are numerous, it is certain that improved employment conditions in the area's coal industry in the 1970s, coupled with declining economic opportunities in the midwestern cities to which so many migrants from Kentucky had earlier traveled, combined to "pull" many persons back to their origins. In the case of Georgia, the economic opportunities that have emerged with the growth of the Atlanta metropolitan area have drawn many migrants to this Sun Belt city. Between 1970 and 1980 the population of the entire Atlanta SMSA increased by 27.2 percent.

The business district of Greenville, South Carolina. In an effort to attract shoppers and business people back into the central city, the main street and a side street have been turned into malls. Greenville is central to the densely populated textile-milling district that extends along the Carolina Piedmont.

Even though Fulton County, where central Atlanta is located, actually experienced a population loss of 2.5 percent, the other fourteen suburban counties of the SMSA gained by 45.4 percent.

Another trend clearly revealed in Table 5.4 is that the population in the rural Appalachian counties increased more rapidly during the 1970s than did that in the urban counties. Indeed, the urban counties of two states, New York and Pennsylvania, actually experienced population losses. Higher gains in rural counties, a reversal of what occurred in the two earlier decades when urban population increases were considerably greater, were characteristic of virtually the entire region. Only in two states, Georgia and South Carolina, were urban-county increases greater, but in both states the rural gains were significantly above the national—and even regional—average. This trend was not unique to Appalachia but part of what has been described as America's "rural renaissance." Many recent studies have analyzed this phenomenon of nonmetropolitan population growth, which began in the early 1970s.[6]

Comparison of Figures 5.2 and 5.3 reveals startling differences in individual county changes in the 1960s and 1970s. In the 1960s 79 percent (351 out of 445) of Appalachia's counties had population growth rates below the national average of 13.4 percent. Nearly all of the counties in the region that had percentage gains higher than the national average

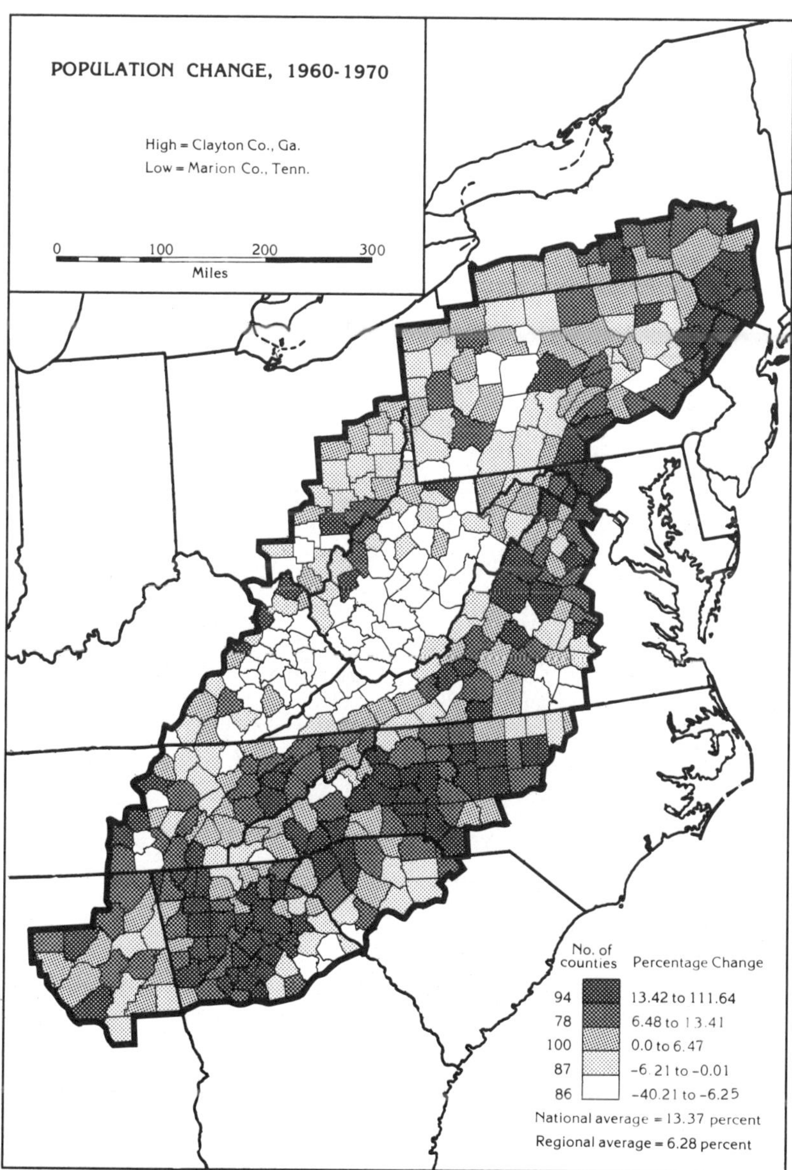
POPULATION CHANGE, 1960-1970
High = Clayton Co., Ga.
Low = Marion Co., Tenn.
0
100
200
300
Miles
No. of counties
Percentage Change
94
13.42 to 111.64
78
6.48 to 13.41
100
0.0 to 6.47
87
-6.21 to -0.01
86
-40.21 to -6.25
National average = 13.37 percent
Regional average = 6.28 percent

**Figure 5.2**

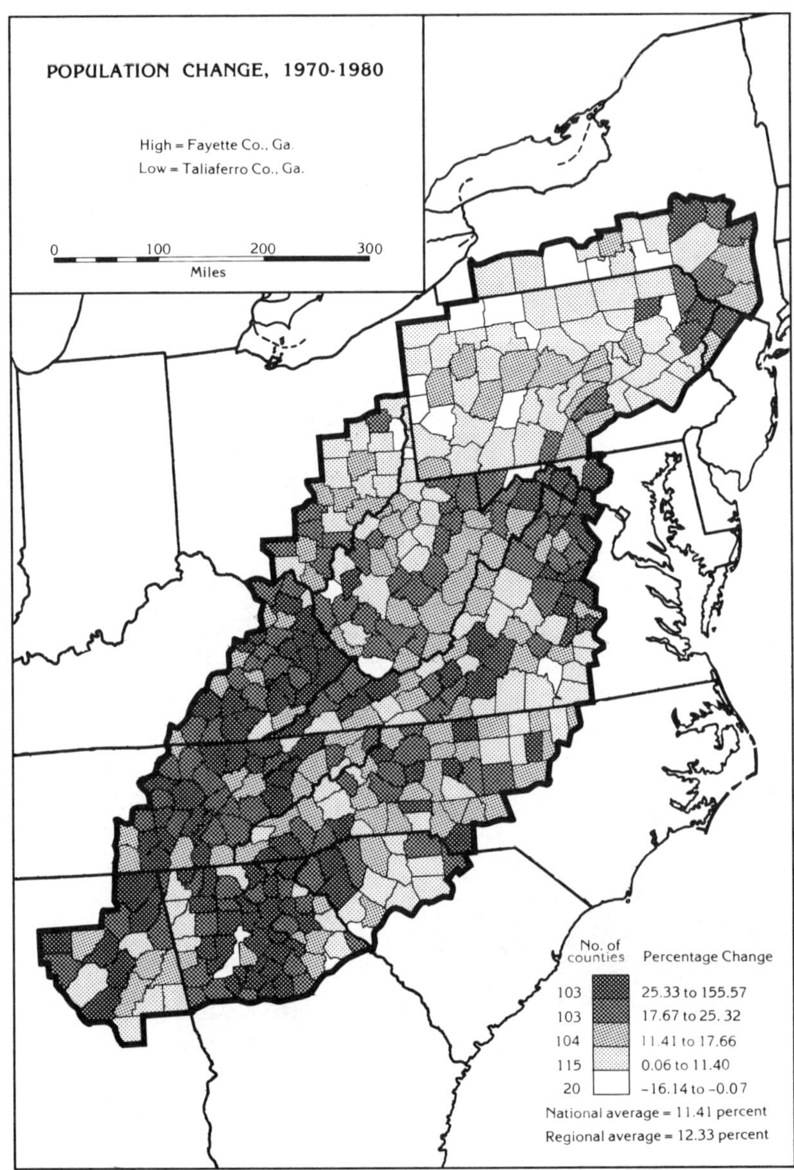
POPULATION CHANGE, 1970-1980
High = Fayette Co., Ga.
Low = Taliaferro Co., Ga.
0 100 200 300
Miles
No. of counties
Percentage Change
103 25.33 to 155.57
103 17.67 to 25.32
104 11.41 to 17.66
115 0.06 to 11.40
20 -16.14 to -0.07
National average = 11.41 percent
Regional average = 12.33 percent

**Figure 5.3**

were metropolitan counties or were located adjacent to metropolitan counties. As already noted, Georgia had one of the highest percentage increases during the 1960–1970 period, and certainly the largest cluster of rapidly growing counties in Appalachia was in Georgia. Nearly all of the counties in the Atlanta metropolitan area, as well as all those located along Interstate 75 north to the Tennessee border and Chattanooga, were high-growth counties in the 1960s. A second major clustering of high-growth counties was found in North Carolina, where all of the state's Appalachian cities, including Charlotte, Winston-Salem, Greensboro, Durham, and High Point, experienced rapid gains. Similarly, smaller clusters of rapid-growth counties associated with expanding metropolitan areas were found in Tennessee (Knoxville) and Virginia (Roanoke, Lynchburg).

Gains also occurred in a few nonmetropolitan counties in areas associated with scenery, second-home development, recreation, and tourism. Examples include counties in northeast Georgia like Hall County, where Lake Sidney Lanier is located, and Lumpkin County; southwest North Carolina's Transylvania (Lake Toxaway and Sapphire Valley) and Jackson counties; Virginia's Shenandoah Valley area (Massanutten Mountain); northeast Pennsylvania's Monroe and Pike counties where the Poconos are located; and southeast New York State's Catskill Mountain counties (Orange, Sullivan, and Ulster). These places are quite accessible to large metropolitan areas, especially since the completion of construction of several interstate highways that crisscross the region.

During the period 1960–1970, 173 counties (39 percent of the regional total) actually experienced population losses. The heaviest losses were located in the Appalachian coal-mining areas of Kentucky, West Virginia, and Virginia. Other heavy losses occurred in rural farm and coal-producing counties in Pennsylvania and Ohio. Finally, most of the rural counties in the Piedmont areas of Virginia, North Carolina, South Carolina, and Georgia also experienced population declines.

The situation in the 1970s was quite the opposite. Only 20 counties in the region, mostly in northern Appalachia, experienced population losses, whereas 310 counties (70 percent) had percentage increases of population in excess of the national average of 11.4 percent (Figure 5.3). The greatest gains in the 1970s occurred in the coal areas of central Appalachia and especially in Kentucky and southwest Virginia. The majority of counties in Alabama, Georgia, Tennessee, North Carolina, and Virginia experienced gains above national and regional averages. On the other hand, most of the counties in the northern Appalachian states of New York, Pennsylvania, and Ohio, as well as in northern West Virginia, experienced percentage increases less than the national average.

## Migration: 1940–1960

Changing trends in population growth or loss can be explained largely by migration. The heavy losses to outmigration during the two decades

Staunton is a Great Valley town in Augusta County, Virginia. Rolling topography has made it possible for the city to extend new subdivisions along radial access roads. (U.S. Department of Agriculture photo.)

between 1940 and 1960 are well known and documented. In the 190 counties of Ford's southern Appalachian region, for example, there was a net migration loss of over 700,000 persons in the 1940s and a further 1.1 million in the 1950s. Although this period has been referred to as one of "the great migration," migration losses to southern Appalachia are not new; southern Appalachia has experienced net migration losses in every decade since 1900.[7] But because of high fertility rates, especially prior to 1960, the region did experience population gain.

The reasons for the heavy outmigration starting in the 1940s are complex, but economic ones were the most important. The heavy losses began with "World War II and the accompanying industrial prosperity and demand for labor,"[8] coupled with sagging or absent economic opportunities in much of Appalachia. In the terminology of Everett Lee, both "pull" and "push" factors combined to move people from their origins.[9] Most of the movement after the 1940s was to large cities both inside and outside the region. Many from eastern Kentucky and West Virginia, for example, moved to cities outside the region: Lexington; Detroit; Cincinnati, Columbus, and Cleveland, Ohio. Today these people still comprise significant populations in such cities and often reside in neighborhoods made up largely of persons of Appalachian origin. For example, Cincinnati's Over-the-Rhine and Chicago's Uptown are areas in which newly arrived low-income persons from central Appalachia have traditionally settled.[10] There is a relatively high proportion of first- and second-generation Appalachians who now live in midwestern cities. In Columbus, for example, about 30 percent of the population has been so classified.[11] Similar percentages for the Ohio cities of Cincinnati, Middletown, Hamilton, and Cleveland were 15, 50, 60, and 13, respectively. In all, one source estimated that in 1980 somewhere between three and eight million central and southern Appalachians resided outside the mountain region.[12]

In the 1950s the outmigration from Appalachia accelerated. This was not, however, "an isolated phenomenon, but part of a national pattern. In the decade 1950–1960, the shift of population from farm to city appears to have been dramatically accelerated throughout the nation, and marginal farming areas, where poverty is chronic, have contributed heavily to the flow of migrants. [Also] mechanization of the mining industry, together with a decline in the market for coal, has brought about severe unemployment in the nation's mining communities."[13] The region has a large share of counties that depend on coal or farming, and these suffered the heaviest losses. Individuals and families continued to leave for the metropolitan areas and industrial employment opportunities. And because of networks of familiarity that had been established earlier, migrants continued to move to cities about which they had knowledge and in which they most likely had family or friends. Thus, outmigration streams were very specific. In fact, "there has been an obvious tendency for the streams to continue from the same places to the same destinations once the streams have been initiated. . . . Entire families from certain hollows have migrated to the same neighborhoods, even to particular streets in the metropolitan areas, as did relatives and friends in the past."[14]

## Migration: 1960–1970

The 1950s and earlier decades were periods of net migration loss, but the outmigration slowed down considerably in the 1960s (Table 5.5). In fact, if only the 100 or so counties in the 445-county region that had gained metropolitan status by 1977 are considered, then we find a part of Appalachia that actually gained population through migration in the 1960s. Clearly, differences between the 1950s and 1960s are quite significant. In the 1960s, many of the people moving to metropolitan Appalachia counties were coming from nearby rural counties.

Between 1965 and 1970, for example, the Appalachian Regional Commission reported that 1.65 million persons left their region but 1.25 million moved into the region.[15] Many of these migrants were persons returning from the same cities they had moved to years before. The importance of this "return migration" is suggested by the fact that 14 percent of all U.S. migration between 1955 and 1960 was return migration. Furthermore, in states with histories of substantial outmigration (as in Appalachia), over one-third of the inmigrants were return migrants.[16] Some returnees had been successful and came back to their origins, while others had met with little success. Although many returned in part because of ties to their places of origin, one study that examined return migration from Cincinnati to eastern Kentucky found that "the primary reason for the decision to return was the migrant's inability to obtain satisfactory employment in the city."[17]

Three State Economic Areas (SEAs), as defined by the Census Bureau, have been selected to illustrate more specifically the characteristics of return migration, as well as the magnitude and directions of the migration

TABLE 5.5
Net Migration, 1950-1970[1]

| Area | Number of Counties | Net Migration (Percent) 1950-60 | 1960-70 |
|---|---|---|---|
| Rural | 327 | -17.6 | -7.2 |
| Urban | 102 | -3.8 | 3.2 |
| Total | 429[2] | -14.3 | -4.7 |

Source: 1950, 1960, and 1970 Census of Population

[1]Net migration figures are averages of counties.

[2]Sixteen counties with independent cities in Virginia not included.

streams from, and to, each of these areas between 1965 and 1970.[18] The three SEAs selected are all rural-oriented, and all experienced net outmigration in the 1965–1970 period. State Economic Areas entirely within the Appalachian portions of North Carolina, Kentucky, and Pennsylvania have been chosen to illustrate something of the differences and similarities of their migration characteristics.

***North Carolina SEA 1.*** This SEA includes 16 counties in the extreme western portion of the state, all located entirely within the Blue Ridge Province. The area is one of considerable natural beauty and is therefore an area where tourism is highly significant to the local economy. Because the major tourist season occurs in the summer months, tourist-related employment is seasonal. The Great Smoky Mountains National Park and such summer resort centers as Blowing Rock and Highlands are located within the SEA. Boone, the county seat of Watauga County and the location of Appalachian State University, is the largest town. Even given the area's natural attractiveness, the SEA experienced net outmigration between 1965 and 1970. During that period some 34,413 persons left the SEA, and 30,644 migrated into the area; thus, there was a net migration loss of 3,769 persons. Gross migration totaled 65,057 persons, or nearly 23 percent of the 1970 population of 283,384. Most of the migration involved movement from or to nearby states (Table 5.6). Thus, over 44 percent of the outmigrants went to other SEAs in North Carolina, and nearly 44 percent of the inmigrants came from other SEAs within the state. Other southeastern states contributed most of the balance of inmigrants and outmigrants. There were seven SEAs that had at least 1,000 migrants who either arrived in, or departed from, North Carolina SEA 1 between 1965 and 1970. These seven SEAs accounted for 34 percent of the inmigration and 39 percent of the area's outmigration. Not surprisingly, adjacent metropolitan Asheville (North Carolina SEA A) was the leading origin and destination, and it was followed by five other North Carolina SEAs, including four that were rural and one—Charlotte—that was urban. Atlanta (Georgia SEA B) was also a favorite destination for migrants from western North Carolina. Atlanta, the Southeast's largest metropolitan area, has been an attractive destination for many migrants, as indicated by the fact that Atlanta was the single leading destination for southern Appalachian migrants in the 1965–1970 period. Over 46,000 migrants moved to Atlanta from forty-three southern Appalachian SEAs. After Atlanta, the leading destinations were Washington, D.C. (29,605 migrants), Detroit (24,387), Birmingham (22,633), Knoxville (16,680), and Chicago (15,357).[19]

***Kentucky SEA 9.*** A 14-county area in the Appalachian Plateaus Province, part of the southern Appalachian coalfield, makes up this SEA. Bituminous-coal mining is the dominant economic activity. The major towns of the area are Pikeville, Hazard, and Middlesboro (the largest). Middlesboro was established in the late nineteenth century by an English corporation and was ultimately supposed to become the Pittsburgh of central Appalachia, based on its coal. The counties of

TABLE 5.6
Leading State and State Economic Area Origins and Destinations of Migrants for North Carolina SEA 1, 1965-1970[1]

| Leading States or SEAs of Origin or Destination[2] | Outmigrants | | Inmigrants | |
|---|---|---|---|---|
| | Number | Percentage of Total | Number | Percentage of Total |
| North Carolina | 15,195 | 44.2 | 13,406 | 43.7 |
| Georgia | 3,048 | 8.9 | 1,795 | 5.9 |
| South Carolina | 2,771 | 8.1 | 1,901 | 6.2 |
| Florida | 2,057 | 6.0 | 2,716 | 8.9 |
| Tennessee | 1,895 | 5.5 | 1,156 | 3.8 |
| Virginia | 1,893 | 5.5 | 1,778 | 5.8 |
| Total for States | 26,859 | 78.2 | 22,752 | 74.3 |
| N.C. SEA A (Asheville) | 2,853 | 8.3 | 2,755 | 9.0 |
| N.C. SEA 2 | 2,814 | 8.2 | 1,625 | 5.3 |
| N.C. SEA 4 | 2,193 | 6.4 | 2,162 | 7.1 |
| N.C. SEA 5 | 1,674 | 4.9 | 1,623 | 5.3 |
| Ga. SEA B (Atlanta) | 1,317 | 3.8 | 662 | 2.2 |
| N.C. SEA D (Charlotte) | 1,296 | 3.8 | 771 | 2.5 |
| N.C. SEA 3 | 1,214 | 3.5 | 890 | 2.9 |
| Total for SEAs | 13,361 | 38.9 | 10,488 | 34.3 |

Source: U.S. Bureau of the Census, U.S. Census of Population: 1970, Subject Reports, Final Report PC (2) -2E, Migration Between State Economic Areas (Washington, D.C.: G.P.O., 1972).

[1]Includes Alleghany, Ashe, Avery, Cherokee, Clay, Graham, Haywood, Henderson, Jackson, Macon, Madison, Mitchell, Swain, Transylvania, Watauga, and Yancey counties.

[2]Only states and SEAs with at least 1,000 outmigrants or inmigrants are included.

eastern Kentucky have traditionally had among the lowest per capita incomes and educational levels in the United States. Employment, and the area's economy in general, has been largely dependent upon the vagaries of the coal industry. In the 1960s, many more people, especially young adults, were leaving the area than were arriving, because of the lack of opportunities in coal and related industries. Between 1965 and 1970, 52,767 migrants left the SEA and 24,598 arrived for a net loss of 28,169. Gross migration amounted to 77,365 persons, or about 23 percent of the 1970 population of 324,124. Many of the migrants from these eastern Kentucky counties moved to the large metropolitan areas (and, it was hoped, to jobs) of Ohio, Michigan, Indiana, and Illinois (Table 5.7). In fact, these four states accounted for over one-half of all outmigrants (and 46 percent of all inmigrants). Detroit, Chicago, and the Ohio cities of Dayton, Cincinnati, and Columbus were the leading metropolitan destinations, along with Lexington and Louisville within the state. Many of these outmigrants were continuing the pattern of moving to areas where friends and families had earlier ventured. This is suggested by the origins of those who migrated to eastern Kentucky between 1965 and 1970; the percentage distributions are similar to those

TABLE 5.7
Leading State and State Economic Area Origins and Destinations of Migrants for Kentucky SEA 9, 1965-1970[1]

| Leading States or SEAs of Origin or Destination[2] | Outmigrants | | Inmigrants | |
|---|---|---|---|---|
| | Number | Percentage of Total | Number | Percentage of Total |
| Kentucky | 13,278 | 25.2 | 5,978 | 24.3 |
| Ohio | 11,955 | 22.7 | 5,613 | 22.8 |
| Indiana | 6,801 | 12.9 | 1,756 | 7.1 |
| Michigan | 6,121 | 11.6 | 2,168 | 8.8 |
| Virginia | 2,049 | 3.9 | 1,292 | 5.3 |
| Illinois | 1,959 | 3.7 | 1,880 | 7.6 |
| Tennessee | 1,934 | 3.7 | 1,001 | 4.1 |
| Florida | 1,446 | 2.7 | 694 | 2.8 |
| West Virginia | 1,163 | 2.2 | 1,568 | 6.4 |
| Total for States | 46,706 | 88.6 | 21,950 | 89.2 |
| Mich. SEA F (Detroit) | 4,229 | 8.0 | 1,581 | 6.4 |
| Ky. SEA 8 | 2,849 | 5.4 | 1,529 | 6.2 |
| Ky. SEA 6 | 2,603 | 4.9 | 740 | 3.0 |
| Ohio SEA C (Dayton) | 2,430 | 4.6 | 931 | 3.8 |
| Ky. SEA E (Lexington) | 2,094 | 4.0 | 739 | 3.0 |
| Ohio SEA K (Cincinnati) | 1,789 | 3.4 | 1,147 | 4.7 |
| Ky. SEA A (Louisville) | 1,477 | 2.8 | 779 | 3.2 |
| Ill. SEA C (Chicago) | 1,312 | 2.5 | 1,714 | 7.0 |
| Ky. SEA 3 | 1,213 | 2.3 | 596 | 2.4 |
| Ohio SEA 3 | 1,194 | 2.3 | 356 | 1.4 |
| Ohio SEA B (Columbus) | 1,140 | 2.2 | 667 | 2.7 |
| Ind. SEA D (Indianapolis) | 1,044 | 2.0 | 286 | 1.2 |
| Tenn. SEA 8 | 1,002 | 1.9 | 400 | 1.6 |
| Total for SEAs | 24,376 | 46.3 | 11,465 | 46.6 |

Source: U.S. Bureau of the Census, U.S. Census of Population: 1970, Subject Reports, Final Report PC (2) -2E, Migration Between State Economic Areas (Washington, D.C.: G.P.O., 1972).

[1]Includes Bell, Breathitt, Boyd, Harlan, Johnson, Knott, Knox, Leslie, Letcher, McCreary, Martin, Perry, Pike, and Whitley counties.

[2]Only states and SEAs with at least 1,000 outmigrants or immigrants are included.

for destinations, and certainly the inmigrants included a substantial percentage of persons who were returning to their origins.

***Pennsylvania SEA 6.*** This SEA includes 7 counties in the eastern part of the state, 5 of which are a part of Pennsylvania's anthracite region. In this area anthracite was, until about 1930, an industry of expanding production and increasing job opportunities. Since that time it has been characterized by dwindling output and declining employment, and by 1960 the anthracite industry had become insignificant as a source of employment.[20] The major towns of these anthracite counties include Pottsville (the largest), Shamokin, Mount Carmel, Shenandoah, and Frackville. The SEA also includes Monroe and Pike counties, both of which border New Jersey. These counties are noted for winter and summer tourist activities associated with the scenic Pocono Mountains, such as skiing. Unlike the five anthracite counties in the SEA, these two counties gained population through inmigration during the 1960s (refer to Figure 5.2). Nevertheless, the SEA experienced a net migration loss of 10,834 persons between 1965 and 1970. The 31,174 inmigrants were more than offset by the 42,008 outmigrants. The gross migration of 73,182 represented nearly 17 percent of the SEA's 1970 population. As was the case with the previous two SEAs, most outmigrants (and inmigrants) went to (or came from) nearby SEAs. Thus, nearly 58 percent of all outmigrants and 55 percent of inmigrants went to other Pennsylvania SEAs (Table 5.8). Note, however, that these percentages are markedly higher than comparable figures for the North Carolina and Kentucky SEAs previously discussed. Pennsylvania SEA 6 is surrounded by metropolitan areas; this is reflected in the specific migrant destinations

TABLE 5.8
Leading State and State Economic Area Origins and Destinations of Migrants for Pennsylvania SEA 6, 1965-1970[1]

| Leading States or SEAs of Origin or Destination[2] | Outmigrants | | Inmigrants | |
|---|---|---|---|---|
| | Number | Percentage of Total | Number | Percentage of Total |
| Pennsylvania | 24,178 | 57.6 | 17,162 | 55.1 |
| New Jersey | 2,797 | 6.7 | 3,740 | 12.0 |
| New York | 2,007 | 4.8 | 3,708 | 11.9 |
| Florida | 1,686 | 4.0 | 427 | 1.4 |
| Maryland | 1,415 | 3.4 | 728 | 2.3 |
| California | 1,228 | 2.9 | 455 | 1.5 |
| Virginia | 1,111 | 2.6 | 364 | 1.2 |
| Total for States | 34,422 | 82.0 | 26,584 | 85.4 |
| Pa. SEA B (Philadelphia) | 5,711 | 13.6 | 3,818 | 12.2 |
| Pa. SEA M (Allentown) | 3,759 | 8.9 | 2,787 | 8.9 |
| Pa. SEA 4 | 2,486 | 5.9 | 2,046 | 6.6 |
| Pa. SEA G (Wilkes-Barre) | 2,395 | 5.7 | 2,017 | 6.5 |
| Pa. SEA H (Harrisburg) | 2,392 | 5.7 | 1,345 | 4.3 |
| Pa. SEA L (Reading) | 1,829 | 4.4 | 765 | 2.5 |
| Pa. SEA 3 | 1,210 | 2.9 | 909 | 2.9 |
| N.J. SEA 1 | 1,030 | 2.5 | 1,267 | 4.1 |
| Pa. SEA K (Lancaster) | 1,019 | 2.4 | 426 | 1.4 |
| N.Y. SEA G (New York City) | 686 | 1.6 | 2,003 | 6.4 |
| Total for SEAs | 22,517 | 53.6 | 17,383 | 55.8 |

Source: U.S. Bureau of the Census, U.S. Census of Population: 1970, Subject Reports, Final Report PC (2) -2E, Migration Between State Economic Areas (Washington, D.C.: G.P.O., 1972).

[1] Includes Carbon, Columbia, Monroe, Montour, Northumberland, Pike, and Schuylkill counties.

[2] Only states and SEAs with at least 1,000 outmigrants or inmigrants are included.

and origins. Over two-fifths of the outmigrants went to such metropolitan areas, and over one-third of the inmigrants came from the same areas. Philadelphia was both the leading origin and destination.

In summary, there are both similarities and differences among the migration patterns of the three rural SEAs examined. First, in all areas there was a relationship between migration and distance; that is, most migrants tended to go to (or come from) places relatively nearby. This seems most pronounced, however, for Pennsylvania SEA 6 and least marked for Kentucky SEA 9. A combination of very limited employment opportunities in eastern Kentucky and the perception that such opportunities existed in midwestern metropolitan areas in the 1960s certainly is a part of the explanation for the large movement to more distant destinations. The fact that family and friends already resided in such cities was also an important incentive.[21] Second, the "streams and counterstreams" notion first stated by Ravenstein and later discussed by Lee and others is certainly in evidence for all three areas.[22] A comparison of the percentages of outmigrants and inmigrants to or from each SEA clearly supports these data. When (and if) published data become available for migration between SEAs for 1975 to 1980, a period of inmigration for most southern and central Appalachian areas, then the origins of these inmigrants will most likely be very similar to the outmigration streams and patterns of earlier periods.

### Migration: 1970–1980

As has already been noted, most of the region experienced a migration reversal during the 1970s. Reasons for this reversal are still somewhat speculative. In the early 1970s the Appalachian Regional Commission recognized the beginnings of the population turnaround in the region and suggested a number of factors that were believed to have contributed to these trends. These included returning service personnel, the impact of development programs such as ARC sponsorship of new and improved highways, the increase in social security and black-lung damage payments, higher unemployment rates and housing shortages in cities, the growth of employment in the region, and the growth of recreation and retirement homes.[23] Other, more recent studies have suggested that the turnaround and especially the high gains in the nonmetropolitan counties of the region can be related to industrial growth and, more specifically, to the growth of nontraditional kinds of industries that require greater investment and skill levels (like machinery and chemicals rather than textiles). Additionally, gains are attributed to the development of retirement and recreation-oriented communities, to the preference by many to reside in nonmetropolitan areas, to kinship ties, and to rapidly rising unemployment in many northern cities.[24] The population turnaround is also related to greatly improved accessibility to both metropolitan counties, which have jobs, and nonmetropolitan counties, which have homes, within the region.

## SOCIOECONOMIC CHARACTERISTICS

### Income Characteristics

An essay on development in the Appalachian region would be incomplete without an examination of regional income characteristics. Until spatial variations in income are known, it would be difficult to suggest an economic planning or policy strategy for regional development.

Recent evaluations of the economic condition in Appalachia have almost uniformly reported improvement. For example, a 1973 report by the Appalachian Regional Commission stated that "the incidence of poverty as defined by the Social Security Administration declined from 31 percent of the population in 1960 to 18 percent in 1970. Although the incidence of poverty in the region remains higher than the 1970 national average of 14 percent, the rate of decline in population living in poverty was more rapid in Appalachia in the last decade than the average national experience."[25] Whereas there is little question that there has been absolute improvement throughout the region, trends indicate that many areas of the Appalachian region are still well below national levels. Between 1949 and 1969, for example, median incomes of families and unrelated individuals for the entire region rose from $2,281 to $8,378, or by 267 percent. It is important to note that national medians for the same twenty-year period increased from $2,619 to $9,590, or by 266 percent—essentially the same as the regional increase. Within the region median income levels varied widely. The 36 Appalachian counties in Kentucky, traditionally the region's poorest state, had a median income of only $1,392 in 1949. Twenty years later this had increased to $4,928, an increase of 254 percent, below both the national and regional averages. In 1969 the median income for Appalachian Kentucky was only 1 percent of the national figure. West Virginia, which like Kentucky is a central Appalachian state heavily dependent on coal mining, experienced the lowest percentage increase in median income between 1949 and 1969: from $2,335 to $7,128, or 205 percent. The only other Appalachian state where median incomes increased by less than the national and regional medians was Pennsylvania. Median incomes in that state rose from $2,743 to $9,073, or by 231 percent. In contrast, Georgia's median income increased from $1,963 in 1949 to $9,275 in 1969, a percentage increase of 372 percent, the region's highest. In the case of Georgia the most dramatic increases occurred in the suburban counties of the Atlanta metropolitan area. Median incomes in Forsyth County, for example, increased from $548 in 1949 to $7,381 in 1969, or by over 1,200 percent! This represents the highest percentage increase for the entire region.[26]

Examination of another income variable, per capita money income, for the more recent eight-year period 1969 to 1977 (the latest period for which information is available) reveals trends both similar to and dissimilar from the earlier twenty-year period. The 1969 and 1977 per capita money-income figures are the estimated amounts per person of total money income received during the respective calendar year.[27] For the United States the 1969 figure was $3,119; in 1977 it had increased to $5,751, or by 84.4 percent. The figures for the Appalachian region were $2,659 in 1969 and $5,086 in 1977, an increase of 91.3 percent.[28] Thus, the regional income was 85.3 percent of the U.S. average in 1969 and increased to 88.4 percent of the average by 1977. In short, the regional gain between 1969 and 1977 was only slightly greater than that of the nation.

There were wide variations in income throughout the Appalachian region in 1977 (Figure 5.4). Per capita money incomes ranged from a low of $2,262 in Clay County, Kentucky, to the regional high of $7,214 in DeKalb County, Georgia, or from 39.3 percent to 125.4 percent of the U.S. average. Only 29 of the 445 Appalachian counties had income averages above that of the nation, and all but 4 of those were a part of a Standard Metropolitan Statistical Area in 1977. The 4 counties included 3 within commuting distance of major metropolitan areas (Sussex in New Jersey and Clarke and Fauquier in northern Virginia) and Albemarle County in Virginia, where Charlottesville and the University of Virginia are located. On the other hand, 224 counties, or 50 percent of all counties, had per capita money incomes less than 75 percent of the national average. Of these, 94 counties had incomes less than two-thirds of the U.S. average. The poorest counties were located in West Virginia, Kentucky, Tennessee, northeast Georgia, rural Piedmont Georgia and South Carolina, extreme western North Carolina, western Virginia, and rural Piedmont Virginia. Comparison of Figure 5.4 with appropriate maps in other chapters suggests that Appalachia's poorest counties are located in the central and southern portion of the region and/or are counties whose economies have been dependent upon either coal mining (especially in the Plateaus) or farming (especially in the Piedmont).

Significant income gains were made throughout most of Appalachia between 1969 and 1977 (Figure 5.5). Only 71 Appalachian counties had a percentage money-income increase below the national average of 84.4 percent. These counties were confined almost entirely to the northern states of New York and Pennsylvania and to scattered nonmetropolitan counties in Georgia. Appalachia's 2 poorest states, Kentucky and West Virginia, experienced the largest gains in per capita money income, 119.1 percent and 107.9 percent, respectively. It should be remembered that these states also had incomes still well below the national average. The resurgence of coal production and the return of former Appalachian residents to eastern Kentucky, West Virginia, and southwestern Virginia were among the reasons for such income gains.

Appalachian counties in New York (64 percent increase), New Jersey (82.5 percent), Pennsylvania (86.5 percent), Maryland (87.3 percent), Ohio (89.4 percent), and Georgia (90.5 percent) had the lowest money-income gains between 1969 and 1977. There were, of course, exceptions

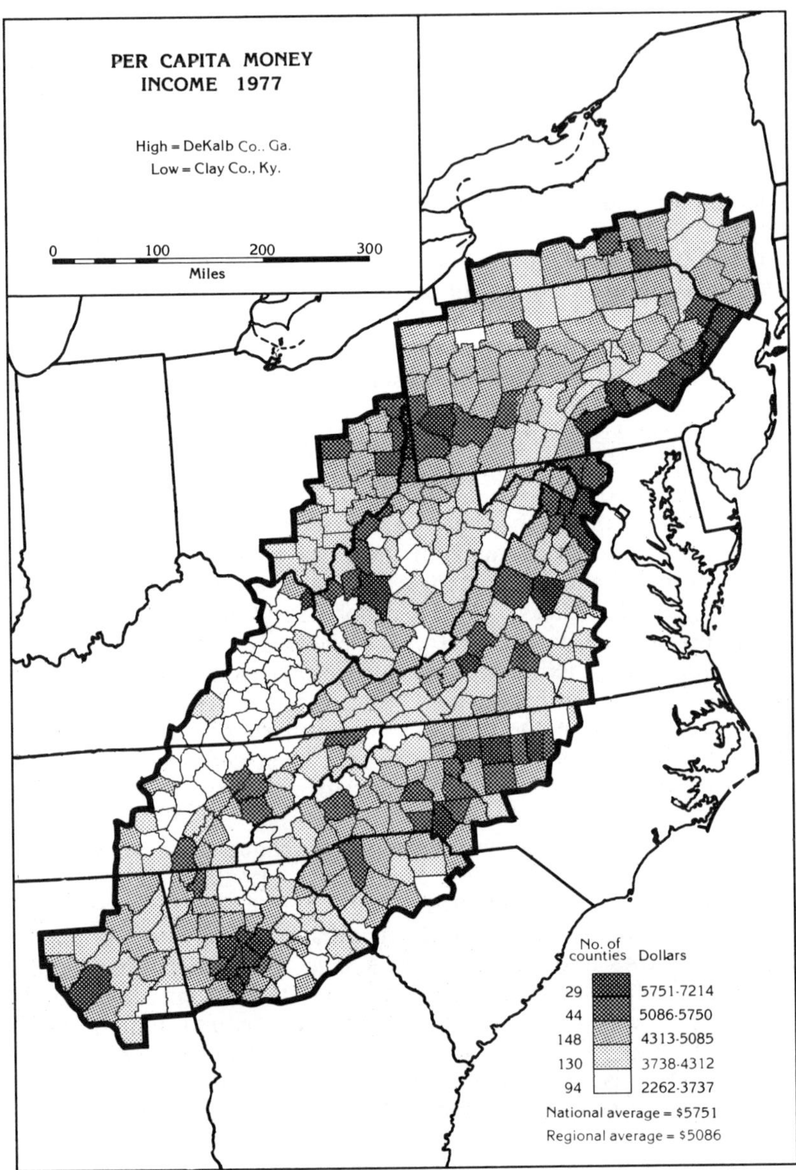
PER CAPITA MONEY
INCOME 1977
High = DeKalb Co., Ga.
Low = Clay Co., Ky.
0
100
200
300
Miles
No. of counties
Dollars
29
5751-7214
44
5086-5750
148
4313-5085
130
3738-4312
94
2262-3737
National average = $5751
Regional average = $5086

**Figure 5.4**

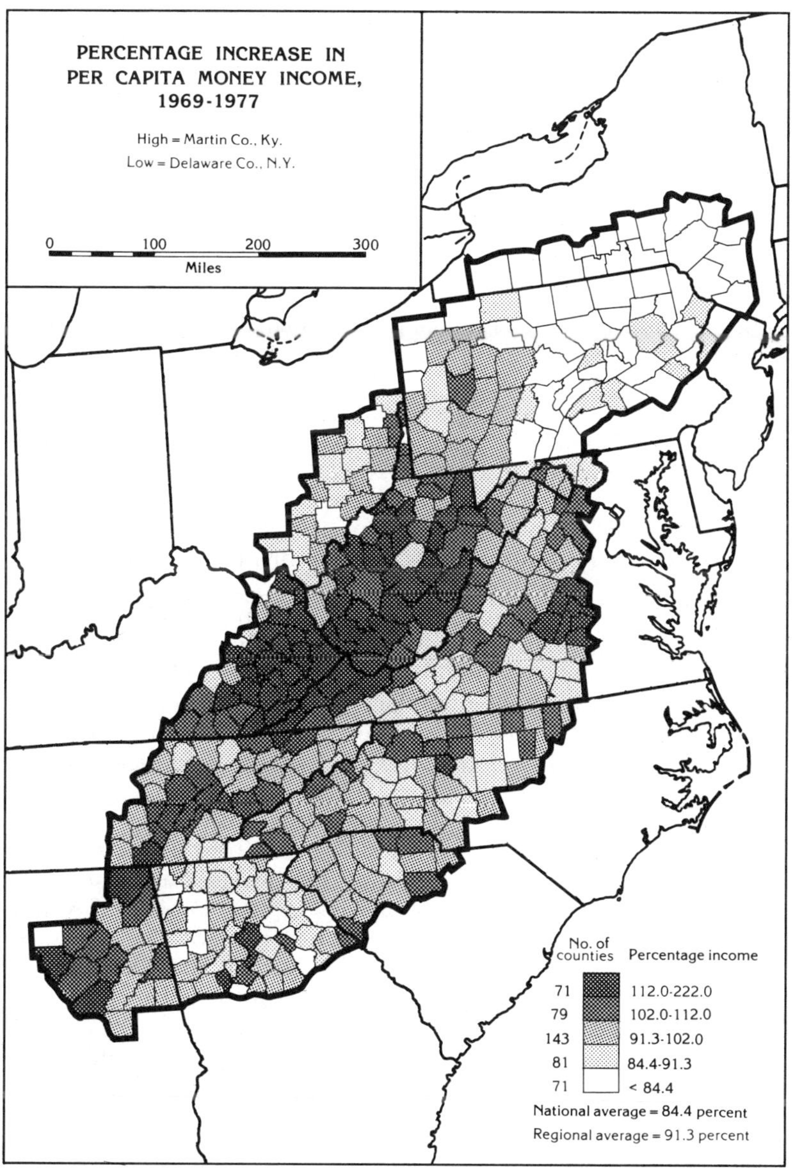
PERCENTAGE INCREASE IN
PER CAPITA MONEY INCOME,
1969-1977
High = Martin Co., Ky.
Low = Delaware Co., N.Y.
0
100
200
300
Miles
No. of counties
Percentage income
71
112.0-222.0
79
102.0-112.0
143
91.3-102.0
81
84.4-91.3
71
< 84.4
National average = 84.4 percent
Regional average = 91.3 percent

**Figure 5.5**

in some of these states. In Georgia, a number of the suburban Atlanta counties (Fayette, Forsyth, Gwinnett, and Henry) had major income gains. And in Ohio, most of the counties along the Ohio River corridor experienced gains well above the national average. On the other hand, not one county in Appalachian New York State had an income gain above the national average, and Delaware County, New York, witnessed a gain of only 55.2 percent, the lowest in the entire region.

## Educational Levels

At least partly responsible for the low incomes in some of the region (especially in the south and central portions) have been the low educational levels of much of the Appalachian population. A comparison of income and educational levels immediately suggests a close correlation (compare Figure 5.6 and Figure 5.4). In Appalachia in 1970 the median number of school years completed by persons twenty-five years or older was 10.0, whereas the median for the nation was 12.2 years. Within the region, there were wide variations that ranged from a low of 7.5 years in Owsley County, Kentucky, to a high of 12.7 years in Tompkins County, New York, the location of Ithaca and Cornell University.

Areas with the highest educational levels included counties that were in metropolitan areas or within commuting distance of a major metropolitan area, had economies and populations dependent in large part on universities or other quaternary activities, and/or were located in northern Appalachia. Albemarle County in Virginia (University of Virginia), Centre County in Pennsylvania (Pennsylvania State University), Tompkins County in New York (Cornell University), Monongalia County in West Virginia (West Virginia University), Montgomery County in Virginia (Virginia Tech and Radford College), Coffee County in Tennessee (Arnold Engineering Development Center), and Anderson County in Tennessee (Oak Ridge) are all examples of counties heavily dependent on quaternary activities and therefore areas with a disproportionate share of individuals with high educational levels. The counties of northern Appalachia had uniformly high educational levels. Only 3 of the 104 counties in New York, Pennsylvania, New Jersey, Ohio, and Maryland had educational levels below the national median of 12.2 years. Thus, over half of the 200 counties in the region with 1970 educational levels above 10.0 years were located in northern Appalachia.

The lowest educational levels were in eastern Kentucky, southwest Virginia, portions of east Tennessee, northern Georgia, and the rural Piedmont areas of both Georgia and Virginia. Educational levels in West Virginia were generally at or above the regional average except in a few counties. The median educational level in 1970 for West Virginia's counties was 9.8 years, as compared to 9.3 years in Appalachian Tennessee and 8.5 years in eastern Kentucky. The populations of rural southern, and especially central, Appalachia remained among the most undereducated people in America.[29] In 1970 James Branscome wrote that "once they are educated and/or trained, Appalachia's young people move

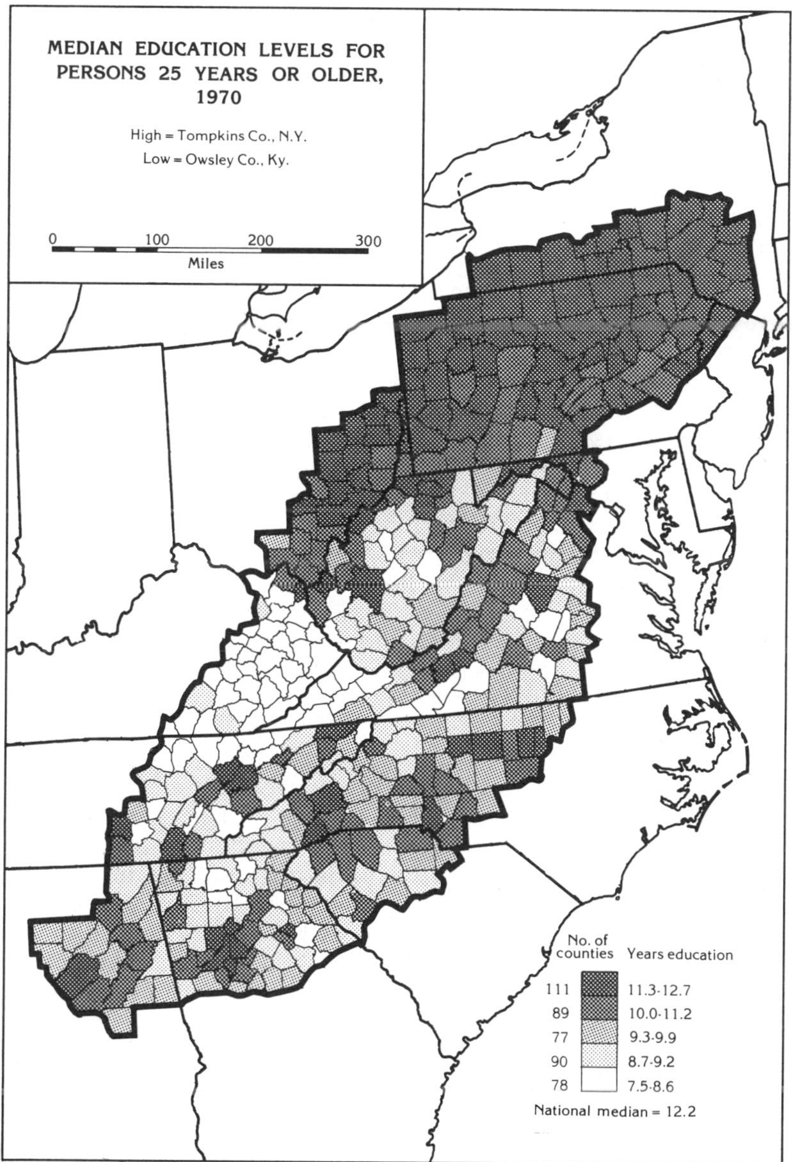
MEDIAN EDUCATION LEVELS FOR PERSONS 25 YEARS OR OLDER, 1970
High = Tompkins Co., N.Y.
Low = Owsley Co., Ky.
0
100
200
300
Miles
No. of counties
Years education
111
11.3-12.7
89
10.0-11.2
77
9.3-9.9
90
8.7-9.2
78
7.5-8.6
National median = 12.2

**Figure 5.6**

away because they believe that nothing can be done to change the way of life they are escaping. . . . In West Virginia, for instance 70 percent of the young people leave before they reach the age of twenty-four. . . . Of young, native Appalachian teachers, nearly 70 percent leave the region after four years of teaching."[30] It is to be hoped that the heavy return migration that occurred during the 1970s has brought back to the region these earlier outmigrants. For it is clear that "educational attainment is one of the most important indicators of human resource potential and a critical component in the development process."[31]

## RACIAL COMPOSITION

The stereotypical perceptions of Appalachia's racial, ethnolinguistic, and religious characteristics are that it is a generally homogeneous region made up almost wholly of white Protestants. As one textbook stated, "one major result of this combined lack of both plantation and urban development was that there was little addition to the early Scots-Irish, English, and German settlers. Appalachia remained overwhelmingly northwest European in ethnic background, and more and more conservative Protestant in religion."[32] Such statements are perhaps more appropriate for the southern and central portions of the region than they are for northern Appalachia. However, even in the southern portion of the region, recent changes in urbanization and migration patterns, as well as the earlier settlement of blacks, East Europeans, and others, suggest that care should be taken in making such generalizations.[33] The region's ethnic history and variation has been discussed in Chapters 3 and 4.

### The Black Population

In terms of racial groups, blacks accounted for the largest minority in the Appalachian region in 1980. The region's blacks numbered over 2.6 million, or 9.9 percent of the total population (compared to 11.7 percent in the United States). Two-thirds of the blacks in Appalachia lived in metropolitan areas, which is significantly higher than the 52 percent of the region's total population who resided in such areas. In addition to metropolitan counties, blacks also accounted for high percentages in the rural Piedmont counties (Figure 5.7), even though there has been a recent history of outmigration from this area as the agricultural economy (e.g., cotton) has declined.[34] The county with the highest percentage of blacks in the entire region—Taliaferro County in Georgia, with nearly 65 percent—is in the Piedmont. This same county also experienced heavy outmigration in *both* the 1960s and the 1970s. In 1980 110 counties in the region had black percentages above the regional average, and nearly all of these counties were located in the southern Piedmont or were adjacent to it. Outside of this area only a few counties had above-average percentages. They included Allegheny County, Pennsylvania (Pittsburgh); Dauphin County, Pennsylvania (Harrisburg); Ham-

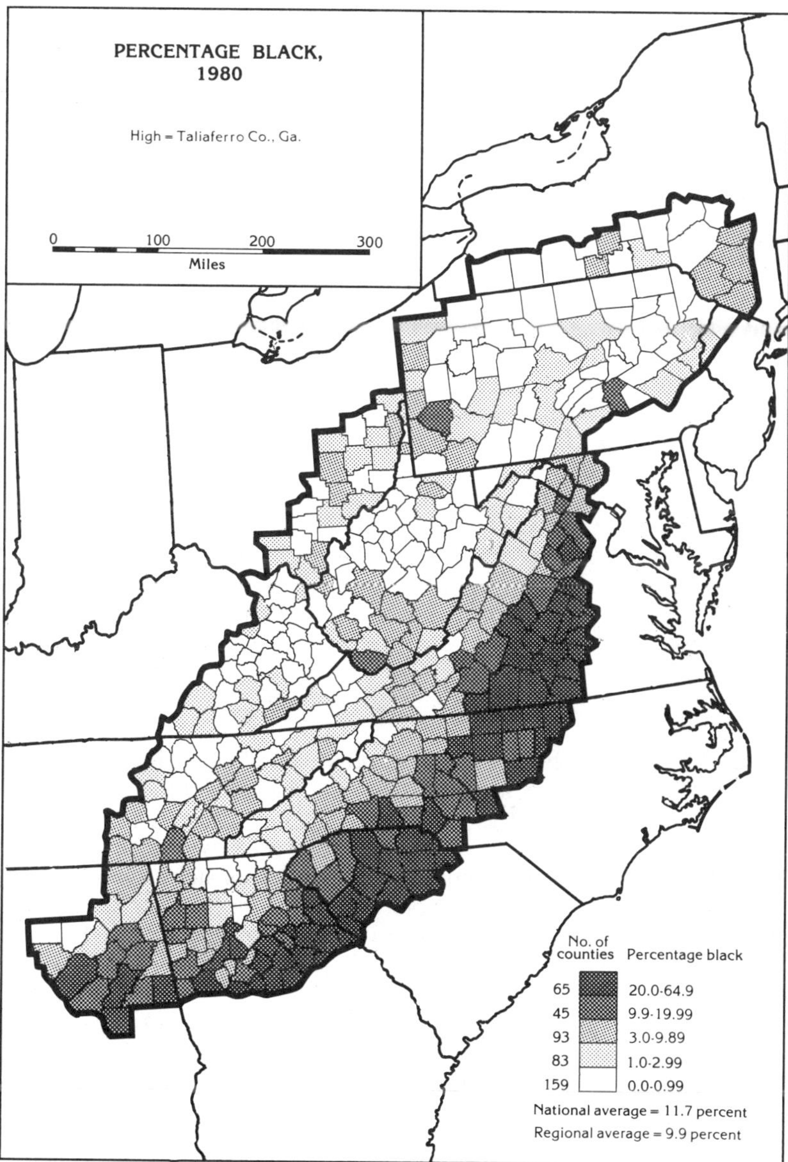
PERCENTAGE BLACK,
1980
High = Taliaferro Co., Ga.
0
100
200
300
Miles
No. of counties
Percentage black
65
20.0-64.9
45
9.9-19.99
93
3.0-9.89
83
1.0-2.99
159
0.0-0.99
National average = 11.7 percent
Regional average = 9.9 percent

**Figure 5.7**

ilton County, Tennessee (Chattanooga); and McDowell County in extreme southern West Virginia. This latter county and other southern West Virginia coal-mining counties have had a history of inmigration since about the 1890s, when both blacks and foreign immigrants were seduced into the coalfields by employment opportunities. Sparsely populated West Virginia had a need for workers as the coal industry expanded, and by 1907 some 35 percent of the mining labor force of this part of West Virginia was black (compared to 17.5 percent for the entire state).[35] Taken together, workers of foreign origin and blacks constituted 79 percent of the mining labor force of southern West Virginia in 1907. Although the percentages have declined since that time, blacks still are a highly significant component of the area's population.

The proportion of blacks in Appalachia in 1980 (9.9 percent) was greater than that in 1970 (9.3 percent), thus the black population gained at a more rapid pace than did the total Appalachian population.[36] Indeed, the black population increased from 2,225,506 in 1970 to 2,608,441 in 1980, or by 17.2 percent (recall that the total regional population increase was 12.3 percent) (Figure 5.8). Blacks in Appalachian urban areas increased from 1,415,667 to 1,720,555, or by 21.5 percent (compared to 10.2 percent for the total regional population), whereas those residents in rural counties numbered 809,839 in 1970 and 887,886 in 1980, an increase of only 9.6 percent (15.8 percent for the region). These figures, of course, imply black outmigration from the nonmetropolitan counties and inmigration to the metropolitan counties. Thus, recent black population changes are dissimilar from the white population changes of the 1970s.

There were some notable exceptions to the general pattern of rapid population increases in metropolitan counties. SMSAs that experienced either an absolute decline of black population or net black outmigration between 1970 and 1980 included Pittsburgh (3.4 percent increase), Altoona (−2.6 percent), Johnstown (−3.1 percent), Charleston (6.6 percent), and Wheeling (0.9 percent), all in Pennsylvania or West Virginia. Those 2 states, along with the Appalachian portions of Kentucky, Ohio, Virginia, and Alabama, experienced either black population declines or only small percentage increases between 1970 and 1980. The figures were 9.1 percent for Alabama (288,971 in 1970 to 315,223 in 1980), 8.4 percent in Virginia (244,738 to 265,248), 7.6 percent for Pennsylvania (245,023 to 263,673), 5.1 percent for Ohio (23,375 to 24,572), −2.9 percent for Kentucky (8,780 to 8,528), and −3.4 percent in West Virginia (67,340 to 65,051). Conversely, the states with the fastest growing black populations were Georgia (34.9 percent; from 476,749 in 1970 to 643,370 in 1980) and North Carolina (18.8 percent; 500,539 to 594,678). Georgia's rapid growth enabled it to surpass North Carolina during the 1970s and become the Appalachian state with the largest black population. This was in part because of the attraction of Atlanta as an inmigrant destination for blacks. The Atlanta metropolitan area's black population increased by nearly 45 percent, from 344,808 in 1970 to 498,821 in 1980. Over

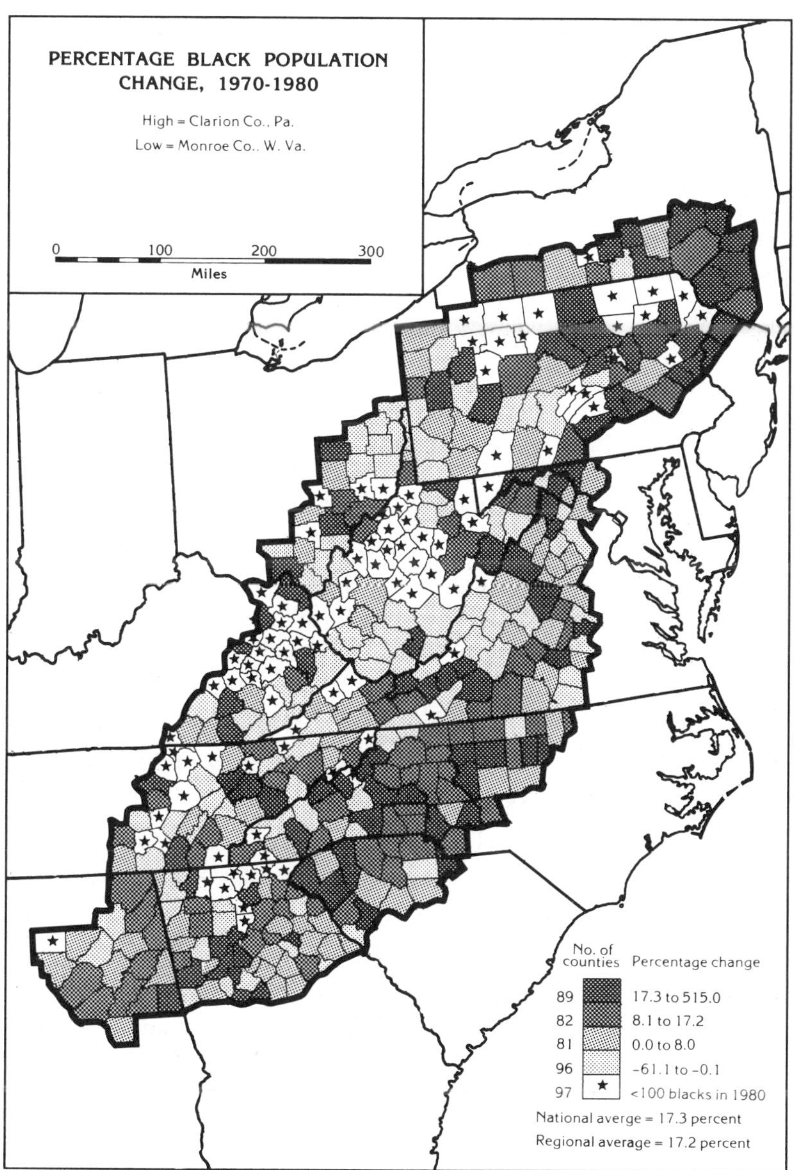
PERCENTAGE BLACK POPULATION
CHANGE, 1970-1980
High = Clarion Co., Pa.
Low = Monroe Co., W. Va.
0
100
200
300
Miles
No. of counties
Percentage change
89
17.3 to 515.0
82
8.1 to 17.2
81
0.0 to 8.0
96
-61.1 to -0.1
97
<100 blacks in 1980
National averge = 17.3 percent
Regional average = 17.2 percent

**Figure 5.8**

87 percent of the total black population in 1980 was concentrated in just two of Atlanta's metropolitan counties, Fulton and DeKalb. Fulton County, with 303,509 blacks in 1980, was the single most populous county in the entire region. At the other extreme, Forsyth County, a part of suburban Atlanta, had a black population that numbered one resident in 1980.

### Other Racial/Ethnic Groups

Other racial groups in Appalachia, though locally or historically important, were few relative to the total population. American Indians numbered 37,219 (0.1 percent of the total regional population) in the 445-county region in 1980. Of the total, 57 percent lived in rural counties and 43 percent were found in the metropolitan areas. This represents a change since 1960, when 77 percent of the region's 8,287 Indians lived in rural counties. The Appalachian state with the largest Indian population was North Carolina, where one-third of the group, mostly Cherokee, resided.[37] Only 7 counties in the region had populations that included at least 1 percent Indian, and 4 of those were in western North Carolina, the heartland of the Cherokee Nation (Table 5.9). In addition to having the highest percentage of Indians in 1980, Swain County also had the greatest number.

Much more recent additions to the region's racial groups are persons of East Asia origin, and in 1980 this group numbered 84,092 (0.3 percent of the regional total). Nearly two-thirds of this group resided in metropolitan areas. The largest numbers were concentrated in central city counties. Allegheny County, Pennsylvania (Pittsburgh) led all counties with 7,737 Asians. It was followed by DeKalb County, Georgia (Atlanta) with 4,633; Fulton County, Georgia (Atlanta) with 2,926; and Mecklenburg County, North Carolina (Charlotte) with 2,804. Other important concentrations of peoples of Asian origin were to be found in nonmetropolitan counties with large universities; presumably Asian professionals were residing there. Only 4 counties in the region had populations that were at least 1 percent Asian, and all were counties with major universities (Tompkins County, New York; Centre County, Pennsylvania; Montgomery County, Virginia; and Monongalia County, West Virginia).

Although not racially distinct from the majority of Appalachians, another new ethnic group has also altered the cultural composition of Appalachia. In 1980 persons of Spanish origin numbered 210,300, or 0.8 percent of the total population. Of the total, nearly 55 percent lived in metropolitan counties. Pennsylvania, with 54,948 persons of Spanish origin (26 percent of the regional total), led all Appalachian states. And in Pennsylvania over 81 percent resided in metropolitan counties. Pennsylvania was followed by Georgia (31,144), New York (26,196), and North Carolina (24,827). Whereas the largest number of people of Spanish origin was in the most populous metropolitan counties, several nonmetropolitan counties also had large numbers (Table 5.10). Indeed,

TABLE 5.9
Appalachian Counties With At Least 1 Percent American Indian Population, 1980

| County | State | Percentage of County Total | Number of Indians |
|---|---|---|---|
| Swain | North Carolina | 24.3 | 2,502 |
| Jackson | North Carolina | 9.3 | 2,412 |
| Graham | North Carolina | 5.3 | 379 |
| Cattaraugus | New York | 1.9 | 1,649 |
| Lumpkin | Georgia | 1.5 | 161 |
| York | South Carolina | 1.2 | 1,254 |
| Cherokee | North Carolina | 1.0 | 189 |

Source: 1980 Census of Population

TABLE 5.10
Appalachian Counties with People of Spanish Origin by Population Rank, 1980

| Rank | | | Total Number of Spanish Origin | County Total |
|---|---|---|---|---|
| *1. | Orange | New York | 11,260 | 4.3 |
| 2. | Berks | Pennsylvania | 9,013 | 2.9 |
| 3. | Allegheny | Pennsylvania | 8,175 | 0.6 |
| 4. | Fulton | Georgia | 7,574 | 1.3 |
| 5. | DeKalb | Georgia | 7,470 | 1.6 |
| 6. | Lehigh | Pennsylvania | 7,065 | 2.6 |
| 7. | Northampton | Pennsylvania | 7,059 | 3.1 |
| *8. | Ulster | New York | 4,931 | 3.1 |
| 9. | Jefferson | Alabama | 4,475 | 0.7 |
| 10. | Mecklenburg | North Carolina | 3,962 | 1.0 |

Source: 1980 Census of Population

*Nonmetropolitan counties

Orange County in New York's Catskill Mountains ranked first in the region.

In some of the remote valleys of east Tennessee and adjacent states there are small groups of people whose racial heritage is conjectured to be a mixture of Indian, black, and white. These people are identified by others as Melungeons. They apparently do not live in segregated communities although they comprise a limited number of families and are often identified as being part of the group by their surnames—Collins, Mullins, Gibson, Goins, Freeman, and Sexton. Some are farmers of long standing, owning their land. Others work as farm laborers or in urban industrial plants. Where coal mining is active, they may work in the mines, as in Wise County, Virginia, and Rhea County, Tennessee.

Edward Price, in examining census schedules, found that Melungeons appeared to have migrated westward into the mountains from a few Piedmont counties on the North Carolina and Virginia border, where a large mixed-blood population is thought to have existed about 1790.[38]

## SUMMARY

We have addressed a number of topics related to Appalachia's population that are particularly relevant to planning for the region's future. For example, we have examined the distribution of income and education in the region, topics basic to understanding of migration trends or to the development of plans and policies for the region. We have also examined population density, distribution, and growth trends in the context of both urban and rural areas. Thus, we have found that whereas Appalachia has become more urbanized since World War II, the recent trend of movement to nonmetropolitan counties has also been significant in the region. This examination of migration trends since World War II has also shown, as is true elsewhere, that the volume and direction of migration remains difficult to predict. Some migration characteristics, such as the predominance of short-distance movement and the importance of the stream and counterstream concept, are evident from analysis of the data and are helpful in estimating future population growth.

Perhaps most importantly, it has been demonstrated that there is significant spatial variation in all of the population characteristics examined: The Appalachia here defined is not homogeneous. The implication of this for the development of regional policy seems obvious. Plans and policies need to address such variations. In short, different strategies are appropriate for different parts of the region.

## NOTES

1. In 1980, the 397 counties of the Appalachian Regional Commission had a population of 20.2 million, or 8.9 percent of the U.S. total. See Jerome Pickard, "A Decade of Change for Appalachia, 1970–1980," *Appalachia* 14 (1981), pp. 1–9.

2. As used throughout this text the terms *metropolitan,* or *urban,* include the populations of all counties within the federal-government–defined Standard Metropolitan Statistical Areas as of December 1977. Briefly, to be included in an SMSA a county must have a central city with a population of fifty thousand or more or must be socially and economically integrated to such a county.

3. By June 1981 twelve new SMSAs (21 counties) had been added that were entirely in the region. These included Anderson, South Carolina; Athens, Georgia; Charlottesville, Virginia; Cumberland, Maryland/West Virginia; Danville, Virginia; Hagerstown, Maryland; Hickory, North Carolina; Newburgh-Middletown, New York; Rock Hill, South Carolina; Salisbury-Concord, North Carolina; and Sharon and State College, both in Pennsylvania.

4. Jerome Pickard, "Appalachia's Decade of Change—A Decade of Immigration," *Appalachia* 15 (1981), p. 24.

5. Gordon F. DeJong, *Appalachian Fertility Decline: Demographic and Sociological Analysis* (Lexington: University of Kentucky Press, 1968), p. 35.

6. See, for example, Peter A. Morrison and Judith P. Wheeler, "Rural Renaissance in America?" *Population Bulletin* 31 (1976), pp. 1–26. Wilbur Zelinsky, "Is Nonmetropolitan America Being Repopulated? The Evidence from Pennsylvania's Minor Civil Divisions," *Demography* 15 (1978), pp. 13–39, and Calvin L. Beale, *The Revival of Population Growth in Nonmetropolitan America,* Economic Research Service Pub. ERS-605 (Washington, D.C.: U.S. Dept. of Agriculture, 1975).

7. James S. Brown and George A. Hillery, Jr., "The Great Migration, 1940–1960," in Thomas R. Ford, ed., *The Southern Appalachian Region: A Survey* (Lexington: University of Kentucky Press, 1962), p. 59.

8. Ibid., p. 54.

9. Everett S. Lee, "A Theory of Migration," *Demography* 3 (1966), pp. 45–57.

10. There is a fairly substantial literature on Appalachians elsewhere. See, for example, William W. Philliber and Clyde B. McCoy, eds., *The Invisible Minority: Urban Appalachians* (Lexington: University Press of Kentucky, 1981); John D. Photiadis, *Social and Socialpsychological Characteristics of West Virginians in Their Own State and in Cleveland, Ohio* (Morgantown: West Virginia University, 1970); and Shane Davies and Gary L. Fowler, "The Disadvantaged Urban Migrant in Indianapolis," *Economic Geography* 48 (1972), pp. 153–167.

11. John Friedl, *Health Care Services and the Appalachian Migrant* (Columbus: Ohio State University, 1978), p. 44.

12. Dwight Billings and David Walls, "Appalachians," in Stephan Thernstrom, ed., *Harvard Encyclopedia of American Ethnic Groups* (Cambridge: Harvard University Press, 1980), pp. 125–128. Excludes northern Appalachians.

13. Brown and Hillery, op. cit. (footnote 7), p. 61.

14. Clyde B. McCoy and James S. Brown, "Appalachian Migration to Midwestern Cities," in Philliber and McCoy, op. cit. (footnote 10), p. 40.

15. Appalachian Regional Commission, *Appalachia—A Reference Book* (Washington, D.C.: Appalachian Regional Commission, 1979), p. 27.

16. B. J. Deaton and K. R. Anschel, "Migration and Return Migration: A New Look at the Eastern Kentucky Migration Stream," *Southern Journal of Agricultural Economics* 6 (1974), p. 185.

17. Ibid., p. 186.

18. A State Economic Area (SEA), a concept first employed in 1950, is a group of counties that have similar social and economic characteristics. Some are agricultural (or mining) oriented; others are metropolitan areas containing a city of at least fifty thousand inhabitants and nearby counties integrated with the central city. Rural SEAs are numbered (e.g., Kentucky SEA 9) and urban SEAs are given letter designations (e.g., New York SEA G). Data presented here were taken from U.S. Bureau of the Census, *Census of Population: 1970, Subject Reports, Final Report PC (2)-2E, Migration Between State Economic Areas* (Washington, D.C.: Government Printing Office, 1972).

19. McCoy and Brown, op. cit. (footnote 14), p. 62.

20. George F. Deasy and Phyllis R. Griess, "Effects of a Declining Mining Economy on the Pennsylvania Anthracite Region," *Annals,* Association of American Geographers, 55 (1965), pp. 239–259.

21. A classic study that investigates outmigration, kinship, and adjustment

from one eastern Kentucky community is Harry K. Schwarzweller, James S. Brown, and J. J. Mangalam, *Mountain Families in Transition: A Case Study of Appalachian Migration* (University Park: Pennsylvania State University Press, 1971).

22. Ravenstein stated that for every "current" (migration stream) there is a "counter-current" (counterstream). The volume of each differs. E. G. Ravenstein, "The Laws of Migration," *Journal of the Royal Statistical Study* 47 (1885), pp. 167–227, and Lee, op. cit. (footnote 9).

23. Appalachian Regional Commission, "Appalachia Is Changing," in Bruce Ergood and Bruce E. Kuhre, eds., *Appalachia: Social Context Past and Present* (Dubuque, Ia.: Kendall/Hunt Publishing Co., 1976), p. 84.

24. See, for example, Fred M. Shelley and Curtis C. Roseman, "Migration Patterns Leading to Population Change in the Nonmetropolitan South," *Growth and Change* 9 (1978), pp. 14–23.

25. Appalachia Regional Commission, 1976, op. cit. (footnote 23), p. 86.

26. U.S. Bureau of the Census, *Census of Population: 1950,* vol. 2, *Characteristics of the Population* (Washington, D.C.: Bureau of the Census, 1952), and U.S. Bureau of the Census, *Census of Population: 1970,* vol. 1, *Characteristics of the Population* (Washington, D.C.: Bureau of the Census, 1973).

27. Total money income is the sum of wages, salaries, self-employment income, social security, railroad-retirement income, public-assistance income, interest, dividends, pensions, unemployment compensation, alimony, and so forth. The total represents the amount of income received before deductions for income taxes, social security, and so forth. Per capita money-income data are reported in U.S. Bureau of the Census, *Census of Population: 1970, Current Population Reports, Series P-25* (Washington, D.C.: Bureau of the Census, 1972).

28. Figures for the Appalachian Regional Commission region were $2,505 in 1969 and $4,830 in 1977 or a 92.8 percent increase. Appalachian Regional Commission, 1979, op. cit. (footnote 15), pp. 20–21.

29. For a discussion of education in southern Appalachia see Orin B. Graff, "The Needs of Education," in Thomas R. Ford, ed., *The Southern Appalachian Region: A Survey* (Lexington: University of Kentucky Press, 1962), pp. 188–200.

30. James Branscome, "Educating Appalachia's Poor," *People's Appalachia* 5 (1970), pp. 5–8.

31. DeJong, op. cit. (footnote 5), p. 23.

32. Stephen S. Birdsall and John W. Florin, *Regional Landscapes of the United States and Canada* (New York: John Wiley & Sons, 1978), p. 145.

33. A useful, short essay on the origins of the southern mountaineer is that by Cratis D. Williams, "Who Are the Southern Mountaineers?" *Appalachian Journal* 1 (1972), pp. 48–55.

34. See, for example, John Fraser Hart, "The Changing Distribution of the American Negro," *Annals,* Association of American Geographers, 50 (1960), pp. 242–266, and George A. Davis and O. Fred Donaldson, *Blacks in the United States: A Geographic Perspective* (Boston: Houghton Mifflin Co., 1975), chaps. 3–4.

35. Mack H. Gillenwater, "Mining Settlements of Southern West Virginia," in Howard G. Adkins, Steve Ewing, and Chester E. Zimolzak, eds., *West Virginia and Appalachia: Selected Readings* (Dubuque, Ia.: Kendall/Hunt Publishing Co., 1977), p. 141.

36. Comparable percentages for 1960 and 1950 were 9.5 and 13.2 respectively.

37. Laurence French and Jim Hornbuckle, eds., *The Cherokee Perspective:*

*Written by Eastern Cherokees* (Boone, N.C.: Appalachian Consortium Press, 1981), pp. 3–43.

38. Edward T. Price, "The Melungeons: A Mixed-Blood Strain of the Southern Appalachians," *Geographical Review* 41 (1951), pp. 251–271. See also Calvin L. Beale, "American Triracial Isolates," *Eugenics Quarterly* 4 (1957), pp. 187–196, and W. H. Gilbert, "Memorandum Concerning the Characteristics of the Larger Mixed-Blood Racial Islands of the Eastern United States," *Social Forces* 24 (1946), pp. 438–447.

# CHAPTER 6

# RESOURCES: RENEWABLE AND NONRENEWABLE

Appalachia has long exported to its neighbors its stores of coal, petroleum, natural gas, metallic ores, timber, and water. But these resources, and others, have not provided many of the region's people with a standard of living that approximates that of the rest of the nation. Herein lies one of the paradoxes of this enigmatic area: chronic imbalance in fiscal well-being across a region of immense resource wealth. Resources can provide the raw materials for sustained regional development and growth. Throughout the region's recent history, though, some resources—such as coal—have been carelessly exploited for short-term gain by the few. Other resources—the seemingly endless hardwood forests, for example—have been abused alike by the people who occupy the land and by outsiders. This tradition of irresponsible resource use is at the root of many of Appalachia's social and economic ills. The region is neither homogeneous in the distribution of resources nor in the governance of their use. Some parts of the region are reasonably prosperous, and a number of urban areas are growing rapidly and are actively diversifying their economic bases. Other sections have experienced prolonged periods of unemployment and environmental and social degradation while surrounded by extensive mineral reserves. This chapter will outline the production and use of four types of resources that have been fundamental to the region's development: forests, agricultural products, water, and coal. Agriculture can be viewed as resource production in the same sense as forestry: Crops utilize soil, climate, and precipitation to yield a primary product that may be processed into food, fiber, or chemical raw materials and thereby provide employment and income.

## RENEWABLE RESOURCES—THE FORESTS

Renewable resources regenerate after use or depletion. Forests grow up again, soils eventually can be restored by vegetation and chemical action on bedrock, and precipitation may clear rivers of acid and the air of dust and noxious gases. Regeneration is not necessarily autogenic, especially in the short term, and restoration may require human intervention. Three issues accompany this condition. Does the public want the resource renewed? Is the renewal process economical? If the resource is reestablished, will it provide a product of some use or value or has technological innovation truncated demand for the resource? Assuming that resources should be renewed at an economical level if possible, those resources that can be restored should be used on a sustained-yield basis to assure future production, a stable economy in the production area, and sufficient time for regeneration.

Of all the items in Appalachia's resource inventory, the hardwood and softwood forests may be the most versatile. Trees contribute to soil formation and help stabilize precipitation runoff. They provide a broad range of raw materials for construction, manufacturing, transportation, and fuel for home and even commercial heating. Forests are also an aesthetic resource for resident and recreational visitor alike. Despite their importance, forests traditionally have been managed counterproductively. To clear land for farming, Indians from New York south to Alabama girdled trees and regularly burned over large areas. By the 1600s, Indians in Virginia's Tidewater and Piedmont had deforested 30 to 40 a. (12.1 to 16.2 h) for each individual in their tribes through clearing and burning. As the fertility of their fields declined, they cleared new land and abandoned the old fields. Burning the woodlands as well as the clearings apparently was so common that reburning of abandoned fields took place with sufficient frequency to hold forest regrowth in check. Travelers noted that throughout the Piedmont and Great Valley there were large expanses of "meadowlands," the product of Indian burning.[1] As white settlers moved beyond the Piedmont and Blue Ridge into the Ridge and Valley they cleared the valley floors for farming, using what timber they needed for building and fencing and burning the rest. By about 1850, most of the forests in the valleys and some of the broader ridges and accessible mountain coves had been removed and replaced by pasture and cultivated fields.[2]

Where iron-ore deposits were found, mining and smelting often preceded farming settlement, and extensive acreages of forest were cut to provide charcoal for the manufacture of iron. Charcoal-fired furnaces were established in northwestern New Jersey before the Revolution and in Pennsylvania and Virginia by 1800. Land speculation for iron ore had begun in upper east Tennessee by 1790.[3] Because pig-iron smelting required large amounts of charcoal, as production increased wide areas of forests were cut over to keep the charcoal ovens going. If the ore deposits were extensive, the hinterland would be recut as soon as regrown trees reached a few inches in diameter. Even in areas where coal was abundant, charcoal was the preferred carbon source: It did not impart the sulfur and other impurities to the iron that coal would, and charcoal iron was therefore considered a superior product that kept an edge if sharpened and was malleable enough to be shaped without breaking. By 1856 there were 560 iron furnaces in the United States—most of them in Appalachia. Of that number, 439 (78 percent) used charcoal, and most of the remainder used clean-burning anthracite.

### Commercial Cutting

The earliest known commercial cutting of timber in the mountains beyond the Ridge and Valley at the latitude of West Virginia was in 1750 when loggers were sent into the Allegheny Mountains to cut red spruce for ship masts.[4] The mountains and Plateaus were the center of the best hardwood stands in the Northern Hemisphere. Oak, beech, maple, hickory, black walnut, and tuliptrees made up more than 80 percent of the stand.[5] Widespread commercial cutting began in New York in the 1820s and 1830s when canals opened access into the region. By 1839, New York was producing 30 percent of the timber cut in the entire country, and in 1849 production in the state peaked. Farther south, large-scale commercial timber cutting from West Virginia to Alabama had to await the railroad. As loggers moved south they were preceded by agents of large timber companies who bought timber rights to vast acreages from local residents. Initial cutting would take place on the upper reaches of major streams that flowed out of the region. Trees were cut in the winter months and were dragged to the stream bank. The logs were carried on spring freshets to sawmills downstream. This process was used extensively in eastern Kentucky, and by 1870 the state was producing over 217 million bd ft of lumber annually and ranked fifteenth in the nation. State production reached a peak in 1907 when thirty thousand men produced 913 million bd ft. By 1925 production had dropped to 207 million bd ft, and employment had declined to ten thousand. In West Virginia, the lumbering boom peaked between 1907 and 1916. At the end of that period, farmers and lumbermen had reduced the state's original forested area of 5.5 million a. (2.2 million h) to 1.5 million a. (606,000 h), and little reforestation was taking place.[6]

The technology of logging during this period was simple and crude. Trees were felled with handsaws and axes, trunks were cut into manageable lengths, and teams of horses dragged the logs to a railroad spur for loading. As much as 60 percent of a horse-logged area could end up as skid trails or covered by deep windrows of slash. The skid trails would erode down to bedrock during heavy rains, and the piles of slash burned easily. Almost every residual tree was pushed down or damaged, thereby slowing the natural reseeding process. The steam engine had a dramatic effect on the region's timber resources, because the steam locomotive made the mountainous areas accessible to economical high-capacity transportation for the first time and the steam-powered sawmill increased the speed with which logs could be cut into dimensional lumber. The steam engine was also incorporated into a cable logging system that gradually replaced horse skidding. A steam-powered winch system gathered logs from a circular cutting area 0.5 mi (0.8 km) across. Logs were skidded along the ground to a central yard where they were loaded on rail cars. Like the horse-sledding system, the steam-cable system produced skid trails and severe soil erosion. Twenty years after logging, as much as 50 percent of the soil on some sites in West Virginia was still severely disturbed.[7] In east Tennessee and western North Carolina, where the Scottish Carolina Land and Lumber Company began logging in 1885, severe erosion of mountain soils often followed logging. Cutover areas may have been burned over by farmers to improve grazing, but burning destroyed deep accumulations of humus, and the unprotected soils washed away. Today, logging-induced erosion is still evident in numerous areas such as the Watauga Valley near Johnson City, Tennessee, and in Tennessee's Unaka Mountains, where thousands of acres are covered by rock cobbles, and scrub brush is all that will grow.[8]

### Lumber and Wood Processing

Despite the assault of nineteenth-century and early twentieth-century commercial lumbering, the region's forestry resources have been steadily reestablished. In central and northern Appalachia, two-thirds of the land is woodland. Forest coverage is greatest in West Virginia, Virginia, and Kentucky, where 75 to 80 percent of the land is tree-covered, and lowest in Ohio and Pennsylvania, where the coverage is about 50 percent.[9] West Virginia had 11.5 million a. (4.65 million h) of commercial forest land in 1975, an amount that had increased 16 percent from 9.9 million a. (3.99 million h) in 1949. The abandonment of farm pastureland to volunteer timber regrowth was responsible for much of this increase. About 83 percent of the timber harvested was from hardwoods, especially oak and hickory. The largest proportion of the annual harvest, about two-thirds, was processed by sawmills into a wide variety of lumber products. The remaining third was processed by pulpmills into a variety of paper and fiberboard products.[10]

In general, the proportion of timber harvested for processing in sawmills as opposed to pulpmills increases from the southern portion of the region to the north. In 1977 (the most recent year for which data are available), there was an average of fourteen lumber and wood-processing firms in each county, but the distribution varied widely, as did the type and quality of wood products produced (Figure 6.1). A dramatic contrast is apparent in Figure 6.1 between the Piedmont—from Virginia south through Alabama—where there were numerous wood processing establishments, and the Plateaus, where there were relatively few. This contrast is illustrated by Kentucky and North

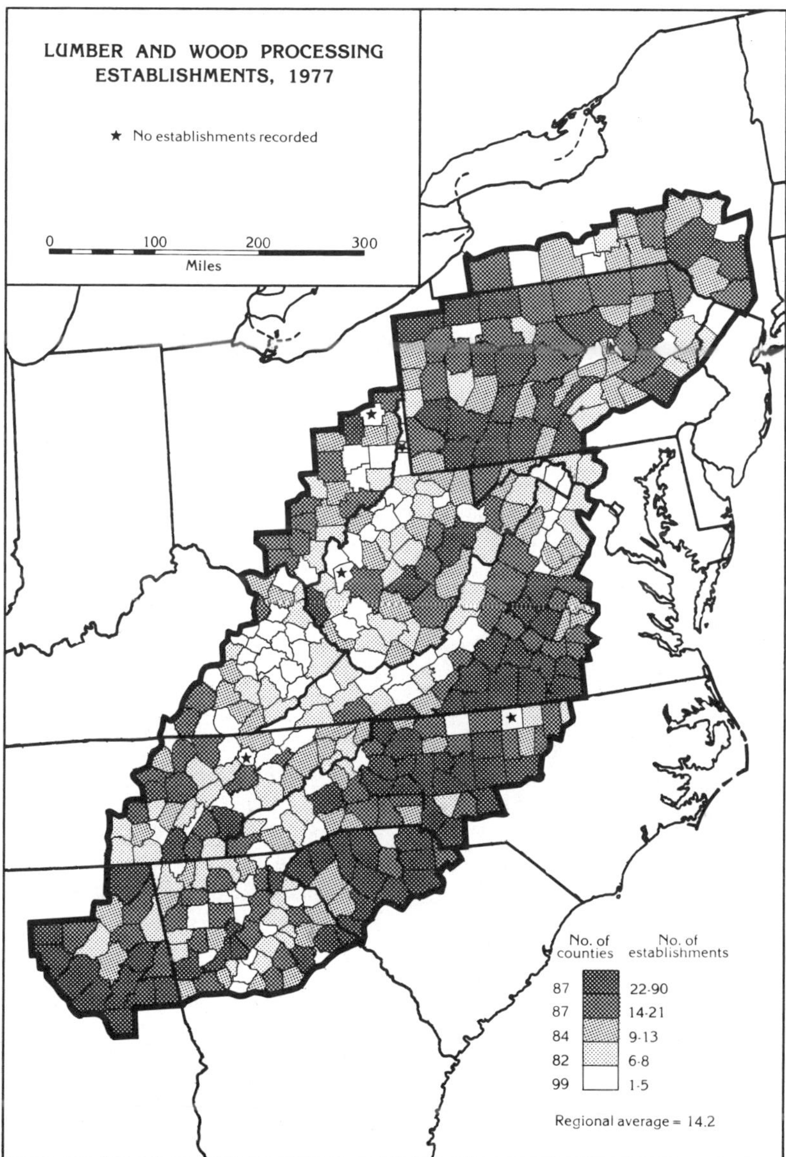


**Figure 6.1**
Source: U.S. Bureau of the Census, *U.S. Census of Manufacturers,* 1977, Geographic Area Series (Washington, D.C.: Bureau of the Census, 1980).

Carolina. In eastern Kentucky, only 3 counties (Pulaski, Rowan, and Wayne) had more than the regional average of fourteen wood-processing establishments per county. Wood processing could be an important source of employment in those counties that are traditionally very low in manufacturing. In Leslie, Knott, and Menifee counties, wood-processing establishments accounted for more than 50 percent of the manufacturing employment. Unfortunately, most of Kentucky's wood plants tended to produce only primary wood products such as rough lumber, mine timbers, cross ties, and pallet stock rather than finished products. The development of secondary wood-processing industries would allow more of the value added to wood by manufacturing to remain in the state.[11]

In North Carolina, 28 of 52 counties (54 percent) had more than the average number of processing plants per county. Five counties had fifty firms or more: Catawba (71), Davidson (90), Guilford (73), Randolph (70), and Wilkes (59). These Piedmont counties are the core of the U.S. high-quality wood-furniture producing region. High Point, the furniture marketing center, is in Randolph County, and factories, many using regionally grown hardwoods, are scattered throughout the area in small towns whose names often bring instant recognition of their product: Thomasville, Hickory, Drexel, and Lenoir, for example. Fine furniture

This stack of black-walnut logs, harvested from the North Carolina Blue Ridge, will be turned into beautiful furniture by Mitchell County craftsmen. Small mountain sawmills may also sell lumber to Piedmont furniture manufacturers.

manufacturing does not continue throughout the Piedmont. Rather, a mix of wood products comes from the high number of establishments in the zone from South Carolina to Alabama—including pulpmills but also including substantial numbers of secondary processing plants.

In Pennsylvania, 32 of 58 counties (55 percent) had more than the regional average number of wood-processing establishments, but only Allegheny County (Pittsburgh) had more than 50 firms. Pennsylvania ranked second in the nation for hardwood lumber output. The state's 684 sawmills produced lumber for a wide range of products including posts, cooperage, bat and handle stock, mine timbers, and veneer logs. Deep mining of coal has been decreasing in southwestern Pennsylvania since the 1960s, so the demand for mine timbers has been decreasing.

### Wood Pulp Production

The production of wood pulp is more geographically restricted than is the processing of lumber from saw logs (Figure 6.2). Across the region 371 counties produced 6.8 million cords of pulpwood in 1979, for a regional average of 20,552 cords per county. Forty counties produced more than 50,000 cords. The most intense concentrations of pulpwood production were on the Virginia Piedmont and the South Carolina Piedmont, which lies at the edge of a pulp-producing zone that stretches southwest into Alabama. Three counties in Alabama (Randolph, Walker, and Winston) produced over 100,000 cords annually, and Fairfield County, South Carolina, produced the highest amount at over 130,000 cords annually. In the north, 12 of Pennsylvania's central and northern counties produced more than the regional average, but compared to the southern states pulp production was modest. Centre County, the state's highest producer—71 percent of the county is in commercial forest—had an output of 51,500 cords. The gradient between the high pulp-producing counties and those with low production or none at all is frequently steep, with only a limited degree of transition. The areas of lowest pulp production tend to be the best agricultural land like the Ridge and Valley of Tennessee and Virginia, rugged mountains like the southern Blue Ridge, or the coalfield counties. Broad areas of Kentucky, West Virginia, and southwestern Pennsylvania have no production.[12]

A second key to understanding the location of pulpwood production is the locational factors associated with pulp-processing mills. A large modern pulpmill can process about 1,000 tn (907 t) of pulpwood each day. According to John Fraser Hart, 1 to 1.5 cords of pulpwood will produce 1 tn (0.907 t) of pulp. One a. (0.4 h) of forest land will produce 1 cord of wood per acre each year if properly managed.[13] A large pulpmill that uses the wood from about 1,000 a.—1.56 sq mi (404 h—4.04 sq km) of land per day will annually consume the wood from 390 sq mi (1,010.1 sq km) if the plant runs 250 days each year. Another way to view this level of production is that the wood from 5 counties, each with an annual production of 50,000 cords, is required to keep one large pulp plant in operation. This implies that for pulp production

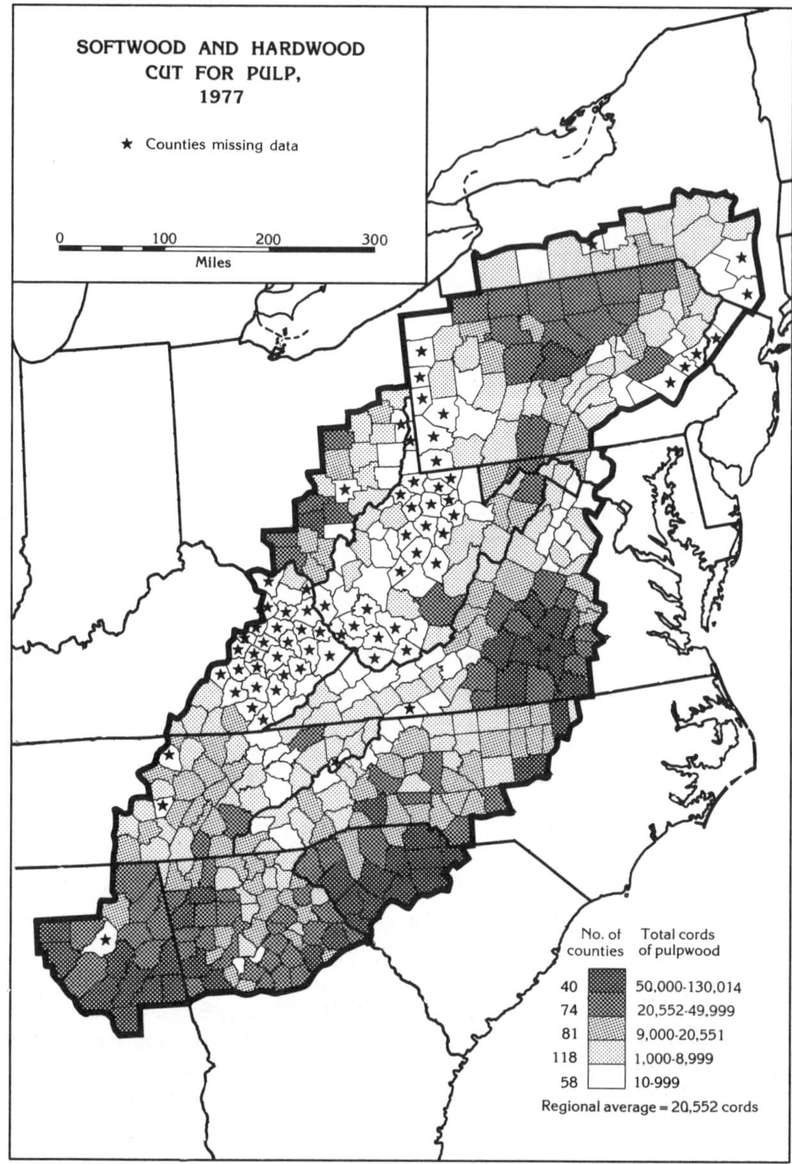


**Figure 6.2**
Source: Robert L. Nevel, Jr., and James T. Bores, *Northeastern Pulpwood, 1979: An Annual Assessment of Regional Timber Output,* Forest Service Resource Bulletin NE-67 (Broomall, Pa.: Northeastern Forest Experiment Station, 1981), and Thomas R. Bellamy and Cecil C. Hutchins, Jr., *Southern Pulpwood Production, 1979,* Forest Service Resource Bulletin SE-57 (Ashville, N.C.: Southeastern Forest Experiment Station, 1981).

to be sustained, the processing company must have access, either through ownership or through lease rights, to extensive acreages of trees at various stages of maturity. In the coal counties where significant acreages of timberland are held by mining corporations, the pulp processors have few entrees. Eastern Kentucky (and West Virginia), where corporate ownership of commercial forest land stands at 25 percent, do not have one operating pulpmill; their production is shipped out of state. Much of the pulpwood cut in eastern West Virginia, for example, goes to two large plants in adjoining states run by the same company: one in Allegany County, Maryland, the other in Alleghany County, Virginia.

Instability in the pattern of pulpwood production is reflected in changes that took place between 1963 and 1979 (Table 6.1). The states with the highest absolute increases in pulp production were the states on the southern Piedmont that already had the highest base production. As the Cotton Belt faded from the Piedmont in the late 1940s and 1950s, much of the cotton land was either purchased by pulp companies and planted to fast-growing pine species or was allowed to revert to woodland by the farmer. By the late 1970s those forests were reaching

TABLE 6.1
Percentage Change in Pulpwood Production: 1963 to 1979
(Roundwood and Residue Materials, All Species)

| State | 1963 (Standard Cords) | 1979 (Standard Cords) | Percentage Change |
|---|---|---|---|
| Alabama | 649,246 | 1,114,305 | 71.6 |
| Georgia | 1,000,147 | 1,411,853 | 41.2 |
| Kentucky | No data | 25,900 | * |
| Maryland | 72,200 | 50,300 | -30.3 |
| New Jersey | No data | 200 | * |
| New York | 15,350 | 51,525 | 235.7 |
| North Carolina | 655,531 | 641,445 | -2.1 |
| Ohio | No data | 280,925 | * |
| Pennsylvania | 493,500 | 615,800 | 24.8 |
| South Carolina | 623,753 | 1,002,489 | 60.7 |
| Tennessee | 479,405 | 366,699 | -23.5 |
| Virginia | 1,042,518 | 1,126,448 | 8.1 |
| West Virginia | 300,325 | 126,300 | -57.9 |
| Total | 5,331,975 | 6,814,189 | Average Change 27.8 |

Source: Herbert A. Knight and Agnes C. Nichols, Southern Pulpwood Production, 1963 (Asheville, N.C.: Southeastern Forest Experiment Station, 1964); Neal P. Kingsley, Pulpwood Production in the Northeast, 1963, Forest Service Resource Bulletin NE=3 (Upper Darby, Pa.: Northeastern Forest Experiment Station, 1966); Thomas R. Bellamy and Cecil C. Hutchins, Jr., Southern Pulpwood Production, 1979, Forest Service Resource Bulletin SE=57 (Asheville, N.C.: Southeastern Forest Experiment Station, 1981); and Robert L. Nevel, Jr., and James T. Bores, Northeastern Pulpwood, 1979: An Annual Assessment of Regional Timber Output, Forest Service Resource Bulletin NE=67 (Broomall, Pa.: Northeastern Forest Experiment Station, 1981).

maturity and furnishing much of the raw material that stimulated the expansion of the southern pulp industry. Production in some states declined sharply, perhaps a response to the increased costs of hauling trees or chips long distances to a mill, as in West Virginia. In the north, New York had the highest percentage increase in pulp production for the period but still remained fourth from the bottom in absolute production. About half of the state of New York is forested, and yet wood processing contributes relatively little to the state's economy (as is the case in Pennsylvania, where only 3 to 4 percent of the manufacturing employment is in wood related industries). The New York forests are second growth, inefficiently managed, and useful primarily for watershed protection and recreation. As a result, 80 percent of New York's timber and wood needs are supplied from other states, Canada, or foreign imports.[14]

### Problems in Forest Productivity

The difficulties that constrain the use of the Appalachian forests for a sustained yield of wood products, watershed protection, and recreation center on the problems of stand quality, application of modern forestry technology, and ownership and taxation patterns. In forest stands that are managed to provide sustained tree yields, even-aged stands provide greater profits than do uneven-aged stands. If even-aged stands are available for harvest, clear-cutting is more profitable than high-grading (cutting only the best trees), and large clear-cuts are more profitable than small ones. The inability of individual or corporate forest landholders to upgrade the tree stands on their lands stems in part from historic exploitation patterns. When extensive areas of virgin timber were logged off around the turn of the century, seed trees were rarely left, and the trees that gradually grew back were often inferior species. In many areas in the Plateau and Blue Ridge, farmers continue to practice a "brush fallow" type of land rotation that neither allows trees to reach maturity nor provides proper management of the so-called weed trees that recolonize abandoned fields and pastures. In areas of coal mining, overcutting by mining companies may not allow trees to stand long enough to mature. Many mine leases allow mine companies to use trees on the surface, up to 12 to 14 in. (30.5 to 35.5 cm) in diameter, for mining purposes. If surface owners sell off the larger trees and the mineral owners or lessees use the smaller trees, virtual clear-cutting results over wide areas. The forest may not be allowed to mature if the miners continue to cut trees before they reach the 12-to-14-in. limit.

Forest fires continue to plague the mountains and play a significant role in reducing much former woodland to brush. In the late 1930s, almost 6 percent of the east Tennessee forest was burned annually by local incendiaries. In Kentucky, about 4 percent of the forest burned each year.[15] The problem continues. In upper east Tennessee, the Cherokee National Forest is regularly set on fire by local people who have complaints against any governmental office from the Forest Service to the Postal Service, a kind of referendum by fire.[16]

Forest productivity traditionally has been limited in part by the type of technology available to harvest trees, but new techniques are reducing environmental damage and allowing the regrowth of even-aged stands. For example, prior to World War II most timber was cut on steep slopes in remote areas, necessitating the construction of the thousands of miles of logging roads that are found everywhere in the eastern forest. On some mountain slopes, up to 25 percent of the land is in roads, land that lies bare to erosion. If the forest is high-graded, the roads must be kept open for frequent harvesting. If clear-cutting in small blocks is permitted, the roads can be planted in a cover crop so that they will revert to woodland about as fast as the harvested area. Clear-cutting, although decried by some conservationists, if done judiciously can actually reduce erosion problems. Clear-cutting coupled with a skyline system that removes trees by cable slings held well above the ground can provide the best combination of techniques to properly manage a given block of forest land for maximum production, sustained yield, environmental balance, and adequate profit.[17]

The ability to accomplish sustained-yield forestry on a significant scale is intensified by a third set of problems: fragmented land ownership and uneven taxation patterns. Throughout most of the region, forest ownership is a mosaic of small holdings. In central Appalachia, about 89 percent of the forested land belongs to farmers or other private owners. Forest industries hold only about 820,000 a. (331,280 h) or about 4 percent. The remaining 7 percent is in national forest or other public ownership. The difficulty of assimilating timber leases from such a profusion of owners is further exacerbated by owner attitudes toward woodland use. A study of private woodland owners in West Virginia found that selling timber ranked very low on the priorities of small landholders. Instead they planned to maintain their woodland—without any selective management—for conservation, as pasture, or to provide timber for their own use.[18] Land taxes in some states do not favor purchase of land for timber management by forest industries. In West Virginia, forest-industry land is taxed 50 percent higher than farm woodland.

These problems place substantial constraints on the development of commercial forestry as an important element in regional development. With the exception of the Piedmont, in Appalachia the scientific management of the region's forests, the sustained yield of high-quality timber products, and employment by primary and secondary wood-processing industries do not seem to be a possibility except in localized areas.

## RENEWABLE RESOURCES—AGRICULTURAL PRODUCTION

The size of the Appalachian region, together with its latitudinal extent and range of climates and geomorphology, suggests that agriculture is as variable within this area as in virtually any comparably sized region in the country. The variations in productivity, farm size, and land values are paralleled by sharp changes in crop and livestock specialization,

TABLE 6.2
Farm Size, Farm Size Change, Value of Land, and Value of Products Sold By Physiographic Province

| Physiographic Province | Number of Counties | Change in Farm Size 1959 to 1978 | Average Farm Size 1978 | Value of Land and Buildings 1978 | Value of All Farm Products Sold 1978 |
|---|---|---|---|---|---|
| | | Percentage Change | Acres Per Farm | $ Per Acre | $ Per Farm |
| Piedmont | 125 | 34.3 | 170.6 | 912.16 | 30,149 |
| Blue Ridge | 39 | 25.4 | 109.4 | 1003.36 | 19,098 |
| Ridge and Valley | 93 | 28.9 | 171.3 | 1007.52 | 28,722 |
| Plateaus | 188 | 33.9 | 159.7 | 701.09 | 15,868 |
| Regional Average | | 32.3 Percent | 160.9 Acres | $850.91 | $22,873 |
| National Average | | 64.0 Percent | 497.0 Acres | $639.00 | $57,470 |

Source: U.S. Bureau of the Census, _1959 Census of Agriculture_, vol. 1, _Counties_ (Washington, D.C.: Bureau of the Census, 1961), and U.S. Bureau of the Census, _1978 Census of Agriculture_, vol. 1, _State and County Data_ (Washington, D.C.: Bureau of the Census, 1980).

changes that in some places occur over short distances. According to the 1978 *Census of Agriculture,* Appalachia's farmlands amounted to 7.9 percent of the national total. Of the region's total land area of 213,217 sq mi (552,232 sq km), approximately 60 percent or 127,800 sq mi (331,002 sq km) was in farms. Within the region are some of the nation's most productive farming counties, and many of the poorest as well. Intensive farming is found wherever soil and slope conditions permit, but much of the land that was cleared for farming by the first generations of settlers has been abandoned and allowed to revert back to trees and brush.

As farmers become more productive they try to obtain more land so that their labor and investments in machinery, buildings, and fertilizers are more efficiently used across more acres. A basic indicator of increasing productivity and efficiency is an increase in farm size over time. In the nation's most productive agricultural areas, farm size grew steadily over the twenty years from 1959 to 1978 (the most recent year for which data are available). But in Appalachia this was not the case. Table 6.2 shows that the regional increase in farm size was almost exactly half of the national average increase. The region's largest increases occurred on the Piedmont, where farm size in about a quarter of the counties increased 50 percent or more from 1959 to 1978. But many counties throughout the region lagged behind, reflecting the limited opportunity for viable farming operations. In each physiographic provincc 60 percent or more of the counties failed to meet even the suppressed regional average farm-size increase or actually declined over the period. Sixty-three counties in the Ridge and Valley (just over two-thirds) either had farm sizes increase less than the regional average or decline. Part of the Ridge and Valley Province contains the fertile and relatively prosperous Great Valley where farm sizes have increased, but much of the remainder of the area is in steep slopes or valley floors that are limited in productivity by their sandstone- and shale-based soils.

In the Plateaus Province, traditionally regarded as the one that has offered the fewest agricultural opportunities and has been least productive in the region, farms in about 55 percent of the counties increased in size less than the regional average or declined. This province had the greatest proportion of its counties decline in farm size (7.2 percent), and the number of counties with stagnating farm growth might have been much larger but for a long tradition of low productivity and land abandonment. Complete land abandonment has been most common on the roughest, most isolated, and inaccessible parts of the Plateaus. Off-farm jobs in coal mines or sawmills may have been available, allowing families to continue living on the farm, while depending on nonfarm employment instead of their hillside fields for their income. Partial or selective abandonment may have resulted when the mule was replaced by the tractor, because mules could negotiate steep slopes that rendered tractors unsafe. Much of the Plateau land was simply not worth the investment in fertilizer and lime, hybrid seed, equipment, fencing, or livestock to make it productive.[19]

In 1978 average farm size across the region was 160.9 a. (65.0 h) as compared to about 497 a. (200.8 h) for the nation. This was about the same size—one-fourth of a square mile—as the acreage allotted to Midwest settlers under the Homestead Act of 1862 as an ideal-sized family farm. Although farm size in other farming regions has steadily increased, Appalachian farms remain small, in part a result of relatively high population pressures on the limited agricultural land resources. The smallest farms were found in the Blue Ridge, where only about 8 percent were above the regional average size. The largest proportion of farms of over 200 a. (80.8 h) (just over 30 percent) was in the Ridge and Valley.

One of the region's few agricultural characteristics that measured higher than the national average in 1978 was farm capitalization as reflected by the value of land and buildings. The regional average value per acre was $211 more than the national average. Blue Ridge farms were some of the highest valued in the region. In almost three-fourths of the counties, the value of land and buildings exceeded the regional average. The highest values were in Henderson ($1,544 per a. or $3,814 per h), Macon ($1,428 or $3,527), Avery ($1,222 or $3,018), and Watauga ($1,013 or $2,502) counties in North Carolina. These extraordinary values for marginal land and small farms, directly attributable to demand by recreational developers, will be reviewed at length in Chapter 7. The comparatively high values in the Piedmont and Ridge and Valley may have resulted from population pressure and nonfarm demand that overvalued the limited amount of rural land desirable for residential use. On the North Carolina Piedmont, for example, the value of land and buildings in Davie and Orange counties was over $1,000 per a. ($2,471 per h). This area is the center of the Piedmont tobacco, textile, and furniture industries. Many of the plants are in small towns, and the countryside is becoming densely populated by nonfarm residents who wish to work in local industrial plants while living in the country. The result is a high rural population density, almost a dispersed city. High land values in this area also may have been maintained by tobacco allotments. Tobacco land, because of the lucrative income obtained from even a small crop, has traditionally been valued higher than adjacent land without an allotment.

Land and building values in the Plateaus were well below average: Over four-fifths of the counties had values below the regional average. This was to be expected in an area of small farms—fewer than 20 percent above 200 a. (80.8 h)—and low productivity. Many counties in the coal districts have below-average values, perhaps because land is usually sold without mineral rights and its value for agriculture is quite low. In a few counties, land speculation or the creation of exclusive hobby farms, rather than agricultural potential, may have created artificially high land value anomalies. Examples include McDowell County, West Virginia, which had the highest land and building value of any county in the region at $2,927 per a. ($7,230 per h) and yet had only

A feeder cattle farm at Hightown, which is central to Highland County in the Ridge and Valley of Virginia. Early farmers preferred chestnut for their stake-and-rider fences because it split evenly. The few such fences still in use are maintained with oak replacement rails.

nine farms. In Mingo County, the value was $1,920 per a. ($4,742 per h) for only five farms. Nearby in Bell and Martin counties in Kentucky, values were below $650 per a. ($1,606 per h).

The intensity of farm land use in 1978 is suggested by the figures shown in Table 6.2 for value of farm products sold. The regional average was only 39.8 percent of the national average. For the region, 280 counties fell below the income level of twenty thousand dollars, the Census Bureau's minimum requirement for a commercial farm. The figure of twenty thousand dollars is used here as a threshold figure to separate the full-time farmers from those who must depend upon off-farm employment for a substantial portion of their income. The Ridge and Valley was the most productive province; the average value of all farm products sold was above thirty-five thousand dollars in almost one-third of the counties. By comparison, the value of products sold exceeded this amount in only about one-fifth of the Blue Ridge counties. The low productivity of Blue Ridge farms reinforces the contention that high land values there are the result of demand by developers. The small hill farms of the Plateaus were the least productive. Here the value of farm produce exceeded thirty-five thousand dollars in fewer than one-tenth of the counties, and over three-fourths had below regional average values.

TABLE 6.3
Selected Agricultural Characteristics: 1978[1]
(Summarized for the Appalachian Portion of Each State)

| State | Number of Counties | Average Farm Size | Tenancy | Milk Cows | Hogs and Pigs | Poultry Sales | Corn for Grain | Tobacco | Cotton | Vegetables | Fruit and Nut Orchards |
|---|---|---|---|---|---|---|---|---|---|---|---|
| | | Acres | Percentage | Number | Number | 000s $ | Acres | Acres | Acres | Acres | Acres |
| AL | 18 | 148.67 | 5.20 | 18,684 | 181,890 | 419,346 | 126,256 | 5 | 37,945 | 9,465 | 607 |
| GA | 59 | 165.75 | 4.87 | 111,100 | 157,100 | 614,951 | 44,411 | 100 | 13,465 | 4,625 | 7,751 |
| KY | 36 | 120.47 | 6.49 | 24,400 | 78,600 | 8,234 | 58,054 | 27,056 | 0 | 1,291 | 842 |
| MD | 4 | 189.00 | 12.35 | 4,300 | 23,100 | 3,717 | 71,988 | 0 | 0 | 2,204 | 7,255 |
| NJ | 2 | 157.50 | 16.70 | 18,000 | 2,100 | 395 | 20,576 | 0 | 0 | 2,498 | 805 |
| NY | 17 | 216.53 | 5.77 | 252,500 | 24,300 | 49,744 | 90,507 | 0 | 0 | 24,695 | 26,135 |
| NC | 52 | 112.00 | 8.45 | 4,900 | 255,800 | 421,624 | 230,324 | 110,429 | 2,764 | 9,246 | 22,446 |
| OH | 23 | 166.79 | 5.57 | 81,300 | 149,800 | 16,588 | 11,985 | 1,858 | 0 | 3,590 | 6,160 |
| PA | 58 | 164.25 | 7.21 | 474,200 | 436,200 | 149,123 | 844,379 | 570 | 0 | 30,435 | 28,633 |
| SC | 16 | 208.25 | 4.46 | 21,900 | 42,700 | 37,405 | 26,186 | 0 | 3,293 | 445 | 20,531 |
| TN | 44 | 117.23 | 5.13 | 140,100 | 253,000 | 61,052 | 155,554 | 31,061 | 2,577 | 19,388 | 2,564 |
| VA | 61 | 200.84 | 7.34 | 151,800 | 238,520 | 80,075 | 270,130 | 63,179 | 0 | 3,732 | 36,141 |
| WV | 55 | 183.51 | 4.55 | 36,100 | 51,600 | 32,694 | 60,883 | 1,344 | 0 | 1,402 | 22,072 |
| Totals | | 160.9 | * | 1,399,284 | 1,894,710 | 1,894,948 | 2,011,233 | 235,602 | 60,044 | 113,016 | 181,942 |

Source: U.S. Bureau of the Census, 1978 Census of Agriculture.

[1]Farms with sales of $2,500 or more.

### Agricultural Patterns

Our understanding of general agricultural patterns can be further refined by examining selected agricultural characteristics at the state level in 1978 (Table 6.3). The region's largest farms were in New York and South Carolina. The smallest were found in Kentucky, Tennessee, and North Carolina. Tenancy has traditionally been the highest in the Piedmont states, but with the decline of cotton farming and the sharecropping system, tenancy in its traditional form has declined. The tenancy rate for both Georgia and South Carolina was less than 5 percent by 1978. Today, consolidation of dispersed fields under the management of a single farmer has produced what Charles Aiken calls the "fragmented neoplantation." The farmer may own one farm, but rents or leases others to make full use of equipment and labor.[20] The highest tenancy rates were in Sussex and Warren counties, New Jersey, and in Maryland. Land values in these two areas were among the highest in the region. In the New Jersey counties, land values averaged almost $2,200 per a. ($5,434 per h) and in Maryland the average value was about $1,170 per a. ($2,890 per h). The high tenancy rates in New Jersey may have resulted from holding acreage in horse farms or other recreational retreats while a tenant is hired to maintain the pastures and buildings, as is done in Loudoun County, Virginia.

Appalachian farms accounted for over 13 percent of the nation's dairy cattle in 1978. The production of dairy products traditionally has been important in Pennsylvania and New York, which together had 51.9 percent of the region's milk cows. Most of the milk output from these two states goes into the massive Grade A fresh-milk market in the Atlantic Coast urban areas. Dairy farmers usually combine some cash crops with their milking operation; for instance, oats or barley may be planted as a nurse crop for alfalfa or clover. Corn is an important forage crop and is often cut green for silage instead of being allowed to ripen as grain. Dairy farms require high investments in livestock, buildings, feed storage facilities, and sanitation equipment to meet state and federal production standards, yet the land they occupy may be only marginally productive. Therefore it is not unexpected that the value of land and buildings in the northern dairy areas may be below the regional average.

Hog production in the region was of minor importance: Just over 3 percent of the nation's hogs were produced here annually. Even if one combined the production of the four highest states—North Carolina, Pennsylvania, Tennessee, and Virginia—their marketed hogs would total only 8 percent of Iowa's annual production. Hogs are raised as feeders and sold to regional packing plants. Their primary feed grain is corn, and this is one reason why the major hog-producing states are also the region's largest corn producers.

One of the region's most significant farm commodities was poultry, especially broilers and turkeys. The region captured over 22 percent of the nation's poultry sales. Broilers are raised in several major clusters

Marshall County, Alabama, is a major poultry-producing area. The long, narrow buildings on these Sand Mountain farms just southeast of Guntersville are broiler houses. (U.S. Department of Agriculture photo.)

on the Georgia and Carolina Piedmont and in northern Alabama. Large co-ops or farm-feed supply companies will provide the chicks, feed, medicines, and some management advice to the farmer who provides buildings and labor. The company often guarantees the farmer a set price per pound and will butcher and market the broilers when they have reached sale weight. Broiler production is attractive for small farmers with off-farm jobs because a small investment and a few hours of work each day will yield a steady income.[21] Poultry is traditionally cheaper to raise if production takes place near the source of feed, yet much of the feed for the southern Appalachian broiler industry comes from the Midwest. James Anderson found that feed transportation costs on river barges and trucks declined from 1955 to 1970 relative to traditional broiler-producing centers such as Delaware, allowing the region's producers a competitive advantage.[22]

Flue-cured–tobacco production is centered in eastern North Carolina and Virginia, and burley tobacco is produced primarily in central Kentucky and Tennessee. The Appalachian upland lies between these two core producing areas and consequently shares production of both tobacco types. About 40 percent—180—of the region's counties produced tobacco in 1978 and accounted for about 24 percent of the nation's total acreage. Burley-tobacco production centers in eastern Kentucky (32 of 36 counties) and Tennessee (38 of 44 counties). The crop is air cured in small barns and is well suited to the small-scale farms found in the region. Federal poundage allotments control production, but a farmer can often produce the full allotment on an acre of land or less. Flue-cured–tobacco production centers on the North Carolina Piedmont (41 of 52 counties). This tobacco, like burley, is used in cigarette manufacture, but unlike burley it is cured in heated barns or sheds. Most tobacco varieties, if grown in limited quantity, require intensive labor only during the spring planting and the late summer harvest, so tobacco is a popular supplemental cash crop for part-time farmers who have full-time jobs off the farm.

Cotton, vegetables, and fruit and nut orchards played a minor role in the Appalachian agricultural economy in 1978, as shown in Table 6.3. The Cotton Belt, which once stretched from North Carolina south and west to Mississippi, had shrunk to a few small islands in the Carolinas, Georgia, and Alabama. Merle Prunty and Charles Aiken attributed this dramatic decline to a series of regional agricultural changes, especially the reinstatement of crop acreage allotments from 1950 onward and the decline of cotton gins. Only in those areas where progressive cotton ginners have worked in concert with operators of fragmented neoplantations has cotton production continued.[23] Vegetable crops offer substantial potential for farmers to augment their incomes, and yet the region had only about 3 percent of the nation's vegetable acreage. In New York and Pennsylvania sweet corn, tomatoes, cabbage, and snap beans occupied the largest proportion of acreage devoted to vegetables. Farther south in Tennessee, snap beans, tomatoes, and turnip

Burley-tobacco harvest in Yancey County, North Carolina. The standing tobacco stalks are cut off near the ground and impaled on a thin stick. After wilting, the sticks are loaded onto a wagon for transport to the curing barn, where the crop is hung and air cured for up to six weeks.

greens were important, and some sweet corn was produced. In each of the 6 states with more than 20,000 a. (8,080 h) of fruit and nut orchards, apples and peaches were the primary fruits grown. In North Carolina, large acreages of pecans were grown on the Piedmont. A few selected areas have specialized in fruit production for decades. Much of Virginia's apple production, for example, is concentrated in the Shenandoah Valley. The valley is shared by Berkeley County, West Virginia, and farmers there derived 55 percent of their agricultural income from fruits and nuts. In North Carolina, apples and peaches were planted intensively around Hendersonville, thereby making Henderson County the seventh-largest producer of apples in the nation. In some areas fruit production has moved onto old Piedmont cotton land. One of the results has been that South Carolina produced more peaches than Georgia, and much of that production was on the Piedmont.

### Commercial Farms and Changes in Farm Income

Commercial farms are defined as those with at least twenty thousand dollars in income annually. Nationally, about 45 percent of all farms as recorded by the 1978 *Census of Agriculture* met this threshold. In Appalachia, only 18.6 percent (or 277,768) of the farms were commercial scale (Figure 6.3). Within the region the problem agricultural area, as

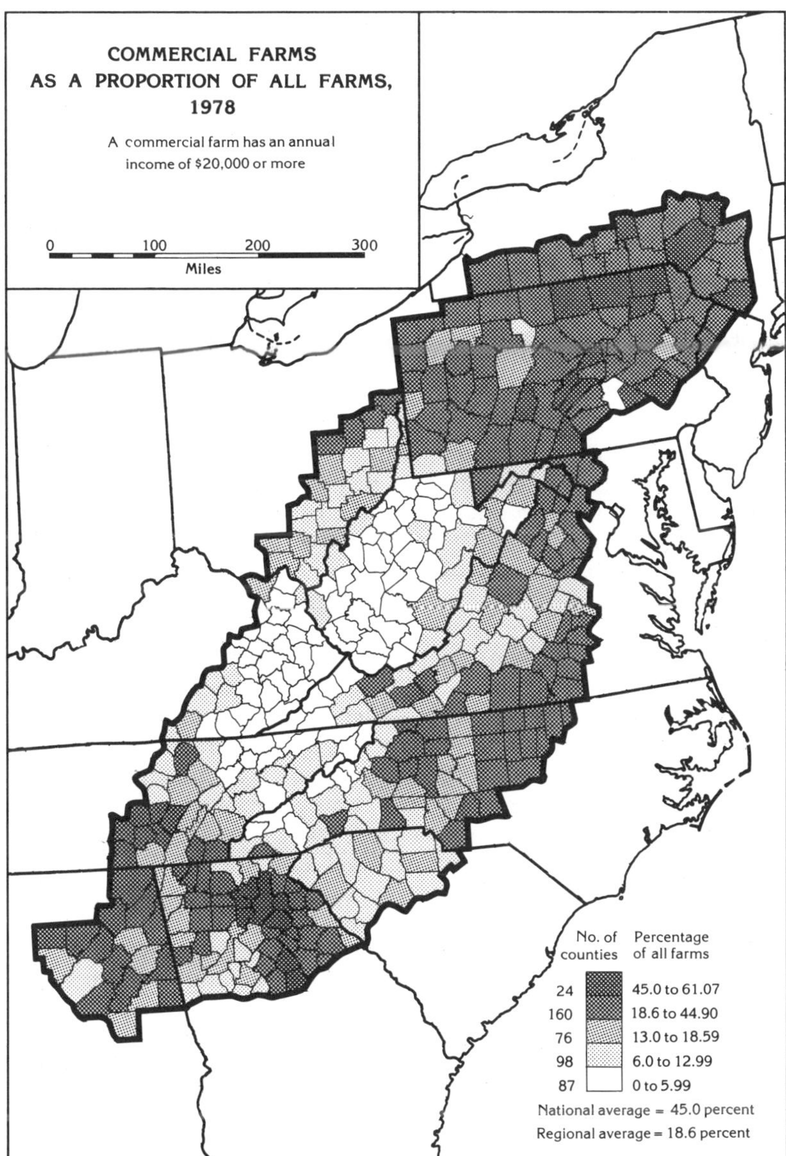


**Figure 6.3**
Source: U.S. Bureau of the Census, *1978 Census of Agriculture,* vol. 1, *State and County Data* (Washington, D.C.: Bureau of the Census, 1980).

suggested by the lowest proportion of commercial farms, was in the eastern Kentucky and West Virginia plateau. In Kentucky, 28 of 36 counties fell below 6 percent commercial farms, or one-third of the regional average. In West Virginia, 34 of 55 counties fit into the same bracket. The steep slopes and shallow soils of these areas simply do not afford adequate farming opportunity, and most of the land in these counties should never have been cleared for cultivation. The small number of commercial farms suggests that substantial numbers of farmers depended upon off-farm employment for a portion of their income: In West Virginia, over 48 percent of the farmers worked two hundred or more days off the farm each year. A sharp contrast in the proportion of commercial farms occurred in south Tennessee. Here, in a number of counties on the Plateau, the proportion of commercial farms approached the regional average, and 10 counties exceeded that figure. The reason is unclear but could have stemmed in part from the presence of the Tennessee Valley Authority and its provision of electricity, cheap fertilizers, and demonstration projects. Agricultural production here was diversified and included dairy (Cumberland County), grain (Coffee County), beef cattle (Van Buren and White counties), and nursery stock (Warren County). The products accounted for at least 30 percent of the total agricultural income in their respective counties.

Across the rest of the region Figure 6.3 shows clusters of counties where the proportion of commercial farms was above average and in 24 counties even exceeded the national average. The densest concentrations of commercial farms occurred in two contrasting areas. On one of them, the glaciated uplands along the Pennsylvania and New York border, large dairy farms provided high gross returns from fluid milk and veal. In Pennsylvania, farmers in Tioga, Bradford, and Susquehanna counties derived over 65 percent of their farm income from dairy products. For dairy farmers in New York's Delaware, Schoharie, and Cortland counties the proportion of income from dairy exceeded 70 percent. On the Georgia Piedmont, just east of Atlanta—the second area—general farming has given way to the production of broilers in the most highly concentrated broiler-producing area in the nation. In 6 counties (Dawson, Forsyth, Hall, Lumpkin, White, and Habersham) farmers derived more than 90 percent of their agricultural income from poultry. On the Piedmont, the zone of commercial-scale farming extended west into northern Alabama. Here cotton gave way to cash grains, livestock, and poultry. Broilers were especially important in Cleburne, Cullman, Randolph, and Winston counties, where 80 percent or more of the farm income was provided by poultry products.

In 1959, the nation's farms produced 30.5 billion dollars worth of agricultural commodities. Of that amount, Appalachia produced 7.1 percent. By 1978 (the most recent data available), national agricultural production was valued at 107.2 billion dollars, and the contribution from Appalachia had fallen to 6.3 percent. The national percentage change for the period was an increase of over 250 percent, whereas the

Appalachian region could manage only a 211 percent increase (Figure 6.4). The reason for the regional lag is twofold. High-quality land around the country has been able to produce greater yields through the application of increasingly sophisticated mechanical, chemical, and genetic technology. Poor mountain land has simply not been worth greater investment even if farming continues. Second, marginal land gradually slips from production as it either is left untended and eventually abandoned or is converted into nonfarm uses such as forestry or residential construction. The result is less land producing fewer commodities.

The areas of greatest change in the southern half of the region are frequently associated with poultry production. Two of the counties with the greatest increase in market value of agricultural products were Union County (918.8 percent) and Wilkes County (698 percent), North Carolina. In both of these counties, more than three-fourths of the agricultural income in 1978 was derived from poultry. High increases in other counties, such as Alleghany County, Virginia, came from increased livestock production on a small agricultural base. Here sales of beef cattle and calves accounted for about 78 percent of the 6.6 million dollar farm income in 1978. In the north the highest percentage change in value of farm products may be attributed to increasing sales of fruits and nuts or poultry, as in Ulster and Sullivan counties respectively in New York, or of dairy products, as in Tompkins and Tioga counties in New York or Elk and Juniata counties in Pennsylvania.

In the central Pennsylvanian plateau, agriculture traditionally has been viewed as a basic pillar of the economy in that it supported many of the region's residents at a subsistence level from the period of initial occupancy until World War II. Farming, however modest, could be depended upon to supplement the diet and provide a bit of cash income. Much of that area remains a poor prospect for modernized agriculture. In other sections—the Piedmont, the Ridge and Valley, and the Plateau of Pennsylvania and New York—agriculture is a much more dynamic source of livelihood and contributes significantly to local economic stability and growth.

## RENEWABLE RESOURCES—WATER

Although the quantity and location of regional water resources were addressed in Chapter 2, an additional dimension of water quality and use will be reviewed here to provide some understanding of the role that water plays in the region's development. Not only is clean water essential to human nourishment, it is required in a number of industrial processes, agriculture, and electrical-power generation in both steam-powered and hydroelectric plants. Unfortunately, running water also provides many communities with their only raw-sewage disposal system.

Water is a renewable resource not only in the sense that it is periodically replenished through precipitation, but also because once it enters the earth-bound phase of the hydrologic cycle it can be purified and be

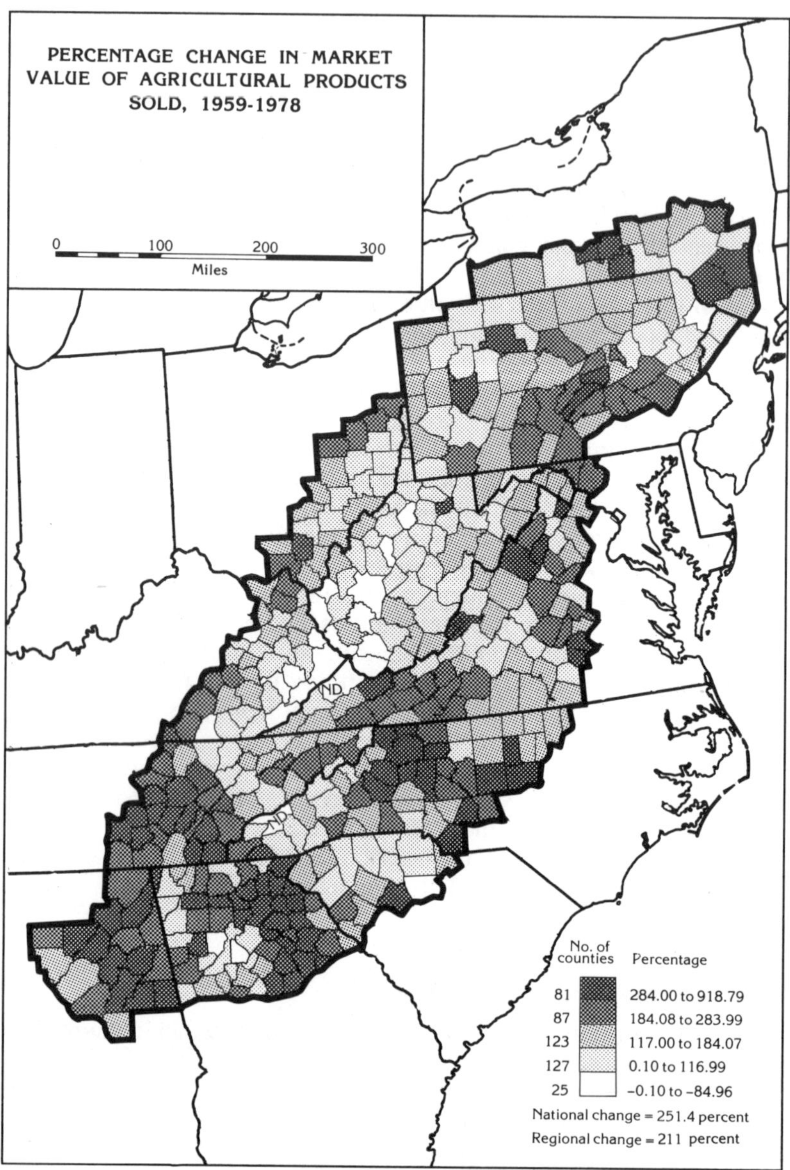


**Figure 6.4**
Source: U.S. Bureau of the Census, *1959 Census of Agriculture* (Washington, D.C.: Bureau of the Census, 1961), and U.S. Bureau of the Census, *1978 Census of Agriculture* (Washington, D.C.: Bureau of the Census, 1980).

used innumerable times. An important measure of water quality is the amount of dissolved solids (calcium magnesium bicarbonate, calcium sulfate, sodium chloride, or materials from industrial or municipal wastes) it contains. Some of these materials enter the water through solution after prolonged contact with soil and bedrock. Concentrations of dissolved solids from this source are usually highest during the dry period of the year when stream flows are lowest. In mountainous areas such as the southern Blue Ridge, dissolved-solid concentrations tend to even out over the course of the year. In general, groundwater will acquire bicarbonates from contact with limestone, dolomite, and glacial drift. Sulfates are dissolved through contact with sandstone and shale. This type of accretion may require several weeks of contact, but large and sudden variations in dissolved-solid content may occur as a stream passes below a municipal or industrial sewage outflow pipe. Acid water from coal mines and brines produced by petroleum well drilling often add significant amounts of hazardous solids in as direct a manner as sewage does.

About 90 percent of Appalachian streams have dissolved-solid concentrations of 300 or fewer parts per million (ppm) and require little treatment other than chlorination before use.[24] Water with fewer than 100 ppm of dissolved solids is considered soft, 100 to 300 ppm moderately hard to hard, and more than 300 ppm very hard. The region's softest water is in the North Carolina Blue Ridge, the Georgia and Alabama Piedmont, and the Pocono Mountains of Pennsylvania. Hard water is found in the limestone and dolomite areas of the Plateaus and the Ridge and Valley. Some of the region's hardest water is found in streams that traverse coal-mining country. Mine wastewater is often acid and may contain high concentrations of calcium and sulfate; dissolved-solid content may range from 100 to 500 ppm on longer streams and may exceed 2,000 ppm in smaller streams that turn red from the formation of sulfuric acid. Three conditions produce acid mine drainage: (1) extensive coal mining in iron sulfide–bearing strata, (2) abundant rainfall and runoff, and (3) low natural alkalinity of stream water. The problem is most severe in the northern and central coalfields, where over 5,700 mi (9,171.3 km) of streams are continually polluted. Here coals are high in sulfur content, yet the streams are low in alkaline materials and are unable to neutralize acid as it accumulates. The problem is perennial once initiated by mining, because groundwater and precipitation percolate through abandoned and inactive mines and mine wastes for years after mining has stopped. The rivers most severely affected are the Susquehanna and Kiskiminetas in Pennsylvania, the Monongahela in West Virginia and Pennsylvania, and the Ohio from Pittsburgh to Wheeling, West Virginia. Numerous smaller streams in heavily mined areas, such as the Big Sandy in Kentucky and the Guyandot in West Virginia, are also affected. Acid water has a deleterious effect on concrete and metal, and because many aquatic animals and plants cannot tolerate low pH (i.e., acid) water, it has limited use for recreational activities such as

TABLE 6.4
Regional Electric Generating Capacity: 1980

| State | Total State Capacity (Megawatts) | Total State Coal Capacity * (Megawatts) | % | Total State Hydroelectric Capacity* (Megawatts) | % | Percentage of Total Capacity in Appalachian Counties | Percentage of Coal Capacity in Appalachian Counties | Percentage of Hydroelectric Capacity** in Appalachian Cos. |
|---|---|---|---|---|---|---|---|---|
| Alabama | 18032.8 | 10659.7 | (56.0) | 2521.1 | (13.2) | 35.9 | 59.3 | 21.9 |
| Georgia | 19429.6 | 10702.1 | (65.1) | 1898.3 | (11.6) | 60.0 | 77.4 | 55.7 |
| Kentucky | 13561.9 | 12488.1 | (92.1 | 742.0 | ( 5.5) | 10.8 | 11.7 | 0 |
| Maryland | 9218.1 | 3031.5 | (32.9) | 476.0 | ( 5.2) | 2.1 | 3.6 | 0 |
| New Jersey | 12653.4 | 1638.2 | (12.4) | 389.4 | ( 3.1) | 0 | 0 | 0 |
| New York | 32550.4 | 2547.0 | ( 7.8) | 4971.5 | (15.3) | 10.6 | 19.8 | 21.9 |
| North Carolina | 16621.0 | 12004.7 | (72.2) | 1934.6 | (11.6) | 61.9 | 77.5 | 67.2 |
| Ohio | 25976.4 | 22130.5 | (85.2) | 1.5 | ( .005) | 42.0 | 48.2 | 0 |
| Pennsylvania | 33964.2 | 19493.8 | (57.4) | 1672.0 | ( 4.9) | 67.7 | 86.5 | 6.6 |
| South Carolina | 11919.9 | 3510.8 | (29.5) | 2268.5 | (19.0) | 37.9 | 10.3 | 42.9 |
| Tennessee | 16293.5 | 9845.0 | (60.4) | 3191.5 | (19.6) | 46.0 | 37.7 | 79.9 |
| Virginia | 11920.2 | 3654.6 | (30.7) | 1054.1 | ( 8.8) | 39.4 | 35.9 | 99.8 |
| West Virginia | 15553.2 | 15272.7 | (98.2) | 264.6 | ( 1.7) | 100 | 100 | 100 |

Source: U.S. Dept. Energy, Inventory of Power Plants in the United States: 1980 Annual; Washington, D.C., 1981.

*Coal and hydro figures will not add up to 100 percent because nuclear, natural gas, and fuel oil power plants are not included.

**Hydroelectric capacity includes power produced by multipurpose and single purpose dam generators and pumped storage generators.

fishing.[25] Extensive treatment is usually required to neutralize the acid and remove iron and other impurities.

Coal mining, especially surface mining, can also contribute heavy sediment loads to streams. Mining, poor agricultural conservation techniques, and urban development are all sources of high sediment concentrations in some streams, which must be removed before the water can be used for most purposes. Sedimentation tends to be lowest in watersheds that are heavily forested; annual loads there may consist of fewer than 20 tn per sq mi (7.0 t per sq km). Other streams in surface-mining areas may have annual sediment loads as high as 3,000 tn per sq mi (1,050.6 t per sq km) of watershed. Sediment may be deposited along streams during high water, necessitating expensive cleanup, or on the stream bottom, thereby reducing channel capacity and aggravating flood potential.[26]

The regional water supply is capable of generating significant quantities of electric power, but the distribution of hydroelectric generating installations is very uneven (Table 6.4). In the southern fourth of the region the Tennessee Valley Authority maintains a number of hydropower sites on the Tennessee River and its tributaries above and below

Norris Dam on the Clinch River in Campbell County, east Tennessee. TVA began construction of the dam in 1933. The two turbine-generators produce about 100,000 kw (about 20 percent less than the power required to operate one large underground coal mine). Norris Lake, 72 mi (115.8 km) long, is the largest of the sixteen major TVA reservoirs that control Tennessee River tributaries.

The Keystone Electric Energy Plant in Indiana County, Pennsylvania. Captive mines nearby provide coal, which is burned in the central furnace building to produce steam. The four cooling towers condense the large volumes of water vapor produced back into water that can either be recycled through the plant or discharged into the stream.

Knoxville. The TVA system is the main reason that almost 80 percent of Tennessee's hydroelectric generating capacity is in the state's Appalachian counties. Although Virginia generates about one-third of the hydroelectric power that Tennessee does, virtually all of it comes from the rivers of the Appalachian section of the state. Each of the states with significant runoff from the southern Blue Ridge and Great Smoky Mountains has taken advantage of its resource and produces substantial amounts of hydroelectric power in its Appalachian counties. The region's largest producer of hydroelectric power is New York, but Tennessee produces about three-fifths more hydroelectricity in its Appalachian counties than does New York.

The pattern of hydroelectric production is different in the coal-producing states. In Kentucky, over 90 percent of the electric power generated within the state comes from coal, and no hydroelectric power is produced in the Plateau counties of the eastern third of the state. In West Virginia, the proportion of power produced by coal-fired steam generators is even higher, over 98 percent. Alabama, Pennsylvania, Ohio, and Tennessee, all coal producers, derive more electric power from coal than from hydroelectric sources. North Carolina and Georgia, although producing little coal, still produce more than 60 percent of their power with coal, much of it imported from Kentucky mines. Whether or not North Carolina and Georgia have significant hydroelectric potential that is underdeveloped is not known. Certainly the construction of reservoirs that would potentially inundate coal-bearing lands, displace large numbers of people, or flood significant acreages of rare level land would not be seriously entertained in most communities. Yet when imported energy costs continue to rise and accidents at nuclear generating plants such as the one at Three Mile Island on the fringe of the region near Harrisburg, Pennsylvania, point up the extreme hazard associated with nuclear-power generation, all reasonable alternatives need to be considered.

## NONRENEWABLE RESOURCES—COAL

Some resources, such as ores and fossil fuels, are nonrenewable—when once used they are gone. Recycling may preserve some materials for additional use, but if coal is burned to produce electricity it is gone forever. The use of nonrenewable resources requires a full understanding of this consequence and planning for economic stability in coal-producing districts prior to the onset of depletion of the resource. The nature of many extractive industries is essentially destructive. Some resources—soil, vegetation, surface water, or groundwater—are severely altered, sometimes permanently, to obtain a more highly valued ore or mineral fuel. Coal is one of these fuels, and some of the methods used to extract it are controversial for their destruction of associated resources.

Coal is mined in some 165 of Appalachia's 445 counties, with production concentrated on the Plateaus or the western third of the region (Figure 6.5). Social and economic life in communities in the Plateaus Province has long been centered on coal mining, and to trace the sequence of heady booms and heartbreaking busts in the cycling of coal demand and production is to gain an understanding of the consequences of dependency on one resource. Both anthracite and bituminous coal have been mined in the region since the 1790s (even earlier in selected areas). Early markets were primarily in home heating, brick making, and blacksmithing. The construction of canals into Pennsylvania made possible the cheap transport of coal, especially anthracite, out of the region to seaboard markets. As the steamboat and railroad gradually eclipsed the canals as transport mediums, they not only improved accessibility to the coal fields but by the 1850s were themselves major consumers of coal. Within the western Pennsylvania coal district, coals were widely available, relatively easy to mine, and an attraction for coke and steel industries that were built at transport access points. Heavy industry developed around some coal-producing points but not others. Pittsburgh, for example, became a major steel center in part because of its river location and its accessibility to growing iron and steel markets in the Midwest, but also because the site was on the thickest section of the Pittsburgh coal seam, one of the most productive

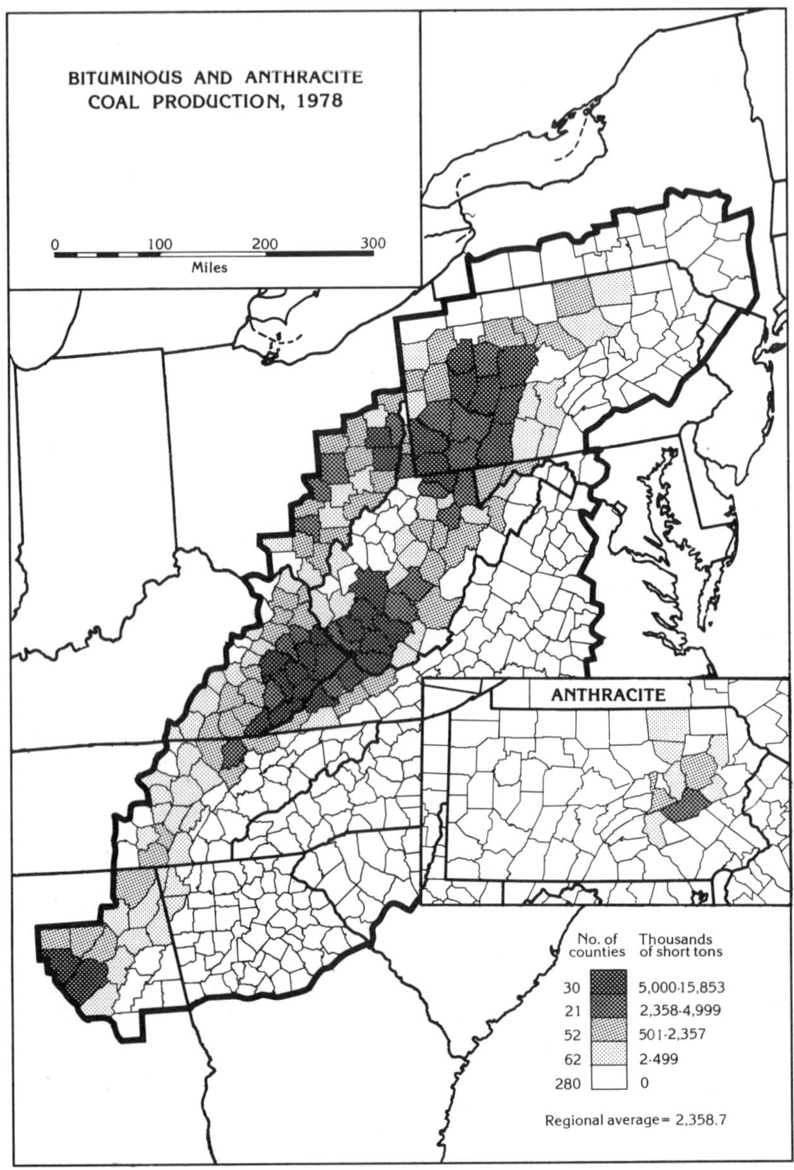


**Figure 6.5**
Source: King Lin, *Coal Data 1978* (Washington, D.C.: National Coal Association, 1980).

of the numerous seams that underlie the region. Johnstown, some 60 mi (96.5 km) east, began as the head of the western branch of the Pennsylvania Canal and supplied local iron ores to Pittsburgh furnaces as well as to its own incipient iron industry. Shortly after 1850, local coals were mined to replace charcoal, and ores from Great Lakes mines were shipped in to replace exhausted local deposits. In the early 1860s, the first elements of the Bessemer Steel Process to be built in the United States were installed in Johnstown's Cambria steel plant, an 8-mile-long (12.9-kilometer-long) complex that became one of the central production units of the Bethlehem Steel Corporation. By 1900, the efficiency of mining and ease of transportation had helped to give coal, together with water power, some 70 percent of the national energy market.[27]

Two decades later, increasingly available petroleum and natural gas provided coal producers strong competition for the domestic heating market. Anthracite was mined with some difficulty and was relatively expensive; as prices continued to rise, the demand in the home-heating market fell, causing a depression in the eastern Pennsylvania fields. Bituminous coals could be sold more readily to industry and electric utilities or exported competitively, and the market for bituminous coal remained somewhat stronger. After World War II, the railroads completed conversion of their coal-fired steam engines to diesel, and the home-heating market for coal continued to decline. By the mid 1960s, coal represented about 80 percent of the total value of Appalachian mineral production, a drop of 7 percent over the twenty years after the war. The only important growth markets for Appalachian bituminous coals in recent years have been exports and domestic demand from electric-power producers. This growth is reflected in an increase of coal tonnage shipped to electrical utilities from 72 million tn (65.3 million t) in 1945 to 490 million tn (444.4 million t) in 1977, or over 71 percent of the U. S. coal production.

Mining has become increasingly mechanized and can no longer be considered a labor-intensive industry. In the nineteenth century, it was not uncommon to have one thousand or more miners in a single mine. Today, it is rare to have five hundred miners in the largest mines, and the average is closer to two hundred.[28] Innovations in automation have lowered employment requirements while maintaining or even increasing productivity. A continuous mining machine costing $430,000 that rips coal from the seam with rotating steel teeth, then loads or conveys it to the mine mouth, can be operated and supported by a crew of about ten miners and three or four major pieces of equipment. A conventional mining crew of up to twelve miners and seven pieces of equipment, using explosives to shatter the coal, may produce somewhat less coal per miner in one eight-hour shift. In the 1950s less than 1 percent of the region's coal was mined by continuous miners, and the average production per person per day stood at about 6.7 tn (6.1 t). By 1978 continuous miners removed 66.5 percent of the coal, and productivity per miner per day was almost 15 tn (13.6 t). Further efficiencies in

TABLE 6.5
Change in Bituminous Coal Production : 1960 to 1978
Underground and Surface Mines

| State | 1960 (000s Short Tons) | 1978 (000s Short Tons) | Percentage Change |
|---|---|---|---|
| Alabama | 13,009 | 14,815 | 13.9 |
| Georgia | 0 | 113 | * |
| Kentucky (Eastern) | 36,259 | 96,233 | 165.4 |
| Maryland | No data | 2,998 | * |
| Ohio | 30,481 | 39,777 | 30.5 |
| Pennsylvania | 63,625 | 81,478 | 28.1 |
| Tennessee | 5,811 | 10,031 | 72.6 |
| Virginia | 22,369 | 31,947 | 42.8 |
| West Virginia | 113,648 | 85,251 | -24.9 |
| Totals | 285,202 | 362,643 | 27.2 |

Source: U.S. Bureau of Mines, Minerals Yearbook, 1960, vol. 2 (Washington, D.C.: Government Printing Office, 1960), and U.S. Department of Energy, Bituminous Coal Production in 1978 (Washington, D.C.: Government Printing Office, 1980).

mining have been gained through surface or strip mining. Surface mines employ fewer miners and yet produce almost twice as much coal per miner per day as do underground mines: In 1978, underground miners produced an average of 14.7 tn (13.3 t) of coal per day compared to the 25.8 tn (23.4 t) produced by a surface miner. In 1950, about a quarter of the coal mined was stripped at the surface; by 1978, the proportion of regional coal mined at the surface had reached just over one-half.

In view of the traditional importance of coal in the regional economy, we must consider whether it can continue to be a catalyst for new development as it was in some parts of the region in the nineteenth century. In the period between 1960 and 1978, Appalachian coal production increased over 27 percent, with the largest absolute and percentage gain coming from eastern Kentucky (Table 6.5). In fact, production increased in each state except West Virginia, where it declined by almost 25 percent. In 1978, the 165 bituminous coal–producing counties had an output of 362.6 million tn (328.9 million t). The average county production was about 2.4 million tn (2.18 million t) (Figure 6.5). Fifty-one counties had above-average production, while 114 were below average. The 51 counties above the regional average produced 289 million tn (262.1 million t), or over 70 percent of the region's coal. County production ranged from a high of 15.9 million tn (14.4 million t) in Pike County, Kentucky, to a low of 4,000 tn (3,628 t) in Dade County, Georgia.

Mining employment is a parallel, though not exact, replication of the coal-production pattern (Figure 6.6). Numerous counties that produce coal—for instance, Fentress and Cumberland counties in Tennessee and Wolfe and Lee counties in Kentucky—have no recorded employees in

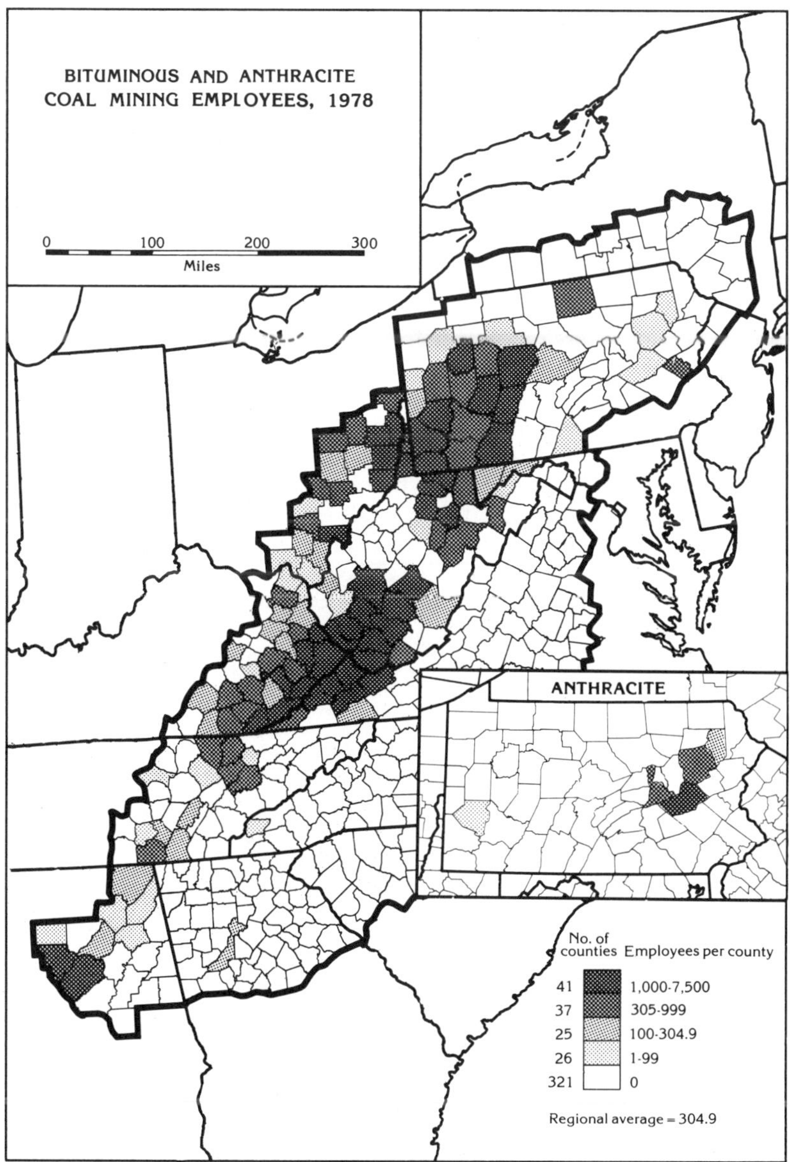


**Figure 6.6**
U.S. Bureau of the Census, *County Business Patterns, 1978* (Washington, D.C.: Government Printing Office, 1980).

coal mining. Employee mobility is quite common in the rural coal fields for two reasons. First, people are increasingly dissatisfied with the quality of life in small coal camps and prefer to live in a larger town to take advantage of shopping, medical services, and social amenities. This may mean that they live in one county and commute to an adjoining county to work. This is the case in Letcher County, Kentucky, where many miners live in Jenkins but drive into Pike County to work in Beth-Elkhorn Corporation's No. 26 mine. Second, strip mines are migratory—some seams may be stripped in a few months, and the equipment is then moved to a new site some distance away. Miners may respond by living in the most desirable location and commuting to the different mine sites.

Some mine employees are not miners at all but are employed in corporate headquarters in administrative positions. Fulton County, Georgia (Atlanta), for example, obviously has no coal mining but does have 175 people employed by coal-mining industries. Allegheny County, Pennsylvania, has no anthracite mines, yet there are some people employed by anthracite companies in the Pittsburgh area. Across the region, bituminous-mining employment decreased by almost 4 percent from 1958 to 1978. The decline was not evenly distributed. Areas with old mines or small mines tended to decline most rapidly, as inefficient operations were shut down. This, at least in part, explains the large percentage changes in Pennsylvania (−33.1 percent) and West Virginia (−22.6 percent). The most rapidly growing sector of mining during the period was strip and auger mining. Much of Ohio's coal is strip mined (71.1 percent), and mining and employment in the state increased over 83 percent over the twenty-year period.[29]

A useful way to assess the overall value of coal production to the regional economy is to examine production stability both in terms of quantity produced and location of production and to examine whether mining employment increases over the same period. We have noted that coal production increased by 27.2 percent (or an average of 496,000 tn—449,872 t—per county) from 1960 to 1978. In order for a coal county to maintain its position relative to the rest of the region, its production would have to increase a like amount. Of 48 counties that ranked above the mean in production increase for the period, 26 experienced comparative growth but 22 went into a comparative decline. In the 23 counties that exceeded the threshold of 1,496,000 tn (1,356,872 t) (Table 6.6), production growth varied from 1.9 million tn (1.7233 million t) in Campbell County, Tennessee, to 9.3 million tn (8.4 million t) in Bell County, Kentucky. The total production in these 23 counties varied from a low of 2.5 million tn (2.27 million t) in Campbell County, Tennessee, to a high of 15.9 million tn (14.4 million t) in Pike County, Kentucky. Together, these 23 counties produced 179 million tn (162.4 million t), or 49.4 percent of the total Appalachian bituminous-coal production in 1978.

It is apparent that coal production is dominated by large mining

TABLE 6.6
Bituminous Coal Producing Counties Experiencing Rapid Production Growth: 1960 to 1978*

| Rank | County | State | 1960 Production (000s Short Tons) | 1978 Production (000s Short Tons) | Percentage Production Increase | Percentage Coal Employment Change 1958-1978 |
|---|---|---|---|---|---|---|
| 1 | Martin | KY | 35 | 8,865 | 25,228.5 | ** |
| 2 | Magoffin | KY | 73 | 2,600 | 3,461.6 | ** |
| 3 | Breathitt | KY | 554 | 5,978 | 979.1 | ** |
| 4 | Muskingum | OH | 591 | 4,764 | 706.1 | 67.2 |
| 5 | Bell | KY | 1,494 | 10,833 | 625.1 | 202.7 |
| 6 | Knott | KY | 1,352 | 5,722 | 323.2 | 14.4 |
| 7 | Jefferson | PA | 974 | 3,866 | 296.9 | -17.1 |
| 8 | Campbell | TN | 643 | 2,493 | 287.7 | 111.3 |
| 9 | Somerset | PA | 2,077 | 6,186 | 197.8 | 16.4 |
| 10 | Armstrong | PA | 2,744 | 6,765 | 146.5 | -28.7 |
| 11 | Clarion | PA | 2,737 | 6,255 | 128.5 | 85.4 |
| 12 | Leslie | KY | 2,291 | 4,989 | 117.8 | -77.9 |
| 13 | Pike | KY | 7,619 | 15,853 | 108.1 | 51.8 |
| 14 | Wise | VA | 5,474 | 11,119 | 103.1 | -12.0 |
| 15 | Indiana | PA | 5,080 | 9,448 | 86.0 | -0.4 |
| 16 | Perry | KY | 4,441 | 7,817 | 76.0 | -14.4 |
| 17 | Clearfield | PA | 6,243 | 10,140 | 62.4 | -13.2 |
| 18 | Belmont | OH | 6,000 | 9,441 | 57.4 | 92.5 |
| 19 | Walker | AL | 3,715 | 5,603 | 50.8 | 52.3 |
| 20 | Harlan | KY | 6,235 | 9,175 | 47.2 | 15.7 |
| 21 | Boone | WV | 6,152 | 8,743 | 42.1 | 2.4 |
| 22 | Monongalia | WV | 6,901 | 8,894 | 28.9 | 2.5 |
| 23 | Buchanan | VA | 10,568 | 13,447 | 27.2 | 21.9 |
| | Totals | | 83,993 | 178,996 | 113.1 | |

Source: U.S. Bureau of Mines, Minerals Yearbook, 1960, vol. 2 (Washington, D.C.: Government Printing O-fice, 1960); U.S. Department of Energy, Bituminous Coal Production in 1978 (Washington, D.C.: Government Printing Office, 1980); U.S. Bureau of the Census, 1958 Census of Mineral Industries, vol. 2, Area Statistics (Washington, D.C.: Bureau of the Census, 1961); and U.S. Bureau of the Census, County Business Patterns, 1978 (Washington, D.C.: Bureau of the Census, 1980).

*To qualify as a rapid growth county, coal production had to exceed the average production increase from 1960 to 1978 by 1,000,000 tons (or the amount of production from one average sized surface or underground mine). The average increase in tonnage per county was 496,000 tons. Therefore, a county had to produce a total tonnage increase of at least 1,496,000 tons to rank as a rapid growth county.

**No employment recorded in 1958.

operations. Small mines cannot effectively utilize modern mining technology, in which one million dollars worth of coal cutting-and-loading machinery is required for just one ten-person crew, nor can the small mine afford the increased employment costs required to comply with the 1969 Coal Mine Safety Act. One must seriously question whether coal will have a positive long-term effect on employment, gross income, or investments in most counties where it is mined or whether the region can create and maintain a stable economy if its future employment is based exclusively on coal. The capital produced by mining could be expected to fund improvements and services and—following the idea of the multiplier effect—to finance a succession of industries within the production area. Coal mining thus should set the stage for the development of other industries that use coal as a raw material, but there is little evidence that this has been the case. In the 23 rapid-growth counties, only Muskingum County, Ohio, and Indiana County, Pennsylvania, had energy-related industry (Standard Industrial Code 35 and others) in 1977, employing a modest total of fifteen hundred people. Those industries normally associated with mining, such as heavy-equipment manufacture, are not attracted to most coal counties because the market is so limited. Nor can local financial institutions participate in encouraging growth by financing equipment purchase or mine construction. The cost of establishing a new underground mine is about $45 per tn (0.907 t) of annual production capacity, so a mine that will produce 1 million tn (907,000 t) per year would cost $45 million to outfit, a cost well beyond the assets of most local banks.[30]

## Mining Technology

The size and location of a coal seam and the topography of the land in which it lies will usually dictate which methods will be used in mining. Thick coal seams (28 in.—71.1 cm—or more) that extend for miles under rolling terrain are very attractive for large underground- or deep-mine development. Various methods may be used to intersect the coal seam, depending on whether it is exposed at the surface or deeply buried, but when it is reached drifts, or tunnels, are simply carved horizontally into the coal. Side corridors are cut back at right angles from the main tunnels, and the corridors are in turn connected by crosscutting passages. The result, when viewed from above, looks like a street map of a midwestern town with square blocks (representing coal to be mined) and streets (representing access tunnels). As coal is removed from the working face, it is brought to the surface by conveyor belts to a tipple where it is washed, sized, and loaded on railroad cars or trucks for shipment.

Mining on the surface may involve two different techniques, depending primarily on the pitch of the slope in which the coal lies. If a coal seam crops out on the surface of a steep hillside, commonly the case in eastern Kentucky, southern West Virginia, Virginia, and Tennessee, it will be contour strip-mined. A heavy bulldozer will remove the vegetation, dirt, and rock—collectively known as overburden—that lie on top of the coal seam and either store the overburden or push it over the edge of the slope. Because bituminous-coal seams lie nearly horizontal the bulldozer can follow the coal-seam outcrop along the side of the hill or mountain and remain at approximately that same elevation. After the coal is exposed it is drilled and blasted loose, and a large front loader moves in to load it onto trucks. The coal is then hauled off the mountain to a tipple, where it is processed for shipment. A variation on this process can be used in gently rolling terrain such as that found in Ohio and parts of western Pennsylvania. Here area strip mining is employed. A trench is dug down through the overburden to

The Pevler Mine preparation plant in Martin County, Kentucky. Bituminous coal from strip and underground mines is carried to holding silos by truck and conveyor. In the preparation building, lower left, coal is washed and sized. Cleaned coal is either loaded on waiting rail cars or conveyed to holding silos. (Photo courtesy of Island Creek Coal Company, Lexington, Kentucky.)

Bituminous-coal strip mining in Indiana County, Pennsylvania. Overburden of soil and rock is set aside during the removal of coal, and the mine eventually will be regraded to approximately the original contour of the slope. Strict reclamation laws and enforcement in Pennsylvania limit the negative effects of new strip mines in that state.

TABLE 6.7
Bituminous Coal Production by Type of Mine in 1978

| State | Type of Mine: Underground | | | Surface | | | |
|---|---|---|---|---|---|---|---|
| | No. of Mines | Short Tons of Coal (000s) | Percentage of Total | No. of Mines | Short Tons of Coal (000s) | Percentage of Total | Average Value Per Short Ton |
| Alabama | 14 | 5,291 | 35.7 | 173 | 9,524 | 64.3 | $ 31.33 |
| Georgia | - | - | - | 3 | 113 | 100.0 | 52.23 |
| Kentucky (Eastern) | 1,060 | 41,625 | 43.3 | 979 | 54,608 | 56.7 | 25.30 |
| Maryland | 5 | 382 | 12.7 | 60 | 2,616 | 87.3 | 19.40 |
| Ohio | 34 | 11,897 | 29.9 | 272 | 27,890 | 71.1 | 21.77 |
| Pennsylvania | 135 | 32,925 | 40.4 | 754 | 48,551 | 59.6 | 27.86 |
| Tennessee | 85 | 4,150 | 41.4 | 146 | 5,882 | 58.6 | 23.21 |
| Virginia | 499 | 21,511 | 67.3 | 250 | 10,435 | 32.7 | 30.50 |
| West Virginia | 740 | 65,216 | 76.4 | 280 | 20,099 | 23.6 | 33.15 |
| Totals | 2,572 | 182,997 | 50.5 | 2,917 | 179,718 | 49.5 | |

Source: U.S. Department of Energy, Bituminous Coal Production in 1978 (Washington, D.C.: Government Printing Office, 1980).

expose the coal seam across one side of the area to be mined. The coal is blasted and removed from the bottom of the trench. As this is done, a mammoth electric-powered dragline will remove the overburden from a second trench parallel to the first. The overburden is dumped into the first trench behind the coal-mining crew. When the process is completed all of the coal is removed from a given area, and the trenches, usually all except the last one, are refilled and graded back to the approximate original contour of the land.

Area strip mining usually leaves little coal behind when mining is complete. Contour strip mining, because it is not economical to remove more than about 1 ft of overburden for every 1 in. of coal-seam thickness, may leave a great deal of coal behind. (This rule of thumb is highly variable according to the type of overburden, price of coal, and other factors.) If the coal seam is near the top of the mountain, the entire seam may be mined by mountain-top removal—a type of area strip mining. If the seam is too far down slope to warrant removing the entire ridge top to expose it, the coal may be mined by auger. A coal auger looks and works like a giant carpenter's brace and bit run by a diesel engine. An auger slightly narrower than the width of the coal seam is screwed into the coal. As the auger works back into the seam, the coal removed is elevated onto trucks, and bit extensions are added to drill the cut deeper. When contour and auger mining is completed, auger holes are sealed, and the empty bench where the coal seam lay and the vertical face or high wall on the ridge side of the bench are back filled.

According to the 1977 federal surface-mine reclamation law, contour strip mines are to be regraded to roughly their original slope to curtail erosion, stream siltation, and acid mine drainage. The regulation is difficult to enforce, and inadequately reclaimed new mines are added to thousands of miles of orphaned or unreclaimed strip mines from older operations, a noxious legacy from the years when strip mining earned its name. Strip mining is predominant today in each coal-mining state except Virginia and West Virginia (Table 6.7). Strip mining has a number of advantages that help account for its increased use. Because fewer miners are employed, the labor cost to produce a given amount of coal is lower than for underground mines. New mines can be opened more quickly and with a much lower investment than deep mines can. If coal seams are too thin or the associated bedrock too brittle for a mine roof in deep mining, stripping may still be possible. Strip mining is also safer than deep mining. In 1977, there were 0.40 deaths per million employee hours in deep mines compared to 0.24 deaths in strip mines (mining still remained one of America's most dangerous occupations).[31]

The price of coal is directly related to its quality, which in turn determines its use. Coal from the Pocahontas seam in southern West Virginia is high quality because it is low in sulfur, pyrites, gas, ash, and other impurities. Consequently it is in demand as coking coal, and its price is high. Ohio coals have higher sulfur content and are usable only for electrical-power generation. The price tends to be much lower, because special sulfur-removal equipment must be installed in power plants using the coal to prevent atmospheric buildups of sulfur that can produce acid rain.

## Coal Mining—Legacy and Future

Coal mining is one of the most controversial issues in contemporary Appalachia. Over the past 130 years mining has been carried on largely unfettered, until the past two decades, by state and federal regulation. Although each state and coal-producing district may present a somewhat different set of mining circumstances—geology, topography, coal quality, market location, law—there has been a dreary similarity in the accumulating results. America's industrial revolution was born in Appalachia—it was in the Pennsylvania anthracite and the Monongahela Valley south of Pittsburgh that large-scale mining techniques were first applied. Little concern was given to the impact these methods had on the people recruited to wrest coal from the ground or on the land that was effectively destroyed in the process.

The anthracite mining country in Schuylkill County, Pennsylvania, illustrates the degree to which problems could develop if regulation and public oversight are not forthcoming to protect those areas that have not yet been fully exploited. Anthracite was mined as early as 1792, with regular boat deliveries to Philadelphia by way of the Pennsylvania Canal by the 1830s. The geology of anthracite was such that individual seams varied from 1 to 6 ft (0.304 to 1.82 m) in thickness. Slate and other rock were interspersed between seams in beds 2 to 18 in. (5.1 to 20.3 cm) thick. Several of these seams and rock partings were mined together as a unit. One of the largest seams was the Mammoth anthracite vein, which measured over 35 ft (10.6 m) in thickness with about 29 ft (8.8 m) of accumulated coal and 6 ft (1.82 m) of refuse rock. Eleven major coal seams of this type were mined. The mining process included bringing the waste rock and coal to the surface, where it was crushed in a breaking mill so that rock could be separated and discarded. Sorting rock was a boy's job—in 1883 over fifteen thousand boys were employed as full-time slate pickers in the breaking mills. Waste rock accumulated in piles near the mines. Today the anthracite fields have an appearance of devastation. Hugh culm piles and abandoned buildings and equipment stand adjacent to the small towns that line valley roads. The removal of thick seams of coal and rock left gaping caverns underground that periodically collapse, resulting in severe subsidence problems and a continuing need to repair damage to roads, underground utilities, and building foundations. Some culm heaps are on fire and send noxious fumes and smoke into the air. In Centralia, a coal seam below the town has been on fire for several years. The fire threatens the health and safety of residents but has so far survived all attempts to put it out.[32]

In the bituminous mining areas, mining often did not get under way until the first two decades of this century, and consequently the accumulation of environmental damage is smaller. It is difficult to mine coal, even using modern technology, without significantly altering environmental quality, not only in the immediate vicinity of a mine but possibly in an entire watershed. For example, coal produced in an underground mine must be washed and graded before it is shipped to buyers. The water used in washing accumulates fine particles of coal and waste rock; regulations prohibit dumping the waste water in surface streams. The alternative has been to build a dam across a valley near the mine and pump the dirty waters into a sludge reservoir behind the dam until the particles settle out or the water evaporates. In February 1972, dams of this type at the head of Buffalo Creek in Logan County, West Virginia, broke (an incident described in Chapter 1). In a similar incident, in December 1981 a slag dam belonging to Eastover Mining Company broke on Ages Creek in Harlan County, Kentucky, filling the valley with black ooze, killing one woman, and damaging homes and property. Although these events were almost ten years apart, they illustrate one facet of an ongoing conflict between coal mining on the one hand and public and environmental well-being on the other. Culm piles and sludge ponds are only two of the problems associated with coal mining. Certainly issues such as black-lung disease, mine safety, and road damage caused by coal trucks must be addressed if coal mining is to become a benign participant in the developmental process. But perhaps the most intractable issue that curtails the positive impact that coal mining could have for the region is mineral ownership and taxation patterns.

## SUMMARY

Many who have extracted Appalachia's resources, as briefly outlined here, have generally lacked compassion for the land they exploited or the people whose lives and livelihoods have been directly linked to sound resource management. In the extractive economy of the coal counties not only are minerals shipped out of state for consumption and support of employment elsewhere, the profits from extraction are also exported. But such transfers only partly explain why investments in industry that would have diversified the economy have not been forthcoming. In some parts of the region, especially the Plateaus, the country is rugged, with limited land available for building sites and tenuous transport connections with outside markets. Some counties have yet to get rail service, in part because the cost of constructing track bed would be prohibitive. Elsewhere, growth and change is an ongoing process. The Piedmont, though ravaged by years of unwise agricultural practices and soil erosion, is now showing signs of an economic recovery. To understand the marked differentials in resource husbandry across the region requires an appreciation of the role of location—in the broad sense of resource distribution and accessibility, and of differences in incentives—in the sense of perceived opportunity for profit and individual or collective responsibility for maintaining human and environmental well-being.

## NOTES

1. Ralph Widner, ed., *Forests and Forestry in the American States* (Washington, D.C.: National Association of State Foresters, 1968), p. 432.
2. Alan H. Strahler, "Forests of the Fairfax Line," *Annals,* Association of American Geographers, 62 (1972), p. 666.
3. Bret Wallach, "The Slighted Mountains of Upper East Tennessee," *Annals,* Association of American Geographers, 71 (1981), p. 363.
4. Widner, op. cit. (footnote 1), p. 312.
5. Ibid., p. 323.
6. Charles H. Ambler, *West Virginia: The Mountain State* (New York: Prentice-Hall, 1940), pp. 482, 513.
7. James H. Patric, *Some Environmental Effects of Cable Logging in Appalachian Forests,* Forest Service General Technical Report NE-55 (Upper Darby, Pa.: Northeastern Forest Experiment Station, 1980), pp. 2–5.
8. Wallach, op. cit. (footnote 3), p. 364, and James N. Kochenderfer and James H. Patric, "Effects of Clearcutting—Past and Present on Water Resources of the Monongahela National Forest," *West Virginia Agriculture and Forestry* 3 (1970), p. 4.
9. George P. Trimble, Jr., et al., *Some Options for Managing Forest Land in the Central Appalachians,* Forest Service General Technical Report NE-12 (Upper Darby, Pa.: Northeastern Forest Experiment Station, 1974), p. 2.
10. *The Forest Resources of West Virginia,* Forest Service Resource Bulletin NE-56 (Broomall, Pa.: Northeastern Forest Experiment Station, 1978), p. 3.
11. Neal P. Kingsley and Douglas S. Powell, *The Forest Resources of Kentucky,* Forest Service Resource Bulletin NE-54 (Broomall, Pa.: Northeastern Forest Experiment Station, 1978), p. 25.
12. Thomas R. Bellamy and Cecil C. Hutchins, Jr., *Southern Pulpwood Production, 1979,* Forest Service Resource Bulletin SE-57 (Asheville, N.C.: Southeast Forest Experiment Station, 1981), pp. 1–2, and Robert L. Nevel, Jr., and James T. Bores, *Northeastern Pulpwood, 1979: An Annual Assessment of Regional Timber Output,* Forest Service Resource Bulletin NE-67 (Broomall, Pa.: Northeastern Forest Experiment Station, 1981), pp. 1–6.
13. John Fraser Hart, "Land Use Change in a Piedmont County," *Annals,* Association of American Geographers, 70 (1980), p. 512.
14. John H. Thompson, ed., *Geography of New York State* (Syracuse, N.Y.: Syracuse University Press, 1966), p. 227.
15. William A. Duerr, *The Economic Problems of Forestry in the Appalachian Region* (Cambridge: Harvard University Press, 1949), p. 120.
16. Wallach, op. cit. (footnote 3), p. 371.
17. Patric, op. cit. (footnote 7), pp. 5–14.
18. Trimble, op. cit. (footnote 9), p. 3.
19. John Fraser Hart, "Abandonment of Farmland on the Appalachian Fringe of Kentucky," *Melanges De Geographie Physique, Humaine, Economique, Appliquee* 1 (1967), p. 358.
20. Charles S. Aiken, "The Fragmented Neoplantation: A New Type of Farm Operation in the Southeast," *Southeastern Geographer* 11 (1971), pp. 43–51.
21. Hart, 1980, op. cit. (footnote 13), p. 507.

22. James R. Anderson, "Specialized Agriculture in the South," *Southeastern Geographer* 10 (1970), p. 21.

23. Merle C. Prunty and Charles S. Aiken, "The Demise of the Piedmont Cotton Region," *Annals,* Association of American Geographers, 62 (1972), pp. 303–304.

24. William J. Schneider et al., *Water Resources of the Appalachian Region: Pennsylvania to Alabama,* Pub. HA-198 (Washington, D.C.: U.S. Geological Survey, 1965), sheet 7.

25. Ibid., sheet 9.

26. Ibid., sheet 8.

27. U.S. Geological Survey, *Mineral Resources of the Appalachian Region,* Professional Paper no. 580 (Washington, D.C.: U.S. Geological Survey, 1968), p. 14.

28. E. Willard Miller, "Mining and Economic Revitalization of the Bituminous Coal Region of Appalachia," *Southeastern Geographer* 18 (1978), p. 89.

29. U.S. Bureau of the Census, *1958 Census of Mineral Industries,* vol. 2, *Area Statistics* (Washington, D.C.: Bureau of the Census, 1961), and U.S. Bureau of the Census, *County Business Patterns, 1978* (Washington, D.C.: Government Printing Office, 1980).

30. For a detailed discussion of these points see Miller, op. cit. (footnote 28), pp. 84–89.

31. National Coal Association, *Coal Data: 1977* (Washington, D.C.: National Coal Association, 1979).

32. John N. Hoffman, *Girard Estate Coal Lands in Pennsylvania, 1801–1884* (Washington, D.C.: Smithsonian Institution Press, 1972), pp. 24–47.

# PART 3

# ISSUES, PROBLEMS, AND SOLUTIONS

# CHAPTER 7

# RECREATION AND DEVELOPMENT

The potential for Appalachian recreational development can be summarized in terms of natural attractions and accessibility. When viewed full length, north to south, the region contains 117 man-made lakes of 500 a. (202 h) or more, catenated behind dams built by the Tennessee Valley Authority, the Corps of Engineers, or various state agencies and utilities. Numerous natural lakes, aligned by glacial scour or sown by glacial ice blocks, dot the Allegheny Plateau in New York and Pennsylvania. Interspersed among the region's ridges and reservoirs are thousands of smaller lakes and farm ponds. The water surface area of these lakes and ponds now approaches 1.5 million a. (606,000 h). About 1.1 million a. (444,000 h) are in public impoundments and private lakes, and ponds provide an additional 300,000 a. (121,200 h). More than 53,000 mi (85,277 km) of rivers and streams traverse the region, and if stream flow is sufficient, at least 10,000 mi (16,090 km) of these rivers are navigable by small water craft.[1]

Scenic uplands are abundant, and nearly two-thirds of the region is wooded. (As a North Carolina mountaineer has said, "The land is turned up on edge so the eye rests on it at every turn.") About one-sixth of the woodland is under state or federal ownership. Many of the nation's largest cities lie adjacent to the region. In fact, the region lies within a single day's driving time of almost 70 percent of the U.S. population. This means, of course, that the potential number of recreational visitors is quite high. The abundance of recreational resources that are easily accessible to large numbers of potential visitors was the primary rationale for the federal government's construction of the 469-mile-long (754.6-kilometer-long) Blue Ridge Parkway and the 80-mile-long (128.7-kilometer-long) Skyline Drive in Shenandoah National Park, as well as the creation of Great Smoky Mountain National Park and numerous other national historic parks and recreation areas. Each of the Appalachian states has established parks in the region, and private recreational facilities cluster near resources and along access routes.

Today, visits to the national park facilities in Appalachia exceed 27

TABLE 7.1
Recreational Visits to Selected Appalachian National Parks and Recreation Areas

| Park or Recreation Area | 1973 Visits (000s) | 1977 Visits (000s) | 1980 Visits (000s) |
|---|---|---|---|
| Blue Ridge Parkway | 11,424 | 12,482 | 13,415 |
| Great Smoky Mountain National Park | 7,586 | 9,174 | 8,441 |
| Shenandoah National Park | 2,308 | 2,789 | 1,699 |
| Harpers Ferry National Historic Park | 936 | 706 | 550 |
| Delaware Water Gap National Recreation Area | 505 | 1,518 | 2,471 |
| Cumberland Gap National Historic Park | 451 | 427 | 486 |
| Totals | 23,210 | 27,096 | 27,062 |

Source: National Park Service. Public Use of the National Park System, Calendar Year Reports, 1974, 1978, 1981, Washington, D.C.

million annually (Table 7.1). The nation's most popular park, Great Smoky Mountain, draws over a million more visitors each year than the better-known national parks of the west—Yellowstone, Yosemite, and Rocky Mountain—combined.

## A RECREATIONAL TRADITION

Although the current volume of recreational use of the Appalachians is impressive, it must be remembered that the region's popularity as a pleasuring place is also historically long standing. As early as the 1790s, residents of Atlantic Coast cities and plantations from New York to Georgia were paying seasonal visits to the mountain highlands, and three distinct resort areas began to emerge over the succeeding decades. In the south, the Carolina Piedmont and Blue Ridge attracted visitors from Georgia and the Carolina Tidewater country; thermal and mineral springs in Virginia's Ridge and Valley drew visitors from the breadth of the coastal lowlands but especially from Maryland, Virginia, and the Carolinas; and the rugged uplands of the Pocono Mountains in Pennsylvania and the Catskills in New York attracted residents of New York City and Philadelphia (Figure 7.1). These early generations of Appalachian recreationalists were not representative of the general population but rather were writers, artists, the wealthy, and the political elite. Their attraction to the region's recreational milieu lay in a variety of philosophical, social, and pragmatic motivations. The people of the coastal cities were not long removed from an Old World, where every acre of land was owned and fenced. Although English tradition, for example, allowed one to cross property owned by others, the village dweller had

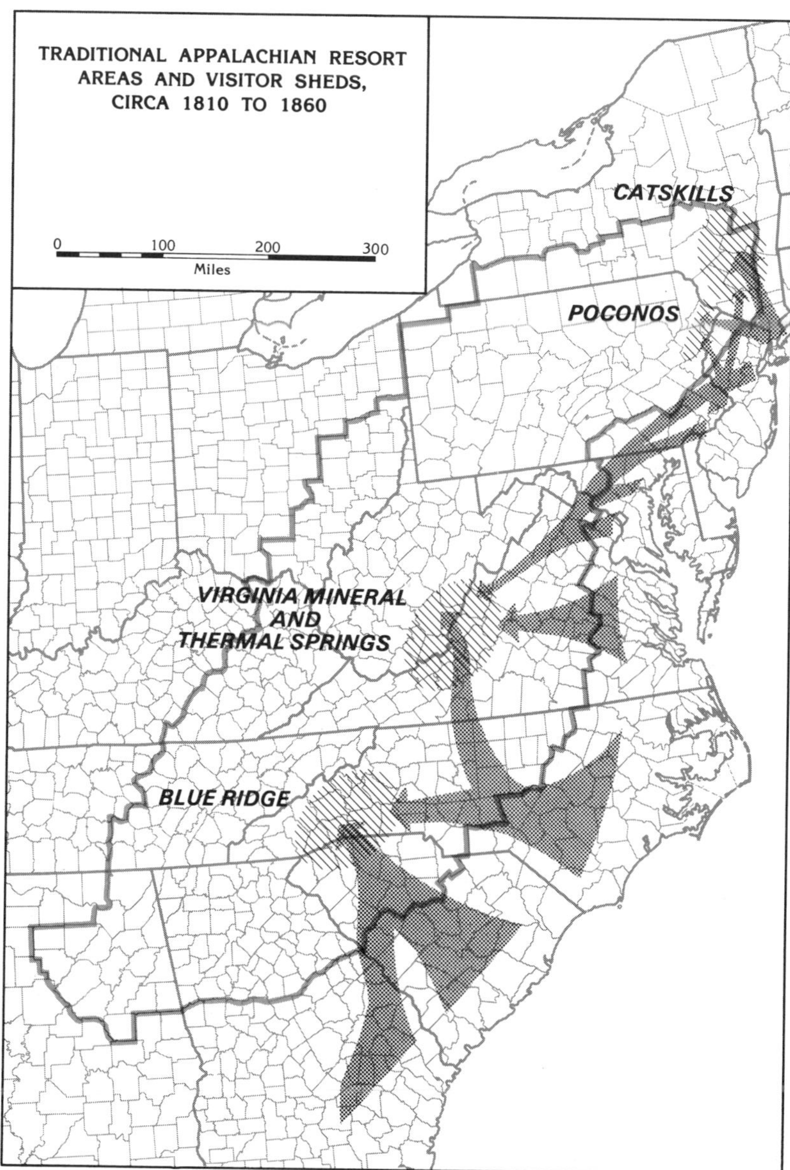
TRADITIONAL APPALACHIAN RESORT AREAS AND VISITOR SHEDS, CIRCA 1810 TO 1860
0
100
200
300
Miles
CATSKILLS
POCONOS
VIRGINIA MINERAL AND THERMAL SPRINGS
BLUE RIDGE

**Figure 7.1**

little open land, other than a tiny village green on which to walk, enjoy nature, or—perhaps—picnic. In the New World, where legal restrictions on use and ownership of land were less onerous, new attitudes toward open space evolved. Individual lawns and grounds around homes and an unobstructed scenic view were landscape qualities highly valued by those who could afford them. The view of a wooded valley or distant mountain became one's slice of wilderness that others could not modify.[2]

As families from the coast began to acquire land in the Appalachian highlands for summer homes and patronize the new mountain resorts, they brought their friends and social traditions with them. The women and children spent several months in the mountains communing with nature and engaging in a continual round of card parties and cotillions, while the men remained at home to manage the plantations. Resort visits might be shortened to a week or two so the family could move on to another resort to meet new people, see and be seen, and begin the social cycle again.

Summer visitors to the mountains also discovered a more pragmatic motive for their travels: health. A number of dread diseases were virtually endemic in the coastal cities and Tidewater plantation country in the early decades of the nineteenth century. Each summer seemed to bring a new cholera or yellow-fever epidemic. Although the causes of illness were not understood at the time, people came to recognize that cities were unhealthy in the summer and that by moving to the mountains they could avoid problems. In the plantation country of the Tidewater South, sluggish rivers and stagnant swamps were breeding grounds for febrile diseases (such as malaria carried by mosquitoes) and miasma; the empoundment of water on riverine plantation rice fields compounded the problem. The moneyed families of the lowlands found that they could escape the "sickly season" by venturing into the mountains, where they found new summer-homes sites, new resorts, and spellbinding scenery.[3] For those who were already ill, the mineral- and thermal-spring resorts of western Virginia offered treatment and remedies.

The three traditional resort areas of the Appalachian highlands evolved somewhat differently, to a great extent because of the contrasts in the resources they were based on and the clientele they served. The resorts of the North Carolina Blue Ridge were established to serve Tidewater planters and the southern urban elite. By the beginning of the nineteenth century, planters were visiting the Piedmont cities of Greenville, Spartanburg, Pendleton, and Winnsboro, where they often purchased land for summer homes or country estates. From these villages they followed the Saluda Gap Road, the state road from Charleston to Greenville, which penetrated into the mountains to Buncombe County, North Carolina, by 1827.[4] A land boom of sorts followed the completion of the road, as planters bought up thousands of acres of mountain land. Slaves were brought to the highlands to clear fields and build houses; churches were established and clergymen were hired. By 1860, summer-home colonies near the route, such as Asheville, Fletcher, and Flat Rock, had new inns or hotels and rows of luxurious residences. Professional developers were quick to recognize that accessibility to the healthful climate and beautiful scenery of the mountains was directly related to the number of potential visitors and buyers, and they seized on the opportunity afforded by the new mountain roads and rails. This is illustrated in some of the first recreational planning evident in the Blue Ridge in 1875. Two developers, Samuel Kelsey and Charles Hutchinson, selected a 1,440-acre (581.8-hectare) tract as the site for an ideal resort location by drawing a straight line on a map between Chicago and Savannah, Georgia, and another line between New York City and New Orleans. They reasoned that their resort, located at the intersection of the two lines in Macon County, North Carolina, would not only be in the heart of the Blue Ridge, but would be midway between north and south and would attract visitors from both regions. They called the village Highlands, and it remains one of North Carolina's most popular summer resorts.[5] By the turn of the century, large inns with resort facilities had been built near Blowing Rock, Cashiers, and Toxaway in North Carolina and at Clayton in Rabun County, Georgia. Smaller hotels, catering to middle-income visitors, also began to appear as railroads penetrated the region.

To the north and west of the Blue Ridge lies a belt of thermal and mineral springs that extends from Saratoga, New York, and Perry County, Pennsylvania, south to Hot Springs, North Carolina, near the Tennessee border (Figure 7.2). All of the distinctly thermal springs in the eastern United States lie within this zone.[6] The largest concentration of springs is in Virginia and West Virginia. All of the Virginia springs are located in the folded rocks of the Ridge and Valley. The alignment of springs stems from water entering a permeable sedimentary rock bed along a relatively high-altitude outcrop on the crest of an anticline. As the water moves under hydraulic head pressure into the adjoining synclinal basin, it is heated to the temperature of the surrounding rock and becomes mineralized. If the water maintains contact with sedimentary formations, it will tend to take up calcium sulfate and sodium chloride. If it passes through crystalline rock, it becomes metallic, arsenical, or sulfated. Volcanic contact will yield carbonated water.[7] The warmed and mineralized water eventually emerges in an outcrop of the same stratum that it entered but at a lower elevation and in an adjacent anticline.

A cluster of springs 25 to 50 mi (40.2 to 80.5 km) northwest of Roanoke was an early attraction for Virginia visitors. Sweet Springs in Alleghany County was resorted to in the 1760s, and by the mid 1790s a resort had opened there. Visitors from Carolina traveled three weeks, over rough roads, to reach the spa. By 1791 the area around Hot Springs and Warm Springs had become so populous that it was made a separate county. The county, following similar locations in Europe, was named Bath, suggesting the central role that the springs played in the area's economy.[8] Hot Springs was promoted by a local physician who extolled the values of its healing baths, treatments, and hotel accommodations.

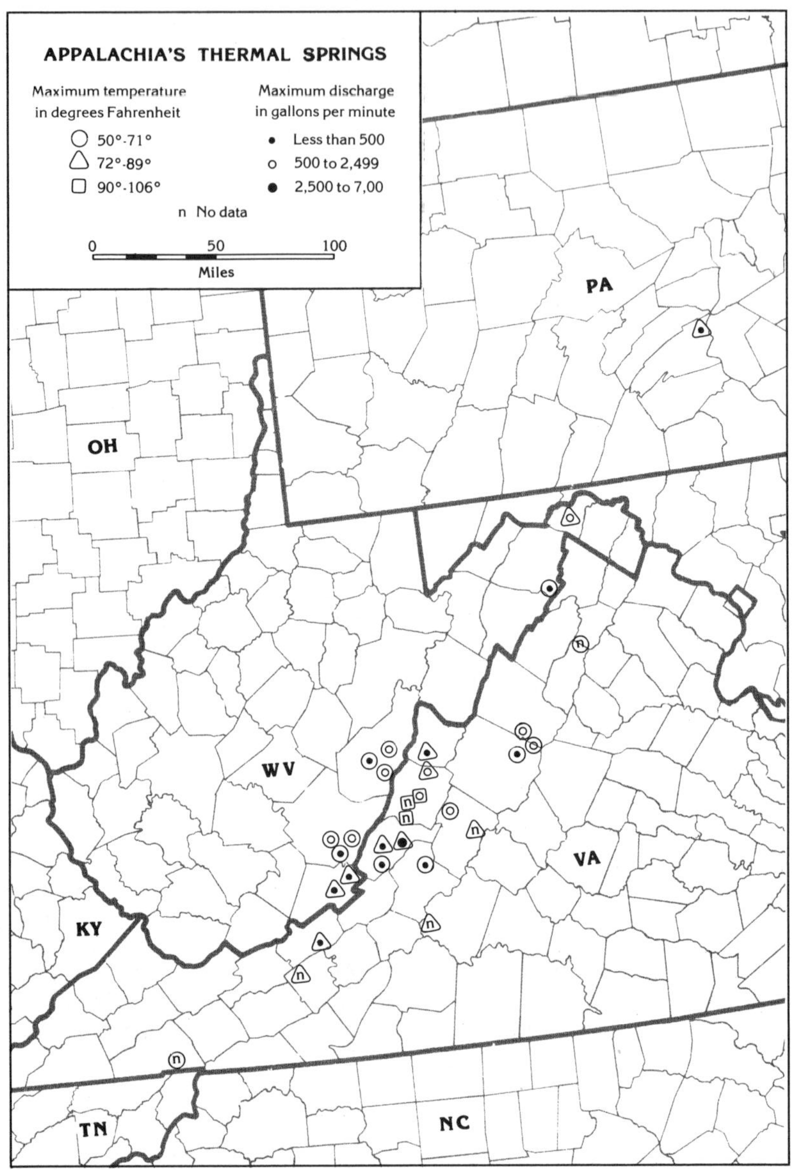


**Figure 7.2**
Based on data in Norah D. Stearns, Harold T. Stearns, and Gerald A. Waring, *Thermal Springs in the United States,* Water-Supply Paper 679-B (Washington, D.C.: U.S. Geological Survey, 1937).

The Bedford Springs Hotel, an early spa in Bedford, Pennsylvania. During the summer, the hotel hosts conventioneers from the large seaboard cities to the east.

Advertising carried promises of cures for afflictions ranging from hepatitis, cholera, and gout to deafness and loss of voice. Other spas advertised cures for special maladies. Patients with multiple ailments traveled a regular 170-mile (273.5-kilometer) circuit of the springs to "take the waters" and, they hoped, obtain a complete cure.[9]

Two great resorts grew around the Virginia springs in Bath County and White Sulphur Springs in Greenbrier County, West Virginia. Hot Springs (eight springs) and Warm Springs (four springs) in Bath County had water temperatures that ranged from 72° F to 106° F (22.2° C to 41.1° C) and a flow volume of 1,200 gal (4,542 l) per minute. White Sulphur Springs, on the other hand, had temperatures of 61° F to 64° F (16.1° C to 17.8° C) and a flow of only 30 gal (113.55 l) per minute. The long-term success of these two resorts seems to stem not from the consistent quality or volume of their resources but from promotion and the maintenance of high-quality services and an image of exclusivity. In 1890, Hot Springs, which had become known as the Homestead during the Civil War, was acquired by the Chesapeake and Ohio Railway (C&O). The hotel was enlarged, and the resort gradually encompassed 17,000 a. (6,868 h) with golf courses, a trout stream, a dairy, and a newspaper. It also employed almost everyone from miles around. Although the C&O has not owned the Homestead since the Depression, the resort has continued to add facilities, such as a commercial airport, and to cultivate an international clientele.[10]

The development of White Sulphur Springs has paralleled that at Hot Springs. White Sulphur gained an early reputation for rather ruthless enforcement of its exclusivity standards. By the 1830s the Greenbrier Valley resort, surrounded by other lesser resorts—Red Sulphur, Green Sulphur, Gray Sulphur, Blue Sulphur, and Salt Sulphur—had become a favorite spa for the southern planters. In the 1850s a new Georgian colonial-style hotel was built near the spring, and the entire resort was acquired by the C&O Railway shortly after the acquisition of the Homestead. In addition to the hotel, today known as the Greenbrier, several rows of cottages were built to accommodate long-term summer visitors. Its railroad station has sidings for private cars, although most visitors today use the airport. Since World War II an estimated 5 percent of Greenbrier County families have held full-time or part-time employment in the resort. The principal clientele of the resort is drawn from the larger cities of the East Coast and Middle West. New York City has been the single largest source of guests.[11]

The third major traditional recreational area in Appalachia is the Catskill and Pocono mountains. The Catskills, lying in portions of Greene, Orange, Sullivan, Ulster, and Delaware counties in southeastern New York, occupy some of the highest elevations along the Allegheny Front. The eastern face of the escarpment stands as much as 3,000 ft (912 m) above the Hudson River, just to the east. The Catskills, and their southern extension into Pennsylvania, the Pocono Mountains, are part of the Allegheny Plateau, much of which has been glaciated. These mountains are rugged and largely forested, with high waterfalls and impressive vistas. The scenery is not only spectacular, especially when juxtaposed against the languid Hudson River, but the area is a scant 100 mi (160.9 km) from New York City. Natural beauty and relatively easy access attracted artists early on—the Hudson River School of landscape painters was one of the early groups of artists, writers, and wealthy travelers to visit the area. With the construction of the Catskill Mountain House on a promontory above the Hudson in 1824, luxurious accommodations were available for the first time. The establishment of this exclusive resort hotel marked the beginning of a sequence of changes in resort visitors, a clientele transition that was based in part on the increasing accessibility of the mountains by more convenient and economical modes of transportation.

In the 1820s and 1830s, the Catskills were patronized primarily by the artists, writers, and social elite of New York City and Philadelphia who were willing to spend eight hours traveling up the Hudson by steamboat and then endure a four-hour stagecoach ride to the hotel. A second exclusive hotel was opened in 1847. Both hotels promoted the healthful climate of the mountains in addition to scenery and an outdoor experience. After the Civil War, this initial stage of travel by steamboat and patronage by the wealthy elite began to change. Up to this point the wealthy largely had dominated visitorship to the resorts. They had the time to travel and obviously could afford the proper equipage or hired help to make the trip reasonably civil. And certainly a measure of status among peers came from the exclusivity of travel to remote or expensive places. In the 1870s a railroad was built into the southern part of the Catskills. New hotels were built near the railroad stations—not large resort hotels but smaller units catering to businessmen. Farmers near the railroad hosted summer visitors in their homes or subdivided their land and built clusters of private summer homes for rent.[12] Improved accessibility and an increase in the number of accommodations, together with intense advertising and promotion, produced an increase in the number of visitors. It was a different group of visitors, to be sure. The wealthy clientele began to abandon the region for more socially and geographically restricted resorts. They were replaced by Protestant businessmen who sent their families for extended summer vacations.

During the first two decades of the twentieth century, with the improvement in roads and the growth of automobile use, the number of visitors to the hotels declined. Services were reduced, new and smaller rooms were added, and some hotels began accepting minorities for the first time. The upper middle class exited and was gradually replaced by middle-income groups and minorities, especially Germans, Italians, Armenians, and Jews. By the late 1920s, the resorts of the Catskills were declining rapidly in popularity, as even the minority groups chose to use their automobiles to travel elsewhere. Today some Catskill resorts are experiencing something of a popularity revival. People are attracted less by the spectacle of nature than by contrived activities and spec-

The relict Hotel Armenia in Haines Falls, New York, was a product of the clientele transition in Catskill resorts when railroads and automobiles provided access to the region's scenic amenities for the middle class.

tatorship. Some hotels retain an ethnic identity—many of the Pocono resorts cater to a Jewish clientele, whereas others have moved to assimilation.[13] The clientele transition process is not inevitable at the level of individual resorts, of course, because resorts can continue to attract primarily wealthy patrons through maintenance of high-quality service and by use of creative marketing. They become unique attractions that create their own demand, and they continue to draw high-income visitors from great distances.

## CONTEMPORARY RECREATIONAL DEVELOPMENT

Recreation is viewed by many local and state governments and some federal agencies as a potentially productive strategy for bringing some measure of economic stability to the depressed areas of Appalachia. Private developers, on the other hand, may recognize the value of employing local people and contributing to the local tax base, but they are less egalitarian than pragmatic in building recreational facilities that will attract visitors and repay investments. These two developmental philosophies are represented in the various interests that have been promoting recreation in the region for a century or more. Regardless of motive, intended purpose, or commitment to local or regional economic

A crossroads grocery store in Towns County, Georgia, has been converted to a real estate office, an "Appalachian Gallery," and other services. As outsiders buy up mountain land for seasonal homes, local people and businesses are displaced.

stability, all development interests—public or private—have found that they must resolve a core of site and situational problems before a recreation-oriented project can be considered economically viable and environmentally compatible.

Recreation is a resource-based activity. Uncommon qualities of place—rugged and scenic uplands, distinctive climate or vegetation, or archeologic and historic significance—are required to attract tourists. The value of these resources to recreational potential depends upon the method and manner of development. Because these resources are restricted to specific locations, they can be developed only if they are made accessible.[14] Appalachian recreational development opportunity is therefore tempered by the restrictions inherent in these characteristics. The region contains a variety of recreational resources and experiences that can only be consumed on site. Further, because only a limited proportion will have an interest in the particular recreational experiences offered by the region or the financial ability to enjoy them, access to the large Midwest and East Coast consumer market is essential for success.

If a sufficient number of tourists patronize a given recreational facility, one important result could be increased local employment. If local people have limited skills and lack the mobility to move to jobs elsewhere, they may provide the basic labor force for a new facility. However, employment in recreational services generally lacks continuity because tourists, although they must go to the resource site, travel according to their own schedule. The result is heavy demand in certain months or days of the week and lower demand at other times. This also means that facilities will be underutilized. To compensate, some specialized, seasonal facilities may close altogether for part of the year. Recent changes in consumer employment patterns and vacation habits also may affect recreational seasonality. People are taking longer vacations, the workweek is getting shorter, and the middle class is generally enjoying higher incomes that allow winter vacations. Skiing, once a sport of the wealthy, is now rapidly gaining popularity with middle-income groups and has diffused from the North into the South along the Appalachian Highlands. High-quality highways now enable outdoor-sport enthusiasts to reach the mountains for weekend recreation virtually year round.

It appears, then, that recreational employment is not a likely panacea for local or state governments seeking some measure of economic stability for Appalachian communities. Much of the work is for women as cooks or maids, and wages for women and men alike tend to be lower than in any other industry. Some of the work is seasonal or part time, and consequently individuals may be paid less than the minimum wage. Because of the problem of employment seasonality and low wages, recreational employment should be considered supplemental to local economies rather than basic.

The reliability of recreational employment is further aggravated by the fact that leisure activities are, perhaps, the segment of a local or regional economy most vulnerable to national economic trends. In a recession, the family vacation is generally the first item cut back when household income or buying power drops. Many recreational facilities—parks, lodges, reservoirs, highways—are built and maintained by public funds. If a faltering national or state economy demands fiscal restraint, recreational construction is often the first area to be reduced.[15] A brief review of governmental and private recreational development throughout the region will illustrate a basic concern for these factors as they contribute to—or detract from—sound, long-term development.

## THE GOVERNMENT AS RECREATIONAL DEVELOPER

The early motive to establish recreational preserves and parks in Appalachia was instigated in large part by public concern for the long-term environmental effects of unfettered lumbering across the region. Beginning in the 1880s, large-scale logging of valuable timber species and extensive burning reduced the wooded uplands to burned-over fields of stumps, exposing the thin soils to severe erosion and the valleys to flooding and siltation. As early as 1900, Congress and the McKinley administration attempted to purchase cutover land in the region for forest reserves to preserve scenic resources in national parks. All of the national parks that had been established at that date were in western states, and eastern politicians were reminded by their constituents of the need for parity. As evidence of the damage caused by clear-cut lumbering accumulated, strong public sentiment developed to preserve timber lands and to gain some measure of control over river-basin flooding. Because the public equated forest reserves with parks, both were thought to serve the same purpose—watershed protection and recreation. The movement to preserve forest lands in southern Appalachia gained strong support from some southern congressmen who wanted the federal government to buy cutover lands and reforest them at federal expense. As a result of a combination of political motivation and continuing environmental damage, the first national forest was established in 1911 in the Monongahela River valley of Pennsylvania and West Virginia.

In 1899, the Appalachian National Park Association was organized in Asheville, North Carolina, with membership from across the nation. The association's objective was to establish a park somewhere in southern Appalachia as a place to experiment in "scientific forestry."[16] The federal government appointed the Southern Appalachian National Park Commission to select a park site. The criteria set by the commission for establishing a park were: (1) the park should be a minimum of 500 sq mi (1,295 sq km) to avoid overcrowding, (2) a substantial part of the area should be in natural forests with scenic rivers and falls, (3) the area should have streams and springs for fishing and camping, (4) the area should function as a natural museum for the preservation of outstanding natural features, and (5) the area should be accessible by railroads and highways.[17] Two areas, from a number of proposals, were selected. The largest of the two was the Great Smoky Mountains, an area of outstanding scenic beauty and diversity of vegetation greater, perhaps, than anywhere else in the eastern United States. The mountains contained 200,000 a. (80,800 h) of largely unknown and virtually unexplored (by outsiders) forest. The second park site was the Blue Ridge in northern Virginia. Although the ridge country was rated as inferior to the Smoky Mountains in scenery and resources, it was located near heavily populated urban areas and consequently was recommended for first establishment under the name Shenandoah. In 1925 President Coolidge signed the bill that authorized the parks.

In the western states the creation of parks and national forests was a relatively straightforward process because much of the land was in the public domain. In the Smoky Mountains, on the other hand, large parcels of land were held by out-of-state speculators or uncooperative lumbermen or were occupied by squatters who held no clear titles but refused to leave their homes. The federal government delegated to the states the responsibility for raising the bulk of the money required to buy the proposed park land. A variety of funding agencies contributed to the project, including the Laure Spelman Rockefeller Memorial Foundation, which granted five million dollars. Land acquisition progressed steadily, and the Great Smoky Mountain National Park was established by Congress in 1934. Two years later Shenandoah National Park, which covered about 100 mi (160.9 km) along the crest of Virginia's Blue Ridge, was established. Skyline Drive was constructed along the crest of the ridge to afford visitors spectacular views of the Piedmont and the Great Valley. Funding was also approved for the completion of the Blue Ridge Parkway in 1936. The parkway had been started in 1933 under the National Industrial Recovery Act and was to connect Skyline Drive to Great Smoky Mountain National Park by a road with broad rights-of-way running along the crest of the Blue Ridge.[18]

Today, the two parks attract over ten million visitors annually (Table 7.1). The majority of park visitors (72 percent in one study) come from the Middle Atlantic and South Atlantic states—the area from New York to Georgia—or from within 300 mi (482.7 km) of the parks. Most visitors are urban or suburban dwellers, and almost half are college graduates with professional careers.[19] The visitors to Great Smoky Mountain National Park tend to be from one of two distinct sheds that are divided by the park itself. Visitors to the Tennessee, or north, side of the park are primarily from northern states along the Interstate 75 travel corridor, with Ohio visitors outnumbering those from all other states. On the south side of the park in Swain County, North Carolina, visitors are primarily from Georgia, Florida, and South Carolina. The

Tourists who leave the Blue Ridge Parkway in western North Carolina to visit Grandfather Mountain or one of the many recreational developments in Watauga and Avery counties provide a ready market for local fruit growers.

creation of this distinctive visitor shed effect is a function partly of distance traveled to reach the park and partly of the difficulty and often congested travel across the mountain barrier and the availability of intervening recreational opportunities on either side of the park.[20]

In general, these parks attract large numbers of visitors for three reasons. First, both parks are close to large population clusters in the eastern states and are served by major interstate highways. Because neither park can be considered remote, visitors can spend more time and money in the vicinity of parks instead of traveling. Consequently, the visitor days for a given person may be greater than at an isolated western park. Second, both parks are "on the way" in median locations. It is a relatively simple matter for someone driving from Michigan to Florida on Interstate 75 to make a short detour through Great Smoky Mountain National Park. Third, both parks, but especially Smoky Mountain, offer a wide range of activities including camping, fishing, hiking trails, historic exhibits, and a reconstructed frontier settlement. Because the modern tourist seeks a wide range of recreational experiences, the volume of visitors to any recreational area tends to be directly proportional to the range of facilities provided.[21]

If the National Park Service can be said to have had a profound effect on recreational development of Appalachia, so has the Tennessee Valley Authority (TVA). The agency was founded in 1933 with the express purpose of controlling flooding, improving navigation, and producing economical electric power through the construction of dams and reservoirs on the Tennessee River and its tributaries. Prior to the establishment of the TVA, recreational development in the Tennessee watershed was largely restricted to the highland resorts of North Carolina and east Tennessee. The recreational resources of the rest of the drainage basin were undeveloped and known only to the few visitors who were willing to cope with poor roads and limited accommodations. The agency recognized early the potential for recreation as a new source of income for the valley. Initially the TVA recreational program was limited to research, planning, and demonstration projects. The agency inventoried recreational resources, planned for recreational development integrating both public and private agencies, and developed model facilities for communities to observe and adopt. Initial planning for recreational use of the flood-control reservoirs focused on local patronage, and benefits were projected to accrue to the counties that immediately bordered the lakes. These counties were all primarily rural with annual income levels substantially below the valley average.[22]

In 1978, more than half of the TVA system was in Appalachia:

| | *Non-Appalachian TVA* | *Appalachian TVA* | *Percentage Appalachian* |
|---|---|---|---|
| Miles of lakeshore | 4,873 | 6,663 | 57.8 |
| Acres of water surface | 314,150 | 338,133 | 51.8 |
| Number of dams | 19 | 27 | 58.7 |

TABLE 7.2
Visits to Tennessee Valley Authority Reservoirs and Associated Sites

| | 1960 | | | 1970 | | | 1978 | | |
|---|---|---|---|---|---|---|---|---|---|
| | Non Appalachian (Visits in 000s) | Appalachian[a] (Visits in 000s) | Percentage Appalachian | Non Appalachian (Visits in 000s) | Appalachian[a] (Visits in 000s) | Percentage Appalachian | Non Appalachian (Visits in 000s) | Appalachian[a] (Visits in 000s) | Percentage Appalachian |
| Summer Cottages[b] | 2,088 | 3,123 | 59.9 | 3,471 | 2,111 | 37.8 | 5,650 | 7,242 | 56.2 |
| Group Camps | 219 | 239 | 52.2 | 754 | 590 | 43.9 | 158 | 378 | 70.5 |
| Commercial Recreational Operations | 5,200 | 7,024 | 57.5 | 4,500 | 6,341 | 58.5 | 3,091 | 9,020 | 74.5 |
| Public Access Areas | 396 | 1,534 | 79.5 | 564 | 2,293 | 80.3 | 6,666 | 11,443 | 63.2 |
| Municipal Parks | 165 | 618 | 78.9 | 351 | 825 | 70.2 | 984 | 994 | 50.3 |
| County Parks | 132 | 1,744 | 93.0 | 155 | 1,647 | 91.4 | 52 | 2,320 | 97.8 |
| State Parks | 3,221 | 1,065 | 24.8 | 8,756 | 2,336 | 21.1 | 11,952 | 6,070 | 33.7 |
| Totals | 11,421 | 15,347 | | 18,551 | 16,143 | | 28,553 | 37,467 | |

Source: TVA statistics, 1981.

[a]The Appalachian segment of the TVA system extends from Guntersville Dam in Alabama upstream and includes tributaries.

[b]Includes both nonestablished homesites and private developments.

By comparison, Lake Ontario, the smallest of the Great Lakes, has 7,500 square miles (19,425 sq km), or 4,800,000 a. (1,939,200 h), of water surface (Table 7.2).[23]

Studies of employment and income generated by recreational activity on the TVA reservoirs reveal that recreation has made a negligible contribution to local communities when compared to the economic benefits derived from manufacturing employment. A case in point is Norris Lake north of Knoxville in eastern Tennessee. Of all visitors to Norris Lake, 69 percent came from three adjoining counties and traveled 50 mi (80.5 km) or less to reach the lake. Their local expenditures per day were small, one-eighth as much as those who traveled more than 100 mi (160.9 km) to the lake. Consequently, income of people in local communities who were employed in recreational services and supply was less than 2 percent of the area's total personal income in 1967. The fact that Norris Lake is a popular recreation site with a large attendance makes these figures all the more sobering. This generalization should apply to other reservoirs in the region as well, and the implication of the Norris Lake case study was that even though the dams and reservoirs attracted millions of visitors each year, the net income gain for people employed in recreational services in the surrounding communities was minimal.[24]

***The Appalachian Trail.*** The Appalachian Trail—a 2,000-mile (3,218-kilometer) footpath along the crest of the Appalachian Front, the Blue Ridge, and the Smoky Mountains—extends from Mt. Katahdin in Maine to Mt. Oglethorpe in Georgia. It was initiated in 1921 by Benton MacKaye of Massachusetts. By 1925, trail clubs along the route had established the Appalachian Trail Conference to coordinate trail maintenance and marking. Today the trail links eight national forests and Shenandoah and Great Smoky Mountain national parks. Although the trail is not directly sponsored by federal or state governments, over 1,100 mi (1,769.8 km) of its route are across state or federal land, and the U.S. Forest Service has attempted to purchase private holdings wherever possible to improve continuity for hikers (the national forests throughout Appalachia are not contiguous units but are pocked with privately owned tracts). In northern Virginia, the trail crosses several private holdings. The owners have blocked the trail with barriers and No Trespassing signs, forcing hikers to use a public road in the adjacent valley bottom. Sections of the trail lie within a day's drive of many of the major metropolitan areas in the eastern states. It is used primarily by college-educated professional and technical people who, because of the nature of hiking and camping, contribute only very small amounts to the recreationally based income of communities along the trail.[25]

## PRIVATE RECREATIONAL DEVELOPMENT: FORM AND PROCESS

Recreation became an important constituent of American life only during the past sixty years. Prior to the 1920s, outdoor recreation was largely experienced only in the traditional resort areas. As the workweek gradually shortened and more leisure time became available to middle-class workers, those with automobiles or train fare could escape the grimy industrial cities on weekends to visit nearby scenic areas. Gradually, private entrepreneurs began to anticipate the recreational-service requirements of tourists by building accommodations and access roads to scenic areas, and landowners began to respond to demands for vacation-home lots by subdividing parcels of their property.[26] Theodore Schmudde has outlined the types of recreational developments that evolved during the 1930s and 1940s to the present.[27] Following his taxonomy we will review the methods of recreational development—land acquisition, building, promoting—and the form of recreational landscape that evolves from the process.

Before World War II, much of the recreational development in the region was accomplished by individuals, who built their own seasonal homes for their own use, or by local entrepreneurs. Developments were usually oriented to a physical resource, such as lakes, streams, falls, or mountain scenery, and were often sited at a parasitic location near a state or national park or a TVA reservoir. There was little evidence of planning, major expenditures, or organized commercial business investment in most projects. A study of land-use changes in a 20-county area in northwestern Virginia from 1937 to 1962 illustrated how this pattern began to change. During World War II residents of metropolitan Washington, D.C., began buying farmland in the northern Virginia mountains for weekend and seasonal homes. By 1962 almost 50 percent of the net change in land use over the preceding fifteen-year study period involved the conversion of farm and forest land to recreation and subdivisions for seasonal housing.[28] After the war, the ballooning demand for recreational facilities and seasonal homes was increasingly filled by planned and promoted business ventures. Large-scale cluster developments evolved, usually near a physical resource, but the role of scenery or lakes and streams was less direct, and natural or primitive sites were of secondary importance. Instead, the emphasis turned to constructed activities such as tennis courts, golf courses, swimming pools, and ski slopes. Developers sought to create projects with an urban character. They found this quality attracted the largest number of visitors, but they also found that this type of development required large amounts of capital to be invested in facilities and services. Profits were realized by subdividing large blocks of rural land into house lots for resale. The tract would be "developed" by means of construction of roads and the installation of utilities. In some instances, the expenditures for promoting and advertising this type of venture exceeded all other costs, including land acquisition and interest.

### Dispersed Development

The process of subdividing rural land for recreational facilities or seasonal housing will often prescribe the form that the development will take. Both process and form have implications for the aesthetics of the facility, the success of the venture in alleviating conflicts with the local environmental balance, and the long-term economic viability of the project. An elementary form of seasonal-housing development is the irregularly dispersed, in which homes are either isolated from one another or are arranged in loosely aligned groups along a road, stream, or lakefront. Lots may be subdivided in small groups or individually by a landowner who provides little additional development; buyers may have to build their own roads and seek utility connections with the nearest public source. This type of subdivision for seasonal housing has taken place around some TVA reservoirs in east Tennessee. At Norris Lake, north of Knoxville, for example, seasonal homes began to appear on isolated lots shortly after Norris Dam was completed in the mid 1930s. Some sites were chosen because of access to waterfronts, others for scenery or simply the solitude of a remote area. This type of development is rarely near a recreationally oriented commercial center. The motivation to engage in dispersed development lies with each individual home owner. Most weekend- or seasonal-home owners in this type of development have permanent residences in nearby urban areas. Speculative building is minimal, and there is little planning or central direction involved.[29] The property for this type of development is frequently obtained through the sale of small farms or wooded portions of abandoned or unproductive farms.

The process of conversion of low-quality farmland to lots for seasonal homes occurs throughout the Appalachian region and is well documented in the Northern Tier counties in Pennsylvania, an area that has a significant share of the regional market for recreational lots and homes. Mary Watson found that Potter County, for example, had a large ratio of seasonal homes to total housing units. She could find no evidence that different types of property—timbered tracts or land with old buildings on it—were more appealing to buyers than others.[30] Local landowners sold mostly small cheap lots, usually less than 1 a. (0.404 h), and advertised in local newspapers or simply reacted to external pressures to sell the land. They were generally unsophisticated in land sales or development techniques. They subdivided their land haphazardly and sold it cheaply because they needed money and had little use for land that produced nothing but a bill for taxes each year.[31] This form of haphazard subdividing occurs when owners sell land parcel by parcel without planning for the consequences. Continued sales lead to highly fragmented ownership patterns, with cheap and unaesthetic improvements and inadequate provisions for services or utilities. In Potter County inexpensive lots of 0.1 a. (0.04 h) were commonly sold and were built up with tar paper shacks or old school buses. Land, once sold to outsiders, is rarely recycled back to the permanent residents.[32] Instead, when absentee owners wish to sell a lot or seasonal home, they will advertise in their urban newspaper, and the sale will likely be to another nonresident.

## Commercial Cluster Development

A second form of recreational development is the commercial cluster. Seasonal homes, motels, and tourist services and attractions are built focused on an existing settlement that is accessible and has some desirable amenities, such as a cool summer climate and beautiful scenery.[33] The clustering process is not new but has precedence in the New York Catskills and the North Carolina Blue Ridge. The western North Carolina towns of Waynesville, Brevard, Tryon, and Saluda began as small lumber towns along the first railroads to penetrate the area or as agricultural service centers along the main highway. Outsiders, attracted by the natural beauty of the region and the amenable weather, began building seasonal homes in and adjacent to these towns in the early 1900s.

Two examples of commercial-cluster developments that illustrate differing methods of exploiting recreational resources and distributing the benefits are Cherokee, North Carolina, and Gatlinburg, Tennessee, 40 mi (64.4 km) to the north. Both towns function as gateways to Great Smoky Mountain National Park, Cherokee at the south entrance on U.S. 441 and Gatlinburg on the north, astride the same highway. The Eastern Cherokee played a role in the establishment of the park by selling 33,000 a. (13,332 h) of tribal lands to be used for the park. Indian laborers helped build the section of U.S. 441 through Cherokee territory to the park site. Today, the town of Cherokee is the center of the 56,500-acre (22,826-hectare) Eastern Cherokee Reservation.[34] The core of the town includes numerous gift shops that sell miniature totem poles and made-in-Taiwan ashtrays, restaurants, motels (some shaped like Plains Indian teepees), and service stations. Occasionally an Indian in a caricature "war bonnet" costume will stand outside the shops (or shoppes) allowing tourists to pay for taking his picture. Beyond this roadside kitsch are a number of cultural attractions that have provided a focal point for income-producing activities and employment of the Indian labor force. A Cherokee museum and historic village attract large numbers of visitors, as does an Indian outdoor play. The Indian Farm Boys Club has used the opportunities provided by these attractions to put together a set of productive economic activities ranging from operating campgrounds to stocking and operating tribal fishing streams. Cherokee has not yet been successful in extending its tourist season into the winter months, and as a result several motels and other recreational businesses are open only during the peak travel season.[35]

Before the creation of Great Smoky Mountain National Park, Gatlinburg was a small settlement in the mountain foothills. The town site is a narrow, confining valley that was easily accessible only after the completion of U.S. 441 from Knoxville to Cherokee. The valley locale has helped restrict tourist-related development to the immediate vicinity of the town. Local landowners became the first recreational entrepreneurs by building motels, restaurants, and gift shops. Since 1960, the Gatlinburg tourist industry has grown very rapidly—the scale of development has been much larger than in Cherokee. By adding a ski lift for the winter season, and a full range of other recreational activities, the town has succeeded in attracting visitors year round. The town offers many ways to spend time and money with evening, as well as weekend, entertainment. Schmudde has found that the town's tourist business and revenues have grown exponentially in recent years. Gross revenues are now comparable to those of other Tennessee cities three or four times the size of Gatlinburg. The fact that gross receipts have risen at a faster rate than park-visitor volume strongly suggests that many tourists now visit Gatlinburg exclusively and largely ignore the park.[36]

Reinforced by this strong economic stimulus, the town is continuing to expand its tourist facilities. National hotel and motel corporations have been attracted and are building large new units. If a cluster development is part of a long-established resort area, national motel chains and large development corporations are more likely to be willing to invest in the area. Established resorts are considered more stable, and development there is more easily financed. Such a resort probably has a national reputation, so an expensive, long-term promotional campaign is not required. A national motel chain generally will not build a new motel with fewer than 100 rooms and wants to maintain at least 75 percent occupancy rate to yield the desired rate of return. By examining the changes in number of hotels and motels and the number of hotel and motel employees for selected recreational areas, one can detect an apparent accommodation replacement process (Table 7.3). In Ulster County, New York, for example, even though the number of motels declined between 1959 and 1978, the number of hotel and motel employees increased by over 240 percent. Small, locally owned motels are either obtaining financing for expansion or are being replaced by larger units built by major motel chains. In the Gatlinburg area (Sevier County), the number of motels increased over 200 percent and employees over 360 percent during the same period. The number of employees per motel is about 8 for Sevier County and 28 for Ulster County. This broad range suggests that most of the established motels in the Gatlinburg area are smaller with fewer rooms and more likely to be locally owned, whereas in Ulster County, in the Catskills, the motels are larger and more likely to be franchised by national chains. Because major motel chains normally expect to derive 80 percent of their income from commercial sources and only 20 percent from tourists, resort-motel developers must promote conventions or seminar business to operate on a break-even basis if there is a substantial off-season period.[37]

Outside of Gatlinburg, near the park boundary, seasonal-home developments are being built, and local investors continue to add amusement equipment, such as cable tramways and a "space needle." Spillover from the Gatlinburg bonanza has now reached Pigeon Forge, located a few miles north on U.S. 441. Here brightly painted motels, snake farms, fantasy lands, and fad "southern" or "hillbilly" restaurants line the

TABLE 7.3
Changes in the Number of Hotels and Motels and Number of Employees in Selected Appalachian Recreational Areas

| State | Recreational Area | County | Number of Hotels & Motels 1959 | Number of Hotels & Motels 1978 | Number of Employees 1959 | Number of Employees 1978 | Percentage Change 1959 to 1978 Hotels | Percentage Change 1959 to 1978 Employees |
|---|---|---|---|---|---|---|---|---|
| NY | Catskills | Delaware | 25 | 26 | 91 | 212 | 4.0 | 133.0 |
| | | Green | 30 | 94 | 84 | 403 | 213.3 | 379.8 |
| | | Orange | 72 | 58 | 494 | 441 | -19.4 | -10.7 |
| | | Sullivan | 80 | 107 | 1,864 | 4,021 | 33.8 | 115.7 |
| | | Ulster | 82 | 80 | 657 | 2,273 | -2.4 | 246.0 |
| NC | Blue Ridge | Avery | 0 | 9 | 0 | 122 | * | * |
| | | Buncombe | 80 | 57 | 573 | 1,158 | -28.8 | 102.1 |
| | | Cherokee | 0 | 0 | 0 | 0 | | |
| | | Clay | 0 | 0 | 0 | 0 | | |
| | | Graham | 0 | 0 | 0 | 0 | | |
| | | Jackson | 14 | 14 | 46 | 111 | 0.0 | 141.3 |
| | | McDowell | 0 | 8 | 0 | 62 | * | * |
| | | Madison | 0 | 0 | 0 | 0 | | |
| | | Mitchell | 0 | 0 | 0 | 0 | | |
| | | Swain | 16 | 32 | 21 | 68 | 100.0 | 223.8 |
| | | Transylvania | 13 | 16 | 30 | 76 | 23.1 | 153.3 |
| | | Watauga | 13 | 27 | 33 | 398 | 107.7 | 1,106.1 |
| | | Yancey | 0 | 0 | 0 | 0 | | |
| PA | Northern Tier | Elk | 0 | 7 | 0 | 50 | * | * |
| | | McKean | 16 | 196 | 12 | 258 | 1,125.0 | 2,050.0 |
| | | Potter | 0 | 9 | 0 | 107 | * | * |
| | | Tioga | 0 | 18 | 0 | 227 | * | * |
| | | Warren | 0 | 13 | 0 | 216 | * | * |
| TN | Smoky Mountain Foothills | Blount | 13 | 15 | 49 | 141 | 15.4 | 187.8 |
| | | Sevier | 44 | 142 | 259 | 1,194 | 222.7 | 361.0 |
| VA | Massanutten Mountain | Page | 0 | 0 | 0 | 0 | | |
| | | Rockingham | 20 | 9 | 125 | 237 | -55.0 | 89.6 |
| | | Shenandoah | 14 | 18 | 53 | 213 | 28.6 | 301.9 |
| | | Warren | 0 | 14 | 0 | 104 | * | * |
| | Regional Average | | 5.1 | 6.1 | 33.9 | 100.8 | -18.1 | 136.9 |

Source: U.S. Bureau of the Census, County Business Patterns, 1959 and 1979 (Washington, D.C.: Government Printing Office, 1961 and 1981).

*Values not calculated.

highway for a mile or more. Pigeon Forge entrepreneurs have found profit in locating close to Gatlinburg—the cluster is a parasite on Gatlinburg just as Gatlinburg has been a parasite on the national park.

Tourist and recreational development in Gatlinburg traditionally has been restricted to a few local families who owned most of the land that was ultimately developed. They have tried to control development and to prevent participation by outsiders. As a result, a few people have prospered by capitalizing on the increase in land values that has occurred, in part, because of the restricted access to the park. They have invested in additional facilities that have added even more to their earning power. Although many townspeople and commuters from nearby are employed by these facilities, the jobs are generally poorly paid. The direct impact of recreational development in Gatlinburg has been considerable, but the indirect impact, as measured by the flow of income and benefits to the community population, is almost nil and certainly has not produced the shared-revenue effect evident in Cherokee.[38]

## Subdivided Tracts

A third form of recreational development in the region is the subdivided tract. Large acreages of rural land are assembled and converted into seasonal-home subdivisions or seasonal-home clubs. Clubs differ from subdivisions in that they provide common recreation facilities to members, such as swimming pools and club rooms. The development site is often resticted to nonowners, and the size and design of the homes may be controlled. The basic resource that attracts tract development may be mountain scenery or other aesthetic attractions, but increasingly the resource may be fabricated—a large lodge, ski slope, golf course, or even a lake.[39] The scale of the subdivided tract is often very large. Developers may acquire land in large units of up to 20,000 a. (8,080 h), and development costs require large capital reserves. Capital in this quantity is usually not available to local residents dependent on small local banks, so the tract is most commonly developed by outside corporations financed by outside institutions.[40]

The primary financial incentive in tract development is the appreciation of land value when it is sold for seasonal-home sites. Examples of concentrations of large tracts can be found throughout the Appalachians. Two intensely developed areas are Cumberland County, Tennessee, and Massanutten Mountain in northwestern Virginia. In Cumberland County, several large tracts have been established on farmland and forested land of the Cumberland Plateau. Although lot sales have lagged behind expected projections, the total number of visitors to the subdivisions each summer has been substantial. In 1973, seventeen thousand families visited one of the developments. The total permanent population of the county was twenty-one thousand, suggesting the possibility of major problems in traffic congestion and demands for services.[41]

Massanutten Mountain in Virginia is a 50-mile-long (80.5-kilometer-long) canoe-shaped mountain lying just west of the Blue Ridge in the Great Valley. Several factors combine to make the mountain and the surrounding countryside appealing to developers. The area is a scant 60 mi (96.5 km) from the heart of the Washington, D.C., metropolitan area. Commuting time to Front Royal, Bentonville, or Luray—three communities along the east side of the mountain—has been one to two hours. That time will shorten appreciably and the inconveniences of small roads will be eliminated when Interstate 66 is completed, connecting the Great Valley route, Interstate 81, with the Washington area. In addition to accessibility, the area had the advantage of being primarily rural farmland surrounded by spectacular scenery. Landowners were willing to sell, and local governments had established no land-use controls or zoning. Tract development began in the late 1950s. By 1973, there

TABLE 7.4
Changes in Seasonal Housing

| State | State Total Seasonal Housing 1950 | Appalachian Seasonal Housing Total 1950 | Appalachian Seasonal Housing as Percentage of State Total 1950 | State Total Seasonal Housing 1980 | Appalachian Seasonal Housing Total 1980 | Appalachian Seasonal Housing as Percentage of State Total 1980 | Appalachian Seasonal Housing Percentage Change 1950-1980 |
|---|---|---|---|---|---|---|---|
| Alabama | 6,307 | 2,052 | 32.5 | 17,363 | 7,607 | 43.8 | 270.7 |
| Georgia | 7,493 | 3,208 | 42.8 | 15,710 | 9,875 | 62.9 | 207.8 |
| Kentucky | 4,586 | 1,107 | 24.1 | 14,117 | 4,830 | 34.2 | 336.3 |
| Maryland | 18,071 | 1,151 | 6.4 | 21,688 | 3,572 | 16.5 | 210.3 |
| New Jersey | 78,320 | 7,450 | 9.5 | 84,395 | 4,087 | 4.8 | -45.1 |
| New York | 161,474 | 41,519 | 25.7 | 168,554 | 45,082 | 26.7 | 8.6 |
| North Carolina | 13,525 | 6,986 | 51.7 | 51,730 | 26,721 | 51.7 | 282.5 |
| Ohio | 23,522 | 3,169 | 13.5 | 30,829 | 5,923 | 19.2 | 86.9 |
| Pennsylvania | 43,071 | 37,233 | 86.4 | 87,099 | 83,067 | 95.3 | 123.1 |
| South Carolina | 7,776 | 544 | 7.0 | 32,261 | 6,415 | 19.9 | 1,079.2 |
| Tennessee | 5,534 | 2,782 | 50.3 | 10,575 | 6,263 | 59.2 | 125.1 |
| Virginia | 9,639 | 3,644 | 37.8 | 22,248 | 11,558 | 52.0 | 217.2 |
| West Virginia | 4,267 | 4,267 | 100.0 | 11,458 | 11,458 | 100.0 | 168.5 |
|  | 383,585 | 115,112 | 30.0 | 568,027 | 226,458 | 39.9 | 96.7 |

Source: U.S. Bureau of the Census, _Census of Housing: 1950_, vol. 1, _General Characteristics_ (Washington, D.C.: Bureau of the Census, 1953), and U.S. Bureau of the Census, _Census of Housing: 1980_, vol. 1, _Characteristics of Housing Units_ (Washington, D.C.: Bureau of the Census, 1983).

were twenty-seven developments on the mountain and an additional thirty or more in the valleys on either side.[42] The scale of development ranged from a fifty-million-dollar ski resort in the south end of Fort Valley in the central section of the mountain to "estates" that were subdivided into 0.5-acre (0.202-hectare) lots without roads, sewerage, or utility easements. Warren County, on the northeast corner of the mountain, did not initiate land-use ordinances to control subdivisions until 1966, after ninety recreational tracts had been created and fifteen thousand lots had been platted and recorded. Much of the land that was divided into lots had natural limitations that should have severely restricted its use for development. The slopes of the mountain and nearby Blue Ridge have shallow soils over steep rock substrata. These conditions make on-site sewage disposal impossible and central sewerage and water systems extremely expensive to operate.[43]

The proportion of seasonal homes in each state built in Appalachian counties is recounted in Table 7.4. In seven states—Alabama, Georgia, Kentucky, Maryland, North Carolina, South Carolina, and Virginia—the proportion of Appalachian seasonal housing increased more than 200 percent from 1950 to 1980. North and South Carolina and Kentucky had the largest increases. The Carolinas have experienced intensive seasonal-home development in the Blue Ridge counties, and the proportion of seasonal-home development in the Appalachian section of these two states either remained stable (North Carolina) or increased dramatically (South Carolina), suggesting that development in the mountains was taking place at a more rapid rate than elsewhere in the state. Kentucky's development has taken place in conjunction with resort development around the reservoirs impounded by dams such as the Lake Cumberland areas in the southeast portion of the state. Several states have at least two major recreational zones. Maryland and Georgia, for example, have the coast or saltwater bays and the mountains as major recreational areas. Each state except New Jersey, North Carolina, and West Virginia increased the proportion of seasonal homes in the mountain counties from 1950 to 1980.

The decline in Appalachian seasonal housing in New Jersey during the thirty-year period may be explained by two related processes that are operating throughout the region. First, in seasonal-home tracts that are associated with large commercial clusters where a range of services is available, or in tracts that are within commuting distance of an urban area, seasonal homes are regularly converted into permanent homes. Owners may retire to their seasonal homes and utilize the services provided by the developer or a nearby commercial cluster. In like manner, people who are willing to commute an hour or more to their jobs may sell their urban homes and move to the country, converting their seasonal homes to permanent homes. Second, small, isolated, or poorly built and maintained seasonal homes may be abandoned or sold to local individuals, who convert them to permanent homes. To a certain extent, the high percentages of decline or increase may be a function of the small number of seasonal homes in 1950.

Counties where the proportion of seasonal homes has declined because retirees and commuters have converted homes into permanent habitations extend across the Piedmont from Pennsylvania south into Virginia and North Carolina. Other areas of rapidly declining seasonal-home concentrations lie within the commuting zone of the region's urban centers such as Atlanta, Knoxville, Pittsburgh, and Binghamton (New York). Small seasonal-home developments, poorly located in undesirable areas, decline through sales to local people for use as permanent homes. This may be seen in the coal-mining districts of eastern Kentucky and southern West Virginia or the anthracite country of eastern Pennsylvania.

Increases in seasonal homes appear in spots or small clusters where attractive recreational resources overcome disadvantages of remoteness or mining and industrialization. A number of counties have sharp increases in seasonal housing where flood-control reservoirs have been built (Knott and Wayne counties, Kentucky; Hall and Franklin counties, Georgia; and Noble, Guernsey, and Morgan counties in Ohio). In Tennessee concentrations of homes appear around TVA reservoirs in Scott, Union, Grainger, and Roane counties. Large areas where contiguous counties have experienced sharp increases in construction of seasonal homes include the Southern Tier counties of New York and the Northern Tier counties of Pennsylvania. Here rolling hills, glacial lakes, and forests—much of northern Pennsylvania is in national or state forest preserves—attract seasonal-home construction. Eastern West Virginia's highlands are undergoing rapid development, in part because of cheap land with spectacular scenery and in part because of access to the Baltimore and Washington, D.C., metropolitan areas. These same factors are likely responsible for the rapid growth of seasonal homes in northern Virginia's Shenandoah Valley–Massanutten Mountain area. Farther south, the Blue Ridge is being heavily developed, beginning in Bedford and Franklin counties in Virginia and extending to the traditional resort counties of Transylvania, Jackson, Macon, and Clay in western North Carolina. Here, large tract developments attract buyers from the eastern Carolina lowlands and as far south as Florida. In some tract developments a majority of the seasonal-home owners may be from the same Carolina or Florida city.

Many recreational tracts throughout the region are poorly planned and developed. Although a majority of the lots may be sold, they may stand open for years as the individual buyers become speculators and try to resell their lots at a profit. The speculative character of lot transactions—together with the perfunctorily developed roads, water and sewerage systems, club houses, golf courses, and other promised amenities—tends to produce subdivisions with few houses and poorly maintained facilities. In 1971 the Pennsylvania Vacation Land Developers Association surveyed buildout rates (the ratio of lots with homes on them to the total number of subdivided lots in a project) in twenty-six recreational subdivisions across the state. The subdivisions contained twenty-five thousand lots of which eighteen thousand had been sold. The overall buildout rate was about 21 percent. Four projects were ten or more years old and had annual buildout rates of 2.5 percent or less.[44] If a project becomes a financial burden and the developer declares bankruptcy, further land-use changes result. The unsold lots are not reaggregated but are sold to a holding company. Any management and regulatory enforcement of county or subdivision codes is now gone, and any further development is largely uncontrolled. Hubert Stroud found that when a resort in the foothills of the Great Smoky Mountains declared bankruptcy in 1970, the enforcement of lot building codes stopped. The few existing well-constructed homes were subsequently surrounded with partially completed shacks and cottages. Roads deteriorated, water lines were laid above ground in some areas, and chronic problems with sewerage and drainage set in.[45]

The reaction against this type of development is strong and well organized in some parts of the region and virtually nonexistent in others. The most vigorous opposition to growth, coupled with support for maintenance of the traditional character of mountain communities, tends to come from the affluent and recent migrants, whereas no-growth sentiment is generally less prevalent among low-income or long-term residents of small, economically depressed areas. To test this idea, Arnold Alanen and Kenard Smith examined the attitudes of the residents of Pocahontas County, West Virginia, toward the building of a large four-season recreational complex (Snowshoe) planned to cost $124 million.[46] The planned project was to be one of the largest skiing and recreational complexes in the eastern United States and would include ski slopes, golf courses, riding stables, tennis courts, a four-hundred-room lodge, thirteen hundred condominium units, and one thousand single-family vacation-home lots. About 79 percent of the respondents were in favor of the development. The strongest opposition came from two groups: The farm families and the white-collar workers at the nearby National Radio Astronomy Observatory tended to oppose the planned complex more than any other groups within the county. In a follow-up study one year after the ski area had been in operation, Alanen and Smith returned to find that the level of acceptance of the resort had actually increased. Especially interesting was the finding that the people who had lived in the region a short time and who had been most opposed to the resort initially were the most supportive one year later; the percentage of approval increased from 79 to 92 percent.[47]

Strong support for new recreational developments may be directly related to the scale of the enterprise and the level of financial commitment. Large developments with strong financial support can, potentially, gain complete control of a development and maintain a high level of aesthetic quality and environmental integrity. The development can become something of a local showplace and stand in dramatic contrast to the pathetic subdivisions that have no redeeming qualities and are designed only for quick profits. On Massanutten Mountain local residents had positive attitudes toward the large ski resort in Fort Valley because the developers were aware of environmental constraints and had cooperated with community leaders. These same residents roundly condemned the smaller subdivision developers who had spoiled the aesthetic qualities of the area and fouled streams with silt and untreated sewage effluent.[48]

## IMPLICATIONS OF RECREATIONAL DEVELOPMENT

The development of recreational resources in Appalachia has long been held by some state and federal government officials and private-sector businesses to be a positive approach to the region's problems of chronic underemployment and low incomes. An example of this prodevelopment attitude is found in a 1975 report on North Carolina's potential for recreational development.[49] County committees, familiar with local resources, made appraisals of the state's recreational potential. Sitting on the committees were representatives of public utilities, county planning boards, economic development commissions, chambers of commerce, newspapers, universities, manufacturing firms, and engineers. After reviewing the natural, scenic, and historic resources of the state, the committees judged 57 counties to have high potential for seasonal-home development (high potential was defined as "great enough to be worthy of future development with few, if any, limitations"). The high-potential zone included 22 counties in the Blue Ridge, such as Avery and Watauga. Addressing the possible benefits of seasonal-home development, the report stated that such development could "provide employment in constructing living quarters, operating and maintaining group camps and cluster developments, and operating other recreational facilities. Local income is enhanced by increasing property taxes and sale of services and supplies as well as through new jobs."[50] The idea that jobs are created, area income enhanced, and local tax base broadened by seasonal-home development is supported by state-wide studies in New England and North Carolina. In these areas an estimated 5 to 10 percent of total state and local real estate taxes are derived from seasonal homes that do not add proportionate demands on the local governments' service loads. The Charles Town–Harpers Ferry development in Jefferson County, West Virginia, is an example. Here motels, restaurants, and two race tracks account for just under 20 percent and seasonal homes for 7 percent of the total county real estate taxes.[51]

The positive effects of recreational development appear to be limited both in type and in location. It cannot be assumed, for example, that tax benefits derived from increased commercial or residential investment will be equally attractive in all locations. Nor can it be assumed that initial benefits of any type will remain stable and not become liabilities over time. In fact, in many Appalachian communities the negative aspects of recreational development far outweigh the positive. The tax issue illustrates the case. When recreational development begins in a rural community, property taxes on new seasonal homes may yield considerable monies for the town or county treasury. But an inevitable result of development is an increase in rural land values as developers bid up the price of land far more than it is worth as farmland. James Branscome and Peggy Matthews discovered that the price of land in North Carolina's Blue Ridge went from $100 an a. to $1,000 an a. (from $241 to $2,471 per h) in five years. Rough, undeveloped land in Macon County sold for $5,000 an a. ($12,355 per h) in the early 1970s and $20,000 an a. ($49,420 per h) at Highlands, North Carolina, if water and sewers were available.[52]

This inflation of land prices in the vicinity of concentrated recreational development is suggested by the data in Table 7.5. Agricultural land values for the entire Appalachian region increased by almost 560 percent from 1959 to 1978. With the exception of the Catskills, where recreational development had influenced land prices prior to this period, the rate of increase of land values in each of the other recreational areas was greater than the regional average. The increasing value of land tends to have a synergistic effect on property taxes and, ultimately, outmigration. As property values increase, rising property taxes on undeveloped farmland or forested land may force the mountain farmer to sell out or to subdivide some property for sale as lots to gain tax relief. Young people find it difficult to purchase a home or a small farm at the higher prices and tax levels, and the likelihood that they will have to migrate from the region increases.[53] Although community members may believe that increased property taxes on recreational developments may stabilize the level and quality of services provided by local governments, the reverse is often the case. In many communities the demand by outsiders for water and sewerage systems, roads, schools, and hospitals outstrips their contributions to the tax base. Even if these services are provided initially, their capacity may be inadequate as recreational development evolves. This was the case in Banner Elk, North Carolina, where two large four-season resorts and numerous smaller tract developments attracted thousands of visitors. A new hospital proved to be too small during the peak seasons, and the cost of treatment rose rapidly for visitor and long-time residents alike.[54]

The role of recreational development in solving the problem of unemployment or underemployment in many communities is not clearly beneficial. Much of the employment available is in low-paying construction or service jobs. Unless resorts operate year round, the duration of employment may be as short as the three-month tourist season. In the large resort developments, construction crews under contract to the developing corporations may be brought into a community during the building phase instead of local contractors being hired. This practice of corporate self-containment may affect the local business community in other ways. The large development may build restaurants, motels, gas stations, a convenience market, furniture store, wine and cheese shop, and clothing stores as part of the recreational complex. While

TABLE 7.5
Changes in the Value of Farmland and Buildings in Selected Appalachian Recreational Areas

| State | Recreational Area | County | Value of Agricultural Land Per Acre In Dollars 1959 | Value of Agricultural Land Per Acre In Dollars 1978 | Percentage Increase In Value 1959-1978 |
|---|---|---|---|---|---|
| New York | Catskills | Delaware | 80 | 577 | 621.3 |
| | | Greene | 140 | 762 | 444.3 |
| | | Orange | 324 | 1,248 | 285.2 |
| | | Sullivan | 215 | 1,070 | 397.7 |
| | | Ulster | 343 | 1,338 | 290.1 |
| | | Average | 220 | 999 | 354.1 |
| North Carolina | Blue Ridge | Avery | 154 | 1,222 | 693.5 |
| | | Buncombe | 283 | 1,181 | 317.3 |
| | | Cherokee | 74 | 836 | 1,029.7 |
| | | Clay | 132 | 1,026 | 677.3 |
| | | Graham | 150 | 1,261 | 740.7 |
| | | Jackson | 122 | 1,542 | 1,163.9 |
| | | McDowell | 156 | 740 | 374.4 |
| | | Madison | 121 | 891 | 636.4 |
| | | Mitchell | 143 | 1,049 | 633.6 |
| | | Swain | 84 | 997 | 1,086.9 |
| | | Transylvania | 184 | 929 | 404.9 |
| | | Watauga | 168 | 1,013 | 502.9 |
| | | Yancey | 152 | 974 | 540.8 |
| | | Average | 148 | 1,051 | 610.1 |
| Pennsylvania | Northern Tier | Elk | 133 | 738 | 454.9 |
| | | McKean | 93 | 646 | 594.6 |
| | | Potter | 57 | 484 | 749.1 |
| | | Tioga | 68 | 554 | 714.7 |
| | | Warren | 87 | 591 | 579.3 |
| | | Average | 88 | 603 | 585.2 |
| Virginia | Massanutten Mt. | Page | 134 | 1,126 | 740.3 |
| | | Rockingham | 216 | 1,567 | 625.5 |
| | | Shenandoah | 126 | 1,008 | 700.0 |
| | | Warren | 121 | 1,198 | 890.1 |
| | | Average | 149 | 1,225 | 722.1 |
| Appalachian Regional Average | | | 128 | 884 | 559.4 |

Source: U.S. Bureau of the Census, 1959 Census of Agriculture, vol. 1, Counties (Washington, D.C.: Bureau of the Census, 1961), and U.S. Bureau of the Census, 1978 Census of Agriculture, vol. 1, State and County Data (Washington, D.C.: Bureau of the Census, 1980).

these facilities attract large numbers of visitors, the net effect is to prevent local business people from participating in the flow of money into the community, and the competition may even force local businesses to close.[55]

The environmental consequences of recreational development can be dramatic and long lasting. When a residential subdivision or resort is built, the land may be at least partially cleared of trees and vegetation, and roads built. Unless great care is taken, the amount of precipitation runoff from denuded slopes will dramatically increase and will result in heavy erosion, sedimentation of streams, flooding, and a lowering of the water table. Bacterial pollution of springs, streams, and lakes may be caused by inadequate septic fields or inferior centralized sewerage systems. According to Robert Gottfried, fewer than half of the land-development projects of the entire region have adequate central sewerage systems.[56] Many mountain soils are too thin or are otherwise unsuited for septic-tank systems to function properly unless the land is subdivided into very large lots to facilitate adequate drainfields. Yet in most of the developments that use septic tanks, 95 percent of the house lots are less than 1 a. (0.404 h) in size.[57] An example of how the local water supply can be altered by increased development is provided by Massanutten Mountain in Warren County, Virginia. A recreational subdivision, initiated in 1959, is gradually building out to full permanent occupancy. In 1968 two wells were sufficient to support the subdivision. A third well was completed in the mid 1970s to meet the steadily increasing demand for water. The water from these wells was once pure enough to be used without treatment. Today, because sewage has percolated down through the limestone bedrock into the water table, heavy chlorination is required before the water can be used.[58]

The visual blight that occurs in and around many recreational developments offends the eye of tourist and long-time resident alike. Uncontrolled commercial strips are built up along highways leading to recreational sites. Garish chalet-style buildings, billboards, and litter mar the scenic views. Wooded hills are defiled by bulldozers scouring out access roads and building pads. When the process is complete, the hills resemble strip mines and the streams below are murky with silt. Only the large, well-financed developments under the control of a corporation or a state or the federal government seem to be capable of controlling the blight that results from the mix of land uses and building design that comes with small-scale development.

The human impact of recreational development is more subtle in many ways than is the environmental degradation, but nevertheless can be profound.[59] Large developments may substantially alter traditional rural and urban settlement patterns. Immigrants may be upper-middle-class or upper-class people from distant cities with different attitudes and values. As seasonal-home owners, the outsiders tend to perceive only those issues that directly affect their proprietary interests. They come to the region to escape urban problems, and they may post their mountain retreat with No Trespassing signs or hire security guards to keep out the "hillbillies." The result is a type of de facto segregation and a dualistic society in which outsiders seek to withdraw from interchange with local residents. To the mountain people, the entire process is an affront. In most mountain communities it is a custom for anyone to cross another's land to hunt, fish, or just walk so long as one does so responsibly. Mountain residents find the outsiders' concept of exclusive use of the land repulsive.[60] In Kentucky's Red River Gorge outsiders have even succeeded in forcing local residents to put up fences

# WHO OWNS WATAUGA'S LAND?

# WHAT DIFFERENCE DOES IT MAKE?

A CONFERENCE

## LAND OWNERSHIP AND COMMUNITY VALUES

TO PRESENT THE FINDINGS OF THE
APPALACHIAN LAND OWNERSHIP STUDY
IN NORTH CAROLINA AND WATAUGA COUNTY

THURSDAY, APRIL 30, 1981

WATAUGA COUNTY COURTHOUSE (COURTROOM)

In some communities where recreational development has placed significant blocks of land in the hands of outsiders, local efforts are underway to curtail further land transfers.

and No Trespassing signs. After a prolonged and well-publicized court fight to prevent the Corps of Engineers from building a dam and flooding the lower reaches of the gorge, thousands of visitors from nearby cities descended on the area. Because private land was interspersed with public national forest land, the local people had to put up fences and signs to keep out unwanted campers and hikers. The fences also restricted the movement of long-time neighbors, and the result was community discord and ill feelings.[61]

Finally, the political character of an area may be altered as a result of recreational development. Several states allow nonresident property owners to vote in local elections on some economic issues. Frequently the priorities of the outsiders are diametrically opposed to those of the local people, and block voting on land-use and utility issues can result. As local businesspeople and developers become more affluent, their economic influence may be manifested in political control of the process that would direct future growth and development. If local people are going to control the way their communities are developed, it is important for them to gain some knowledge of the political process involved in land-use control. Community planning and zoning are often viewed as tools of developers, be they local businesspeople or outside corporations. But zoning regulations can be just as effectively used to keep out undesirable development and maintain traditional values. As long as local communities are quiescent and wait to be exploited by outsiders, it will be very difficult for them to control the direction or type of development that occurs.

## NOTES

1. U.S. Dept. of Interior, *Report for Development of Water Resources in Appalachia,* app. F, "Recreation and Aesthetics" (Atlanta, Ga.: U.S. Dept. of the Interior, 1968), pp. F-xii–F-12.

2. Margaret Mead, "Outdoor Recreation in the Context of Emerging American Cultural Values: Background Consideration," in *Trends in American Living and Outdoor Recreation,* Study Report 22 (Washington, D.C.: Outdoor Recreation Resources Review Commission, 1962), pp. 3–4.

3. Lawrence Fay Brewster, *Summer Migration and Resorts of South Carolina Low-Country Planters* (Durham, N.C.: Duke University Press, 1947), pp. 4, 53, 63.

4. Ibid., p. 63.

5. Jeffrey W. Neff, "A Geographic Analysis of the Characteristics and Development Trends of the Non-Metropolitan Tourist-Recreation Industry of Southern Appalachia," (Ph.D. dissertation, Department of Geography, University of Tennessee, 1975), pp. 34–36.

6. Norah D. Stearns, Harold T. Stearns, and Gerald A. Waring, *Thermal Springs in the United States,* Water Supply Paper 679-B (Washington, D.C.: U.S. Geological Survey, 1937), pp. 74–75.

7. David Lowenthal, "Tourists and Thermalists," *Geographical Review* 52 (1962), p. 125.

8. Andrew Hepburn, *Great Resorts of North America* (New York: Doubleday & Co., 1965), p. 3.

9. Lowenthal, op. cit. (footnote 7), p. 126.

10. Hepburn, op. cit. (footnote 8), p. 5.

11. Jesse H. Wheeler, Jr., *Land use in Greenbrier County, West Virginia,* Department of Geography Research Paper no. 15 (Chicago: University of Chicago, 1950), pp. 51, 86, 130.

12. James W. Darlington, "Railroads and the Evolution of the Catskill Mountain Resort Area, 1870–1920," paper presented at the Association of American Geographers Annual Meeting, Los Angeles, 1981, p. 3.

13. Betsy Blackmar et al., *Resorts of the Catskills* (New York: St. Martin's Press, 1979), p. 96.

14. Appalachian Regional Commission, *Recreation as an Industry,* Appalachian Research Report no. 2 (Washington, D.C.: Appalachian Regional Commission, 1966), p. 13.

15. Ibid., pp. 14–15.

16. John Ise, *Our National Park Policy* (Baltimore: Johns Hopkins Press, 1961), pp. 249–251.

17. Ibid., p. 253.

18. Ibid., p. 416.

19. Glenn E. Haas, *Recreation and Parks: A Social Study of Shenandoah National Park,* Scientific Monograph Series, no. 10 (Washington, D.C.: National Park Service, 1977), pp. 21–33.

20. Neff, op. cit. (footnote 5), p. 79, and Robert L. S. Cole, Jr., and Lisle Serles Mitchell, "Attendance as a Negative Function of Distance, Great Smoky Mountains National Park Campgrounds," *Southeastern Geographer* 9 (1969), p. 20.

21. Appalachian Regional Commission, op. cit. (footnote 14), p. 19.

22. Robert M. Howes, "Recreational Opportunities from Reservoir Construction," *Economic Geography* 15 (1939), pp. 250–252, and U.S. House of Representatives, *Recreational Development of the Tennessee River System* (Washington, D.C.: 76th Congress, 3d session, 1940, Document no. 565), pp. 1–9.

23. TVA statistics compiled by TVA in 1981. John W. Morris, "The Potential of Tourism," in Thomas R. Ford, ed., *The Southern Appalachian Region: A Survey* (Lexington: University of Kentucky Press, 1962), p. 40.

24. Charles B. Garrison, "A Case Study of the Local Economic Impact of Reservoir Recreation," *Journal of Leisure Research* 6 (1974), pp. 7–19.

25. Judith Buckley Murray, *Appalachian Trail Users in the Southern National Forests: Their Characteristics, Attitudes, and Management Preferences,* Forest Service Research Paper SE-116 (Washington, D.C.: U.S. Dept. of Agriculture, 1974), pp. 6–7.

26. Richard Lee Ragatz, "Vacation Homes in the Northeastern United States: Seasonality in Population Distribution," *Annals,* Association of American Geographers, 60 (1970), p. 449.

27. Theodore H. Schmudde, "The Making of Recreational Places in East Tennessee," in Ole Gade, ed., *Planning Frontiers in Rural America* (Washington, D.C.: Papers of the Boone Conference, U.S. Senate Committee on Agriculture and Forestry, 1976), pp. 47–52.

28. Hugh A. Johnson, J. Raymond Carpenter, and Henry W. Dill, Jr., *Exurban Development in Selected Areas of the Appalachian Mountains,* Economic Research Service Pub. ERS-429 (Washington, D.C.: U.S. Dept. of Agriculture, 1969), p. vii.

29. Schmudde, op. cit. (footnote 27), p. 48.
30. Mary Keys Watson, "The Recreational Real Estate Market in Rural Property," *Journal of Leisure Research* 11 (1979), pp. 16–20.
31. R. J. Burby and S. F. Weiss, *Public Policy and Shoreline Landowner Behavior,* Report no. 38 (Chapel Hill: Water Resources Research Institute of the University of North Carolina, 1970), pp. 1–4.
32. Watson, op. cit. (footnote 30), p. 24.
33. Schmudde, op. cit. (footnote 27), p. 49.
34. Laurence French and Jim Hornbuckle, eds., *The Cherokee Perspective: Written By Eastern Cherokees* (Boone, N.C.: Appalachian Consortium Press, 1981), pp. 26–29.
35. Appalachian Regional Commission, op. cit. (footnote 14), p. 43.
36. Schmudde, op. cit. (footnote 27), p. 49.
37. William W. Lyons, "Attracting Investment in Recreation and Travel," *Appalachia* 3 (1970), p. 7.
38. Appalachian Regional Commission, op. cit. (footnote 14), p. 72.
39. Schmudde, op. cit. (footnote 27), p. 49.
40. Hubert B. Stroud, "Amenity Land Developments as an Element of Geographic Change: A Case Study," (Ph.D. dissertation, Department of Geography, University of Tennessee, 1974), p. 125.
41. Schmudde, op. cit. (footnote 27), p. 30.
42. Ken Ringle, "Land Rush Changes Massanutten Rural Life," *Washington Post* (Sept. 4, 1973), pp. A1, A14.
43. William E. Shands and Patricia Woodson, *The Subdivision of Virginia's Mountains,* rev. ed. (Washington, D.C.: Central Atlantic Environmental Center, 1974), p. 31.
44. American Society of Planning Officials, *Subdividing Rural America: Impacts of Recreational Lot and Second Home Development* (Washington, D.C.: Council on Environmental Quality, 1976), p. 25.
45. Stroud, op. cit. (footnote 40), p. 125.
46. Arnold R. Alanen and Kenard E. Smith, "Growth Versus No-Growth Issues, with an American Appalachian Perspective," *Tijdschrift voor Econ. en Soc. Geografie* 68 (1977), p. 30.
47. Arnold R. Alanen and Kenard E. Smith, "Adolescent Impressions of Rural Development in an Appalachian County," in Sue Weidemann and James R. Anderson, eds., *Priorities of Environmental Design Research* (Washington, D.C.: Environmental Design Research Association, 1976), p. 77.
48. Ringle, op. cit. (footnote 42), p. A14.
49. U.S. Department of Agriculture, *An Appraisal of North Carolina's Potential for Outdoor Recreation Development* (Raleigh, N.C.: Soil Conservation Service, 1975), p. 30.
50. Ibid., p. 6.
51. Appalachian Regional Commission, op. cit. (footnote 14), p. 51.
52. James Branscome and Peggy Matthews, "Selling the Mountains," *Southern Exposure* 2 (1974), p. 124.
53. Robert R. Gottfried, *Distributional Implications of Recreation-Led Growth: Appalachia,* PB-257660 (Chapel Hill, N.C.: U.S. Dept. of Commerce, National Technical Information Service, 1975), pp. 69–76.
54. Branscome and Matthews, op. cit. (footnote 52), p. 218.
55. Ibid., p. 126.
56. Gottfried, op. cit. (footnote 53), p. 79.
57. Ibid., p. 82.

58. Shands and Woodson, op. cit. (footnote 43), p. 23.

59. Edgar Bingham, "The Impact of Recreational Development on Pioneer Life Styles in Southern Appalachia," in Helen M. Lewis, Linda Johnson, and Donald Askins, eds., *Colonialism in Modern America: The Appalachian Case* (Boone, N.C.: Appalachian Consortium Press, 1978), p. 57.

60. Gottfried, op. cit. (footnote 53), p. 86.

61. Mary E. Beebe, "Recreation, Exploitation, and Expropriation in the Red River Gorge of Kentucky," paper presented at the Society for Applied Anthropology Annual Meeting, Denver, 1980, pp. 4–6.

# CHAPTER 8

# MANUFACTURING

Manufacturing plays a prominent role in the economy of Appalachia. Over one-fourth of the region's employed civilian labor force worked in manufacturing jobs in 1980, as compared to about one-fifth in the nation as a whole. By comparison, mining and agriculture, traditional employment sources in the region, together accounted for approximately 7 percent of the regional labor force in 1980.

An assessment of the changes in manufacturing between 1958 and 1977 suggests that the region maintained its position in manufacturing vis-à-vis the United States. In 1977 the Appalachian manufacturing labor force of more than 2.7 million workers accounted for 14.8 percent of total U.S. manufacturing employment, compared to 14.6 percent in 1958. Between 1958 and 1977 the region's manufacturing employment increased at a slightly more rapid rate (21.5 percent) than did that of the nation (20.3 percent). Similarly, the Appalachian region had 10.9 percent (38,108 establishments) of all manufacturing establishments in the United States in 1977. In this instance, too, the 1958 to 1977 change was more rapid in Appalachia (21.1 percent) than in the United States (17.6 percent). Over 13 percent (14,878) of all manufacturing establishments employing twenty or more workers in 1977 were located in the region. The regional gain in these larger establishments was 29.5 percent compared to a national gain of 19.8 percent. In 1977, Appalachia accounted for 11.5 percent of the total value added by manufacturing in the United States.[1] However, the 1958 to 1977 percentage change for this measure of manufacturing was more rapid for the United States (314 percent) than it was for the region (302 percent). This is not surprising, for—as we shall see—a large proportion of Appalachia's factories are the kind that process raw materials from the farm, forest, or mine; that is, they are primary manufacturing establishments. Such industries include low-wage, labor-intensive factories that produce textile, apparel, wood, and furniture products.

Although manufacturing is important, there is a very uneven spatial distribution of manufacturing activity throughout the region. Moreover, several recent trends have begun to alter the traditional spatial pattern of manufacturing within the region, trends that are occurring nationally

TABLE 8.1
Manufacturing Employment, Manufacturing Establishments, and Value Added by Manufacture for Leading SMSAs, 1977

| SMSA | Mfg. Employment (thousands) | Percentage of Regional Total | Mfg. Establishments (Number) | Percentage of Regional Total | Value Added ($ million) | Percentage of Regional Total |
|---|---|---|---|---|---|---|
| Pittsburgh | 239.7 | 8.8 | 2,662 | 7.0 | 6,478.4 | 9.6 |
| Greensboro-Winston-Salem-High Point | 144.2 | 5.3 | 1,741 | 4.6 | 4,285.3 | 6.4 |
| Atlanta | 128.7 | 4.7 | 2,758 | 7.2 | 4,222.8 | 6.3 |
| Allentown-Bethlehem-Easton | 106.8 | 3.9 | 1,183 | 3.1 | 2,731.8 | 4.0 |
| Greenville-Spartanburg | 104.8 | 3.8 | 983 | 2.6 | 2,129.7 | 3.2 |
| Charlotte-Gastonia | 87.1 | 3.2 | 1,401 | 3.7 | 1,885.1 | 2.8 |
| Northeast Pennsylvania | 70.9 | 2.6 | 1,266 | 3.3 | 1,327.8 | 2.0 |
| Birmingham | 64.5 | 2.4 | 1,084 | 2.8 | 1,595.7 | 2.4 |
| Johnson City-Kingsport-Bristol | 54.5 | 2.0 | 429 | 1.1 | 1,505.0 | 2.2 |
| Chattanooga | 53.9 | 2.0 | 671 | 1.8 | 1,290.0 | 1.9 |
| Reading | 50.1 | 1.8 | 667 | 1.8 | 1,378.8 | 2.0 |
| Harrisburg | 40.4 | 1.6 | 495 | 1.3 | 1,164.2 | 1.7 |
| Knoxville | 39.6 | 1.5 | 546 | 1.4 | 1,174.8 | 1.7 |
| Binghamton | 39.6 | 1.5 | 389 | 1.0 | 1,081.2 | 1.6 |
| TOTAL | 1,224.8 | 45.1 | 16,275 | 42.7 | 32,250.6 | 47.8 |

Source: U.S. Bureau of the Census, U.S. Census of Manufacturers, 1977, Geographic Area Series (Washington, D.C.: Bureau of the Census, 1980).

and are also reflected in the region's changing population patterns. Two of these changes are the movement of manufacturing to the Sun Belt, as the southern portion of the United States is sometimes called, and the growth in the importance of manufacturing in nonmetropolitan areas.[2]

## THE SPATIAL DISTRIBUTION OF MANUFACTURING

Appalachian Pennsylvania, North Carolina, and Georgia accounted for the majority of the region's manufacturing in 1977. Together the Appalachian portions of the 3 states made up nearly 60 percent of the region's manufacturing employment, manufacturing establishments, and the value added by manufacturing. The Appalachian counties of South Carolina, Tennessee, and Virginia each accounted for an additional 7 to 8 percent of the region's manufacturing employment. The other Appalachian states were less important, and the share of manufacturing contributed by the coal-mining areas of central Appalachia (Kentucky and West Virginia) was very small indeed.

The majority of manufacturing employment, manufacturing establishments, and value added by manufacturing was found in the region's 105 metropolitan counties. However, in Appalachia the share of manufacturing employment in nonmetropolitan counties is significantly higher than the 29 percent average for the nation.[3]

As one would expect, the largest cities accounted for the greatest share of manufacturing (Table 8.1). The 66 counties that made up the region's fourteen most important manufacturing Standard Metropolitan Statistical Areas (SMSAs) accounted for over two-fifths of all manufacturing employment, establishments, and value added. The Pittsburgh SMSA led in two categories; nearly 9 percent of all manufacturing employment was located in the 4 counties of the Pittsburgh SMSA. The 15-county Atlanta SMSA, which ranked third in employment and value added behind the Greensboro–Winston-Salem–High Point, North Carolina, SMSA, was first in number of manufacturing establishments.

Several indices can be used to measure the importance of manufacturing in any given area relative to some established norm. One such index is the location quotient, which is actually a ratio of ratios. The location quotient for manufacturing employment for each county is determined by dividing its percentage of employment in manufacturing by the national percentage (8.17 percent for 1977). Thus, if a county had a location quotient exceeding 1.0, it had more than its share of the nation's manufacturing employment.

The location quotient for the Appalachian region in 1977 was 1.26, meaning that the region's share of manufacturing employment was about one-quarter greater than that of the total U.S. population. A map of the location quotient by county reveals the relative concentration of manufacturing (see Figure 8.1; this and all other figures in this chapter

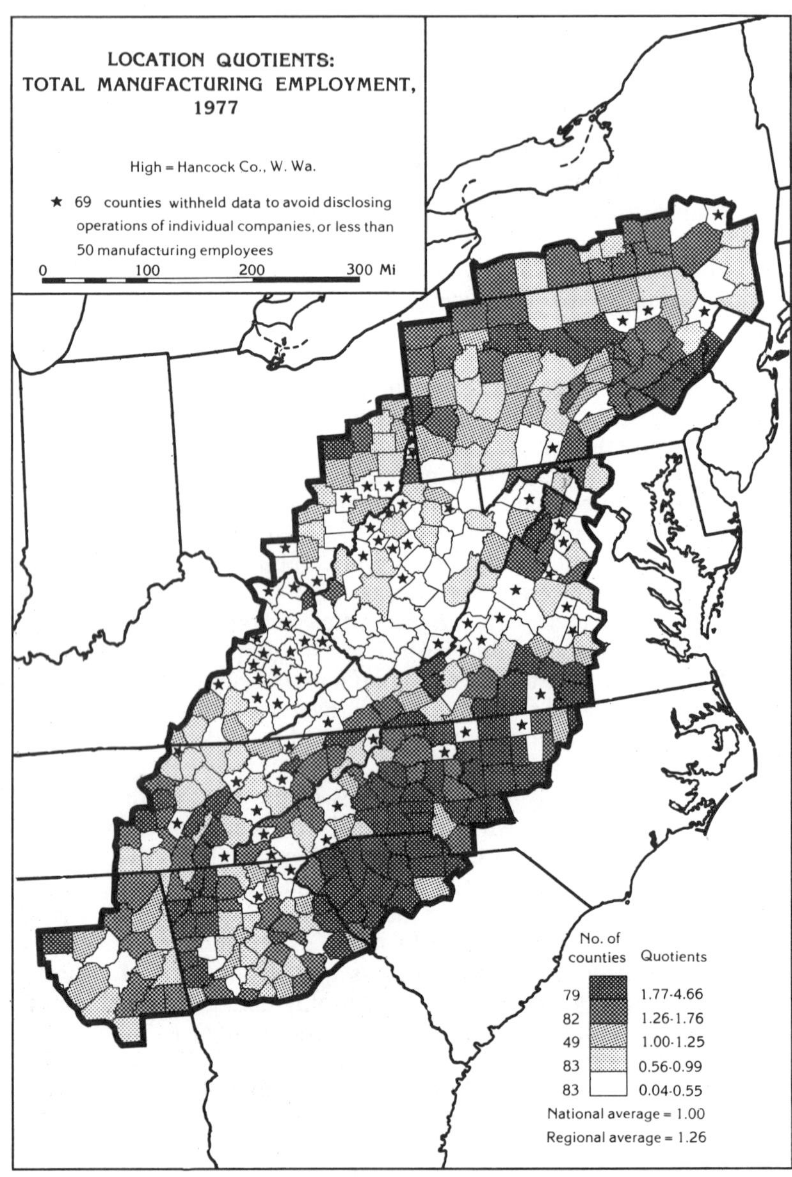
LOCATION QUOTIENTS:
TOTAL MANUFACTURING EMPLOYMENT,
1977
High = Hancock Co., W. Wa.
★ 69 counties withheld data to avoid disclosing operations of individual companies, or less than 50 manufacturing employees
0 100 200 300 Mi
No. of counties
Quotients
79 1.77-4.66
82 1.26-1.76
49 1.00-1.25
83 0.56-0.99
83 0.04-0.55
National average = 1.00
Regional average = 1.26

**Figure 8.1**

are based on data obtained from the U.S. *Census of Manufacturers*, 1958 and 1977). Nearly 43 percent of the 376 counties for which data were available in 1977 had location quotients above both the national and regional average.[4] In 1977 manufacturing was most concentrated in the Piedmont counties of the Carolinas and southern Virginia where the textile and apparel industries were highly significant; in southeast Tennessee; in northwest Georgia; and in eastern, central, and northwestern Pennsylvania. West Virginia's Hancock County (where Weirton is located), on the Ohio River and contiguous to the Pittsburgh SMSA, had the region's highest concentration of manufacturing employment. In summary, the greatest concentration of manufacturing employment was found in the southern Appalachian counties, and a large share of the high-employment counties there were nonmetropolitan (compare Figures 5.1 and 8.1).

In considering the spatial distribution of manufacturing in the Appalachian region it is also important to examine the technical level of industry. Appalachia, and especially its southern areas, is perceived to have industries with low technical levels. Most "generalizations about the structure of southern manufacturing include its lack of a diversified industrial base and the dominance of low wage, low value-added, low capital investment, and slow growth industries."[5] Indeed, popular preconceptions about manufacturing development, in central and southern Appalachia at least, were that such areas could not support manufacturing at all because of the isolation, poverty, and low educational levels that were characteristic of the region and its people.[6]

One of several measures that can be used to demonstrate the level of manufacturing sophistication is value added per manufacturing employee. Nationally, the value added per manufacturing employee was $31,603 in 1977, whereas the regional figure was only $24,712. This lends support to the notion of a lower technical level of manufacturing in the region. Nearly one-third of the 376 counties for which data were available had higher ratios than the regional average, but only 41 of the counties were above the national average (Figure 8.2). These 41 counties were scattered across the region. Although they included metropolitan counties, such as those in the Atlanta SMSA, nearly two-thirds were nonmetropolitan, including Jefferson County in West Virginia's eastern panhandle, which had the highest value added per manufacturing employee. Counties with low ratios were located predominantly in the southern and central portions of the region. Thus, the majority of counties in North Carolina, South Carolina, Alabama, Tennessee, and West Virginia were well below the regional average. As we shall see, the types of manufacturing establishments in these areas included a large share of those producing food products, textiles, lumber and wood, apparel, and furniture and fixtures. These are manufacturing categories that include industries described as laggard, or growing very slowly, by Robert Estall.[7]

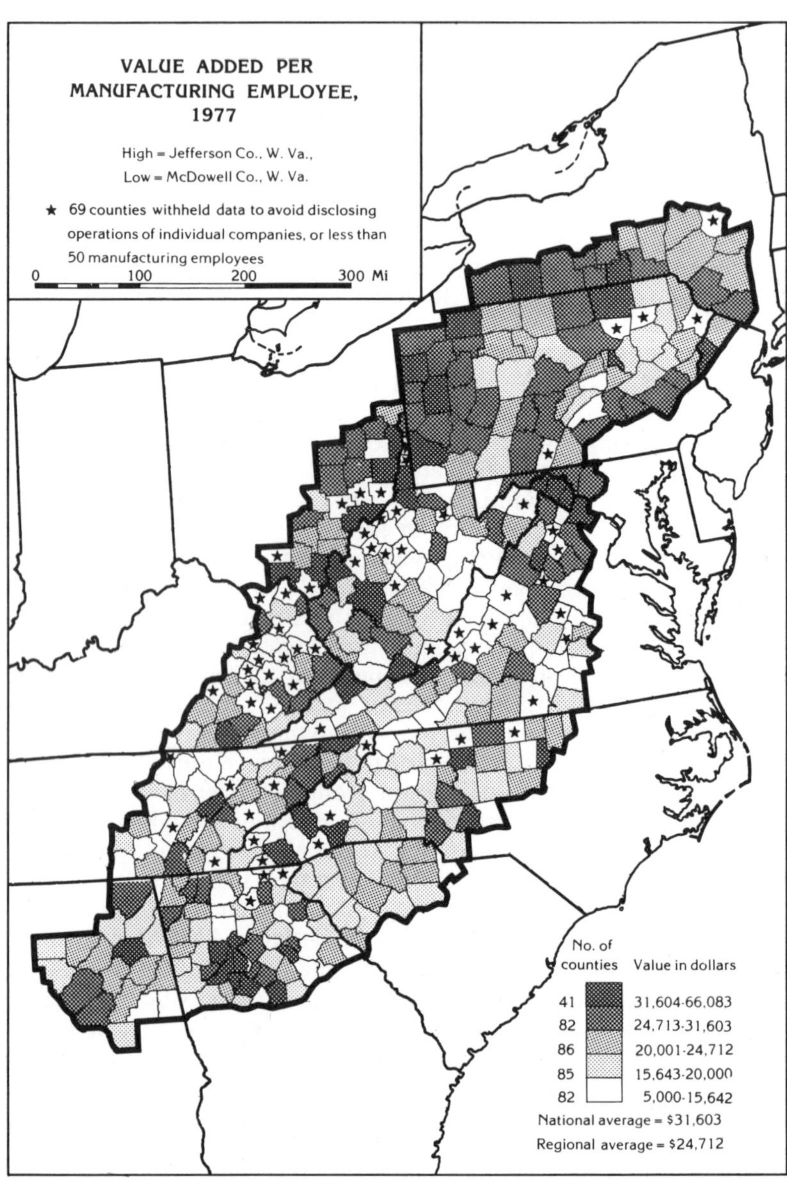
VALUE ADDED PER
MANUFACTURING EMPLOYEE,
1977
High = Jefferson Co., W. Va.,
Low = McDowell Co., W. Va.
★ 69 counties withheld data to avoid disclosing operations of individual companies, or less than 50 manufacturing employees
0 100 200 300 Mi
No. of counties
Value in dollars
41 31,604-66,083
82 24,713-31,603
86 20,001-24,712
85 15,643-20,000
82 5,000-15,642
National average = $31,603
Regional average = $24,712

**Figure 8.2**

## CHANGE IN MANUFACTURING: 1958–1977

Manufacturing employment between 1958 and 1977 increased by 21.5 percent in Appalachia, from 2.25 million to over 2.7 million workers. But this growth was not uniformly distributed throughout the region. Some areas enjoyed healthy gains, some had only very moderate increases, and others actually suffered losses in manufacturing employment. Of the 358 counties for which data were available or in which there were at least one hundred industrial workers, 67 (or 19 percent) experienced a loss of manufacturing jobs (Figure 8.3). The majority of counties that suffered losses or experienced less than the average regional growth were located in northern or central Appalachia, or they were metropolitan counties in which central cities were located (e.g., Atlanta's Fulton County, Birmingham's Jefferson County). Conversely, nearly all the counties in which rapid advances in manufacturing employment occurred were located in southern Appalachian states, both in the nonmetropolitan counties and the suburban metropolitan counties of these states. All of the suburban metropolitan counties south and east of downtown Atlanta, for example, experienced rapid gains in manufacturing employment. Clayton County, which had the region's most rapid gain in manufacturing employment, had a tenfold increase to about forty-seven hundred manufacturing employees.[8] A comparison of changes in manufacturing employment with changes in total population reveals that both were rather closely related; in short, factories followed the movement of population.

In addition to this shift of manufacturing from the north, or Snow Belt, to the Sun Belt, manufacturing also migrated to nonmetropolitan counties in both northern and southern Appalachia, with the most rapid gains occurring in southern Appalachia's nonmetropolitan counties (Table 8.2). This trend also corresponded rather closely to recent population shifts. In the region as a whole, manufacturing employment increased by over 35 percent in nonmetropolitan counties and by less than 12 percent in metropolitan counties. The percentage increases in both the number of large establishments (those employing twenty or more workers) and in value added by manufacturing was also greater in the nonmetropolitan counties. Only total number of manufacturing establishments increased at a greater rate in urban areas. Examination of individual states reveals, with but few exceptions, that manufacturing employment increased more rapidly (or losses were slower) in the states' nonmetropolitan counties. The exceptions were New Jersey, South Carolina, and Virginia—in the latter 2 states employment gains in the rural counties exceeded regional and national averages.

A number of reasons have been cited for the recent shift of industry to both the Sun Belt and to nonmetropolitan counties. In the case of the Sun Belt, and especially its southeast portion, these reasons include lower energy costs, a milder climate, availability of water, availability of qualified labor, more favorable attitudes toward industry (e.g., less unionization and "right-to-work" laws), cheaper and more-accessible

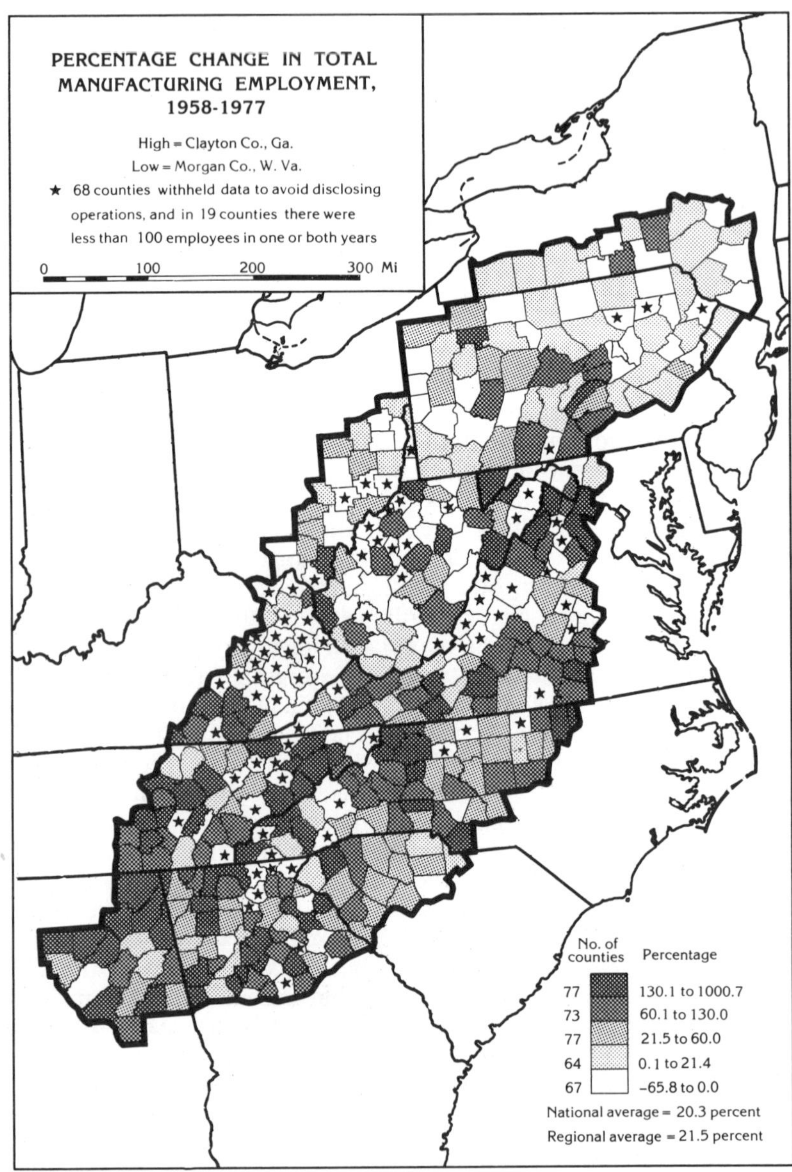
PERCENTAGE CHANGE IN TOTAL MANUFACTURING EMPLOYMENT, 1958-1977
High = Clayton Co., Ga.
Low = Morgan Co., W. Va.
★ 68 counties withheld data to avoid disclosing operations, and in 19 counties there were less than 100 employees in one or both years
0 100 200 300 Mi
No. of counties
Percentage
77 130.1 to 1000.7
73 60.1 to 130.0
77 21.5 to 60.0
64 0.1 to 21.4
67 -65.8 to 0.0
National average = 20.3 percent
Regional average = 21.5 percent

**Figure 8.3**

TABLE 8.2
Percentage Change in Manufacturing Employment, Manufacturing Establishments, and Value Added by Manufacture by State and Urban-Rural Areas, 1958-1977

| State | Manufacturing Employment | Total Manufacturing Establishments | Establishments with 20 or More Employees | Value Added by Manufacture |
|---|---|---|---|---|
| Alabama | 23.7 | 41.2 | 53.9 | 241.7 |
| Rural | 120.0 | 50.0 | 118.6 | 755.1 |
| Urban | 5.0 | 37.6 | 37.8 | 185.8 |
| Georgia | 52.1 | 69.0 | 69.6 | 492.0 |
| Rural | 68.1 | 56.4 | 76.3 | 557.0 |
| Urban | 38.4 | 79.4 | 64.4 | 453.6 |
| Kentucky | 107.5 | -3.6 | 64.9 | 664.7 |
| Rural | 136.9 | -9.7 | 54.4 | 1,746.3 |
| Urban | 68.7 | 54.4 | 111.1 | 195.0 |
| Maryland | 0.04 | 1.9 | 0.0 | 325.9 |
| Rural | 0.04 | 1.9 | 0.0 | 325.9 |
| Urban | - | - | - | - |
| New Jersey | 19.7 | 35.5 | 33.8 | 369.9 |
| Rural | 14.2 | 54.8 | 12.5 | 252.4 |
| Urban | 21.0 | 24.2 | 43.4 | 393.7 |
| New York | -6.6 | -5.8 | -8.5 | 220.2 |
| Rural | -2.2 | -7.0 | -9.4 | 222.5 |
| Urban | -12.8 | -2.0 | -6.3 | 216.9 |
| North Carolina | 45.8 | 40.2 | 48.7 | 380.1 |
| Rural | 62.4 | 30.9 | 48.8 | 489.8 |
| Urban | 32.2 | 48.7 | 48.6 | 320.8 |
| Ohio | -11.1 | 4.7 | 4.6 | 212.5 |
| Rural | -6.7 | 5.2 | 10.4 | 223.1 |
| Urban | -22.6 | 2.7 | -12.5 | 191.7 |
| Pennsylvania | 2.2 | 2.0 | 7.5 | 219.1 |
| Rural | 13.1 | 0.7 | 17.9 | 340.3 |
| Urban | -1.9 | 2.7 | 3.0 | 202.9 |
| South Carolina | 47.6 | 59.9 | 76.4 | 490.0 |
| Rural | 31.6 | 38.7 | 59.0 | 438.1 |
| Urban | 69.5 | 92.0 | 95.4 | 552.5 |
| Tennessee | 46.6 | 36.4 | 61.0 | 416.9 |
| Rural | 94.4 | 40.5 | 93.6 | 535.7 |
| Urban | 20.8 | 32.5 | 39.3 | 351.1 |
| Virginia | 44.6 | 15.0 | 36.3 | 367.1 |
| Rural | 35.3 | 9.4 | 36.5 | 319.2 |
| Urban | 74.7 | 34.8 | 35.7 | 512.8 |
| West Virginia | -19.4 | -2.2 | 12.3 | 209.0 |
| Rural | 4.9 | -2.1 | 27.8 | 366.2 |
| Urban | -32.4 | -2.3 | -2.7 | 155.7 |
| TOTAL | 21.5 | 21.1 | 29.5 | 302.1 |
| Rural | 35.2 | 15.6 | 35.6 | 369.2 |
| Urban | 11.7 | 26.6 | 24.8 | 263.9 |

Source: U.S. Bureau of the Census, U.S. Census of Manufacturers, 1958, vol. 3, Area Statistics (Washington, D.C.: Bureau of the Census, 1961), and U.S. Bureau of the Census, U.S. Census of Manufacturers, 1977, Geographic Area Series (Washington, D.C.: Bureau of the Census, 1980).

land, and a greatly improved and expanded transportation network.[9] In short, the situation for industry was better in the Sun Belt than in the traditional manufacturing belt of the north. A recent survey, in which businesses ranked the 48 contiguous states on thirty-one criteria of business climate, listed 8 Sun Belt states among the top 10.[10]

Although there is regional variation, probably the single most important reason for industrial expansion into nonmetropolitan counties has been the availability of low-cost labor in such counties.[11] Unemployment and underemployment rates in many of Appalachia's nonmetropolitan counties have traditionally been high, thereby assuring a (largely unskilled) labor pool that has attracted industry. The extent to which such areas can continue to meet labor demand is limited. In the nonmetropolitan counties of Appalachian Pennsylvania, for example, the lack of a labor supply is the major factor discouraging future industrial growth.[12]

Another reason cited as important in explaining the recent location of industry in nonmetropolitan counties is that employers often believe that the labor force in such areas has a stronger "work ethic," learns quickly, and thus ultimately will have a higher productivity.[13] Certainly increased accessibility of nonmetropolitan counties to both workers and raw materials as a result of the construction of interstate highways has also been a major contributing force to nonmetropolitan industrialization. And finally, local officials and civic leaders in some nonmetropolitan counties have been very active and successful in their attempts to attract industry. They have made available industrial sites and parks, as well as facilities such as buildings.

In southern Appalachia, one such county that has been successful in attracting industry is Hamblen County, Tennessee, where manufacturing employment increased by over 150 percent (from 5,150 to 13,000 workers) between 1958 and 1977. Morristown, the county seat, has two industrial parks, one of which is filled with industries that have recently been attracted because of its industrial facilities and the active recruitment of industry by town leaders.[14] Among the recent plants to open in Morristown are factories that produce cosmetic packaging, truck gears, and aluminum pistons. The latter is a German-owned and -managed plant. The opening of foreign plants is becoming increasingly common throughout Appalachia. The earliest manufacturing plants in Morristown included a furniture factory that came in the 1930s and a synthetic textile plant that opened in the 1940s. Industries such as these are the types that traditionally have been associated with most of southern Appalachia. In short, diversification is beginning to occur in southern nonmetropolitan counties like Hamblen, although traditional industries, like furniture products, are still important.

Although many northern Appalachian counties have experienced either declines or only slow growth in manufacturing employment, there are exceptions. In Appalachian Ohio, for example, Hocking County increased its employment by nearly 50 percent, from over fifteen hundred to twenty-three hundred employees. On the other hand, in Appalachian

Ohio as a whole, manufacturing employment declined by over 11 percent between 1958 and 1977, and in nonmetropolitan counties by nearly 7 percent (Table 8.2). Civic leaders in Logan, the county seat, have been moderately successful in attracting industry that includes two Goodyear plants (although they laid off five hundred workers beginning in 1979), clay-product plants, and a file-folder company, among others.[15]

Many nonmetropolitan counties, of course, do not have a diversified industrial base. Frequently a single plant or industry will dominate manufacturing in a rural county seat or county. Many examples can be found throughout the region, like the textile industry in the southern Piedmont or the stone, clay, and glass industry in rural Pennsylvania. In some cases the dominance of a single industry has discouraged the growth of other forms of manufacturing.[16]

The majority of plants that have been established recently in counties like Hamblen and Hocking are called branch plants and generally employ between fifty and five hundred workers. In Appalachian Kentucky over 70 percent of all manufacturing employment is in branch plants, rather than indigenous industries.[17] Branch plants have headquarters that are located in other places, usually large metropolitan centers. Therefore headquarters of branch plants in Appalachia are in the major metropolitan centers of the nation's manufacturing belt, an area that includes much of the northeastern quarter of the United States. The extent to which local economies are affected in the long run by such plants is not yet clear. For example, one study on corporate dominance in 8 rural counties in Appalachian Tennessee found "that the corporate and input-output linkages of forty-nine establishments extend beyond the rural areas and regional cities to the detriment of the area."[18] On the other hand, "recent evidence indicates that branch plants of metropolitan manufacturing corporations have been more significant to contributing to employment growth and stability in nonmetropolitan areas than previously reported."[19] Certainly the impact of branch plants depends in part on local conditions and the types of plants opened.

## THE STRUCTURE OF MANUFACTURING

The industrial structure of a region can be examined through investigation of the major types of manufacturing industry as defined according to the Standard Industrial Classification (SIC) system. For manufacturing there are twenty two-digit SIC major groups numbered 20 to 39 (Table 8.3).[20] As previously noted, various criteria are utilized to determine the importance of manufacturing. For this discussion of types of manufacturing we have chosen to employ simply the number of manufacturing establishments in order to measure the importance of each industrial group in the region. Also, we will use this same measure to show the spatial distribution of selected kinds of manufacturing throughout the region.

It could be argued that criteria like employment or value added are

TABLE 8.3
Manufacturing Establishments by SIC Code, 1977

| SIC Code | Industry Group | Manufacturing Establishments in Region | Percentage in Rural Counties | Percentage of U.S. Total | Three Leading States (with percentage of total in Appalachia in state) | | |
|---|---|---|---|---|---|---|---|
| 20 | Food and kindred products | 2,745 | 47.5 | 10.3 | PA (33.9) | NC (13.2) | GA (10.9) |
| 21 | Tobacco products | 40 | 47.5 | 17.5 | NC (42.5) | PA (27.5) | VA (15.0) |
| 22 | Textile mill products | 2,717 | 60.8 | 37.7 | NC (43.7) | GA (21.2 | SC (11.1) |
| 23 | Apparel and related products | 3,059 | 46.0 | 11.5 | PA (43.3) | NC (14.3) | GA (11.7) |
| 24 | Lumber and wood products | 6,293 | 72.9 | 16.9 | NC (17.7) | PA (16.6) | VA (14.3) |
| 25 | Furniture and fixtures | 1,575 | 53.0 | 15.4 | NC (37.8) | TN (13.4) | PA (12.6) |
| 26 | Paper and allied products | 676 | 37.6 | 10.3 | PA (22.8) | NC (20.6) | GA (17.5) |
| 27 | Printing and publishing | 4,212 | 38.6 | 8.5 | PA (25.6) | NC (15.7) | GA (15.3) |
| 28 | Chemicals and allied products | 1,242 | 33.6 | 10.2 | PA (23.4) | GA (17.3) | NC (15.4) |
| 29 | Petroleum and coal products | 307 | 44.3 | 13.9 | PA (35.5) | GA (13.7) | NY ( 9.8) |
| 30 | Rubber and plastic products | 1,026 | 45.5 | 8.6 | PA (24.3) | NC (19.3) | GA (14.7) |
| 31 | Leather and leather products | 287 | 53.7 | 9.3 | PA (28.6) | TN (15.0) | NY (12.2) |
| 32 | Stone, clay, and glass products | 2,619 | 54.7 | 14.8 | PA (25.8) | GA (12.1) | NC (11.9) |
| 33 | Primary metal industries | 882 | 34.6 | 12.0 | PA (41.8) | AL (10.8 | NC ( 7.5) |
| 34 | Fabricated metal products | 2,827 | 33.9 | 8.4 | PA (34.9) | NC (12.7) | GA (10.8) |
| 35 | Machinery, except electrical | 4,090 | 42.7 | 8.5 | PA (29.9) | NC (16.2) | GA ( 9.7) |
| 36 | Electrical machinery | 1,080 | 39.5 | 7.2 | PA (32.6) | VA (12.3) | GA (11.9) |
| 37 | Transportation equipment | 653 | 43.2 | 6.4 | PA (27.4) | GA (14.9) | NC (12.6) |
| 38 | Instruments and related products | 480 | 37.9 | 6.4 | PA (32.1) | GA (11.9) | NC (11.5) |
| 39 | Miscellaneous manufacturing | 1,080 | 37.8 | 6.3 | PA (29.0) | NC (15.6) | GA (13.6) |
| | TOTAL | 37,890 | 48.2 | 10.9 | PA (27.1) | NC (18.3) | GA (13.0) |

Source: U.S. Bureau of the Census, Census of Manufacturers, 1977, Geographic Area Series (Washington, D.C.: Bureau of the Census, 1980).

more suitable measures in that "logically [the number of manufacturing establishments] is of little significance in measuring a region's industrialization because it fails to recognize very meaningful attributes of factories. For example, a factory with only three employees is the equal of a factory employing 5,000 people. Each is one factory."[21] On the other hand, the number of establishments is the least confidential of all the criteria. That is, authorities will often withhold information on value of employment in order to avoid disclosing figures for individual companies, but they will almost always divulge information regarding number of establishments (in Appalachia, for example, employment data were withheld for 69 of the 445 counties). Furthermore, studies have clearly demonstrated there is a close correlation between number of establishments and every other common measure of manufacturing available.[22] And finally, the discussion is about different types of manufacturing (rather than total manufacturing) and therefore the variation in number of employees per establishment is less important.

Nearly 11 percent of all manufacturing establishments in the United States were located in the Appalachian region in 1977. The percentage of establishments in Appalachia was higher than this average for eight categories of manufacturing. For instance, nearly 40 percent of all U.S. textile mills were located in the Appalachian region in 1977. Similarly, the Appalachian region had a higher-than-average percentage of primary metal industries and of the establishments manufacturing tobacco products; lumber and wood products; furniture and fixtures; stone, clay, and glass products; petroleum and coal products; and apparel and related products. In short, these eight manufacturing categories were more concentrated in Appalachia than were the other major SIC groups.

Reasons for the heavier concentration of these manufacturing categories in Appalachia, of course, vary according to type of industry, and we shall address specific factors in the next section. In general, however, the primary reasons for the location of industry in the region are related to: (1) historical factors; (2) the presence of natural resources including coal, petroleum and natural gas, stone, forests, and water; and (3) the availability of low-cost labor. Factors that perhaps until recently have retarded industrial development in Appalachia include the rough terrain of the region, which has been "a formidable barrier to access and transportation and an inhospitable setting for town and plant development and even for farming. . . . Appalachia was therefore literally by-passed by the bulk of the people and enterprises in a developing America in favor of surrounding areas."[23] With a few exceptions (such as Pittsburgh), early centers of manufacturing activity developed around the margins of the region, and these centers gorged themselves on Appalachia's rich and varied natural resources. It has been a region of resource extraction and export; in short, an "internal colony."[24]

Within Appalachia the distribution of industry by manufacturing category varied markedly. At one extreme were manufacturing types like textiles and tobacco products that were highly concentrated in only a few areas. For example, over three-quarters of all textile mills were located in North Carolina, Georgia, and South Carolina in 1977. Moreover, within these states the majority of establishments were located in the counties of the Piedmont where cheap labor was available. At the other extreme were industries that tended to be much more widely distributed. For example, lumber and wood-product establishments, which are resource-oriented, were nearly ubiquitous in Appalachia (refer to Figure 6.1). Not surprisingly, almost 73 percent of such establishments were located in nonmetropolitan counties rather than in the region's 105 metropolitan counties (Table 8.3).

Pennsylvania was the leading Appalachian state in all but four of the twenty SIC categories. In those four groups (tobacco products, textile mill products, lumber and wood products, and furniture and fixtures), North Carolina was the Appalachian leader. Taken together, Pennsylvania and North Carolina accounted for over 45 percent of the total manufacturing establishments in the Appalachian region. Ohio, Kentucky, West Virginia, New Jersey, and Maryland did not rank among the top 3 states in a single one of the twenty manufacturing categories.

Examination of changes in number of manufacturing establishments that have occurred in the SIC categories reveal both similarities and differences in comparison with national trends (Table 8.4). The number of establishments in four categories (SIC codes 20, 21, 24, and 31) declined in both Appalachia and the United States. On the other hand, the number of textile mills and establishments that produce apparel and related products increased in Appalachia but declined in the remainder of the United States. In each of the other fourteen major categories there was an increase in the number of establishments, and in every category except one (stone, clay, and glass products), the percentage increase was greater in the Appalachian region than in the nation.

As already noted, increases in manufacturing have generally been more rapid in the southern portion of Appalachia and in the region's nonmetropolitan counties. The rapid increase in some of the more technically sophisticated, higher-paying types of industry (e.g., SIC codes 30, 35, 36, and 38), especially in southern Appalachia, suggests that manufacturing is becoming more diversified. Southern Appalachia is in the youthful stage of the industrial cycle whereby "markets are typically expanding rapidly and the relative locational advantages of the region are being suddenly recognized."[25] This reflects what is happening in the American South more generally. Thus,

> The US South has evidenced . . . a generally increasing diversity of manufacturing employment [since 1947] . . . in that part of the South not historically considered the textile South. The increased diversity can be attributed to the expansion of food processing and apparel, but also, particularly since 1967, to the growth of high-technology industries such as metal fabricating, machinery, electrical machinery, and transportation equip-

TABLE 8.4
Percentage Change in Total Manufacturing Establishments by SIC Code for Appalachia and the United States, 1958-1977

| SIC Code | Industry Group | Appalachia (Percentage Change) | United States (Percentage Change) |
|---|---|---|---|
| 20 | Food and kindred products | -44.2 | -36.0 |
| 21 | Tobacco products | -51.2 | -54.8 |
| 22 | Textile mill products | 19.3 | -6.2 |
| 23 | Apparel and related products | 40.4 | -9.5 |
| 24 | Lumber and wood products | -15.7 | -1.3 |
| 25 | Furniture and fixtures | 33.6 | 0.7 |
| 26 | Paper and allied products | 73.3 | 24.2 |
| 27 | Printing and publishing | 50.6 | 40.7 |
| 28 | Chemicals and allied products | 27.4 | 7.6 |
| 29 | Petroleum and coal products | 62.4 | 37.2 |
| 30 | Rubber and plastics products | 305.5 | 167.7 |
| 31 | Leather and leather products | -20.1 | -32.2 |
| 32 | Stone, clay, and glass products | 17.2 | 18.1 |
| 33 | Primary metal industries | 15.9 | 14.4 |
| 34 | Fabricated metal products | 66.2 | 36.0 |
| 35 | Machinery, except electrical | 108.8 | 61.5 |
| 36 | Electrical machinery | 135.3 | 85.1 |
| 37 | Transportation equipment | 99.7 | 54.0 |
| 38 | Instruments and related products | 182.4 | 112.2 |
| 39 | Miscellaneous Manufacturing | 54.9 | 20.9 |

Source: U.S. Bureau of the Census, U.S. Census of Manufacturers, 1958, vol. 3, Area Statistics (Washington, D.C.: Bureau of the Census, 1961), and U.S. Bureau of the Census, U.S. Census of Manufacturers, 1977, Geographic Area Series (Washington, D.C.: Bureau of the Census, 1980).

ment. The results, though not of themselves conclusive, support the hypothesis that the more recent comparative shifts represent a basic change in the evolution of the national space economy.[26]

## SELECTED INDUSTRIES

Several categories of manufacturing are associated closely with at least some portion of the Appalachian region. In this section we will examine the historical geography and current standing of several key industries that have had significant impact on the region.

### The Iron and Steel Industry

In the United States the first iron furnace was built in 1629 in Massachusetts, and by the early nineteenth century small ironworks were found throughout the East, particularly in Pennsylvania. The earliest ironworks in America needed a steady supply of charcoal, so that the iron could be smelted. Because forests were found everywhere the industry was initially attracted to minable ore deposits. Iron was discovered early on in central Pennsylvania's Nittany Valley, and by 1820 some forty furnaces existed in the area around Bellefonte, then the largest town in the region. Such small operations each had "a handful of workmen who dug iron and a little lime in summer, chopped wood for charcoal in winter, and hoped their crude cast ingots would fetch enough to keep them alive. Whether or not it supported the workmen is hard to say, but iron supported the town—and grandly."[27] Development during this early period was based on the existence of local markets supplied by comparatively small furnaces and "as entry to such a trade was easy so, too, elimination was frequent."[28] The decline of the small ironworks was because of local conditions and changes that occurred in other parts of the world. Locally, forests were used up because a "good-sized furnace—which employed perhaps fifty men—consumed an acre of hardwood forest per day."[29] At the world scale, new technical developments from Europe altered the iron-making process. A new puddling furnace, in which coal (and later coke) replaced charcoal as fuel, was initiated in 1784. The process "reduced the cost of manufacture and yielded a larger quantity and more uniform grade of iron."[30] The U.S. iron industry altered its technology only slowly, and even by 1850 about one-half of America's pig iron was still fueled by charcoal. Puddling began in Pennsylvania in 1817 (and in New England in 1835). There were various reasons for the continued smallness and technical backwardness of the iron industry in the United States. They included "competition from Britain, higher labour costs, lack of mineral fuel, and transportation difficulties in a widely dispersed economy."[31]

In 1856, as mentioned earlier, a method was developed by Henry Bessemer in which large quantities of steel, a much more durable and resistant metal than iron, could be made from pig iron. This and later, more refined methods (e.g., the open-hearth process of William Siemans) of steel manufacture not only revolutionized the industry but also greatly affected the future location, because the relative inputs had changed. After coal replaced charcoal as the major fuel in iron-making,

> The weight of the coal needed exceeded the combined weights of the other materials . . . so the pull of the coalfield was great enough to insure the location of the plants there. As technology improved, the quantity of coal was reduced and, during the second half of the 19th century, coal suppliers lost their dominant position. At first this had the effect of making iron ore deposits away from the coalfields viable locations for iron and steel plants. . . . But the reduction in the importance of coal also increased the pull of the market.[32]

The output of steel in relation to iron rose rapidly and ultimately, of course, surpassed iron production. Although the United States was slow to catch up with England and Germany, the world's early production leaders, by 1890 U.S. production of iron and steel exceeded that of Britain and thus the United States became the leading producer. And it was Appalachian Pennsylvania, first under the stimulus of the anthracite furnaces in the eastern part of the state beginning in the 1840s and later of the coke blast furnaces of western Pennsylvania, that led America to supremacy.[33] By the twentieth century the leading iron and steel production region was Pittsburgh.

In 1790 Pittsburgh was a quiet little village of fewer than four hundred people but "by 1810 it had grown to nearly 5,000 and was the scene of continual bustle and hurry as thousands of pioneers rode or walked into town from the east to demand boats, household goods, and supplies for the trip down the Ohio."[34] During this period three industries—boat building, clothing, and metal—led Pittsburgh into the industrial era. Although no iron ore was found in the immediate vicinity of Pittsburgh, river transportation facilitated the growth of a secondary metal-products industry (e.g., nails, iron kettles) based on the import of bar and pig iron from elsewhere in Pennsylvania, like the Juniata Valley. Pittsburgh did have large quantities of bituminous coal nearby, and the iron and steel industry flourished there when coal became the industry's major input.

The first ironworks in western Pennsylvania was constructed in 1790 on Jacob's Creek, a tributary of the Youghiogheny, and Fayette County became the first boom area of furnace construction in the region.[35] In Pittsburgh, the first rolled iron was manufactured in 1812, and by 1829 eight mills were found in or near the town. Iron and steel production in Pittsburgh and its environs grew rapidly because of the nearness of coal, the availability of water, and the extensive and well-integrated river and canal transportation system. Large parcels of flat land were also prime requisites in selecting sites for plants, and although such sites were limited in the area because of the rugged terrain, flat land in the major river valleys was available. Thus, steel mills are located on much of the best flat land in western Pennsylvania, as on the floodplains of Pittsburgh and Johnstown. In Johnstown, which in many ways is Pittsburgh in miniature, the steel industry occupies more land space in the congested Conemaugh Valley than all other manufacturing combined. Today, about one-half of Johnstown's manufacturing labor force works in the steel industry, which in this city is completely dominated by the Bethlehem Steel Corporation.

The Pittsburgh iron and steel district, which includes the triangular area outlined by the cities of Youngstown (Ohio), Wheeling (West Virginia), and Johnstown, became the world's greatest iron and steel region by the latter part of the nineteenth century. At the peak of its dominance in 1914, the region produced about 70 percent of the total U.S. output, and it was not until the 1920s that it produced less than one-half of the national output. Although still the nation's premier producing region, the Pittsburgh district accounted for only about one-third of the steel output by 1960.[36] Possibly the single most important reason for the diffusion of the steel industry to other areas of the United States has been the growth of major new markets.

Within the Appalachian region, Pittsburgh was clearly the leader in

Rolling mills, part of a large Bethlehem Steel facility, encroach on the business district in Johnstown, Pennsylvania. Furnaces and other fabrication plants line the Little Conemaugh floodplain into the distance. A flood on Stoney Creek, off the photograph to the right, killed twenty-two hundred people in 1889. A second major flood occurred in 1936, and in July 1977 a flood filled two Bethlehem coal mines with water and forced the closing of coke ovens, blast furnaces, and open hearths.

primary metal industries in 1977 (Table 8.5). The 84,900 employees in primary metal industries in the Pittsburgh SMSA accounted for 7.6 percent of the nation's total employment in this manufacturing category. Perhaps more significantly, the 73,500 workers in SIC subgroup 331 (those employed in blast furnaces and basic steel products) in the Pittsburgh SMSA made up nearly 14 percent of the national work force in that industry. Pittsburgh reflects the changes that have taken place in America's steel industry in recent decades. Because of foreign and domestic competition as well as a lagging economy, employment in the primary metal industries declined from 117,800 to 84,900, or by 28 percent, between 1958 and 1977 in the four-county Pittsburgh SMSA. Employment in blast furnaces and basic steel products (SIC code 331) declined by nearly 36 percent during the same time period.

Within the Appalachian region Birmingham, Alabama, was the second SMSA in employment in primary metal industries in 1977 (although it ranked third behind Allentown-Bethlehem-Easton in value added). The modern industry in Birmingham dates to the 1870s. The unique locational

TABLE 8.5
Employment, Establishments, and Value Added in Primary Metal Industries (SIC Code 33) for Ten Leading SMSAs, 1977

| | Employment (thousands) | Establishments Total | Establishments 20 or More Employees | Value Added ($ Million) |
|---|---|---|---|---|
| Pittsburgh | 84.9 | 156 | 99 | 2,781.0 |
| Birmingham | 20.3 | 66 | 48 | 445.9 |
| Allentown-Bethlehem-Easton | 15.0 | 28 | 18 | 465.6 |
| Huntington-Ashland | 10.2 | 12 | 7 | 300.9 |
| Reading | 7.6 | 39 | 30 | 265.4 |
| Chattanooga | 5.2 | 23 | 13 | 103.7 |
| Atlanta | 4.4 | 37 | 18 | 151.0 |
| Wheeling | 1.4 | 11 | 7 | 47.5 |
| Johnson City-Kingsport-Bristol | 1.2 | 13 | 7 | 31.8 |
| Anniston | 1.1 | 11 | 6 | 20.4 |

Source: U.S. Bureau of the Census, Census of Manufacturers, 1977, Geographic Area Series (Washington, D.C.: Bureau of the Census, 1980).

A complex of steel mills on the west side of the Monongahela River near Duquesne, Pennsylvania. Many of the mills in this highly concentrated steel-producing area are too old or too small to produce a competitively priced product and are being shut down.

factors that led to the establishment of a major iron and steel industry in Birmingham included nearby extensive deposits of coking coal, iron ore, and limestone. These three inputs, and water, rarely occur together anywhere in the world. As a result, Birmingham today leads the entire south in steel production.

### The Textile and Apparel Industries

The textile and apparel industries (SIC codes 22 and 23) are closely related and concentrated in two or three areas of Appalachia. Therefore it is appropriate that they be discussed together. The location of both industries in the United States has historically been oriented toward the major national markets. Both industries were initially highly concentrated in the northeastern states: the textile industry in New England and the apparel industry in the northeastern megalopolis centered on New York City. Although these areas are still important, both industries—especially textiles—have migrated to other locations as the population center of the United States has moved westward.

In the early 1880s, textile mills began to appear in the southern Piedmont; by 1925 this region surpassed New England and the Middle Atlantic states in total production. In the south the manufacture of cotton textiles was most important, but more recently synthetics have also become significant. Today the textile area of the Piedmont, which extends from Virginia to Georgia (Figure 8.4), accounts for nearly all the nation's employment in cotton mills and a majority of the employment in mills producing man-made fibers. Only in woolens does the Northeast have the greatest share of employment.[37]

There are a number of reasons for the migration and growth of the cotton textile industry in the Piedmont. One often cited, for example, is that the industry was simply moving closer to its raw material. But as cotton production became less important in the South, the industry still throve. Thus this explanation is at best only partially adequate. A second factor was that new markets were opening up in the West and South, and thus the Piedmont was closer to the new population center of the country. A 1954 study demonstrated that Greenville, South Carolina, had an advantage over Lewiston, Maine, in terms of transportation costs for finished cotton piece goods. Lewiston controlled only a small portion of the national market in terms of areal extent (although the area did include the Northeast's major population centers). It was found that Greenville could deliver goods cheaper in the Southeast, of course, and to all markets west of the Mississippi River.[38] A third reason that the Piedmont was attractive to the textile industry was the easy access to water power. Dams and generators were constructed on small streams to provide power for the mills.

Such advantages were important in the southern Piedmont as an impetus to the industry initially, but the "more significant factor in explaining the growth of the southern textile industry is the sizable differential in labor cost between northern and southern mills."[39] Since

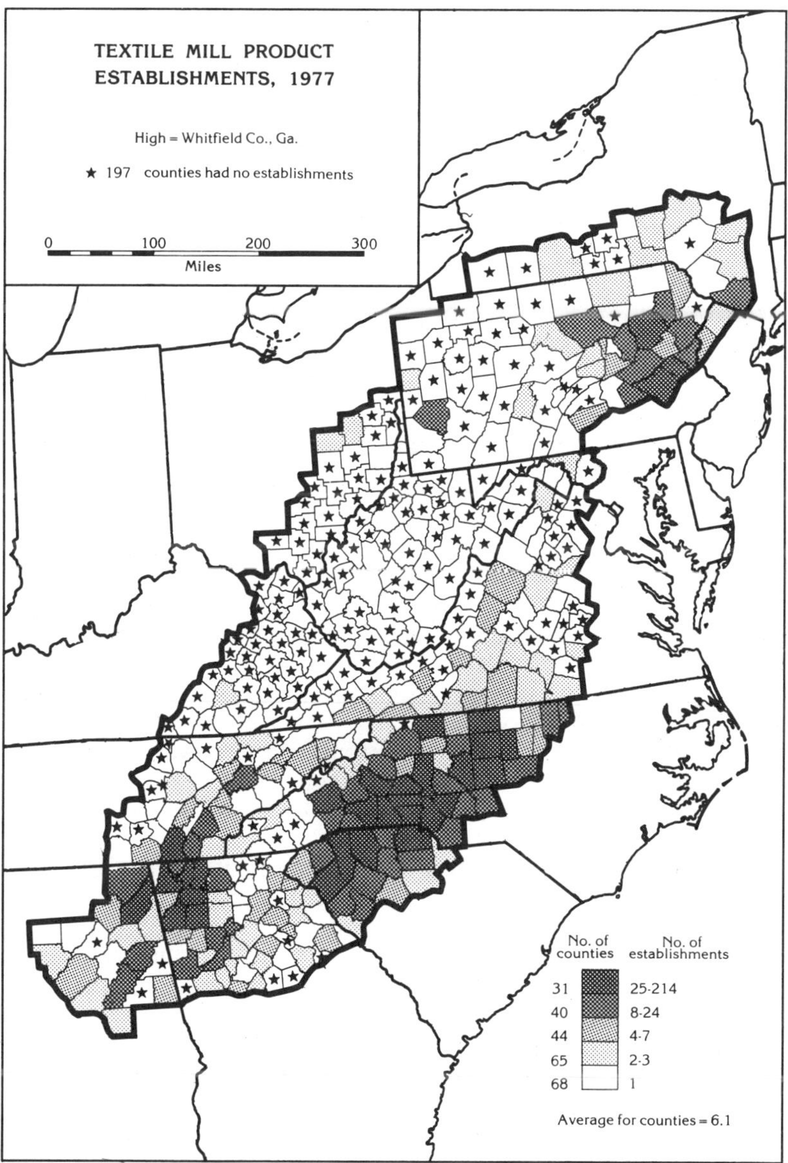
TEXTILE MILL PRODUCT
ESTABLISHMENTS, 1977
High = Whitfield Co., Ga.
★ 197 counties had no establishments
0
100
200
300
Miles
No. of counties
No. of establishments
31
25-214
40
8-24
44
4-7
65
2-3
68
1
Average for counties = 6.1

**Figure 8.4**

TABLE 8.6
Average Hourly Earnings of Production Workers in Manufacturing Industries for Selected States and SMSAs, 1950 and 1980

| State or SMSA | Average Hourly Earnings ($) 1950 | 1980 | Percent Increase 1950-1980 |
|---|---|---|---|
| Alabama* | 1.18 | 6.85 | 481 |
| Birmingham | 1.35 | 7.76 | 475 |
| Georgia* | 1.08 | 6.09 | 464 |
| Atlanta | 1.22 | 7.20 | 490 |
| Binghamton, New York | 1.48 | 6.89 | 366 |
| North Carolina* | 1.10 | 5.68 | 416 |
| Charlotte | 1.16 | 5.69 | 391 |
| Pennsylvania* | 1.43 | 8.03 | 462 |
| Johnstown | 1.56 | 8.74 | 460 |
| Pittsburgh | 1.63 | 9.82 | 503 |
| Scranton | 1.18 | 6.05 | 413 |
| South Carolina* | 1.11 | 5.86 | 428 |
| Tennessee* | 1.18 | 6.42 | 444 |
| Chattanooga | 1.21 | 6.42 | 431 |

Source: Compiled from Bureau of Labor Statistics, Employment, Hours, and Earning -- State and Area Data, 1947-1950; and Employment and Earnings, February 19, 1982.

*Includes entire state.

wages and salaries represent 25 percent of the value of the product, the South, with lower costs and an adequate labor supply, seemed a logical location for the industry. Southern workers were less skilled but they learned quickly and cost less. They were also less inclined to join unions. Today, manufacturing workers in southern Appalachia and the South generally still earn less than workers in the North, and the gap does not appear to have narrowed very much between 1950 and 1980 (Table 8.6).

As shown in Figure 8.4, the Piedmont areas of North Carolina and South Carolina had the greatest concentration of textile mills in Appalachia in 1977. The Carolinas accounted for nearly 55 percent of all textile mills in the Appalachian region, and most of the establishments were located in nonmetropolitan counties (Table 8.3). Frequently nonmetropolitan counties and towns in the Piedmont have been dominated by the textile industry. Over three-quarters of the total manufacturing work force of fifty-five hundred in Rock Hill, South Carolina, for example, was employed in the textile industry. The livelihood of the Saluda River town of Piedmont, a few miles south of Greenville, South Carolina, on State Route 20 (near Interstate 85), has revolved around one muslin-producing textile mill, the Piedmont Manufacturing Company. Piedmont is an example of a company town; as late as 1950 the Piedmont Manufacturing Company owned all the homes and many of the retail businesses in this town of twenty-five hundred.[40]

Another major textile subregion within Appalachia includes northwest Georgia and several nearby counties in Alabama and Tennessee. Appalachia's leading county in number of mills is located here, Whitfield County, Georgia, which had 214 mills that averaged 70 employees each in 1977, up from 53 in 1958. Whereas the number of textile mills has decreased in the nation and shown only moderate gain in the region (Table 8.4), Whitfield County not only increased the number of mills but also its employment in textiles, from 9,000 workers in 1958 to 18,600 in 1977, or by over 106 percent! In 1977 nearly four-fifths of all manufacturing workers were employed in the county's textile mills. Whitfield County and Dalton, the county seat, are known today principally for the tufted carpets and rugs produced there. Anyone who has traveled on Interstate 75 between Chattanooga and Atlanta can attest to the numerous billboards and factory outlets that line the highway, advertising carpets at wholesale prices. The tufted-textile industry had its beginnings in Dalton in 1895 when tufted bedspreads were produced in local cottage industries. By 1940 it had changed from a cottage industry to modern tufted-textile manufacturing, and by 1970 over 60 percent of the nation's domestic value of tufted products were produced in and around Dalton.[41]

A third textile subregion is in eastern Pennsylvania, where about 240 mills, or nearly 9 percent of the regional total, were located in 1977. As in the Piedmont, the industry began to migrate to this area in the 1880s and by the 1930s had become the dominant industry in cities like Scranton. The textile industry in eastern Pennsylvania is a good example of industrial parasitism: Historically about four-fifths of the workers have been women, mostly the daughters and wives of the men who worked in the region's anthracite mines.

In the United States the location of the apparel industry is rather closely correlated with the major urban markets, especially New York City. This is because the industry, which produces a tremendous variety of sizes, styles, and qualities of clothing, needs to be near the style centers, a skilled labor supply, and major markets. Thus within the region it is not surprising that eastern Pennsylvania, on the margin of the northeastern megalopolis, is the premier apparel-producing subregion (Figure 8.5). A secondary apparel subregion has emerged in the southern Piedmont. As we have already seen, this area, in addition to its nearness to national markets, is the nation's premier textile region, and thus the raw materials necessary to apparel are readily available.

## Furniture and Fixtures

In some respects the history of the furniture industry is similar to that of the textile industry. Originally established in New England, the industry migrated southwestward to the southern Piedmont as the nation's population center moved west. In the southern Piedmont the industry, with factories that averaged fifty to one hundred workers, found powerful attractions including "less costly labor, lower taxes, and Appalachian

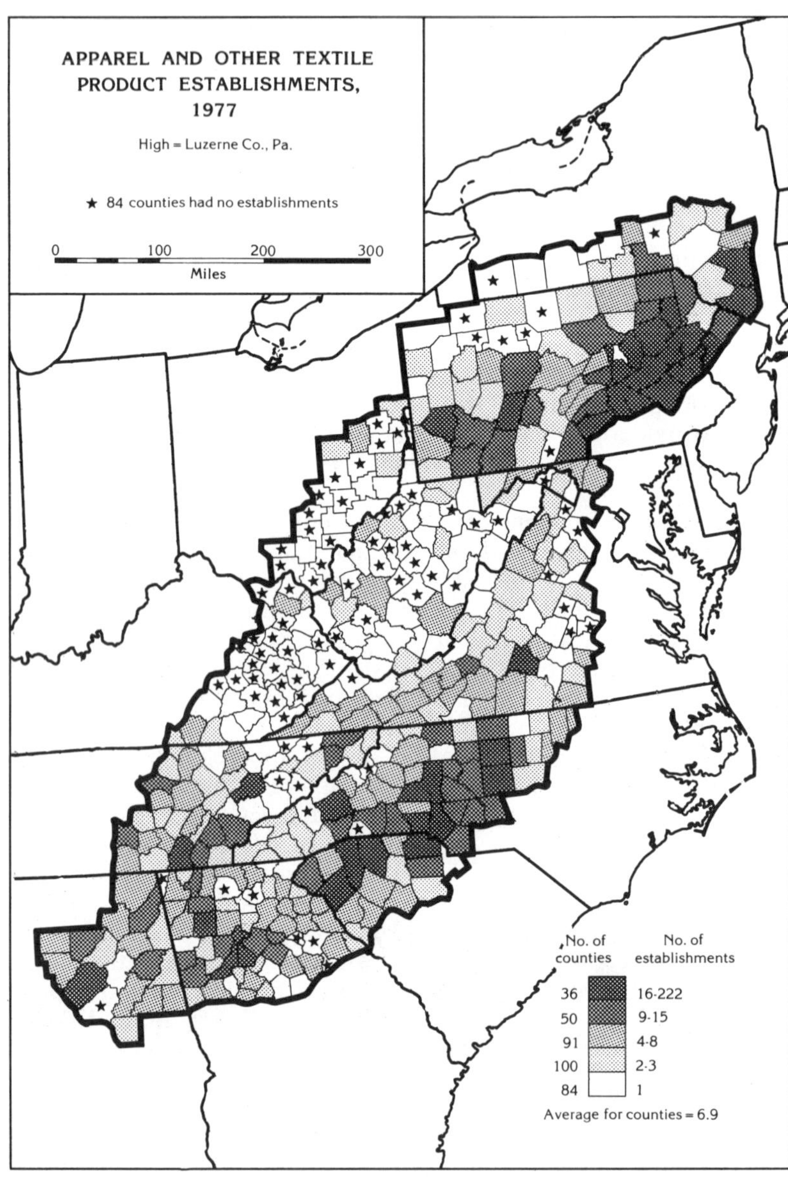
APPAREL AND OTHER TEXTILE
PRODUCT ESTABLISHMENTS,
1977
High = Luzerne Co., Pa.
★ 84 counties had no establishments
0
100
200
300
Miles
No. of counties
No. of establishments
36
16-222
50
9-15
91
4-8
100
2-3
84
1
Average for counties = 6.9

**Figure 8.5**

hardwood forests. The advantage of hardwood is their strength; most softwoods make poor furniture."[42]

North Carolina was the nation's leading furniture producer in 1977 and clearly the major producing area in Appalachia (Figure 8.6). Although the furniture industry does not dominate individual counties to the extent that the textile industry does, it accounts for a large share of the manufacturing in some counties. Appalachia's leading county in 1977 was Catawba County, North Carolina, where Hickory is located. The 135 furniture factories in the county employed 14,100 workers, or nearly 40 percent of the county's manufacturing labor force. The 1977 work force in the furniture industry represented an increase of 160 percent over that in 1958. Outside of North Carolina most of the region's major furniture-producing counties were located within major markets, that is, they were counties within the Pittsburgh, Atlanta, or Birmingham SMSAs. One exception was the aforementioned Hamblen County in Tennessee, where some 4,000 workers, or 35 percent of the county's manufacturing labor force, were employed in furniture factories.

### Stone, Clay, and Glass Products

Nearly 15 percent of the nation's establishments that manufacture stone, clay, and glass products were located in the Appalachian region in 1977. Pennsylvania, Georgia, North Carolina, and Ohio were the leading producing states for these resource-oriented industrics (Figure 8.7). In western Pennsylvania the industry is centered around Allegheny County, which had more establishments than any other single county in the region. Over thirteen thousand workers were employed in this major group in the Pittsburgh SMSA, and of this total about six thousand were employed in the manufacture of glass and glassware alone. In Appalachian Pennsylvania and Ohio, the industry is based on extensive deposits of sand and gravel, limestone, clay, and crushed stone. Pennsylvania, where 227 quarries were found in 54 counties, ranked first nationally in crushed-stone production.[43] Beaver County, Pennsylvania, was the state's leading producer of sand and gravel, accounting for 11 percent of the total production.

Similarly, the North Carolina stone, clay, and glass-products industry is based on local raw materials. The state ranked second in the nation in the production of clay and shale and led in the production of brick from these materials. North Carolina also led the country in feldspar and scrap-mica production. The most valuable single mineral commodity, however, is stone, with North Carolina ranked twelfth in the nation in 1978, accounting for 4 percent of total U.S. output.[44] The majority of these commodities were found in the Appalachian portion of the state.

Georgia ranked first nationally in the production of kaolin, dimension granite, and crushed granite and second in the production of crushed marble, dimension marble, crude mica, and feldspar. With the exception of kaolin, virtually the total production of these commodities was in the Appalachian portion of the state. Elbert County in northeast Georgia

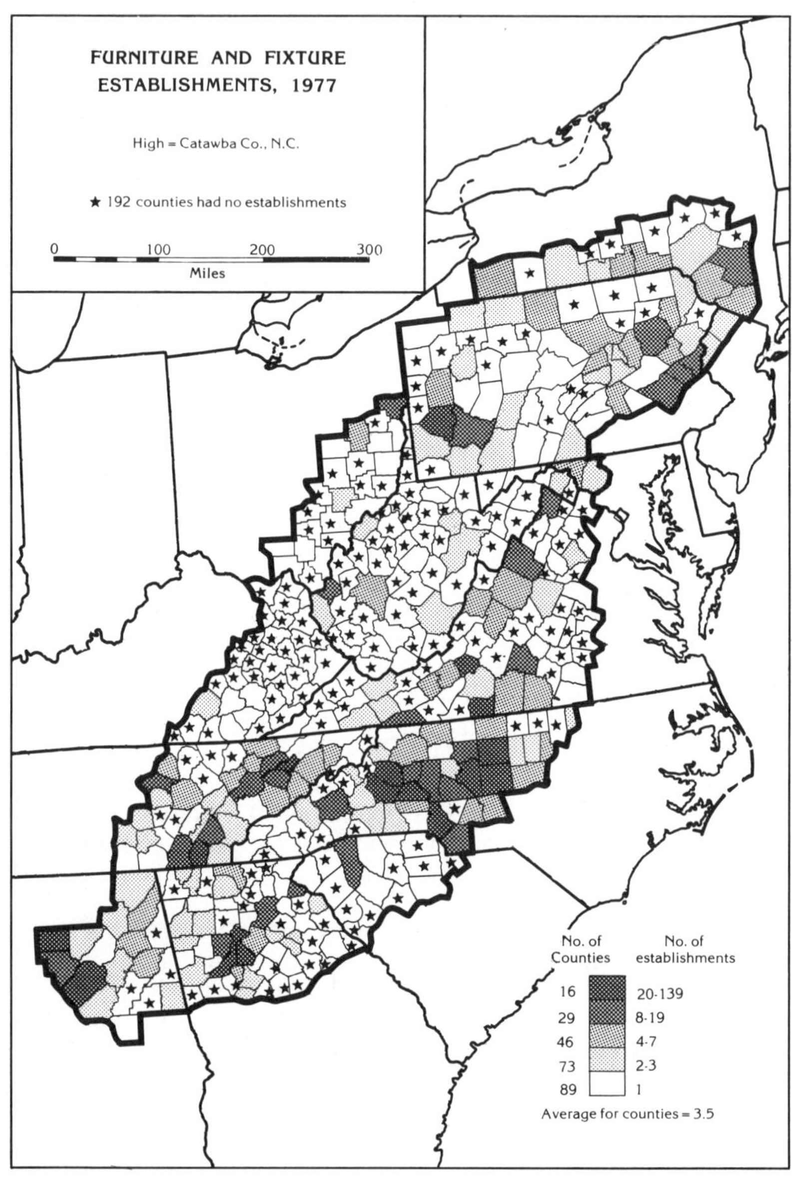
FURNITURE AND FIXTURE
ESTABLISHMENTS, 1977
High = Catawba Co., N.C.
★ 192 counties had no establishments
0
100
200
300
Miles
No. of Counties
No. of establishments
16
20-139
29
8-19
46
4-7
73
2-3
89
1
Average for counties = 3.5

**Figure 8.6**

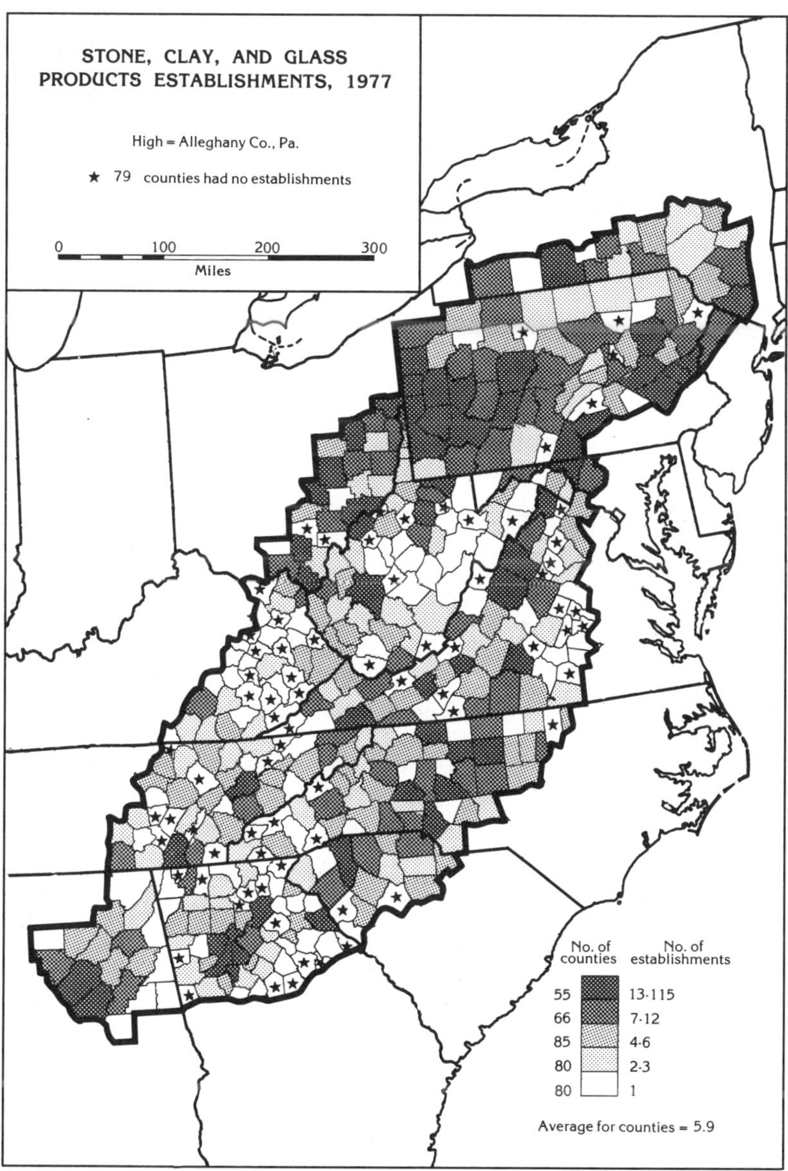
STONE, CLAY, AND GLASS
PRODUCTS ESTABLISHMENTS, 1977
High = Alleghany Co., Pa.
★ 79 counties had no establishments
0
100
200
300
Miles
No. of counties
No. of establishments
55
13-115
66
7-12
85
4-6
80
2-3
80
1
Average for counties = 5.9

Figure 8.7

was the entire region's second leading county in the number of establishments manufacturing stone, clay, and glass products. Approximately fifteen hundred workers, or more than one-half of the county's total labor force, were employed in eighty cut-stone–product establishments (SIC code 3281) that were engaged in the cutting, shaping, and finishing of granite, principally for memorial markers. Most of Georgia's granite production (which accounts for one-third of the nation's total output) is from the Elberton granite district that includes Elbert, Oglethorpe, Hart, Wilkes, and Lincoln counties. The first quarry in the district, and one of the state's first, opened near Elberton in 1882. By 1978, thirty-six quarries were in operation in the district, and these furnished high-quality granite to the area's wholesale manufacturers.[45]

### Other Industries

Some industries do not have a wide distribution throughout Appalachia, but rather are important locally. One example is the tobacco-products industry, which manufactures cigarettes, cigars, chewing tobacco, and pipe tobacco. Appalachia accounted for nearly one-fifth of the nation's total tobacco-products establishments in 1977, and within the region, North Carolina, Pennsylvania, and Virginia accounted for 85 percent of the regional total (Table 8.3).

Another locally important industry is primary aluminum manufacturing (SIC code 3334). The industry became important to Appalachia during World War I when the first two aluminum plants were built at Alcoa, Tennessee, and Badin, North Carolina. The single most important locational consideration for the manufacture of aluminum is access to cheap electric power. Production of 1 tn (0.907 t) of aluminum requires 20,000 kwhr of electricity—enough to service a family of six in an eight-room house for ten years.[46] Because of these enormous electric-power requirements, aluminum factories have been located near cheap hydroelectric power sources, such as those provided in the Tennessee River Valley. Seven of the nation's thirty-two plants manufacturing primary aluminum were in the Appalachian region in 1977, and these accounted for over one-fifth of the nation's total employment (28,600 workers) in the industry. Two plants were located in northern Alabama, and one each was located in the Appalachian portions of Tennessee, Ohio, North Carolina, and West Virginia.

## SUMMARY

Historically, manufacturing in Appalachia has been oriented toward the region's natural resources. The first industries included mostly primary manufacturing establishments that processed the region's lumber, tobacco, cotton, stone, or coal or utilized the region's abundant power resources such as water and coal. Abundant cheap labor has been another factor critical to the location of industry, and today this remains a most significant reason for the location of industry, especially in the nonmetropolitan counties of southern and central Appalachia. As access to and within the region continues to improve, it can be expected that the number of manufacturing establishments will continue to increase, especially in the southern portion of Appalachia. The types of manufacturing in southern and central Appalachia should become more sophisticated and will include largely branch plants, both U.S. and foreign, that will improve the skill level of the labor force. As has occurred elsewhere, manufacturing in Appalachia, now in an early stage of development, will gradually move to the later stages of the industrial cycle.

Continued industrial development is important to Appalachia because it provides an employment alternative for areas that have long been dependent upon one or two primary commodities. This is especially true of the coal-mining areas of central Appalachia, although it also applies to the areas heavily dependent upon forests, farming, and other minerals or building stones. Furthermore, development strategies should consider the importance of establishing a more diversified industrial base in those areas historically dependent upon one industry like textiles, furniture, or cut stone—all low-wage and low-technology resource-oriented industries that process primary commodities. Providing diversified employment opportunities, of course, establishes a more stable economic environment that is better able to cope with economic vagaries. The effect of dependence upon one or a few commodities, and the long-term impact of this upon the economy, can be seen through study of any Third World nation.

## NOTES

1. All data on manufacturing are taken from either U.S. Bureau of the Census, *U.S. Census of Manufacturers, 1958*, vol. 3, *Area Statistics* (Washington, D.C.: Bureau of the Census, 1961) or U.S. Bureau of the Census, *U.S. Census of Manufacturers, 1977*, Geographic Area Series (Washington, D.C.: Bureau of the Census, 1980). Value added is "probably the most meaningful value measuring stick, since it specifically measures the change in form or substance accomplished by manufacturing." In brief, it is the difference between value of materials used (including purchased parts) and value of the product leaving the factory. E. Willard Miller, *A Geography of Manufacturing* (Englewood Cliffs, N.J.: Prentice-Hall, 1962), pp. 14–15.

2. The Sun Belt, according to one source, includes fifteen states extending from Virginia to California. Sun Belt states partly in Appalachia include North Carolina, South Carolina, Georgia, Alabama, and Virginia. See Jeanne C. Biggar, "The Sunning of America: Migration to the Sunbelt," *Population Bulletin* 34 (1979), pp. 1–42. For discussion of various facets of manufacturing in non-metropolitan areas, see Richard E. Lonsdale and H. L. Seyler, *Nonmetropolitan Industrialization* (New York: John Wiley & Sons, 1979).

3. Lonsdale and Seyler, op. cit. (footnote 2), p. 3.

4. Data on manufacturing employment (and other variables) were not available for 69 of Appalachia's 445 counties because information was often withheld in order to avoid disclosing statistics for individual companies. A few

counties with significant manufacturing employment (or value added) opted to employ the disclosure rule. Thus, manufacturing employment for Buncombe County, North Carolina (Asheville), with 238 establishments was not available. The number of manufacturing establishments, on the other hand, was available for every county.

5. James O. Wheeler, "Regional Manufacturing Structure in the Southeastern United States, 1973," *Southeastern Geographer* 14 (1974), p. 67.

6. Charles L. Quittmeyer and Lorin A. Thompson, "The Development of Manufacturing," in Thomas R. Ford, ed., *The Southern Appalachian Region: A Survey* (Lexington: University of Kentucky Press, 1962), p. 123.

7. One source ranks the major industry groups according to the following criteria: rate of employment growth, size of employment growth, rate of growth of value added, and the index of industrial production. The industries cited in the text all rank low according to these criteria and are thus described as "laggard" or slow-growth industries. Robert Estall, *A Modern Geography of the United States* (Baltimore: Penguin Books, 1972), pp. 258–261.

8. In the 1977 *Census of Manufacturers* number of employees is rounded off to the nearest hundred, whereas in the 1958 *Census of Manufacturers* the exact number of employees is given. Thus, the figure for percentage change is not as accurate as it could be, especially in those counties with few employees in 1977.

9. Biggar, op. cit. (footnote 2), pp. 24–26.

10. Ira Black, "Sunbelt: Myth or Mecca?" *Iron Age* 219 (March 7, 1977), pp. 51–52.

11. Steven R. Kale and Richard E. Lonsdale, "Factors Encouraging and Discouraging Plant Location in Nonmetropolitan Areas," in Lonsdale and Seyler, op. cit. (footnote 2), pp. 47–56.

12. E. Willard Miller, "Manufacturing in Nonmetropolitan Pennsylvania" (Harrisburg, Dept. of Commerce, Commonwealth of Pennsylvania, 1980, unpublished report), p. 62.

13. Kale and Lonsdale, op. cit. (footnote 11), pp. 49–50.

14. Anne Newman, "The Recruiters and the Recruited: How One Town Filled an Industrial Park," *Appalachia* 15 (1981), pp. 6–19.

15. "Appalachian Views: An Ohio Mayor Speaks," *Appalachia* 14 (1981), pp. 24–27.

16. Miller, 1980, op. cit. (footnote 12), p. 5.

17. Robert C. Cromley and Thomas R. Leinbach, "Patterns of Manufacturing in Nonmetropolitan Kentucky, 1968–78," *Kentucky Economy* 5 (1981), p. 10.

18. Theodore Klimasewski, "Corporate Dominance of Manufacturing in Appalachia," *Geographical Review* 68 (1978), p. 94.

19. Rodney A. Erickson and Thomas R. Leinbach, "Characteristics of Branch Plants Attracted to Nonmetropolitan Areas," in Lonsdale and Seyler, op. cit. (footnote 2), pp. 57–58.

20. These can be further subdivided into 144 three-digit SIC groups numbered 201 to 399 (e.g., 203 for "canned and frozen foods" or 332 for "iron and steel foundries") and 452 four-digit industries numbered 2011 to 3999 (e.g., 2035 for "pickles and sauces" or 3322 for "malleable iron foundries").

21. Miller, 1962, op. cit. (footnote 1), p. 13.

22. The correlation coefficients are all above 0.90. See John W. Alexander and James B. Lindberg, "Measurements of Manufacturing: Coefficients of Correlation," *Journal of Regional Science* 3 (1961), pp. 71–81, and Joel L. Morrison,

Morton W. Scripter, and Robert H. T. Smith, "Basic Measures of Manufacturing in the United States, 1958," *Economic Geography* 44 (1958), pp. 296–311.

23. U.S. Geological Survey, *Mineral Resources of the Appalachian Region*, Geological Survey Professional Paper no. 580 (Washington, D.C.: U.S. Geological Survey, 1968), p. 4.

24. See, for example, Helen Lewis, Linda Johnson, and Donald Askins, eds., *Colonialism in Modern America: The Appalachian Case* (Boone, N.C.: Appalachian Consortium Press, 1978).

25. James O. Wheeler and Peter O. Muller, *Economic Geography* (New York: John Wiley & Sons, 1981), p. 204.

26. James S. Fisher, "Structural Adjustments in the Southern Manufacturing Sector," *The Professional Geographer* 33 (1981), pp. 472–473.

27. Peirce F. Lewis, "Small Town in Pennsylvania," *Annals*, Association of American Geographers, 62 (1972), p. 337.

28. Kenneth Warren, *The American Steel Industry, 1850–1970: A Geographical Interpretation* (Oxford: Clarendon Press, 1973), p. 11.

29. Lewis, op. cit. (footnote 27), p. 339.

30. Miller, 1962, op. cit. (footnote 1), p. 283.

31. Warren, op. cit. (footnote 28), p. 11.

32. David M. Smith, *Industrial Location: An Economic Geographical Approach* (New York: John Wiley & Sons, 1971), p. 347.

33. Miller, 1962, op. cit. (footnote 1), p. 284.

34. Raymond E. Murphy and Marion Murphy, *Pennsylvania: A Regional Geography* (Harrisburg: Pennsylvania Book Service, 1937), p. 110.

35. Warren, op. cit. (footnote 28), p. 27.

36. Smith, op. cit. (footnote 32), p. 347.

37. John W. Alexander and Lay James Gibson, *Economic Geography* (Englewood Cliffs, N.J.: Prentice-Hall, 1979), p. 233.

38. Smith, op. cit. (footnote 32), pp. 305–306.

39. Miller, 1962, op. cit. (footnote 1), p. 447.

40. Ibid., p. 92.

41. John McGregor and Robert H. Maxey, "The Dalton, Georgia, Tufted Textile Concentration," *Southeastern Geographer* 14 (1974), pp. 133–144.

42. Alexander and Gibson, op. cit. (footnote 37), p. 243.

43. Bureau of Mines, *Minerals in the Economy of Pennsylvania* (Washington, D.C.: Government Printing Office, 1979), p. 7.

44. Bureau of Mines, *Minerals in the Economy of North Carolina* (Washington, D.C.: Government Printing Office, 1979), pp. 1–3.

45. Bureau of Mines, *Minerals in the Economy of Georgia* (Washington, D.C.: Government Printing Office, 1979).

46. Alexander and Gibson, op. cit. (footnote 37), p. 254.

# CHAPTER 9

# TRANSPORT PATTERNS, PROGRESS, AND ISSUES

*Thomas R. Leinbach*

Transportation generally has been viewed as a primary ingredient in regional and national development. Improvement in the conditions of accessibility is critical for a variety of reasons. In purely economic terms supply and demand points may be connected, raw materials may be collected, and finished products distributed. In addition, lower shipping costs and an overall reduction in resource requirements for the production process are achieved.[1] Highways, for example, serve as a public good to be enjoyed by those living in or traveling through the area.[2] Improved transport also may encourage existing industry and the location of new firms, facilitate commuting to work, and permit access to resources. These basic influences have been recognized in setting out the transportation objectives for a development strategy in Appalachia, for "the key to an accelerated rate of economic growth involves the efficient movement of people and goods within, to and from the Region."[3]

It is clear that transportation has been, and will continue to be, important in the development of the region. Over the past decade, however, a new view of transportation's role in development has emerged. That view maintains that transportation, while undeniably important, must not be assigned the role of catalytic agent. In other words, physical infrastructure and services, while necessary, do not cause development to take place.[4] Rather the role assigned to this sector should be a facilitative or permissive one. Moreover it is now recognized that previous investments in transportation may have been excessive and out of proportion to that required. In addition there is growing evidence to support an earlier view that various effects, not all positive, may be produced on an economy as transportation is improved.[5]

Transportation has been linked to the growth-center notion of regional development, which maintains that lagging regions can be efficiently developed by concentrating investment in specific nodes. Transportation is often viewed as critical in such a strategy, since it is maintained that the network is a vital factor in the spread of growth to surrounding areas. Yet such "trickle down" effects are essentially based upon a multiplier effect, a notion that states that the growth of an area is dependent upon the ability to market goods outside the region and the development of a basic industry through competitive advantage. A strong argument maintains, however, that the need for transportation is a derived demand based on the need for links joining production and market nodes. If the basic sector does not exist or a market for goods and services does not emerge, then transportation-system additions will not stimulate development. Critical too in the development of regions is the cost difference between various modes of transportation. Here haulage distance, nature of demand, and bulk all influence the selection of a particular form of carriage.[6] Typically, of course, water and rail, where available, have been utilized to ship heavy and bulky goods. Highway, rail, and water are often in competition with each other and may attempt to attract traffic by offering distinctive services coupled with lower costs. The role of transportation in regional development has been discussed in order to point up the conflict that has developed over the importance of transportation as a policy instrument. A clear position is that of the ARC, which maintains that transportation plays a leading role in development and that this sector is the prime mechanism. Against this view are the cautionary attitudes of numerous planners, economists, and geographers who believe that the importance and role of transportation should be more carefully qualified.

## HIGHWAYS IN REGIONAL DEVELOPMENT

It has long been suggested that isolation is a major factor contributing to Appalachia's relative economic stagnation. In order to minimize costs, it has been argued, major highways were built to bypass the region. Poor local transportation discouraged commerce and industrial development and prevented many communities from securing large employers because of the limited market access.

The Appalachian Regional Development Act of 1965 provided the authorization for the construction of an Appalachian development highway system (ADHS) and local access roads to serve the region. The highway system was intended to be built in conjunction with the interstate network and other federal-aid highways in order to open up areas with development potential that had been suppressed because of a lack of adequate access (Figure 9.1).

Construction on the developmental highway system was to be limited to 2,900 mi (4,666.1 km); an additional limit of 1,400 mi (2,252.6 km) was set on the construction of local access roads. The latter were intended to serve specific commercial, recreational, industrial, residential, or other facilities. The facilitation of school consolidation programs was suggested as an appropriate focus of the local access road program. The ARC was to transmit to the secretary of transportation the corridor locations of the development highways, local access roads to be constructed, and priorities for segment construction. Over two billion dollars were initially

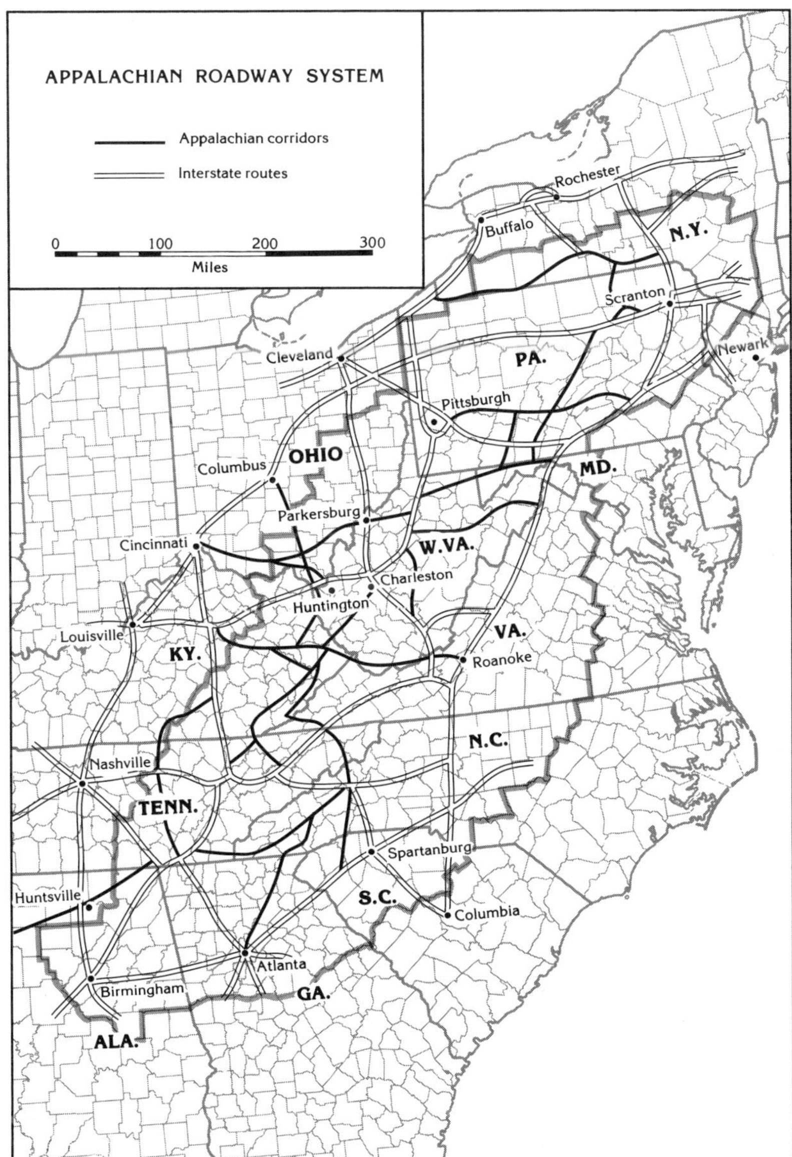


**Figure 9.1**
From Appalachian Regional Commission, *Appalachian Highway Program: Progress, Impacts, and Planning for the Future* (Washington, D.C.: ARC, 1975).

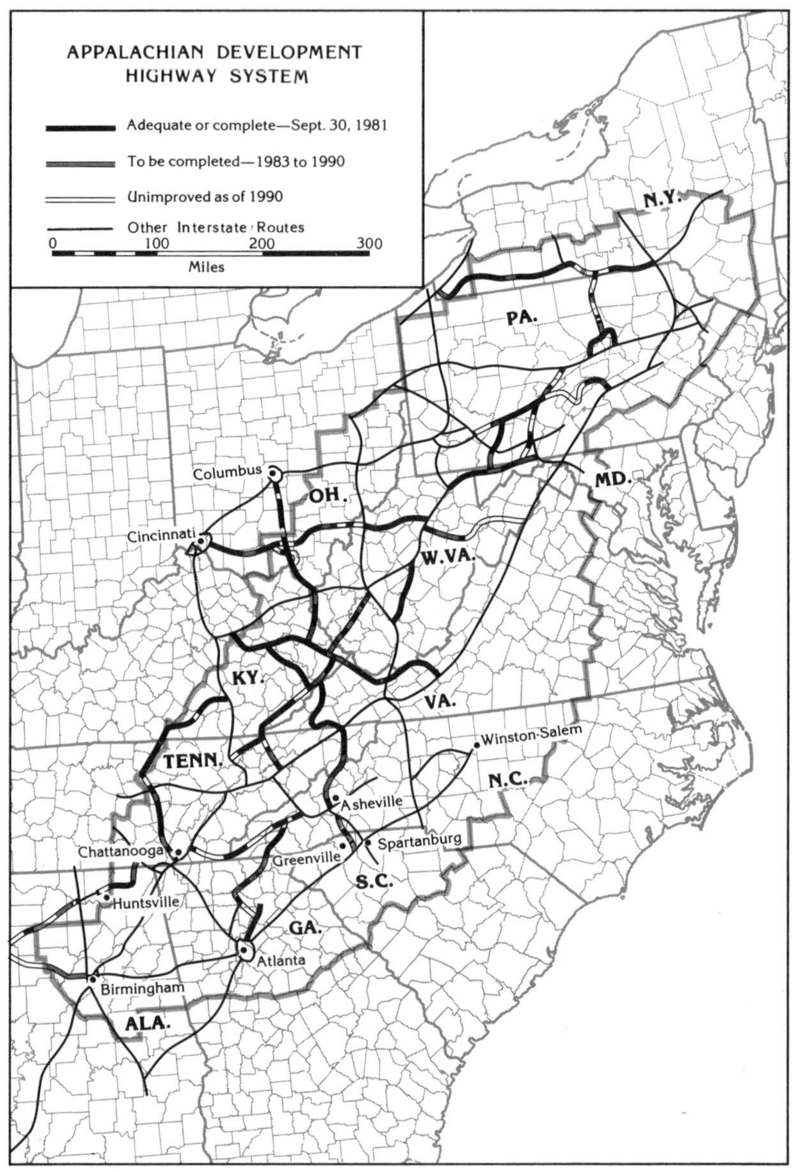


**Figure 9.2**
From "Appalachian Highways Are Catalysts of Change," *Appalachia* 15 (Nov.–Dec. 1981 and Jan.–Feb. 1982), p. 2.

authorized to be spent for transportation development purposes from 1971 through 1981.

The ADHS is composed of a series of twenty-four individual corridors (Figure 9.2) and includes both existing highways and new construction. The total mileage is 3,025 (4,867.2 km). By late 1980, 1,565 of the total corridor mi (2,518.1 km) in the system were completed, and another 235 mi (378.1 km) were under construction. Another 1,224 mi (1,969.4 km) were in some stage of engineering and land acquisition. A total of $2.45 billion in federal funds and $1.5 billion in state funds had been committed to the construction. An additional $430 million in federal funds had been authorized through 1981.[7]

The completion phase of the development highway system has occurred much sooner in some areas than others (Table 9.1). Virginia, North Carolina, and New York have finished over 70 percent of their segments, whereas Alabama, South Carolina, and Mississippi have much smaller portions completed. If the average percentage of construction completed over all the states is weighted by the total miles of construction finished in each state, the weighted average is 58 percent. Thus, on the average, over 40 percent of the basic highway grid needed to be completed as of late 1980. Georgia and Pennsylvania have construction completion averages that are well under the overall average. Overall the access road program has progressed more satisfactorily, evidently because of the smaller lengths of required construction and the lower costs. The weighted-average completion rate was just over 77 percent. Progress in Georgia, Mississippi, New York, and West Virginia has lagged well behind the other states in the region.

The logic, utility, and impact of the ADHS has been the subject of various investigations from a variety of perspectives over the past fifteen years. One researcher rejected the idea that Appalachia has suffered from a lack of access. Overall, J. M. Munro contended, the region was better supplied with interstate highways than the country as a whole, and the same conclusion applied to rural highways.[8] Another argument contended that a case was not adequately made for highway construction as the best means of alleviating poverty in the region. Further, the so-called planning process did not seek to maximize potential benefits but rather simply filled in gaps left by the interstate system and merely attempted to insure that each state received a fair share of funds. For example, the states of Alabama and South Carolina, it was claimed, were allocated 50 percent of the access road funds since they did not participate in the development highway program.[9] The data in Table 9.1, however, clearly show that Alabama had over $45 million obligated for development through 1980 highway construction, although South Carolina had much less. Alabama and South Carolina do have large approved mileages in the access program, but the amount obligated through 1980 was approximately 28 percent of the total, not 50 percent.

A major criticism in the early 1970s focused upon the use of the ADHS as an instrument for the redistribution of income and the basis

TABLE 9.1
Appalachian Development Highway System and Access Roads
(As of September 30, 1980)

| State | Highway Development | | | | Access Roads | | | |
|---|---|---|---|---|---|---|---|---|
| | Construction Required* | Construction Completed | %** | Dollars Obligated through 1980 (000) | Miles Approved | Construction Completed | %** | Dollars Obligated through 1980 (000) |
| Alabama | 244.2 | 40.4 | 17 | 45,271 | 210.1 | 186.4 | 89 | 21,464 |
| Georgia | 134.6 | 37.9 | 28 | 65,900 | 36.9 | 16.7 | 45 | 13,321 |
| Kentucky | 433.2 | 295.2 | 68 | 429,702 | 15.2 | 11.1 | 73 | 4,194 |
| Maryland | 81.4 | 50.0 | 62 | 71,017 | 7.6 | 6.8 | 89 | 2,174 |
| Mississippi | 116.8 | 22.8 | 20 | 44,885 | 181.7 | 107.1 | 59 | 19,787 |
| New York | 219.5 | 158.8 | 72 | 220,734 | 9.1 | 3.5 | 38 | 3,145 |
| North Carolina | 203.6 | 148.4 | 73 | 127,958 | 23.9 | 20.6 | 86 | 6,329 |
| Ohio | 201.1 | 102.5 | 51 | 105,396 | 44.7 | 35.9 | 80 | 5,150 |
| Pennsylvania | 453.5 | 154.1 | 34 | 344,687 | 102.4 | 83.1 | 81 | 14,385 |
| South Carolina | 11.8 | 1.7 | 14 | 4,383 | 121.7 | 98.5 | 81 | 14,443 |
| Tennessee | 331.8 | 180.6 | 54 | 268,328 | 57.3 | 43.0 | 75 | 10,480 |
| Virginia | 190.8 | 137.5 | 72 | 112,289 | 22.4 | 18.2 | 81 | 4,676 |
| West Virginia | 410.6 | 235.5 | 57 | 571,218 | 49.4 | 21.8 | 44 | 8,127 |
| Total | 3,032.9 | 1,565.4 | 48 | 2,411,768 | 882.4 | 652.7 | 71 | 127,675 |
| | | | 58 | (weighted average) | | | 77 | |

Source: Appalachian Regional Commission Annual Report, 1980.

*Only 3,025 miles are authorized for ARC funding.

**Percentage completed of construction required or miles approved.

for providing social services to needy areas. The conclusion drawn was that redistribution was in favor of urban and suburban centers at the expense of rural districts. Thus if the provision of social services was tied to the highway program, those services would be provided to states having the tax resources required by a matching-funds strategy of investment. The outcome suggested was that inequities—instead of being decreased by the program—would be increased.[10] Still another study that examined the role of highways in West Virginia concluded that the ADHS has influenced the pattern of retail firms and employment. A major finding was that the level of prior development of each county relative to other areas served by a highway link is of importance.[11] The ARC has also produced numerous studies and figures that point to the significant impact of the highway system.[12] More recently, for example, a comprehensive survey showed that more than 400,000 new jobs have been created along or near the Appalachian corridors. In addition, a major share of the region's industrial growth, it was claimed, can be linked to the corridor system: Almost 60 percent of new manufacturing plants employing 50 or more persons (801 plants with 182,000 employees) that have located in Appalachia since 1965 selected sites within thirty minutes of an existing or planned corridor. The fact that over 0.79 billion tn-mi (1.15 billion t-km) of coal moved over the system in 1980 was also cited as a measure of the system's contribution to regional development.[13] Even though these data are forceful and impressive, it is important to recall the fact that transportation is merely a permissive agent and only one service among many required.

In July 1981, the House Appropriations Committee asked the ARC for a plan to "finish up" the highway program. The request was made in light of the huge $7 billion amount required to complete all the remaining segments. The response to the request proposed that a "finish up" program would complete only the *critically important* segments with a federal ceiling of $2.27 billion on the construction. The highest-priority linkages, 550 mi (884.9 km) of the 1,303 unimproved mi (2,096.5 km) in the ADHS, would include those within each state that carry the highest overall traffic, contribute most to regional economic development, eliminate the most restrictive gaps, and carry the most coal and would complete the most-critical state-line crossings. The result would be a 2,351-mi (3,781.8-k) system as opposed to the full 3,033-mi (4,880.1-k) planned system. Under the "finish up" program a number of corridors in the ADHS would remain unimproved. Among these are corridors in Mississippi, Alabama, West Virginia, Pennsylvania, and Kentucky (Figure 9.2).[14]

## THE RAIL SYSTEM

Rail transportation is critical to the region and has undergone some significant changes over the past decade. The objective in this section is to define the pattern of rail facilities as well as the traffic handled

TABLE 9.2
Rail Mileage Within the Appalachian Region, by State

| State | Mileage |
|---|---|
| Alabama | 3,285 |
| Georgia | 1,029 |
| Kentucky | 948 |
| Maryland | 275 |
| Mississippi | 915 |
| New York | 1,238 |
| North Carolina | 890 |
| Ohio | 1,876 |
| Pennsylvania | 5,358 |
| South Carolina | 331 |
| Tennessee | 1,466 |
| Virginia | 978 |
| West Virginia | 2,972 |
| Total | 21,561 |

Source: Estimated from data in Railroad Atlas of the United States, Rand McNally, 1971.

by the system. Subsequently, rail service and various rail issues will be discussed.

There are approximately 21,000 mi (33,789 km) of rail line within the Appalachian region. This total represents about 11 percent of the total U.S. rail mileage. The distribution of the mileage by state is shown in Table 9.2 (these mileages represent only the ARC-region portion of the states listed). The total mileage is accounted for by twenty Class I railroads and roughly an equal number of Class II railroads (annual revenue less than five million dollars) operating minor amounts of trackage in Appalachia. Of the twenty Class I railroads, only a few are truly significant.[15] Among these are the CSX Corporation, Norfolk and Western, the Southern Railroad, and the Illinois Central Gulf. With reference to these, several recent mergers are significant. The CSX Corporation was formed by the merger of the Chessie System and the Seaboard Coast Line Industries in November 1980.[16] Included under the system are the Chesapeake and Ohio, Baltimore and Ohio, and Western Maryland (all formerly the Chessie System) and Seaboard Coast Line, Louisville and Nashville, Clinchfield, and Georgia Railroad (all formerly Family Lines). The CSX Corporation and its affiliated railroads clearly dominate the railway mileage of the region with over 23,000 mi (37,007 km) (Table 9.3). A variety of benefits solidified the merger. The unification, which joins two major coal haulers, is the first rail system to link the industrial Northeast, the Great Lakes region, and the Southeast and as such provides shippers with many opportunities for single-system

TABLE 9.3
Major Rail Firm Mileage Operated, by State*

| State | CSX | Norfolk and Western | Southern | Illinois Central Gulf |
|---|---|---|---|---|
| Alabama | 1,969 | | 964 | 442 |
| Georgia | 3,774 | | 903 | |
| Kentucky | 2,520 | 128 | 133 | 690 |
| Maryland | 607 | 40 | | |
| Mississippi | 74 | | 46 | 3,064 |
| New York | 209 | 268 | | |
| North Carolina | 2,606 | 170 | 1,283 | |
| Ohio | 2,088 | 3,552 | | |
| Pennsylvania | 1,148 | 240 | | |
| South Carolina | 2,568 | | 1,000 | |
| Tennessee | 1,737 | | 683 | 659 |
| Virginia | 1,504 | 2,948 | 681 | |
| West Virginia | 2,628 | 1,607 | | |
| Total | 23,432 | 8,953 | 5,693 | 4,855 |

Source: Resource Planning Associates, Transportation Development Program for Appalachia, November, 1974.

*Totals and individual state mileage reflect both ARC and non-ARC areas.

service (Figure 9.3). The Chessie was primarily an east-west railroad with routes linking eastern coalfields to the industrial basins of Ohio and Michigan. Seaboard operated on a predominantly north-south axis with routes stretching along the eastern seaboard into Florida. Wider markets for existing coal-mining operations, more efficient car utilization through reduced empty backhaul movements, and new and expanded piggyback services between major markets in the South and Northeast were additional benefits of the merger. The reduction of costs and interchange delays and the improved quality and frequency of general freight service were also important.

An additional merger, that of the Norfolk and Western (N&W) and the Southern Railway Systems (Norfolk, Southern) on June 1, 1982, has resulted in a combined trackage of over 14,000 mi (22,526 km) extending from Omaha in the West to northern Florida and New Orleans in the South (Figure 9.4).[17] The heart of the N&W's operations has been providing rail service to coal fields. Coal transportation provided over 50 percent of the line's revenues in 1980, and transportation of motor vehicles and parts, the next-largest contributor, represented 9 percent of revenue.[18] The N&W benefits from having tracks that run from the mines of West Virginia, Kentucky, and Pennsylvania directly to its pier at Hampton Roads, Virginia. Besides this geographic advantage there is virtually no competition, except for barge transport on the Ohio

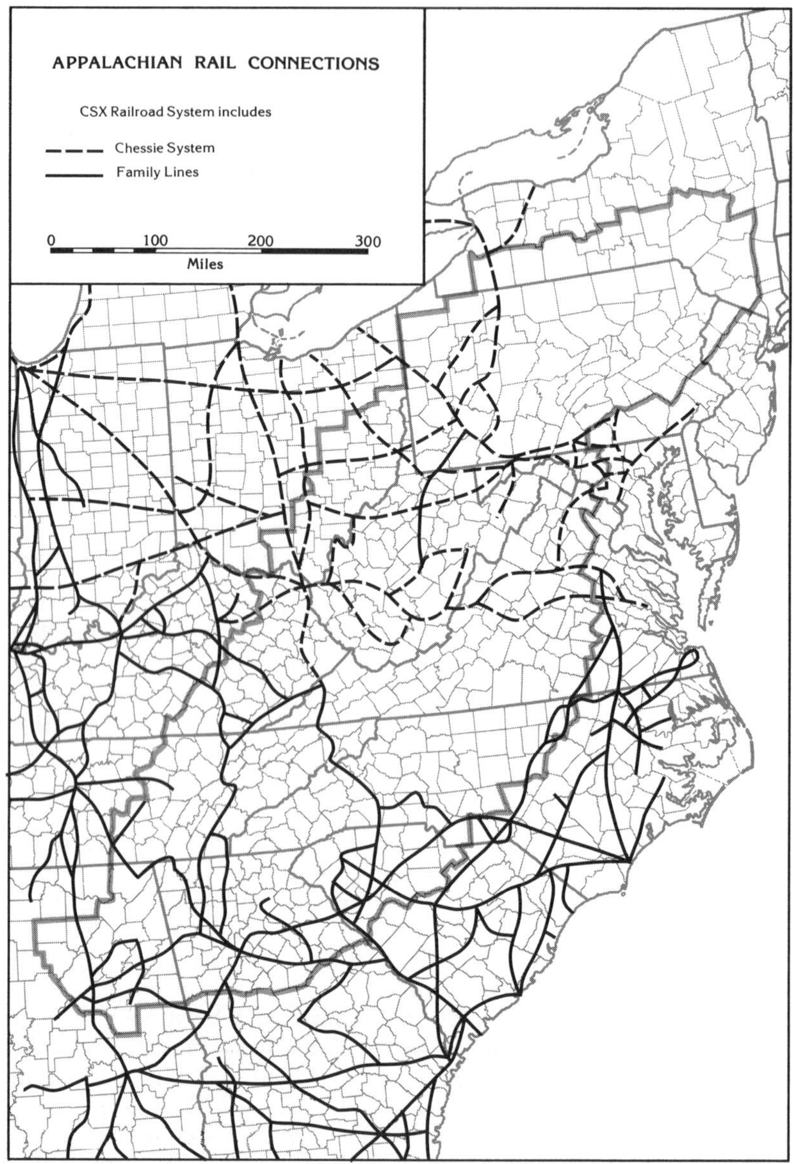


**Figure 9.3**
Information generalized from Rand McNally and Co., "Principal Railroads in the United States, Southern Canada, and Northern Mexico," n.d., and CSX Corporation, "CSX Rail System" (Richmond, Va.: CSX Research Dept., n.d.).

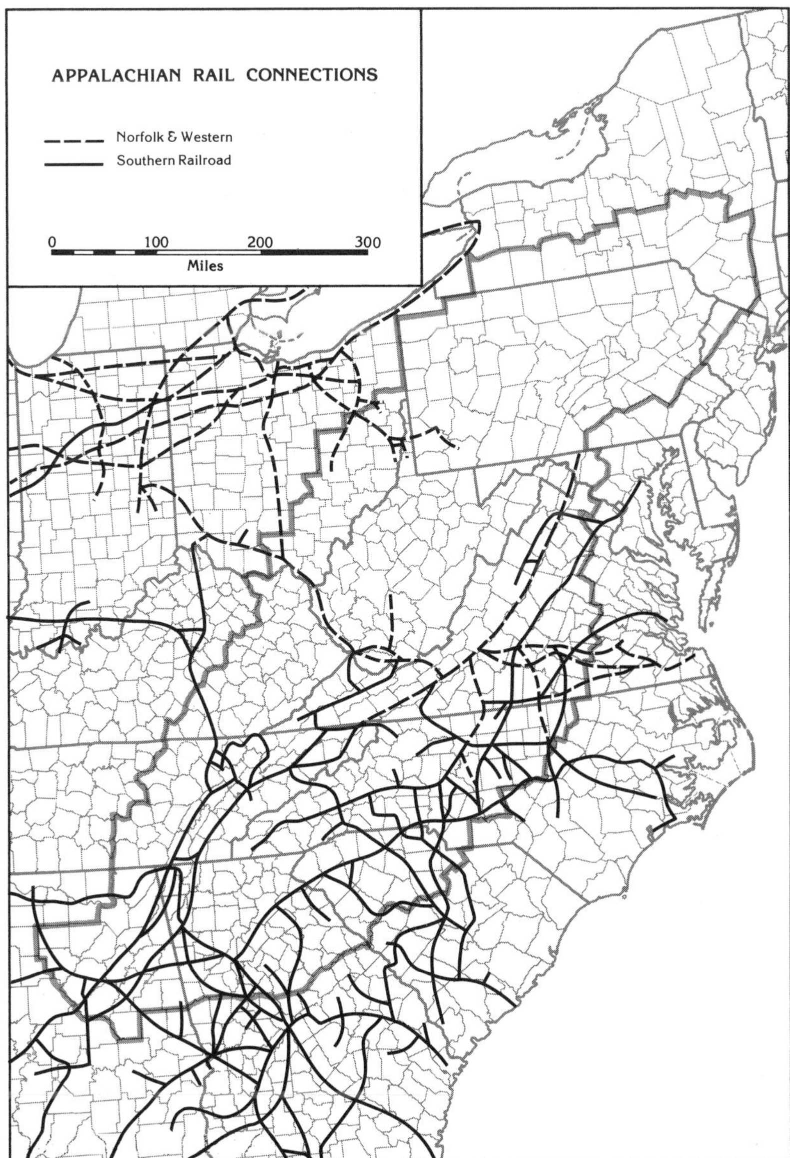


**Figure 9.4**
Information generalized from Rand McNally and Co., "Principal Railroads in the United States, Southern Canada, and Northern Mexico," n.d.

River, by other modes of transportation for coal shipment. Thus coal transportation represents a relatively stable earning source. In contrast the N&W shipment of auto parts faces stiff competition from the trucking industry and also has fallen off with the slump in the industry. The merger with the Southern system creates a railroad that competes directly with the CSX Corporation, which operates in the same territory and serves many of the same markets. The merger has joined two strong companies and will enable them to compete more effectively by controlling more points of origin and destination in the Middle West and Southeast. Under deregulation railroads benefit when they control points of origin and destination, because this allows them to offer shippers low-cost service along single rail lines between two cities. Shippers face higher costs when they use two linking railroads. Essentially mergers are stimulated by the desires of railroads to control as many origin and destination points as possible. Outside the Appalachian region (in the Midwest and some parts of the Northeast), the N&W and the Southern are expected to face stiff competition from CSX and from the Consolidated Rail Corporation (Conrail). Since the demand for coal is on the rise, particularly among European countries with the decline of the Polish source, the earnings potential looks very positive. To expand these earnings the N&W has streamlined operations and revamped scheduling to increase export coal shipments. The demurrage or waiting time for ships at Hampton Roads, for example, has been decreased from thirty to five days. At the same time the system has recently pumped cash into maintenance of equipment and trackage.

## Rail Usage in the Region

Analysis of origin and destination tonnages on the region's rail system reveals a wide range in volumes (Table 9.4). Of the nearly 0.5 billion tn (453.5 million t) of rail freight moved in the region in the early 1970s, 290 million tn (263 million t) represented originations of Appalachian products, and 177 million tn (160.5 million t) terminated within the region. Pennsylvania, West Virginia, and Kentucky dominated the total tonnage figures. The commodity type that accounted for the highest origination tonnage in the majority of the states was coal, as follows:

| | *tn* | *t* |
|---|---|---|
| Alabama | 3,466 | 3,143.6 |
| Kentucky | 46,203 | 41,906.0 |
| Maryland | 560 | 507.9 |
| Ohio | 14,970 | 13,477.8 |
| Pennsylvania | 31,411 | 28,489.7 |
| Tennessee | 4,485 | 4,067.9 |
| Virginia | 28,198 | 25,575.6 |
| West Virginia | 68,421 | 62,057.8 |

TABLE 9.4
Total Volume of Shipments Originated or Terminated by the Appalachian Region's Rail System
(000s of tons)

| State* | Tonnage Originated | Tonnage Terminated | Total Tonnage |
|---|---|---|---|
| Alabama | 17,513 | 16,060 | 33,573 |
| Georgia | 3,928 | 8,581 | 12,509 |
| Kentucky | 48,474 | 6,454 | 54,928 |
| Maryland | 1,413 | 1,386 | 2,799 |
| Mississippi | 2,597 | 1,680 | 4,277 |
| New York | 1,211 | 4,209 | 5,420 |
| North Carolina | 3,170 | 8,451 | 11,621 |
| Ohio | 22,081 | 12,204 | 34,285 |
| Pennsylvania | 64,413 | 60,247 | 124,660 |
| South Carolina | 1,624 | 4,428 | 6,052 |
| Tennessee | 14,164 | 18,740 | 32,904 |
| Virginia | 31,635 | 7,771 | 39,406 |
| West Virginia | 78,008 | 27,269 | 105,277 |
| Total | 290,231 | 177,480 | 467,711 |

Source: 1972 Rail Waybill data provided by the Federal Railroad Administration to ARC; and Resource Planning Associates, Transportation Development Program for Appalachia, 1974.

*Data reflect only Appalachian region portion of state.

Lumber and wood products accounted for the greatest volume in four states:[19]

| | *tn* | *t* |
|---|---|---|
| Georgia | 867 | 786.4 |
| Mississippi | 1,040 | 943.3 |
| North Carolina | 874 | 792.7 |
| South Carolina | 353 | 320.1 |

Other bulk commodity types that dominated the flow patterns were stone, clay and glass, primary metals, chemicals, and nonmetallic minerals. In only two states, North Carolina and New York, were food and kindred products major items in the rail-flow patterns. The data point up the relatively lower importance of the rail system to manufactured goods and agricultural products originating in the region vis-à-vis bulk commodities. Nearly two-thirds of the Appalachian rail use for outgoing shipment was for coal movement.

Coal also accounted for a significant proportion of the commodity terminations. Coal was the major commodity in the flow patterns terminating in these states:[20]

| | *tn* | *t* |
|---|---|---|
| Alabama | 6,303 | 5,716.8 |
| Georgia | 3,991 | 3,619.8 |
| Kentucky | 3,161 | 2,867.0 |
| New York | 2,150 | 1,950.0 |
| North Carolina | 3,135 | 2,843.4 |
| Tennessee | 7,669 | 6,955.8 |
| Virginia | 7,033 | 6,378.9 |
| West Virginia | 19,319 | 17,522.3 |

In the remaining states the highest commodity terminations were as follows:

| | *tn* | *t* |
|---|---|---|
| Maryland: lumber and wood | 259 | 234.9 |
| Mississippi: chemicals | 439 | 398.2 |
| Ohio: metallic ores | 4,126 | 3,742.3 |
| Pennsylvania: metallic ores | 21,151 | 19,184.0 |
| South Carolina: nonmetallic minerals | 982 | 890.7 |

Coal for use in industry and for electric utilities is obviously important both domestically and internationally. The strong demand for this commodity and its role in the region's economy has stimulated considerable activity and impact that is worth examining more closely.

## The Coal-Export Boom

By the year 2000, U.S. coal exports may exceed today's huge exports of grain. In light of this surge in demand, U.S. ports are launching a major expansion of export capacity. Total investment in coal terminals may reach four billion dollars within the near future. Across the country forty-five new terminals are being built or planned at twenty-nine harbors on three coasts. All of this activity will produce a coal loading capacity in excess of 625 million tn (567 million t) per year. The Department of Energy predicts that 250 million tn (226.8 million t) will be shipped abroad each year by the end of the century. Today's export level is 110 million tn (99.8 million t).[21] The growth in coal shipments will provide employment, incomes for local businesses, and tax revenues for the harbor areas. The two major East Coast ports, Hampton Roads and Baltimore, will become larger through investments in terminal facilities by the Virginia Port Authority and by Consolidation Coal (a subsidiary of Conoco) respectively, as well as by other investors.

Until 1979 nearly all exports were metallurgical coal used in the manufacture of steel. The future growth in demand from Europe and Asia will be for steam coal to be burned by utilities to generate power. Low sulfur and high energy contents are the critical properties of good-quality steam coal. Many governments limit the sulfur content to 1 percent or less as an antipollution measure. The higher the Btu's per pound, the more valuable is the coal. For example, a firm must purchase, transport, and handle 300 tn (272.1 t) of 8,000 Btu coal to get the same energy that is obtained from 200 tn (181.4 t) of 12,000 Btu coal. Recent spot prices value Wyoming and Idaho coal (8,000 Btu and 1 percent sulfur) at $7.50 per tn ($8.26 per t), Illinois coal (10,500 Btu and 3 percent sulfur) at $19 per tn ($20.95 per t), and southern West Virginia and eastern Kentucky coal (12,000 Btu and 1 percent sulfur) at $35 per tn ($38.59 per t).[22] The latter commodity is in great demand.

Critical, too, in the export process are transportation costs from mine to port. The Chessie line and the N&W charge $15 to $16 per tn ($16.54 to $17.64 per t) to place Appalachian coal aboard ship at Hampton Roads. Rates at Baltimore and Mobile are $14 and $10 respectively. These export rail rates give these three ports a major advantage over competitors. Despite the vast quantities of western coal, the Great Plains deposits are low in energy content and must travel over 1,000 mi (1,609 km) to the nearest port. In contrast the low-sulfur, high-energy-content coal of Appalachia (18.7 billion tns—16.9 billion tns) is situated within easy reach of the East Coast.[23] As a result of this locational advantage the Chesapeake Bay ports command a strong economic position in a competitive battle among ports throughout the country.

Both the Chessie system and the N&W will obtain a share of the new terminal capacity at Hampton Roads, which now has an export loading capacity of over 50 million tn (45.4 million t) a year and which is expected to add up to 90 million tn (81.6 million t). Baltimore is expanding even faster than Hampton Roads and could lure away traffic with its current capacity of 36 million tn (32.7 million t) a year. In addition Baltimore has obtained federal authorization to deepen its channel, and if financing can be obtained, the port could move into a lead position. Such dredging would allow Baltimore the advantage of being able to use supercolliers, huge 1,000-foot (304-meter) coal ships, and thus being able to deliver coal to Europe and perhaps even Asia at a considerably lower cost.[24] In addition to these ports, others—some at considerable distances from the Appalachian coal fields—are also planning to enter the competition. Both Mobile and New Orleans are preparing to upgrade capacities. The Mississippi River outlet, despite its cost disadvantage, has been able to lure vessels that have encountered considerable service delays in the eastern ports. If vessels are forced to wait in port, they must pay a demurrage, or waiting charge, that can amount to fifteen thousand dollars per day and can offset the locational advantage of the Chesapeake ports.[25] In addition, New Orleans is well situated to handle the lower-quality midwestern coal that arrives on the inland waterway system that drains from lower Illinois into the Mississippi and the Gulf. The survival and advantage of terminals handling export coal will depend upon the ability of operators to obtain long-term commitments in order to avoid operation below capacity, as well as reasonable handling charges despite the necessity to recover heavy capital costs.

The economic recession and oil glut of 1982 have deflated overseas demand for coal. Long-term export forecasts therefore have been scaled down considerably. As a consequence, on the East and Gulf coasts ambitious port and terminal projects are being postponed.[26] Whether or not the major expansions are ever realized will depend largely upon the level of export demand, which is itself a function of oil prices and supplies as well as alternative energy sources and conservation practices.

## Finances and Revenues of Railroads Operating in the Region

The recent bankruptcy of major railroads has focused attention upon issues associated with the economic viability of this mode. The reorganization of the Penn Central, Reading, Lehigh Valley, and Erie Lackawanna railroads points up the failure to achieve efficient operations and the regional impact that may result. This is especially so since rail revenues are critical to the Appalachian region. The amount of revenue in Appalachia, both origination and termination, in 1972 was estimated to be $2.5 billion and represented nearly 20 percent of national rail freight revenues for that year.[27] Appalachia has a high degree of rail dependency in comparison to other regions of the nation; that is, other carriers are not available as a result of cost, infrequent scheduling, or both. The state of Pennsylvania in 1972 accounted for roughly 30 percent of the total revenue ($745 million). West Virginia accounted for another 20 percent ($492 million), and Kentucky accounted for 10 percent ($236 million).[28]

The region has a diverse mixture of railroads operating within its boundaries: Some of the systems are quite profitable, whereas others have had to be reorganized as a result of weak financial conditions. The Seaboard Coast Line, Norfolk and Western, Southern, and Chesapeake and Ohio ranked eighth, sixth, seventh, and thirteenth respectively out of sixty-one Class I railroads in terms of 1973 freight revenues.[29] These lines ranked tenth, fourth, second, and seventh in ordinary income. The Illinois Central Gulf ranked eleventh and sixth on these two measures. On the other hand, the Penn Central ranked first and fifty-seventh, the Western Maryland thirty-second and twenty-fourth, the Lehigh Valley thirtieth and fifty-sixth, and the Monongahela sixtieth and forty-ninth.

The declining health of certain railroads in the region has resulted in a neglect of maintenance on facilities—especially track condition. Poor earnings obviously prevent a system from providing the maintenance required to achieve adequate standards. Also related to the financial conditions of the railroads is the factor of capacity utilization. For example, the daily car mileage is substantially lower in the region than it is in the West.[30] Although this is accounted for by longer shipping runs in the latter, the lower use is nonetheless significant in income production. In addition, existing rail line capacity in the region tends to be underutilized. In some areas usage is only 25 to 30 percent of capacity. All of these issues are affected by the Regional Rail Reorganization Act (RRR Act) of 1973, which attempted to improve the operating efficiency of lines by various measures. One of the suggestions has been simply to eliminate excess trackage and stations.

### The Railway Abandonment Problem

The inability of the railroads to reorganize under traditional means led Congress to pass the RRR Act. This legislation essentially addressed the railroad problem as one of excess branch lines and track. Faced with massive abandonments of branch lines, 18 states reacted to preserve essential services. A major study undertaken by the Council of State Governments and supported by the Economic Development Administration identified the problem of rail abandonment and rural development and presented alternatives available to states in coping with abandonment problems.[31]

Research completed by federal, state, and regional governments shows that rail abandonments in rural areas do produce substantial impact. The impact involves not only socioeconomic issues (loss of equipment, income, and taxes), but environmental (air, water, land, and noise pollution) as well. The recommendations and solutions to the problem of discontinued service are varied.[32] Several suggestions are clear. States should take an active role in rail abandonment proceedings that affect them. In addition they should preserve vital rail links to areas with natural and economic resources that have the potential for future expansion or development. Moreover, development programs should cooperate in locating new industry on marginal branch lines.

The alternatives to rail abandonment are important, for they are applicable to a variety of small Appalachian communities that have low-density lines. The most popular alternative to abandonment is the creation of a short-line railroad.[33] A major advantage of a short line is lower operating cost because of lower labor cost. Such lines are usually more flexible than larger railroads; for example, new services are possible and cars may be moved with only minimal delays. The major disadvantage is size: Short lines are frequently too small to be efficient. The lack of operational economics can partly be alleviated by the concept of regional subsystems, which involves tying two or more short lines together. The tie need not be a merger but merely an agreement to share equipment, facilities, and services. Numerous other alternatives exist. Among these are reduced service levels, subsidization of short-term losses, and finally state acquisition and subsequent leasing.

Rail abandonment most commonly has negative rural development impacts.[34] Although it does not mean that an area will not develop if it lacks rail service, it will reduce the comparative advantage of the site. Negative impacts are likely to be most damaging in areas with natural resources that have not been developed or fully developed. Here a subsidy program may be merited. Other strategies are appropriate given specific circumstances. Rail access is certainly not a prerequisite for development, but the efficient operation of such service may encourage development.

However, despite the impact on small communities, the fact remains that we will not have a strong national rail system until railroads are allowed to do efficiently what they do best. Railroads are very cost effective in handling large volumes of traffic between fixed points. Railroads are not very efficient at handling sparse traffic over branch lines, and such tasks can probably be more efficiently performed by the trucking industry. It is really too soon to predict the impact of deregulation on both small rural communities and regional economies. The competitive process has been stimulated and regulation relaxed. The next few years will provide the answers.

## INLAND WATERWAYS IN APPALACHIA

As discussed in Chapter 2, the major waterways in the region include the Ohio, Susquehanna, and Tennessee rivers, their tributaries, and the Black Warrior River. The navigable waterways include nearly 400 mi

Pineville, Kentucky, lies at the point where the Cumberland River has cut a water gap through Pine Mountain. This easy water-level passage allowed early migrants to move across the wind gap in Cumberland Mountain a few miles to the southeast and follow the river into the Appalachian Plateaus without crossing the formidable Pine Mountain.

From its headwaters in western North Carolina, the New River flows north and west across the grain of the Ridge and Valley and Appalachian Plateaus into West Virginia. Long a major barrier to east-west transportation, the river was recently crossed by the New River Gorge Bridge. The 1,700-foot (516.8-meter) steel main span is the world's longest, and at over 875 ft (266 m) above the river, it is the second-highest bridge in the nation. The bridge, in Fayette County, West Virginia, will allow a highway link between Interstates 77, 64, and 79. Steel girders for the bridge were fabricated in Ambridge, Pennsylvania by the American Bridge Company. That plant closed in 1984 putting many of the townspeople out of work. (Photo courtesy of Gerald Ratliff, West Virginia State Government Public Information Office.)

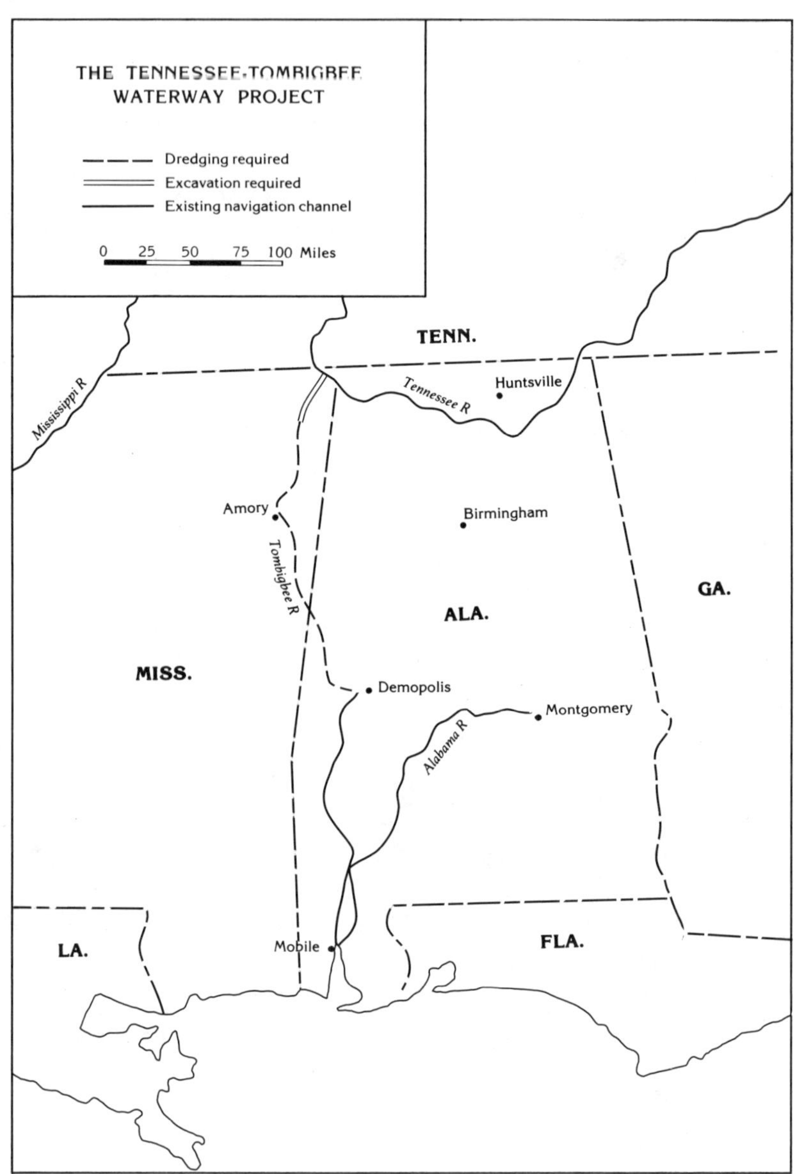
THE TENNESSEE-TOMBIGBEE
WATERWAY PROJECT
Dredging required
Excavation required
Existing navigation channel
0 25 50 75 100 Miles
TENN.
Mississippi R
Tennessee R
Huntsville
Amory
Birmingham
Tombigbee R
GA.
ALA.
MISS.
Demopolis
Montgomery
Alabama R
LA.
Mobile
FLA.

**Figure 9.5**

(643.6 km) on the Ohio from Pittsburgh to Manchester, Ohio. The Ohio River provides a major transportation corridor through southern Ohio and West Virginia. Industrial activity throughout the corridor has a significant impact on jobs and income flows in northern Appalachia.[35]

Approximately 400 mi of the Tennessee River are within Appalachia, and this river also provides a major lane of transportation for eastern Tennessee and northern Alabama. Over 180 mi (289.6 km) on the Black Warrior River are located in Appalachian Alabama, providing a link with the Gulf of Mexico through the Tombigbee River system.

Inland-waterway transport provides an important industrial transport link between leading production points of northern Appalachia and a corridor of shipment for eastern Tennessee and northern Alabama. A major project still uncompleted is the Tennessee-Tombigbee Waterway (Figure 9.5).[36] For more than two centuries entrepreneurs and engineers have explored the possibilities for a canal cutting through northeastern Mississippi, to link the Tennessee River to the north with the Tombigbee River to the south as a passage from the Gulf port of Mobile to the cities and towns of the Tennessee Valley. Most cost-benefit studies have revealed unfavorable evidence, and there is still considerable doubt that enough barge traffic would use the route to justify the cost of 200 mi (321.8 km) of channel improvement and 50 mi (80.5 km) of canals, locks, and dams. The project would allow barges to make the trip from Mobilc to inland Appalachian cities such as Knoxville, Tennessee, hauling in chemicals, oil, and raw ore and hauling out coal, lumber, steel, and grain. The only way a barge can now reach Knoxville from the Gulf is to move up the Mississippi from New Orleans, cross over into the Ohio at Cairo, Illinois, then move into the Tennessee at Paducah, Kentucky. Knoxville would be 800 mi (1,287.2 km) and five days closer to the sea via the new system. Speculation abounds as to the benefits to be reaped by Mobile. Clearly much of the freight downstream will be coal from Appalachia. This fact disturbs the railroads, which generally charge three times as much as barges to move freight (this is in part because barge operators pay no fee for use of the waterways).

Construction on the project began in 1972 at Gainseville, Alabama, following extensive litigation based upon environmental considerations. The first river port on the Mississippi system, the Yellow Creek complex, has been completed. The waterway is certain to exert a major influence on flows and industrial location patterns in this segment of northeastern Mississippi.[37]

### Commodity Flows for the Appalachian Waterways

A basic summary of the commodity flows gives some evidence of the nature and importance of the commerce that is carried out on the system (Table 9.5). Data are for the entire river system, not merely for the Appalachian counties that contribute to the flow. The figures do, however, provide some indication of the relative magnitude of various commodities moved over the waterways. For the Ohio River system as

TABLE 9.5
Appalachian Waterways: 1972 Total Annual Traffic and Principal Commodities

| | Net Tons (000s) | | Ton Miles (000,000s) |
|---|---|---|---|
| Monongahela River | 38,624 | | 1,527 |
| Coal/Lignite | | 30,587 | |
| Iron/Steel | | 1,955 | |
| Allegheny River | 5,425 | | 80 |
| Coal/Lignite | | 2,670 | |
| Sand/Gravel | | 1,651 | |
| Kanawha River | 14,501 | | 815 |
| Coal/Lignite | | 7,412 | |
| Sand/Gravel | | 1,594 | |
| Chemicals | | 2,940 | |
| Alcohols | | 646 | |
| Tennessee River | 28,529 | | 3,755 |
| Coal/Lignite | | 11,964 | |
| Sand/Gravel | | 4,090 | |
| Gasoline | | 1,652 | |
| Chemicals | | 895 | |
| Ohio River | 138,848 | | 32,055 |
| Grain | | 2,698 | |
| Coal/Lignite | | 65,088 | |
| Crude Petroleum | | 7,811 | |
| Sand/Gravel | | 17,171 | |
| Sulphur | | 2,074 | |
| Chemicals | | 6,727 | |
| Gasoline | | 10,934 | |
| Fuel Oil | | 3,869 | |
| Asphalt tar | | 1,755 | |
| Cement | | 1,283 | |
| Black Warrior, Warrior, Tombigbee | 14,491 | | 3,816 |
| Iron Ore | | 2,889 | |
| Coal/Lignite | | 6,405 | |
| Crude Petroleum | | 1,172 | |
| Sand/Gravel | | 883 | |

Source: Resource Planning Associates, Transportation Development Program for Appalachia, 1974.

a whole, coal accounted for over 60 percent of outbound tonnage and 43 percent of inbound tons in 1972. Shipments on the Ohio are focused around iron and steel production in the Pittsburgh area and power generating facilities along the river. The relatively low ton miles, given the net tons, support this conclusion and may be compared, for example, with the Tennessee River and its net tons and ton miles. The Tennessee River accounted for roughly one-third of total tonnage generated in the region. Coal predominated in regional commodity flows and accounted for about one-third of total traffic in the area.[38]

### Inland-Waterway Issues

Inland-waterway transport has not received due attention as a component of transportation and development planning in Appalachia. Several reasons explain this apparent oversight. Inland-waterway transportation is primarily tied to interstate commerce, and thus related navigation is a responsibility of the federal government. Many agencies are involved in waterway development both regionally and nationally. There is also considerable difficulty inherent in any attempt to assess economic impact of the waterways and potential improvements where criteria for regional delineation do not provide optimal regional boundaries. Thus any appraisal efforts must take into account the entire river system and economic region.[39] Still another problem with respect to inland-waterway transportation planning is that the waterways are related to water policy, transportation policy, and public expenditure or federal budget policy. The question to be resolved is what criteria shall be applicable to an appraisal of future waterway development.[40] All of the issues mentioned must be resolved if waterway transport is to become a more efficient contributor to the region's transportation system. Obviously, in addition, the huge costs entailed in most waterway improvements are not warmly entertained by budget decision makers, especially in tight money situations.

## THE ROLE OF AIR SERVICE IN THE REGION

The availability of air service to and from and indeed within a region plays an important role in regional development. Access to such services influences industrial and commercial, as well as residential, location decisions. Surveys show that the absence of scheduled airline service may limit the ability of nonmetropolitan areas to attract new industries.[41] Some companies ignore a location beyond a certain distance from an airport. Even if scheduled service is not available, the presence of an airstrip so that private aircraft may be utilized could be influential.

The air industry is composed of three major types of carriers—trunk lines, local service, and commuters. Trunk lines are the major long-haul carriers that provide nationwide service. The basic requirement is a high volume of traffic for economically viable service. Large aircraft—jets almost exclusively—and long runways are also distinguishing characteristics. The major domestic trunk lines are TWA, American, Eastern, United, and Delta. The local-service, or regional, carriers generally serve specific regions and act as feeders into the major carriers. Examples are USAir (formerly Allegheny) and Piedmont. Finally, the commuter lines are operations that use smaller planes (up to thirty passengers) and require much shorter runways. These airlines are a relatively recent development in the industry and are the primary sources of service for the smaller, often remote, communities that do not warrant trunk or regional service because of insufficient traffic.[42]

Under the deregulation bill passed by Congress in 1978, airlines are given much more flexibility in entering and leaving markets. Consequently, since that time service patterns have changed and will continue to change as carriers test the markets across the country. Both major and smaller urban areas in Appalachia are of course served by both trunk and regional carriers, although there have been some shifts in service in light of the new regulations. A dramatic shift has come about as a result of the higher-order carriers' careful selection of markets. Essentially aided by opportunities opened up by air deregulation, commuter airlines have embarked on a surge of activity, moving into markets that their bigger competitors find uneconomical. The roughly 250 commuter airlines have become a critical link in the nation's transportation system, providing some five hundred communities with their only air service.

Air-service needs in the ARC region are accommodated by a system of over sixty airports. In 1982 the bulk of this service was to small hub and nonhub airports (Figure 9.6), respectively defined by the Federal Aviation Administration as communities that enplane 0.05 to 0.24 percent and less than 0.05 percent of the total enplaned passengers nationwide in scheduled and nonscheduled service. The service levels of these airports have been significantly affected by airline deregulation.

Air trip patterns in the region are dominated by the demand for travel to major cities east of the Mississippi River. For most of the communities four cities—New York, Chicago, Washington, D.C., and Atlanta—are the major destinations, accounting for nearly one-third of all air trips generated by Appalachian communities. Ten other major metropolitan areas in the east are also quite important in terms of travel demand. Among these are Boston, Pittsburgh, and Philadelphia. Overall fourteen cities account for 50 percent of the passenger traffic.[43]

Appalachia's air passengers are heavily dependent on the network of connecting flights provided by the national system. Over 70 percent of air trips originating within the region require connections with two or more flights, whereas the national average is only 35 percent. Seventy-five percent of all air passengers generated by the region move through the airports at Atlanta, Pittsburgh, Chicago, Washington, D.C., and New York. The high concentration points up the critical importance of a few airports to the air service of Appalachia. Generally deregulation has further concentrated the route patterns and has heightened the dependence on connecting services and these several large airports.[44]

Prior to deregulation the region was served by registered carriers that accounted for over 90 percent of the traffic. Nine of the sixteen small hubs were served by trunk airlines, and twenty-four of the thirty-eight nonhub communities were served by certificated carriers. Between 1973 and 1978, the region's traffic grew at the rate of 5.1 percent per year as compared to the national rate of 5.8 percent. By 1978 the northern

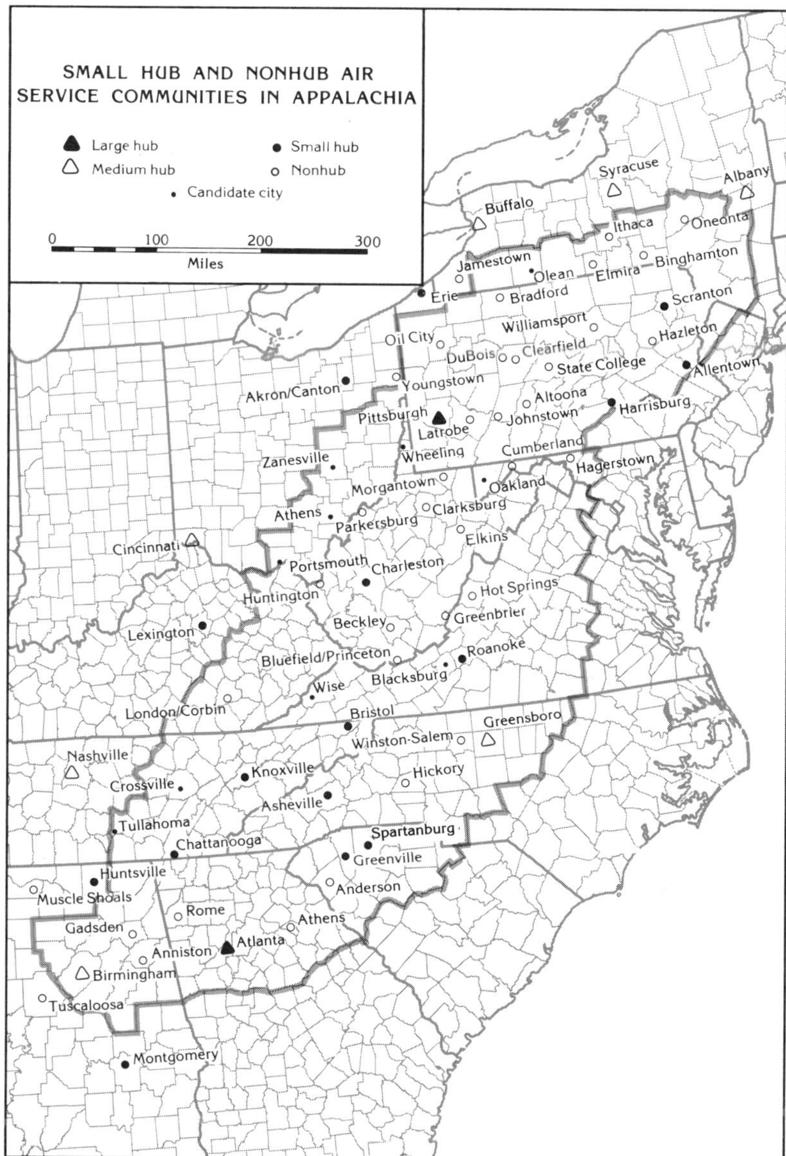


**Figure 9.6**
From Appalachian Regional Commission and Simat, Helliesen, and Eichner, Inc., *The Effects of Airline Deregulation Upon Air Service in Appalachia* (Washington, D.C.: ARC, 1982), p. 49.

portions of Appalachia were served by a number of reasonably well established commuter airlines. However, in the middle and southern section of the region, commuter airlines were only weakly developed. This was because local carriers provided service to many small communities.[45]

In the period since deregulation, Appalachia's air-service levels have been reduced by 25 percent, and air fares have more than doubled. Clearly these impacts were due not only to deregulation but also to rising fuel prices, poor economic conditions, and an air traffic controllers strike. A basic change, however, has occurred under deregulation: a contraction of certificated-carrier routes and an increased dependence on commuter airlines. Commuter airlines now provide over 60 percent of the region's total aircraft departures and nearly one-quarter of the seat capacity. The further impact of deregulation is measured by the elimination of certificated air service at small hubs. Among these Akron/Canton, Asheville, Charleston, and Chattanooga were abandoned by major carriers. Service levels at these nodes declined by more than 30 percent.[46]

The net effect of carrier terminations, route realignments, and service changes at Appalachia's small-hub cities was a greatly reduced level of service concentrated into fewer city markets. Intraregional markets and one-stop points experienced the greatest losses in service. Overall air traffic has declined about 10 percent; commuter traffic has increased by 34 percent. While the current recession in the U.S. economy has depressed air travel demand, the reduced traffic at Appalachian airports is largely attributable to deregulation.

### Issues in Air Transportation

It is clear that under deregulation trunk and regional carriers will not be forced into serving uneconomical markets. The question of how beneficial third-level carrier, or commuter, service would be to more communities and how beneficial it is to communities already served has not been adequately answered. The impact of new service to new communities should be investigated on a case-by-case basis. Impact must be measured not only by business and industry locational decisions but also with respect to multiplier effects, employment, and service availability (medical, recreational, and governmental). The cost of operating commuters may be less than operating certified carriers, but the cost to users may seem high.[47] This is so because the commuter does not receive government subsidies and rates are not regulated. If service is too expensive, too inconvenient, or just not an accepted mode of travel, then air service will have a poor probability for success. Another major problem with the small operations has been safety. The increased rate of accidents with the rapid growth of these operations is alarming.[48] Still other considerations are the physical issues of proper equipment, runways, and access roads. The full potential of this type of service cannot of course be realized without basic financial support. This has traditionally come from high-risk investors, local communities, and the owners themselves.[49] Detailed marketing and facility surveys must be utilized to determine whether this mode is a viable policy instrument in Appalachian regional development.

## ADDITIONAL CONCERNS

A variety of transportation-related problems and issues face the Appalachian region today. Although several of these are urban in nature (e.g., mass transit), the focus here is upon those major problems that are of a more integral nature and have broader implications for regional development. In addition to those issues that have been treated above, two others seem worth discussing as part of this chapter.

### Coal-Road Transport Impacts

Appalachia represents a key source of energy, for in 1974 8 of the 13 states in the region accounted for 62 percent of the nation's total coal production. In addition the region's reserves are 25 percent of the nation's total coal reserves.[50] The ability to accommodate increased production and to move the coal efficiently from producers to consumers by the transportation systems within the region thus becomes a critical issue.

The ARC has conducted an energy policy study to assess the effects of coal movement on the highway system in the region. The critical importance of the highway system to coal movements is indicated in Table 9.6. In 1974, 58 percent of all coal produced was transported by truck from the mines. The impact of these movements was felt over 14,300 mi (23,008.7 km) of roadway. Projections of increased production show that in the current period roughly 17,000 mi (27,353 km) of highway are affected.

TABLE 9.6
Tons of Coal Moved by Transport Mode (in Million Tons): 1974

| State | Truck | | | | Rail Only | Water Only | Other | Total |
|---|---|---|---|---|---|---|---|---|
| | Truck Only | Truck to Rail | Truck to Water | Total | | | | |
| Alabama | 2.6 | 5.7 | 3.0 | 11.3 | 5.0 | 1.4 | 1.8 | 19.6 |
| Kentucky | 4.6 | 68.5 | 1.0 | 74.1 | 11.1 | - | - | 85.1 |
| Maryland | 1.0 | 1.4 | - | 2.4 | - | - | - | 2.2 |
| Ohio | 11.5 | 3.7 | 2.7 | 17.9 | 14.7 | 3.2 | 5.5 | 41.3 |
| Pennsylvania | 18.7 | 25.5 | 2.1 | 46.3 | 20.8 | 13.3 | 7.2 | 87.6 |
| Tennessee | 2.3 | 2.5 | .8 | 5.6 | 3.7 | - | - | 9.2 |
| Virginia | .008 | 29.4 | - | 29.4 | 7.2 | - | - | 36.6 |
| West Virginia | 3.1 | 5.6 | 25.6 | 34.3 | 56.4 | 2.2 | 5.6 | 98.5 |
| Total | 43.8 | 142.3 | 35.2 | 221.3 | 118.9 | 20.1 | 20.1 | 380.1 |

Source: Assessment of the Effects of Coal Movement on the Highways in the Appalachian Region, ARC, November, 1977.

The serious nature of this impact is revealed by data collected from the ARC study. In 1980 nearly twelve hundred bridges and 7,000 mi (11,263 km) of road were judged inadequate to meet the present volume of coal-truck traffic. These inadequacies affect not only coal traffic but also all other traffic that must use the deteriorating structures. The cost of bridge replacements and roadway reconstruction and rehabilitation in the region is estimated to range from $591 to $726 million and $4.9 billion respectively.[51] The states do not have sufficient federal, state, and local funds to meet these needs on coal haul roads under either current or increased levels of coal-truck movements. Regulatory activities and mode diversion will not be able to provide significant immediate relief, and thus long-term coal transportation solutions must be examined. Roadway-improvement measures and measures to divert coal must be pursued rather than regulatory type policies. The magnitude of the costs means that a variety of funding sources must be explored. Coal severance taxes and highway-user taxes appear to be the only reliable revenue sources. Both of these must be studied in greater detail to determine various impacts, which include the potential revenue contribution of each, specific tax structures to encourage diversion of coal movements, and other special assessment options.[52]

Coal-movement diversion measures are very limited and rail abandonment, especially in Pennsylvania and Ohio, has intensified the coal-road problem. Many newly opened coal-mining areas in Appalachia lack adequate coal-preparation and rail-loading facilities. Attempts to encourage private-sector provision of these may aid the larger transport problem. In addition, the public sector might use financial and institutional inducements to encourage the formation of cooperatives among smaller, independent producers in these areas.[53]

## Rural Transportation

A final major transportation problem in the region is that involving transit for rural people. Numerous studies of the needs of the rural poor and the elderly highlight transportation to and from jobs, schools, service agencies, and health care as problems.[54] Both the poor and the elderly often have no alternative to the automobile as a means of travel. The increased cost of gasoline, despite a temporary respite in 1981–1982 as a result of a world oil glut, will continue to affect rural residents who commute by private automobile. Indeed the ARC has recognized these deficiencies and has advocated the improvement and consolidation of rural public-transportation services as a major transportation objective in the overall regional development strategy.

Analysis of rural transportation systems suggests that there are no easy solutions to intercity and local travel problems of transport-disadvantaged people. Several alternatives to private auto travel should be considered, however. Although intercity travel is to some extent an important requirement—for health care, for example—the more common need to the transport-disadvantaged is to a local center of economic and social activity, as well as intown services.[55]

Rural areas, unlike urban areas, cannot depend on a "captive" ridership, because low population density cannot generate large volumes of traffic in specific corridors. Origins are usually more dispersed, although destinations may be concentrated. But even destination locations are distributed spatially to favor auto users rather than transit-service users. Intercity bus transportation has declined significantly in rural areas away from interstate highways and other major arteries. The reason is simply the lack of sufficient passenger volumes to make such operations economical. The solutions to the renewal of bus service to smaller communities that lie off the preferred routes are temporary subsidization and bus shelters on major highways. In a real sense almost no public transportation exists in many small towns and adjacent rural areas.[56]

Research on rural transit systems has recently shed some light on the problem and has provided suggestions for improvement. The Department of Transportation (DOT) has experimented with various systems to provide transportation to local people but nearly all would collapse without public funding. The fundamental problems in designing subsidized services exist in weighing costs and benefits. Demand-responsive (door-to-door) service is almost a requirement given the scattered origins and nature of trips and users. But the level of demand must be considered in producing a system that will be cost efficient. Service must be reliable yet minimal. Several considerations that are related to the success of rural transit operations have emerged. Prior reservations or monthly subscription services are effective methods of assuring use of vehicles. Contracts with social-services agencies, schools, employers, and shopping centers could represent stable revenue sources and would benefit both provider and user. Equipment utilized must be scaled to demand, or rural transit systems will fail. In addition, use of volunteer and paid part-time drivers and dispatchers can be important. Possible transit use of school buses, postal vehicles, and other types of vehicles must be explored. Other measures must be investigated as well.[57] Car-pool locations and mobile units of various services are examples of ways to relieve the problem of immobility. Above all, the ability to communicate the need for transportation to others is critical in providing and maintaining a demand-responsive system.[58]

## NOTES

1. Gerald Kraft et al., *The Role of Transportation in Regional Economic Development* (Lexington, Mass.: Lexington Books, 1971), p. 7.
2. Niles Hansen, *The Future of Nonmetropolitan America* (Lexington, Mass.: Lexington Books, 1973), pp. 19–32.
3. Appalachian Regional Commission, *Appalachia: Goals, Objectives, and Development Strategies* (Washington, D.C.: Appalachian Regional Commission, December 1977), pp. 28–30.
4. Thomas R. Leinbach, *Transportation and Development Issues* (Englewood

Cliffs, N.J.: Prentice-Hall, forthcoming).

5. George Wilson, "Towards a Theory of Transport and Development," in B. S. Hoyle, ed., *Transport and Development* (London: Macmillan, 1973), pp. 208–230.

6. Philip Locklin, *Economics of Transportation*, 7th ed. (Homewood, Ill.: Richard D. Irvin, 1972).

7. Appalachian Regional Commission, *1980 Annual Report* (Washington, D.C.: Appalachian Regional Commission, 1981), pp. 15–18.

8. J. M. Munro, "Planning the Appalachian Development Highway System: Some Critical Questions," *Land Economics* 45 (1969), pp. 149–161.

9. Robert A. Weiss, "The Distribution of Benefits of the Appalachian Development Highway System," (Ph.D. dissertation, Department of Economics, University of Wisconsin, 1972), pp. 13–26.

10. Howard Gauthier, "The Appalachian Development Highway System: Development for Whom?" *Economic Geography* 49 (1973), pp. 103–108.

11. Robert Shawcroft, "The Role of Highways in Regional Development: A Review of the Appalachian Highway System and Case Study of West Virginia" (seminar paper, Department of Geography, University of Washington, Seattle, 1977). For the broader view of the impact of interstate highways the interested reader should turn to Hansen, op. cit. (footnote 2); James P. Miller, "Interstate Highways and Job Growth in Nonmetropolitan Areas: A Reassessment," *Transportation Journal* 19 (1979), pp. 78–81; and Daniel Lichter and Glen V. Fuguitt, "Demographic Response to Transportation Innovation: The Case of the Interstate Highway," *Social Forces* 59 (1980), pp. 492–512.

12. Appalachian Regional Commission, *Appalachian Highway Program: Progress, Impacts, and Planning for the Future* (Washington, D.C.: Appalachian Regional Commission, December 1975). See also M. H. Coogan, "Two Appalachian Corridors, Ten Years Later," *Appalachia* 12 (1979), pp. 13–26.

13. "Appalachian Highways Are Catalysts of Change," *Appalachia* 15 (1981), p. 10.

14. Ibid., pp. 8–17.

15. Resource Planning Associates, *Transportation Development Program for Appalachia* (Washington, D.C.: Appalachian Regional Commission, November 1974), p. III-36.

16. Ernest Holsendolph, "Chessie-Seaboard Merger is Set," *New York Times* (September 25, 1980), pp. D6–D7.

17. Agis Salpukas, "N & W–Southern Merger Set," *New York Times* (March 26, 1982), p. 33.

18. Leslie Wayne, "A Surprising Move by N & W," *New York Times* (September 3, 1981), p. 29.

19. Resource Planning Associates, op. cit. (footnote 15), p. III-41.

20. Ibid., p. III-43.

21. David White, "The Coal Export Gamble," *Fortune* 104 (December 14, 1981), pp. 122–136.

22. Ibid., p. 124.

23. Ibid., p. 128.

24. Ibid., p. 129.

25. Ibid., p. 133.

26. Susan Carey, "Planned Expansion in Coal Loading Ports is Scaled Back as the Export Boom Wanes," *Wall Street Journal* (March 30, 1982), p. 14.

27. Resource Planning Associates, op. cit. (footnote 15), p. III-40.

28. Ibid., p. III-44.

29. Ibid., p. III-45.
30. Ibid., p. III-51.
31. William Black and James Runke, *The States and Rural Rail Preservation: Alternative Strategies* (Lexington, Ky.: Council of State Governments, 1975), p. 2.
32. Ibid., pp. 6–14, and Robert D. Hershey, Jr., "Little Railroads That Think They Can," *New York Times* (September 18, 1983), p. 30.
33. Black and Runke, *The States and Rural Rail Preservation,* pp. 74–79.
34. Ibid., p. 52.
35. Resource Planning Associates, op. cit. (footnote 15), p. III-54.
36. Drummond Ayres, "A Canal Project in South Caps 200 Year Dream," *New York Times* (June 22, 1976), p. 19, and William E. Schmidt, "Southern River Project Stirs Economic Hopes," *New York Times* (September 28, 1983), p. 10.
37. Resource Planning Associates, op. cit. (footnote 15), p. III-65.
38. Ibid., p. III-57.
39. Ibid., p. III-65.
40. Ibid., p. III-65.
41. Stephen R. Kale and Richard E. Lonsdale, "Factors Encouraging and Discouraging Plant Location in Nonmetropolitan Areas," in Richard E. Lonsdale and H. L. Seyler, eds., *Nonmetropolitan Industrialization* (New York: Winston Halsted, 1979), pp. 47–56.
42. Jonathan Mayer, "Local and Commuter Airlines in the United States," *Traffic Quarterly* 31 (1977), pp. 333–350.
43. Appalachian Regional Commission, *The Effects of Airline Deregulation upon Air Service in Appalachia* (Washington, D.C.: Appalachian Regional Commission, January 1982), p. 22.
44. Ibid., p. 24.
45. Ibid., pp. 28–29.
46. Ibid., p. 36.
47. Resource Planning Associates, op. cit. (footnote 15), p. III-80.
48. Ernest Holsendolph, "Use of Commuter Airlines Grows as Does Crash Rate," *New York Times* (June 21, 1980), pp. 1, 7.
49. Resource Planning Associates, op. cit. (footnote 15), p. III-82.
50. Appalachian Regional Commission, *An Assessment of the Effects of Coal Movement on the Highways in the Appalachian Region*, Research Triangle Institute, Final Report (Raleigh: North Carolina State University, 1977), p. i.
51. Ibid., p. vi.
52. Ibid., p. xvi.
53. Ibid., p. xvi, and Hal S. Maggied, *Transportation for the Poor: Research in Rural Mobility* (Boston: Kluwer Nijhoff Publishing, 1982).
54. Malcolm J. Moseley, *Accessibility: The Rural Challenge* (London: Methuen, 1979), and National Area Development Institute, Lexington, Kentucky, *Meeting Rural Transportation Needs*, prepared for the Committee on Agriculture and Forestry, U.S. Senate, 94th Congress, 1st session, February 10, 1975 (Washington, D.C.: Government Printing Office, 1975).
55. U.S. Dept. of Agriculture, Economic Research Service, *Transportation in Rural America* (Washington, D.C.: Government Printing Office, 1975), p. 184.
56. Ibid., pp. 185–186.
57. Moseley, op. cit. (footnote 54), pp. 115–161.
58. Economic Research Service, op. cit. (footnote 55), pp. 187–191.

# CHAPTER 10

# REGIONAL DEVELOPMENT: PAST, PRESENT, AND FUTURE

It is clear from our examination of Appalachia that this region is extremely diverse, whether one considers its physical, cultural, or economic attributes. In terms of regional development, then, it seems rather obvious that problems within the region cannot be solved by a common development strategy. Instead alternative strategies that are conceived must be based on evaluation of the characteristics, problems, and goals of various subregions within Appalachia. Identification of subregions for development purposes is a difficult task but one that needs to be addressed. Appalachian development schemes have evolved in the context of subregions that are either very large (and thus too diverse) or very small. For example, as pointed out in Chapter 1, the Appalachian Regional Commission (ARC) has defined three large subregions called Northern, Central, and Southern Appalachia. On the other hand, development schemes are often defined and administered at a much smaller scale, either by individual counties or by Local Development Districts (LDDs). LDDs consist of a small number of counties; the ARC subdivided its region into some seventy LDDs each averaging 5 to 6 counties. In short, scale is a very important consideration in devising development plans. We will return to this question, and that of subregions, toward the end of the chapter.

It seems appropriate, however, to first discuss two other topics. First, we need to review the region's problems and offer some explanation as to why these problems exist. We have, of course, described major regional problems such as poverty, underdevelopment, and environmental degradation, but we have not yet offered explanations for these problems. We will do so now through examination of a number of arguments that have been advanced by social scientists. Clearly, before regional development strategies can be discussed, we need to understand *what* the problems are and *why* they exist, as well as *where* they are located.

Second, we will examine some of the specific development schemes that have affected the Appalachian region and attempt to evaluate their successes and failures. Probably the best-known projects have been those fostered by federal agencies, including the Appalachian Regional Commission and the Tennessee Valley Authority, and it is such examples that are of primary interest here. These public projects, as well as numerous development schemes, have brought change to the region, and it is inevitable that change will continue, for better or worse.

## EXPLANATIONS FOR APPALACHIAN POVERTY

The characteristic of Appalachia cited most often by residents and nonresidents alike is poverty.[1] We have already seen that although there are pockets of wealth (chiefly the major metropolitan areas), even today much of the region's per capita income and education remains well below national levels. Other characteristics often associated with the region include economic underdevelopment and environmental degradation. Although such negative characteristics are mentioned more frequently by those who do not consider themselves Appalachians, even persons who do perceive themselves as residents of the region often cite them.[2] These, then, are the major "problems" of the region.

On the other hand, we have seen also that the region has a rich natural-resource base that includes fuels, minerals, abundant water, forests, wildlife, and natural beauty. Areas with plentiful resources generally become affluent, but this has not occurred in Appalachia. What, then, accounts for this resource-wealth paradox?

Since the recognition in the late nineteenth century that Appalachia was an area beset by problems, a number of "theories" have been espoused that attempt to explain the reasons for the problems. These include what we shall call the ancestry, environment, population, cultural, and infrastructure schools of thought. Some of the arguments, it should be noted, were explanations for the problems of that portion of our region that Campbell called the Southern Highlands (as shown in Chapter 1). Certainly, however, some of the explanations for poverty have relevance to much of the remainder of Appalachia as well.

### Ancestry

One of the first to argue that the poverty and backwardness of Appalachia's people were derived from their ancestry was historian John Fiske.[3] Writing in 1897, Fiske suggested the poor Appalachians were descendants of convicts and indentured servants who had reached America's shores some decades before. What was especially striking to Fiske and later social scientists (and novelists) was the apparent physical homogeneity of the region's people. This trait also led to studies on inbreeding and genetic deficiency. In the 1920s Arthur Estabrook and Nathaniel Hirsch elaborated on the "genetic deficiency" argument. Hirsch concluded that Kentucky mountaineers were from "one of the purest strains in the world, yet they possess physical traits which reveal that the compounding and intermixture of racial strains has not yet after six generations of intermarriage proceeded to the extent of blending the component elements."[4] More recently Harry Caudill stated in *Night Comes to the Cumberlands*: "for many decades there flowed from Merry England . . . honest men who could not pay their debts, pickpockets, and thieves. . . . It is apparent that such human refuse . . . was incapable of developing the kind of stable society under construction in the Puritan North. . . . [Some] . . . ran away to the interior. . . . And here we have the people . . . who were the first to earn for themselves the title of 'Southern mountaineers' . . . whose descendents have . . . spread throughout the entire mountain range, along every winding creek. . . ."[5]

In an essay on the origins of the southern mountaineer, Cratis Williams disagreed with this idea and concluded, "Placed against these views is the more tenable one that he was part and parcel of the whole Westward Movement and settled in the mountains because he sought fertile soil for his crops, good range land for his cattle, delicious drinking water from permanent springs, and coverts for the wildlife that would afford him the pleasures and profits derived from hunting."[6]

**Environment**

About the same time that Fiske's work was published, others suggested that explanations for Appalachia's poverty could be found through study of the region's isolation. Isolation was related to rugged topography and the resultant lack of transportation and communications links. Those who did venture into the region to live were thus cut off from the rest of America. Geographer Ellen Churchill Semple was one of the first to write on this subject (as it applies to eastern Kentucky), and William Goodell Frost also helped to popularize the theme.[7] In the early twentieth century the idea of environmental determinism was popular in the social sciences, and it offered a ready explanation for human conditions, especially in regions where development lagged.

The notion of isolation remains important as an explanation for Appalachian problems and in recent planning and development efforts for the region. For example, in 1964 the President's Appalachian Regional Commission viewed it as the principal obstacle to growth: "Development activity in Appalachia cannot proceed until regional isolation has been overcome."[8] The subsequent heavy investment in road building by the ARC was an attempt to reduce the region's isolation.

Mary Jean Bowman and Warren Haynes, in their well-known work on eastern Kentucky, viewed isolation as the first, and the major, "problem" of that area: "The key variables that make East Kentucky the distinctive area that it is are closely associated with one thing—isolation."[9] However, the authors noted that "isolation is never complete; it is a matter of degree. Even within the area defined as East Kentucky the frequency and intensities of interaction between local people and people outside the mountains vary considerably. Examination of mountain gradients in degree of isolation is therefore an important part of

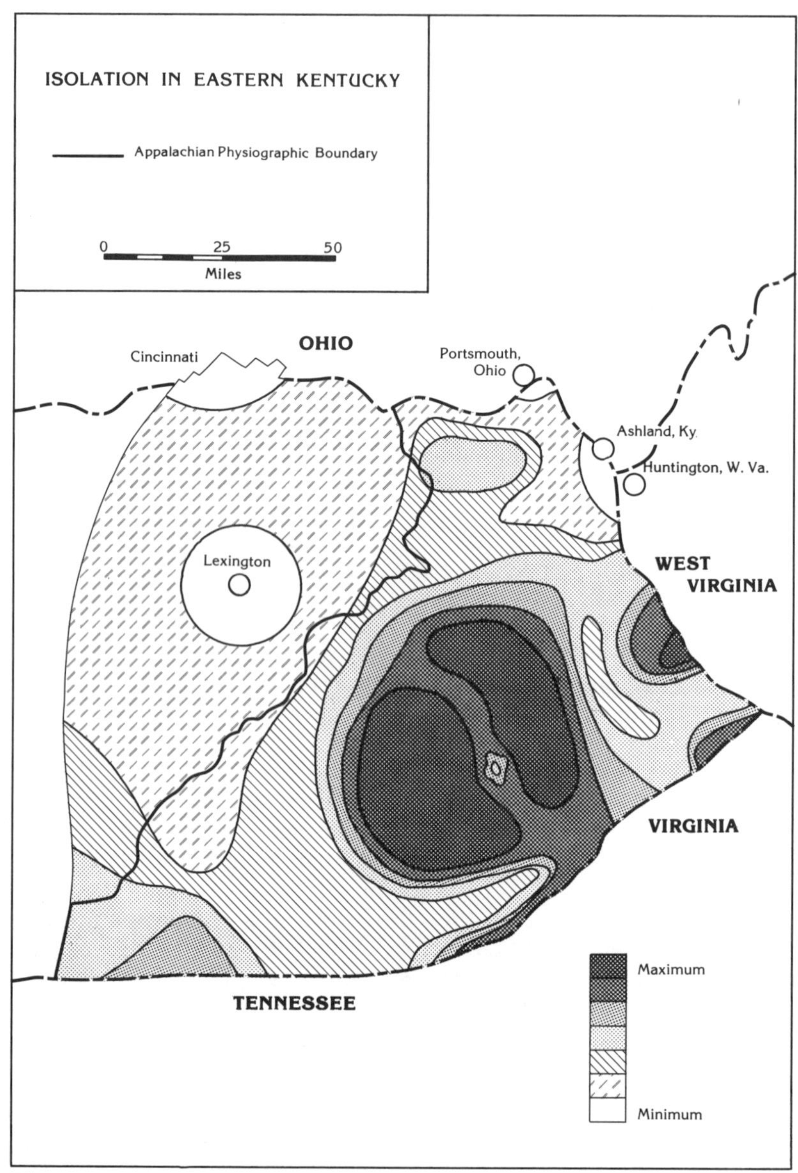


**Figure 10.1**
From Mary Jean Bowman and W. Warren Haynes, *Resources and People in East Kentucky* (Baltimore: Johns Hopkins Press, 1963), p. 30.

the picture of what East Kentucky is."[10] The authors presented a map of isolation contours that suggests differences in degree of isolation in eastern Kentucky (Figure 10.1).

More recently, and at a larger scale, Brian Berry demonstrated that much of Appalachia and two other areas (Southwest deserts and the central and northern Rockies) are isolated from the United States if one uses the 350 principal commuting areas of major urban centers as a means to determine isolation. "The areas of Appalachia outside these important commuting fields in which a majority of persons were so isolated were concentrated in West Virginia, eastern Kentucky, and southwestern Virginia coalfields; southeastern Ohio; north central West Virginia; and the Cumberland River Valley area of Tennessee and Kentucky" (Figure 10.2).[11] Berry's advice contributed to the decision by the ARC to develop the urban-rural growth strategy by way of Appalachian Development Highways.

Donald Rothblatt, in tracing the history of Appalachian development, also concluded that regional isolation is a crucial factor in understanding regional problems. After the Civil War, when national attention turned toward Appalachia because of its vast hardwood forests and bituminous coal, the construction of routeways (especially railroads) into the region quickened, but "for the sole purpose of resource exploitation."[12] Even by the end of the 1870–1930 period when Appalachia underwent a "vast structural transformation associated with regional economic development,"[13] the region still lagged far behind the rest of the nation, in large part because of its geographic isolation.

## Population

Another argument advanced as an explanation for the region's poverty and underdevelopment was that the region was overcrowded. In 1935 the U.S. Department of Agriculture issued a publication on the problems of southern Appalachia and concluded that "the basic problems of the region . . . grew out of maladjustments in land use and in the relation of population to land."[14] In short, in much of the region there was an "excess of population in relation to the economic opportunities to be found there under prevailing conditions."[15]

Rupert Vance also cited population pressure as a primary explanation for Appalachia's lack of development. This pressure "results in the division of fertile fields among heirs until the time comes when fields are too small to offer subsistence and 'young sons have pushed out beyond the mountain rim; others have retreated back up the slopes to the shelter of a cabin and a cleared patch.'"[16]

Recall that in Chapter 5 we commented on what is a surprisingly high population density in rural Appalachia given the region's ruggedness. Such high densities are not a recent phenomenon, as attested to by William Bradley in describing the situation in a part of eastern Kentucky in 1918 where "every creek at all capable of growing corn (the one stable crop) had a population far in excess of its power to support. . . .

ZONES OF APPALACHIA LYING OUTSIDE
METROPOLITAN COMMUTING ZONES
0
100
200
Miles
Source: Berry, 1973, p. 47.

**Figure 10.2**

Many of these people . . . were crowded into one and two room cabins, sometimes without windows."[17] Indeed, those who travel into some of the valleys and hollows of Appalachia today are often amazed at the high densities of population and the intensive use of what appears to be rather marginal land.

## Culture

In searching for explanations for Appalachian poverty, one could conclude that culture-based theories have predominated in the literature. Generally, such explanations tend to identify subcultural traits (or behaviors) and compare these against some "norm," usually the larger American culture. What is often concluded is that a distinctive Appalachian subculture exists, because its people exhibit different (i.e., "deficient") traits from those of the American mainstream. The studies that have assumed this cultural explanation for poverty vary in the degree to which the traits observed can be characterized as "negative" or "positive." Studies of Appalachia that emphasize the negative aspects of the culture grow out of Oscar Lewis's Culture of Poverty model that identifies "the internal deficiencies of the lower-class subculture as the source of the problem."[18] The model and the studies based on it then go on to identify and describe such "deficiencies."

The Culture of Poverty model has come under increasing criticism. Those who find fault with it argue that the model tells us nothing of why conditions of poverty exist: It presumes that such a "culture of poverty" exists and then proceeds to fill in its description, having little concern with either the cause of poverty or the content of what is transmitted from generation to generation. "The assumption is that middle-class or dominant American values are not transmitted in Appalachia."[19] Nonetheless, recognition and understanding of this school of thought is important because "one could dismiss all of this as nothing but academic folly if it were not for the fact that those persons and agencies concerned with relieving the above conditions often accept the Culture of Poverty model."[20]

One of the first attempts to determine whether or not a distinctive Appalachian subculture existed was an essay by Thomas Ford entitled "The Passing of Provincialism."[21] Ford's study examined how closely Appalachians have clung to what he identified as traditional cultural traits. The traits, or themes, he selected were individualism and self-reliance, traditionalism, fatalism, and fundamentalism in religious outlook. Ford's conclusions "essentially disproved the existence of a unique Appalachian subculture, but his essay served to focus attention on the cultural values he tested";[22] it "answered 'no' to the question of cultural obsolesence. His findings clearly support the passing of provincialism, not the tenacity of a subculture. Ford concluded that the region had become 'progressive-minded' and 'achievement-oriented' to a high degree."[23]

One of the most influential works on Appalachian culture was Jack

Weller's *Yesterday's People.* In it Weller, a Presbyterian missionary from outside Appalachia, identified values of the southern Appalachian folk culture based on his study of one coal community in West Virginia. He saw that culture as changing, but as one that historically differed from that of the rest of the United States. In comparing the southern Appalachian subculture with that of middle-class America, Weller identified thirty-four ways in which the two differed. For example, the middle-class American is free to determine his or her goals, is strongly motivated by status, readily joins groups, and uses government and law to achieve goals. The southern Appalachian, on the other hand, is fatalistic, is oriented toward existence, is not status seeking, rejects joining groups, and is antagonistic toward government and law.[24] In short, southern Appalachians have a deficient culture that needs to accept the values of the larger culture if it is to solve its problems. Weller made use of Ford's study in discussing Appalachian values, but his conclusions do not agree with those of Ford. Since the publication of Weller's book a substantial number of observers have accepted his findings.[25]

On the other hand, a number of studies have emphasized the distinctiveness of an Appalachian subculture, but from a positive perspective. One study of this genre is John Stephenson's *Shiloh: A Mountain Community.*[26] Like Weller's works, Stephenson's was a single-community study, and thus one needs to be careful in transferring the findings to a larger population. Stephenson saw Appalachians as contented rather than fatalistic and present-oriented rather than regressive. Loyal Jones identified religion, individualism, hospitality, family solidarity, personalism, love of place, sense of beauty, sense of humor, and patriotism as key positive values shown by Appalachian people.[27]

Whether or not distinctive cultural values exist such as those described—whether positive or negative—is debatable. We have already discussed the findings of the Ford essay in this regard. In addition, Dwight Billings has also demonstrated that cultural explanations for regional poverty may be overemphasized. In his study that compared respondents from Appalachian and non-Appalachian parts of North Carolina, it was found that the value differences were "attributable to rurality rather than to a distinctive mountain culture."[28] His conclusion was that "there has been an overemphasis on cultural explanations. Attitudinal characteristics do not explain the lack of development in the mountain counties surveyed. . . . A situational analysis of Appalachian poverty recommends itself as an alternative to the cultural explanation . . . [that] views the behavioral characteristics of the poor as adaptations to environment and circumstances."[29]

## Infrastructure Lag

In 1973 Brian Berry wrote that "technological change and market shifts are not peculiar to Appalachia but are occurring all over the United States. However, other parts of the nation have shown themselves to be capable of responding to those changes. They have reached a stage in their development which enables them to attract and develop new types of economic activity to replace the old. But regions such as Appalachia did not develop the social and economic infrastructure for this kind of flexibility."[30]

Such an infrastructure was not developed because of the long history of control over Appalachian land and labor by a few dominant economic activities. As we have seen, the sectors that have dominated the Appalachian economy have been lumber, railroads, mining, and primary industry. These economic activities are closely interrelated and generally have been controlled by persons from outside the region, although recently local cities have also played a role. In short, it is argued that local economics and political institutions in much of the region are closely tied to those who control the region's economy.[31] The power of this group, especially the absentee owners, is seen as maintaining the prevailing order of inequality through institutional barriers. Those who control the region are viewed as colonizers, and proponents of this argument have elaborated on what is termed the "internal colonialism" model. As applied to Appalachia it means "the process by which dominant outside industrial interests establish control and continue to prevent autonomous development of the subordinate internal colony. The model suggests that need for an anticolonial movement and a radical structuring of society, with a redistribution of resources to the poor and the powerless."[32]

Probably the first person to formally apply the idea to a part of Appalachia (Kentucky's Cumberland Plateau) was Harry Caudill in *Night Comes to the Cumberlands*.[33] He expanded on and popularized this idea in subsequent writings, and others soon followed this example. These later proponents saw parallels between what had occurred in Appalachia and colonialism in Third World nations or between Appalachia and the process of internal colonization of minority groups, such as blacks in America. Those who have applied this model to Appalachia include Helen Lewis and her associates, Emil Malizia, Keith Dix, and others.[34]

Although it has relevance elsewhere in the region, the issue of internal colonialism is most closely associated with coal mining in the subregion the ARC defined as Central Appalachia. Within this area the most volatile historic and contemporary problems stemming from outside control relate to mineral (and timber) ownership and taxation patterns. Industrial corporations sent agents into the central and southern mining districts before the turn of the century. Mineral rights were often purchased from illiterate farmers for as little as \$0.25 to \$0.50 per a. (\$0.62 to \$1.24 per h). The farmers signed broad-form deeds that gave the holder the right to remove the coal at any time and in virtually any manner. Today many of those deeds, as well as general land and mineral ownership, are in the hands of a relatively few individuals and corporations. Often these owners are absentees who do not live in the county. In 1981, the Appalachian Land Ownership Task Force conducted

TABLE 10.1
Land and Mineral Rights Ownership in Selected Counties*
(Based on 1978 Tax Records)

| State | County | Percentage of Surface Land Owned by Corporations | Percentage of Mineral Rights Owned by Corporations | Percentage of Surface Land Owned by Absentees | Percentage of County Mineral Rights Owned by Absentees | Mineral Taxes Paid Per Acre by Corporations (Dollars) | Percentage County Property Taxes Paid by Corporations |
|---|---|---|---|---|---|---|---|
| AL | Walker | 25.9 | 49.3 | 29.1 | 45.3 | .04 | 2.9 |
| KY | Bell | 27.1 | 9.3 | 48.3 | 14.0 | .002 | 19.1 |
| | Breathitt | 13.9 | 43.2 | 45.9 | 45.0 | .006 | 25.3 |
| | Harlan | 55.2 | 35.0 | 57.6 | - | - | 25.1 |
| | Knott | 35.8 | - | 57.6 | - | - | 20.5 |
| | Martin | 39.8 | 59.6 | 57.2 | 90.9 | .0009 | 7.4 |
| | Perry | 25.4 | 64.1 | 40.6 | 61.0 | .001 | 9.3 |
| | Pike | 14.7 | 25.4 | 26.4 | 26.2 | .01 | 5.9 |
| TN | Campbell | 57.5 | 7.4 | 58.3 | 7.2 | .58 | 5.6 |
| VA | Buchanan | 30.6 | 65.6 | 43.5 | 68.4 | 1.34-.92 | 38.9 |
| | Wise | 45.2 | 38.6 | 54.6 | 35.3 | .69-.32 | 9.3 |

*Counties selected experienced rapid coal production growth during the 1960 to 1978 period (see Table 6.6) and were also sample counties in the Appalachian Land Ownership Task Force survey of regional land ownership patterns. See their publication Land Ownership Patterns and Their Impacts on Appalachian Communities: A Survey of 80 Counties. Center for Appalachian Studies, Boone, North Carolina, 1981.

a survey of regional land ownership. In a review of 1978 tax records in 80 sample counties in 6 Appalachian states, the survey established that the ownership of land and minerals in the region was highly concentrated in the hands of a few owners. Only 1 percent of the local population, together with absentee holders, corporations, and governmental agencies, controlled about 53 percent of the total land surface in the sample counties. Although some thirty thousand owners held part of the 20 million a. (8.08 million h) of land in these counties, only fifty private owners and ten governmental agencies held 41 percent, or about 8.2 million (3.31 million h). Nearly three-fourths of the surface acres and four-fifths of the mineral acres surveyed were owned by absentees. Seventy percent of the mineral rights in the sample were owned by corporations (forty-six of the top fifty owners were corporations). Nineteen were principally coal and coal-land corporations, others were oil, timber, and steel companies, and four were railroads.

If one looks again at the list of counties with rapidly growing coal production and selects those that were covered by the land-ownership survey, it is apparent that the control of the land and minerals in those counties is not in the hands of local individuals (Table 10.1). In 7 of the 11 counties, more than half of the surface land or mineral rights is owned by corporations or absentees. This suggests that profits from mining operations on this land flow outside the county or region to be invested elsewhere. A related problem is underassessment of taxes on land and minerals held by corporations. In Kentucky, the mineral taxes paid on unmined coal land were often $0.001 per acre ($0.0027 per h) or less. In 1978, the Kentucky General Assembly passed a bill that set a uniform tax of about $0.002 per acre ($0.0049 per h) on unmined coal land. West Virginia, by comparison, has an average mineral tax of $1.09 per acre ($2.69 per h) or five hundred times the Kentucky tax. This disparity has two possible impacts. First, West Virginia collects much more tax money that can be applied directly to solving some of the problems associated with coal mining. Second, coal production has declined in West Virginia over the past two decades, whereas production in Kentucky has surged.

The roster of tax payments into county coffers is brief. In Martin County, Kentucky, the county with the most rapid increase in coal production between 1960 and 1978 (Table 6.6), the taxes paid by corporations amounted to $0.0009 per acre ($0.0022 per h). Corporations contributed just over 7 percent of the property taxes in the county. This means that the revenues that support the school system, road construction and maintenance, and all other county and local services came from local individuals, many of them miners (2,210 in 1978).[35] If extraction of nonrenewable resources is to provide a basis for long-term stability and development, then a significant proportion of the income generated by the resource should be invested in the region to provide alternative future employment. Coal mining does not appear to meet this requirement at present, but the opportunity exists for change. Bituminous-coal reserves for the region exceed 262 trillion tn (237.6 trillion t). At the present rate of production these reserves will last over seven hundred years.[36] The opportunity to rectify the imbalance and inequity in the tax structure seems apparent. Even a small tax on land and minerals would have a substantial long-term impact.

### Recent Explanations

From one or a combination of the explanations for poverty just described there have emerged recent statements as to why Appalachia's problems persist. David Walls and Dwight Billings suggested a comprehensive theory of social change that involves aspects of several of the above arguments and that "synthesize[s] and integrate[s] a humanistic approach to culture, the technical aspects of regional development, and an appropriate critique of domination at the present period."[37] Walls suggested an alternative to the internal colonialism model because Appalachia does not fit the strict definition of an internal colony: The region is not a separate political entity from the United States nor are its people citizens apart. Rather, central and southern Appalachia (at least) should be viewed as an internal periphery within an advanced capitalist society. In this way the problems (and solutions) of Appalachia are put in a more realistic framework. Thus, for example, "if the heart of the problem is defined as private ownership of the coal industry, then the possibility of public ownership, perhaps even limited to regional basis, is suggested."[38]

## EVALUATION OF DEVELOPMENT PROGRAMS

The many and varied development programs that have been established to solve Appalachia's problems have been based upon one or a combination of the explanations for regional poverty discussed above. For example, the great expansion of social services that took place in the 1960s through agencies like the Office of Economic Opportunity (OEO) was rationalized in part through the Culture of Poverty ideas. In Appalachia the War on Poverty declared by President Johnson in his 1964 State of the Union message included such programs as adult basic education, rural loans, and Project Headstart. Some of the programs did have limited local success, but as one critic has observed, "the statistics told of minimal impact."[39] One basic failing of such programs was that they did not speak to the basic structural problems of the region, that is, there was "no intention of changing the relationship between the poor and rich."[40]

Other major government-sponsored programs intended to improve conditions in the region included those provided by the TVA Act of 1933 and the Appalachian Regional Development Act of 1965. It is to the impact of these two "models" of public investment that we now turn.

## TVA

In 1933 President Roosevelt signed the TVA Act, a bill that had twice before been vetoed (by Presidents Coolidge and Hoover). The bill established a single government agency with its own capital and its own income and gave it broad powers to serve the Tennessee River Valley in the areas of flood control, navigation, electric-power generation, land-use planning, and reforestation. Although the agency was public, it had many of the attributes of a private corporation. It was a novel idea for government at the time and one that was either bitterly opposed or staunchly supported. Its ultimate purpose was to improve the social and economic well-being of the regional population it was to serve. The Tennessee Valley in the early 1930s was a region of extreme poverty. Its farms suffered from widespread soil erosion and recurrent floods, and the river itself was difficult to navigate because of its irregular flow, immense soil load, and the existence of frequent rapids and sand bars. At Muscle Shoals in northern Alabama, for example, navigation was not possible because the river dropped some 100 ft (30.4 m) in the course of 20 mi (32.2 km).

The drainage basin of the Tennessee River covers a total area of over 40,000 sq mi (103,600 sq km) and includes 125 counties, about one-half of which overlap with the ARC region. (The actual power service area of the TVA covers some 90,000 sq mi—233,100 sq km—in 201 counties.) Over 25,000 sq mi (64,750 sq km) of the drainage basin are within the Appalachian region. Portions of 6 Appalachian states are included within the Tennessee drainage basin: Tennessee, Kentucky, Virginia, North Carolina, Georgia, and Alabama. Within Appalachia the Tennessee cities of Bristol, Kingsport, Chattanooga, and Knoxville are within the TVA service area, with administrative headquarters in Knoxville. By the 1970s, TVA operated thirty-two major dams in the Tennessee Valley, of which twenty-one were built by the agency. Most of the dams were located in the Appalachian region. The primary purposes of the dams were to control floods and improve navigation. It was the third major activity, the production and sale of electric power, that caused the most problems initially, as well as more recently. In the early years, privately owned power companies saw competition from the TVA as an abhorrence. More recently, the controversy has centered on the issue of environmental degradation.

Recent evaluations of the TVA nearly all agree that the agency's first twenty years were highly successful in terms of the benefits it brought to the region and its people. Certainly there were some negative impacts. The 125,000 people who were forced to leave their land between 1933 and 1953 because of dam construction and reservoir impoundment did not see the agency so positively. But on the whole the early record was good. Employment was provided; people were trained for skilled jobs; river traffic increased tremendously; some 212,000 a. (85,648 h) of land was reforested; farms became more productive because the TVA educated farmers and provided fertilizer produced at its own fertilizer development center at Muscle Shoals; per capita income rose from 44 percent to 60 percent of the national average; and manufacturing employment opportunities increased 20 percent faster than in the nation.[41] Harry Caudill, who has not been particularly enamored with government programs in Appalachia, said that TVA "achieved genuine miracles in a startlingly short space of time."[42] Caudill saw the early TVA years as a model for the "Southern Mountain Authority" that he proposed in *Night Comes to the Cumberlands.*

Since the 1950s the achievements of the TVA have been subject to more criticism. During that decade the agency began a vast expansion in power requirements for homes, industries, and especially for defense activities. The most notable energy user by far was the Atomic Energy Commission, which by 1955 consumed one-half of the TVA output at its Oak Ridge and Paducah (Kentucky) uranium enrichment plants. In order to supply the added electric power, the TVA constructed huge coal-fired electric plants. By the 1960s only about one-quarter of the power purchased from the authority came from its dams, whereas in 1950 the figure had been 90 percent. Coal, of course, was needed to operate the plants, and the TVA began using cheap coal that was high in sulfur content. Much of it was strip-mined from its own reserves or purchased from private coal producers. The TVA, for example, purchased the total output of Peabody Coal's, western Kentucky strip mines. By 1968 the authority was using over 5 percent of the total national output of coal, making it the nation's single largest user of stripped coal.[43] Little attention was paid to what strip mining was doing to the land, and many protests were forthcoming because of the environmental degradation that ensued in western Kentucky and in Appalachia. Furthermore, the high-sulfur coal used polluted the region's air. By the mid 1970s officials of the Environmental Protection Agency (EPA) estimated that "TVA emits 14 percent of all utility sulfur dioxide nationally and 52 percent of the poison in eight states of the South."[44] TVA resisted the EPA's demands to clean up its emissions by installing scrubbers and instead built taller smoke stacks so that the contaminants would be dispersed over a wider area (and thus not cleaned up but diffused). The scrubbers eventually installed were, in fact, very effective.

Other environmental criticisms brought against the authority included its movement into nuclear-power generation in the 1960s. Many public protests arose, but the agency was "insensitive to a growing body of public opinion"[45] and plants like the one at Brown's Ferry, Alabama, were constructed. Much public opposition also arose to new dam plans for the Little Tennessee (where the much publicized Tellico Dam was to be built) and French Broad rivers. In short, a large segment of the public, especially those locally affected, began to view the TVA as a destroyer of natural resources, rather than the caretaker it once had been.

Other criticisms that were leveled against the TVA included its purchase of nonunion strip-mined coal so as to drive coal prices down; a regressive rate policy whereby the largest users paid the lowest prices; increased electric costs after the introduction of coal-fired plants (which, of course, hurt the small user the most); and its passive approach in the area of human-resource development.

By the mid 1970s the people of the TVA region had average incomes that were about 75 percent of the national average or "about the same figure as for all of Appalachia."[46] Thus, gains in socioeconomic status in the Tennessee Valley from the early 1950s to the present have not been as rapid as during the first twenty years of the authority's existence. Naturally, there are many reasons for this. For example, even though the proportion employed in manufacturing increased (from 12 percent of the work force in 1933 to one-third in the early 1970s), a large share of the industrial workers, as discussed in Chapter 8, are employed in low-wage industries like apparel, textiles, and furniture. Whatever the reasons, "it must . . . have come as a shock to many people to discover that most of the area where the TVA has been operating for the past forty years [was to be] included in [the ARC] poverty program."[47]

## ARC

The decade of the 1960s was not a fortuitous time for the establishment of new federal programs to help Appalachia, in large part because criticism of the TVA was rapidly increasing. Nevertheless a wide variety of problems had been identified by those in political power, including the governors of the Appalachian states. Not the least of these problems were the natural and man-made disasters that occurred, such as flooding and landslides. Because of these, and as a direct result of the devastating spring floods of 1963, President Kennedy in April of that year established the President's Appalachian Regional Commission (PARC). The charge of the commission was to prepare a plan to deal with the region's poverty so that conditions would be improved. The plan devised "attempted to induce growth of private investment in the region largely through construction of physical infrastructure facilities."[48] Like the TVA, heavy investment was put into public works (over 75 percent of all funds requested for 1965), and minimal funding was allocated to human-resource development (18.5 percent). One reason for this was overlap with other War on Poverty programs of the Johnson administration. A major criticism of the PARC report and subsequent ARC budgets has been the small proportion of funds for human-resource programs. With Appalachia's serious problem in the area of human-resource development, "it seems appropriate to question the wisdom of the allocation of public funds which invests heavily in large-scale physical projects with very long-term benefits, rather than aids the Appalachians more directly through education, training, and health programs."[49]

The commission adopted a growth-center strategy and the construction of the Appalachian Development Highway System (ADHS) as the means of regional development. A growth center was defined as one community or an agglomeration of communities providing a range of social, cultural, employment, trade, and service functions for the community and the rural hinterland. The Appalachian states defined some 70 multicounty areas in the region called Local Development Districts. After delimiting these districts, the next task was to determine where growth was most likely to occur. To aid in this, the ARC developed a three-tier hierarchy of urban centers that were classified according to the function of each center within both the development district and the entire region. In this manner, 23 regional centers, 68 primary centers, and 122 secondary centers were selected. The very largest centers, like Pittsburgh, Knoxville, and Binghamton, required only limited assistance. The primary centers were to receive the majority of urban service investment (e.g., sewage treatment, water supply, airports, roads) to strengthen their competitive advantage. These were the key growth centers in the strategy and included places like Cooperstown, New York; Clearfield-Dubois, Pennsylvania; Buckhannon, West Virginia; Hazard-Whitesburg, Kentucky; Dayton, Tennessee; and Boone, North Carolina. The smallest centers, called secondary centers, were selected as sites for health and vocational-educational institutions.[50]

A growth-center strategy was adopted because investment in designated growth centers, rather than a dispersed investment strategy, was economically more efficient. The physical infrastructure necessary for successful implementation of such a strategy, it was generally agreed, was a development highway system that would make it possible for people living anywhere in the region to commute to new jobs and services created in the growth centers. Also, heavy investment in a highway system was perceived as the best way to lessen regional isolation. So it was that the 1964 ARC report called for improved access to and within the region by construction of nearly 2,200 mi (3,539.8 km) of major highways through remote areas with development potential. Additionally, some 500 mi (804.5 km) of local access roads were to be built to serve industries, recreational sites, and schools. Subsequently the mileage for both the development highways (or "corridor" highways) and the local access roads were increased to 2,900 mi (4,666.1 km) and 1,400 mi (2,252.6 km), respectively. By mid 1975 more than one-half of the corridor highways had been completed or were under construction. The importance of roads to the ARC is evident in its budgets, although the proportion allocated to roads has decreased somewhat since the early years of the commission. Through mid 1978, 60 percent ($2.1 billion out of $3.5 billion) of all ARC appropriations has been allocated for highways.[51]

There have been many evaluations of the ADHS since 1965, and it is useful to summarize the criticisms. John Munro, for example, stated that there was no convincing evidence to prove that the highway system that existed in 1965 was inadequate. The corridor system developed for the most part followed the heavily traveled, noninterstate routes in the region, and their adequacy had been established. In short, "the transportation system does not seem to be an important cause of Appalachian depression."[52] Furthermore, the direct costs of the ADHS had been only vaguely estimated and varied considerably at different times. Little care was taken in planning the system; both the costs and benefits had not been carefully studied or specified.[53] Gauthier suggested that too much money went into transportation development and insufficient amounts into human services. A reason for this, of course, was that road projects are quite tangible, cannot be moved from the region, and are politically safe. Gauthier also showed that corridors were only being completed in part and were not linking the urban centers in Appalachia, thus "obtaining a patchwork of isolated highway segments which provide no regional basis for coordinated development."[54] Unfortunately, individual states establish their own construction priorities. Another study evaluating transportation in Appalachia between 1960 and 1970 concluded there was little evidence that economic growth was related to accessibility; "instead, the important factors which have led to this economic growth may be simple population growth and urbanization."[55]

Evaluating the overall impact of the ARC is difficult, and the evaluations have been mixed. Aside from the commission itself, which of course supports its program in its publications, there are others who have given the ARC good marks. Monroe Newman, an economist who helped start the ARC and was subsequently a consultant for the commission, concluded that the ARC has received generally favorable evaluations from most commentators.[56] Rothblatt's 1971 assessment of the ARC was also generally favorable, and he concluded that "it appears the Commission's greatest value to the region is its role of innovator in the Appalachian planning process."[57] It is difficult to measure any of the benefits of the ARC, according to Rothblatt, and it may be that the "principal unrealized benefits of Appalachian planning have been the political and social gains of widespread local participation and some control of the Appalachian program."[58] Finally, Niles Hansen wrote that "despite the difficulties [e.g., too great an emphasis on highway construction], . . . the ARC is the most promising regional development institution in the United States."[59]

On the reverse side of the coin, there are those who view the impact of the ARC as very limited, or negative. In addition to being criticized for what it has accomplished, the ARC is often criticized for what it has not done. We have seen, for example, that the commission has not accomplished very much in the area of human services. And perhaps most important, it has not addressed questions that to many are at the heart of problems in some parts of Appalachia. In short, the questions of energy and, more specifically, the coal industry have not been dealt with at all (or at least not until very recently when the ARC participated in a study on land ownership patterns in the region; see Note 35). Al Smith, federal cochairman of the ARC, said, "There was a time when the word [*coal*] wasn't mentioned at ARC apparently for fear of offending coal operators or their congressmen."[60] David Whisnant, one of the harshest critics of the commission, has written that it is "a nearly unmitigated disaster in every aspect. ARC is conventional, business-oriented, status quo, federalism. . . . Pressing problems of strip-mining, black lung and other occupational diseases, secondary and higher education, housing, and community-based primary health care have been dealt with belatedly and gingerly if at all. The energy question has been sidestepped entirely."[61]

In 1983 it appears that the commission will be eliminated, or at least greatly diminished, as a result of the Reagan administration economic cutbacks. Inevitably, studies will be forthcoming further evaluating the impact of the commission on the region. Still, questions will remain about the impact, because there are so many other factors that have affected Appalachian development (e.g., the coal industry). One impact the ARC has had about which there is little argument—it has greatly increased awareness and knowledge about the Appalachian region for both residents and nonresidents.

## WHITHER THE REGION?

This is an appropriate point to return to our discussion in Chapter 1 of the Appalachian region and regionalism. Recall that the two themes central to our work are regional diversity and regional development. It should now be clear that because of diversity, no single development strategy for the entire Appalachian region—however it is defined—is appropriate. Rather, different subregional strategies must be developed that are appropriate to the characteristics and problems of each subregion. It has been suggested that ARC subregions are ill defined and do not serve very well as planning units. At the macrolevel the ARC defined first four and then three subregions that were very large and diverse. Each of these subregions has its own development strategy.[62] At the microscale there are the nearly seventy multicounty LDDs. Each LDD was established around at least one designated growth center, and it was through such districts that the ARC implemented its "coordinated investment strategy" whereby funds would be allocated to those areas with the greatest growth potential. Several problems were associated with the LDD concept. First, the LDD boards were made up of all major elected officials in the counties, and as a result local citizens complained that the LDD was "an impediment to local will. . . . They contend that it is hard enough to deal with their own 'courthouse gang'; merge six or eight together in a single LDD and 'you simply don't have a chance.'"[63] Second, some counties were poorly grouped together, and consequently there was no unifying factor for the LDD. For example, foothill counties were grouped with mountain counties and coal counties with noncoal counties. Spinelli stated that "the Appalachian region was divided arbitrarily without any overall standardized method and with different interpretations of the goals of subregionalization among the participating states."[64] Perhaps the major difficulty with the ARC subregional delimitation, and for that matter with the ARC region as a whole, was that there was no sense of regional identity among the people. According to Primack, "Successful attempts at regionalism have two common factors: They have had the tools and the mandate with which to proceed . . . in Appalachia, regional mechanisms have tried to operate in a vacuum of citizen awareness and support."[65]

If, then, the ARC planning and administrative subregions were poorly defined, what are the alternatives? There have been considerable criticisms made of the ARC subregions, as well as suggestions for more appropriate ones. Our final task will be to examine the topic of alternative regionalisms.

Instead of the present LDDs, Primack suggested that "districts should be developed according to common realities, according to economic and social factors which might produce a certain jurisdictional cohesiveness. To combine units sheerly on the basis of geography (the north fork of a river), or politics (there's a congressional district there), is shortsighted if the real goal is to use common facilities for the common solution of common problems."[66] Based on this statement, one logical choice for multicounty subregions would be to utilize those defined by the Census Bureau and called State Economic Areas (SEAs). Such areas consist of single counties or groups of counties that have similar social and economic characteristics (recall that southern Appalachia as defined by the Ford study used SEAs). The SEAs, however, are uniform regions (they are either urban or nonurban) rather than nodal regions, and most critics argue that subregions should be nodal, or functional, rather than uniform, since development occurs most rapidly around growth centers and diffuses outward to rural hinterlands. Besides, as Pickard argued, "the first great truth that a regional geographer finds out about Appalachia . . . [is] that it is a collection of nodal regions."[67]

For planning and development purposes it is useful to subdivide Appalachia into macrolevel subregions initially and then subdivide these large areas into smaller ones. Stephen Fuller said there are two Appalachias: "One is clearly depressed but not underdeveloped. The conditions characteristic of this portion of the region call for a growth strategy. The other subregion is underdeveloped and has conditions which necessitate a development strategy."[68] Pickard suggested three zones in the region, which he calls the expanded developed zone (characterized by economic diversity including manufacturing), the developed zone of stagnation or depression (e.g., much of Appalachian Pennsylvania), and the primitive zone.[69] The latter includes both the coal areas, like eastern Kentucky, and noncoal areas. These are uniform subregions and correspond roughly to the ARC's southern, northern, and central subregions, respectively. After defining such large subregions, the next step is to identify smaller, nodal subregions.

In defining nodal subregions the question of including counties (cities) on the periphery of, and outside, Appalachia must be considered, because—as we have seen—much of the region is heavily oriented toward such centers. John Friedmann early recognized this and suggested that transportation and communications facilities should be planned to take advantage of such "extra-regional" linkages. The fact that so many Appalachians resided in cities like Cincinnati, Detroit, Chicago, and Lexington was further evidence that the development effort should be expanded to areas outside the geographic region normally thought of as Appalachia. According to Friedmann, "the region itself should be restructured and, as it were, apportioned among the metropolitan regions of its perimeter."[70] Hoover suggested that "Appalachia should be regarded as a succession of hinterlands to various major centers located mainly outside the region as officially defined. . . ."[71] Hoover went on to suggest that if the most promising areas for future growth are metropolitan centers with population in six figures (as studies suggest), "then the appropriate units for programs of employment creation are regions with such centers as focal points."[72] Clearly, this implies development-planning subregions that transcend the boundaries of physiographic or cultural Appalachia (perhaps identified, for example, on the basis of commuting fields). Finally, Rothblatt believed that "With respect to functional linkage of economic activities and migration flows, the region presented is equally deficient. In order to meet this criterion, the region should have been either enlarged to include those metropolitan areas for which Appalachia acts as a migration shed (e.g., Cincinnati, Chicago, Cleveland, Dayton, and Baltimore) or broken down into a series of areas each linked to the urban center which it serves as a hinterland."[73]

Definition of "rational" (from an economic viewpoint) planning subregions such as those reviewed would be opposed by many. Certainly many residents and students of Appalachian culture and folkways would argue that such a regionalization would further destroy what remains of the unique cultural character in segments of the region, in that "outside" influences would further penetrate and alter the region. The fact is that the region is changing and will continue to do so. New industries, recreational homes, retirement areas, and returning migrants are only part of the evidence of the change taking place as a result of outside influences. Since change is inevitable, it would seem that more appropriate development strategies should be initiated to both accommodate and facilitate change. One change that is necessary to improve the living conditions of the poorest of the region's residents—those in the coal-producing counties and many of the remote rural counties—is the definition of more appropriate planning subregions, attaching the poor areas to the nodal regions their resource wealth (e.g., coal) is sent to. If we wish to see the people of this region improve their social and economic well-being to a level approaching the national norm, then it is imperative that the responsibility for that improvement be shared by those who withdraw the region's wealth for their own uses.

## NOTES

1. Richard Ulack and Karl Raitz, "Perceptions of Appalachia," *Environment and Behavior* 14 (1982), pp. 725–752.

2. Ibid.

3. John Fiske, *Old Virginia and Her Neighbors* (Boston: Houghton, Mifflin, 1897).

4. Nathaniel D. M. Hirsch, "An Experimental Study of the East Kentucky Mountains," *Genetic Psychology Monographs* 3 (1928), p. 229. See also Arthur H. Estabrook, "Blood Seeks Environment (Presidential Address)," *Eugenical News* (1926), pp. 106–114.

5. Harry M. Caudill, *Night Comes to the Cumberlands: A Biography of a Depressed Area* (Boston: Little, Brown and Co., 1963), pp. 5–6.

6. Cratis D. Williams, "Who Are the Southern Mountaineers?" *Appalachian Journal* 1 (1972), p. 50.

7. Ellen Churchill Semple, "The Anglo-Saxons of the Kentucky Mountains: A Study in Anthropogeography," *Geographical Journal* 17 (1901), pp. 588–623, and William Goodell Frost, "Our Contemporary Ancestors in the Southern Mountains," *Atlantic Monthly* 83 (1899), pp. 311–319.

8. President's Appalachian Regional Commission (P.A.R.C.), *Appalachia* (Washington, D.C.: Government Printing Office, 1964), p. 32.

9. Mary Jean Bowman and W. Warren Haynes, *Resources and People in East Kentucky: Problems and Potentials of a Lagging Economy* (Baltimore: Johns Hopkins Press, 1963), p. 244.

10. Ibid., p. 25.

11. Brian J. L. Berry, *Growth Centers in the American Urban System* (Cambridge, Mass.: Ballinger Publishing Company, 1973), p. 45.

12. Donald N. Rothblatt, *Regional Planning: The Appalachian Experience* (Lexington, Mass.: D. C. Heath and Co., 1971), p. 9.

13. Ibid., p. 16.

14. U.S. Department of Agriculture, *Economic and Social Problems and Conditions of the Southern Appalachians*, Misc. Pub. no. 205 (Washington, D.C.: U.S. Dept. of Agriculture, 1935), p. 2.

15. Ibid., p. 5.

16. Rupert B. Vance, *Human Geography of the South*, 1935, cited in Williams, op. cit. (footnote 6), p. 53.

17. William Bradley, "The Women on Troublesome," *Scribner's* 63 (1918), p. 320.

18. David S. Walls and Dwight B. Billings, "The Sociology of Southern Appalachia," *Appalachian Journal* 5 (1977), p. 132.

19. Helen M. Lewis and Edward E. Knipe, "The Colonialism Model: The Appalachian Case," in Helen M. Lewis, Linda Johnson, and Donald Askins, eds., *Colonialism in Modern America: The Appalachian Case* (Boone, N.C.: Appalachian Consortium Press, 1978), p. 14.

20. Ibid., pp. 14–15.

21. Thomas R. Ford, "The Passing of Provincialism," in Thomas R. Ford, ed., *The Southern Appalachian Region: A Survey* (Lexington: University of Kentucky Press, 1962), chap. 2.

22. Stephen L. Fisher, "Victim-Blaming in Appalachia: Cultural Theories and the Southern Mountaineers," in Bruce Ergood and Bruce E. Kuhre, eds.,

*Appalachia: Social Context Past and Present* (Dubuque, Ia.: Kendall/Hunt Publishing Co., 1976), p. 140.

23. Dwight Billings, "Culture and Poverty in Appalachia: A Theoretical Discussion and Empirical Analysis," *Social Forces* 53 (1974), p. 316.

24. Jack E. Weller, *Yesterday's People: Life in Contemporary Appalachia* (Lexington: University of Kentucky Press, 1965), pp. 161–163.

25. Richard A. Ball, "Poverty Case: The Analgesic Subculture of the Southern Appalachians," *American Sociological Review* 33 (1968), pp. 885–895, and David H. Looff, *Appalachia's Children: The Challenge of Mental Health* (Lexington: University Press of Kentucky, 1971).

26. John B. Stephenson, *Shiloh: A Mountain Community* (Lexington: University Press of Kentucky, 1968).

27. Loyal Jones, "Appalachian Values," in Ergood and Kuhre, op. cit. (footnote 22), pp. 101–105.

28. Billings, op. cit. (footnote 23), p. 319.

29. Ibid., pp. 320–321.

30. Berry, op. cit. (footnote 11), p. 43.

31. See John Gaventa, *Power and Powerlessness: Quiescence and Rebellion in an Appalachian Valley* (Urbana: University of Illinois Press, 1980).

32. David S. Walls, "Central Appalachia: A Peripheral Region Within an Advanced Capitalist Society," *Journal of Sociology and Social Welfare* 4 (1976), p. 234.

33. Caudill, op. cit. (footnote 5), p. 325.

34. Lewis and Knipe, op. cit. (footnote 19); Emil Malizia, "Economic Imperialism: An Interpretation of Appalachian Underdevelopment," *Appalachian Journal* 1 (1973), pp. 130–137; and Keith Dix, "Appalachia: Third World Pillage," *Antipode: A Radical Journal of Geography* 5 (1973), pp. 25–30.

35. Appalachian Land Ownership Task Force, *Land Ownership Patterns and Their Impacts on Appalachian Communities: A Survey of 80 Counties* (Boone, N.C.: Center for Appalachian Studies, 1981). The approximate amount of coal may be calculated by multiplying area times thickness times density. A 36 in. (91.4 cm) seam of coal under 1 a. (0.405 h) of land, at a density of 1,800 tn per a. ft (1.32 t per cu m), would contain 5,400 tn (4,898.9 t) of bituminous coal. If this coal was valued at the average West Virginia price (about $33.00 per tn—$36.30 per t), the total value of that coal would be $178,200 ($177,830). The value for that seam under 640 a. (259.2 h) or 1 sq mi (2.6 sq km) would be $114,048,000 ($113,811,200).

36. John Calhoun Wells, Jr., "Poverty Amidst Riches: Why People Are Poor in Appalachia," (Ph.D. dissertation, Department of Urban Planning and Policy Development, Rutgers University, 1977), p. 144.

37. Walls and Billings, op. cit. (footnote 18), p. 134.

38. David Walls, "Internal Colony or Internal Periphery? A Critique of Current Models and an Alternative Formulation," in Lewis, Johnson, and Askins, eds., op. cit. (footnote 19), p. 340.

39. David E. Whisnant, *Modernizing the Mountaineer: People, Power, and Planning in Appalachia* (New York: Burt Franklin & Company, 1980), p. 107.

40. Ibid.

41. James Branscome, *The Federal Government in Appalachia* (New York: Field Foundation, 1977), p. 14.

42. Caudill, op. cit. (footnote 5), p. 367.

43. Whisnant, op. cit. (footnote 39), p. 50.

44. Branscome, op. cit. (footnote 41), p. 18.

45. Whisnant, op. cit. (footnote 39), p. 52.

46. Branscome, op. cit. (footnote 41), p. 21.

47. J. H. Paterson, *North America: A Geography of the United States and Canada* (New York: Oxford University Press, 1975), p. 221.

48. Rothblatt, op. cit. (footnote 12), p. 59.

49. Ibid.

50. Bruce Ryan, "The Criteria for Selecting Growth Centers in Appalachia," *Proceedings*, Association of American Geographers, 2 (1970), pp. 118–123.

51. William H. Miernyk, "The Tools of Regional Development Policy," *Growth and Change* 11 (1980), p. 5.

52. John M. Munro, "Planning the Appalachian Development Highway System: Some Critical Questions," *Land Economics* 45 (1969), p. 157.

53. Ibid., p. 161.

54. Howard Gauthier, "The Appalachian Development Highway System: Development for Whom?" *Economic Geography* 49 (1973), p. 106.

55. Powel Crosley V, "The Role of Accessibility in the Development of Appalachia: 1960–1970," (Master's Thesis, Department of Geography, University of South Carolina, 1978), p. 70.

56. Monroe Newman, "The Future of Multistate Regional Commissions," *Growth and Change* 11 (1980), p. 15.

57. Rothblatt, op. cit. (footnote 12), p. 194.

58. Ibid.

59. Niles M. Hansen, "A Review of the Appalachian Regional Commission Program," (paper, University of Texas, Austin, 1969), p. 5.

60. *Louisville Courier-Journal*, Sunday, June 7, 1981, p. A-16.

61. Whisnant, op. cit. (footnote 39), p. xxi.

62. "The New Appalachian Subregions and Their Development Strategies," *Appalachia* 8 (1974), pp. 10–27.

63. Phil Primack, "Hidden Traps of Regionalism," in Lewis, Johnson, and Askins, eds., op. cit. (footnote 19), p. 298.

64. Michael Ambrose Spinelli, "A Definition of the Economic Subregions of Appalachia Using Factor Analysis," (Ph.D. dissertation, Department of Economics, West Virginia University, 1971), p. 14.

65. Primack, op. cit. (footnote 63), pp. 295–296.

66. Ibid., p. 303.

67. Jerome P. Pickard, "An Analysis of Regional Structure in Appalachia," (unpublished manuscript).

68. Stephen Souther Fuller, "The Appalachian Experiment: Growth or Development?" (Ph.D. dissertation, Department of Sociology, Cornell University, 1969), p. 6.

69. Pickard, op. cit. (footnote 67).

70. John Friedmann, "Poor Regions and Poor Nations: Perspectives on Problems in Appalachia," *Southern Economic Journal* 32 (1966), p. 472.

71. Edgar M. Hoover, *An Introduction to Regional Economics* (New York: Alfred A. Knopf, 1975), p. 289.

72. Ibid.

73. Rothblatt, op. cit. (footnote 12), p. 55.

# BIBLIOGRAPHY


Aiken, Charles S. "The Fragmented Neoplantation: A New Type of Farm Operation in the Southeast." *Southeastern Geographer* 11 (1971):43–51.

Alanen, Arnold R., and Smith, Kenard E. "Adolescent Impressions of Rural Development in an Appalachian County." In *Priorities of Environmental Design Research*, edited by Sue Weidemann and James R. Anderson. Washington, D.C.: Environmental Design Research Association, 1976.

________. "Growth Versus No-Growth Issues, with an American Appalachian Perspective." *Tijdschrift voor Econ. en Soc. Geografie* 68 (1977):30–42.

Alexander, John W., and Gibson, Lay James. *Economic Geography*. Englewood Cliffs, N.J.: Prentice-Hall, 1979.

Alexander, John W., and Lindberg, James B. "Measurements of Manufacturing: Coefficients of Correlation." *Journal of Regional Science* 3 (1961):71–81.

Ambler, Charles H. *West Virginia: The Mountain State*. New York: Prentice-Hall, 1940.

American Society of Planning Officials. *Subdividing Rural America: Impacts of Recreational Lot and Second Home Development*. Washington, D.C.: Council on Environmental Quality, 1976.

Anderson, James R. "Specialized Agriculture in the South." *Southeastern Geographer* 10 (1970):13–27.

"Appalachian Highways Are Catalysts of Change." *Appalachia* 15 (1981):8–17.

Appalachian Land Ownership Task Force. *Land Ownership Patterns and Their Impacts on Appalachian Communities: A Survey of 80 Counties*. Boone, N.C.: Center for Appalachian Studies, 1981.

Appalachian Regional Commission (ARC). *Recreation as an Industry*. Appalachian Research Report no. 2. Washington, D.C.: ARC, 1966.

________. "The New Appalachian Subregions and Their Development Strategies." *Appalachia* 8 (1974):10–27.

________. *Appalachian Highway Program: Progress, Impacts, and Plannning for the Future*. Washington, D.C.: ARC, 1975.

________. "Appalachia Is Changing." In *Appalachia: Social Context Past and Present*, edited by Bruce Ergood and Bruce E. Kuhre. Dubuque, Ia.: Kendall/Hunt Publishing Co., 1976.

________. *Appalachia: Goals, Objectives, and Development Strategies*. Washington, D.C.: ARC, 1977.

________. *An Assessment of the Effects of Coal Movement on the Highways in the Appalachian Region*. Final Report. Research Triangle Institute, Raleigh: North Carolina State University, 1977.

———. *Appalachia—A Reference Book.* Washington, D.C.: ARC, 1979.

———. *1980 Annual Report.* Washington, D.C.: ARC, 1981.

———. *The Effects of Airline Deregulation Upon Air Service in Appalachia.* Washington, D.C.: ARC, 1982.

"Appalachian Views: An Ohio Mayor Speaks." *Appalachia* 14 (1981):24–27.

Arensberg, Conrad M. "American Communities." *American Anthropologist* 57 (1955):1143–1162.

Atwood, W. W. *The Physiographic Provinces of North America.* Boston: Ginn & Co., 1940.

Babu, S. P. et al. *Suitability of West Virginia Coals to Coal-Conversion Processes.* Coal-Geology Bulletin no. 1. Morgantown: West Virginia Geological and Economic Survey, 1973.

Baldwin, John L. *Weather Atlas of the United States.* 1968. Reprint. Detroit: Gale Research Co., 1975.

Ball, Richard A. "Poverty Case: The Analgesic Subculture of the Southern Appalachians." *American Sociological Review* 33 (1968):885–895.

Barnum, Darold T. *The Negro in the Bituminous Coal Mining Industry.* Industrial Research Unit, Report no. 14. Philadelphia: University of Pennsylvania, 1970.

Beale, Calvin L. "American Triracial Isolates." *Eugenics Quarterly* 4 (1957):187–196.

———. *The Revival of Population Growth in Nonmetropolitan America.* Economic Research Service Pub. ERS-605. Washington, D.C.: U.S. Dept. of Agriculture, 1975.

Beebe, Mary E. "Recreation, Exploitation, and Expropriation in the Red River Gorge of Kentucky." Paper presented at the Society for Applied Anthropology Annual Meeting, Denver, 1980.

Bellamy, Thomas R., and Hutchins, Cecil C., Jr. *Southern Pulpwood Production, 1979.* Forest Service Resource Bulletin SE-57. Asheville, N.C.: Southeastern Forest Experiment Station, 1981.

Bellows, David. "Appalachian Blacks: A Demographic Analysis." Department of Sociology, Rutgers University, 1974. Mimeographed.

Berry, Brian J. L. *Growth Centers in the American Urban System.* Cambridge, Mass.: Ballinger Publishing Co., 1973.

Biggar, Jeanne C. "The Sunning of America: Migration to the Sunbelt." *Population Bulletin* 34 (1979):1–42.

Billings, Dwight. "Culture and Poverty in Appalachia: A Theoretical Discussion and Empirical Analysis." *Social Forces* 53 (1974):315–323.

———. *Planters and the Making of a "New South": Class, Politics, and Development in North Carolina, 1865–1900.* Chapel Hill: University of North Carolina Press, 1979.

Billings, Dwight, and Walls, David. "Appalachians." In *Harvard Encyclopedia of American Ethnic Groups,* edited by Stephen Thernstrom. Cambridge: Harvard University Press, 1980.

Billington, Ray A. *Westward Expansion: A History of the American Frontier.* 3d ed. New York: Macmillan Co., 1967.

Bingham, Edgar. "The Impact of Recreational Development on Pioneer Life Styles in Southern Appalachia." In *Colonialism in Modern America: The Appalachian Case,* edited by Helen M. Lewis, Linda Johnson, and Donald Askins. Boone, N.C.: Appalachian Consortium Press, 1978.

Birdsall, Stephen S., and Florin, John W. *Regional Landscapes of the United States and Canada.* New York: John Wiley & Sons, 1978.

Black, Ira. "Sunbelt: Myth or Mecca?" *Iron Age* 219 (March 7, 1977):51–52.

Black, William, and Runke, James. *The States and Rural Rail Preservation: Alternative Strategies.* Lexington, Ky.: Council of State Governments, 1975.

Blackmar, Betsy et al. *Resorts of the Catskills.* New York: St. Martins Press, 1979.

Borchert, John R. "American Metropolitan Evolution." *Geographical Review* 57 (1967):301–325.

Bowman, Mary Jean, and Haynes, W. Warren. *Resources and People in East Kentucky: Problems and Potentials of a Lagging Economy.* Baltimore: Johns Hopkins Press, 1963.

Bradley, William. "The Women on Troublesome." *Scribner's* 63 (1918):320.

Branscome, James. "Educating Appalachia's Poor." *People's Appalachia* 5 (1970):5–8.

________. *The Federal Government in Appalachia.* New York: Field Foundation, 1977.

Branscome, James, and Matthews, Peggy. "Selling the Mountains." *Southern Exposure* 2 (1974):122–129.

Braun, E. Lucy. *Deciduous Forests of Eastern North America.* 1950. Reprint. New York: Hafner Press, 1974.

Brewster, Lawrence Fay. *Summer Migrations and Resorts of South Carolina Low-Country Planters.* Durham, N.C.: Duke University Press, 1947.

Brooks, Maurice. *The Appalachians.* Boston: Houghton Mifflin Co., 1965.

Brosky, Alphonse F. "Building a Town for a Mountain Community: A Glimpse of Jenkins and Nearby Villages." *Coal Age* 23 (1923):554–563.

Brown, James S., and Hillery, George A., Jr. "The Great Migration, 1940–1960." In *The Southern Appalachian Region: A Survey*, edited by Thomas R. Ford. Lexington: University of Kentucky Press, 1962.

Brown, Ralph H. *Historical Geography of the United States.* New York: Harcourt, Brace and World, 1948.

Brownell, Joseph W. "The Cultural Midwest." *Journal of Geography* 59 (1960):81–85.

Burby, R. J., and Weiss, S. F. *Public Policy and Shoreline Landowner Behavior.* Report no. 38. Chapel Hill: Water Resources Research Institute of the University of North Carolina, 1970.

Campbell, John C. *The Southern Highlander and His Homeland.* Lexington: University of Kentucky Press, 1969. Originally published by the Russell Sage Foundation in 1921.

Carney, George O. "Bluegrass Grows All Around: The Spatial Dimensions of a Country Music Style." In *The Sounds of People and Places*, edited by George O. Carney. Washington, D.C.: University Press of America, 1978.

________. "Country Music and the South: A Cultural Geography Perspective." *Journal of Cultural Geography* 1 (1980):16–33.

Caudill, Harry M. *Night Comes to the Cumberlands: A Biography of a Depressed Area.* Boston: Little, Brown and Co., 1963.

*Churches and Church Membership in the U.S., 1971.* Washington, D.C.: Glenmary Research Center, 1974. Prepared for the National Council of Churches.

Cole, Robert L. S., Jr., and Mitchell, Lisle Serles. "Attendance as a Negative Function of Distance, Great Smoky Mountains National Park Campgrounds." *Southeastern Geographer* 9 (1969):13–24.

Coogan, M. H. "Two Appalachian Corridors, Ten Years Later." *Appalachia* 12 (1979):13–26.

Cook, Frederick A.; Brown, Larry D.; and Oliver, Jack E. "The Southern Appalachians and the Growth of Continents." *Scientific American* 243 (1980):156–168.

Core, Earl L. *Vegetation of West Virginia.* Parsons, W. Va.: McClain Printing Co., 1966.

Cox, Kevin R., and Zannaras, Georgia. "Designative Perceptions of Macrospaces: Concepts, a Methodology, and Applications." In *Image and Environment: Cognitive Mapping and Spatial Behavior*, edited by Roger M. Downs and David Stea. Chicago: Aldine, 1973.

Cromley, Robert C., and Leinbach, Thomas R. "Patterns of Manufacturing in Nonmetropolitan Kentucky, 1968–78." *Kentucky Economy* 5 (1981):10–13.

Crosley, Powel, V. "The Role of Accessibility in the Development of Appalachia: 1960–1970." Master's thesis, Department of Geography, University of South Carolina, 1978.

Darlington, James W. "Railroads and the Evolution of the Catskill Mountain Resort Area, 1870–1920." Paper presented at the Association of American Geographers Annual Meeting, Los Angeles, 1981.

Davies, Shane, and Fowler, Gary L. "The Disadvantaged Urban Migrant in Indianapolis." *Economic Geography* 48 (1972):153–167.

Davis, George A., and Donaldson, O. Fred. *Blacks in the United States: A Geographic Perspective.* Boston: Houghton Mifflin Co., 1975.

Deasy, George F., and Griess, Phyllis R. "Effects of a Declining Mining Economy on the Pennsylvania Anthracite Region." *Annals*, Association of American Geographers, 55 (1965):239–259.

Deaton, B. J., and Anschel, K. R. "Migration and Return Migration: A New Look at the Eastern Kentucky Migration Stream." *Southern Journal of Agricultural Economics* 6 (1974):185–191.

DeJong, Gordon F. *Appalachian Fertility Decline: Demographic and Sociological Analysis.* Lexington: University of Kentucky Press, 1968.

Distilled Spirits Council of the United States. Letter to author.

Dix, Keith. "Appalachia: Third World Pillage." *Antipode: A Radical Journal of Geography* 5 (1973):25–30.

Duerr, William A. *The Economic Problems of Forestry in the Appalachian Region.* Cambridge: Harvard University Press, 1949.

Dunaway, Wayland F. "Pennsylvania as an Early Distributing Center of Population." *Pennsylvania Magazine of History and Biography* 55 (1931):134–169.

Durand, Loyal, Jr. "'Mountain Moonshining' in East Tennessee." *Geographical Review* 46 (1956):168–181.

Dykeman, Wilma, and Stokely, Jim. *Highland Homeland: The People of the Great Smokies.* Washington, D.C.: U.S. Dept. of the Interior, 1978.

Eller, Ronald D. *Miners, Millhands, and Mountaineers: Industrialization of the Appalachian South, 1880–1930.* Knoxville: University of Tennessee Press, 1982.

Ergood, Bruce. "Toward a Definition of Appalachia." In *Appalachia: Social Context Past and Present*, edited by Bruce Ergood and Bruce E. Kuhre. Dubuque, Ia.: Kendall/Hunt Publishing Co., 1976.

Erickson, Rodney A., and Leinbach, Thomas R. "Characteristics of Branch Plants Attracted to Nonmetropolitan Areas." In *Nonmetropolitan Industrialization*, edited by Richard E. Lonsdale and H. L. Seyler. New York: John Wiley & Sons, 1979.

Estabrook, Arthur H. "Blood Seeks Environment (Presidential Address)," *Eugenical News* (1926):106–114.

Estall, Robert. *A Modern Geography of the United States.* Baltimore: Penguin Books, 1972.

Evans, E. Estyn. "The Scotch-Irish in the New World: An Atlantic Heritage." *Journal of the Royal Society of Antiquaries of Ireland* 95 (1965):39–49.

———. "Cultural Relics of the Ulster-Scots in the Old West of North America." *Ulster Folklife* 11 (1966):33–38.

———. "The Scotch-Irish: Their Cultural Adaptation and Heritage in the American Old West." In *Essays in Scotch-Irish History,* edited by E.R.R. Green. London: Routledge & Kegan Paul, 1969.

Feld, Rose C. "What I Found in Lynch, Kentucky." *Success* (March 1926):58–59, 114–119.

Fenneman, Nevin M. "Physiographic Boundaries Within the United States." *Annals,* Association of American Geographers, 4 (1914):84–134.

———. *Physiography of Eastern United States.* New York: McGraw-Hill Book Co., 1938.

Fisher, George W. et al., editors. *Studies of Appalachian Geology: Central and Southern.* New York: Interscience Publishers, 1970.

Fisher, James S. "Structural Adjustments in the Southern Manufacturing Sector." *The Professional Geographer* 33 (1981):466–474.

Fisher, Stephen L. "Victim-Blaming in Appalachia: Cultural Theories and the Southern Mountaineers." In *Appalachia: Social Context Past and Present,* edited by Bruce Ergood and Bruce E. Kuhre. Dubuque, Ia: Kendall/Hunt Publishing Co., 1976.

Fiske, John. *Old Virginia and Her Neighbours.* Boston: Houghton, Mifflin, 1897.

Ford, Thomas P. "Status, Residence, and Fundamentalist Religious Beliefs in the Southern Appalachians." *Social Forces* 39 (1960):41–49.

Ford, Thomas R. "The Passing of Provincialism." In *The Southern Appalachian Region: A Survey,* edited by Thomas R. Ford. Lexington: University of Kentucky Press, 1962.

Ford, Thomas R., ed. *The Southern Appalachian Region: A Survey.* Lexington: University of Kentucky Press, 1962.

*The Forest Resources of West Virginia.* Forest Service Resource Bulletin NE-56. Broomall, Pa.: Northeastern Forest Experiment Station, 1978.

Foth, Henry D., and Schafer, John W. *Soil Geography and Land Use.* New York: John Wiley & Sons, 1980.

French, Laurence, and Hornbuckle, Jim, editors. *The Cherokee Perspective: Written by Eastern Cherokees.* Boone, N.C.: Appalachian Consortium Press, 1981.

Friedl, John. *Health Care Services and the Appalachian Migrant.* Columbus: Ohio State University, 1978.

Friedmann, John. "Poor Regions and Poor Nations: Perspectives on Problems in Appalachia." *Southern Economic Journal* 32 (1966):465–473.

Frost, William Goodell. "Our Contemporary Ancestors in the Southern Mountains." *Atlantic Monthly* 83 (1899):311–319.

———. *For the Mountains: An Autobiography.* New York: Revell, 1937.

Fuller, Stephen Souther. "The Appalachian Experiment: Growth or Development?" Ph.D. dissertation, Department of Sociology, Cornell University, 1969.

Garrison, Charles B. "A Case Study of the Local Economic Impact of Reservoir Recreation." *Journal of Leisure Research* 6 (1974):7–19.

Gastil, Raymond D. *Cultural Regions of the United States.* Seattle: University of Washington Press, 1975.

Gauthier, Howard. "The Appalachian Development Highway System: Devel-

opment for Whom?" *Economic Geography* 49 (1973):103–108.
Gaventa, John. *Power and Powerlessness: Quiescence and Rebellion in an Appalachian Valley.* Urbana: University of Illinois Press, 1980.
Gersmehl, Phil. "Factors Leading to Mountaintop Grazing in the Southern Appalachians." *Southeastern Geographer* 10 (1970):67–72.
Gilbert, W. H. "Memorandum Concerning the Characteristics of the Larger Mixed-Blood Racial Islands of the Eastern United States." *Social Forces* 24 (1946):438–447.
Gillenwater, Mack H. "Mining Settlements of Southern West Virginia." In *West Virginia and Appalachia: Selected Readings,* edited by Howard G. Adkins, Steven Ewing, and Chester E. Zimolzak. Dubuque, Ia.: Kendall/Hunt Publishing Co., 1977.
Gillespie, Paul F. *Foxfire 7.* New York: Anchor Books, 1982.
Glassie, Henry. "The Appalachian Log Cabin." *Mountain Life and Work* 39 (1963):5–14.
_______. "The Old Barns of Appalachia." *Mountain Life and Work* 41 (1965):21–30.
_______. *Pattern in the Material Folk Culture of the Eastern United States.* Philadelphia: University of Pennsylvania Press, 1968.
Gottfried, Robert R. *Distributional Implications of Recreation-Led Growth: Appalachia.* PB-Z57660. Chapel Hill, N.C.: U.S. Dept. of Commerce, National Technical Information Service, 1975.
Govan, Gilbert E., and Livingood, James W. *The Chattanooga Country: 1540–1951.* New York: E. P. Dutton and Co., 1952.
Graff, Orin B. "The Needs of Education." In *The Southern Appalachian Region: A Survey,* edited by Thomas R. Ford. Lexington: University of Kentucky Press, 1962.
Griffin, Paul F. et al. *Anglo-America: A Systematic and Regional Geography.* Palo Alto, Ca.: Fearon Publishers, 1968.
Guyot, Arnold. "On the Appalachian Mountain System." *American Journal of Science and Arts* 31 (1861):157–187.
Haas, Glenn E. *Recreation and Parks: A Social Study of Shenandoah National Park.* Scientific Monograph Series no. 10. Washington, D.C.: National Park Service, 1977.
Hale, Ruth F. "A Map of Vernacular Regions in America." Ph.D. dissertation, Department of Geography, University of Minnesota, 1971.
Halvorson, Peter L., and Newman, William M. *Atlas of Religious Change in America: 1952–1971.* Washington, D.C.: Glenmary Research Center, 1978.
Hansen, Niles M. "A Review of the Appalachian Regional Commission Program." University of Texas, 1969. Paper.
_______. *The Future of Nonmetropolitan America.* Lexington, Mass.: Lexington Books, 1973.
Hart, John Fraser. "The Changing Distribution of the American Negro." *Annals,* Association of American Geographers, 50 (1960):242–266.
_______. "Abandonment of Farmland on the Appalachian Fringe of Kentucky." *Melanges De Geographie Physique, Humaine, Economique, Appliquee* 1 (1967):352–360.
_______. "Loss and Abandonment of Cleared Farm Land in the Eastern United States." *Annals,* Association of American Geographers, 58 (1968):417–440.
_______. "Land Rotation in Appalachia." *Geographical Review* 67 (1977): 148–166.

———. "Land Use Change in a Piedmont County." *Annals*, Association of American Geographers, 70 (1980):492–527.

Hepburn, Andrew. *Great Resorts of North America*. New York: Doubleday & Co., 1965.

Hirsch, Nathaniel D. M. "An Experimental Study of the East Kentucky Mountains." *Genetic Psychology Monographs* 3 (1928):229.

Hoffman, John N. *Girard Estate Coal Lands in Pennsylvania, 1801–1884*. Washington, D.C.: Smithsonian Institution Press, 1972.

Hoover, Edgar M. *An Introduction to Regional Economics*. New York: Alfred A. Knopf, 1975.

Howes, Robert M. "Recreational Opportunities from Reservoir Construction." *Economic Geography* 15 (1939):250–255.

Hudson, Charles. *The Southeastern Indians*. Knoxville: University of Tennessee Press, 1976.

Hunt, Charles B. *Natural Regions of the United States and Canada*. San Francisco: W. H. Freeman and Co., 1974.

Ise, John. *Our National Park Policy*. Baltimore: Johns Hopkins Press, 1961.

Jackson, George Pullen. *White Spirituals in the Southern Uplands*. Chapel Hill: University of North Carolina Press, 1933.

Jakle, John A. "Salt on the Ohio Valley Frontier, 1770–1820." *Annals*, Association of American Geographers, 59 (1969):687–709.

Janssen, Raymond E. "The Teays River, Ancient Precursor of the East." *The Scientific Monthly* 77 (1953):306–314.

Jennings, Francis. "Susquehannock." *Handbook of North American Indians*. Vol. 15, *Northeast*. Washington, D.C.: Smithsonian Institution, 1978.

Johnson, Hugh A.; Carpenter, J. Raymond; and Dill, W., Jr. *Exurban Development in Selected Areas of the Appalachian Mountains*. Economic Research Service Pub. ERS-429. Washington, D.C.: U.S. Department of Agriculture, 1969.

Johnson, Ole S. *The Industrial Store*. Atlanta: Research Division, School of Business Administration, University of Georgia, 1952.

Jones, Loyal. "Appalachian Values." In *Appalachia: Social Context Past and Present*, edited by Bruce Ergood and Bruce E. Kuhre. Dubuque, Ia.: Kendall/Hunt Publishing Co., 1976.

———. "The Foxfire Phenomenon." *Appalachian Notes* 1 (1973):9–12.

Kale, Steven R., and Lonsdale, Richard E. "Factors Encouraging and Discouraging Plant Location in Nonmetropolitan Areas." In *Nonmetropolitan Industrialization*, edited by Richard E. Lonsdale and H. L. Seyler. New York: Winston Halsted, 1979.

Kellogg, Paul U. "Monongah." *Charities* 19 (1907):1313–1328.

Kingsley, Neal P. *Pulpwood Production in the Northeast, 1963*. Forest Service Resource Bulletin NE-3. Upper Darby, Pa.: Northeastern Forest Experiment Station, 1966.

Kingsley, Neal P., and Powell, Douglas S. *The Forest Resources of Kentucky*. Forest Service Resource Bulletin NE-54. Broomall, Pa.: Northeastern Forest Experiment Station, 1978.

Kirkland, Edward C. *A History of American Economic Life*. 3d ed. New York: Appleton-Century-Crofts, Inc., 1951.

Klimasewski, Theodore. "Corporate Dominance of Manufacturing in Appalachia." *Geographical Review* 68 (1978):94–102.

Kniffen, Fred, and Glassie, Henry. "Building in Wood in the Eastern United States: A Time-Place Perspective." *Geographical Review* 56 (1966):40–66.

Knight, Herbert A., and Nichols, Agnes C. *Southern Pulpwood Production, 1979*. Forest Service Resource Bulletin SE-57. Asheville, N.C.: Southeastern Forest Experiment Station, 1981.

Kochenderfer, James N., and Patric, James H. "Effects of Clearcutting—Past and Present on Water Resources of the Monongahela National Forest." *West Virginia Agriculture and Forestry* 3 (1970):4–11.

Kraft, Gerald et al. *The Role of Transportation in Regional Economic Development*. Lexington, Mass.: Lexington Books, 1971.

Kurath, Hans. *A Word Geography of the Eastern United States*. Ann Arbor: University of Michigan Press, 1949.

LaFarge, Oliver. "Myths that Hide the American Indian." *American Heritage* 7 (1956):4–19.

Laing, James T. "The Negro Miner in West Virginia." *Social Forces* 14 (1936):416–422.

Lee, Everett S. "A Theory of Migration." *Demography* 3 (1966):45–57.

Leighton, George R. *America's Growing Pains: The Romance, Comedy, and Tragedy of Five Great Cities*. New York: Harper and Brothers, 1939.

Leinbach, Thomas R. *Transportation and Development Issues*. Englewood Cliffs, N.J.: Prentice-Hall, forthcoming.

Lewis, Helen M.; Johnson, Linda; and Askins, Donald. *Colonialism in Modern America: The Appalachian Case*. Boone, N.C.: Appalachian Consortium Press, 1978.

Lewis, Helen M., and Knipe, Edward E. "The Colonialism Model: The Appalachian Case." In *Colonialism in Modern America: The Appalachian Case*, edited by Helen M. Lewis, Linda Johnson, and Donald Askins. Boone, N.C.: Appalachian Consortium Press, 1978.

Lewis, Peirce F. "Small Town in Pennsylvania." *Annals*, Association of American Geographers, 62 (1972):323–351.

Lewis, Peirce, and Marsh, Ben. "Slices Through Time: The Physical and Cultural Landscapes of Central and Eastern Pennsylvania." In *The Philadelphia Region: Selected Essays and Field Trip Itineraries*, edited by Roman A. Cybriwsky. Washington, D.C.: Association of American Geographers, 1979.

Leyburn, James G. *The Scotch-Irish: A Social History*. Chapel Hill: University of North Carolina Press, 1962.

Lichter, Daniel, and Fuguitt, Glen V. "Demographic Response to Transportation Innovation: The Case of the Interstate Highway." *Social Forces* 59 (1980):492–512.

Lin, King. *Coal Data 1978*. Washington, D.C.: National Coal Assn., 1980.

Locklin, Philip. *Economics of Transportation*. 7th ed. Homewood, Ill.: Richard D. Irvin, 1972.

Lonsdale, Richard E., and Seyler, H. L. *Nonmetropolitan Industrialization*. New York: Winston Halsted, 1979.

Looff, David H. *Appalachia's Children: The Challenge of Mental Health*. Lexington: University Press of Kentucky, 1971.

Lowenthal, David. "Tourists and Thermalists." *Geographical Review* 52 (1962):124–127.

Lyons, William W. "Attracting Investment in Recreation and Travel." *Appalachia* 3 (1970):6–10.

McCoy, Clyde B., and Brown, James S. "Appalachian Migration to Midwestern Cities." In *The Invisible Minority: Urban Appalachians*, edited by William

W. Philliber and Clyde B. McCoy. Lexington: University Press of Kentucky, 1981.

McGregor, John, and Maxey, Robert H. "The Dalton, Georgia, Tufted Textile Concentration." *Southeastern Geographer* 14 (1974):133–144.

Malizia, Emil. "Economic Imperialism: An Interpretation of Appalachian Underdevelopment." *Appalachian Journal* 1 (1973):130–137.

Mangus, Arthur R. *Rural Regions of the United States.* Washington, D.C.: Government Printing Office, 1940.

Marschner, Francis J. *Boundaries and Records in the Territory of Early Settlement from Canada to Florida.* Washington, D.C.: Agricultural Research Service, 1960.

Mathews, Lois K. *The Expansion of New England.* New York: Houghton Mifflin Co., 1909.

Mayer, Jonathan. "Local and Commuter Airlines in the United States." *Traffic Quarterly* 31 (1977):333–350.

Mead, Margaret. "Outdoor Recreation in the Context of Emerging American Cultural Values: Background Considerations." In *Trends in American Living and Outdoor Recreation.* Study Report 22. Washington, D.C.: Outdoor Recreation Resources Review Commission, 1962.

Meinig, D. W. "Geography of Expansion, 1785–1855." In *Geography of New York State,* edited by John H. Thompson. Syracuse, N.Y.: Syracuse University Press, 1966.

Merk, Frederick. *History of the Westward Movement.* New York: Alfred A. Knopf, 1978.

Miernyk, William H. "The Tools of Regional Development Policy." *Growth and Change* 11 (1980):2–6.

Miller, E. Willard. *A Geography of Manufacturing.* Englewood Cliffs, N.J.: Prentice-Hall, 1962.

———. "Mining and Economic Revitalization of the Bituminous Coal Region of Appalachia." *Southeastern Geographer* 18 (1978):81–92.

———. "Manufacturing in Nonmetropolitan Pennsylvania." Report issued by the Dept. of Commerce, Commonwealth of Pennsylvania, Harrisburg, 1980.

Miller, James P. "Interstate Highways and Job Growth in Nonmetropolitan Areas: A Reassessment." *Transportation Journal* 19 (1979):78–81.

Mitchell, Robert D. "The Shenandoah Valley Frontier." *Annals,* Association of American Geographers, 62 (1972):461–486.

———. *Commercialism and Frontier: Perspectives on the Early Shenandoah Valley.* Charlottesville: University Press of Virginia, 1977.

Morris, John W. "The Potential of Tourism." In *The Southern Appalachian Region: A Survey,* edited by Thomas R. Ford. Lexington: University of Kentucky Press, 1967.

Morrison, Joel L.; Scripter, Morton W.; and Smith, Robert H. T. "Basic Measures of Manufacturing in the United States, 1958." *Economic Geography* 44 (1958):296–311.

Morrison, Peter A., and Wheeler, Judith P. "Rural Renaissance in America?" *Population Bulletin* 31 (1976):1–26.

Moseley, Malcolm J. *Accessibility: The Rural Challenge.* London: Methuen, 1979.

Munro, John M. "Planning the Appalachian Development Highway System:

Some Critical Questions." *Land Economics* 45 (1969):149–161.

Murphy, Raymond E., and Murphy, Marion. *Pennsylvania: A Regional Geography*. Harrisburg: Pennsylvania Book Service, 1937.

Murray, Judith Buckley. *Appalachian Trail Users in the Southern National Forests: Their Characteristics, Attitudes, and Management Preferences*. Forest Service Research Paper SE-116. Washington, D.C.: U.S. Dept. of Agriculture, 1974.

National Area Development Institute, Lexington, Kentucky. *Meeting Rural Transportation Needs*. Prepared for the Committee on Agriculture and Forestry, U.S. Senate, 94th Cong., 1st session, February 10, 1975 (Washington, D.C.: U.S. Government Printing Office, 1975).

Neff, Jeffrey W. "A Geographic Analysis of the Characteristics and Development Trends of the Non-Metropolitan Tourist-Recreation Industry of Southern Appalachia." Ph.D. dissertation, Department of Geography, University of Tennessee, 1975.

Nevel, Robert L., Jr., and Bores, James T. *Northeastern Pulpwood, 1979: An Annual Assessment of Regional Timber Output*. Forest Service Resource Bulletin NE-67. Broomall, Pa.: Northeastern Forest Experiment Station, 1981.

"The New Appalachian Subregions and Their Development Strategies." *Appalachia* 8 (1974):10–27.

Newman, Anne. "The Recruiters and the Recruited: How One Town Filled an Industrial Park." *Appalachia* 15 (1981):6–19.

Newman, Monroe. "The Future of Multistate Regional Commissions." *Growth and Change* 11 (1980):14–18.

Newton, Milton. "Cultural Preadaptation and the Upland South." In *Man and Cultural Heritage,* vol. 5, *Geoscience and Man*, edited by H. J. Walker and W. G. Haag. Baton Rouge: Louisiana State University Press, 1974.

Otto, J. S., and Anderson, N. E. "Slash-and-Burn Cultivation in the Highland South: A Problem in Comparative Agricultural History." *Comparative Studies in Society and History* 24 (1982):131–147.

Paterson, J. H. *North America: A Geography of the United States and Canada*. New York: Oxford University Press, 1975.

Patric, James H. *Some Environmental Effects of Cable Logging in Appalachian Forests*. Forest Service General Technical Report NE-55. Upper Darby, Pa.: Northeastern Forest Experiment Station, 1980.

Philliber, William W., and McCoy, Clyde B., editors. *The Invisible Minority: Urban Appalachians*. Lexington: University Press of Kentucky, 1981.

Phillips, Kevin R. *The Emerging Republican Majority*. Garden City, N.Y.: Doubleday & Co., 1970.

Photiadis, John D. *Social and Socialpsychological Characteristics of West Virginians in Their Own State and in Cleveland, Ohio*. Morgantown: West Virginia University, 1970.

Photiadis, John, and Maurer, B. B. *Religion in an Appalachian State*. Appalachian Center Research Report no. 6. Morgantown: West Virginia University, 1974.

Pickard, Jerome P. "An Analysis of Regional Structure in Appalachia." Manuscript.

———. "Appalachia's Decade of Change—A Decade of Immigration." *Appalachia* 15 (1981):24–28.

———. "A Decade of Change for Appalachia, 1970–1980." *Appalachia* 14 (1981):1–9.

Porter, Frank W. "From Back Country to County: The Delayed Settlement of Western Maryland." *Maryland Historical Magazine* 70 (1975):329–349.

Powell, H. Benjamin. "The Pennsylvania Anthracite Industry." *Pennsylvania History* 47 (1980):3–28.

Powell, John Wesley. *Physiographic Regions of the United States.* New York: American Book Co., 1895.

President's Appalachian Regional Commission (P.A.R.C.). *Appalachia.* Washington, D.C.: Government Printing Office, 1964.

Price, Edward T. "The Melungeons: A Mixed-Blood Strain of the Southern Appalachians." *Geographical Review* 41 (1951):251–271.

———. "The Central Courthouse Square in the American County Seat." *Geographical Review* 58 (1968):29–60.

Primack, Phil. "Hidden Traps of Regionalism." In *Colonialism in Modern America: The Appalachian Case,* edited by Helen M. Lewis, Linda Johnson, and Donald Askins. Boone, N.C.: Appalachian Consortium Press, 1978.

Prpic, George J. "The Croatian Immigrants in Pittsburgh." In *The Ethnic Experience in Pennsylvania,* edited by John E. Bodnar. Lewisburg, Pa.: Bucknell University Press, 1973.

Prunty, Merle C., and Aiken, Charles S. "The Demise of the Piedmont Cotton Region." *Annals,* Association of American Geographers, 62 (1972):283–306.

Quittmeyer, Charles L., and Thompson, Lorin A. "The Development of Manufacturing." In *The Southern Appalachian Region: A Survey,* edited by Thomas R. Ford. Lexington: University of Kentucky Press, 1962.

Ragatz, Richard Lee. "Vacation Homes in the Northeastern United States: Seasonality in Population Distribution." *Annals,* Association of American Geographers, 60 (1970):447–455.

Raitz, Karl, and Ulack, Richard. "Appalachian Vernacular Regions." *Journal of Cultural Geography* 2 (1981):106–119.

———. "Cognitive Maps of Appalachia." *Geographical Review* 71 (1981):201–213.

Raitz, Karl; Ulack, Richard; and Cromley, Robert. "An Automated Method for Cognitive Map Analysis." *Cartographia* 18 (1981):36–50.

Ravenstein, E. G. "The Laws of Migration." *Journal of the Royal Statistical Study* 47 (1885):167–227.

Rayback, Robert. "The Indian." In *Geography of New York State,* edited by John H. Thompson. Syracuse, N.Y.: Syracuse University Press, 1966.

Resource Planning Associates. *Transportation Development Program for Appalachia.* Washington, D.C.: ARC, 1974.

Rice, Otis K. *The Allegheny Frontier: West Virginia Beginnings, 1730–1830.* Lexington: University Press of Kentucky, 1970.

Riddel, Frank J., editor. *Appalachia: Its People, Heritage, and Problems.* Dubuque, Ia.: Kendall/Hunt Publishing Co., 1974.

Ringle, Ken. "Land Rush Changes Massanutten Rural Life." *Washington Post,* (Sept. 4, 1973):A1, A14.

Rodechko, James. "Irish-American Society in the Pennsylvania Anthracite Region: 1870–1880." In *The Ethnic Experience in Pennsylvania,* edited by John E. Bodnar. Lewisburg, Pa.: Bucknell University Press, 1973.

Rothblatt, Donald N. *Regional Planning: The Appalachian Experience.* Lexington, Mass.: D. C. Heath and Co., 1971.

Ryan, Bruce. "The Criteria for Selecting Growth Centers in Appalachia."

*Proceedings,* Association of American Geographers, 2 (1970):118–123.

Sadie, Stanley. *The New Grove Dictionary of Music and Musicians.* London: Macmillan, 1980.

Sale, Randall D., and Karn, Edwin D. *American Expansion: A Book of Maps.* Homewood, Ill.: Dorsey Press, 1962.

Schmudde, Theodore H. "The Making of Recreational Places in East Tennessee." In *Planning Frontiers in Rural America,* edited by Ole Gade. Washington, D.C.: Papers of the Boone Conference, U.S. Senate Committee on Agriculture and Forestry, 1976.

Schneider, William J. et al. *Water Resources of the Appalachian Region: Pennsylvania to Alabama.* Pub. HA-198. Washington, D.C.: U.S. Geological Survey, 1965.

Schwarzweller, Harry K.; Brown, James S.; and Mangalam, J. J. *Mountain Families in Transition: A Case Study of Appalachian Migration.* University Park: Pennsylvania State University Press, 1971.

Semple, Ellen Churchill. "The Anglo-Saxons of the Kentucky Mountains: A Study in Anthropogeography." *Geographical Journal* 17 (1901): 588–623.

________. *American History and Its Geographic Conditions.* New York: Houghton, Mifflin, and Co., 1903.

Shands, William E., and Woodson, Patricia. *The Subdivision of Virginia's Mountains.* Rev. ed. Washington, D.C.: Central Atlantic Environmental Center, 1974.

Shaw, Earl B. *Anglo-America: A Regional Geography.* New York: John Wiley & Sons, 1959.

Shawcroft, Robert. "The Role of Highways in Regional Development: A Review of the Appalachian Highway System and Case Study of West Virginia." Department of Geography, University of Washington, 1977. Paper.

Shelley, Fred M., and Roseman, Curtis C. "Migration Patterns Leading to Population Change in the Nonmetropolitan South." *Growth and Change* 9 (1978):14–23.

Smith, David M. *Industrial Location: An Economic Geographical Approach.* New York: John Wiley & Sons, 1971.

Smith, J. Russell, and Phillips, M. Ogden. *North America: Its People and the Resources, Development, and Prospects of the Continent as the Home of Man.* New York: Harcourt, Brace and Co., 1940.

Smith, T. Lynn. "The Emergence of Cities." In *The Urban South,* edited by Rupert B. Vance and Nicholas J. Demersth. Chapel Hill: University of North Carolina Press, 1954.

Spinelli, Michael Ambrose. "A Definition of the Economic Subregions of Appalachia Using Factor Analysis." Ph.D. dissertation, Department of Economics, West Virginia University, 1971.

Stearns, Norah D.; Stearns, Harold T.; and Waring, Gerald A. *Thermal Springs in the United States.* Water-Supply Paper 679-B. Washington, D.C.: U.S. Geological Survey, 1937.

Stephenson, John B. *Shiloh: A Mountain Community.* Lexington: University of Kentucky Press, 1968.

Strahler, Alan H. "Forests of the Fairfax Line." *Annals,* Association of American Geographers, 62 (1972):664–684.

Strahler, Arthur N., and Strahler, Alan H. *Geography and Man's Environment.* New York: John Wiley & Sons, 1977.

Stroud, Hubert B. "Amenity Land Developments as an Element of Geographic Change: A Case Study." Ph.D. dissertation, Department of Geography, University of Tennessee, 1974.

Taylor, James W. *Alleghania: A Geographical and Statistical Memoir.* St. Paul: James Davenport, 1862.

Thompson, John H., ed. *Geography of New York State.* Syracuse, N.Y.: Syracuse University Press, 1966.

Thornbury, William D. *Regional Geomorphology of the United States.* New York: John Wiley & Sons, 1965.

Tooker, Elizabeth. "Iroquois Since 1820." *Handbook of North American Indians.* Vol. 15, *Northeast.* Washington, D.C.: Smithsonian Institution, 1978.

Trigger, Bruce G. "Early Iroquoian Contacts with Europeans." *Handbook of North American Indians.* Vol. 15, *Northeast.* Washington, D.C.: Smithsonian Institution, 1978.

Trimble, George P. et al. *Some Options for Managing Forest Land in the Central Appalachians.* Forest Service General Technical Report NE-12. Upper Darby, Pa.: Northeastern Forest Experiment Station, 1974.

Trimble, Stanley W. *Man-Induced Soil Erosion on the Southern Piedmont, 1700–1970.* Milwaukee: Soil Conservation Society of America, 1974.

Turner, Frederick Jackson. *Frontier and Section: Selected Essays of Frederick Jackson Turner.* Englewood Cliffs, N.J.: Prentice-Hall, 1961.

Turner, William. "A Demographic Profile of Blacks in Appalachia: Selected Social and Economic Characteristics." Department of Sociology, University of Kentucky, 1982. Manuscript.

Ulack, Richard, and Raitz, Karl. "Appalachia: A Comparison of the Cognitive and Appalachian Regional Commission Regions." *Southeastern Geographer* 21 (1981):40–53.

———. "Perceptions of Appalachia." *Environment and Behavior* 14 (1982):725–752.

U.S. Bureau of Agricultural Economics. *Economic and Social Problems and Conditions of Southern Appalachians.* Misc. Pub. no. 205. Washington, D.C.: U.S. Dept. of Agriculture, 1935.

U.S. Bureau of the Census. *Census of Housing: 1980.* Vol. 1, *Characteristics of Housing Units.* Washington, D.C.: Bureau of the Census, 1983.

———. *Census of Housing: 1950.* Vol. 1, *General Characteristics.* Washington, D.C.: Bureau of the Census, 1953.

———. *Census of Housing: 1970.* Washington, D.C.: Bureau of the Census, 1972.

———. *Census of Population: 1950.* Vol. 2, *Characteristics of the Population.* Washington, D.C.: Bureau of the Census, 1952.

———. *Census of Population: 1970.* Vol. 1, *Characteristics of the Population.* Washington, D.C.: Bureau of the Census, 1973.

———. *Census of Population: 1970, Current Population Reports, Series P-25.* Washington, D.C.: Bureau of the Census, 1972.

———. *Census of Population: 1970.* Subject Reports, Final Report PC (2)-2E, *Migration Between State Economic Areas.* Washington, D.C.: Government Printing Office, 1972.

———. *County Business Patterns, 1978.* Washington, D.C.: Government Printing Office, 1980.

———. *1958 Census of Mineral Industries.* Vol. 2, *Area Statistics.* Washington, D.C.: Bureau of the Census, 1961.

_______. *1959 Census of Agriculture.* Vol. 1, *Counties.* Washington, D.C.: Bureau of the Census, 1961.

_______. *1978 Census of Agriculture.* Vol. 1, *State and County Data.* Washington, D.C.: Bureau of the Census, 1980.

_______. *U.S. Census of Manufacturers, 1958.* Vol. 3, *Area Statistics.* Washington, D.C.: Bureau of the Census, 1961.

_______. *U.S. Census of Manufacturers, 1977.* Geographic Area Series. Washington, D.C.: Bureau of the Census, 1980.

U.S. Bureau of Mines. *Minerals in the Economy of Georgia.* Washington, D.C.: Government Printing Office, 1979.

_______. *Minerals in the Economy of North Carolina.* Washington, D.C.: Government Printing Office, 1979.

_______. *Minerals in the Economy of Pennsylvania.* Washington, D.C.: Government Printing Office, 1979.

_______. *Minerals in the Economy of Tennessee.* Washington, D.C.: Government Printing Office, 1979.

_______. *Minerals Yearbook, 1960,* vol. 2. Washington, D.C.: Government Printing Office, 1960.

U.S. Department of Agriculture. *An Appraisal of North Carolina's Potential for Outdoor Recreation Development.* Raleigh N.C.: Soil Conservation Service, 1975.

_______. *Economic and Social Problems and Conditions of the Southern Appalachians.* Misc. Pub. no. 205. Washington, D.C.: Department of Agriculture, 1935.

_______. Economic Research Service. *Transportation in Rural America.* Washington, D.C.: Government Printing Office, 1975.

U.S. Department of Energy. *Bituminous Coal Production in 1978.* Washington, D.C.: Government Printing Office, 1980.

U.S. Department of Interior, Bureau of Outdoor Recreation. *Report for Development of Water Resources in Appalachia.* Appendix F, "Recreation and Aesthetics." Atlanta, Ga.: 1968.

U.S. Geological Survey. *Mineral Resources of the Appalachian Region.* Professional Paper no. 580. Washington, D.C.: U.S. Geological Survey, 1968.

U.S. House of Representatives. *Recreation Development of the Tennessee River System.* Washington, D.C.: 76th Congress, 3rd Session, 1940, Document no. 565.

Van Noppen, Ina W., and Van Noppen, John J. *Western North Carolina Since the Civil War.* Boone, N.C.: Appalachian Consortium Press, 1973.

Wallach, Bret. "The Slighted Mountains of Upper East Tennessee." *Annals,* Association of American Geographers, 71 (1981):359–373.

Walls, David S. "Central Appalachia: A Peripheral Region Within an Advanced Capitalist Society." *Journal of Sociology and Social Welfare* 4 (1976):232–246.

_______. "On the Naming of Appalachia." In *An Appalachian Symposium: Essays Written in Honor of Cratis D. Williams,* edited by J. W. Williamson. Boone, N.C.: Appalachian State University Press, 1977.

_______. "Internal Colony or Internal Periphery? A Critique of Current Models and an Alternative Formulation." In *Colonialism in Modern America: The Appalachian Case,* edited by Helen M. Lewis, Linda Johnson, and Donald Askins. Boone, N.C.: Appalachian Consortium Press, 1978.

Walls, David S., and Billings, Dwight B. "The Sociology of Southern Appalachia." *Appalachian Journal* 5 (1977):131–144.

Warren, Kenneth. *The American Steel Industry, 1860–1970: A Geographical Interpretation.* Oxford: Clarendon Press, 1973.

Warzeski, Walter C. "The Rusin Community in Pennsylvania." In *The Ethnic Experience in Pennsylvania,* edited by John E. Bodnar. Lewisburg, Pa.: Bucknell University Press, 1973.

Watson, Mary Keys. "The Recreational Real Estate Market in Rural Property." *Journal of Leisure Research* 11 (1979):15–27.

Watts, Ann DeWitt. "Does the Appalachian Regional Commission Really Represent a Region?" *Southeastern Geographer* 18 (1978):19–36.

Weatherford, W. D., editor. *Religion in the Appalachian Mountains.* Berea, Ky.: Berea College, 1955.

Weber, Michael P. "Occupational Mobility of Ethnic Minorities in Nineteenth-Century Warren, Pennsylvania." In *The Ethnic Experience in Pennsylvania,* edited by John E. Bodnar. Lewisburg, Pa.: Bucknell University Press, 1973.

Weiss, Robert A. "The Distribution of Benefits of the Appalachian Development Highway System." Ph.D. dissertation, Department of Economics, University of Wisconsin, 1972.

Weller, Jack E. *Yesterday's People: Life in Contemporary Appalachia.* Lexington: University of Kentucky Press, 1965.

Wells, John Calhoun, Jr. "Poverty Amidst Riches: Why People Are Poor in Appalachia." Ph.D. dissertation, Department of Urban Planning and Policy Development, Rutgers University, 1977.

Wertenbaker, Thomas J. *The Founding of American Civilization: The Middle Colonies.* New York: Charles Scribners & Sons, 1938.

Wheeler, James O. "Regional Manufacturing Structure in the Southeastern United States, 1973." *Southeastern Geographer* 14 (1974):67–83.

Wheeler, James O., and Muller, Peter O. *Economic Geography.* New York: John Wiley & Sons, 1981.

Wheeler, Jesse H., Jr. *Land Use in Greenbrier County, West Virginia.* Department of Geography Research Paper no. 15. Chicago: University of Chicago, 1950.

Whisnant, David E. *Modernizing the Mountaineer: People, Power, and Planning in Appalachia.* New York: Burt Franklin & Co., 1980.

White, C. Langdon et al. *Regional Geography of Anglo-America.* 5th ed. Englewood Cliffs, N.J.: Prentice-Hall, 1979.

White, David. "The Coal Export Gamble." *Fortune* 104 (1981):122–136.

Widner, Ralph, editor. *Forests and Forestry in the American States.* Washington, D.C.: National Association of State Foresters, 1968.

Williams, Cratis. "Moonshining in the Mountains." *North Carolina Folklore* 15 (1967):11–17.

———. "Who Are the Southern Mountaineers?" *Appalachian Journal* 1 (1972):48–55.

Willis, Bailey. "The Northern Appalachians." *National Geographic Monographs,* no. 6. New York: American Book Co., 1895.

Wilms, Douglas C. "Cherokee Settlement Patterns in Nineteenth Century Georgia." *Southeastern Geographer* 14 (1974):46–53.

Wilson, George. "Towards a Theory of Transport and Development." In *Transport and Development,* edited by B. S. Hoyle. London: Macmillan, 1973.

Wolfe, Thomas. *Look Homeward Angel.* New York: Charles Scribners & Sons, 1929.

Woodruff, James F. "Debris Avalanches as an Erosional Agent in the Appalachian Mountains." *Journal of Geography* 70 (1971):399–406.

Zelinsky, Wilbur. "Where the South Begins: The Northern Limit of the Cis-Appalachian South in Terms of Settlement Landscape." *Social Forces* 30 (1951):172–178.

_______. "An Approach to the Religious Geography of the United States: Patterns of Church Membership in 1952." *Annals,* Association of American Geographers, 51 (1961):139–193.

_______. *The Cultural Geography of the United States.* Englewood Cliffs, N.J.: Prentice-Hall, 1973.

_______. "The Pennsylvania Town: An Overdue Geographical Account." *Geographical Review* 67 (1977):127–147.

_______. "Is Nonmetropolitan America Being Repopulated? The Evidence from Pennsylvania's Minor Civil Divisions." *Demography* 15 (1978):13–39.

# INDEX

Acadian orogeny, 41
Acid mine drainage. *See* Coal, and water pollution
Acid soils, 63
Acid water, 213, 215
ADHS. *See* Appalachian Development Highway System
Adirondack Mountains, 11, 42, 69(fig.)
Ages Creek (Ky.), 229
Agriculture, 3, 16, 23, 24, 32, 39, 72, 84, 100–101, 178, 189, 271
  commercial, 208–211
  crops, 204(table), 205–208. *See also individual crops*
  farm size, 199, 200(table), 201, 202, 204(table), 205
  farm types, 115–116, 124–125, 205, 210–211
  income, 210, 212(fig.)
  Indian, 89, 91, 190
  and land values, 202–203, 205
  modernization, 146, 201, 205, 211
  and precipitation, 56
  production, 201, 204(table), 210–211
  sharecropping, 205
  and soils, 63, 65, 210
  specialization, 101, 199
  *See also* Livestock; *under individual states*
Agriculture, Department of, 19, 23, 26, 135, 339
Aiken, Charles S., 205, 207
Airline deregulation (1978), 326, 328
Akron (Ohio), 328
Alabama, 2, 11, 14, 19, 23, 32(table), 109
  ADHS, 307, 308(table), 309
  agriculture, 205, 210
  Blacks in, 180
  caves, 49
  coal, 50, 51, 129, 214(table), 216, 220(table), 223(table), 226(table)
  counties, 152(table)
  electricity, 214(table), 216
  forests, 72
  iron ore, 75
  land ownership, 344(table)
  manufacturing, 278(table), 288–290, 292(table), 293, 298
  minerals, 73, 75
  in Piedmont Province, 43
  population, 152(table), 158(table), 163, 180
  pulp and paper, 195, 197(table)
  railroads, 310–311(tables), 314, 315(table), 316
  religions, 135
  in Ridge and Valley Province, 46, 48, 49
  settlement, 95
  SMSAs, 153(fig.)
  soils, 63, 64(fig.)
  Spanish-origin population in, 183(table)
  temperature, 52(fig.), 53
  thunderstorms, 56
  tourism, 258(table), 259
  water, 213
Alanen, Arnold R., 261
Albany (N.Y.), 4(fig.), 89
Albemarle County (Va.), 173, 176
Alcoa (Tenn.), 298
Alfalfa, 205
Alfisols, 63, 64(fig.), 65
Algonquin Indians, 87, 88(fig.), 89
Alkaline water, 213
Allegany County (Md.), 197
Alleghany County (Va.), 197, 211, 239
Alleghenian orogeny. *See* Appalachian orogeny
Allegheny, 23
*Allegheny,* 11
Allegheny County (Pa.), 178, 182, 183(table), 195, 222, 295, 297(fig.)
Allegheny-Cumberland Plateaus, 19
Allegheny Front, 49–50, 51, 67, 70, 94

Allegheny Mountains, 50, 51, 56, 67, 69(fig.), 70, 191
Allegheny Plateaus, 11, 50, 56, 67, 68, 69(fig.), 70, 71, 235, 242
Allegheny River, 60, 61(fig.), 97(illus.), 107, 127, 324(table)
Allentown (Pa.), 49, 153(fig.), 154(table), 170(table), 272(table), 288, 289(table)
Alluvial valleys, 60, 98, 136
Altamaha River, 61(fig.), 63
Altoona (Pa.), 180
Aluminum, 298
  clay, 65
American (airline), 325
Amish, 48, 115, 130
Anabaptists, 138
Anderson, James R., 207
Anderson County (Tenn.), 176
Anthracite Region, 49
Anticlines, 79, 239
Antrim (Pa.), 116
Apalachee Indians, 11
Apalachicola River, 61(fig.), 62
Appalachia
  air service, 325–329
  Asians in, 182
  attitudes toward, 145–146
  birth rate, 159
  Blacks in, 2, 22, 129–130, 178–182
  boundaries, 2, 9, 16, 17(fig.), 18, 29, 30–32
  climates, 2, 39, 51–56
  cognitive outsiders, 28(fig.), 29
  counties, 32(table), 151, 161–162(figs.), 163, 173
  cultural diversity, 1, 2–3, 19, 22, 29, 33, 113, 117, 127, 143, 145–146, 184, 341–342
  cultural hearths, 113, 114(fig.)
  dams, 62, 235, 347, 348. *See also* Slag dams
  death rate, 159
  developed zone of stagnation, 353
  development, 1–2, 3, 40, 171, 244–267, 303–304, 309, 319–320, 325, 328–329, 330–331, 335–336, 339, 346–354
  diets, 1
  disease, 238
  drainage, 2, 39, 46, 48, 58(table), 59–60, 70
  economy, 1, 3, 24, 32, 100–109, 165, 178, 189, 343. *See also* Agriculture; Lumber; Mining; *individual industries*
  education, 176–178
  electricity, 214(table), 215–217, 347
  ethnic groups, 3, 178, 182–184, 336. *See also* Indians; *individual states,* settlement
  expanded development zone, 353
  fauna, 72
  fertility rates, 159
  flora, 2
  forests, 65, 67–72, 84, 189, 190–199, 235, 246, 247
  geology, 40–43, 79
  geomorphology, 2
  governmental regionalization, 23–26, 246–251, 336, 346–352
  and government policy, 3
  highways. *See* Appalachian Development Highway System
  income, 172–176
  industrialization, 2, 3, 5, 24, 101, 171, 309
  infrastructure lag, 342–346
  inland sea, 41
  insiders, 28(fig.), 29
  isolation, 3, 22, 337–339
  labor force, 271, 272(table), 274(fig.), 277–281, 289(table), 298, 299, 349
  lakes, 235
  land use, 251–262, 339, 341, 343–345
  land values, 202–203, 263, 264(table), 343
  manufacturing, 271–299
  maps, 4, 10, 12–13, 20
  migration, 155–156, 159–160, 163–171, 178, 180, 184
  mountain ranges, 11, 18, 19, 40–41
  music, 1, 138–140, 141(fig.)
  name origin, 11
  natural resources, 40, 57, 73–84, 189–208, 211–230, 298–299, 336, 339
  perceptions of, 26–29, 341
  physiography, 11, 14–16, 18, 21, 22, 43–51
  population, 1, 3, 32, 151, 152(table), 154(table), 155–166, 178–184, 336–337, 339, 341
  population density, 155, 339, 341
  poverty, 172, 336–346
  precipitation, 39, 53, 55(fig.), 56, 57
  primitive zone, 353
  rail system, 309–320
  recreation, 2, 3, 48, 56, 163, 235–267
  regions, 1, 2, 9, 11–33, 335, 352–354
  religions, 115, 127, 130–136, 178
  reservoirs, 62
  residential outsiders, 28(fig.), 29
  rivers, 58(table), 60–63, 105, 320–324

routes, 62–63, 71, 72, 87, 89, 94–100, 114(fig.), 115, 119, 120(fig.)
rural, 1, 3, 24, 152(table), 158(table), 160, 184, 277, 279(table), 280, 309, 319, 320, 330–331
settlement, 2, 3, 21, 22, 29, 42, 59, 71, 72, 84, 87, 90–100, 113, 115–122, 125, 130, 145
sociocultural regionalizations, 18–22, 119, 121, 125, 130–146, 151, 184, 189, 354
soils, 2, 39–40, 56, 63–65, 66(cutline), 89, 265
speech patterns, 136–138
square miles, 32, 151
states, 151, 152(table). *See also individual states*
subculture, 341–342
subregions, 3, 14, 15(fig.), 335, 353–354
temperature range, 52(fig.), 53
topography, 39, 42, 43–51, 283. *See also* Appalachian Plateaus Province; Blue Ridge Province; Piedmont Province; Ridge and Valley Province
tourism, 3, 46, 48, 163, 236, 238–244
transportation, 3, 39, 62, 101–109, 246, 280, 303–331
unemployment, 165
urban, 1, 3, 24, 32, 101, 102(fig.), 103, 105, 109, 119, 145, 151, 152(table), 153(fig.), 154(table), 155, 158(table), 166, 180, 184, 277, 279(table)
wages, 292
water supply, 39, 40, 57–63, 189, 211, 213–217
Appalachian America, 19
Appalachian Development Highway System (ADHS), 304, 306(fig.), 307–309, 339, 350–351
Appalachian Front, 90, 98, 105, 251
Appalachian Highlands, 14, 47, 56
Appalachian Land Ownership Task Force, 343, 345
Appalachian Mountains, 40–41
Appalachian National Park Association (1899), 247
Appalachian orogeny, 41
Appalachian-Ozark Region, 18
Appalachian Plateaus Province, 14, 15(fig.), 18, 23
agriculture, 146, 198, 299(table), 201, 203
boundaries, 49–50
coal, 51, 82, 217, 229
counties, 156(table)
drainage, 51, 59
electricity, 216
elevations, 50–51
forests, 67, 69(fig.)
geology, 42, 50
lumbering, 192
migration, 51
minerals, 73, 74, 75
population, 156(table)
routes, 98
settlement, 51, 94, 117, 123, 129
steel, 51
topography, 44(fig.), 49–51
urban, 51
water, 213
Appalachian Ranges, 11
Appalachian Regional Commission (ARC), 2, 3, 23–26, 30, 32, 159, 166, 172, 336
and development, 171, 304, 330–331, 337, 339, 349–352
impact, 351–352
regions, 32(table), 184(n1), 335, 352–353
and transportation, 304, 309, 326, 329–330, 350, 351–352
Appalachian Regional Development Act. *See* Public Law 89-4
Appalachian State University (Boone, N.C.), 167
*Appalachia* report (1964), 24
Appalachian Studies Center (U. of Ky.), 5
Appalachian Trail, 251
Appalachian Trail Conference, 251
Apparel industry. *See* Textile industry
ARC. *See* Appalachian Regional Commission
Arizona, 65
Ark. *See* Flat boat
Arkansas, 16, 18, 32
Armagh (Pa.), 116
Armenians, 243
Arnold Engineering Development Center (Tenn.), 176
Asbury, Francis, 133
Ash, 68
Ashe County (N.C.), 60
Asheville (N.C.), 4(fig.), 21, 46, 102(fig.), 107, 109, 167, 168(table), 238, 328
SMSA, 153(fig.)
Asians. *See* Appalachia, Asians in
Association of American Geographers, 14

Atlanta (Ga.), 4(fig.), 16, 32, 45, 102(fig.), 107, 108, 326
income, 172, 176
manufacturing, 272(table), 273, 277, 289(table), 292(table), 295
population, 108, 109, 154(table), 159–160, 167, 168(table), 180, 182
SMSA, 153(fig.), 154(table), 155, 159–160, 163, 172, 176, 182, 272(table), 273, 275, 295
Atlantic Ocean, 57, 58(table), 59, 60
Atlantic Seaboard, 21
Atomic Energy Commission, 348
Atwood, W. W., 14
Augusta (Ga.), 45
Augusta County (Va.), 116, 164(cutline)
Avery County (N.C.), 202, 262

Badin (N.C.), 298
Bagpipe bands, 140
Balds, 71
Balsam, 68
Baltimore, Lord, 19
Baltimore (Md.), 2, 32, 71, 95, 103, 105, 107, 316, 317, 354
Baltimore and Ohio Railroad, 71, 105, 108, 310
Banjo, 140
Banner Elk (N.C.), 263
Baptists, 131(fig.), 132, 133, 134–135, 136
Barge transport, 311, 314, 323
Barley, 205
Barns, 123–124
Barnum, Darold T., 129
Basswood, 68
Bath County (Va.), 239, 242
Beaver County (Pa.), 295
Bedford County (Va.), 260
Bedford Springs (Pa.), 49
Beech, 68, 70, 71, 191
Bell County (Ky.), 203, 222, 223(table), 344(table)
Bellefonte (Pa.), 285
Berea College (Ky.), 34(n17)
Berkeley County (W.Va.), 208
Berks County (Pa.), 183(table)
Berkshire Mountains, 115
Berry, Brian J. L., 339, 342
Bessemer, Henry, 108, 286
Bessemer Steel Process, 219, 286
Beth-Elkhorn Corporation, 222
Bethlehem (Pa.), 288, 289(table)
Bethlehem Steel Corporation, 219, 287
Bibb County (Ala.), 73
Bicarbonates, 213
Big Black Mountain (Ky.), 51
Big Levels, 70
Big Sandy River, 60, 61(fig.), 100, 213
Billings, Dwight, 342, 346
Binghampton (N.Y.), 4(fig.), 51, 103, 153(fig.), 154(table), 272(table), 292(table)
Birch, 70
Birdsall, Stephen S., 16
Birmingham (Ala.), 4(fig.), 21, 23, 32, 49, 75, 79, 102(fig.), 107, 109
manufacturing, 272(table), 288–290, 292(table), 295
population, 109, 154(table), 155, 167
SMSA, 153(fig.), 154(table), 155, 272(table), 295
Bison, 72
Black bears, 72
Blackjack oak, 72
Black oak, 72
Black spruce, 70
Black walnut, 191
Black Warrior coalfield (Ala.), 51
Black Warrior River, 320, 323, 324(table)
Blowing Rock (N.C.), 46, 167, 239
Bluegrass music, 138, 140, 141(fig.)
Bluegrass region. *See under* Kentucky
Blue Ridge frontal scarp, 45, 46
Blue Ridge Mountains, 23, 41, 53, 67, 93, 216, 247
Blue Ridge Parkway, 46, 235, 236(table)
Blue Ridge Province, 1, 14, 15(fig.), 18, 19, 47, 195, 251
agriculture, 146, 198, 200(table), 201, 202, 203
borders, 45–46
counties, 156(table), 167
drainage, 46, 59
elevations, 45, 46
forests, 68, 69(fig.), 71
geology, 41, 73
minerals, 73
national parks, 46
population density, 155, 156(table)
settlement, 100, 123, 129
topography, 44(fig.), 45–46
tourism, 46, 109, 167, 236, 238, 239, 260
urban, 46, 109
water, 213
Bog rosemary, 68
Bogs, 68, 70
Boone, Daniel, 51, 62, 95
Boone (N.C.), 167, 350
Boonesborough (Ky.), 95, 96(fig.)
Bootlegging, 140, 142–143
Borchert, John, 103, 107

Born-again Christians, 135
Boston (Mass.), 107, 326
Bowman, Mary Jean, 337
Braddock's Road, 95, 96(fig.)
Bradford County (Pa.), 210
Bradley, William, 339
Branch plants, 281
Branscome, James, 176, 263
Brass, 79
Brasstown Bald (Ga.), 46
Brethren, Church of the, 130, 132, 135
Brevard (N.C.), 254
Bridges, 330
Brines, 213
Bristol (Tenn.), 4(fig.), 49, 272(table), 289(table), 347
Bristol (Va.), 49, 153(fig.), 154(table)
Broad River, 58(table), 61(fig.), 63
Brownell, Joseph W., 9
Brown's Ferry (Ala.), 348
Brush-fallow. *See* Slash-and-burn
Buckbean, 68
Buckeye, 71. *See also* Sweet buckeye
Buckhannon (W. Va.), 350
Buffalo (N.Y.), 4(fig.), 105
Buffalo Creek (W. Va.), 57, 229
Building methods, 122–124
Buncombe County (N.C.), 238
Burkes Garden (Va.), 49
Burley tobacco, 207, 208(illus.)
Bus transportation, 331

Cabbage, 207
Calcium magnesium chloride, 213
Calcium sulfate, 213, 239
California, 65, 170(table)
Calvinist doctrine, 133, 135
Cambrian limestone, 79
Cambria steel plant (Johnstown, Pa.), 219
Campbell, John C., 19, 20(fig.), 336
Campbell County (Tenn.), 222, 223(table), 344(table)
Canada, 11, 16, 42, 46, 198
Canals, 62, 103, 105, 108
C&O. *See* Chesapeake and Ohio Railway
Cannon County (Tenn.), 23
Carbon, 79, 80, 108
Carbonate rocks, 41
Carney, George O., 138
Carolina Piedmont, 45, 95, 98, 109, 119, 129, 133, 195, 207, 236
Carolina Regulators, 90
Carolina slate belt, 41
Cartersville fault line, 45
Cashiers (N.C.), 239
Cataract. *See* Great Falls
Catawba County (N.C.), 194, 295, 296(fig.)
Catawba River, 58(table), 63
Catholics, 130, 131(fig.), 132
Catskill Mountain House (N.Y.), 243
Catskill Mountains, 30, 32, 42, 50, 98, 115, 163, 183, 236, 237(fig.), 242–244
Cattaraugus County (N.Y.), 183(table)
Cattle, 101, 204(table), 205
  beef, 210, 211
Caudill, Harry M., 337, 343, 348
Caves, 49
Cayuga Indians, 87, 88(fig.)
Celtic dispersed farm, 115, 125
Cement, 73
Cementon (Pa.), 73
Census, Bureau of the, 19, 166, 203, 353
*Census of Agriculture,* 201, 208
*Census of Manufacturers,* 275
Central Appalachian subregion, 24, 25(fig.), 343
Centralia (Pa.), 228
Central Lowland, 14, 50
Centre County (Pa.), 176, 182, 195
Chalcopyrite, 75
Charcoal, 71, 75, 190–191, 286
Charleston (S.C.), 4(fig.), 21, 32, 51, 102, 105, 107, 119
Charleston (W. Va.), 4(fig.), 60, 153(table), 180
Charles Town–Harpers Ferry development (W. Va.), 262
Charlotte (N.C.), 4(fig.), 16, 32, 45, 109, 153(fig.), 154(table), 163, 167, 168(table), 292(table)
Charlottesville (Va.), 173
Chattahoochee River, 58(table), 61(fig.), 62, 107
Chattanooga (Tenn.), 4(fig.), 21, 32, 49, 102(fig.), 107–108, 109, 153(fig.), 154(table), 163, 272(table), 289(table), 292(table), 326, 347
Chautaugua County (N.Y.), 30
Cheat River, 100
Chemical Valley, 60
Cherokee (N.C.), 46, 91, 254, 257
Cherokee County (N.C.), 183(table)
Cherokee Indians, 75, 88(fig.), 90–91, 100, 182, 254
Cherokee Lake, 62
Cherokee National Forest (Tenn.), 198
Chesapeake and Ohio Canal Company (1827), 105

Chesapeake and Ohio Railway (C&O), 71, 242, 310, 318
Chesapeake Bay, 21, 60, 62, 317
Chessie System, 310, 311, 312(fig.), 317
Chestnut, 68, 71, 72, 109
Chestnut oak, 71
Chicago (Ill.), 167, 168, 169(table), 326, 354
  Uptown neighborhood, 165
Chillicothe (Ohio), 43
Chilton County (Ala.), 73
Chimneys, 123
Chlorination, 213
Cholera, 238, 242
Churches of Christ, 134
Church of God, 132, 135, 138
Cincinnati (Ohio), 4(fig.), 30, 165, 166, 168, 169(table), 354
  Over-the-Rhine neighborhood, 135, 165
Civil War, 22, 108
Clarion County (Pa.), 181(fig.), 223(table)
Clay, 63, 65. *See also* Stone, clay, and glass industry
Clay County (Ky.), 173, 174(fig.)
Clay County (N.C.), 260
Clayton (Ga.), 239
Clayton County (Ga.), 277, 278(fig.)
Clearfield-Dubois (Pa.), 350
Cleburne County (Ala.), 210
Cleveland (Ohio), 4(fig.), 165, 354
Clinchfield (RR). *See* CSX Corporation
Clinch River, 48, 60, 61(fig.), 215(cutline)
Clingmans Dome (Tenn.), 46
Coal, 22, 24, 32, 75, 79–82, 83(illus.), 108, 189, 282(table), 283, 285(table), 286, 343, 345, 354
  and air pollution, 316–317, 348
  anthracite, 49, 78(fig.), 79–80, 81(illus.), 107, 126, 169, 217, 218(table), 219, 223–224, 228
  bituminous, 42, 50, 51, 78(fig.), 79, 82, 83(illus.), 107, 217, 218(table), 219, 220, 222, 223(table), 224, 226(table), 228–229, 287, 346
  deposits, 41, 42, 49, 78(fig.), 79, 82, 219, 224, 228
  and electric power, 214(table), 219, 348
  exports, 316–318
  fires, 228
  and forests, 197, 198
  mechanization, 165, 219
  mine explosion (1907), 127
  miners, 126–127, 129–130, 183, 219–220, 221(fig.), 223(table)
  production, 217, 218(fig.), 219, 220, 222, 226(table)
  quality, 227–228, 316–317
  technology, 224, 227–228, 229
  transportation, 217, 219, 228, 311, 314, 315–318, 323, 324, 329–330
  and unionization, 126, 129
  and water pollution, 57, 84, 213, 214
Coal Mine Safety Act (1969), 223
Clover, 205
Coastal Plain, 43, 45, 50
Coffee County (Tenn.), 176, 210
Coke, 286
Coke blast furnaces, 287
Columbia (S.C.), 16, 45
Columbus (Ohio), 135, 165, 168, 169(table)
Commercial cluster, 254–257
Commercial farms, 208–211
Conemaugh River, 105
Conemaugh section, 50
Conemaugh Valley, 287
Conglomerate, 41, 42, 48, 74
Congregationalists, 130, 133
Coniferous forests, 63, 65, 68
Connecticut, 92
Connecticut River, 115
Conrail. *See* Consolidated Rail Corporation
Consolidated Rail Corporation (Conrail), 314
Consolidation Coal (company), 316
Coolidge, Calvin, 247, 347
Cooperstown (N.Y.), 350
Coosa Valley, 48
Copper, 75, 76(fig.)
Copper oxide, 79
Corn, 32, 53, 107, 204(table), 205, 207, 208. *See also* Maize
Cornell University (Ithaca, N.Y.), 176
Corner-notching, 123
Corps of Engineers, 235, 267
Cortland County (N.Y.), 210
Cotton, 98, 107, 129, 178, 204(table), 205, 207
  Belt, 65, 129, 197, 207
Council of State Governments, 319
Country music, 138, 140, 141(fig.)
County-seat town, 121–122
County units, 121, 152(table)
Courthouse-town system, 121–122
Coves, 41
Cox, Kevin R., 26
Crab Orchard Mountains, 51
Cranberry, 68

Croats, 126
Crossroads hamlets, 121, 122
Crossville (Tenn.), 51
Crystalline rocks, 45, 239
CSX Corporation (RR), 310–311, 314
Cullman County (Ala.), 210
Culm piles, 228
*Cultural Geography of the United States, The* (Zelinsky), 21
Culture of Poverty model (Lewis), 341
Cumberland (Md.), 95, 102(fig.), 105, 106(illus.)
Cumberland, Lake, 259
Cumberland County (Pa.), 46
Cumberland County (Tenn.), 210, 220, 257
Cumberland Gap, 51, 62, 94, 95, 100
Cumberland Gap National Historical Park (Ky.-Tenn.-Va.), 236(table)
Cumberland Mountains, 50–51, 68, 69(fig.), 70, 84
Cumberland Plateau, 50, 56, 69(fig.), 70, 100, 109
Cumberland River, 58(table), 60, 61(fig.), 94
Cumberland Road, 63, 95, 103
Cumberland Valley, 48, 89, 339
Czechs, 126

Dade County (Ga.), 220
Dahlonega Plateau, 45
Dairy products, 205, 210. *See also* Cattle
Dalton (Ga.), 293
Dauphin County (Pa.), 178
Davidson County (N.C.), 194
Davie County (N.C.), 202
Dawson County (Ga.), 210
Dayton (Ohio), 135, 168, 169(table), 354
Dayton (Tenn.), 350
Deciduous trees, 65, 70
Deer, 72
Deforestation, 190
DeKalb County (Ga.), 173, 174(fig.), 182, 183(table)
Delaware, 207
Delaware County (N.Y.), 175(fig.), 176, 210, 242
Delaware Indians, 88(fig.), 89, 90
Delaware River, 47, 58(table), 61(fig.), 62, 103, 107
Delaware Valley, 21, 115, 116
Delaware Water Gap National Recreation Area (N.J.-Pa.), 236(table)
Delta (airline), 325
Dendritic stream patterns, 59
Derry (Pa.), 116
Des Moines (Ia.), 133
De Soto, Hernando, 11
Detroit (Mich.), 165, 167, 168, 169(table)
Developmental ecology, 2
Devonian period, 41
Diesel engines, 219
Disciples of Christ, 132, 135
Dix, Keith, 343
Dolomite, 213
DOT. *See* Transportation, Department of
Douglas Lake, 62
Dove-tailing, 123
Drumlins, 43
Ducktown (Tenn.), 75
  Desert, 75, 77(illus.)
Dulcimer, 140
Dunkards, 115, 138
Durham (N.C.), 163
Dutch Reformed Church, 133
Dutch settlers, 89, 113
Dystrochrepts, 63

Eastern (airline), 325
Eastern Cherokee Reservation (N.C.), 254
East Europeans, 22, 126
Easton (Pa.), 102(fig.), 153(fig.), 154(table), 272(table), 288, 289(table)
Eastover Mining Company, 229
Ecology. *See* Developmental ecology
Economic Development Administration, 319
Elbert County (Ga.), 295, 298
Elberton granite district (Ga.), 298
Elk, 72
Elk County (Pa.), 211
Elmira (N.Y.), 103, 153(fig.)
Endless Mountains, 48, 84, 98, 115
Energy, Department of, 316
English law, 121
English settlers, 2, 22, 62, 90, 113, 115, 122, 123, 125, 130, 138
Environmental determinism, 39
Environmental Protection Agency (EPA), 348
EPA. *See* Environmental Protection Agency
Episcopalians, 130, 133
Erie, Lake, 108. *See also* Great Lakes
Erie Canal (1825), 103, 105, 108
Erie County (Pa.), 30
Erie Indians, 88(fig.), 89

Erie Lackawanna (RR), 318
Erosion, 43, 45, 63, 79, 84, 192
Estabrook, Arthur H., 336
Estall, Robert, 275
Evans, E. Estyn, 116, 123

Fairfield County (S.C.), 195
Fall Line, 32, 45, 62
Family Lines (RR), 310, 312(fig.)
Faulting, 40, 41, 79
Faults, 51
Feldspar, 109, 295
Fenneman, Nevin M., 14, 30, 32, 43, 46, 47, 50
Fentress County (Tenn.), 220
Fermanagh (Pa.), 116
Ferns, 70
Fiddle, 140
Finger Lakes, 43, 100
Fire Baptized Baptists, 134
Firs, 67, 68, 71
Fiske, John, 336, 337
Flat boat, 101
Flax, 101
Flint River, 58(table), 61(fig.)
Flood-control reservoirs, 260
Floods, 56, 57
Florida, 11, 168–169(tables), 170(table)
Florin, John W., 16
Flour, 107
Flue cured tobacco, 207
Fodder, 65, 204(table)
Folding, 40, 41, 42, 50, 79
Folk music. *See* Appalachia, music
Forbes Road, 95, 96(fig.)
Ford, Thomas R., 19, 20(fig.), 21, 133, 165, 341, 342, 353
Ford Foundation, 19
Forebay barns. *See* Pennsylvania barns
Forest fires, 198
Forest reserves, 246
Forestry, 3, 189, 198–199
Forests. *See under* Appalachia; *individual states*
Forest Service, 251
Forsyth County (Ga.), 172, 182, 210
Forsyth County (N.C.), 132
Fort Dusquesne, 97(illus.)
Fort Pitt, 60, 95, 97(illus.)
Fort Valley (Va.), 259, 262
*Foxfire* project, 135, 145
*Foxfire Book, The,* 145
Frackville (Pa.), 169
"Fragmented neoplantation" system, 205
Franklin County (Va.), 260
Fraser fir, 71
Fraternal clubs, 127
Freight, 101, 103, 105. *See also* Appalachia, transportation; Coal, transportation
French and Indian War (1763), 90, 93
French Broad River, 60, 61(fig.), 98, 348
French Broad Valley, 95
French Huguenots, 113
French settlers, 125
Friedmann, John, 354
Frost, William Goodell, 19, 337
Frost-free period, 53, 54(fig.)
Fruit, 101. *See also* Orchards
Fuller, Stephen Souther, 353
Fulton County (Ga.), 160, 182, 183(table), 222
Fundamentalists, 134–135, 142–143
Furniture, 194–195, 202, 282(table), 283, 284, 285(table), 293, 295, 296(fig.)
Fur trade, 89

Gainesville (Ala.), 323
Gainesville (Ga.), 46
Gant, Oliver, 113
Gaspé Peninsula, 11
Gastil, Raymond D., 21–22
Gatlinburg (Tenn.), 46, 254–257
Gauley River, 43, 60, 61(fig.)
Gauthier, Howard, 351
Genessee country, 100
Genessee Road, 89, 96(fig.)
George III (king of England), 59
Georgia, 14, 16, 19, 23, 29, 32(table), 251
  ADHS, 307, 308(table)
  agriculture, 205, 207, 208, 210
  Asians in, 182
  Blacks in, 178, 179(fig.), 180, 182
  in Blue Ridge Province, 46
  coal, 220, 226(table)
  education, 176
  electricity, 214(table), 216, 217
  fauna, 72
  forests, 68, 72
  gold, 75, 91
  highest peak, 46
  income, 172, 173, 176
  Indians, 75, 91, 183(table)
  manufacturing, 273, 275, 279(table), 284, 292(table), 293, 295–298
  minerals, 73, 75
  orchards, 72
  in Piedmont Province, 43, 45
  population, 152(table), 158(table), 159, 160, 163, 168(table), 180

pulpwood, 197(table)
railroads, 310–311(tables), 315, 316
rural, 152(table), 158(table), 160, 163, 279(table)
SEA, 167, 168(table)
settlement, 75, 94, 98, 100
soils, 64(fig.), 65
Spanish-origin population in, 182, 183(table)
springs, 49
tourism, 239, 258(table), 259–260
urban, 152(table), 153(fig.), 154(table), 155, 158(table), 160, 279(table)
water, 213
Georgia Railroad. *See* CSX Corporation
Georgia Territory, 95
Germans, 243
German settlers, 2, 22, 62, 113, 115, 116, 117, 118(fig.), 119, 121, 122–123, 124, 125, 130, 138
Glacial drift, 42, 213
Glacial till, 63
Glaciation, 42–43, 49, 67
Glades, 70
Glassie, Henry, 123
Glass industry, 74. *See also* Stone, clay, and glass industry
Gneiss, 41
Gold, 75, 76(fig.), 91
Gorges, 60
Gospel music, 138, 140
Gottfried, Robert R., 265
Gout, 242
Graham County (N.C.), 183(table)
Granite, 41, 73, 295, 298
Grazing, 71, 125
Great Falls, 62
Great Lakes, 56, 89, 105, 115, 219, 251
Great Revivals, 133
Great Smoky Mountains, 46, 67, 216, 247, 251
Great Smoky Mountains National Park (N.C.-Tenn.), 46, 71, 167, 235, 236, 248–249, 251, 254
Great Valley, 2, 42, 48, 49, 62, 66(illus.), 93, 98, 103, 201
Great Valley Road, 95, 96(fig.), 100
Greenbrier County (W. Va.), 242
Greenbrier River, 60, 70
Greenbrier Valley, 51
Green County (Ky.), 30
Greene County (N.Y.), 242
Green Mountains, 115
Greensboro (N.C.), 4(fig.), 45, 153(fig.), 154(table), 163, 272(table), 273
Greenville (S.C.), 33, 45, 109, 153(fig.), 154(table), 160(illus.), 272(table), 290
Griffin, Paul F., 16, 18
Ground moraine, 42
Groundwater, 213
Growing seasons, 53, 54(fig.)
Guilford County (N.C.), 194
Gulf Coastal Plain, 14, 18, 50
Guyandot River, 213
Guyot, Arnold, 11
Gypsum, 74

Habersham County (Ga.), 210
Hagerstown (Md.), 4(fig.), 102(fig.), 119
Hagerstown Valley, 48
Hale, Ruth F., 26
Half-timber houses, 122
Hall County (Ga.), 163, 210
Hamblen County (Tenn.), 280, 281, 295
Hamilton (Ohio), 165
Hamilton County (Tenn.), 178, 180
Hampton Roads (Va.), 311, 314, 316, 317
Hancock County (W. Va.), 274(fig.), 275
Handicrafts, 145
Hansen, Niles M., 351
Hard water, 213
Hardwood forests, 65, 68, 70, 71, 109, 190, 191
Harlan County (Ky.), 223(table), 229, 344(table)
Harmony singing, 138, 140
Harpers Ferry (Md.), 46, 62
Harpers Ferry (W. Va.), 119
Harpers Ferry National Historic Park (W. Va.), 236(table)
Harrisburg (Pa.), 4(fig.), 32, 49, 57, 62, 101, 102(fig.), 105
manufacturing, 272(table)
population, 103, 154(table), 170(table)
SMSA, 153(fig.), 154(table), 272(table)
state capital (1812), 103
Harrodsburg (Ky.), 95, 96(fig.)
Hart, John Fraser, 195
Hawthorn, 68
Haynes, W. Warren, 337
Hazard-Whitesburg (Ky.), 350
"Head Right," 92
Healing, 135
Heath shrubs, 71
Hemlock, 68, 70
Hemlock–white pine–northern hardwoods region, 68, 69(fig.)
Hemp, 101
Hepatitis, 242

Henderson County (N.C.), 202, 208
Hickory, 70, 72, 191
Hickory (N.C.), 295
Highland Rim, 18
Highlands (N.C.), 167, 239
Highlands Appalachia subregion, 24, 25(fig.)
High Point (N.C.), 153(fig.), 154(table), 163, 194, 272(table), 273
High-pressure systems, 53
Hillsboro (W. Va.), 70
Hirsch, Nathaniel D. M., 336
Hocking County (Ohio), 280, 281
Hogs. *See* Swine
Holston, Stephen, 60
Holston River, 48, 60, 61(fig.), 98
Holston Valley, 98
Homestead. *See* Hot Springs (Va.)
Homestead Act (1862), 202
Hoover, Edgar M., 354
Hoover, Herbert, 347
Horizontal-log building, 122, 123
Horses, 101, 205
Hot springs, 49, 236, 237(fig.), 239–242
Hot Springs (N.C.), 239
Hot Springs (Va.), 49, 239, 242
Hudson-Champlain Section, 47
Hudson River, 47, 48, 61(fig.), 108, 115, 242, 243
Hudson River school of landscape painters, 243
Hudson Valley, 2, 14, 16, 18, 22, 30, 87, 113, 137(fig.)
Human migration, 42, 90, 92, 93. *See also* Appalachia, migration; Appalachia, routes
Hungarians, 126
"Hunky towns," 127
Hunt, Charles B., 14
Huntington (W. Va.), 4(fig.), 21, 51, 153(fig.), 154(table), 289(table)
Hurricane Agnes (1972), 57
Hutchinson, Charles, 239
Hydroelectric capacity, 214(table), 215–217, 298

Ice Age. *See* Pleistocene epoch
Igneous rock, 41, 42, 73, 75
Illinois, 168, 169(table)
Illinois Central Gulf (RR), 310, 311(table), 318
Inceptisols, 63–65
Indiana, 168, 169(table)
Indiana County (Pa.), 223(table), 224
Indianapolis (Ind.), 169(table)
Indian Farm Boys Club (N.C.), 254
Indians, 11, 71, 72, 75, 87–93, 100, 115, 125, 254
  population (1980), 182, 183(table)
Industrial wastes, 213
Inland waterways, 317, 320–325
Interfluvial uplands, 72
Interior Low Plateaus, 18, 50
"Internal colonialism" model, 343, 346
Iowa, 205
Irish, 113, 126, 127. *See also* Scotch-Irish settlers
Irish potato famines (1840s), 126
Iron furnaces, 71, 75, 101, 190–191, 285–287
  first (1629), 285
  *See also* Steel manufacturing
Iron ore, 71, 75, 76(fig.), 79, 190–191, 219
Iron oxides, 65
Iron sulfide, 213
Iroquois Confederacy, 89, 115
Iroquois Indians, 87–89, 91, 92
Isopleth map, 26, 27(fig.)
Italians, 243
Italian workmen, 74(cutline)
Ithaca (N.Y.), 4(fig.), 176

Jackson, Andrew, 91
Jackson County (N.C.), 163, 183(table), 260
Jacob's Creek, 287
James River, 46, 58(table), 61(fig.), 63
Jefferson, Thomas, 91
Jefferson County (Ala.), 183(table)
Jefferson County (Tenn.), 79
Jefferson County (W. Va.), 262, 275, 276(fig.)
Jews, 130, 243, 244
Johnson, Lyndon B., 346, 349
Johnson City (Tenn.), 49, 153(fig.), 154(table), 192, 272(table), 289(table)
Johnstown (Pa.), 4(fig.), 51, 105, 127, 128(illus.), 153(fig.), 180, 219, 287, 292(table)
Jones, Loyal, 342
Jonesboro Road, 96(fig.)
Juniata County (Pa.), 211
Juniata River, 57, 62, 101, 105
Juniata Valley, 287

Kames, 43
Kanawha River, 43, 60, 61(fig.), 324(table)
Kanawha section, 50, 145
Kanawha Valley, 136
Kaolin, 109, 295

Karst topography, 49, 70
Katahdin, Mt. (Me.), 251
Kelsey, Samuel, 239
Kennedy, John F., 23, 26, 349
Kentucky, 18, 19, 23, 24, 29, 30, 32(table), 48, 337–339, 353
  ADHS, 308(table), 309
  agriculture, 205, 207, 210
  in Appalachian Plateaus Province, 50, 51
  Blacks in, 180
  Bluegrass region, 62, 94, 95, 98, 100
  coal, 50, 82, 108, 127, 129, 159, 168, 214(table), 216, 217, 220, 222, 223(table), 226(table), 229, 348
  education, 168, 176
  electricity, 214(table), 216
  forests, 68, 70, 192, 197, 198
  highest point, 51
  income, 168, 172, 173, 318
  iron ore, 75
  land ownership, 344(table)
  land values, 203
  manufacturing, 273, 279(table), 284
  migration, 165, 166, 168
  oil, 82
  population, 109, 152(table), 158(table), 159, 163, 180, 336–337
  pulpwood, 197
  railroads, 310–311(tables), 314, 315(table), 316, 318
  religions, 133
  SEA, 167–169, 170, 171
  settlement, 93–94, 100, 127, 129
  soils, 63, 64(fig.)
  taxes, 345
  timber, 191
  tourism, 258(table), 259–260, 265
  water, 213
  wood processing, 192, 194
Kentucky River, 58(table), 60, 61(fig.), 94, 100
King, Philip, 40
Kings Mountain (N.C.), 41
Kingsport (Tenn.), 49, 153(fig.), 154(table), 272(table), 289(table), 347
Kishacoquillas Valley, 48
Kiskiminetas River, 213
Kittatinny Ridge, 48, 101
"Knob" belt, 18, 50
Knott County (Ky.), 194, 223(table), 344(table)
Knoxville (Tenn.), 4(fig.), 21, 32, 49, 102(fig.), 105, 107, 109, 153(fig.), 154(table), 163, 167, 272(table), 323, 347
Kumbrabow State Forest (W. Va.), 56
Kurath, Hans, 136, 138

Lamar County (Ala.), 23
Lancaster (Pa.), 119, 170(table)
Landmass uplift and erosion, 43
Land rights, 92–94
Land subsidence, 84
*Laube,* 124
LDDs. *See* Local Development Districts
Leached soils, 63, 65
Lead oxide, 79
Lebanon Valley, 48
Lee, Everett S., 165, 171
Lee County (Ky.), 220
Lehigh County (Pa.), 73, 74, 154(table), 183(table)
Lehigh River, 107
Lehigh Valley, 48, 132
Lehigh Valley (RR), 318
Leslie County (Ky.), 194, 223(table)
Letcher County (Ky.), 222
Lewis, Helen M., 343
Lewis, Oscar, 341
Lewis, Peirce, 117
Lewisburg (W. Va.), 70
Lewiston (Me.), 290
Lexington (Ky.), 4(fig.), 165, 168, 169(table)
Licking River, 58(table), 60, 61(fig.), 100
Lignite, 79
Lime, 79
Limestone, 42, 48, 49, 65, 70, 73, 75, 79, 213
Lithosphere, 40
Little Levels, 70
Little Tennessee River, 348
Livestock, 101, 204(table), 205–207, 210, 211
Loblolly pine, 72
Local Development Districts (LDDs), 335, 350, 352, 353
Logan (Ohio), 281
Logan County (W. Va.), 229
Logging technology, 191–192, 199
Log houses, 122–123
London Company, 92
Loudoun County (Va.), 205
Louisiana Purchase (1803), 91
Louisville (Ky.), 18, 107, 168, 169(table)
Louisville and Nashville (RR). *See* CSX Corporation
Lowland Piedmont, 45
Lowland South, 21
Low-pressure system, 53

Lumber, 32, 65, 68, 71, 72, 109, 191–195, 282(table), 283, 284, 285(table), 315, 316, 343
Lumber City (Ga.), 63
Lumpkin County (Ga.), 163, 183(table), 210
Luray Cave (Va.), 49
Lutherans, 130, 131(fig.), 133
Luzerne County (Pa.), 107, 126, 154(table), 155, 294(fig.)
Lynch (Ky.), 127
Lynchburg (Va.), 46, 153(fig.), 163

McDowell County (W. Va.), 180, 202, 276(fig.)
MacKaye, Benton, 251
Macon (Ga.), 45, 107
Macon County (N.C.), 202, 239, 260
Macon County (Tenn.), 30
Maine, 251
Maize, 101. *See also* Corn
Malizia, Emil, 343
Maple, 191
Marathon Basin region (Texas), 18
Marble, 73, 74(illus.), 295
Marschner, F. J., 23
Marsh, Ben, 117
Martin County (Ky.), 203, 223(table), 344(table), 345
Maryland, 19, 23, 29, 32(table)
  ADHS, 308(table)
  agriculture, 205
  coal, 220(table), 226(table)
  education, 176
  electricity, 214(table)
  forests, 67
  income, 173
  iron furnaces, 75
  manufacturing, 279(table), 284
  Panhandle, 67
  population, 152(table), 158(table), 170(table)
  pulpwood, 197(table)
  railroads, 310–311(tables), 314, 315(table), 316
  religions, 130, 132
  in Ridge and Valley Province, 48
  roads, 95
  SEA, 170(table)
  settlement, 93, 116, 119
  tourism, 258(table), 259–260
Mason and Dixon Line, 19, 119
Massachusetts, 132, 285
Massanutten Cave (Va.), 49
Massanutten Mountain (Va.), 48, 66(illus.), 163, 257, 260, 262, 265
Matthews, Peggy, 263
Maysville (Ky.), 95
Mecklenburg County (N.C.), 182, 183(table)
Medicinal plants, 70
Melungeons, 183–184
Menifee County (Ky.), 194
Mennonites, 115, 130, 138
Mercer County (W. Va.), 29
Mesophytic forest, 68–71
Metal industries, 282(table), 283, 285(table), 287, 289(table), 315, 316
Metals, 75–77, 79
Metamorphic rock, 41, 73
Methodists, 130, 131(fig.), 132–133, 135, 138
Metropolitan commuting zones, 339, 340(fig.)
Mexico, Gulf of, 46, 53, 56, 57, 58(table), 59, 60, 323
Miasma, 238
Mica, 109, 295
Michigan, 75, 168, 169(table)
Mid-Atlantic cultural hearth, 113, 114(fig.), 115, 119, 120(fig.), 122, 133, 136, 138, 140
Middletown (Ohio), 165
Middle West cultural area, 21
Midland culture area, 21
Mid-West culture area, 120(fig.)
Milk, 205, 210
Mineral rights, 108–109, 343–345
Minerals, 73–84, 109
Mineral springs, 49, 236, 237(fig.), 239
Mining, 3, 73, 82, 271, 343. *See also* Coal
Minnesota, 75
Mississippi, 23, 32(table), 95, 307, 308(table), 309, 310–311(tables), 315(table), 316, 323
Mississippian period, 41
Mississippi River, 59, 60, 61(fig.)
Mississippi Valley, 108
Missouri, 16, 32
Mitchell, Robert D., 101
Mitchell, Mt., 46
Mixed-blood population. *See* Melungeons
Mobile (Ala.), 317, 323
Mohawk Indians, 87, 88(fig.)
Mohawk River, 11, 61(fig.)
Mohawk Turnpike, 96(fig.)
Mohawk Valley, 2, 14, 16, 18, 22, 30, 89, 91, 98, 100, 103, 115
Mollies. *See* Molly Maguires
Molly Maguires (vigilance committee), 126
Monadnocks, 41, 45

Monongah (W. Va.), 127
Monongahela (RR), 318
Monongahela River, 60, 61(fig.), 63, 97(illus.), 100, 107, 127, 213, 324(table)
Monongahela Valley, 228, 247
Monongalia County (W. Va.), 176, 182, 223(table)
Monroe County (Ohio), 26
Monroe County (Pa.), 155, 163, 169
Monroe County (W. Va.), 181(fig.)
Montgomery County (Va.), 176, 182
Moravians, 130, 132, 136
Morgan County (W. Va.), 74, 278(fig.)
Morristown (Tenn.), 280
Mountain lions, 72
Mountain Region of the South, 19
Mount Carmel (Pa.), 169
Mungo County (W. Va.), 203
Munro, John M., 307, 350
Muscle Shoals (Ala.), 348
  rapids, 107, 347
Music symbols, 138
Muskingum County (Ohio), 223(table), 224

N&W. *See* Norfolk and Western
Nantahala mountain range, 71
Nanticoke Indians, 88(fig.), 89
Nashville (Tenn.), 4(fig.), 18, 108
Nashville Basin, 94
Nashville Road, 96(fig.)
National forests, 68, 198, 199, 247
National parks, 46, 71, 72, 235–236, 246–249, 251
National Park Service, 249
National Radio Astronomy Observatory, 261
National Road. *See* Cumberland Road
Natural Bridge (Va.), 49
Natural gas, 82, 219
Nelson (Ga.), 74(cutline)
New England, 22, 47, 92, 113, 115, 286, 290
New England cultural hearth, 113, 114(fig.), 115, 121, 136
Newer Appalachians, 42
Newfoundland (Canada), 11, 18
New Jersey, 32(table), 152(table), 158(table), 159, 170(table), 173, 176, 197(table), 205, 214(table), 258(table), 259, 277, 279(table), 284
New-Kanawha river valley, 100
Newman, Monroe, 351
New Orleans (La.), 317
New River, 11, 43, 47, 60, 61(fig.), 321(cutline)
Newton, Milton, 119, 121, 145
New York Central Railroad (1853), 108
New York City, 32, 103, 105, 107, 170(table), 242, 290, 293, 326
New York State, 2, 11, 14, 23, 30, 32(table)
  ADHS, 307, 308(table)
  agriculture, 25, 205, 207, 210, 211
  in Appalachian Plateaus Province, 50
  Asians in, 182
  cultural region, 21, 22
  education, 176
  electricity, 214(table), 216
  elevations, 67
  fauna, 72
  forests, 67, 72, 198
  frost-free period, 53
  geology, 42–43, 67
  income, 173, 176
  Indians, 89, 183(table)
  lakes, 235
  land values, 264(table)
  manufacturing, 279(table)
  in Piedmont Province, 43
  population, 103, 152(table), 158(table), 160, 163
  precipitation, 53, 56
  pulpwood, 197(table), 198
  railroads, 310–311(tables), 315, 316
  religions, 130, 131(fig.)
  SEA, 170(table)
  settlement, 92, 98, 100, 115
  soils, 63, 64(fig.)
  Spanish-origin population in, 182, 183
  speech, 136, 137(fig.)
  temperature, 52(fig.), 53, 67
  thunderstorms, 56
  timber, 191
  tourism, 236, 237(fig.), 239, 242–244, 255, 256(table), 258(table), 259–260
  urban, 152(table), 153(fig.), 158(table), 160, 163, 279(table)
  vegetation, 67
  *See also* Southern Tier
*Night Comes to the Cumberlands* (Caudill), 337, 343, 348
Nittany Valley, 48, 285
Noble County (Ohio), 26
Nolichucky River, 60, 98
Nonmetallic minerals, 73–74
Nonrenewable resources, 217–229, 345
Norfolk (Va.), 105
Norfolk and Western (N&W) (RR), 310, 311, 313(fig.), 314, 317, 318
Norris Dam (Tenn.), 215(illus.), 253
Norris Lake, 62, 215(cutline), 251, 253

Northampton County (Pa.), 73, 74, 183(table)
North Carolina, 16, 19, 23, 29, 32(table)
ADHS, 307, 308(table)
agriculture, 205, 207, 208, 211
in Blue Ridge Province, 46
economy, 167
electricity, 214(table), 216, 217
forests, 68, 71
geology, 43
income, 173
Indians, 182, 183(table)
land values, 202, 264(table)
manufacturing, 273, 275, 279(table), 284, 292, 295, 298
minerals, 73
population, 152(table), 155, 158(table), 159, 163, 167, 168(table), 180
precipitation, 53, 56
pulpwood, 197(table)
railroads, 310–311(tables), 315, 316
religions, 132
SEA, 167, 168(table), 170
settlement, 94, 100, 116, 117(table)
snowfall, 56
soils, 64(fig.), 192
Spanish-origin population in, 182, 183(table)
speech, 136, 137(fig.), 138
tourism, 167, 238–239, 254, 256(table), 258(table), 259–260, 262–263
urban, 109, 154(table), 155, 158(table), 163, 279(table)
water, 213
wood processing, 192, 194
Northern Appalachia subregion, 24, 25(fig.)
Notching techniques, 122–123
Nuclear power, 217
Nuts. *See* Orchards

Oak, 68, 70, 71, 191
Oak-chestnut forest, 69(fig.), 71–72
Oak-pine forest, 69(fig.), 72–73
Oak Ridge (Tenn.), 176, 348
Oats, 205
Ochrepts, 63
Ocmulgee River, 58(table), 63
Oconee River, 58(table), 61(fig.), 63
OEO. *See* Office of Economic Opportunity
Off-farm employment, 210
Office of Economic Opportunity (OEO), 346
Oglethorpe, Mt. (Ga.), 251
Ohio, 23, 26, 29, 30, 32(table), 75, 339
ADHS, 308(table)
in Appalachian Plateaus Province, 51
coal, 220(table), 222, 223(table), 224, 226(table), 228, 330
education, 126
electricity, 214(table), 216
forests, 192
income, 173, 176
manufacturing, 279(table), 280–281, 284, 295, 298
population, 152(table), 158(table), 159, 163, 168, 169(table), 180
pulpwood, 197(table)
religions, 133, 135
SEA, 169(table)
settlement, 100
SMSAs, 153(fig.)
soils, 63
speech, 136, 137(fig.)
tourism, 258(table), 260
Ohio River, 23, 48, 57, 58(table), 60, 61(fig.), 74, 107, 127, 213, 311, 314, 320, 323, 324
Falls, 107
Forks, 94, 95, 98, 100
Ohio Valley, 90, 100, 105
Oil, 78(fig.), 82, 213, 219, 282(table), 283, 285(table)
first well (1859), 82
Oklahoma, 11, 16
Old Elizabethan English, 138
Older Appalachians, 41
Oneida Indians, 87, 88(fig.)
Onondaga Indians, 87, 88(fig.)
Ontario, Lake, 251. *See also* Great Lakes
Ontario Plain, 103
"On the Appalachian Mountain System" (Guyot), 11
Orange County (N.C.), 202
Orange County (N.Y.), 163, 183
Orchards, 65, 68, 72, 204(table), 207, 208, 211
Ordovician limestone, 48, 75, 79
Ordovician period, 41
Oriskany sandstone, 74
Orogeny, 41, 42, 43, 50, 73
Otsego Lake, 62
Ouachitas. *See* Ozark-Ouachita Uplands
Owego (N.Y.), 103, 104(illus.)
Owsley County (Ky.), 176
Ozark-Ouachita Uplands, 16, 18
Ozarks, 18, 22

Paducah (Ky.), 348

Painters. *See* Mountain lions
Paleozoic era, 41, 42
Panthers. *See* Mountain lions
PARC. *See* President's Appalachian Regional Commission
"Passing of Provincialism, The" (Ford), 341
PCA. *See* Pennsylvania Culture Area
Peabody Coal (company), 348
Peat, 82
Pee Dee River, 58(table), 61(fig.), 63
Peneplain, 43, 45
Penn, William, 19, 90, 93
Penn Central (RR), 318
Penn's Colony, 115
Pennsylvania, 1, 23, 29, 30, 32(table), 353
  ADHS, 307, 308(table), 309
  agriculture, 101, 115, 205, 207, 210, 211
  in Appalachian Plateaus Province, 50
  Asians in, 182
  Blacks in, 178, 180, 181(fig.)
  in Blue Ridge Province, 46
  canals, 105
  capital. *See* Harrisburg
  cement, 73
  coal, 49, 75, 79–80, 81(illus.), 82, 126, 169, 195, 214(table), 216, 217–219, 220(table), 222, 223(table), 224, 226(table), 228, 330
  colony (1681), 90
  cultural regions, 21, 22. *See also* Pennsylvania Culture Area
  education, 176
  electricity, 214(table), 216
  elevations, 67
  fauna, 72
  flood (1972), 57
  floods (1889, 1936), 288(cutline)
  forests, 67, 68, 70, 71, 72, 192
  income, 172, 173, 318
  iron and steel industry, 285–288, 289(table)
  iron ore, 75
  lakes, 235
  land use, 253
  land values, 264(table)
  manufacturing, 272(table), 273, 275, 279(table), 281, 284, 285, 288, 289(table), 292(table), 293
  minerals, 74, 75
  oil, 82
  population, 152(table), 154(table), 155, 158(table), 159, 160, 163, 170–171, 180, 181(fig.)
  precipitation, 53
  pulp and paper, 195, 197(table)
  railroads, 310–311(tables), 314, 315(table), 316, 318, 330
  religions, 130, 131(fig.), 132, 133
  in Ridge and Valley Province, 1, 47, 48, 49, 126
  roads, 95
  rural, 152(table), 158(table), 163, 279(table)
  SEA, 169–171
  settlement, 92, 93, 98, 115, 116, 117–119
  soils, 63, 64(fig.), 65
  springs, 49, 240(fig.)
  State University, 176
  temperature, 67
  thunderstorms, 56
  tourism, 169–170, 236, 237(fig.), 239, 242, 244, 256(table), 258(table), 259–261
  urban, 122, 152(table), 153(fig.), 155, 158(table), 160, 279(table)
  water, 213
  wood processing, 195
Pennsylvania barns, 124, 125(illus.)
Pennsylvania Culture Area (PCA), 119, 124, 132
Pennsylvania Dutch, 115
Pennsylvanian period, 79
Pennsylvania Portage and Canal System (1834), 105, 219, 228
Pennsylvania Railroad (1852), 108
Pennsylvania Road, 95, 103
Pennsylvania Vacation Land Developers Association, 260
Pentacostal Holiness, 134, 135
Permian period, 41
Perry County (Pa.), 239
Philadelphia (Pa.), 2, 21, 22, 32, 45, 71, 95, 103, 105, 107, 108, 115, 122, 326
  geology, 42
  population, 170(table), 171
Philadelphia Wagon Road, 119, 120(fig.)
Phillips, Kevin R., 22
Photiadis, John, 135
*Physiography of Eastern United States* (Fenneman), 14, 15(fig.), 44(fig.)
*Physiography of Western United States* (Fenneman), 14
Pickard, Jerome P., 353
Pickens County (Ala.), 23
Pickens County (Ga.), 73
Piedmont (airline), 325
Piedmont (S.C.), 292
Piedmont Manufacturing Company, 292
Piedmont Plateaus, 11, 22

Piedmont Province, 14, 15(fig.), 16, 32, 40, 47
  agriculture, 16, 72, 200(table), 202, 208, 210
  Blacks in, 178
  boundaries, 43, 45
  counties, 45, 156(table)
  drainage, 59
  economy, 229
  elevations, 53
  forests, 68, 69(fig.), 72
  geology, 41, 45, 73
  lumbering, 192
  manufacturing, 290
  minerals, 73, 75
  population, 156(table), 163
  routes, 62
  settlement, 117, 123, 129
  soils, 65, 72, 229
  topography, 43–45
  urban, 16, 45
  water, 213
  *See also* Lowland Piedmont; Upland Piedmont
Pietists, 115, 130
Pigeon Forge (N.C.), 255–256
Pike County (Ky.), 220, 222, 223(table), 344(table)
Pike County (Pa.), 163, 169
Pine, 65, 68, 70, 72
Pine Mountain, 51, 84, 94
Pittsburgh (Pa.), 4(fig.), 16, 32, 48, 51, 95, 102(fig.), 105, 107, 108, 127, 326
  Golden Triangle, 97(illus.)
  industry, 217, 219, 272(table), 273, 287–288, 289(table), 292(table), 295, 324
  population, 107, 108, 154(table), 180
  rivers, 60, 97(illus.)
  SMSA, 153(fig.), 154(table), 155, 272(table), 273, 275, 288, 295
Place names, 11, 86(n56), 92
Plantation South, 21, 117, 129, 238
Plate tectonics, 40, 41
Pleistocene epoch, 42–43, 49, 67
Plutonic. *See* Igneous rock
Pocahontas County (W. Va.), 70, 261
Pocono Mountains, 163, 170, 213, 236, 237(fig.), 242, 244
Point Pleasant (W. Va.), 60
Poison drinking, 135
Poles, 126
Polish Falcons, 127
Polk County (Tenn.), 79
Pollution, 57, 75, 77(illus.), 84, 265. *See also* Coal, and air pollution; Coal, and water pollution
Portland (Pa.), 73
Portsmouth (Ohio), 60
Potomac River, 45, 46, 58(table), 61(fig.), 62, 63, 95, 103, 105, 107
Potter County (Pa.), 253
Pottsville (Pa.), 169
Pottsville Escarpment, 50, 70, 73
Poultry, 204(table), 205–207, 210, 211
Powell, John Wesley, 11
Powell River, 48, 60, 61(fig.)
Precambrian, 73
Presbyterians, 115, 130, 132, 133, 136
President's Appalachian Regional Commission (PARC), 349
Price, Edward T., 122, 184
Primack, Phil, 353
Primitive Baptist, 134, 138
Proclamation Line (1763), 59, 96(fig.)
Proselytism, 133
Protestant sects, 155, 178
Prunty, Merle C., 207
Public Law 89-4 (1965), 23, 24, 304, 346
Public Law 90-103 (1967), 23
Puddling furnace, 286
Pulaski County (Ky.), 194
Pulp and paper, 65, 68, 72, 192, 195–198, 282(table), 285(table)

Quakers, 115, 116, 117(fig.), 130, 132, 133, 136
Qualla Boundary (N.C.), 91
Quartz, 74
Quartzite, 74
Quebec Province (Canada), 11

Rabun County (Ga.), 239
Rabun Gap–Nacoochee School (Ga.), 145
Raccoons, 72
Radford College (Va.), 176
Railroads, 62, 71, 100, 103, 107–109, 219, 242, 243, 309–320, 323, 343
  gauge standardization, 108
Raitz-Ulack region, 4(fig.), 29–33, 151, 159
Randolph County (Ala.), 195, 210
Randolph County (N.C.), 194
Randolph County (W. Va.), 56, 70
Rappahannock River, 45, 58(table), 61(fig.)
Ravenstein, E. G., 171
Reading (Pa.), 47, 153(fig.), 154(table), 170(table), 272(table), 289(table)

Reading (RR), 318
Reading Prong, 47
Red maple, 68
Red oak, 68, 71, 72
Red River Gorge (Ky.), 265, 267
Red spruce, 71, 191
Regional Rail Reorganization (RRR) Act (1973), 319
Renewable resources, 190–217
Republican Party, 22
Resorts. *See* Appalachia, recreation; Appalachia, tourism
Retirement living, 3
Return migration, 166, 171
Revolutionary War, 90, 91, 92
Rhea County (Tenn.), 183
Rhododendron, 70, 71
Richmond (Va.), 45, 107
Ridge and Valley Province, 14, 15(fig.), 18, 23, 29, 40, 105
  agriculture, 48, 49, 195, 200(table), 202, 203
  boundaries, 46–47
  caves, 49
  coal, 49, 79, 80
  counties, 156(table)
  drainage, 48, 49, 59, 95
  elevations, 48
  forests, 67, 68, 69(fig.), 71
  geology, 41, 42, 48, 49, 73
  minerals, 73, 74, 79
  population density, 155, 156(table)
  routes, 48, 62
  settlement, 48, 123
  soils, 65
  springs, 49, 239
  topography, 44(fig.), 46–49
  tourism, 49
  urban, 49
  water, 213
Ridgeley sandstone, 74
River birch, 72
River towns, 101
Roads, 62. *See also* Appalachian Development Highway System
Roanoke (Va.), 4(fig.), 21, 46, 49, 109, 119, 153(fig.), 163
Roanoke Gap, 136
Roanoke River, 46, 58(table), 61(fig.), 63
Rockbridge County (Va.), 116
Rockefeller, Laure Spelman, Memorial Foundation, 247
Rock Hall (S.C.), 292
Rockland County (N.Y.), 43
Rogers, Mt. (Va.), 46
Roosevelt, Franklin D., 49, 347
Roosevelt, Franklin D., Jr., 24
Root zones, 63, 65
Rothblatt, Donald N., 339, 351, 354
Rowan County (Ky.), 194
RRR. *See* Regional Rail Reorganization Act
Runoff, 56, 57, 70, 190, 213, 216
"Rural renaissance," 160
Ruthenians, 126
Rye, 101

Saddle notching, 123
Sail-Wagon era (1790–1830), 103, 105
St. Lawrence River, 14, 61(fig.)
St. Lawrence Valley, 46
St. Louis (Mo.), 132
Salem (N.C.), 102(fig.), 105
Salt, 98, 100
Saluda (N.C.), 97(illus.), 109, 254
Saluda Gap, 95
  Road, 238
Saluda River, 58(table), 61(fig.), 63
Saluda Trail, 95, 96(fig.)
Sand and gravel, 43, 74, 75
Sand Mountain, 51
Sandstone, 41, 42, 48, 50, 63, 73, 74, 79, 213
Santee River, 61(fig.), 63
Sapphire Valley, 163
Saprolite, 63
Saratoga (N.Y.), 239
Savannah (Ga.), 4(fig.), 105, 107
Savannah River, 61(fig.), 98
Sawmills, 191, 192, 195
Schist, 41
Schmudde, Theodore H., 252, 255
Schoharie County (N.Y.), 210
Schunemuck Ridge, 48
Schuylkill (Pa.), 126
Schuylkill County (Pa.), 228
Schuylkill River, 57, 107
*Schwalbenschwanz*. *See* Dove-tailing
Scotch-Irish settlers, 2, 22, 113, 115, 116–117, 118(fig.), 119, 121, 122, 123, 124–125, 130
Scottish Carolina Land and Lumber Company, 192
Scranton (Pa.), 4(fig.), 49, 155, 292(table), 293
SEA. *See* State Economic Areas
Seaboard Coast Line Industries, 318. *See also* CSX Corporation
Seasonal housing, 3, 48, 163, 238, 250(table), 252–253, 254, 257–262, 265, 267
Second homes. *See* Seasonal housing

Sedimentry rock, 41, 42, 43, 45, 73, 75, 79, 80, 82, 239
Sediment loads, 215
Semple, Ellen Churchill, 337
Seneca Indians, 87, 88(fig.)
Sequatchie Valley, 51
Sequoyah, 91
Serbs, 126
"Settlement landscape," 9, 21
Sevier County (N.C.), 255
Sewage, 213
Shale, 42, 56, 63, 73, 79, 213, 295
Shamokin (Pa.), 169
Shape-note singing, 138, 139(fig.), 140
Shawnee Indians, 88(fig.), 89, 90
Shenandoah (Pa.), 169
Shenandoah Cave (Va.), 49
Shenandoah National Park (Va.), 46, 72, 235, 236(table), 247, 248, 249, 251
Shenandoah River, 61(fig.), 62, 66(illus.)
Shenandoah Valley, 29, 42, 48, 62, 95, 101, 116, 119, 132, 208, 260
Sherman, William Tecumseh, 108
Shifting cultivation, 72
*Shiloh: A Mountain Community* (Stephenson), 342
SIC. *See* Standard Industrial Classification
Sidney Lanier, Lake, 163
Siemans, William, 286
Silt, 75
Silurian iron ore, 75
Silurian period, 42, 75
Silverbell, 71
Sinkholes, 49, 70
Skiing, 48, 56, 246, 255, 261, 262
Skyline Drive, 235, 248
Slag dams, 229
Slash-and-burn, 125, 198
Slate, 41, 73–74
Slatedale (Pa.), 74
Slateford (Pa.), 74
Slatington (Pa.), 74, 86(n56)
Slaves, 22. *See also* Appalachia, Blacks in
Slide Mountain, 50
Slovaks, 126
Smith, Al, 351
Smith, Kenard E., 261
SMSAs. *See* Standard Metropolitan Statistical Areas
Smyth County (Va.), 74
Snake handling, 135
Snap beans, 207
Snow Belt, 277
Snowfall, 56
Social Security Administration, 172
Sodium chloride, 213, 239
Soft water, 213
Soils. *See under* Appalachia; *individual states*
Sour gum, 68
South, 21, 22, 133, 284, 290–292. *See also* Plantation South; Upland South
South Carolina, 1, 16, 19, 29, 32(table)
  ADHS, 307, 308(table)
  agriculture, 205, 208
  electricity, 214(table)
  forests, 68
  income, 173
  Indians, 183(table)
  manufacturing, 273, 275, 277, 279(table), 284, 292
  orchards, 72
  population, 152(table), 158(table), 160, 163, 168(table)
  pulp and paper, 195, 197(table)
  railroads, 310–311(tables), 315(table), 316
  SEA, 168(table)
  settlement, 94, 116, 117(table)
  soils, 64(fig.)
  speech, 137(fig.), 138
  tourism, 258(table), 259–260
Southern Appalachian National Park Commission, 247
*Southern Appalachian Region, The: A Survey* (Ford), 19, 20(fig.), 21
Southern Appalachia subregion, 24, 25(fig.)
*Southern Highlander and His Homeland, The* (Campbell), 19, 20(fig.)
Southern Highlands, 22, 336
Southern mountaineers, 337
Southern Mountains, 22
Southern Railroad, 310, 311, 313(fig.), 314, 318
Southern Railway Systems, 311
Southern Tier (NYS), 22, 103, 108, 260
spanish-origin population, 182–183
Spartanburg (S.C.), 4(fig.), 45, 272(table)
Speaking in tongues, 134, 135
Sphagnum mosses, 68, 70
Spinelli, Michael Ambrose, 352
Spruce, 67, 71
Spruce Knob Mountain (W. Va.), 50
Squatter settlements, 93, 98
Standard Industrial Classification (SIC), 281, 282(table), 284, 288, 289(table), 290, 298

Standard Metropolitan Statistical Areas (SMSAs), 151, 153(fig.), 154(table), 155, 173, 180, 184(n2), 272(table), 273
State Economic Areas (SEA), 19, 21, 166–171, 353
  defined, 185(n18)
State forests, 56
State parks, 235, 250(table)
Steamboat-Iron Horse era (1830–1870), 107
Steamboats, 103, 107, 243
Steam engines, 107, 108, 191–192
Steel manufacturing, 22, 51, 108, 217, 285–290
Steel-Rail era (1870–1920), 108
Stephenson, John B., 342
Stone, clay, and glass industry, 281, 282(table), 283, 284, 285(table), 295, 297(fig.), 298, 315
Stone Mountain (Ga.), 41
Stream patterns, 59
Stroud, Hubert B., 261
Stroudsburg (Pa.), 155
Subdivided tracts, 257, 259–262
Subduction, 40
Sugar maple, 68, 70, 71
Sulfates, 213
Sulfides, 75
Sulfur, 75, 191, 228, 316
Sulfur dioxide, 348
Sulfuric acid, 75
Sulfur oxides, 75
Sullivan County (N.Y.), 163, 211, 242
Summer homes. *See* Seasonal housing
Sun Belt, 159, 277, 280, 299(n2)
Sunbury (Pa.), 101
Sundew, 68
Surface-mine reclamation law (1977), 227
Surface strip mines, 82, 83(illus.), 129, 220, 222, 224, 227, 348
Susquehanna Company, 92
Susquehanna County (Pa.), 210
Susquehanna River, 45, 57, 58(table), 60, 61(fig.), 62, 101, 103, 105, 107, 213, 320
Susquehanna Valley, 21, 57, 89, 115, 137(fig.)
Susquehannock Indians, 88(fig.), 89
Sussex County (N.J.), 205
Suturing. *See* Orogeny
Swain County (N.C.), 182, 183(table), 248
Swamps, 79, 82
Sweet buckeye, 68
Sweetgum, 72
Sweet Springs (Va.), 239
Swine, 101, 204(table), 205
Swiss settlers, 113, 115
Sycamore, 72
Synclines, 73, 79

Taconian orogeny, 41
Taconic Mountains, 115
Taliaferro County (Ga.), 178, 179(fig.)
Tamarack, 70
Teays River system, 43
Tectonic activity, 40–41, 42, 79
Tellico Dam, 348
Tennessee, 18, 19, 23, 24, 30, 32(table), 339
  ADHS, 308(table)
  agriculture, 205, 207, 210
  in Appalachian Plateaus Province, 51
  Blacks in, 178, 180
  in Blue Ridge Province, 46
  caves, 49
  coal, 220, 222, 223(table), 226(table)
  copper, 75
  education, 176
  electricity, 214(table), 216
  forests, 71, 198
  gold, 75
  highest mountain, 46
  income, 173
  iron, 75
  isolation, 107
  land ownership, 344(table)
  manufacturing, 273, 275, 279(table), 280, 281, 292(table), 293, 295, 298
  minerals, 73, 75, 79
  population, 152(table), 158(table), 163, 168–169(tables). *See also* Melungeons
  pulpwood, 197(table)
  railroads, 310–311(tables), 314, 315(table), 316
  religions, 133, 135
  in Ridge and Valley Province, 48, 49
  roads, 95
  SEA, 168–169(tables)
  settlement, 95, 98, 100, 117
  snowfall, 56
  soils, 63, 64(fig.), 65, 107, 192
  tourism, 254–257, 258(table), 259–260
  urban, 152(table), 153(fig.), 154(table), 158(table), 163, 279(table)
Tennessee drainage basin, 347
Tennessee River, 47, 58(table), 60, 61(fig.), 94, 98, 105, 107, 215, 320, 323, 324, 347
Tennessee-Tombigbee Waterway project, 322(fig.), 323

Tennessee Valley Authority (TVA) (1933), 2, 3, 26, 60, 62, 215–216, 235, 336, 346
 and agriculture, 210, 348
 dams, 347, 348
 electricity, 347, 348, 349
 impact, 347–349
 and industry, 298
 and recreation, 249–251
 and seasonal housing, 253, 260
Texas, 11, 18, 65
Textile industry, 202, 275, 281, 282(table), 283, 284, 285(table), 290–293, 294(fig.)
Thermal springs. *See* Hot springs
Three Mile Island (Pa.), 217
Thrust faults, 51
Thunderstorms, 56
Tidewater. *See under* Virginia
Timber, 191–192, 199
Timber wolves, 72
Tioga County (N.Y.), 211
Tioga County (Pa.), 210
Titusville (Pa.), 82
Tobacco, 32, 101, 107, 202, 204(table), 207, 282(table), 283, 284, 285(table), 298
Tomatoes, 207
Tombigbee River, 323, 324(table). *See also* Tennessee-Tombigbee Waterway project
Tompkins County (N.Y.), 176, 182
Town forms, 119, 121–122
Toxaway (N.C.), 239
Toxaway, Lake, 163
Trail of Tears (1838), 91
Transportation, Department of (DOT), 331
Transylvania County (N.C.), 163, 260
Trellised stream patterns, 59
Triassic period, 41, 45, 73
Tri-racial groups. *See* Melungeons
Truck garden crops, 65
Tryon (N.C.), 109, 154
Tug Fork, 60
Tuliptree, 68, 70, 71, 191
Turner, Frederick Jackson, 121
Turnip greens, 207–208
Tuscaloosa (Ala.), 23
Tuscarora Indians, 88(fig.), 89, 90
Tuscarora quartzite, 74
Tuscarora sandstone, 42, 48
TVA. *See* Tennessee Valley Authority
TWA (airline), 325
Tygart River, 100
Tyrone (Pa.), 116

Ukrainians, 126
Ulster County (N.Y.), 163, 183(table), 211, 242, 255
Ultisols, 63, 64(fig.), 65, 72
Unaka Mountains, 71, 192
Union County (N.C.), 211
Union County (Tenn.), 73
United (airline), 325
United States
 cultural regionalizations, 21
 eastern highest peak, 46
 income, 173
 manufacturing, 271
 physiographic divisions, 14
 population, 158(table)
 population density, 155
University of Kentucky, 5
Upland Piedmont, 1, 18, 32, 45
Upland South, 21, 115
 cultural hearth, 119, 120(fig.), 121–122, 140, 145
Upper South, 21
USAir (airline), 325
Utica (N.Y.), 89

Valley of East Tennessee, 48, 98, 100
Valley of Virginia, 48
Value added, 271, 275, 276(fig.), 279(table), 289(table)
Van Buren County (Tenn.), 210
Vance, Rupert B., 339
Veal, 210
Vegetables, 101, 204(table), 207–208
Vegetational boundaries, 67
Virgin forest, 68
Virginia, 1, 2, 19, 23, 24, 29, 32(table), 339
 ADHS, 307, 308(table)
 agriculture, 205, 207, 208, 211
 in Appalachian Plateaus Province, 50
 Asians in, 182
 Blacks in, 180
 caves, 49
 coal, 129, 214(table), 220(table), 223(table), 226(table)
 education, 176
 electricity, 214(table), 216
 forests, 70, 72, 192
 geology, 43
 highest peak, 46
 income, 173
 iron furnaces, 75
 land ownership, 344(table)
 land use, 252, 257
 land values, 264(table)
 manufacturing, 273, 275, 277, 279(table), 298

minerals, 74
population, 109, 152(table), 158(table), 163, 168–169(tables), 170(table), 180
pulpwood, 197(table)
railroads, 310–311(tables), 314, 315(table), 316
religions, 130, 131(fig.), 132, 133, 135
in Ridge and Valley Province, 48, 49
SEA, 168–169(tables), 170(table)
settlement, 92, 93, 94, 116, 117, 127, 129
soils, 63, 64(fig.), 65
speech, 136, 137(fig.)
springs, 49, 239, 240(fig.), 242
Tech, 176
Tidewater, 21, 22, 129, 238
tourism, 239, 242, 256(table), 257–259, 260
University of, 173, 176
urban, 152(table), 153(fig.), 158(table), 163, 279(table)
Virginia Port Authority, 316
V-notching, 123
Volunteer pines and oaks, 72
Vulcanism, 40, 41

Walden Ridge, 51
Walker County (Ala.), 195, 223(table), 344(table)
Walls, David S., 19, 34(n17), 346
Warm Springs (Ga.), 49
Warm Springs (Va.), 239, 242
War of 1812, 91
War on Poverty, 346, 349
Warren County (N.J.), 205
Warren County (Tenn.), 210
Warren County (Va.), 259, 265
Washington County (Tenn.), 73
Washington County (Va.), 74
Washington, D.C., 32, 167, 257, 326
Watauga County (N.C.), 167, 202, 262
Watauga River, 98
Watauga Valley, 192
Waterfalls, 62, 243
Water gaps, 42, 46, 48, 51, 59, 62, 94
Watson, Mary Keys, 269
Watts Bar Lake, 62
Wayne County (Ky.), 194
Waynesville (N.C.), 254
Weathering, 63
Weed trees, 68, 198
Weirton (W. Va.), 275
Weller, Jack E., 341–342
Welsh, 113, 125
West Chesapeake Tidewater cultural hearth, 113, 114(fig.), 117, 123
Westerly winds, 53
Western and Atlantic Railraod, 108
Western Maryland (RR), 318. *See also* CSX Corporation
West Virginia, 2, 19, 23, 24, 29, 32(table), 339
ADHS, 307, 308(table), 309
agriculture, 202–203, 208, 210
in Appalachian Plateaus Province, 50, 51
Asians in, 182
Blacks in, 180, 181(fig.)
coal, 82, 108–109, 127, 180, 214(table), 216, 220, 222, 223(table), 226(table), 227, 229
Eastern Panhandle, 74
education, 176, 178
electricity, 214(table), 216
flood (1972), 57
forests, 67, 70, 71, 192, 197, 199
geology, 42, 43
gorges, 60
highest peak, 50
income, 172, 173, 318
iron ore, 75
land values, 202–203
livestock, 70
lumber, 191
manufacturing, 273, 275, 279(table), 284, 298
migration, 165, 169(table), 180
minerals, 74, 75
Northern Panhandle, 74
oil, 82
population, 109, 152(table), 158(table), 163, 169(table), 180, 181(fig.)
precipitation, 56
pulpwood, 197, 198
railroads, 310–311(tables), 314, 315(table), 316, 318
religions, 133, 135
in Ridge and Valley Province, 49
SEA, 169(table)
settlement, 94, 100, 126, 127
soils, 64(fig.), 192
speech, 136, 137(fig.), 138
springs, 49, 239, 240(fig.), 242
state forest, 56
taxes, 345
tourism, 242, 258(table), 259–260, 261
University, 176
water, 213
Wheat, 101, 103, 107

Wheeling (W. Va.), 4(fig.), 51, 95, 102(fig.), 108, 153(fig.), 180, 287, 289(table)
Whiskey, 101, 144(fig.). *See also* Bootlegging
Whisnant, David E., 29, 352
White County (Ga.), 210
White County (Tenn.), 210
White oak, 68, 71, 72
White pine, 68
White Sulphur Springs (W. Va.), 49, 242
Whitetailed deer, 72
Whitfield County (Ga.), 293
Wigginton, Eliot, 145
Wilderness Trail (Road), 51, 62, 95, 96(fig.), 98
Wilkes-Barre (Pa.), 4(fig.), 49, 92, 102(fig.), 107, 108, 155, 170(table)
Wilkes County (N.C.), 194, 211
Williams, Cratis D., 337
Williamsport (Pa.), 153(fig.)
Willis, Bailey, 49
Wind gaps, 42, 46, 48, 51, 94
  defined, 59
Winston County (Ala.), 195, 210
Winston-Salem (N.C.), 4(fig.), 45, 119, 132, 153(fig.), 154(table), 163, 272(table), 273
Wise County (Va.), 183, 223(table), 344(table)
Wolfe, Thomas, 113
Wolfe County (Ky.), 220
Wolves. *See* Timber wolves
Workingmen's Benevolent Association, 126
Works Progress Administration, 23, 26
Wyoming Valley, 49, 92

Yadkin River, 61(fig.), 62, 63
Yellow birch, 68, 71
Yellow Creek complex, 323
Yellow-fever, 238
Yellow pine, 72
Yellow-poplar. *See* Tuliptree
Yeoman South, 21
*Yesterday's People* (Weller), 342
York (Pa.), 119
York County (S.C.), 183(table)
Youghiogheny River, 63, 287
Youngstown (Ohio), 287

Zane's Trace, 95, 96(fig.)
Zannaras, Georgia, 26
Zelinsky, Wilbur, 9, 21, 22, 119
Zigzag mountains, 47–48
Zinc, 75, 76(fig.), 79

## Other Titles of Interest from Westview Press

†*Rural Education: In Search of a Better Way*, edited by Paul M. Nachtigal

†*Poverty in Rural America: A Case Study*, Janet M. Fitchen

†*The Myth of the Family Farm: Agribusiness Dominance of U.S. Agriculture*, Ingolf Vogeler

†*The Family in Rural Society*, Raymond T. Coward and William M. Smith

†*Rural Society in the U.S.: Issues for the 1980s*, edited by Don A. Dillman and Daryl J. Hobbs

†*Politics in the Rural States: People, Parties, and Processes*, Frank M. Bryan

*The Impact of Population Change on Business Activity in Rural America*, Kenneth M. Johnson

*The Socioeconomic Impact of Resource Development: Methods for Assessment*, F. Larry Leistritz and Steven H. Murdock

*Coping with Rapid Growth in Rural Communities*, edited by Bruce A. Weber and Robert E. Howell

†Available in hardcover and paperback.

# About the Book and Authors

*Appalachia: A Regional Geography*
*Land, People, and Development*

Karl B. Raitz and Richard Ulack
with Thomas R. Leinbach

Although Appalachia has long been recognized as one of the most distinctive subregions in North America and has been studied widely as an "underdeveloped problem area," this book is the first to provide a comparative and analytical geographical perspective on the entire Appalachian region rather than on portions of it. The authors highlight the diversity of the region and examine its varying levels of economic development, identifying problem areas as they go. They also review developmental difficulties in light of historical resource use and present patterns of resource control. Based on the most recently available census data, 40 tables and 62 maps complement the narrative, along with 40 photographs.

The book is ideal for college courses on the Appalachian region, but is also designed to be useful for local, state, and federal government offices responsible for dealing with Appalachia's special needs. Even casual visitors to the region will find much information here that will help them interpret and better understand what they see.

Dr. Karl B. Raitz has been with the Geography Department at the University of Kentucky since 1970. Professor Raitz served 5 years as department chairman and is currently director of graduate studies, as well as book review editor for *Professional Geographer*.

Dr. Richard Ulack is associate professor in the Geography Department at the University of Kentucky, but spent 1982 and part of 1983 teaching in the Philippines on a Fulbright Fellowship grant, which was augmented by grants from the National Geographical Society and the National Science Foundation in support of his own research on migration, population problems, and regional development.

Thomas R. Leinbach is also a professor of geography at the University of Kentucky.